INDEX OF PLAYS

INDEX OF PLAYLETS

A complete index of all Prefaces and Plays appears at the end of Volume VI. Most of the Prefatory and Post-script material adjoins the play which it interprets. When Prefaces are not connected, they can be located by referring to the Table of Contents of the Volume in which the play appears.

D1060500

BERNARD SHAW

COMPLETE PLAYS
WITH PREFACES

VOLUME V

THE CROWNING YEARS

BERNARD SHAW

COMPLETE PLAYS

WITH PREFACES

Volume V

DODD, MEAD & COMPANY

NEW YORK

1963

© 1962 by The Public Trustee as Executor
of the Estate of George Bernard Shaw.
All Rights Reserved.

WHY SHE WOULD NOT. Copyright 1956, The Public Trustee as Executor of the Estate of George Bernard Shaw. SHAKES VERSUS SHAV. Copyright 1949, George Bernard Shaw. Copyright 1951, The Public Trustee as Executor of the Estate of George Bernard Shaw. THE SIX OF CALAIS. Copyright 1934, 1936, George Bernard Shaw. Copyright 1961, The Public Trustee as Executor of the Estate of George Bernard Shaw. ANNAJANSKA, THE BOLSHEVIK EMPRESS. Copyright 1919, 1930, 1948, George Bernard Shaw. Copyright 1957, The Public Trustee as Executor of the Estate of George Bernard Shaw. AUGUSTUS DOES HIS BIT. Copyright 1919, 1930, 1948, George Bernard Shaw. Copyright 1957, The Public Trustee as Executor of the Estate of George Bernard Shaw. THE INCA OF PERUSALEM. Copyright 1919, 1930, 1948, George Bernard Shaw. Copyright 1957, The Public Trustee as Executor of the Estate of George Bernard Shaw. O'FLAHERTY V.C. Copyright 1919, 1930, 1948, George Bernard Shaw. Copyright 1957, The Public Trustee as Executor of the Estate of George Bernard Shaw. THE MUSIC-CURE. Copyright 1926, George Bernard Shaw. Copyright 1954, The Public Trustee as Executor of the Estate of George Bernard Shaw. THE SHEWING-UP OF BLANCO POSNET. Copyright 1909, Brentano's. Copyright 1911, 1913, 1930, 1941, George Bernard Shaw. Copyright 1957, The Public Trustee as Executor of the Estate of George Bernard Shaw. THE ADMIRABLE BASH-VILLE. Copyright 1901, Herbert S. Stone & Co. Copyright 1913, Brentano's. Copyright 1941, George Bernard Shaw. ANDROCLES AND THE LION. Copyright 1913, 1916, 1930, 1941, 1944, George Bernard Shaw. Copyright 1957, The Public Trustee as Executor of the Estate of George Bernard Shaw. ON THE ROCKS. Copyright 1934, George Bernard Shaw. Copyright 1961, The Public Trustee as Executor of the Estate of George Bernard Shaw. GENEVA. Copyright 1938, 1946, George Bernard Shaw. HOW HE LIED TO HER HUSBAND. Copyright 1907, 1913, 1930, 1941, George Bernard Shaw. Copyright 1957, The Public Trustee as Executor of the Estate of George Bernard Shaw. VILLAGE WOOING. Copyright 1934, George Bernard Shaw. Copyright 1961, The Public Trustee as Executor of the Estate of George Bernard Shaw. PLAYLET ON THE BRITISH PARTY SYSTEM. Copyright 1944, George Bernard Shaw.

All rights fully protected and reserved. No part of this book may be reproduced in any form and no performance thereof may be given without written permission of the author's agent.

LIBRARY OF CONGRESS CATALOG CARD NUMBER: 62-13608

PRINTED IN THE UNITED STATES OF AMERICA

CONTENTS

CONTENTS

WHY SHE WOULD NOT

A COMEDIETTA

Written in 1950
Only five of the six scenes finished
First Performance not recorded

WHY SHE WOULD NOT
A LITTLE COMEDY

A PATH *through a wood. A fine summer afternoon. A lady, good-looking, well dressed, and not over thirty, is being conducted along the path by a burly and rather dangerous-looking man, middle aged, ugly, dressed in a braided coat and mutton pie cap which give him the air of being a hotel porter or commissionaire of some sort.*

THE LADY [*stopping*] Where are we now? I should hardly call this a short cut.

THE MAN [*truculently*] I'm damned if I know. Two miles from anywhere.

THE LADY. But you must know. You are a forest guide.

THE MAN. Guide my foot! I'm no bloody guide. How much money have you got on you?

THE LADY. Why?

THE MAN. Because I mean to have it off you, see? Hand over.

THE LADY. Do you mean to rob me? You said you were a guide; and we agreed for seven-and-sixpence. I meant to give you ten shillings if you were civil; but now I will give you your seven-and-sixpence and not a penny more. If you dare try to rob me I'll call the police.

THE MAN. Call away. There isnt a copper within five miles. Are them pearls round your neck real? Whether or no I mean to have them. You have three pounds in notes in your handbag: I saw them when you paid the taxi. Are you going to hand over quietly or shall I have to take them? It'll hurt a bit.

A YOUNG MALE VOICE [*very affable*] Is there anything amiss? Can I help?

The Man and the Lady start violently, not having noticed the newcomer until he arrives between them. He is a likeable looking juvenile in a workman's cap, but otherwise might by his clothes be an artisan off duty or a gentleman. His accent is that of a wellbred man.

3

WHY SHE WOULD NOT

THE MAN [*ferociously*] Who the hell are you?

THE NEWCOMER. Nobody but a tramp looking for a job.

THE MAN. Well, dont you come interfering with me. Get out of here, double quick.

THE NEWCOMER [*sunnily*] I'm in no hurry. The lady might like me to stay. If she wants a witness I'm on the job.

THE LADY. Oh yes: please stay. This man is trying to rob me.

THE NEWCOMER. Oh dear! That wont do, you know, matey. Thou shalt not steal.

THE MAN [*with exaggerated fierceness*] Who are you calling matey? Listen here. Are you going to get out or have I to sling you out?

THE NEWCOMER [*gaily*] You can try. I'm game for a scrap. Fists, catch as catch can, up and down wrestling, or all three together? Be quick. The mounted police patrol will pass at six. Take off your coat; and come on.

THE MAN [*he is an abject coward*] Easy, governor, easy. I dont want no fighting. All I asked of the lady was my money for guiding her.

THE NEWCOMER [*to the Lady*] Give it to him and get rid of him.

THE LADY. I never refused to give it to him. Here it is. [*She gives the Man five shillings*].

THE MAN [*humbly*] Thank you, lady. [*He hurries away, almost running*].

THE LADY. How brave of you to offer to fight that big man!

THE NEWCOMER. Bluff, dear lady, pure bluff. A bully is not always a coward; but a big coward is almost always a bully. I took his measure; that is all. Where do you want to go to?

THE LADY. To Timbertown. I live there. I am Miss White of Four Towers: a very famous old house. I can reward you handsomely for rescuing me when I get home.

THE NEWCOMER. I know the way. A mile and a half. Can you walk it?

THE LADY. Yes of course. I can walk ten miles.

THE NEWCOMER. Right O! Follow me.

They go off together.

SCENE II

A T *the gates of a pretentious country house surrounded by a high stone wall and overshadowed by heavy elm trees. The wall is broken by four sham towers with battlemented tops.*

The Newcomer and the Lady arrive. She opens her bag and takes out a key to unlock the wicket.

THE LADY. Here we are. This is my house.

THE NEWCOMER [*looking at it*] Oh. Is it?

He is not as much impressed as she expected. She fingers the cash pocket in her bag, and is obviously embarrassed.

THE NEWCOMER. You are safe at home now. I must hurry into the town to get a night's lodging. Goodnight, lady. [*He turns to go*].

THE LADY. O please wait a moment. I hardly know——

THE NEWCOMER. How much to tip me, eh?

THE LADY. Well, I must reward you. You have done me a great service. I promised——

THE NEWCOMER. You did. But rescuing ladies from robbers is not my profession: it is only my amusement as an amateur. But you can do something for me. You said your name was White. Your people are the greatest timber merchants and woodmen in the county. Well, I'm a carpenter of sorts. Could you get me a job in the timber yard at three pound ten a week? I cant live on less.

THE LADY. Oh, I'm sure I can. My grandfather is

chairman of the Board. My brother is manager. What is your name? Where do you live?

THE NEWCOMER. My name is Henry Bossborn. I live nowhere, or where I can: I have no address. I'll call on Thursday at your kitchen door: you can leave word with your maid if there is any news for me. Good night.

THE LADY [*very graciously*] Au revoir.

BOSSBORN. Not necessarily. Adieu: remember me.

He goes decisively. She unlocks the wicket and goes home.

SCENE III

T*HE boardroom of White Sons and Bros. Ltd. In the chair old Reginald White, still keen and attentive, but mostly silent. Jasper White, domineering but not quite up to his father's mark, Montgomery Smith, counting-house chief, and two clerks who make notes but say nothing, and three or four members of the Board, silent lookers-on. Bossborn, looking quite smart in a clean white collar and well brushed suit, is before them, bareheaded.*

OLD REGINALD. Well, Bossborn, you have done a plucky service to my granddaughter, Miss Serafina White, who holds many shares in this concern.

BOSSBORN. Oh, nothing, sir. I could have killed the fellow.

OLD REGINALD. The lady says he was twice your size and weight. We must find you a job. You want one, dont you?

BOSSBORN. I want three pound ten a week, sir. I must live.

OLD REGINALD. You are a white collar case, I suppose. We shall have to make room for you in the counting house.

BOSSBORN. No, sir, manual worker, carpenter on the wages list. Three pound ten and the usual bonus, same as the rest in the carpenters' shop.

OLD REGINALD. Oh well, if you prefer it: that will be easy. [*To Jasper*] Tell him his duties.

JASPER [*much more distant and peremptory*] Youll be here at six on Monday morning, and clock in sharp to the minute. We dont allow unpunctuality here. The foreman will direct you to a place on the bench, where you will be expected to work—to work, mind you, not to dawdle—until eleven, when you can knock off for five minutes for a cup of tea. Half an hour off for a meal at one. Work again at the bench until four. Overtime wages one and a half. Five day week: nothing on Saturdays. A week's notice if you are a slacker. Thats all. You can go.

BOSSBORN. I'm very grateful to you gentlemen for offering me this job. But I'm afraid it will not suit me. I must take to the road again.

JASPER. Why? It is what you ask for.

BOSSBORN. I'm not that sort of man. I cant clock in, and work at regular hours at the bench. I cant do what you call work at all. It is not in my nature. I must come when I like and go when I like and stay away when I like. I get up at eight, breakfast at nine, and read the papers until ten. I've never in my life got up at five in the morning.

JASPER. In short, you are an unemployable walking gentleman. You expect to be paid three pound ten a week for doing nothing.

BOSSBORN. Three pound ten and the bonus. Not exactly for doing nothing. I ask to have the run of the works and just loaf round to see if there is anything I can do.

SMITH. Well, of all the—! Just to snoop round and find out all our trade secrets and sell them to the next timber yard.

OLD REGINALD. We have no secrets here. All the world is welcome to learn the ways of White Ltd. Straightforward work and first quality. Let those who can copy us and welcome.

SMITH. Yes, sir, we know that. But this young fellow can make a living by going from one firm to another, taking a job and being sacked as a slacker at a fortnight's notice; then going on to the next shop and doing it again.

BOSSBORN. I can meet you on that. Take me on for a fortnight on my own terms. If at the end of the fortnight you find me worth keeping for another week you pay me for the whole three weeks; but if you find me no use I get no wages at all, nothing but the sack.

OLD REGINALD. How is that, Mr Smith?

SMITH. Well, sir, if you want a sleeping partner, this is the man for you. That is all I can say.

OLD REGINALD [rising] We'll try him. Come with me, Bossborn: my granddaughter is waiting in my private room to hear how you have got on.

BOSSBORN. Good morning, gentlemen. [He follows old Reginald out].

SMITH. The old man is going dotty. You really ought to take over, Mr Jasper.

JASPER. Let him have his way. We shall soon be rid of this rotter.

SCENE IV

THE drawingroom of Four Towers, overcrowded with massive early Victorian furniture, thick curtains, small but heavy tables crowded with nicnacs, sea shells, stuffed birds in glass cases, carpets and wall paper with huge flower designs, movement obstructed and light excluded in every possible way.

Two years have elapsed since the incident in the wood. Bossborn, now a very smart city man, matured and important looking, is being entertained by Serafina.

BOSSBORN. Twice round the world!

SERAFINA. Yes, twice. And a winter in Durban.

BOSSBORN. Why twice?

SERAFINA. Once for sightseeing. But life in a pleasure

ship is so easy and comfortable and careless and social that at the end of the trip you just stick to the ship and start again for another round-the-world cruise, mostly with the same people. Quite a lot of them spend their lives going round and round. It costs only about a thousand a year; and everything is done for you.

BOSSBORN. Then why did you come back here?

SERAFINA. Homesick. For me there is no place like Four Towers. Besides, I had to come back after father's death to settle about his will and all that. I shall never leave dear Four Towers again. I was born here; and I shall die here.

BOSSBORN. Hmmm! There are better places.

SERAFINA. Not for me. Nowhere on earth. But never mind that now. What about yourself? I hear you have made terrible changes in the company, and that you and Jasper are on very bad terms. You have pensioned off poor old Smith and dismissed four clerks who had been with us for sixteen years and never had a word against them.

BOSSBORN. Their work is done by a girl with a calculating and invoicing typewriter as big as herself. Smith was twenty-five years out of date. The waste of labor all over the place was frightful.

SERAFINA. Before I went away Jasper said that either you or he would have to go when father retired. We Whites like to be masters in our own house. I like to be mistress in mine.

BOSSBORN. Oh, that is all over. Ive trained Jasper in my methods, and am now in business on my own.

SERAFINA. Have you set up in opposition to us?

BOSSBORN. Not at all. I'm still a director and shareholder. My own business is land agency, dealer in real estate, private banking, building, and so on. Anything there is money in and that I understand.

SERAFINA. How wonderful! And only two years ago you were a tramp looking for a job.

9

BOSSBORN. And you got one for me. What can I do for you in return?

SERAFINA. Well, there is something you could perhaps advise me on. My old nurse and housekeeper thinks there is something wrong with the drainage here; and the gardener thinks that two of the four towers are not quite safe. Would you greatly mind if I asked you to have a look round and tell me if there is really anything wrong, and if so what I ought to do about it?

BOSSBORN. I need not look round. I have had my eye on Four Towers for some time; and I know it inside and out. There is no drainage.

SERAFINA. No drainage! But there must be.

BOSSBORN. Absolutely none. The sewage has been simply soaking into the soil for heaven knows how many years. None of the towers are worth repairing. The one thing to be done is to blow them up, get rid of that prison wall, cut down those trees that shut out the sunlight, and knock down this ugly, unhealthy, troublesome, costly house. It is not fit to live in. I'll build you a modern house with a beautiful view in a better situation. This neighbourhood was fashionable fifty years ago: it is now east end. I'll build six prefabricated villas lettable at moderate rents to replace your four rotten old towers and bring you in a tidy addition to your income.

SERAFINA [*rising in boiling wrath*] Mr Bossburn: leave my house.

BOSSBORN. Oh! [*rising*] Why?

SERAFINA. I can hardly speak. My house! My house, the great house of Timbertown. My beautiful house, built by my people and never lived in by anyone else. I was born here. And you dare—!! Go; or I will call my servants to shew you out. And never approach my door again: it will be shut in your face.

BOSSBURN [*quite unmoved*] Think it over! I'll call again in a month. [*He goes promptly*].

Serafina rings the bell and strides about the room,

10

raging, then rings again violently three times. Her old
nurse-housekeeper rushes in, alarmed.

NURSE. What's the matter, dearie?

SERAFINA. If that man calls here again, shut the door
in his face. Slam it. Set the dog on him if he wont go.
Tell the maids.

NURSE. Oh, we couldnt do that. Hes such a gentleman. We'll say you are not at home.

SERAFINA. Youll obey my orders. Gentleman! Do
you know what he has done?

NURSE. No, dearie. It must be something dreadful to
put you into a state like this. What was it?

SERAFINA. He said that my house—Four Towers!—
is ugly, unhealthy, troublesome, not fit to live in. My
house! The house I was born in.

NURSE [*unimpressed*]. Well, you know, dearie, it *is*
troublesome. We cant do without seven housemaids, and
they are always complaining and wont stay long. There
are always one or two of them sick. Theres no life in the
house with all those stairs to drag scuttles of coal up and
down because there is no proper heating, only the old open
grates. And the place is so dark with all those trees, and
nothing to look at but a stone wall. In the kitchen they
are always wondering why you live here instead of moving into a nice new house with every convenience.

SERAFINA [*astounded*] So you—you!—agree with
him!

NURSE. Oh no, dearie, I could never agree with anyone against you. I know you think the world of the old
house. But you can hardly blame the gentleman for saying what everybody says. He is such a nice gentleman.
Think it over, dearie.

SCENE V

T*HE lounge in an ultra modern country house dated 1950, contrasting strangely with Four Towers. As before, Serafina hostess and Bossborn visitor.*

BOSSBORN. Well, what is the matter today? Why have you sent for me?

SERAFINA. I want to have it out with you about my Thursday at-homes. You have stopped coming to them. Why?

BOSSBORN. Have I? Well, you see, I am full up of business all day. I have my own business to attend to all the forenoon, and in the afternoon there are Board meetings of directors and the County Council, and appointments of all sorts. Much as I like to turn up at your at-homes for the pleasure of seeing you I simply cannot find time for society and small talk. I am, unfortunately, a very busy man.

SERAFINA. How charmingly you pay out that budget of lies! A busy man can always find time to do anything he really wants to do, and excuses for everything he doesnt.

BOSSBORN. That is true. Ive not thought about it. To be quite frank, I dislike the society of ladies and gentlemen. They bore me. I am not at home among them. You know I am only an upstart tramp.

SERAFINA. Very clever. But a much bigger lie. I dont know where you got your courtly manners and the way you speak and carry your London clothes; but I know you are a cut above me socially, and look down on us poor provincials and tradespeople.

BOSSBORN. Well, suppose it is so. Let us assume that I was brought up as a court page, and was so bored by it that I broke loose from it, threw myself on the streets penniless just as Kropotkin when he grew out of being Tsar Alexander's page, chose an infantry regiment in Siberia instead of the Imperial Guards at the top of the tree in

12

Petersburg. Such things happen. You may pretend that it happened to me. But if so does not this prove that I am not a snob?

SERAFINA. At last you may be telling the truth. But if you are not a snob why have you stopped coming to my at-homes? Answer me that.

BOSSBORN. Whats the use of answering if you will not believe a word I say? You seem to know the truth, whatever it may be. It is for you to tell it to me.

SERAFINA. The reason you have stopped coming is that you think I want to marry you.

BOSSBORN. Oh, nonsense!

SERAFINA. It is not nonsense. Do stop lying. It would be a social promotion for me. My old nurse, with her talk about your being a very nice gentleman, selected you for my husband from the time she first saw you. Everybody thinks I ought to get married before I am too old. If you came always to my at-homes they would think you are the man. That is what you are afraid of. You need not be afraid. I have sent for you to tell you that nothing on earth could induce me to marry you. So there. You can come as often as you like. I have no designs on you.

BOSSBORN. But have I offended you in any way? Are my manners inconsiderate?

SERAFINA. No. Your manners are perfect.

BOSSBORN. You just dont like me. Simply natural antipathy, eh?

SERAFINA. Not in the least. I like you and admire you more than any man I have ever known. You are a wonder.

BOSSBORN. Then why?

SERAFINA. I am afraid of you.

BOSSBORN. Afraid of Me!!! Impossible. How? Why? Are you serious?

SERAFINA. Yes: afraid of you. Everybody is afraid of you.

BOSSBORN. Is there any use in saying that you have no reason to be afraid of me?

13

WHY SHE WOULD NOT

SERAFINA. Yes I have. I like to be mistress in my own house, as I was in Four Towers.

BOSSBORN. But you would be mistress in my house if we married.

SERAFINA. No one will ever be mistress in any house that you are in. Only your slaves and your bedfellow.

BOSSBORN. This bewilders me. Have I ever forced you to do anything you did not want to do?

SERAFINA. No; for I always had to do what you wanted me to do. I was happy at Four Towers: I loved it: I was born there and mistress of it and of myself: it was sacred to me. I turned you out of it for daring to say a word against it. Where is it now? And where am I? Just where you put me: I might as well have been a piece of furniture. Here in this house of your choosing and your building I have heard my four towers being blown up, bang, bang, bang, bang, striking on my heart like an earthquake; and I never lifted my finger to stop you as I could have done if I had been my own mistress. At the works, where my grandfather always had the last word until he died, you came; and with Jasper and Smith and all the rest against you, you turned the whole place inside out: poor old Smith and his clerks had to retire; Jasper had to knuckle under; our splendid old craftsmen had to learn new machines or be sacked and replaced by American mechanics.

BOSSBORN. Yes yes yes; but they consented: they were willing. I doubled, trebled, quadrupled the product and the profit. You could not live in Four Towers now because you are so enormously more comfortable and civilized here. You can all do far more as you like with the leisure my reforms give you than you could before I came. Leisure is the only reality of freedom. I coerce nobody: I only point out the way.

SERAFINA. Yes: your way, not our way.

BOSSBORN. Neither my way nor yours. The way of the world. Some people call it God's way.

14

WHY SHE WOULD NOT

SERAFINA. Anyhow I will live my own life, not yours.
If I marry, my choice will not be a Bossborn.

BOSSBORN. Is that final?

SERAFINA. Yes. Friendship only.

BOSSBORN. So be it. Good day to you.

He rises and goes out promptly, as before.

SHAKES VERSUS SHAV

A PUPPET PLAY

Written in 1949

First Performed Malvern 1949

PREFACE

THIS in all actuarial probability is my last play and the climax of my eminence, such as it is. I thought my career as a playwright was finished when Waldo Lanchester of the Malvern Marionette Theatre, our chief living puppet master, sent me figures of two puppets, Shakespear and myself, with a request that I should supply one of my famous dramas for them, not to last longer than ten minutes or thereabouts. I accomplished this feat, and was gratified by Mr Lanchester's immediate approval.

I have learnt part of my craft as conductor of rehearsals (producer, they call it) from puppets. Their unvarying intensity of facial expression, impossible for living actors, keeps the imagination of the spectators continuously stimulated. When one of them is speaking or tumbling and the rest left aside, these, though in full view, are invisible, as they should be. Living actors have to learn that they too must be invisible while the protagonists are conversing, and therefore must not move a muscle nor change their expression, instead of, as beginners mostly do, playing to them and robbing them of the audience's undivided attention.

Puppets have also a fascination of their own, because there is nothing wonderful in a living actor moving and speaking, but that wooden headed dolls should do so is a marvel that never palls.

And they can survive treatment that would kill live actors. When I first saw them in my boyhood nothing delighted me more than when all the puppets went up in a balloon and presently dropped from the skies with an appalling crash on the floor.

Nowadays the development of stagecraft into filmcraft may destroy the idiosyncratic puppet charm. Televised puppets could enjoy the scenic backgrounds of the cinema. Sound recording could enable the puppet master to give all his attention to the strings he is manipulating, the dialogue being spoken by a company of first-rate speakers as in the theatre. The old puppet master spoke all the parts himself in accents which he differentiated by Punch-and-Judy squeaks and the like. I can imagine the puppets simu-

19

lating living performers so perfectly that the spectators will be completely illuded. The result would be the death of puppetry; for it would lose its charm with its magic. So let reformers beware.

Nothing can extinguish my interest in Shakespear. It began when I was a small boy, and extends to Stratford-upon-Avon, where I have attended so many bardic festivals that I have come to regard it almost as a supplementary birthplace of my own.

No year passes without the arrival of a batch of books contending that Shakespear was somebody else. The argument is always the same. Such early works as Venus and Adonis, Lucrece, and Love's Labour's Lost, could not possibly have been written by an illiterate clown and poacher who could hardly write his own name. This is unquestionably true. But the inference that Shakespear did not write them does not follow. What does follow is that Shakespear was not an illiterate clown but a well read grammar-schooled son in a family of good middle-class standing, cultured enough to be habitual playgoers and private entertainers of the players.

This, on investigation, proves to be exactly what Shakespear was. His father, John Shakespear, Gent, was an alderman who demanded a coat of arms which was finally granted. His mother was of equal rank and social pretension. John finally failed commercially, having no doubt let his artistic turn get the better of his mercantile occupation, and leave him unable to afford a university education for William, had he ever wanted to make a professional scholar of him.

These circumstances interest me because they are just like my own. They were a considerable cut above those of Bunyan and Cobbett, both great masters of language, who nevertheless could not have written Venus and Adonis nor Love's Labour's Lost. One does not forget Bunyan's "The Latin I borrow." Shakespear's standing was nearer to Ruskin's, whose splendid style owes much more to his mother's insistence on his learning the Bible by heart than to his Oxford degree.

20

SHAKES VERSUS SHAV

So much for Bacon-Shakespear and all the other fables founded on that entirely fictitious figure Shaxper or Shagsper the illiterate bumpkin.

Enough too for my feeling that the real Shakespear might have been myself, and for the shallow mistaking of it for mere professional jealousy.

Ayot Saint Lawrence,
1949

SHAKES VERSUS SHAV

*SHAKES enters and salutes the audience with a flour-
ish of his hat.*

SHAKES. Now is the winter of our discontent
Made glorious summer by the Malvern sun.
I, William Shakes, was born in Stratford town,
Where every year a festival is held
To honour my renown not for an age
But for all time. Hither I raging come
An infamous impostor to chastize,
Who in an ecstasy of self-conceit
Shortens my name to Shav, and dares pretend
Here to reincarnate my very self,
And in your stately playhouse to set up
A festival, and plant a mulberry
In most presumptuous mockery of mine.
Tell me, ye citizens of Malvern,
Where I may find this caitiff. Face to face
Set but this fiend of Ireland and myself;
And leave the rest to me. [*Shav enters*]. Who art thou?
That rearst a forehead almost rivalling mine?

SHAV. Nay, who art thou, that knowest not these features
Pictured throughout the globe? Who should I be
But G. B. S.?

SHAKES. What! Stand, thou shameless fraud.
For one or both of us the hour is come.
Put up your hands.

SHAV. Come on.

*They spar. Shakes knocks Shav down with a straight
left and begins counting him out, stooping over him and
beating the seconds with his finger.*

SHAKES. Hackerty-backerty one, Hackerty-backerty two,
Hackerty-backerty   three . . . Hackerty-backerty
nine—
*At the count of nine Shav springs up and knocks Shakes
down with a right to the chin.*

SHAV [*counting*] Hackerty-backerty one, . . . Hackerty-
backerty ten. Out.

SHAKES. Out! And by thee! Never. [*He rises*]. Younger
you are

23

SHAKES VERSUS SHAV

By full three hundred years, and therefore carry
A heavier punch than mine; but what of that?
Death will soon finish you; but as for me,
Not marble nor the gilded monuments
Of princes—

SHAV.   —shall outlive your powerful rhymes.
So you have told us: I have read your sonnets.

SHAKES. Couldst write Macbeth?

SHAV. No need. He has been bettered
By Walter Scott's Rob Roy. Behold, and blush.

Rob Roy and Macbeth appear, Rob in Highland tartan and kilt with claymore, Macbeth in kingly costume.

MACBETH. Thus far into the bowels of the land
Have we marched on without impediment.
Shall I still call you Campbell?

ROB [*in a strong Scotch accent*] Caumill me no Caumills.
Ma fet is on ma native heath: ma name's Macgregor.

MACBETH. I have no words. My voice is in my sword. Lay
on, Rob Roy;
And damned be he that proves the smaller boy.

He draws and stands on guard. Rob draws; spins round several times like a man throwing a hammer; and finally cuts off Macbeth's head at one stroke.

ROB. Whaur's your Wullie Shaxper the noo?

Bagpipe and drum music, to which Rob dances off.

MACBETH [*headless*] I will return to Stratford: the hotels
Are cheaper there. [*He picks up his head, and goes off with it under his arm to the tune of British Grenadiers*].

SHAKES. Call you this cateran
Better than my Macbeth, one line from whom
Is worth a thousand of your piffling plays.

SHAV. Quote one. Just one. I challenge thee. One line.

SHAKES. "The shardborne beetle with his drowsy hum."

SHAV. Hast never heard of Adam Lindsay Gordon?

SHAKES. A name that sings. What of him?

SHAV.   He eclipsed
Thy shardborne beetle. Hear his mighty lines. [*Reciting*]

"The beetle booms adown the glooms
And bumps among the clumps."
SHAKES [*roaring with laughter*] Ha ha! Ho ho! My lungs
like chanticleer
Must crow their fill. This fellow hath an ear.
How does it run? "The beetle booms—
SHAV. Adown the glooms—
SHAKES. And bumps—
SHAV. Among the clumps." Well done, Australia!
Shav laughs.
SHAKES. Laughest thou at thyself? Pullst thou my leg?
SHAV. There is more fun in heaven and earth, sweet William,
Than is dreamt of in your philosophy.
SHAKES. Where is thy Hamlet? Couldst thou write King
Lear?
SHAV. Aye, with his daughters all complete. Couldst thou
Have written Heartbreak House? Behold my Lear.
*A transparency is suddenly lit up, shewing Captain
Shotover seated, as in Millais' picture called North-West
Passage, with a young woman of virginal beauty.*
SHOTOVER [*raising his hand and intoning*] I built a house
for my daughters and opened the doors thereof
That men might come for their choosing, and their betters
spring from their love;
But one of them married a numskull: the other a liar
wed;
And now she must lie beside him even as she made her
bed.
THE VIRGIN. "Yes: this silly house, this strangely happy
house, this agonizing house, this house without founda-
tions. I shall call it Heartbreak House."
SHOTOVER. Enough. Enough. Let the heart break in silence.
The picture vanishes.
SHAKES. You stole that word from me: did I not write
"The heartache and the thousand natural woes
That flesh is heir to"?
SHAV.   You were not the first
To sing of broken hearts. I was the first

SHAKES VERSUS SHAV

That taught your faithless Timons how to mend them.

SHAKES. Taught what you could not know. Sing if you can
My cloud capped towers, my gorgeous palaces,
My solemn temples. The great globe itself,
Yea, all which it inherit, shall dissolve—

SHAV. —and like this foolish little show of ours
Leave not a wrack behind. So you have said.
I say the world will long outlast our day.
Tomorrow and tomorrow and tomorrow
We puppets shall replay our scene. Meanwhile,
Immortal William dead and turned to clay
May stop a hole to keep the wind away.
Oh that that earth which kept the world in awe
Should patch a wall t' expel the winter's flaw!

SHAKES. These words are mine, not thine.

SHAV. Peace, jealous Bard.
We both are mortal. For a moment suffer
My glimmering light to shine.

A light appears between them.

SHAKES. Out, out, brief candle! [*He puffs it out*].
Darkness. The play ends.

THE END

26

THE SIX OF CALAIS

A MEDIAEVAL WAR STORY IN ONE ACT

by Jean Froissart, Auguste Rodin and Bernard Shaw

Written in 1934

First Performed London 1934

PREFATORY TO THE SIX OF CALAIS

THE most amusing thing about the first performance of this little play was the exposure it elicited of the quaint illiteracy of our modern London journalists. Their only notion of a king was a pleasant and highly respectable gentleman in a bowler hat and Victorian beard, shaking hands affably with a blushing football team. To them a queen was a dignified lady, also Victorian as to her coiffure, graciously receiving bouquets from excessively washed children in beautiful new clothes. Such were their mental pictures of Great Edward's grandson and his queen Philippa. They were hurt, shocked, scandalized at the spectacle of a medieval soldier-monarch publicly raging and cursing, crying and laughing, asserting his authority with thrasonic ferocity and the next moment blubbering like a child in his wife's lap or snarling like a savage dog at a dauntless and defiant tradesman: in short, behaving himself like an unrestrained human being in a very trying situation instead of like a modern constitutional monarch on parade keeping up an elaborate fiction of living in a political vacuum and moving only when his ministers pull his strings. Edward Plantagenet the Third had to pull everybody else's strings and pull them pretty hard, his father having been miserably killed for taking his job too lightly. But the journalist critics knew nothing of this. A King Edward who did not behave like the son of King Edward the Seventh seemed unnatural and indecent to them, and they rent their garments accordingly.

They were perhaps puzzled by the fact that the play has no moral whatever. Every year or so I hurl at them a long play full of insidious propaganda, with a moral in every line. They never discover what I am driving at: it is always too plainly and domestically stated to be grasped by their subtle and far flung minds; but they feel that I am driving at something: probably something they had better not agree with if they value their livelihoods. A play of mine in which I am not driving at anything more

than a playwright's direct business is as inconceivable by
them as a medieval king.

Now a playwright's direct business is simply to provide the theatre with a play. When I write one with
the additional attraction of providing the twentieth century with an up-to-date religion or the like, that luxury
is thrown in gratuitously; and the play, simply as a play,
is not necessarily either the better or the worse for it.
What, then, is a play simply as a play?

Well, it is a lot of things. Life as we see it is so hap-
hazard that it is only by picking out its key situations and
arranging them in their significant order (which is never
how they actually occur) that it can be made intelligible.
The highbrowed dramatic poet wants to make it intelligible
and sublime. The farce writer wants to make it funny. The
melodrama merchant wants to make it as exciting as some
people find the police news. The pornographer wants to
make it salacious. All interpreters of life in action, noble
or ignoble, find their instrument in the theatre; and all
the academic definitions of a play are variations of this
basic function.

Yet there is one function hardly ever alluded to now,
though it was made much too much of from Shakespear's
time to the middle of the nineteenth century. As I write
my plays it is continually in my mind and very much to
my taste. This function is to provide an exhibition of the
art of acting. A good play with bad parts is not an impossibility; but it is a monstrosity. A bad play with good
parts will hold the stage and be kept alive by the actors
for centuries after the obsolescence of its mentality would
have condemned it to death without them. A great deal
of the British Drama, from Shakespear to Bulwer Lytton,
is as dead as mutton, and quite unbearable except when
heroically acted; yet Othello and Richelieu can still draw
hard money into the pay boxes; and The School For
Scandal revives again and again with unabated vigor.
Rosalind can always pull As You Like It through in spite

PREFATORY TO THE SIX OF CALAIS

of the sententious futility of the melancholy Jaques; and Millamant, impossible as she is, still produces the usual compliments to the wit and style of Congreve, who thought that syphilis and cuckoldry and concupiscent old women are things to be laughed at.

The Six of Calais is an acting piece and nothing else. As it happened, it was so well acted that in the eighteenth century all the talk would have been about Siddons as Philippa. But the company got no thanks except from the audience: the critics were prostrated with shock, damn their eyes!

I have had to improve considerably on the story as told by that absurd old snob Froissart, who believed that "to rob and pill was a good life" if the robber was at least a baron. He made a very poor job of it in my opinion.

ON THE HIGH SEAS,
28th May 1935.

THE SIX OF CALAIS

A.D. 4th August 1347. Before the walls of Calais on the last day of the siege. The pavilion of Edward III, King of England, is on your left as you face the walls. The pavilion of his consort Philippa of Hainault is on your right. Between them, near the King's pavilion, is a two-seated chair of state for public audiences. Crowds of tents cover the background; but there is a clear way in the middle through the camp to the great gate of the city with its drawbridge still up and its flag still flying.

The Black Prince, aged 17, arrives impetuously past the Queen's tent, a groom running after him.

THE PRINCE. Here is the King's pavilion without a single attendant to announce me. What can the matter be?

A child's scream is heard from the royal pavilion; and John of Gaunt, aged 7, dashes out and is making for his mother's tent when the Prince seizes him.

THE PRINCE. How now, Johnny? Whats the matter?

JOHN [*struggling*] Let me go. Father is in a frightful wax.

THE PRINCE. I shall be in a wax myself presently. [*Releasing him*] Off with you to mother. [*The child takes refuge in the Queen's pavilion*].

THE KING'S VOICE. Grrr! Yah! Why was I not told? Gogswoons, why was I not told? [*Edward III, aged 35, dashes from his pavilion, foaming*]. Out! [*The groom flies for his life*]. How long have you been here? They never tell me anything. I might be a dog instead of a king.

THE PRINCE [*about to kneel*] Majesty—

THE KING. No no: enough of that. Your news. Anything from Scotland? Anything from Wales?

THE PRINCE. I—

THE KING [*not waiting for the answer*] The state of things here is past words. The wrath of God and all his saints is upon this expedition.

THE PRINCE. I hope not, sir. I—

32

THE SIX OF CALAIS

THE KING [*raging on*] May God wither and blast this accursed town! You would have thought that these dogs would have come out of their kennels and grovelled for mercy at my summons. Am I not their lawful king, ha?

THE PRINCE. Undoubtedly, sir. They—

THE KING. They have held me up for twelve months! A whole year!! My business ruined! My plans upset! My money exhausted! Death, disease, mutiny, a dog's life here in the field winter and summer. The bitch's bastard who is in command of their walls came to demand terms from me! to demand terms!!! looked me straight in the eyes with his head up as if I—I, his king! were dirt beneath his feet. By God, I will have that head: I will kick it to my dogs to eat. I will chop his insolent herald into four quarters—

THE PRINCE [*shocked*] Oh no, sir: not a herald: you cannot do that.

THE KING. They have driven me to such extremity that I am capable of cutting all the heralds in Christendom into their quarterings. [*He sits down in his chair of state and suddenly becomes ridiculously sentimental*]. I have not told you the worst. Your mother, the Queen, my Philippa, is here: here! Edward, in her delicate state of health. Even that did not move them. They want her to die: they are trying to murder her and our innocent unborn child. Think of that, boy: oh, think of that [*he almost weeps*].

THE PRINCE. Softly, father: that is not their fault: it is yours.

THE KING. Would you make a jest of this? If it is not their fault it shall be their misfortune; for I will have every man, woman, and child torn to pieces with red hot pincers for it.

THE PRINCE. Truly, dear Sir, you have great cause to be annoyed; but in sober earnest how does the matter stand? They must be suffering the last extremity of famine. Their walls may hold out; but their stomachs cannot.

33

Cannot you offer them some sort of terms to end the business? Money is running short. Time is running short. You only make them more desperate by threatening them. Remember: it is good policy to build a bridge of silver for a flying foe.

THE KING. Do I not know it? Have I not been kind, magnanimous? Have I not done all that Christian chivalry could require of me? And they abuse my kindness: it only encourages them: they despise me for it.

THE PRINCE. What terms have you offered them?

THE KING. I have not threatened the life of a single knight. I have said that no man of gentle condition and noble blood shall be denied quarter and ransom. It was their knightly duty to make a show of arms against me. But [*rising wrathfully*] these base rascals of burgesses: these huckstering hounds of merchants who have made this port of Calais a nest of pirates: these usurers and tradesmen: these rebel curs who have dared to take up arms against their betters: am I to pardon their presumption? I should be false to our order, to Christendom, if I did not make a signal example.

THE PRINCE. By all means, sir. But what have you demanded?

THE KING. Six of the most purseproud of their burgesses, as they call themselves—by God, they begin to give themselves the airs of barons—six of them are to come in their shirts with halters round their necks for me to hang in the sight of all their people. [*Raising his voice again and storming*] They shall die the dog's death they deserve. They shall—

A court lady comes in.

THE COURT LADY. Sir: the Queen. Sssh!

THE KING [*subsiding to a whisper*] The Queen! Boy: not a word here. Her condition: she must not be upset: she takes these things so amiss: be discreet, for heaven's sake.

THE SIX OF CALAIS

*Queen Philippa, aged 33, comes from her pavilion,
attended.*

THE QUEEN. Dear child: welcome.

THE PRINCE. How do you, lady mother? [*He kisses
her hand*].

THE KING [*solicitously*] Madam: are you well
wrapped up? Is it wise to come into the cold air here? Had
they better not bring a brazier and some cushions, and a
hot drink—a posset—

THE QUEEN [*curtseying*] Sir: beloved: dont fuss. I
am very well; and the air does me good. [*To the Prince*]
You must cheer up your father, my precious. He will
fret about my health when it is his own that needs care.
I have borne him eleven children; and St Anne be my
witness they have cost less looking after than this one
big soldier, the greatest baby of them all. [*To the King*]
Have you put on your flannel belly band, dearest?

THE KING. Yes, yes, yes, my love: do not bother about
me. Think of yourself and our child—

THE QUEEN. Oh, leave me to take care of myself and
the child. I am no maternal malingreuse I promise you.
And now, sir sonny, tell me all your news. I—

She is interrupted by a shrill trumpet call.

THE KING. What is that? What now?

*John of Gaunt, who has been up to the town gates to
see the fun, runs in excitedly.*

JOHN OF GAUNT [*bending his knee very perfunctorily*]
Sire: they have surrendered: the drawbridge is down. The
six old men have come out in their shirts with ropes round
their necks.

THE KING [*clouting him*] Sssh! Hold your tongue,
you young devil.

THE QUEEN. Old men in their shirts in this weather!!
They will catch cold.

THE KING. It is nothing, madam my love: only the
ceremony of surrender. You must go in: it is not fitting

THE SIX OF CALAIS

that these half naked men should be in your presence. I
will deal with them.

THE QUEEN. Do not keep them too long in the cold,
dearest sir.

THE KING [*uxoriously waving her a kiss*] My love!

*The Queen goes into her pavilion; and a group of
noblemen attendant on the King, including Sir Walter
Manny and the Lords Derby, Northampton, and Arundel,
issue from their tents and assemble behind the chair of
state, where they are joined by the Black Prince, who
stands at the King's right hand and takes charge of John
of Gaunt.*

THE KING. Now for these swine, these bloodsuckers.
They shall learn—[*shouting*] Fetch me these fellows in
here. Drag them in. I'll teach them to hold me up here
for twelve months. I'll—

*The six burgesses, hustled by men-at-arms, enter in
their shirts and halters, each carrying a bunch of massive
iron keys. Their leader, Eustache de St Pierre, kneels at
the King's feet. Four of his fellow victims, Piers de Wissant, Jacques de Wissant, Jean d'Aire, and Gilles
d'Oudebolle, kneel in pairs behind him, and, following
his example, lay their keys on the ground. They are deeply
cast down, bearing themselves like condemned men, yet
maintaining a melancholy dignity. Not so the sixth, Piers
de Rosty (nicknamed Hardmouth), the only one without
a grey or white beard. He has an extraordinarily dogged
chin with a few bristles on it. He deliberately separates
himself from the rest by passing behind the royal chair to
the King's right and planting himself stiffly erect in an attitude of intense recalcitrance. The King, scowling fiercely
at St Pierre and the rest, does not notice this until Peter
flings down his keys with a violence which suggests that he
would very willingly have brained Edward with them.*

THE KING. On your knees, hound.

PETER. I am a good dog, but not of your kennel,
Neddy.

THE SIX OF CALAIS

THE KING. Neddy!!!!

PETER. Order your own curs: I am a free burgess and take commands from nobody.

Before the amazed monarch can retort, Eustache appeals to Peter.

EUSTACHE. Master Peter: if you have no regard for yourself, remember that our people, our wives and children, are at the mercy of this great king.

PETER. You mistake him for his grandfather. Great! [*He spits*].

EUSTACHE. Is this your promise to be patient?

PETER. Why waste civilities on him, Master Mayor? He can do no worse than hang us; and as to the town, *I* would have burnt it to the last brick, and every man, woman and child along with it, sooner than surrender. I came here to make up the tale of six to be hanged. Well, he can hang me; but he shall not outface me. I am as good a dog as he, any day in the week.

THE PRINCE. Fie, fellow! is this a way for one of thy degree to speak to an anointed king? Bear thyself as befits one of thy degree in the royal presence, or by Holy Paul—

PETER. You know how we have borne ourselves in his royal presence these twelve months. We have made some of you skip. Famine and not you, has beaten us. Give me a square meal and a good sword and stake all on a fair single combat with this big bully, or his black whelp here if he is afraid of me; and we shall see which is the better dog of the two.

THE KING. Drag him to his knees. Hamstring him if he resists.

Three men-at-arms dash at Peter and drag him to his knees. They take his halter and tie his ankles and wrists with it. Then they fling him on his side, where he lies helpless.

THE KING. And so, Master Burgess—

PETER. Bow-wow-wow!

37

THE SIX OF CALAIS

THE KING [*furious*] Gag him. Gogswoons, gag him. *They tear a piece of linen from the back of his shirt, and bind his mouth with it. He barks to the last moment. John of Gaunt laughs ecstatically at this performance, and sets off some of the soldiers.*

THE KING. If a man laughs I will have him flayed alive.

Dead silence.

THE KING. And now, fellows, what have ye to say to excuse your hardy and stubborn resistance for all these months to me, your king?

EUSTACHE. Sir, we are not fellows. We are free burgesses of this great city.

THE KING. Free burgesses! Are you still singing that song? Well, I will bend the necks of your burgesses when the hangman has broken yours. Am I not your overlord? Am I not your anointed king?

EUSTACHE. That is your claim, sir; and you have made it good by force of arms. We must submit to you and to God.

THE KING. Leave God out of this! What hast thou or thy like to do with God?

EUSTACHE. Nothing, sir: we would not so far presume. But with due respect to your greatness I would humbly submit to your Majesty that God may have something to do with us, seeing that he created us all alike and redeemed us by the blood of his beloved son.

THE KING [*to the Prince*] Can you make head or tail of this, boy? Is he accusing me of impiety? If he is, by God—

EUSTACHE. Sir, is it for me to accuse you of anything? Here we kneel in the dust before you, naked and with the ropes on our necks with which you will presently send us into the presence of our maker and yours. [*His teeth chatter*].

THE KING. Ay: you may well tremble. You have cause.

EUSTACHE. Yes: I tremble; and my teeth chatter: the

38

few I have left. But you gentlemen that see our miserable plight, I call on your generosity as noblemen, on your chivalry as good knights, to bear witness for us that it is the cold of the morning and our naked condition that shakes us. We kneel to implore your King's mercy for our wretched and starving townsfolk, not for ourselves.

THE KING. Whose fault is it that they are starving? They have themselves to thank. Why did they not open their gates to me? Why did they take arms against their anointed king? Why should I have mercy on them or on you?

EUSTACHE. Sir: one is merciful not for reasons, but for the love of God, at whose hand we must all sue for mercy at the end of our days.

THE KING. You shall not save yourself by preaching. What right have you to preach? It is for churchmen and learned divines to speak of these mysteries, not for trades-men and usurers. I'll teach you to rebel against your bet-ters, whom God has appointed to keep you in obedience and loyalty. You are traitors; and as traitors you shall die. Thank my mercy that you are spared the torments that traitors and rebels suffer in England. [*Rising*] Away with them to the hangman; and let our trumpeters summon the townspeople to the walls to take warning from their dangling corpses.

The three men-at-arms begin to lift Peter. The others lay hands on his five colleagues.

THE KING. No: let that hound lie. Hanging is too good for him.

The Queen hurries in with her ladies in great concern. The men-at-arms release the burgesses irresolutely. It is evident that the Queen's arrival washes out all the King's orders.

THE QUEEN. Sir, what is this they tell me?

THE KING [*hurrying across to intercept her*] Madam: this is no place for you. I pray you, retire. The business is one in which it becomes you not to meddle.

THE QUEEN [*evading him and passing on to inspect the*

burgesses] But these gentlemen. They are almost naked. It is neither seemly nor sufficient. They are old: they are half frozen: they should be in their beds.

THE KING. They soon will be. Leave us, madam. This is business of State. They are suffering no more than they deserve. I beg and pray you—I command you—

THE QUEEN. Dear sir, your wishes are my law and your commands my duty. But these gentlemen are very cold.

THE KING. They will be colder presently; so you need not trouble about that. Will it please you, madam, to withdraw at once?

THE QUEEN. Instantly, my dear lord. [*To Eustache*] Sir: when his Majesty has ended his business with you, will you and your friends partake of some cups of hot wine in my pavilion? You shall be furnished with gowns.

THE KING [*choking with wrath*] Hot w—!

EUSTACHE. Alas, madam, when the King has ended his business with us we shall need nothing but our coffins. I also beg you to withdraw and hasten our despatch to that court where we shall not be held guilty for defending our hearths and homes to the last extremity. The King will not be baulked of his revenge; and we are shriven and ready.

THE QUEEN. Oh, you mistake, sir: the King is incapable of revenge: my husband is the flower of chivalry.

EUSTACHE. You little know your husband, madam. We know better what to expect from Edward Plantagenet.

THE KING [*coming to him threateningly past his consort*] Ha! do you, Master Merchant? You know better than the Queen! You and your like know what to expect from your lords and rulers! Well, this time you shall not be disappointed. You have guessed aright. You shall hang, every man of you, in your shirts, to make mirth for my horseboys and their trulls.

THE QUEEN. Oh no—

THE KING [*thundering*] Madam: I forbid you to speak.

I bade you go: you would not; and now you shall see what
I would have spared you had you been obedient. By God,
I will be master in my own house and king in my own
camp. Take these fellows out and hang them in their white
beards.

*The King takes his place on his chair of state with his
arms folded implacably. The Queen follows him slowly
and desolately. She takes her place beside him. The dead
silence is very trying.*

THE QUEEN [*drooping in tears and covering her face
with her hands*] Oh!

THE KING [*flinching*] No no no no NO. Take her
away.

THE QUEEN. Sir: I have been always a great trouble
to you. I have asked you for a thousand favors and graces
and presents. I am impatient and ungrateful, ever asking, asking, asking. Have you ever refused me even once?

THE KING. Well, is that a reason why I should give
and grant, grant and give, for ever? Am I never to have
my own way?

THE QUEEN. Oh, dearest sir, when next I ask you for
a great thing, refuse me: teach me a lesson. But this is such
a little thing. [*Heartbroken*] I cannot bear your refusing
me a little thing.

THE KING. A little thing! You call this a little thing!

THE QUEEN. A very very little thing, sir. You are the
King: you have at your disposal thousands of lives: all our
lives from the noblest to the meanest. All the lives in that
city are in your hand to do as you will with in this your
hour of victory: it is as if you were God himself. You said
once that you would lead ten kings captive to my feet.
Much as I have begged from you I have never asked for
my ten kings. I ask only for six old merchants, men beneath your royal notice, as my share of the spoils of your
conquest. Their ransom will hardly buy me a new girdle;
and oh, dear sir, you know that my old one is becoming
too strait for me. Will you keep me begging so?

41

THE SIX OF CALAIS

THE KING. I see very well that I shall not be allowed my own way. [*He begins to cry*].

THE QUEEN [*throwing her arms round him*] Oh, dear sir, you know I would die to spare you a moment's distress. There, there, dearest! [*She pets him*].

THE KING [*blubbering*] I am never allowed to do anything I want. I might as well be a dog as a king. You treat me like a baby.

THE QUEEN. Ah no: you are the greatest of kings to me, the noblest of men, my dearest lord and my dearest dearest love. [*Throwing herself on her knees*] Listen: do as you will: I will not say another word: I ask nothing.

THE KING. No: you ask nothing because you know you will get everything. [*He rises, shouting*] Take those men out of my sight.

THE PRINCE. What shall we do with them, sir?

THE KING [*flinging himself back into his seat*] Ask the Queen. Banquet them: feast them: give them my crown, my kingdom. Give them the clothes off my back, the bread out of my mouth, only take them away. Will you go, curses on you.

The five burgesses kneel gratefully to the Queen.

EUSTACHE [*kissing her hand*] Madam: our ransom shall buy you a threefold girdle of gold and a cradle of silver.

THE KING. Aye, well, see that it does: see that it does.

The burgesses retire, bowing to the Queen, who, still on her knees, waves her hand graciously to them.

THE QUEEN. Will you not help me up, dear sir?

THE KING. Oh yes, yes [*raising her*]: you should be more careful: who knows what harm you may have done yourself flopping on your knees like that?

THE QUEEN. I have done myself no harm, dear sir; but you have done me a world of good. I have never been better nor happier in my life. Look at me. Do I not look radiant?

THE KING. And how do I look? Like a fool.

42

THE SIX OF CALAIS

JOHN OF GAUNT. Sir: the men-at-arms want to know what they are to do with this fellow?

THE KING. Aye, I forgot him. Fetch him here.

The three men-at-arms carry Peter to the King, and fling him down. The King is now grinning. His paroxysm of tears has completely discharged his ill temper. It dawns on him that through Peter he may get even with Philippa for his recent domestic defeat.

THE QUEEN. Oh, the poor man has not even a proper shirt to wear. It is all torn: it is hardly decent.

THE KING. Look well at this man, madam. He defied me. He spat at me. There is no insult that he did not heap on me. He looked me in the face and spoke to me as if I were a scullion. I swear to you by the Holy Rood, he called me Neddy! Donkeys are called Neddy. What have you to say now? Is he, too, to be spared and petted and fed and have a gown from you?

THE QUEEN [*going to Peter*] But he is blue with cold. I fear he is dying. Untie him. Lift him up. Take that bandage off his mouth. Fie fie! I believe it is the tail of his shirt.

THE KING. It is cleaner than his tongue.

The men-at-arms release Peter from his bonds and his gag. He is too stiff to rise. They pull him to his feet.

PETER [*as they lift him groaning and swearing*] Ah-ooh-oh-ow!

THE KING. Well? Have you learnt your lesson? Are you ready to sue for the Queen's mercy?

PETER. Yah! Henpecked! Kiss mammy!

THE KING [*chuckles*]!!

THE QUEEN [*severely*] Are you mad, Master Burgess? Do you not know that your life is in the King's hand? Do you expect me to recommend you to his mercy if you forget yourself in this unseemly fashion?

PETER. Let me tell you, madam, that I came here in no ragged shirt. I have a dozen shirts of as fine a web as ever went on your back. Is it likely that I, a master mercer,

43

would wear aught but the best of the best to go to my grave in?

THE QUEEN. Mend your manners first, sir; and then mend your linen; or you shall have no countenance from me.

PETER. I have naught to do with you, madam, though I well see who wears the breeches in this royal household. I am not skilled in dealing with fine handsome ladies. Leave me to settle my business with your henpecked husband.

THE QUEEN. You shall suffer for this insolence. [*To the King*] Will you, my lord, stand by and hear me spoken to in this tone by a haberdasher?

THE KING [*grinning*] Nay: I am in a merciful mood this morning. The poor man is to be pitied, shivering there in his shirt with his tail torn off.

PETER. Shivering! You lie in your teeth, though you were fifty kings. No man alive shall pity Peter Hardmouth, a dog of lousy Champagne.

THE KING [*going to him*] Ha! A dog of Champagne! Oh, you must pardon this man, madam; for my grandmother hailed from that lousy province; so I also am a dog of Champagne. We know one another's bark. [*Turning on him with bristling teeth*] Eh?

PETER [*growling in his face like a dog*] Grrrr!!!

THE KING [*returning the growl chin to chin*] Grrrr!!!!!!

They repeat this performance, to the great scandal of the Queen, until it develops into a startling imitation of a dog fight.

THE QUEEN [*tearing the two dogs asunder*] Oh, for shame, sir! And you, fellow: I will have you muzzled and led through the streets on a chain and lodged in a kennel.

THE KING. Be merciful, lady. I have asked you for many favors, and had them granted me too, as the world, please God, will soon have proof. Will you deny me this?

THE QUEEN. Will you mock my condition before this

44

insolent man and before the world? I will not endure it.

THE KING. Faith, no, dearest: no mockery. But you have no skill in dealing with the dogs of lousy Champagne. We must pity this poor trembling fellow.

THE QUEEN [*angrily*] He is not trembling.

PETER. No, by all the saints in heaven and devils in hell. Well said, lass.

He nudges her, to her extreme indignation.

THE KING. Hear that, dearest: he calls thee lass. Be kind to him. He is only a poor old cur who has lost half his teeth. His condition would move a heart of stone.

PETER. I may be an old cur; but if I had sworn to hang the six of us as he swore, no shrew should scold me out of it, nor any softbosomed beauty wheedle me out of it. Yah, cry baby! Give her your sword and sit in the corner with her distaff. The grey mare is the better horse here. Do your worst, dame: I like your spunk better than his snivel.

THE QUEEN [*raging*] Send him away, sir. He is too ugly; and his words are disgusting. Such objects should be kept out of my sight: would you have me bear you a monster? Take him away.

THE KING. Away with him. Hurt him not; but let him not come into the Queen's presence. Quick there. Off with him.

The men-at-arms lay hands on Peter who struggles violently.

PETER. Hands off me, spaniels. Arrr! Grrr! [*As they drag him out overpowere*d] Gee-up, Neddy. [*He finishes with a spirited imitation of a donkey's bray*].

THE KING. That is how they build men in Champagne. By the Holy Rood I care not if a bit of him gets into our baby.

THE QUEEN. Oh, for shame! for shame! Have men no decency?

The King snatches her into his arms, laughing bois-terously. The laugh spreads to all the soldiers and cour-

THE SIX OF CALAIS

tiers. The whole camp seems in a hilarious uproar.

THE QUEEN. No no: for shame! for shame!

The King stops her mouth with a kiss. Peter brays
melodiously in the distance.

ANNAJANSKA, THE BOLSHEVIK EMPRESS

FROM THE RUSSIAN OF GREGORY BLESSIPOFF
(ANNAJANSKA, THE WILD GRAND DUCHESS)
A REVOLUTIONARY ROMANCELET

Written in 1917

First Performed London 1918

ANNAJANSKA is frankly a bravura piece. The modern variety theatre demands for its "turns" little plays called sketches, to last twenty minutes or so, and to enable some favorite performer to make a brief but dazzling appearance on some barely passable dramatic pretext. Miss Lillah McCarthy and I, as author and actress, have helped to make one another famous on many serious occasions, from Man and Superman to Androcles; and Mr Charles Ricketts has not disdained to snatch moments from his painting and sculpture to design some wonderful dresses for us. We three unbent as Mrs Siddons, Sir Joshua Reynolds, and Dr Johnson might have unbent, to devise a "turn" for the Coliseum variety theatre. Not that we would set down the art of the variety theatre as something to be condescended to, or our own art as elephantine. We should rather crave indulgence as three novices fresh from the awful legitimacy of the highbrow theatre.

Well, Miss McCarthy and Mr Ricketts justified themselves easily in the glamor of the footlights, to the strains of Tchaikovsky's 1812. I fear I did not. I have received only one compliment on my share; and that was from a friend who said "it is the only one of your works that is not too long." So I have made it a page or two longer, according to my own precept: EMBRACE YOUR REPROACHES: THEY ARE OFTEN GLORIES IN DISGUISE.

ANNAJANSKA, THE BOLSHEVIK EMPRESS

T HE *General's office in a military station on the east
front in Beotia. An office table with a telephone, writing
materials, official papers, etc., is set across the room. At
the end of the table, a comfortable chair for the General. Behind
the chair, a window. Facing it at the other end of the table, a
plain wooden bench. At the side of the table, with its back to the
door, a common chair, with a typewriter before it. Beside the
door, which is opposite the end of the bench, a rack for caps and
coats. There is nobody in the room.*

*General Strammfest enters, followed by Lieutenant Schneide-
kind. They hang up their cloaks and caps. Schneidekind takes a
little longer than Strammfest, who comes to the table.*

STRAMMFEST. Schneidekind.

SCHNEIDEKIND. Yes, sir.

STRAMMFEST. Have you sent my report yet to the government? [*He sits down*].

SCHNEIDEKIND [*coming to the table*] Not yet, sir. Which
government do you wish it sent to? [*He sits down*].

STRAMMFEST. That depends. Whats the latest? Which of
them do you think is most likely to be in power tomorrow
morning?

SCHNEIDEKIND. Well, the provisional government was
going strong yesterday. But today they say that the prime
minister has shot himself, and that the extreme left fellow
has shot all the others.

STRAMMFEST. Yes: thats all very well; but these fellows
always shoot themselves with blank cartridge.

SCHNEIDEKIND. Still, even the blank cartridge means
backing down. I should send the report to the Maximilian-
ists.

STRAMMFEST. Theyre no stronger than the Oppido-
shavians; and in my own opinion the Moderate Red Revo-
lutionaries are as likely to come out on top as either of them.

SCHNEIDEKIND. I can easily put a few carbon sheets in
the typewriter and send a copy each to the lot.

STRAMMFEST. Waste of paper. You might as well send

51

reports to an infant school. [*He throws his head on the table with a groan*].

SCHNEIDEKIND. Tired out, sir?

STRAMMFEST. O Schneidekind, Schneidekind, how can you bear to live?

SCHNEIDEKIND. At my age, sir, I ask myself how can I bear to die?

STRAMMFEST. You are young, young and heartless. You are excited by the revolution: you are attached to abstract things like liberty. But my family has served the Panjandrums of Beotia faithfully for seven centuries. The Panjandrums have kept our place for us at their courts, honored us, promoted us, shed their glory on us, made us what we are. When I hear you young men declaring that you are fighting for civilization, for democracy, for the overthrow of militarism, I ask myself how can a man shed his blood for empty words used by vulgar tradesmen and common laborers: mere wind and stink. [*He rises, exalted by his theme*]. A king is a splendid reality, a man raised above us like a god. You can see him; you can kiss his hand; you can be cheered by his smile and terrified by his frown. I would have died for my Panjandrum as my father died for his father. Your toiling millions were only too honored to receive the toes of our boots in the proper spot for them when they displeased their betters. And now what is left in life for me? [*He relapses into his chair discouraged*]. My Panjandrum is deposed and transported to herd with convicts. The army, his pride and glory, is paraded to hear seditious speeches from penniless rebels, with the colonel actually forced to take the chair and introduce the speaker. I myself am made Commander-in-Chief by my own solicitor: a Jew, Schneidekind! a Hebrew Jew! It seems only yesterday that these things would have been the ravings of a madman: today they are the commonplaces of the gutter press. I live now for three objects only: to defeat the enemy, to restore the Panjandrum, and to hang my solicitor.

SCHNEIDEKIND. Be careful, sir: these are dangerous

views to utter nowadays. What if I were to betray you?

STRAMMFEST. What!

SCHNEIDEKIND. I wont, of course: my own father goes on just like that; but suppose I did?

STRAMMFEST [*chuckling*] I should accuse you of treason to the Revolution, my lad; and they would immediately shoot you, unless you cried and asked to see your mother before you died, when they would probably change their minds and make you a brigadier. Enough. [*He rises and expands his chest*]. I feel the better for letting myself go. To business. [*He takes up a telegram; opens it; and is thunderstruck by its contents*]. Great heaven! [*He collapsed into his chair*]. This is the worst blow of all.

SCHNEIDEKIND. What has happened? Are we beaten?

STRAMMFEST. Man: do you think that a mere defeat could strike me down as this news does: I, who have been defeated thirteen times since the war began? O, my master, my master, my Panjandrum! [*He is convulsed with sobs*].

SCHNEIDEKIND. They have killed him?

STRAMMFEST. A dagger has been struck through his heart—

SCHNEIDEKIND. Good God!

STRAMMFEST. —and through mine, through mine.

SCHNEIDEKIND [*relieved*] Oh: a metaphorical dagger. I thought you meant a real one. What has happened?

STRAMMFEST. His daughter, the Grand Duchess Anna-janska, she whom the Panjandrina loved beyond all her other children, has—has—[*he cannot finish*].

SCHNEIDEKIND. Committed suicide?

STRAMMFEST. No. Better if she had. Oh, far far better.

SCHNEIDEKIND [*in hushed tones*] Left the Church?

STRAMMFEST [*shocked*] Certainly not. Do not blaspheme, young man.

SCHNEIDEKIND. Asked for the vote?

STRAMMFEST. I would have given it to her with both hands to save her from this.

SCHNEIDEKIND. Save her from what? Dash it, sir, out

53

with it.

STRAMMFEST. She has joined the Revolution.

SCHNEIDEKIND. But so have you, sir. Weve all joined the Revolution. She doesnt mean it any more than we do.

STRAMMFEST. Heaven grant you may be right! But that is not the worst. She has eloped with a young officer. Eloped, Schneidekind, eloped!

SCHNEIDEKIND [not particularly impressed] Yes, sir.

STRAMMFEST. Annajanska, the beautiful, the innocent, my master's daughter! [He buries his face in his hands].

The telephone rings.

SCHNEIDEKIND [taking the receiver] Yes: G.H.Q. Yes. . . . Dont bawl: I'm not a general. Who is it speaking? . . . Why didnt you say so? dont you know your duty? Next time you will lose your stripe. . . . Oh, theyve made you a colonel, have they? Well, theyve made me a field-marshal: now what have you to say? . . . Look here: what did you ring up for? I cant spend the day here listening to your cheek. . . . What! the Grand Duchess! [Strammfest starts]. Where did you catch her?

STRAMMFEST [snatching the telephone and listening for the answer] Speak louder, will you: I am a General . . . I know that, you dolt. Have you captured the officer that was with her? . . . Damnation! You shall answer for this: you let him go: he bribed you. . . . You must have seen him: the fellow is in the full dress court uniform of the Panderobajensky Hussars. I give you twelve hours to catch him or . . . whats that you say about the devil? Are you swearing at me, you . . . Thousand thunders! [To Schneidekind] The swine says that the Grand Duchess is a devil incarnate. [Into the telephone] Filthy traitor: is that the way you dare speak of the daughter of our anointed Panjandrum? I'll—

SCHNEIDEKIND [pulling the telephone from his lips] Take care, sir.

STRAMMFEST. I wont take care: I'll have him shot. Let go that telephone.

SCHNEIDEKIND. But for her own sake, sir—

STRAMMFEST. Eh?

SCHNEIDEKIND. For her own sake they had better send her here. She will be safe in your hands.

STRAMMFEST [*yielding the receiver*] You are right. Be civil to him. I should choke [*he sits down*].

SCHNEIDEKIND [*into the telephone*] Hullo. Never mind all that: it's only a fellow here who has been fooling with the telephone. I had to leave the room for a moment. Wash out; and send the girl along. We'll jolly soon teach her to behave herself here. . . . Oh, youve sent her already. Then why the devil didnt you say so, you— [*he hangs up the telephone angrily*]. Just fancy: they started her off this morning: and all this is because the fellow likes to get on the telephone and hear himself talk now that he is a colonel. [*The telephone rings again. He snatches the receiver furiously*] Whats the matter now? . . . [*To the General*] It's our own people downstairs. [*Into the receiver*] Here! do you suppose Ive nothing else to do than to hang on to the telephone all day? . . . Whats that? Not men enough to hold her! What do you mean? [*To the General*] She is there, sir.

STRAMMFEST. Tell them to send her up. I shall have to receive her without even rising, without kissing her hand, to keep up appearances before the escort. It will break my heart.

SCHNEIDEKIND [*into the receiver*] Send her up. . . . Tcha! [*He hangs up the receiver*]. He says she is half way up already: they couldnt hold her.

The Grand Duchess bursts into the room, dragging with her two exhausted soldiers hanging on desperately to her arms. She is enveloped from head to foot by a fur-lined cloak, and wears a fur cap.

SCHNEIDEKIND [*pointing to the bench*] At the word Go, place your prisoner on the bench in a sitting posture; and take your seats right and left of her. Go.

The two soldiers make a supreme effort to force her to sit down. She flings them back so that they are forced to sit on the bench to save themselves from falling backwards over it, and

55

is herself dragged into sitting between them. The second soldier, holding on tight to the Grand Duchess with one hand, produces papers with the other, and waves them towards Schneidekind, who takes them from him and passes them on to the General. He opens them and reads them with a grave expression.

SCHNEIDEKIND. Be good enough to wait, prisoner, until the General has read the papers on your case.

THE GRAND DUCHESS [*to the soldiers*] Let go. [*To Strammfest*] Tell them to let go, or I'll upset the bench backwards and bash our three heads on the floor.

FIRST SOLDIER. No, little mother. Have mercy on the poor.

STRAMMFEST [*growling over the edge of the paper he is reading*] Hold your tongue.

THE GRAND DUCHESS [*blazing*] Me, or the soldier?

STRAMMFEST [*horrified*] The soldier, madam.

THE GRAND DUCHESS. Tell him to let go.

STRAMMFEST. Release the lady.

The soldiers take their hands off her. One of them wipes his fevered brow. The other sucks his wrist.

SCHNEIDEKIND [*fiercely*] 'ttention!

The two soldiers sit up stiffly.

THE GRAND DUCHESS. Oh, let the poor man suck his wrist. It may be poisoned. I bit it.

STRAMMFEST [*shocked*] You bit a common soldier!

GRAND DUCHESS. Well, I offered to cauterize it with the poker in the office stove. But he was afraid. What more could I do?

SCHNEIDEKIND. Why did you bite him, prisoner?

THE GRAND DUCHESS. He would not let go.

STRAMMFEST. Did he let go when you bit him?

THE GRAND DUCHESS. No. [*Patting the soldier on the back*] You should give the man a cross for his devotion. I could not go on eating him; so I brought him along with me.

STRAMMFEST. Prisoner—

THE GRAND DUCHESS. Dont call me prisoner, General Strammfest. My grandmother dandled you on her knee.

THE BOLSHEVIK EMPRESS

STRAMMFEST [*bursting into tears*] O God, yes. Believe me, my heart is what it was then.

THE GRAND DUCHESS. Your brain also is what it was then. I will not be addressed by you as prisoner.

STRAMMFEST. I may not, for your own sake, call you by your rightful and most sacred titles. What am I to call you?

THE GRAND DUCHESS. The Revolution has made us comrades. Call me comrade.

STRAMMFEST. I had rather die.

THE GRAND DUCHESS. Then call me Annajanska; and I will call you Peter Piper, as grandmamma did.

STRAMMFEST [*painfully agitated*] Schneidekind: you must speak to her: I cannot—[*he breaks down*].

SCHNEIDEKIND [*officially*] The Republic of Beotia has been compelled to confine the Panjandrum and his family, for their own safety, within certain bounds. You have broken those bounds.

STRAMMFEST [*taking the word from him*] You are—I must say it—a prisoner. What am I to do with you?

THE GRAND DUCHESS. You should have thought of that before you arrested me.

STRAMMFEST. Come, come, prisoner! do you know what will happen to you if you compel me to take a sterner tone with you?

THE GRAND DUCHESS. No. But I know what will happen to you.

STRAMMFEST. Pray what, prisoner?

THE GRAND DUCHESS. Clergyman's sore throat.

Schneidekind splutters: drops a paper; and conceals his laughter under the table.

STRAMMFEST [*thunderously*] Lieutenant Schneidekind.

SCHNEIDEKIND [*in a stifled voice*] Yes, sir. [*The table vibrates visibly*].

STRAMMFEST. Come out of it, you fool: youre upsetting the ink.

Schneidekind emerges, red in the face with suppressed mirth.

57

STRAMMFEST. Why dont you laugh? Dont you appreciate Her Imperial Highness's joke?

SCHNEIDEKIND [*suddenly becoming solemn*] I dont want to, sir.

STRAMMFEST. Laugh at once, sir. I order you to laugh.

SCHNEIDEKIND [*with a touch of temper*] I really cant, sir. [*He sits down decisively*].

STRAMMFEST [*growling at him*] Yah! [*He turns impressively to the Grand Duchess*] Your Imperial Highness desires me to address you as comrade?

THE GRAND DUCHESS [*rising and waving a red handkerchief*] Long live the Revolution, comrade!

STRAMMFEST [*rising and saluting*] Proletarians of all lands, unite. Lieutenant Schneidekind: you will rise and sing the Marseillaise.

SCHNEIDEKIND [*rising*] But I cannot, sir. I have no voice, no ear.

STRAMMFEST. Then sit down; and bury your shame in your typewriter [*Schneidekind sits down*]. Comrade Annajanska: you have eloped with a young officer.

THE GRAND DUCHESS [*astounded*] General Strammfest: you lie.

STRAMMFEST. Denial, comrade, is useless. It is through that officer that your movements have been traced. [*The Grand Duchess is suddenly enlightened, and seems amused. Strammfest continues in a forensic manner*] He joined you at the Golden Anchor in Hakonsburg. You gave us the slip there; but the officer was traced to Potterdam, where you rejoined him and went alone to Premsylople. What have you done with that unhappy young man? Where is he?

THE GRAND DUCHESS [*pretending to whisper an important secret*] Where he has always been.

STRAMMFEST [*eagerly*] Where is that?

THE GRAND DUCHESS [*impetuously*] In your imagination. I came alone. I am alone. Hundreds of officers travel every day from Hakonsburg to Potterdam. What do I know about them?

STRAMMFEST. They travel in khaki. They do not travel in full dress court uniform as this man did.

SCHNEIDEKIND. Only officers who are eloping with grand duchesses wear court uniform: otherwise the grand duchesses could not be seen with them.

STRAMMFEST. Hold your tongue. [*Schneidekind, in high dudgeon, folds his arms and retires from the conversation. The General returns to his paper and to his examination of the Grand Duchess*] This officer travelled with your passport. What have you to say to that?

THE GRAND DUCHESS. Bosh! How could a man travel with a woman's passport?

STRAMMFEST. It is quite simple, as you very well know. A dozen travellers arrive at the boundary. The official collects their passports. He counts twelve persons; then counts the passports. If there are twelve, he is satisfied.

THE GRAND DUCHESS. Then how do you know that one of the passports was mine?

STRAMMFEST. A waiter at the Potterdam Hotel looked at the officer's passport when he was in his bath. It was your passport.

THE GRAND DUCHESS. Stuff! Why did he not have me arrested?

STRAMMFEST. When the waiter returned to the hotel with the police the officer had vanished; and you were there with your own passport. They knouted him.

THE GRAND DUCHESS. Oh! Strammfest: send these men away. I must speak to you alone.

STRAMMFEST [*rising in horror*] No: this is the last straw: I cannot consent. It is impossible, utterly, eternally impossible, that a daughter of the Imperial House should speak to anyone alone, were it even her own husband.

THE GRAND DUCHESS. You forget that there is an exception. She may speak to a child alone. [*She rises*] Strammfest: you have been dandled on my grandmother's knee. By that gracious action the dowager Panjandrina made you a child forever. So did Nature, by the way. I order you to speak to

59

me alone. Do you hear? I order you. For seven hundred years no member of your family has ever disobeyed an order from a member of mine. Will you disobey me?

STRAMMFEST. There is an alternative to obedience. The dead cannot disobey. [*He takes out his pistol and places the muzzle against his temple*].

SCHNEIDEKIND [*snatching the pistol from him*] For God's sake, General—

STRAMMFEST [*attacking him furiously to recover the weapon*] Dog of a subaltern, restore that pistol, and my honor.

SCHNEIDEKIND [*reaching out with the pistol to the Grand Duchess*] Take it: quick: he is as strong as a bull.

THE GRAND DUCHESS [*snatching it*] Aha! Leave the room, all of you except the General. At the double! lightning! electricity! [*she fires shot after shot, spattering bullets about the ankles of the soldiers. They fly precipitately. She turns to Schneidekind, who has by this time been flung on the floor by the General*] You too. [*He scrambles up*]. March [*he flies to the door*].

SCHNEIDEKIND [*turning at the door*] For your own sake, comrade—

THE GRAND DUCHESS [*indignantly*] Comrade! You!!! Go. [*She fires two more shots. He vanishes*].

STRAMMFEST [*making an impulsive movement towards her*] My Imperial Mistress—

THE GRAND DUCHESS. Stop. I have one bullet left, if you attempt to take this from me [*putting the pistol to her temple*].

STRAMMFEST [*recoiling, and covering his eyes with his hands*]. No no: put it down: put it down. I promise everything: I swear anything; put it down, I implore you.

THE GRAND DUCHESS [*throwing it on the table*] There!

STRAMMFEST [*uncovering his eyes*] Thank God!

THE GRAND DUCHESS [*gently*] Strammfest: I am your comrade. Am I nothing more to you?

STRAMMFEST [*falling on his knee*] You are, God help me, all that is left to me of the only power I recognize on earth. [*He kisses her hand*].

60

THE GRAND DUCHESS [*indulgently*] Idolater! When will you learn that our strength has never been in ourselves, but in your illusions about us? [*She shakes off her kindliness, and sits down in his chair*] Now tell me, what are your orders? And do you mean to obey them?

STRAMMFEST [*starting like a goaded ox, and blundering fretfully about the room*] How can I obey six different dictators, and not one gentleman among the lot of them? One of them orders me to make peace with the foreign enemy. Another orders me to offer all the neutral countries 48 hours to choose between adopting his views on the single tax and being instantly invaded and annihilated. A third orders me to go to a damned Socialist Conference and explain that Beotia will allow no annexations and no indemnities, and merely wishes to establish the Kingdom of Heaven on Earth throughout the universe. [*He finishes behind Schneidekind's chair*].

THE GRAND DUCHESS. Damn their trifling?

STRAMMFEST. I thank Your Imperial Highness from the bottom of my heart for that expression. Europe thanks you.

THE GRAND DUCHESS. M'yes; but—[*rising*] Strammfest: you know that your cause—the cause of the dynasty—is lost.

STRAMMFEST. You must not say so. It is treason, even from you. [*He sinks, discouraged, into the chair, and covers his face with his hand*].

THE GRAND DUCHESS. Do not deceive yourself, General: never again will a Panjandrum reign in Beotia. [*She walks slowly across the room, brooding bitterly, and thinking aloud*]. We are so decayed, so out of date, so feeble, so wicked in our own despite, that we have come at last to will our own destruction.

STRAMMFEST. You are uttering blasphemy.

THE GRAND DUCHESS. All great truths begin as blasphemies. All the king's horses and all the king's men cannot set up my father's throne again. If they could, you would have done it, would you not?

61

STRAMMFEST. God knows I would!

THE GRAND DUCHESS. You really mean that? You would keep the people in their hopeless squalid misery? you would fill those infamous prisons again with the noblest spirits in the land? you would thrust the rising sun of liberty back into the sea of blood from which it has risen? And all because there was in the middle of the dirt and ugliness and horror a little patch of court splendor in which you could stand with a few orders on your uniform, and yawn day after day and night after night in unspeakable boredom until your grave yawned wider still, and you fell into it because you had nothing better to do. How can you be so stupid, so heartless?

STRAMMFEST. You must be mad to think of royalty in such a way. I never yawned at court. The dogs yawned; but that was because they were dogs: they had no imagination, no ideals, no sense of honor and dignity to sustain them.

THE GRAND DUCHESS. My poor Strammfest: you were not often enough at court to tire of it. You were mostly soldiering; and when you came home to have a new order pinned on your breast, your happiness came through looking at my father and mother and at me, and adoring us. Was that not so?

STRAMMFEST. Do you reproach me with it? I am not ashamed of it.

THE GRAND DUCHESS. Oh, it was all very well for you, Strammfest. But think of me, of me! standing there for you to gape at, and knowing that I was no goddess, but only a girl like any other girl! It was cruelty to animals: you could have stuck up a wax doll or a golden calf to worship; it would not have been bored.

STRAMMFEST. Stop; or I shall renounce my allegiance to you. I have had women flogged for such seditious chatter as this.

THE GRAND DUCHESS. Do not provoke me to send a bullet through your head for reminding me of it.

STRAMMFEST. You always had low tastes. You are no

true daughter of the Panjandrums: you are a changeling, thrust into the Panjandrina's bed by some profligate nurse. I have heard stories of your childhood: of how—

THE GRAND DUCHESS. Ha, ha! Yes: they took me to the circus when I was a child. It was my first moment of happiness, my first glimpse of heaven. I ran away and joined the troupe. They caught me and dragged me back to my gilded cage; but I had tasted freedom; and they never could make me forget it.

STRAMMFEST. Freedom! To be the slave of an acrobat! to be exhibited to the public! to—

THE GRAND DUCHESS. Oh, I was trained to that. I had learnt that part of the business at court.

STRAMMFEST. You had not been taught to strip yourself half naked and turn head over heels—

THE GRAND DUCHESS. Man: I wanted to get rid of my swaddling clothes and turn head over heels. I wanted to, I wanted to, I wanted to. I can do it still. Shall I do it now?

STRAMMFEST. If you do, I swear I will throw myself from the window so that I may meet your parents in heaven without having my medals torn from my breast by them.

THE GRAND DUCHESS. Oh, you are incorrigible. You are mad, infatuated. You will not believe that we royal divinities are mere common flesh and blood even when we step down from our pedestals and tell you ourselves what a fool you are. I will argue no more with you: I will use my power. At a word from me your men will turn against you: already half of them do not salute you; and you dare not punish them: you have to pretend not to notice it.

STRAMMFEST. It is not for you to taunt me with that if it is so.

THE GRAND DUCHESS [haughtily] Taunt! I condescend to taunt! To taunt a common General! You forget yourself, sir.

STRAMMFEST [dropping on his knee submissively] Now at last you speak like your royal self.

THE GRAND DUCHESS. Oh, Strammfest, Strammfest, they have driven your slavery into your very bones. Why did you

63

not spit in my face?

STRAMMFEST [*rising with a shudder*] God forbid!

THE GRAND DUCHESS. Well, since you will be my slave, take your orders from me. I have not come here to save our wretched family and our bloodstained crown. I am come to save the Revolution.

STRAMMFEST. Stupid as I am, I have come to think that I had better save that than save nothing. But what will the Revolution do for the people? Do not be deceived by the fine speeches of the revolutionary leaders and the pamphlets of the revolutionary writers. How much liberty is there where t h e y have gained the upper hand? Are they not hanging, shooting, imprisoning as much as ever we did? Do they ever tell the people the truth? No: if the truth does not suit them they spread lies instead, and make it a crime to tell the truth.

THE GRAND DUCHESS. Of course they do. Why should they not?

STRAMMFEST [*hardly able to believe his ears*] Why should they not!

THE GRAND DUCHESS. Yes: why should they not? We did it. You did it, whip in hand: you flogged women for teaching children to read.

STRAMMFEST. To read sedition. To read Karl Marx.

THE GRAND DUCHESS. Pshaw! How could they learn to read the Bible without learning to read Karl Marx? Why do you not stand to your guns and justify what you did, instead of making silly excuses. Do you suppose *I* think flogging a woman worse than flogging a man? I, who am a woman myself!

STRAMMFEST. I am at a loss to understand your Imperial Highness. You seem to me to contradict yourself.

THE GRAND DUCHESS. Nonsense! I say that if the people cannot govern themselves, they must be governed by somebody. If they will not do their duty without being half forced and half humbugged, somebody must force them and humbug them. Some energetic and capable minority must al-

64

ways be in power. Well, I am on the side of the energetic minority whose principles I agree with. The Revolution is as cruel as we were; but its aims are my aims. Therefore I stand for the Revolution.

STRAMMFEST. You do not know what you are saying. This is pure Bolshevism. Are you, the daughter of a Panjandrum, a Bolshevist?

THE GRAND DUCHESS. I am anything that will make the world less like a prison and more like a circus.

STRAMMFEST. Ah! You still want to be a circus star.

THE GRAND DUCHESS. Yes, and be billed as the Bolshevik Empress. Nothing shall stop me. You have your orders, General Strammfest: save the Revolution.

STRAMMFEST. What Revolution? Which Revolution? No two of your rabble of revolutionists mean the same thing by the Revolution. What can save a mob in which every man is rushing in a different direction?

THE GRAND DUCHESS. I will tell you. The war can save it.

STRAMMFEST. The war?

THE GRAND DUCHESS. Yes, the war. Only a great common danger and a great common duty can unite us and weld these wrangling factions into a solid commonwealth.

STRAMMFEST. Bravo! War sets everything right: I have always said so. But what is a united people without a united army? And what can *I* do? I am only a soldier. I cannot make speeches: I have won no victories: they will not rally to my call [*again he sinks into his chair with his former gesture of discouragement*].

THE GRAND DUCHESS. Are you sure they will not rally to mine?

STRAMMFEST. Oh, if only you were a man and a soldier!

THE GRAND DUCHESS. Suppose I find you a man and a soldier?

STRAMMFEST [*rising in a fury*] Ah! the scoundrel you eloped with! You think you will shove this fellow into an army command, over my head. Never.

THE GRAND DUCHESS. You promised everything. You

65

swore anything. [*She marches as if in front of a regiment*]. I know that this man alone can rouse the army to enthusiasm.

STRAMMFEST. Delusion! Folly! He is some circus acrobat; and you are in love with him.

THE GRAND DUCHESS. I swear I am not in love with him. I swear I will never marry him.

STRAMMFEST. Then who is he?

THE GRAND DUCHESS. Anybody in the world but you would have guessed long ago. He is under your very eyes.

STRAMMFEST [*staring past her right and left*] Where?

THE GRAND DUCHESS. Look out of the window.

He rushes to the window, looking for the officer. The Grand Duchess takes off her cloak and appears in the uniform of the Panderobajensky Hussars.

STRAMMFEST [*peering through the window*] Where is he? I can see no one.

THE GRAND DUCHESS. Here, silly.

STRAMMFEST [*turning*] You! Great Heavens! The Bolshevik Empress!

AUGUSTUS DOES HIS BIT

AN UNOFFICIAL DRAMATIC TRACT ON WAR SAVING
AND COGNATE TOPICS BY THE AUTHOR OF THE
INCA OF PERUSALEM
(A TRUE TO LIFE FARCE)

Written in 1916

First Performed London 1917

I WISH to express my gratitude for certain good offices which Augustus secured for me in January 1917. I had been invited to visit the theatre of war in Flanders by the Commander-in-Chief: an invitation which was, under the circumstances, a summons to duty. Thus I had occasion to spend some days in procuring the necessary passports and other official facilities for my journey. It happened just then that the Stage Society gave a performance of this little play. It opened the heart of every official to me. I have always been treated with distinguished consideration in my contacts with bureaucracy during the war; but on this occasion I found myself *persona grata* in the highest degree. There was only one word when the formalities were disposed of; and that was "We are up against Augustus all day." The shewing-up of Augustus scandalized one or two innocent and patriotic critics who regarded the prowess of the British army as inextricably bound up with Highcastle prestige. But our Government departments knew better: their problem was how to win the war with Augustus on their backs, well-meaning, brave, patriotic, but obstructively fussy, self-important, imbecile, and disastrous.

Save for the satisfaction of being able to laugh at Augustus in the theatre, nothing, as far as I know, came of my dramatic reduction of him to absurdity. Generals, admirals, Prime Ministers and Controllers, not to mention Emperors, Kaisers and Tsars, were scrapped remorselessly at home and abroad, for their sins or services, as the case might be. But Augustus stood like the Eddystone in a storm, and stands so to this day. He gave us his word that he was indispensable; and we took it.

AUGUSTUS DOES HIS BIT

THE *Mayor's parlor in the Town Hall of Little Pifflington. Lord Augustus Highcastle, a distinguished member of the governing class, in the uniform of a colonel,
and very well preserved at 45, is comfortably seated at a writing
table with his heels on it, reading The Morning Post. The door
faces him, a little to his left, at the other side of the room. The
window is behind him. In the fireplace, a gas stove. On the table
a bell button and a telephone. Portraits of past Mayors, in robes
and gold chains, adorn the walls. An elderly clerk with a short
white beard and whiskers, and a very red nose, shuffles in.*

AUGUSTUS [*hastily putting aside his paper and replacing his
feet on the floor*] Hullo! Who are you?

THE CLERK. The staff [*a slight impediment in his speech
adds to the impression of incompetence produced by his age and
appearance*].

AUGUSTUS. You the staff! What do you mean, man?

THE CLERK. What I say. There aint anybody else.

AUGUSTUS. Tush! Where are the others?

THE CLERK. At the front.

AUGUSTUS. Quite right. Most proper. Why arnt you at
the front?

THE CLERK. Over age. Fiftyseven.

AUGUSTUS. But you can still do your bit. Many an older
man is in the G.R.'s, or volunteering for home defence.

THE CLERK. I have volunteered.

AUGUSTUS. Then why are you not in uniform?

THE CLERK. They said they wouldnt have me if I was
given away with a pound of tea. Told me to go home and
not be an old silly. [*A sense of unbearable wrong, til now only
smouldering in him, bursts into flame*]. Young Bill Knight, that
I took with me, got two and sevenpence. I got nothing. Is it
justice? This country is going to the dogs, if you ask me.

AUGUSTUS [*rising indignantly*] I do not ask you, sir; and I
will not allow you to say such things in my presence. Our
statesmen are the greatest known to history. Our generals
are invincible. Our army is the admiration of the world.

71

[*Furiously*] How dare you tell me that the country is going to the dogs!

THE CLERK. Why did they give young Bill Knight two and sevenpence, and not give me even my tram fare? Do you call that being great statesmen? As good as robbing me, I call it.

AUGUSTUS. Thats enough. Leave the room. [*He sits down and takes up his pen, settling himself to work. The clerk shuffles to the door. Augustus adds, with cold politeness*] Send me the Secretary.

THE CLERK. I'm the Secretary. I cant leave the room and send myself to you at the same time, can I?

AUGUSTUS. Dont be insolent. Where is the gentleman I have been corresponding with: Mr Horatio Floyd Beamish?

THE CLERK [*returning and bowing*] Here. Me.

AUGUSTUS. You! Ridiculous. What right have you to call yourself by a pretentious name of that sort?

THE CLERK. You may drop the Horatio Floyd. Beamish is good enough for me.

AUGUSTUS. Is there nobody else to take my instructions?

THE CLERK. It's me or nobody. And for two pins I'd chuck it. Dont you drive me too far. Old uns like me is up in the world now.

AUGUSTUS. If we were not at war, I should discharge you on the spot for disrespectful behavior. But England is in danger; and I cannot think of my personal dignity at such a moment. [*Shouting at him*] Dont you think of yours, either, worm that you are; or I'll have you arrested under the Defence of the Realm Act, double quick.

THE CLERK. What do I care about the realm? They done me out of two and seven—

AUGUSTUS. Oh, damn your two and seven! Did you receive my letters?

THE CLERK. Yes.

AUGUSTUS. I addressed a meeting here last night—went straight to the platform from the train. I wrote to you that I should expect you to be present and report yourself. Why

72

did you not do so?

THE CLERK. The police wouldnt let me on the platform.

AUGUSTUS. Did you tell them who you were?

THE CLERK. They knew who I was. Thats why they wouldnt let me up.

AUGUSTUS. This is too silly for anything. This town wants waking up. I made the best recruiting speech I ever made in my life; and not a man joined.

THE CLERK. What did you expect? You told them our gallant fellows is falling at the rate of a thousand a day in the big push. Dying for Little Pifflington, you says. Come and take their places, you says. That aint the way to recruit.

AUGUSTUS. But I expressly told them their widows would have pensions.

THE CLERK. I heard you. Would have been all right if it had been the widows you wanted to get round.

AUGUSTUS [*rising angrily*] This town is inhabited by dastards. I say it with a full sense of responsibility, dastards! They call themselves Englishmen; and they are afraid to fight.

THE CLERK. Afraid to fight! You should see them on a Saturday night.

AUGUSTUS. Yes: they fight one another; but they wont fight the Germans.

THE CLERK. They got grudges again one another: how can they have grudges again the Huns that they never saw? Theyve no imagination: thats what it is. Bring the Huns here; and theyll quarrel with them fast enough.

AUGUSTUS [*returning to his seat with a grunt of disgust*] Mf! Theyll have them here if theyre not careful. [*Seated*] Have you carried out my orders about the war saving?

THE CLERK. Yes.

AUGUSTUS. The allowance of petrol has been reduced by three quarters?

THE CLERK. It has.

AUGUSTUS. And you have told the motor-car people to come here and arrange to start munition work now that

73

their motor business is stopped?

THE CLERK. It aint stopped. Theyre busier than ever.

AUGUSTUS. Busy at what?

THE CLERK. Making small cars.

AUGUSTUS. New cars!

THE CLERK. The old cars only do twelve miles to the gallon. Everybody has to have a car that will do thirtyfive now.

AUGUSTUS. Cant they take the train?

THE CLERK. There aint no trains now. Theyve tore up the rails and sent them to the front.

AUGUSTUS. Psha!

THE CLERK. Well, we have to get about somehow.

AUGUSTUS. This is perfectly monstrous. Not in the least what I intended.

THE CLERK. Hell—

AUGUSTUS. Sir!

THE CLERK [*explaining*] Hell, they says, is paved with good intentions.

AUGUSTUS [*springing to his feet*] Do you mean to insinuate that hell is paved with m y good intentions—with the good intentions of His Majesty's Government?

THE CLERK. I dont mean to insinuate anything until the Defence of the Realm Act is repealed. It aint safe.

AUGUSTUS. They told me that this town had set an example to all England in the matter of economy. I came down here to promise the Mayor a knighthood for his exertions.

THE CLERK. The Mayor! Where do *I* come in?

AUGUSTUS. You dont come in. You go out. This is a fool of a place. I'm greatly disappointed. Deeply disappointed. [*Flinging himself back into his chair*] Disgusted.

THE CLERK. What more can we do? Weve shut up everything. The picture gallery is shut. The museum is shut. The theatres and picture shows is shut: I havnt seen a movy picture for six months.

AUGUSTUS. Man, man: do you w a n t to see picture shows when the Hun is at the gate?

74

AUGUSTUS DOES HIS BIT

THE CLERK [*mournfully*] I dont now, though it drove me melancholy mad at first. I was on the point of taking a pennorth of rat poison—

AUGUSTUS. Why didnt you?

THE CLERK. Because a friend advised me to take to drink instead. That saved my life, though it makes me very poor company in the mornings, as [*hiccuping*] perhaps youve noticed.

AUGUSTUS. Well, upon my soul! You are not ashamed to stand there and confess yourself a disgusting drunkard.

THE CLERK. Well, what of it? We're at war now; and everything's changed. Besides, I should lose my job here if I stood drinking at the bar. I'm a respectable man and must buy my drink and take it home with me. And they wont serve me with less than a quart. If youd told me before the war that I could get through a quart of whisky in a day, I shouldnt have believed you. Thats the good of war: it brings out powers in a man that he never suspected himself capable of. You said so yourself in your speech last night.

AUGUSTUS. I did not know that I was talking to an imbecile. You ought to be ashamed of yourself. There must be an end of this drunken slacking. I'm going to establish a new order of things here. I shall come down every morning before breakfast until things are properly in train. Have a cup of coffee and two rolls for me here every morning at half-past ten.

THE CLERK. You cant have no rolls. The only baker that baked rolls was a Hun; and he's been interned.

AUGUSTUS. Quite right, too. And was there no Englishman to take his place?

THE CLERK. There was. But he was caught spying; and they took him up to London and shot him.

AUGUSTUS. Shot an Englishman!

THE CLERK. Well, it stands to reason if the Germans wanted a spy they wouldnt employ a German that everybody would suspect, dont it?

AUGUSTUS [*rising again*] Do you mean to say, you scoun-

75

drel, that an Englishman is capable of selling his country to the enemy for gold?

THE CLERK. Not as a general thing I wouldnt say it; but theres men here would sell their own mothers for two coppers if they got the chance.

AUGUSTUS. Beamish: it's an ill bird that fouls its own nest.

THE CLERK. It wasnt me that let Little Pifflington get foul. *I* dont belong to the governing classes. I only tell you why you cant have no rolls.

AUGUSTUS [*intensely irritated*] Can you tell me where I can find an intelligent being to take my orders?

THE CLERK. One of the street sweepers used to teach in the school until it was shut up for the sake of economy. Will he do?

AUGUSTUS. What! You mean to tell me that when the lives of the gallant fellows in our trenches, and the fate of the British Empire, depend on our keeping up the supply of shells, you are wasting money on sweeping the streets?

THE CLERK. We have to. We dropped it for a while; but the infant death rate went up something frightful.

AUGUSTUS. What matters the death rate of Little Pifflington in a moment like this? Think of our gallant soldiers, not of your squalling infants.

THE CLERK. If you want soldiers you must have children. You cant buy em in boxes, like toy soldiers.

AUGUSTUS. Beamish: the long and short of it is, you are no patriot. Go downstairs to your office; and have that gas stove taken away and replaced by an ordinary grate. The Board of Trade has urged on me the necessity for economizing gas.

THE CLERK. Our orders from the Minister of Munitions is to use gas instead of coal, because it saves material. Which is it to be?

AUGUSTUS [*bawling furiously at him*] Both! Dont criticize your orders: obey them. Yours not to reason why: yours but to do and die. Thats war. [*Cooling down*] Have you anything else to say?

76

THE CLERK. Yes: I want a rise.

AUGUSTUS [*reeling against the table in his horror*] A rise! Horatio Floyd Beamish: do you know that we are at war?

THE CLERK [*feebly ironical*] I have noticed something about it in the papers. Heard you mention it once or twice, now I come to think of it.

AUGUSTUS. Our gallant fellows are dying in the trenches; and you want a rise!

THE CLERK. What are they dying for? To keep me alive, aint it? Well, whats the good of that if I'm dead of hunger by the time they come back?

AUGUSTUS. Everybody else is making sacrifices without a thought of self; and you—

THE CLERK. Not half, they aint. Wheres the baker's sacrifice? Wheres the coal merchant's? Wheres the butcher's? Charging me double: thats how they sacrifice themselves. Well, I want to sacrifice myself that way too. Just double next Saturday: double and not a penny less; or no secretary for you [*he stiffens himself shakily, and makes resolutely for the door*].

AUGUSTUS [*looking after him contemptuously*] Go: miserable pro-German.

THE CLERK [*rushing back and facing him*] Who are you calling a pro-German?

AUGUSTUS. Another word, and I charge you under the Act with discouraging me. Go.

The clerk blenches and goes out, cowed.

The telephone rings.

AUGUSTUS [*taking up the telephone receiver*] Hallo . . . Yes: who are you? . . . oh, Blueloo, is it? . . . Yes: theres nobody in the room: fire away . . . What? . . . A spy! . . . A woman! . . . Yes: I brought it down with me. Do you suppose I'm such a fool as to let it out of my hands? Why, it gives a list of all our anti-aircraft emplacements from Ramsgate to Skegness. The Germans would give a million for it —what? . . . But how could she possibly know about it? I havnt mentioned it to a soul, except, of course, dear Lucy.

. . . Oh, Toto and Lady Popham and that lot: they dont count: theyre all right. I mean that I havnt mentioned it to any Germans. . . . Pooh! Dont you be nervous, old chap. I know you think me a fool; but I'm not such a fool as all that. If she tries to get it out of me I'll have her in the Tower before you ring up again. [*The clerk returns*]. Sh-sh! Somebody's just come in: ring off. Goodbye. [*He hangs up the receiver*].

THE CLERK. Are you engaged? [*His manner is strangely softened*].

AUGUSTUS. What business is that of yours? However, if you will take the trouble to read the society papers for this week, you will see that I am engaged to the Honorable Lucy Popham, youngest daughter of—

THE CLERK. That aint what I mean. Can you see a female?

AUGUSTUS. Of course I can see a female as easily as a male. Do you suppose I'm blind?

THE CLERK. You dont seem to follow me, somehow. Theres a female downstairs: what you might call a lady. She wants to know can you see her if I let her up.

AUGUSTUS. Oh, you mean am I disengaged. Tell the lady I have just received news of the greatest importance which will occupy my entire attention for the rest of the day, and that she must write for an appointment.

THE CLERK. I'll ask her to explain her business to me. *I* aint above talking to a handsome young female when I get the chance [*going*].

AUGUSTUS. Stop. Does she seem to be a person of consequence?

THE CLERK. A regular marchioness, if you ask me.

AUGUSTUS. Hm! Beautiful, did you say?

THE CLERK. A human chrysanthemum, sir, believe me.

AUGUSTUS. It will be extremely inconvenient for me to see her; but the country is in danger; and we must not consider our own comfort. Think how our gallant fellows are suffering in the trenches! Shew her up. [*The clerk makes for the door, whistling the latest popular love ballad*]. Stop whistling instantly, sir. This is not a casino.

THE CLERK. Aint it? You just wait til you see her. [*He goes out*].

Augustus produces a mirror, a comb, and a pot of moustache pomade from the drawer of the writing-table, and sits down before the mirror to put some touches to his toilet.

The clerk returns, devotedly ushering a very attractive lady, brilliantly dressed. She has a dainty wallet hanging from her wrist. Augustus hastily covers up his toilet apparatus with The Morning Post, and rises in an attitude of pompous condescension.

THE CLERK [*to Augustus*] Here she is. [*To the lady*] May I offer you a chair, lady? [*He places a chair at the writing-table opposite Augustus, and steals out on tiptoe*].

AUGUSTUS. Be seated, madam.

THE LADY [*sitting down*] Are you Lord Augustus Highcastle?

AUGUSTUS [*sitting also*] Madam: I am.

THE LADY [*with awe*] The great Lord Augustus?

AUGUSTUS. I should not dream of describing myself so, madam; but no doubt I have impressed my countrymen —and [*bowing gallantly*] may I say my countrywomen—as having some exceptional claims to their consideration.

THE LADY [*emotionally*] What a beautiful voice you have!

AUGUSTUS. What you hear, madam, is the voice of my country, which now takes a sweet and noble tone even in the harsh mouth of high officialism.

THE LADY. Please go on. You express yourself so wonderfully!

AUGUSTUS. It would be strange indeed if, after sitting on thirty-seven Royal Commissions, mostly as chairman, I had not mastered the art of public expression. Even the Radical papers have paid me the high compliment of declaring that I am never more impressive than when I have nothing to say.

THE LADY. I never read the Radical papers. All I can tell you is that what we women admire in you is not the politician, but the man of action, the heroic warrior, the *beau sabreur.*

79

AUGUSTUS DOES HIS BIT

AUGUSTUS [*gloomily*] Madam. I beg! Please! My military exploits are not a pleasant subject, unhappily.

THE LADY. Oh, I know, I know. How shamefully you have been treated! What ingratitude! But the country is with you. The women are with you. Oh, do you think all our hearts did not throb and all our nerves thrill when we heard how, when you were ordered to occupy that terrible quarry in Hulluch, and you swept into it at the head of your men like a sea-god riding on a tidal wave, you suddenly sprang over the top shouting "To Berlin! Forward!"; dashed at the German army single-handed; and were cut off and made prisoner by the Huns.

AUGUSTUS. Yes, madam; and what was my reward? They said I had disobeyed orders, and sent me home. Have they forgotten Nelson in the Baltic? Has any British battle ever been won except by a bold individual initiative? I say nothing of professional jealousy: it exists in the army as elsewhere; but it is a bitter thought to me that the recognition denied me by my own country—or rather by the Radical cabal in the Cabinet which pursues my family with rancorous class hatred—that this recognition, I say, came to me at the hands of an enemy—of a rank Prussian.

THE LADY. You dont say so!

AUGUSTUS. How else should I be here instead of starving to death in Ruhleben? Yes, madam: the Colonel of the Pomeranian regiment which captured me, after learning what I had done, and conversing for an hour with me on European politics and military strategy, declared that nothing would induce him to deprive my country of my services, and set me free. I offered, of course, to procure the release in exchange of a German officer of equal quality; but he would not hear of it. He was kind enough to say he could not believe that a German officer answering to that description existed. [*With emotion*] I had my first taste of the ingratitude of my own country as I made my way back to our lines. A shot from our front trench struck me in the head. I still carry the flattened projectile as a trophy [*he throws it on*

80

the table: the noise it makes testifies to its weight]. Had it penetrated to the brain I might never have sat on another Royal Commission. Fortunately we have strong heads, we Highcastles. Nothing has ever penetrated to our brains.

THE LADY. How thrilling! How simple! And how tragic! But you will forgive England? Remember: England! Forgive her.

AUGUSTUS [*with gloomy magnanimity*] It will make no difference whatever to my services to my country. Though she slay me, yet will I, if not exactly trust in her, at least take my part in her government. I am ever at my country's call. Whether it be the embassy in a leading European capital, a governor-generalship in the tropics, or my humble mission here to make Little Pifflington do its bit, I am always ready for the sacrifice. Whilst England remains England, wherever there is a public job to be done you will find a Highcastle sticking to it. And now, madam, enough of my tragic personal history. You have called on business. What can I do for you?

THE LADY. You have relatives at the Foreign Office, have you not?

AUGUSTUS [*haughtily*] Madam: the Foreign Office is staffed by my relatives exclusively.

THE LADY. Has the Foreign Office warned you that you are being pursued by a female spy who is determined to obtain possession of a certain list of gun emplacements—

AUGUSTUS [*interrupting her somewhat loftily*] All that is perfectly well known to this department, madam.

THE LADY [*surprised and rather indignant*] Is it? Who told you? Was it one of your German brothers-in-law?

AUGUSTUS [*injured, remonstrating*] I have only three German brothers-in-law, madam. Really, from your tone, one would suppose that I had several. Pardon my sensitiveness on that subject; but reports are continually being circulated that I have been shot as a traitor in the courtyard of the Ritz Hotel simply because I have German brothers-in-law. [*With feeling*] If you had a German brother-in-law, madam,

81

you would know that nothing else in the world produces so strong an anti-German feeling. Life affords no keener pleasure than finding a brother-in-law's name in the German casualty list.

THE LADY. Nobody knows that better than I. Wait until you hear what I have come to tell you: you will understand me as no one else could. Listen. This spy, this woman—

AUGUSTUS [*all attention*] Yes?

THE LADY. She is a German. A Hun.

AUGUSTUS. Yes, yes. She would be. Continue.

THE LADY. She is my sister-in-law.

AUGUSTUS [*deferentially*] I see you are well connected, madam. Proceed.

THE LADY. Need I add that she is my bitterest enemy?

AUGUSTUS. May I— [*he proffers his hand. They shake, fervently. From this moment onward Augustus becomes more and more confidential, gallant, and charming*].

THE LADY. Quite so. Well, she is an intimate friend of your brother at the War Office, Hungerford Highcastle: Blueloo as you call him: I dont know why.

AUGUSTUS [*explaining*] He was originally called The Singing Oyster, because he sang drawing-room ballads with such an extraordinary absence of expression. He was then called the Blue Point for a season or two. Finally he became Blueloo.

THE LADY. Oh, indeed: I didnt know. Well, Blueloo is simply infatuated with my sister-in-law; and he has rashly let out to her that this list is in your possession. He forgot himself because he was in a towering rage at its being entrusted to you: his language was terrible. He ordered all the guns to be shifted at once.

AUGUSTUS. What on earth did he do that for?

THE LADY. I cant imagine. But this I know. She made a bet with him that she would come down here and obtain possession of that list and get clean away into the street with it. He took the bet on condition that she brought it straight back to him at the War Office.

AUGUSTUS. Good heavens! And you mean to tell me that Blueloo was such a dolt as to believe that she could succeed? Does he take me for a fool?

THE LADY. Oh, impossible! He is jealous of your intellect. The bet is an insult to you: dont you feel that? After what you have done for our country—

AUGUSTUS. Oh, never mind that. It is the idiocy of the thing I look at. He'll lose his bet; and serve him right!

THE LADY. You feel sure you will be able to resist the siren? I warn you, she is very fascinating.

AUGUSTUS. You need have no fear, madam. I hope she will come and try it on. Fascination is a game that two can play at. For centuries the younger sons of the Highcastles have had nothing to do but fascinate attractive females when they were not sitting on Royal Commissions or on duty at Knightsbridge barracks. By Gad, madam, if the siren comes here she will meet her match.

THE LADY. I feel that. But if she fails to seduce you—

AUGUSTUS [*blushing*] Madam!

THE LADY [*continuing*]—from your allegiance—

AUGUSTUS. Oh, that!

THE LADY. —she will resort to fraud, to force, to anything. She will burgle your office: she will have you attacked and garotted at night in the street.

AUGUSTUS. Pooh! I'm not afraid.

THE LADY. Oh, your courage will only tempt you into danger. She may get the list after all. It is true that the guns are moved. But she would win her bet.

AUGUSTUS [*cautiously*] You did not say that the guns were moved. You said that Blueloo had ordered them to be moved.

THE LADY. Well, that is the same thing, isnt it?

AUGUSTUS. Not quite—at the War Office. No doubt those guns will be moved: possibly even before the end of the war.

THE LADY. Then you think they are there still! But if the German War Office gets the list—and she will copy it before she gives it back to Blueloo, you may depend on it—all is lost.

AUGUSTUS [*lazily*] Well, I should not go as far as that. [*Lowering his voice*] Will you swear to me not to repeat what I am going to say to you; for if the British public knew that I had said it, I should be at once hounded down as a pro-German.

THE LADY. I will be silent as the grave. I swear it.

AUGUSTUS [*again taking it easily*] Well, our people have for some reason made up their minds that the German War Office is everything that our War Office is not—that it carries promptitude, efficiency, and organization to a pitch of completeness and perfection that must be, in my opinion, destructive to the happiness of the staff. My own view— which you are pledged, remember, not to betray—is that the German War Office is no better than any other War Office. I found that opinion on my observation of the characters of my brothers-in-law: one of whom, by the way, is on the German general staff. I am not at all sure that this list of gun emplacements would receive the smallest attention. You see, there are always so many more important things to be attended to. Family matters, and so on, you understand.

THE LADY. Still, if a question were asked in the House of Commons—

AUGUSTUS. The great advantage of being at war, madam, is that nobody takes the slightest notice of the House of Commons. No doubt it is sometimes necessary for a Minister to soothe the more seditious members of that assembly by giving a pledge or two; but the War Office takes no notice of such things.

THE LADY [*staring at him*] Then you think this list of gun emplacements doesnt matter!!

AUGUSTUS. By no means, madam. It matters very much indeed. If this spy were to obtain possession of the list, Blueloo would tell the story at every dinner-table in London; and—

THE LADY. And you might lose your post. Of course.

AUGUSTUS [*amazed and indignant*] *I* lose my post! What are you dreaming about, madam? How could I possibly be

84

spared? There are hardly Highcastles enough at present to fill half the posts created by this war. No: Blueloo would not go that far. He is at least a gentleman. But I should be chaffed; and, frankly, I dont like being chaffed.

THE LADY. Of course not. Who does? It would never do. Oh never, never.

AUGUSTUS. I'm glad you see it in that light. And now, as a measure of security, I shall put that list in my pocket. [*He begins searching vainly from drawer to drawer in the writing-table*]. Where on earth—? What the dickens did I—? Thats very odd: I— Where the deuce—? I thought I had put it in the— Oh, here it is! No: this is Lucy's last letter.

THE LADY [*elegiacally*] Lucy's Last Letter! What a title for a picture play!

AUGUSTUS [*delighted*] Yes: it is, isnt it? Lucy appeals to the imagination like no other woman. By the way [*handing over the letter*] I wonder could you read it for me? Lucy is a darling girl; but I really cant read her writing. In London I get the office typist to decipher it and make me a typed copy; but here there is nobody.

THE LADY [*puzzling over it*] It is really almost illegible. I think the beginning is meant for "Dearest Gus."

AUGUSTUS [*eagerly*] Yes: that is what she usually calls me. Please go on.

THE LADY [*trying to decipher it*] "What a"—"what a" —oh yes: "what a forgetful old"—something—"you are!" I cant make out the word.

AUGUSTUS [*greatly interested*] Is it blighter? That is a favorite expression of hers.

THE LADY. I think so. At all events it begins with a B. [*Reading*] "What a forgetful old"—[*she is interrupted by a knock at the door*].

AUGUSTUS [*impatiently*] Come in. [*The clerk enters, clean shaven and in khaki, with an official paper and an envelope in his hand*]. What is this ridiculous mummery, sir?

THE CLERK [*coming to the table and exhibiting his uniform to both*] Theyve passed me. The recruiting officer come for

85

me. Ive had my two and seven.

AUGUSTUS [*rising wrathfully*] I shall not permit it. What
do they mean by taking my office staff? Good God! they will
be taking our hunt servants next. [*Confronting the clerk*]
What did the man mean? What did he say?

THE CLERK. He said that now you was on the job we'd
want another million men, and he was going to take the old-
age pensioners or anyone he could get.

AUGUSTUS. And did you dare to knock at my door and
interrupt my business with this lady to repeat this man's
ineptitudes?

THE CLERK. No. I come because the waiter from the
hotel brought this paper. You left it on the coffee-room
breakfast-table this morning.

THE LADY [*intercepting it*] It is the list. Good heavens!

THE CLERK [*proffering the envelope*] He says he thinks this
is the envelope belonging to it.

THE LADY [*snatching the envelope also*] Yes! Addressed to
you. Lord Augustus! [*Augustus comes back to the table to look
at it*] Oh, how imprudent! Everybody would guess its importance with your name on it. Fortunately I have some
letters of my own here [*opening her wallet*]. Why not hide it
in one of my envelopes? then no one will dream that the
enclosure is of any political value. [*Taking out a letter, she
crosses the room towards the window, whispering to Augustus as
she passes him*] Get rid of that man.

AUGUSTUS [*haughtily approaching the clerk, who humor-
ously makes a paralytic attempt to stand at attention*] Have you
any further business here, pray?

THE CLERK. Am I to give the waiter anything; or will you
do it yourself?

AUGUSTUS. Which waiter is it? The English one?

THE CLERK. No: the one that calls hisself a Swiss.
Shouldnt wonder if he'd made a copy of that paper.

AUGUSTUS. Keep your impertinent surmises to yourself,
sir. Remember that you are in the army now; and let me
have no more of your civilian insubordination. Attention!

Left turn! Quick march!

THE CLERK [*stolidly*] I dunno what you mean.

AUGUSTUS. Go to the guard-room and report yourself for disobeying orders. Now do you know what I mean?

THE CLERK. Now look here. I aint going to argue with you—

AUGUSTUS. Nor I with you. Out with you.

He seizes the clerk; and rushes him through the door. The moment the lady is left alone, she snatches a sheet of official paper from the stationery rack; folds it so that it resembles the list; compares the two to see that they look exactly alike; whips the list into her wallet; and substitutes the facsimile for it. Then she listens for the return of Augustus. A crash is heard, as of the clerk falling downstairs.

Augustus returns and is about to close the door when the voice of the clerk is heard from below:

THE CLERK. I'll have the law of you for this, I will.

AUGUSTUS [*shouting down to him*] Theres no more law for you, you scoundrel. Youre a soldier now. [*He shuts the door and comes to the lady*]. Thank heaven, the war has given us the upper hand of these fellows at last. Excuse my violence; but discipline is absolutely necessary in dealing with the lower middle classes.

THE LADY. Serve the insolent creature right! Look! I have found you a beautiful envelope for the list, an unmistakable lady's envelope. [*She puts the sham list into her envelope and hands it to him*].

AUGUSTUS. Excellent. Really very clever of you. [*Slyly*] Come: would you like to have a peep at the list [*beginning to take the blank paper from the envelope*]?

THE LADY [*in the brink of detection*] No no. Oh, p l e a s e, no.

AUGUSTUS. Why? It wont bite you [*drawing it out further*].

THE LADY [*snatching at his hand*] Stop. Remember: if there should be an inquiry, you must be able to swear that you never shewed that list to a mortal soul.

AUGUSTUS. Oh, that is a mere form. If you are really curious—

THE LADY. I am not. I couldnt bear to look at it. One of my dearest friends was blown to pieces by an aircraft gun; and since then I have never been able to think of one without horror.

AUGUSTUS. You mean it was a real gun, and actually went off. How sad! how sad! [*He pushes the sham list back into the envelope, and pockets it*].

THE LADY. Ah! [*great sigh of relief*]. And now, Lord Augustus, I have taken up too much of your valuable time. Goodbye.

AUGUSTUS. What! Must you go?

THE LADY. You are so busy.

AUGUSTUS. Yes; but not before lunch, you know. I never can do much before lunch. And I'm no good at all in the afternoon. From five to six is my real working time. Must you really go?

THE LADY. I must, really. I have done my business very satisfactorily. Thank you ever so much [*she proffers her hand*].

AUGUSTUS [*shaking it affectionately as he leads her to the door, but first pressing the bell button with his left hand*] Goodbye. Goodbye. So sorry to lose you. Kind of you to come; but there was no real danger. You see, my dear little lady, all this talk about war saving, and secrecy, and keeping the blinds down at night, and so forth, is all very well; but unless it's carried out with intelligence, believe me, you may waste a pound to save a penny; you may let out all sorts of secrets to the enemy; you may guide the Zeppelins right on to your own chimneys. Thats where the ability of the governing class comes in. Shall the fellow call a taxi for you?

THE LADY. No, thanks: I prefer walking. Goodbye. Again, many, many thanks.

She goes out. Augustus returns to the writing-table smiling, and takes another look at himself in the mirror. The clerk returns with his head bandaged, carrying a poker.

THE CLERK. What did you ring for? [*Augustus hastily drops the mirror*]. Dont you come nigh me or I'll split your head with this poker, thick as it is.

AUGUSTUS. It does not seem to me an exceptionally thick poker. I rang for you to shew the lady out.

THE CLERK. She's gone. She run out like a rabbit. I ask myself, why was she in such a hurry?

THE LADY'S VOICE [*from the street*] Lord Augustus. Lord Augustus.

THE CLERK. She's calling you.

AUGUSTUS [*running to the window and throwing it up*] What is it? Wont you come up?

THE LADY. Is the clerk there?

AUGUSTUS. Yes. Do you want him?

THE LADY. Yes.

AUGUSTUS. The lady wants you at the window.

THE CLERK [*rushing to the window and putting down the poker*] Yes, maam? Here I am, maam. What is it, maam?

THE LADY. I want you to witness that I got clean away into the street. I am coming up now.

The two men stare at one another.

THE CLERK. Wants me to witness that she got clean away into the street!

AUGUSTUS. What on earth does she mean?

The lady returns.

THE LADY. May I use your telephone?

AUGUSTUS. Certainly. Certainly. [*Taking the receiver down*] What number shall I get you?

THE LADY. The War Office, please.

AUGUSTUS. The War Office!?

THE LADY. If you will be so good.

AUGUSTUS. But— Oh, very well. [*Into the receiver*] Hallo. This is the Town Hall Recruiting Office. Give me Colonel Bogey, sharp.

A pause.

THE CLERK [*breaking the painful silence*] I dont think I'm awake. This is a dream of a movy picture, this is.

AUGUSTUS [*his ear at the receiver*] Shut up, will you? [*Into the telephone*] What?...[*To the lady*] Whom do you want to get on to?

89

THE LADY. Blueloo.

AUGUSTUS [*into the telephone*] Put me through to Lord Hungerford Highcastle. . . . I'm his brother, idiot. . . . That you, Blueloo? Lady here at Little Pifflington wants to speak to you. Hold the line. [*To the lady*] Now, madam [*he hands her the receiver*].

THE LADY [*sitting down in Augustus's chair to speak into the telephone*] Is that Blueloo? . . . Do you recognize my voice? . . . Ive won our bet. . . .

AUGUSTUS. Your bet!

THE LADY [*into the telephone*] Yes: I have the list in my wallet. . . .

AUGUSTUS. Nothing of the kind, madam. I have it here in my pocket. [*He takes the envelope from his pocket; draws out the paper; and unfolds it*].

THE LADY [*continuing*] Yes: I got clean into the street with it. I have a witness. I could have got to London with it. Augustus wont deny it. . . .

AUGUSTUS [*contemplating the blank paper*] Theres nothing written on this. Where is the list of guns?

THE LADY [*continuing*] Oh, it was quite easy. I said I was my sister-in-law and that I was a Hun. He lapped it up like a kitten. . . .

AUGUSTUS. You dont mean to say that—

THE LADY [*continuing*] I got hold of the list for a moment and changed it for a piece of paper out of his stationery rack: it was quite easy [*she laughs; and it is clear that Blueloo is laughing too*].

AUGUSTUS. What!

THE CLERK [*laughing slowly and laboriously, with intense enjoyment*] Ha ha! Ha ha ha! Ha! [*Augustus rushes at him: he snatches up the poker and stands on guard*]. No you dont.

THE LADY [*still at the telephone, waving her disengaged hand behind her impatiently at them to stop making a noise*] Sh-sh-sh-sh-sh!!! [*Augustus, with a shrug, goes up the middle of the room. The lady resumes her conversation with the telephone*] What? . . . Oh yes: I'm coming up by the 12.35: why

90

not have tea with me at Rumpelmeister's? . . . Rum-pel-meister's. You know: they call it Robinson's now. . . . Right. Ta ta. [*She hangs up the receiver, and is passing round the table on her way towards the door when she is confronted by Augustus*].

AUGUSTUS. Madam: I consider your conduct most unpatriotic. You make bets and abuse the confidence of the hardworked officials who are doing their bit for their country whilst our gallant fellows are perishing in the trenches—

THE LADY. Oh, the gallant fellows are not all in the trenches, Augustus. Some of them have come home for a few days hard-earned leave; and I am sure you wont grudge them a little fun at your expense.

THE CLERK. Hear! Hear!

AUGUSTUS [*amiably*] Ah, well! For my country's sake—!

THE INCA OF PERUSALEM

AN ALMOST HISTORICAL COMEDIETTA BY
"A MEMBER OF THE ROYAL LITERARY SOCIETY"

Written in 1916

First Performed Birmingham 1916

I MUST remind the reader that this playlet was written when its principal character, far from being a fallen foe and virtually a prisoner in our victorious hands, was still the Caesar whose legions we were resisting with our hearts in our mouths. Many were so horribly afraid of him that they could not forgive me for not being afraid of him: I seemed to be trifling heartlessly with a deadly peril. I knew better; and I have represented Caesar as knowing better himself. But it was one of the quaintnesses of popular feeling during the war that anyone who breathed the slightest doubt of the absolute perfection of German organization, the Machiavellian depth of German diplomacy, the omniscience of German science, the equipment of every German with a complete philosophy of history, and the consequent hopelessness of overcoming so magnificently accomplished an enemy except by the sacrifice of every recreative activity to incessant and vehement war work, including a heartbreaking mass of fussing and cadging and bluffing that did nothing but waste our energies and tire our resolution, was called a pro-German.

Now that this is all over, and the upshot of the fighting has shewn that we could quite well have afforded to laugh at the doomed Inca, I am in another difficulty. I may be supposed to be hitting Caesar when he is down. That is why I preface the play with this reminder that when it was written he was not down. To make quite sure, I have gone through the proof sheets very carefully, and deleted everything that could possibly be mistaken for a foul blow. I have of course maintained the ancient privilege of comedy to chasten Caesar's foibles by laughing at them, whilst introducing enough obvious and outrageous fiction to relieve both myself and my model from the obligations and responsibilities of sober history and biography. But I should certainly put the play in the fire instead of publishing it if it contained a word against our defeated enemy that I would not have written in 1913.

95

PROLOGUE

THE *tableau curtains are closed. An English archdeacon comes through them in a condition of extreme irritation. He speaks through the curtains to someone behind them.*

THE ARCHDEACON. Once for all, Ermyntrude, I cannot afford to maintain you in your present extravagance. [*He goes to a flight of steps leading to the stalls and sits down disconsolately on the top step. A fashionably dressed lady comes through the curtains and contemplates him with patient obstinacy. He continues, grumbling*] An English clergyman's daughter should be able to live quite respectably and comfortably on an allowance of £150 a year, wrung with great difficulty from the domestic budget.

ERMYNTRUDE. You are not a common clergyman: you are an archdeacon.

THE ARCHDEACON [*angrily*] That does not affect my emoluments to the extent of enabling me to support a daughter whose extravagance would disgrace a royal personage. [*Scrambling to his feet and scolding at her*] What do you mean by it, Miss?

ERMYNTRUDE. Oh really, father! Miss! Is that the way to talk to a widow?

THE ARCHDEACON. Is that the way to talk to a father? Your marriage was a most disastrous imprudence. It gave you habits that are absolutely beyond your means—I mean beyond my means: you have no means. Why did you not marry Matthews: the best curate I ever had?

ERMYNTRUDE. I wanted to; and you wouldnt let me. You insisted on my marrying Roosenhonkers-Pipstein.

THE ARCHDEACON. I had to do the best for you, my child. Roosenhonkers-Pipstein was a millionaire.

ERMYNTRUDE. How did you know he was a millionaire?

THE ARCHDEACON. He came from America. Of course he was a millionaire. Besides, he proved to my solicitors that he had fifteen million dollars when you married him.

ERMYNTRUDE. His solicitors proved to me that he had sixteen millions when he died. He was a millionaire to the

97

last.

THE ARCHDEACON. O Mammon, Mammon! I am punished now for bowing the knee to him. Is there nothing left of your settlement? Fifty thousand dollars a year it secured to you, as we all thought. Only half the securities could be called speculative. The other half were gilt-edged. What has become of it all?

ERMYNTRUDE. The speculative ones were not paid up; and the gilt-edged ones just paid the calls on them until the whole show burst up.

THE ARCHDEACON. Ermyntrude: what expressions!

ERMYNTRUDE. Oh bother! If you had lost ten thousand a year what expressions would you use, do you think? The long and the short of it is that I cant live in the squalid way you are accustomed to.

THE ARCHDEACON. Squalid!

ERMYNTRUDE. I have formed habits of comfort.

THE ARCHDEACON. Comfort!!

ERMYNTRUDE. Well, elegance if you like. Luxury, if you insist. Call it what you please. A house that costs less than a hundred thousand dollars a year to run is intolerable to me.

THE ARCHDEACON. Then, my dear, you had better become lady's maid to a princess until you can find another millionaire to marry you.

ERMYNTRUDE. Thats an idea. I will [*She vanishes through the curtains*].

THE ARCHDEACON. What! Come back, Miss. Come back this instant. [*The lights are lowered*]. Oh, very well: I have nothing more to say. [*He descends the steps into the auditorium and makes for the door, grumbling all the time*]. Insane, senseless extravagance! [*Barking*] Worthlessness!! [*Muttering*] I will not bear it any longer. Dresses, hats, furs, gloves, motor rides: one bill after another: money going like water. No restraint, no self-control, no decency. [*Shrieking*] I say, no decency! [*Muttering again*] Nice state of things we are coming to! A pretty world! But I simply will not bear it. She can

THE INCA OF PERUSALEM

do as she likes. I wash my hands of her: I am not going to die in the workhouse for any good-for-nothing, undutiful, spendthrift daughter; and the sooner that is understood by everybody the better for all par—[*He is by this time out of hearing in the corridor*].

THE PLAY

A HOTEL *sitting room. A table in the centre. On it a telephone. Two chairs at it, opposite one another. Behind it, the door. The fireplace has a mirror in the mantelpiece.*

A spinster Princess, hatted and gloved, is ushered in by the Hotel Manager, spruce and artificially bland by professional habit, but treating his customer with a condescending affability which sails very close to the east wind of insolence.

THE MANAGER. I am sorry I am unable to accommodate Your Highness on the first floor.

THE PRINCESS [*very shy and nervous*] Oh please dont mention it. This is quite nice. Very nice. Thank you very much.

THE MANAGER. We could prepare a room in the annexe—

THE PRINCESS. Oh no. This will do very well.

She takes off her gloves and hat; puts them on the table; and sits down.

THE MANAGER. The rooms are quite as good up here. There is less noise; and there is the lift. If your Highness desires anything, there is the telephone—

THE PRINCESS. Oh, thank you, I dont want anything. The telephone is so difficult: I am not accustomed to it.

THE MANAGER. Can I take any order? Some tea?

THE PRINCESS. Oh, thank you. Yes: I should like some tea, if I might—if it would not be too much trouble.

He goes out. The telephone rings. The Princess starts out of her chair, terrified, and recoils as far as possible from the instrument.

THE PRINCESS. Oh dear! [*It rings again. She looks scared. It rings again. She approaches it timidly. It rings again. She retreats hastily. It rings repeatedly. She runs to it in desperation and puts the receiver to her ear*]. Who is there? What do I do? I am not used to the telephone: I dont know how—What! Oh, I can hear you speaking quite distinctly. [*She sits down, delighted, and settles herself for a conversation*]. How wonderful! What! A lady? Oh! a person. Oh yes: I know. Yes,

100

THE INCA OF PERUSALEM

please, send her up. Have my servants finished their lunch yet? Oh no: please dont disturb them: I'd rather not. It doesnt matter. Thank you. What? Oh yes, it's quite easy. I had no idea—am I to hang it up just as it was? Thank you. [*She hangs it up*].

Ermyntrude enters, presenting a plain and staid appearance in a long straight waterproof with a hood over her head gear. She comes to the end of the table opposite to that at which the Princess is seated.

THE PRINCESS. Excuse me. I have been talking through the telephone; and I heard quite well, though I have never ventured before. Wont you sit down?

ERMYNTRUDE. No, thank you, Your Highness. I am only a lady's maid. I understood you wanted one.

THE PRINCESS. Oh no: you mustnt think I want one. It's so unpatriotic to want anything now, on account of the war, you know. I sent my maid away as a public duty; and now she has married a soldier and is expecting a war baby. But I dont know how to do without her. Ive tried my very best; but somehow it doesnt answer: everybody cheats me; and in the end it isnt any saving. So Ive made up my mind to sell my piano and have a maid. That will be a real saving, because I really dont care a bit for music, though of course one has to pretend to. Dont you think so?

ERMYNTRUDE. Certainly I do, Your Highness. Nothing could be more correct. Saving and self-denial both at once; and an act of kindness to me, as I am out of place.

THE PRINCESS. I'm so glad you see it in that way. Er— you wont mind my asking, will you?—how did you lose your place?

ERMYNTRUDE. The war, Your Highness, the war.

THE PRINCESS. Oh yes, of course. But how—

ERMYNTRUDE [*taking out her handkerchief and shewing signs of grief*] My poor mistress—

THE PRINCESS. Oh p l e a s e say no more. Dont think about it. So tactless of me to mention it.

ERMYNTRUDE [*mastering her emotion and smiling through*

IOI

her tears] Your Highness is too good.

THE PRINCESS. Do you think you could be happy with me? I attach such importance to that.

ERMYNTRUDE [*gushing*] Oh, I know I shall.

THE PRINCESS. You must not expect too much. There is my uncle. He is very severe and hasty; and he is my guardian. I once had a maid I liked very much; but he sent her away the very first time.

ERMYNTRUDE. The first time of what, Your Highness?

THE PRINCESS. Oh, something she did. I am sure she had never done it before; and I k n o w she would never have done it again, she was so truly contrite and nice about it.

ERMYNTRUDE. About what, Your Highness?

THE PRINCESS. Well, she wore my jewels and one of my dresses at a rather improper ball with her young man; and my uncle saw her.

ERMYNTRUDE. Then he was at the ball too, Your Highness?

THE PRINCESS [*struck by the inference*] I suppose he must have been. I wonder! You know, it's very sharp of you to find that out. I hope you are not too sharp.

ERMYNTRUDE. A lady's maid has to be. Your Highness. [*She produces some letters*]. Your Highness wishes to see my testimonials, no doubt. I have one from an Archdeacon. [*She proffers the letters*].

THE PRINCESS [*taking them*] Do archdeacons have maids? How curious!

ERMYNTRUDE. No, Your Highness. They have daughters. I have first-rate testimonials from the Archdeacon and from his daughter.

THE PRINCESS [*reading them*] The daughter says you are in every respect a treasure. The Archdeacon says he would have kept you if he could possibly have afforded it. Most satisfactory, I'm sure.

ERMYNTRUDE. May I regard myself as engaged then, Your Highness?

THE PRINCESS [*alarmed*] Oh, I'm sure I dont know. If

102

you like, of course; but do you think I ought to?

ERMYNTRUDE. Naturally I think Your Highness ought to, most decidedly.

THE PRINCESS. Oh well, if you think that, I daresay youre quite right. Youll excuse my mentioning it, I hope; but what wages—er—?

ERMYNTRUDE. The same as the maid who went to the ball. Your Highness need not make any change.

THE PRINCESS. M'yes. Of course she began with less. But she had such a number of relatives to keep! It was quite heartbreaking: I had to raise her wages again and again.

ERMYNTRUDE. I shall be quite content with what she began on; and I have no relatives dependent on me. And I am willing to wear my own dresses at balls.

THE PRINCESS. I am sure nothing could be fairer than that. My uncle cant object to that: can he?

ERMYNTRUDE. If he does, Your Highness, ask him to speak to me about it. I shall regard it as part of my duties to speak to your uncle about matters of business.

THE PRINCESS. Would you? You must be frightfully courageous.

ERMYNTRUDE. May I regard myself as engaged, Your Highness? I should like to set about my duties immediately.

THE PRINCESS. Oh yes, I think so. Oh certainly. I—

A waiter comes in with the tea. He places the tray on the table.

THE PRINCESS. Oh, thank you.

ERMYNTRUDE [*raising the cover from the tea cake and looking at it*] How long has that been standing at the top of the stairs?

THE PRINCESS [*terrified*] Oh please! It doesnt matter.

THE WAITER. It has not been waiting. Straight from the kitchen, madam, believe me.

ERMYNTRUDE. Send the manager here.

THE WAITER. The manager! What do you want with the manager?

ERMYNTRUDE. He will tell you when I have done with him. How dare you treat Her Highness in this disgraceful

103

manner? What sort of pothouse is this? Where did you learn to speak to persons of quality? Take away your cold tea and cold cake instantly. Give them to the chambermaid you were flirting with whilst Her Highness was waiting. Order some fresh tea at once; and do not presume to bring it yourself: have it brought by a civil waiter who is accustomed to wait on ladies, and not, like you, on commercial travellers.

THE WAITER. Alas, madam, I am not accustomed to wait on anybody. Two years ago I was an eminent medical man. My waiting-room was crowded with the flower of the aristocracy and the higher bourgeoisie from nine to six every day. But the war came; and my patients were ordered to give up their luxuries. They gave up their doctors, but kept their week-end hotels, closing every career to me except the career of a waiter. [*He puts his fingers on the teapot to test its temperature, and automatically takes out his watch with the other hand as if to count the teapot's pulse*]. You are right: the tea i s cold: it was made by the wife of a once fashionable architect. The cake is only half toasted: what can you expect from a ruined west-end tailor whose attempt to establish a second-hand business failed last Tuesday week? Have you the heart to complain to the manager? Have we not suffered enough? Are our miseries nev—[*the manager enters*] Oh Lord! here he is. [*The waiter withdraws abjectly, taking the tea tray with him*].

THE MANAGER. Pardon. Your Highness; but I have received an urgent inquiry for rooms from an English family of importance; and I venture to ask you to let me know how long you intend to honor us with your presence.

THE PRINCESS [*rising anxiously*] Oh! am I in the way?

ERMYNTRUDE [*sternly*] Sit down, madam. [*The Princess sits down forlornly. Ermyntrude turns imperiously to the Manager*]. Her Highness will require this room for twenty minutes.

THE MANAGER. Twenty minutes!

ERMYNTRUDE. Yes: it will take fully that time to find a proper apartment in a respectable hotel.

THE INCA OF PERUSALEM

THE MANAGER. I do not understand.

ERMYNTRUDE. You understand perfectly. How dare you offer Her Highness a room on the second floor?

THE MANAGER. But I have explained. The first floor is occupied. At least—

ERMYNTRUDE. Well? At least?

THE MANAGER. It is occupied.

ERMYNTRUDE. Dont you dare tell Her Highness a falsehood. It is not occupied. You are saving it up for the arrival of the five fifteen express, from which you hope to pick up some fat armaments contractor who will drink all the bad champagne in your cellar at 25 francs a bottle, and pay twice over for everything because he is in the same hotel with Her Highness, and can boast of having turned her out of the best rooms.

THE MANAGER. But Her Highness was so gracious. I did not know that Her Highness was at all particular.

ERMYNTRUDE. And you take advantage of Her Highness's graciousness. You impose on her with your stories. You give her a room not fit for a dog. You send cold tea to her by a decayed professional person disguised as a waiter. But dont think you can trifle with me. I am a lady's maid; and I know the ladies' maids and valets of all the aristocracies of Europe and all the millionaires of America. When I expose your hotel as the second-rate little hole it is, not a soul above the rank of a curate with a large family will be seen entering it. I shake its dust off my feet. Order the luggage to be taken down at once.

THE MANAGER [appealing to the Princess] Can Your Highness believe this of me? Have I had the misfortune to offend Your Highness?

THE PRINCESS. Oh no. I am quite satisfied. Please—

ERMYNTRUDE. Is Your Highness dissatisfied with m e?

THE PRINCESS [intimidated] Oh no: please dont think that. I only meant—

ERMYNTRUDE [to the Manager] You hear. Perhaps you think Her Highness is going to do the work of teaching you

105

your place herself, instead of leaving it to her maid.

THE MANAGER. Oh please, mademoiselle. Believe me: our only wish is to make you perfectly comfortable. But in consequence of the war, all royal personages now practise a rigid economy, and desire us to treat them like their poorest subjects.

THE PRINCESS. Oh yes, You are quite right—

ERMYNTRUDE [*interrupting*] There! Her Highness forgives you; but dont do it again. Now go downstairs, my good man, and get that suite on the first floor ready for us. And send some proper tea. And turn on the heating apparatus until the temperature in the rooms is comfortably warm. And have hot water put in all the bedrooms—

THE MANAGER. There are basins with hot and cold taps.

ERMYNTRUDE [*scornfully*] Yes: there would be. I suppose we must put up with that: sinks in our rooms, and pipes that rattle and bang and guggle all over the house whenever anyone washes his hands. *I* know.

THE MANAGER [*gallant*] You are hard to please, mademoiselle.

ERMYNTRUDE. No harder than other people. But when I'm not pleased I'm not too ladylike to say so. Thats all the difference. There is nothing more, thank you.

The Manager shrugs his shoulders resignedly; makes a deep bow to the Princess; goes to the door; wafts a kiss surreptitiously to Ermyntrude; and goes out.

THE PRINCESS. It's wonderful! How have you the courage?

ERMYNTRUDE. In Your Highness's service I know no fear. Your Highness can leave all unpleasant people to me.

THE PRINCESS. How I wish I could! The most dreadful thing of all I have to go through myself.

ERMYNTRUDE. Dare I ask what it is, Your Highness?

THE PRINCESS. I'm going to be married. I'm to be met here and married to a man I never saw. A boy! A boy who never saw me! One of the sons of the Inca of Perusalem.

ERMYNTRUDE. Indeed? Which son?

THE INCA OF PERUSALEM

THE PRINCESS. I dont know. They havnt settled which. It's a dreadful thing to be a princess: they just marry you to anyone they like. The Inca is to come and look at me, and pick out whichever of his sons he thinks will suit. And then I shall be an alien enemy everywhere except in Perusalem, because the Inca has made war on everybody. And I shall have to pretend that everybody has made war on him. It's too bad.

ERMYNTRUDE. Still, a husband is a husband. I wish I had one.

THE PRINCESS. Oh, how can you say that! I'm afraid youre not a nice woman.

ERMYNTRUDE. Your Highness is provided for. I'm not.

THE PRINCESS. Even if you could bear to let a man touch you, you shouldnt say so.

ERMYNTRUDE. I shall not say so again, Your Highness, except perhaps to the man.

THE PRINCESS. It's too dreadful to think of. I wonder you can be so coarse. I really dont think youll suit. I feel sure now that you know more about men than you should.

ERMYNTRUDE. I am a widow, Your Highness.

THE PRINCESS [*overwhelmed*] Oh, I BEG your pardon. Of course I ought to have known you would not have spoken like that if you were not married. That makes it all right, doesnt it? I'm so sorry.

The Manager returns, white, scared, hardly able to speak.

THE MANAGER. Your Highness: an officer asks to see you on behalf of the Inca of Perusalem.

THE PRINCESS [*rising distractedly*] Oh, I cant, really. Oh, what shall I do?

THE MANAGER. On important business, he says, Your Highness. Captain Duval.

ERMYNTRUDE. Duval! Nonsense! The usual thing. It is the Inca himself, incognito.

THE PRINCESS. Oh, send him away. Oh, I'm so afraid of the Inca. I'm not properly dressed to receive him; and he is so particular: he would order me to stay in my room for a week. Tell him to call tomorrow: say I'm ill in bed. I cant: I wont: I darent: you must get rid of him somehow.

ERMYNTRUDE. Leave him to me, Your Highness.

THE PRINCESS. Youd never dare!

ERMYNTRUDE. I am an Englishwoman, Your Highness, and perfectly capable of tackling ten Incas if necessary. I will arrange the matter. [*To the Manager*] Shew Her Highness to her bedroom; and then shew Captain Duval in here.

THE PRINCESS. Oh thank you so much. [*She goes to the door. Ermyntrude, noticing that she has left her hat and gloves on the table, runs after her with them*]. Oh, thank you. And oh, please, if I must have one of his sons, I should like a fair one that doesnt shave, with soft hair and a beard. I couldnt bear being kissed by a bristly person. [*She runs out, the Manager bowing as she passes. He follows her*].

Ermyntrude whips off her waterproof; hides it; and gets herself swiftly into perfect trim at the mirror, before the Manager, with a large jewel case in his hand, returns, ushering in the Inca.

THE MANAGER. Captain Duval.

The Inca, in military uniform, advances with a marked and imposing stage walk; stops; orders the trembling Manager by a gesture to place the jewel case on the table, dismisses him with a frown; touches his helmet graciously to Ermyntrude; and takes off his cloak.

THE INCA. I beg you, madam, to be quite at your ease, and to speak to me without ceremony.

ERMYNTRUDE [*moving haughtily and carelessly to the table*] I hadnt the slightest intention of treating you with ceremony. [*She sits down: a liberty which gives him a perceptible shock*]. I am quite at a loss to imagine why I should treat a perfect stranger named Duval: a captain! almost a subaltern! with the smallest ceremony.

THE INCA. That is true. I had for the moment forgotten my position.

ERMYNTRUDE. It doesnt matter. You may sit down.

THE INCA [*frowning*] What!

ERMYNTRUDE. I said, you...may...sit...down.

108

THE INCA. Oh. [*His moustache droops. He sits down*].

ERMYNTRUDE. What is your business?

THE INCA. I come on behalf of the Inca of Perusalem.

ERMYNTRUDE. The Allerhöchst?

THE INCA. Precisely.

ERMYNTRUDE. I wonder does he feel ridiculous when people call him the Allerhöchst.

THE INCA [*surprised*] Why should he? He is the Allerhöchst.

ERMYNTRUDE. Is he nice looking?

THE INCA. I—er. Er—I. I—er. I am not a good judge.

ERMYNTRUDE. They say he takes himself very seriously.

THE INCA. Why should he not, madam? Providence has entrusted to his family the care of a mighty empire. He is in a position of half divine, half paternal responsibility towards sixty millions of people, whose duty it is to die for him at the word of command. To take himself otherwise than seriously would be blasphemous. It is a punishable offence—severely punishable—in Perusalem. It is called Incadisparagement.

ERMYNTRUDE. How cheerful! Can he laugh?

THE INCA. Certainly, madam. [*He laughs, harshly and mirthlessly*]. Ha ha! Ha ha ha!

ERMYNTRUDE [*frigidly*] I asked could the Inca laugh. I did not ask could you laugh.

THE INCA. That is true, madam. [*Chuckling*] Devilish amusing, that! [*He laughs, genially and sincerely, and becomes a much more agreeable person*]. Pardon me: I am now laughing because I cannot help it. I am amused. The other was merely an imitation: a failure, I admit.

ERMYNTRUDE. You intimated that you had some business?

THE INCA [*producing a very large jewel case, and relapsing into solemnity*] I am instructed by the Allerhöchst to take a careful note of your features and figure, and, if I consider them satisfactory, to present you with this trifling token of His Imperial Majesty's regard. I do consider them satisfactory. Allow me [*he opens the jewel case and presents it*]!

THE INCA OF PERUSALEM

ERMYNTRUDE [*staring at the contents*] What awful taste he must have! I cant wear that.

THE INCA [*reddening*] Take care, madam! This brooch was designed by the Inca himself. Allow me to explain the design. In the centre, the shield of Arminius. The ten surrounding medallions represent the ten castles of His Majesty. The rim is a piece of the telephone cable laid by His Majesty across the Shipskeel canal. The pin is a model in miniature of the sword of Henry the Birdcatcher.

ERMYNTRUDE. Miniature! It must be bigger than the original. My good man, you dont expect me to wear this round my neck: it's as big as a turtle. [*He shuts the case with an angry snap*]. How much did it cost?

THE INCA. For materials and manufacture alone, half a million Perusalem dollars, madam. The Inca's design constitutes it a work of art. As such, it is now worth probably ten million dollars.

ERMYNTRUDE. Give it to me [*she snatches it*]. I'll pawn it and buy something nice with the money.

THE INCA. Impossible, madam. A design by the Inca must not be exhibited for sale in the shop window of a pawnbroker. [*He flings himself into his chair, fuming*].

ERMYNTRUDE. So much the better. The Inca will have to redeem it to save himself from that disgrace; and the poor pawnbroker will get his money back. Nobody would buy it, you know.

THE INCA. May I ask why?

ERMYNTRUDE. Well, look at it! Just look at it! I ask you!

THE INCA [*his moustache drooping ominously*] I am sorry to have to report to the Inca that you have no soul for fine art. [*He rises sulkily*]. The position of daughter-in-law to the Inca is not compatible with the tastes of a pig. [*He attempts to take back the brooch*].

ERMYNTRUDE [*rising and retreating behind her chair with the brooch*] Here! you let that brooch alone. You presented it to me on behalf of the Inca. It is mine. You said my appearance was satisfactory.

THE INCA OF PERUSALEM

THE INCA. Your appearance is n o t satisfactory. The Inca would not allow his son to marry you if the boy were on a desert island and you were the only other human being on it [*he strides up the room*].

ERMYNTRUDE [*calmly sitting down and replacing the case on the table*] How could he? There would be no clergyman to marry us. It would have to be quite morganatic.

THE INCA [*returning*] Such an expression is out of place in the mouth of a princess aspiring to the highest destiny on earth. You have the morals of a dragoon. [*She receives this with a shriek of laughter. He struggles with his sense of humor*]. At the same time [*he sits down*] there is a certain coarse fun in the idea which compels me to smile [*he turns up his moustache and smiles*].

ERMYNTRUDE. When I marry the Inca's son, Captain, I shall make the Inca order you to cut off that moustache. It is too irresistible. Doesnt it fascinate everyone in Perusalem?

THE INCA [*leaning forward to her energetically*] By all the thunders of Thor, madam, it fascinates the whole world.

ERMYNTRUDE. What I like about you, Captain Duval, is your modesty.

THE INCA [*straightening up suddenly*] Woman: do not be a fool.

ERMYNTRUDE [*indignant*] Well!

THE INCA. You must look facts in the face. This moustache is an exact copy of the Inca's moustache. Well, does the world occupy itself with the Inca's moustache or does it not? Does it ever occupy itself with anything else? If that is the truth, does its recognition constitute the Inca a coxcomb? Other potentates have moustaches: even beards and moustaches. Does the world occupy itself with those beards and moustaches? Do the hawkers in the streets of every capital on the civilized globe sell ingenious cardboard representations of t h e i r faces on which, at the pulling of a simple string, the moustaches turn up and down, so—[*he makes his moustache turn up and down several times*]? No! I say No. The Inca's moustache is so watched and studied that it has made his face the political barometer of the whole continent. When that moustache goes up, culture rises with it. Not what you call culture; but Kultur, a word so much more significant that I hardly understand it myself except when I am in specially good form. When it goes down, millions of men perish.

ERMYNTRUDE. You know, if I had a moustache like that, it would turn my head. I should go mad. Are you quite sure the Inca isnt mad?

THE INCA. How can he be mad, madam? What is sanity? The condition of the Inca's mind. What is madness? The condition of the people who disagree with the Inca.

ERMYNTRUDE. Then I am a lunatic because I dont like that ridiculous brooch.

THE INCA. No, madam: you are only an idiot.

ERMYNTRUDE. Thank you.

THE INCA. Mark you: it is not to be expected that you should see eye to eye with the Inca. That would be presumption. It is for you to accept without question or demur the assurance of your Inca that the brooch is a masterpiece.

ERMYNTRUDE. My Inca! Oh, come! I like that. He is not my Inca yet.

THE INCA. He is everybody's Inca, madam. His realm will yet extend to the confines of the habitable earth. It is his divine right; and let those who dispute it look to themselves. Properly speaking, all those who are now trying to shake his world predominance are not at war with him, but in rebellion against him.

ERMYNTRUDE. Well, he started it, you know.

THE INCA. Madam, be just. When the hunters surround the lion, the lion will spring. The Inca had kept the peace for years. Those who attacked him were steeped in blood, black blood, white blood, brown blood, yellow blood, blue blood. The Inca had never shed a drop.

ERMYNTRUDE. He had only talked.

THE INCA. Only talked! Only talked! What is more glorious than talk? Can anyone in the world talk like him? Madam: when he signed the declaration of war, he said to his foolish generals and admirals, 'Gentlemen: you will all be sorry for this.' And they are. They know now that they had better have relied on the sword of the spirit: in other words, on their Inca's talk, than on their murderous cannons. The world will one day do justice to the Inca as the man who kept the peace with nothing but his tongue and his moustache. While he talked: talked just as I am talking now to you, simply, quietly, sensibly, but GREATLY, there was peace; there was prosperity; Perusalem went from success to success. He has been silenced for a year by the roar of trinitrotoluene and the bluster of fools; and the world is in ruins. What a tragedy! [*He is convulsed with grief*].

ERMYNTRUDE. Captain Duval: I dont want to be unsympathetic; but suppose we get back to business.

THE INCA. Business! What business?

ERMYNTRUDE. Well, my business. You want me to marry one of the Inca's sons: I forget which.

THE INCA. As far as I can recollect the name, it is His Imperial Highness Prince Eitel William Frederick George Franz Josef Alexander Nicholas Victor Emmanuel Albert Theodore Wilson—

ERMYNTRUDE [*interrupting*] Oh, please, please, maynt I have one with a shorter name? What is he called at home?

THE INCA. He is usually called Sonny, madam. [*With great charm of manner*] But you will please understand that the Inca has no desire to pin you to any particular son. There is Chips and Spots and Lulu and Pongo and the Corsair and the Piffler and Jack Johnson the Second, all unmarried. At least not seriously married: nothing, in short, that cannot be arranged. They are all at your service.

ERMYNTRUDE. Are they all as clever and charming as their father?

THE INCA [*lifts his eyebrows pityingly; shrugs his shoulders; then, with indulgent paternal contempt*] Excellent lads, madam. Very honest affectionate creatures. I have nothing against them. Pongo imitates farmyard sounds—cock-crowing and that sort of thing—extremely well. Lulu plays Strauss's

113

Sinfonia Domestica on the mouth organ really screamingly. Chips keeps owls and rabbits. Spots motor bicycles. The Corsair commands canal barges and steers them himself. The Piffler writes plays, and paints most abominably. Jack Johnson trims ladies' hats, and boxes with professionals hired for that purpose. He is invariably victorious. Yes: they all have their different little talents. And also, of course, their family resemblances. For example, they all smoke; they all quarrel with one another; and they none of them appreciate their father, who, by the way, is no mean painter, though the Piffler pretends to ridicule his efforts.

ERMYNTRUDE. Quite a large choice, eh?

THE INCA. But very little to choose, believe me. I should not recommend Pongo, because he snores so frightfully that it has been necessary to build him a sound-proof bedroom: otherwise the royal family would get no sleep. But any of the others would suit equally well—if you are really bent on marrying one of them.

ERMYNTRUDE. If! What is this? I never wanted to marry one of them. I thought you wanted me to.

THE INCA. I did, madam; but [confidentially, flattering her] you are not quite the sort of person I expected you to be; and I doubt whether any of these young degenerates would make you happy. I trust I am not shewing any want of natural feeling when I say that from the point of view of a lively, accomplished, and beautiful woman [Ermyntrude bows] they might pall after a time. I suggest that you might prefer the Inca himself.

ERMYNTRUDE. Oh, Captain, how could a humble person like myself be of any interest to a prince who is surrounded with the ablest and most far-reaching intellects in the world?

THE INCA [explosively] What on earth are you talking about, madam? Can you name a single man in the entourage of the Inca who is not a born fool?

ERMYNTRUDE. Oh, how can you say that! There is Admiral von Cockpits—

THE INCA [rising intolerantly and striding about the room]
114

Von Cockpits! Madam: if Von Cockpits ever goes to heaven, before three weeks are over, the Angel Gabriel will be at war with the man in the moon.

ERMYNTRUDE. But General Von Schinkenburg—

THE INCA. Schinkenburg! I grant you, Schinkenburg has a genius for defending market gardens. Among market gardens he is invincible. But what is the good of that? The world does not consist of market gardens. Turn him loose in pasture and he is lost. The Inca has defeated all these generals again and again at manœuvres; and yet he has to give place to them in the field because he would be blamed for every disaster—accused of sacrificing the country to his vanity. Vanity! Why do they call him vain? Just because he is one of the few men who are not afraid to live. Why do they call themselves brave? Because they have not sense enough to be afraid to die. Within the last year the world has produced millions of heroes. Has it produced more than one Inca? [*He resumes his seat*].

ERMYNTRUDE. Fortunately not, Captain. I'd rather marry Chips.

THE INCA [*making a wry face*] Chips! Oh no: I wouldnt marry Chips.

ERMYNTRUDE. Why?

THE INCA [*whispering the secret*] Chips talks too much about himself.

ERMYNTRUDE. Well, what about Snooks?

THE INCA. Snooks? Who is he? Have I a son named Snooks? There are so many—[*wearily*] so many—that I often forget. [*Casually*] But I wouldnt marry him, anyhow, if I were you.

ERMYNTRUDE. But hasnt any of them inherited the family genius? Surely, if Providence has entrusted them with the care of Perusalem—if they are all descended from Bedrock the Great—

THE INCA [*interrupting her impatiently*] Madam: if you ask me, I consider Bedrock a grossly overrated monarch.

ERMYNTRUDE [*shocked*] Oh, Captain! Take care! Incadisparagement.

THE INCA. I repeat, grossly overrated. Strictly between ourselves, I do not believe all this about Providence entrusting the care of sixty million human beings to the abilities of Chips and the Piffler and Jack Johnson. I believe in individual genius. That is the Inca's secret. It must be. Why, hang it all, madam, if it were a mere family matter, the Inca's uncle would have been as great a man as the Inca. And—well, everybody knows what the Inca's uncle was.

ERMYNTRUDE. My experience is that the relatives of men of genius are always the greatest duffers imaginable.

THE INCA. Precisely. That is what proves that the Inca is a man of genius. His relatives are duffers.

ERMYNTRUDE. But bless my soul, Captain, if all the Inca's generals are incapables, and all his relatives duffers, Perusalem will be beaten in the war; and then it will become a republic, like France after 1871, and the Inca will be sent to St Helena.

THE INCA [triumphantly] That is just what the Inca is playing for, madam. It is why he consented to the war.

ERMYNTRUDE. What!

THE INCA. Aha! The fools talk of crushing the Inca; but they little know their man. Tell me this. Why did St Helena extinguish Napoleon?

ERMYNTRUDE. I give it up.

THE INCA. Because, madam, with certain rather remarkable qualities, which I should be the last to deny, Napoleon lacked versatility. After all, any fool can be a soldier: we know that only too well in Perusalem, where every fool is a soldier. But the Inca has a thousand other resources. He is an architect. Well, St Helena presents an unlimited field to the architect. He is a painter: need I remind you that St Helena is still without a National Gallery? He is a composer: Napoleon left no symphonies in St Helena. Send the Inca to St Helena, madam, and the world will crowd thither to see his works as they crowd now to Athens to see the Acropolis, to Madrid to see the pictures of Velasquez, to Bayreuth to

116

see the music dramas of that egotistical old rebel Richard
Wagner, who ought to have been shot before he was forty,
as indeed he very nearly was. Take this from me: hereditary
monarchs are played out: the age for men of genius has
come: the career is open to the talents: before ten years have
elapsed every civilized country from the Carpathians to the
Rocky Mountains will be a Republic.

ERMYNTRUDE. Then goodbye to the Inca.

THE INCA. On the contrary, madam, the Inca will then
have his first real chance. He will be unanimously invited by
those Republics to return from his exile and act as Super-
president of all the republics.

ERMYNTRUDE. But wont that be a come down for him?
Think of it! after being Inca, to be a mere President!

THE INCA. Well, why not! An Inca can do nothing. He is
tied hand and foot. A constitutional monarch is openly called
an india-rubber stamp. An emperor is a puppet. The Inca is
not allowed to make a speech: he is compelled to take up a
screed of flatulent twaddle written by some noodle of a minister and read it aloud. But look at the American President!
He is the Allerhöchst, if you like. No, madam, believe me,
there is nothing like Democracy, American Democracy.
Give the people voting papers: good long voting papers,
American fashion; and while the people are reading the
voting papers the Government does what it likes.

ERMYNTRUDE. What! You too worship before the statue
of Liberty, like the Americans?

THE INCA. Not at all, madam. The Americans do not
worship the statue of Liberty. They have erected it in the
proper place for a statue of Liberty: on its tomb [*he turns
down his moustaches*].

ERMYNTRUDE [*laughing*] Oh! Youd better not let them
hear you say that, Captain.

THE INCA. Quite safe, madam: they would take it as a
joke. [*He rises*]. And now, prepare yourself for a surprise.
[*She rises*]. A shock. Brace yourself. Steel yourself. And do
not be afraid.

117

THE INCA OF PERUSALEM

ERMYNTRUDE. Whatever on earth can you be going to tell me, Captain?

THE INCA. Madam: I am no captain. I—

ERMYNTRUDE. You are the Inca in disguise.

THE INCA. Good heavens! how do you know that? Who has betrayed me?

ERMYNTRUDE. How could I help divining it, Sir? Who is there in the world like you? Your magnetism—

THE INCA. True: I had forgotten my magnetism. But you know now that beneath the trappings of Imperial Majesty there is a Man: simple, frank, modest, unaffected, colloquial: a sincere friend, a natural human being, a genial comrade, one eminently calculated to make a woman happy. You, on the other hand, are the most charming woman I have ever met. Your conversation is wonderful. I have sat here almost in silence, listening to your shrewd and penetrating account of my character, my motives, if I may say so, my talents. Never has such justice been done me: never have I experienced such perfect sympathy. Will you—I hardly know how to put this—will you be mine?

ERMYNTRUDE. Oh, Sir, you are married.

THE INCA. I am prepared to embrace the Mahometan faith, which allows a man four wives, if you will consent. It will please the Turks. But I had rather you did not mention it to the Inca-ess, if you dont mind.

ERMYNTRUDE. This is really charming of you. But the time has come for me to make a revelation. It is your Imperial Majesty's turn now to brace yourself. To steel yourself. I am not the princess. I am—

THE INCA. The daughter of my old friend Archdeacon Daffodil Donkin, whose sermons are read to me every evening after dinner. I never forget a face.

ERMYNTRUDE. You knew all along!

THE INCA [*bitterly, throwing himself into his chair*] And you supposed that I, who have been condemned to the society of princesses all my wretched life, believed for a moment that any princess that ever walked could have your intelligence!

118

THE INCA OF PERUSALEM

ERMYNTRUDE. How clever of you, Sir! But you cannot afford to marry me.

THE INCA [*springing up*] Why not?

ERMYNTRUDE. You are too poor. You have to eat war bread. Kings nowadays belong to the poorer classes. The King of England does not even allow himself wine at dinner.

THE INCA [*delighted*] Haw! Ha ha! Haw! haw! [*he is convulsed with laughter, and finally has to relieve his feelings by waltzing half round the room*].

ERMYNTRUDE. You may laugh, Sir; but I really could not live in that style. I am the widow of a millionaire, ruined by your little war.

THE INCA. A millionaire! What are millionaires now, with the world crumbling?

ERMYNTRUDE. Excuse me: mine was a hyphenated millionaire.

THE INCA. A highfalutin millionaire, you mean. [*Chuckling*] Haw! ha ha! really very nearly a pun, that. [*He sits down in her chair*].

ERMYNTRUDE [*revolted, sinking into his chair*] I think it quite the worst pun I ever heard.

THE INCA. The best puns have all been made years ago: nothing remained but to achieve the worst. However, madam [*he rises majestically; and she is about to rise also*]. No: I prefer a seated audience [*she falls back into her seat at the imperious wave of his hand*]. So [*he clicks his heels*]. Madam: I recognize my presumption in having sought the honor of your hand. As you say, I cannot afford it. Victorious as I am, I am hopelessly bankrupt; and the worst of it is, I am intelligent enough to know it. And I shall be beaten in consequence, because my most implacable enemy, though only a few months further away from bankruptcy than myself, has not a ray of intelligence, and will go on fighting until civilization is destroyed, unless I, out of sheer pity for the world, condescend to capitulate.

ERMYNTRUDE. The sooner the better, Sir. Many fine young men are dying while you wait.

119

THE INCA [*flinching painfully*] Why? Why do they do it?

ERMYNTRUDE. Because you make them.

THE INCA. Stuff! How can I? I am only one man; and they are millions. Do you suppose they would really kill each other if they didnt want to, merely for the sake of my beautiful eyes? Do not be deceived by newspaper claptrap, madam. I was swept away by a passion not my own, which imposed itself on me. By myself I am nothing. I dare not walk down the principal street of my own capital in a coat two years old, though the sweeper of that street can wear one ten years old. You talk of death as an unpopular thing. You are wrong: for years I gave them art, literature, science, prosperity, that they might live more abundantly; and they hated me, ridiculed me, caricatured me. Now that I give them death in its frightfullest forms, they are devoted to me. If you doubt me, ask those who for years have begged our taxpayers in vain for a few paltry thousands to spend on Life: on the bodies and minds of the nation's children, on the beauty and healthfulness of its cities, on the honor and comfort of its worn-out workers. They refused; and because they refused, death is let loose on them. They grudged a few hundreds a year for their salvation: they now pay millions a day for their own destruction and damnation. And this they call m y doing! Let them say it, if they dare, before the judgment-seat at which they and I shall answer at last for what we have left undone no less than for what we have done. [*Pulling himself together suddenly*] Madam: I have the honor to be your most obedient [*he clicks his heels and bows*].

ERMYNTRUDE. Sir! [*she curtsies*].

THE INCA [*turning at the door*] Oh, by the way, there is a princess, isnt there, somewhere on the premises?

ERMYNTRUDE. There is. Shall I fetch her?

THE INCA [*dubious*] Pretty awful, I suppose, eh?

ERMYNTRUDE. About the usual thing.

THE INCA [*sighing*] Ah well! What can one expect? I dont think I need trouble her personally. Will you explain to her about the boys?

THE INCA OF PERUSALEM

ERMYNTRUDE. I am afraid the explanation will fall rather flat without your magnetism.

THE INCA [*returning to her and speaking very humanly*] You are making fun of me. Why does everybody make fun of me? Is it fair?

ERMYNTRUDE [*seriously*] Yes: it is fair. What other defence have we poor common people against your shining armor, your mailed fist, your pomp and parade, your terrible power over us? Are these things fair?

THE INCA. Ah, well, perhaps, perhaps. [*He looks at his watch*]. By the way, there is time for a drive round the town and a cup of tea at the Zoo. Quite a bearable band there: it does not play any patriotic airs. I am sorry you will not listen to any more permanent arrangement; but if you would care to come—

ERMYNTRUDE [*eagerly*] Ratherrrrr. I shall be delighted.

THE INCA [*cautiously*] In the strictest honor, you understand.

ERMYNTRUDE. Dont be afraid. I promise to refuse any incorrect proposals.

THE INCA [*enchanted*] Oh! Charming woman: how well you understand men!

He offers her his arm: they go out together.

O'FLAHERTY V.C.

A REMINISCENCE OF 1915
(A RECRUITING PAMPHLET)

Written in 1915

First Performed on the Western Front Belgium 1917

IT may surprise some people to learn that in 1915 this little play was a recruiting poster in disguise. The British officer seldom likes Irish soldiers; but he always tries to have a certain proportion of them in his battalion, because, partly from a want of common sense which leads them to value their lives less than Englishmen do (lives are really less worth living in a poor country), and partly because even the most cowardly Irishman feels obliged to outdo an Englishman in bravery if possible, and at least to set a perilous pace for him, Irish soldiers give impetus to those military operations which require for their spirited execution more devilment than prudence.

Unfortunately, Irish recruiting was badly bungled in 1915. The Irish were for the most part Roman Catholics and loyal Irishmen, which means that from the English point of view they were heretics and rebels. But they were willing enough to go soldiering on the side of France and see the world outside Ireland, which is a dull place to live in. It was quite easy to enlist them by approaching them from their own point of view. But the War Office insisted on approaching them from the point of view of Dublin Castle. They were discouraged and repulsed by refusals to give commissions to Roman Catholic officers, or to allow distinct Irish units to be formed. To attract them, the walls were covered with placards headed REMEMBER BELGIUM. The folly of asking an Irishman to remember anything when you want him to fight for England was apparent to everyone outside the Castle: FORGET AND FORGIVE would have been more to the point. Remembering Belgium and its broken treaty led Irishmen to remember Limerick and its broken treaty; and the recruiting ended in a rebellion, in suppressing which the British artillery quite unnecessarily reduced the centre of Dublin to ruins, and the British commanders killed their leading prisoners of war in cold blood morning after morning with an effect of long drawn out ferocity. Really it was only the usual childish petulance in which John Bull does things in a week that disgrace him for a century, though

125

he soon recovers his good humor, and cannot understand why the survivors of his wrath do not feel as jolly with him as he does with them. On the smouldering ruins of Dublin the appeals to remember Louvain were presently supplemented by a fresh appeal. IRISHMEN: DO YOU WISH TO HAVE THE HORRORS OF WAR BROUGHT TO YOUR OWN HEARTHS AND HOMES? Dublin laughed sourly.

As for me, I addressed myself quite simply to the business of obtaining recruits. I knew by personal experience and observation what anyone might have inferred from the records of Irish emigration, that all an Irishman's hopes and ambitions turn on his opportunities of getting out of Ireland. Stimulate his loyalty, and he will stay in Ireland and die for her; for, incomprehensible as it seems to an Englishman, Irish patriotism does not take the form of devotion to England and England's king. Appeal to his discontent, his deadly boredom, his thwarted curiosity and desire for change and adventure, and, to escape from Ireland, he will go abroad to risk his life for France, for the Papal States, for secession in America, and even, if no better may be, for England. Knowing that the ignorance and insularity of the Irishman is a danger to himself and to his neighbours, I had no scruple in making that appeal when there was something for him to fight which the whole world had to fight unless it meant to come under the jack boot of the German version of Dublin Castle.

There was another consideration, unmentionable by the recruiting sergeants and war orators, which must nevertheless have helped them powerfully in procuring soldiers by voluntary enlistment. The happy home of the idealist may become common under millennial conditions. It is not common at present. No one will ever know how many men joined the army in 1914 and 1915 to escape from tyrants and taskmasters, termagants and shrews, none of whom are any the less irksome when they happen by ill-luck to be also our fathers, our mothers, our wives and our children. Even at their amiablest, a holiday from them may be a tempting

change for all parties. That is why I did not endow O'Flaherty V.C. with an ideal Irish colleen for his sweetheart, and
gave him for his mother a Volumnia of the potato patch
rather than an affectionate parent from whom he could not
so easily have torn himself away.

I need hardly say that a play thus carefully adapted to its
purpose was voted utterly inadmissible; and in due course
the British Government, frightened out of its wits for the
moment by the rout of the Fifth Army, ordained Irish Conscription, and then did not dare to go through with it. I still
think my own line was the more businesslike. But during
the war everyone except the soldiers at the front imagined
that nothing but an extreme assertion of our most passionate
prejudices, without the smallest regard to their effect on
others, could win the war. Finally the British blockade won
the war; but the wonder is that the British blockhead did not
lose it. I suppose the enemy was no wiser. War is not a
sharpener of wits; and I am afraid I gave great offence by
keeping my head in this matter of Irish recruiting. What
can I do but apologize, and publish the play now that it can
no longer do any good?

O'FLAHERTY V.C.

*A*T *the door of an Irish country house in a park. Fine summer weather: the summer of* 1915. *The porch, painted white, projects into the drive; but the door is at the side and the front has a window. The porch faces east; and the door is in the north side of it. On the south side is a tree in which a thrush is singing. Under the window is a garden seat with an iron chair at each end of it.*

The last four bars of God Save the King are heard in the distance, followed by three cheers. Then the band strikes up It's a Long Way to Tipperary and recedes until it is out of hearing.

Private O'Flaherty V.C. comes wearily southward along the drive, and falls exhausted into the garden seat. The thrush utters a note of alarm and flies away. The tramp of a horse is heard.

A GENTLEMAN'S VOICE. Tim! Hi! Tim! [*He is heard dismounting*].

A LABORER'S VOICE. Yes, your honor.

THE GENTLEMAN'S VOICE. Take this horse to the stables, will you?

A LABORER'S VOICE. Right, your honor. Yup there. Gwan now. Gwan. [*The horse is led away*].

General Sir Pearce Madigan, an elderly baronet in khaki, beaming with enthusiasm, arrives. O'Flaherty rises and stands at attention.

SIR PEARCE. No, no, O'Flaherty: none of that now. Youre off duty. Remember that though I am a general of forty years service, that little Cross of yours gives you a higher rank in the roll of glory than I can pretend to.

O'FLAHERTY [*relaxing*] I'm thankful to you, Sir Pearce; but I wouldnt have anyone think that the baronet of my native place would let a common soldier like me sit down in his presence without leave.

SIR PEARCE. Well, youre not a common soldier, O'Flaherty: youre a very uncommon one; and I'm proud to have you for my guest here today.

O'FLAHERTY. Sure I know, sir. You have to put up with a

lot from the like of me for the sake of the recruiting. All the quality shakes hands with me and says theyre proud to know me, just the way the king said when he pinned the Cross on me. And it's as true as I'm standing here, sir, the queen said to me "I hear you were born on the estate of General Madigan," she says; "and the General himself tells me you were always a fine young fellow." "Bedad, Mam," I says to her, "if the General knew all the rabbits I snared on him, and all the salmon I snatched on him, and all the cows I milked on him, he'd think me the finest ornament for the county jail he ever sent there for poaching."

SIR PEARCE [*laughing*] Youre welcome to them all, my lad. Come [*he makes him sit down again on the garden seat*]! sit down and enjoy your holiday [*he sits down on one of the iron chairs: the one at the doorless side of the porch*].

O'FLAHERTY. Holiday, is it? I'd give five shillings to be back in the trenches for the sake of a little rest and quiet. I never knew what hard work was til I took to recruiting. What with the standing on my legs all day, and the shaking hands, and the making speeches, and—whats worse—the listening to them, and the calling for cheers for king and country, and the saluting the flag til I'm stiff with it, and the listening to them playing God Save the King and Tipperary, and the trying to make my eyes look moist like a man in a picture book, I'm that bet that I hardly get a wink of sleep. I give you my word, Sir Pearce, that I never heard the tune of Tipperary in my life til I came back from Flanders; and already it's drove me to that pitch of tiredness of it that when a poor little innocent slip of a boy in the street the other night drew himself up and saluted and began whistling it at me, I clouted his head for him, God forgive me.

SIR PEARCE [*soothingly*] Yes, yes: I know. *I* know. One does get fed up with it: Ive been dog tired myself on parade many a time. But still, you know, theres a gratifying side to it, too. After all, he is our king; and it's our own country, isnt it?

O'FLAHERTY. Well, sir, to you that have an estate in it, it

would feel like your country. But the divil a perch of it ever I owned. And as to the king, God help him, my mother would have taken the skin off my back if I'd ever let on to have any other king than Parnell.

SIR PEARCE [*rising, painfully shocked*] Your mother! What are you dreaming about, O'Flaherty? A most loyal woman. Always most loyal. Whenever there is an illness in the Royal Family, she asks me every time we meet about the health of the patient as anxiously as if it were yourself, her only son.

O'FLAHERTY. Well, she's my mother; and I wont utter a word agen her. But I'm not saying a word of lie when I tell you that old woman is the biggest kanatt from here to the cross of Monasterboice. Sure she's the wildest Fenian and rebel, and always has been, that ever taught a poor innocent lad like myself to pray night and morning to St Patrick to clear the English out of Ireland the same as he cleared the snakes. Youll be surprised at my telling you that now, maybe, Sir Pearce?

SIR PEARCE [*unable to keep still, walking away from O'Flaherty*] Surprised! I'm more than surprised, O'Flaherty. I'm overwhelmed. [*Turning and facing him*] Are you—are you joking?

O'FLAHERTY. If youd been brought up by my mother, sir, youd know better than to joke about her. What I'm telling you is the truth; and I wouldnt tell it to you if I could see my way to get out of the fix I'll be in when my mother comes here this day to see her boy in his glory, and she after thinking all the time it was against the English I was fighting.

SIR PEARCE. Do you mean to say you told her such a monstrous falsehood as that you were fighting in the German army?

O'FLAHERTY. I never told her one word that wasnt the truth and nothing but the truth. I told her I was going to fight for the French and for the Russians; and sure who ever heard of the French or the Russians doing anything to the English but fighting them? That was how it was, sir. And sure the poor woman kissed me and went about the house

singing in her old cracky voice that the French was on the
sea, and theyd be here without delay, and the Orange will
decay, says the Shan Van Vocht.

SIR PEARCE [*sitting down again, exhausted by his feelings*]
Well, I never could have believed this. Never. What do you
suppose will happen when she finds out?

O'FLAHERTY. She mustnt find out. It's not that she'd half
kill me, as big as I am and as brave as I am. It's that I'm fond
of her, and cant bring myself to break the heart in her. You
may think it queer that a man should be fond of his mother,
sir, and she having bet him from the time he could feel to
the time she was too slow to ketch him; but I'm fond of her;
and I'm not ashamed of it. Besides, didnt she win the Cross
for me?

SIR PEARCE. Your mother! How?

O'FLAHERTY. By bringing me up to be more afraid of running away than of fighting. I was timid by nature; and when
the other boys hurted me, I'd want to run away and cry.
But she whaled me for disgracing the blood of the O'Flahertys until I'd have fought the divil himself sooner than
face her after funking a fight. That was how I got to know
that fighting was easier than it looked, and that the others
was as much afeard of me as I was of them, and that if I only
held out long enough theyd lose heart and give up. Thats
the way I came to be so courageous. I tell you, Sir Pearce, if
the German army had been brought up by my mother, the
Kaiser would be dining in the banqueting hall at Buckingham Palace this day, and King George polishing his jack
boots for him in the scullery.

SIR PEARCE. But I dont like this, O'Flaherty. You cant go
on deceiving your mother, you know. It's not right.

O'FLAHERTY. Cant go on deceiving her, cant I? It's little
you know what a son's love can do, sir. Did you ever notice
what a ready liar I am?

SIR PEARCE. Well, in recruiting a man gets carried away.
I stretch it a bit occasionally myself. After all, it's for king
and country. But if you wont mind my saying it, O'Flaherty,

I think that story about your fighting the Kaiser and the twelve giants of the Prussian guard singlehanded would be the better for a little toning down. I dont ask you to drop it, you know; for it's popular, undoubtedly; but still, the truth is the truth. Dont you think it would fetch in almost as many recruits if you reduced the number of guardsmen to six?

O'FLAHERTY. Youre not used to telling lies like I am, sir. I got great practice at home with my mother. What with saving my skin when I was young and thoughtless, and sparing her feelings when I was old enough to understand them, Ive hardly told my mother the truth twice a year since I was born; and would you have me turn round on her and tell it now, when she's looking to have some peace and quiet in her old age?

SIR PEARCE [*troubled in his conscience*] Well, it's not my affair, of course, O'Flaherty. But hadnt you better talk to Father Quinlan about it?

O'FLAHERTY. Talk to Father Quinlan, is it! Do you know what Father Quinlan says to me this very morning?

SIR PEARCE. Oh, youve seen him already, have you? What did he say?

O'FLAHERTY. He says "You know, dont you" he says "that it's your duty, as a Christian and a good son of the Holy Church, to love your enemies?" he says. "I know it's my juty as a soldier to kill them" I says. "Thats right, Dinny," he says: "quite right. But" says he "you can kill them and do them a good turn afterwards to shew your love for them" he says; "and it's your duty to have a mass said for the souls of the hundreds of Germans you say you killed" says he; "for many and many of them were Bavarians and good Catholics" he says. "Is it me that must pay for masses for the souls of the Boshes?" I says. "Let the King of England pay for them" I says; "for it was his quarrel and not mine."

SIR PEARCE [*warmly*] It is the quarrel of every honest man and true patriot, O'Flaherty. Your mother must see that as clearly as I do. After all, she is a reasonable, well disposed woman, quite capable of understanding the right and the wrong of the war. Why cant you explain to her what the war is about?

o'flaherty. Arra, sir, how the divil do I know what the war is about?

sir pearce [*rising again and standing over him*] What! O'Flaherty: do you know what you are saying? You sit there wearing the Victoria Cross for having killed God knows how many Germans; and you tell me you dont know why you did it!

o'flaherty. Asking your pardon, Sir Pearce. I tell you no such thing. I know quite well why I kilt them. I kilt them because I was afeard that, if I didnt, theyd kill me.

sir pearce [*giving it up and sitting down again*] Yes, yes, of course; but have you no knowledge of the causes of the war? of the interests at stake? of the importance—I may almost say—in fact I will say—the sacred rights for which we are fighting? Dont you read the papers?

o'flaherty. I do when I can get them. Theres not many newsboys crying the evening paper in the trenches. They do say, Sir Pearce, that we shall never beat the Boshes until we make Horatio Bottomley Lord Leftnant of England. Do you think thats true, sir?

sir pearce. Rubbish, man! theres no Lord Lieutenant in England: the king is Lord Lieutenant. It's a simple question of patriotism. Does patriotism mean nothing to you?

o'flaherty. It means different to me than what it would to you, sir. It means England and England's king to you. To me and the like of me, it means talking about the English just the way the English papers talk about the Boshes. And what good has it ever done here in Ireland? It's kept me ignorant because it filled up my mother's mind, and she thought it ought to fill up mine too. It's kept Ireland poor, because instead of trying to better ourselves we thought we was the fine fellows of patriots when we were speaking evil of Englishmen that was as poor as ourselves and maybe as good as ourselves. The Boshes I kilt was more knowledg-able men than me: and what better am I now that Ive kilt them? What better is anybody?

SIR PEARCE [*huffed, turning a cold shoulder to him*] I am sorry the terrible experience of this war—the greatest war ever fought—has taught you no better, O'Flaherty.

O'FLAHERTY [*preserving his dignity*] I dont know about it's being a great war, sir. It's a big war; but thats not the same thing. Father Quinlan's new church is a big church: you might take the little old chapel out of the middle of it and not miss it. But my mother says there was more true religion in the old chapel. And the war has taught me that may be she was right.

SIR PEARCE [*grunts sulkily*]!!

O'FLAHERTY [*respectfully but doggedly*] And theres another thing it's taught me too, sir, that concerns you and me, if I may make bold to tell it to you.

SIR PEARCE [*still sulkily*] I hope it's nothing you oughtnt to say to me, O'Flaherty.

O'FLAHERTY. It's this, sir: that I'm able to sit here now and talk to you without humbugging you; and thats what not one of your tenants or your tenants' childer ever did to you before in all your long life. It's a true respect I'm shew-ing you at last, sir. Maybe youd rather have me humbug you and tell you lies as I used, just as the boys here, God help them, would rather have me tell them how I fought the Kaiser, that all the world knows I never saw in my life, than tell them the truth. But I cant take advantage of you the way I used, not even if I seem to be wanting in respect to you and cocked up by winning the Cross.

SIR PEARCE [*touched*] Not at all, O'Flaherty. Not at all.

O'FLAHERTY. Sure whats the Cross to me, barring the little pension it carries? Do you think I dont know that theres hundreds of men as brave as me that never had the luck to get anything for their bravery but a curse from the sergeant, and the blame for the faults of them that ought to have been their betters? Ive learnt more than youd think, sir; for how would a gentleman like you know what a poor ignorant conceited creature I was when I went from here into the wide world as a soldier? What use is all the lying, and pretending, and humbugging, and letting on, when the day comes to you that your comrade is killed in the trench beside you, and you dont as much as look round at him until you trip over his poor body, and then all you say is to ask why the hell the stretcher-bearers dont take it out of the way. Why should I read the papers to be humbugged and lied to by them that had the cunning to stay at home and send me to fight for them? Dont talk to me or to any soldier of the war being right. No war is right; and all the holy water that Father Quinlan ever blessed couldnt make one right. There, sir! Now you know what O'Flaherty V.C. thinks; and youre wiser so than the others that only knows what he done.

SIR PEARCE [*making the best of it, and turning good-humoredly to him again*] Well, what you did was brave and manly, anyhow.

O'FLAHERTY. God knows whether it was or not, better than you nor me, General. I hope He wont be too hard on me for it, anyhow.

SIR PEARCE [*sympathetically*] Oh yes: we all have to think seriously sometimes, especially when we're a little run down. I'm afraid weve been overworking you a bit over these recruiting meetings. However, we can knock off for the rest of the day; and tomorrow's Sunday. Ive had about as much as I can stand myself. [*He looks at his watch*]. It's teatime. I wonder whats keeping your mother.

O'FLAHERTY. It's nicely cocked up the old woman will be having tea at the same table as you, sir, instead of in the kitchen. She'll be after dressing in the heighth of grandeur; and stop she will at every house on the way to shew herself off and tell them where she's going, and fill the whole parish with spite and envy. But sure, she shouldnt keep you waiting, sir.

SIR PEARCE. Oh, thats all right: she must be indulged on an occasion like this. I'm sorry my wife is in London: she'd

136

have been glad to welcome your mother.

o'flaherty. Sure, I know she would, sir. She was always a kind friend to the poor. Little her ladyship knew, God help her, the depth of divilment that was in us: we were like a play to her. You see, sir, she was English: that was how it was. We was to her what the Pathans and Senegalese was to me when I first seen them: I couldnt think, somehow, that they were liars, and thieves, and backbiters, and drunkards, just like ourselves or any other Christians. Oh, her ladyship never knew all that was going on behind her back: how would she? When I was a weeshy child, she gave me the first penny I ever had in my hand; and I wanted to pray for her conversion that night the same as my mother made me pray for yours; and—

sir pearce [scandalized] Do you mean to say that your mother made you pray for m y conversion?

o'flaherty. Sure and she wouldnt want to see a gentleman like you going to hell after she nursing your own son and bringing up my sister Annie on the bottle. That was how it was, sir. She'd rob you; and she'd lie to you; and she'd call down all the blessings of God on your head when she was selling you your own three geese that you thought had been ate by the fox the day after youd finished fattening them, sir; and all the time you were like a bit of her own flesh and blood to her. Often has she said she'd live to see you a good Catholic yet, leading victorious armies against the English and wearing the collar of gold that Malachi won from the proud invader. Oh, she's the romantic woman is my mother, and no mistake.

sir pearce [in great perturbation] I really cant believe this, O'Flaherty. I could have sworn your mother was as honest a woman as ever breathed.

o'flaherty. And so she is, sir. She's as honest as the day.

sir pearce. Do you call it honest to steal my geese?

o'flaherty. She didnt steal them, sir. It was me that stole them.

sir pearce. Oh! And why the devil d i d you steal them?

137

o'flaherty. Sure we needed them, sir. Often and often we had to sell our own geese to pay you the rent to satisfy your needs; and why shouldnt we sell your geese to satisfy ours?

sir pearce. Well, damn me!

o'flaherty [*sweetly*] Sure you had to get what you could out of us; and we had to get what we could out of you. God forgive us both!

sir pearce. Really, O'Flaherty, the war seems to have upset you a little.

o'flaherty. It's set me thinking, sir; and I'm not used to it. It's like the patriotism of the English. They never thought of being patriotic until the war broke out; and now the patriotism has took them so sudden and come so strange to them that they run about like frightened chickens, uttering all manner of nonsense. But please God theyll forget all about it when the war's over. Theyre getting tired of it already.

sir pearce. No, no: it has uplifted us all in a wonderful way. The world will never be the same again, O'Flaherty. Not after a war like this.

o'flaherty. So they all say, sir. I see no great differ myself. It's all the fright and the excitement; and when that quiets down theyll go back to their natural divilment and be the same as ever. It's like the vermin: itll wash off after a while.

sir pearce [*rising and planting himself firmly behind the garden seat*] Well, the long and the short of it is, O'Flaherty, I must decline to be a party to any attempt to deceive your mother. I thoroughly disapprove of this feeling against the English, especially at a moment like the present. Even if your mother's political sympathies are really what you represent them to be, I should think that her gratitude to Gladstone ought to cure her of such disloyal prejudices.

o'flaherty (*over his shoulder*) She says Gladstone was an Irishman, sir. What call would he have to meddle with Ireland as he did if he wasnt?

SIR PEARCE. What nonsense! Does she suppose Mr Asquith is an Irishman?

O'FLAHERTY. She wont give him any credit for Home Rule, sir. She says Redmond made him do it. She says you told her so.

SIR PEARCE [*convicted out of his own mouth*] Well, I never meant her to take it up in that ridiculous way. [*He moves to the end of the garden seat on O'Flaherty's left*] I'll give her a good talking to when she comes. I'm not going to stand any of her nonsense.

O'FLAHERTY. It's not a bit of use, sir. She says all the English generals is Irish. She says all the English poets and great men was Irish. She says the English never knew how to read their own books until we taught them. She says we're the lost tribes of the house of Israel and the chosen people of God. She says that the goddess Venus, that was born out of the foam of the sea, came up out of the water in Killiney Bay off Bray Head. She says that Moses built the seven churches, and that Lazarus was buried in Glasnevin.

SIR PEARCE. Bosh! How does she know he was? Did you ever ask her?

O'FLAHERTY. I did, sir, often.

SIR PEARCE. And what did she say?

O'FLAHERTY. She asked me how did I know he wasnt, and fetched me a clout on the side of my head.

SIR PEARCE. But have you never mentioned any famous Englishman to her, and asked her what she had to say about him?

O'FLAHERTY. The only one I could think of was Shakespear, sir; and she says he was born in Cork.

SIR PEARCE [*exhausted*] Well, I give it up [*he throws himself into the nearest chair*] The woman is—Oh, well! No matter.

O'FLAHERTY [*sympathetically*] Yes, sir: she's pigheaded and obstinate: theres no doubt about it. She's like the English: they think theres no one like themselves. It's the same with the Germans, though theyre educated and ought to

139

know better. Youll never have a quiet world til you knock
the patriotism out of the human race.

SIR PEARCE. Still, we—

O'FLAHERTY. Whisht, sir, for God's sake: here she is.

*The General jumps up. Mrs O'Flaherty arrives, and comes
between the two men. She is very clean, and carefully dressed
in the old fashioned peasant costume: black silk sunbonnet with a
tiara of trimmings, and black cloak.*

O'FLAHERTY [*rising shyly*] Good evening, mother.

MRS O'FLAHERTY [*severely*] You hold your whisht, and
learn behavior while I pay my juty to his honor. [*To Sir
Pearce, heartily*] And how is your honor's good self? And
how is her ladyship and all the young ladies? Oh, it's right
glad we are to see your honor back again and looking the
picture of health.

SIR PEARCE [*forcing a note of extreme geniality*] Thank you,
Mrs O'Flaherty. Well, you see weve brought you back your
son safe and sound. I hope youre proud of him.

MRS O'FLAHERTY. And indeed and I am, your honor. It's
the brave boy he is; and why wouldnt he be, brought up
on your honor's estate and with you before his eyes for a
pattern of the finest soldier in Ireland. Come and kiss your
old mother, Dinny darlint. [*O'Flaherty does so sheepishly*].
Thats my own darling boy. And look at your fine new uniform stained already with the eggs youve been eating and
the porter youve been drinking. [*She takes out her handkerchief; spits on it; and scrubs his lapel with it*]. Oh, it's the un-
tidy slovenly one you always were. There! It wont be seen
on the khaki: it's not like the old red coat that would shew
up everything that dribbled down on it. [*To Sir Pearce*] And
they tell me down at the lodge that her ladyship is staying
in London, and that Miss Agnes is to be married to a fine
young nobleman. Oh, it's your honor that is the lucky and
happy father! It will be bad news for many of the young
gentlemen of the quality round here, sir. Theres lots thought
she was going to marry young Master Lawless—

SIR PEARCE. What! that—that—that bosthoon!

O'FLAHERTY V.C.

MRS O'FLAHERTY [*hilariously*] Let your honor alone for finding the right word! A big bosthoon he is indeed, your honor. Oh, to think of the times and times I have said that Miss Agnes would be my lady as her mother was before her! Didnt I, Dinny?

SIR PEARCE. And now, Mrs O'Flaherty, I daresay you have a great deal to say to Dennis that doesnt concern me. I'll just go in and order tea.

MRS O'FLAHERTY. Oh, why would your honor disturb yourself? Sure I can take the boy into the yard.

SIR PEARCE. Not at all. It wont disturb me in the least. And he's too big a boy to be taken into the yard now. He has made a front seat for himself. Eh? [*He goes into the house*].

MRS O'FLAHERTY. Sure he has that, your honor. God bless your honor! [*The General being now out of hearing, she turns threateningly to her son with one of those sudden Irish changes of manner which amaze and scandalize less flexible nations, and exclaims*] And what do you mean, you lying young scald, by telling me you were going to fight agen the English? Did you take me for a fool that couldnt find out, and the papers all full of you shaking hands with the English king at Buckingham Palace?

O'FLAHERTY. I didnt shake hands with him: he shook hands with me. Could I turn on the man in his own house, before his own wife, with his money in my pocket and in yours, and throw his civility back in his face?

MRS O'FLAHERTY. You would take the hand of a tyrant red with the blood of Ireland—

O'FLAHERTY. Arra hold your nonsense, mother: he's not half the tyrant you are, God help him. His hand was cleaner than mine that had the blood of his own relations on it, may be.

MRS O'FLAHERTY [*threateningly*] Is that a way to speak to your mother, you young spalpeen?

O'FLAHERTY [*stoutly*] It is so, if you wont talk sense to me. It's a nice thing for a poor boy to be made much of by kings and queens, and shook hands with by the heighth of his country's nobility in the capital cities of the world, and then to come home and be scolded and insulted by his own mother. I'll fight for who I like; and I'll shake hands with what kings I like; and if your own son is not good enough for you, you can go and look for another. Do you mind me now?

MRS O'FLAHERTY. And was it the Belgians learned you such brazen impudence?

O'FLAHERTY. The Belgians is good men; and the French ought to be more civil to them, let alone their being half murdered by the Boshes.

MRS O'FLAHERTY. Good men is it. Good men! to come over here when they were wounded because it was a Catholic country, and then to go to the Protestant Church because it didnt cost them anything, and some of them to never go near a church at all. Thats what you call good men!

O'FLAHERTY. Oh, youre the mighty fine politician, arnt you? Much you know about Belgians or foreign parts or the world youre living in, God help you!

MRS O'FLAHERTY. Why wouldnt I know better than you? Amment I your mother?

O'FLAHERTY. And if you are itself, how can you know what you never seen as well as me that was dug into the continent of Europe for six months, and was buried in the earth of it three times with the shells bursting on the top of me? I tell you I know what I'm about. I have my own reasons for taking part in this great conflict. I'd be ashamed to stay at home and not fight when everybody else is fighting.

MRS O'FLAHERTY. If you wanted to fight, why couldnt you fight in the German army?

O'FLAHERTY. Because they only get a penny a day.

MRS O'FLAHERTY. Well, and if they do itself, isnt there the French army?

O'FLAHERTY. They only get a hapenny a day.

MRS O'FLAHERTY [*much dashed*] Oh murder! They must be a mean lot, Dinny.

O'FLAHERTY [*sarcastic*] Maybe youd have me join the Turkish army, and worship the heathen Mahomet that put a corn in his ear and pretended it was a message from the heavens when the pigeon come to pick it out and eat it. I went where I could get the biggest allowance for you; and little thanks I get for it!

MRS O'FLAHERTY. Allowance, is it! Do you know what the thieving blackguards did on me? They came to me and they says, "Was your son a big eater?" they says. "Oh, he was that" says I: "ten shillings a week wouldnt keep him." Sure I thought the more I said the more theyd give me. "Then" says they, "thats ten shillings a week off your allowance" they says, "because you save that by the king feeding him." "Indeed!" says I: "I suppose if I'd six sons, youd stop three pound a week from me, and make out that I ought to pay you money instead of you paying me." "Theres a fallacy in your argument" they says.

O'FLAHERTY. A what?

MRS O'FLAHERTY. A fallacy: thats the word he said. I says to him, "It's a Pharisee I'm thinking you mean, sir; but you can keep your dirty money that your king grudges a poor old widow; and please God the English will be bet yet for the deadly sin of oppressing the poor"; and with that I shut the door in his face.

O'FLAHERTY [furious] Do you tell me they knocked ten shillings off you for my keep?

MRS O'FLAHERTY [soothing him] No, darlint: they only knocked off half a crown. I put up with it because Ive got the old age pension; and they know very well I'm only sixty-two; so Ive the better of them by half a crown a week anyhow.

O'FLAHERTY. It's a queer way of doing business. If theyd tell you straight out what they was going to give you, you wouldnt mind; but if there was twenty ways of telling the truth and only one way of telling a lie, the Government would find it out. It's in the nature of governments to tell lies.

Teresa Driscoll, a parlor maid, comes from the house.

TERESA. Youre to come up to the drawing room to have your tea, Mrs O'Flaherty.

MRS O'FLAHERTY. Mind you have a sup of good black tea

for me in the kitchen afterwards, acushla. That washy draw-ing room tea will give me the wind if I leave it on my stomach. [*She goes into the house, leaving the two young people alone together*].

o'FLAHERTY. Is that yourself, Tessie? And how are you?

TERESA. Nicely, thank you. And hows yourself?

o'FLAHERTY. Finely, thank God. [*He produces a gold chain*]. Look what Ive brought you, Tessie.

TERESA [*shrinking*] Sure I dont like to touch it, Denny. Did you take it off a dead man?

o'FLAHERTY. No: I took it off a live one; and thankful he was to me to be alive and kept a prisoner in ease and comfort, and me left fighting in peril of my life.

TERESA [*taking it*] Do you think it's real gold, Denny?

o'FLAHERTY. It's real German gold, anyhow.

TERESA. But German silver isnt real, Denny.

o'FLAHERTY [*his face darkening*] Well, it's the best the Bosh could do for me, anyhow.

TERESA. Do you think I might take it to the jeweller next market day and ask him?

o'FLAHERTY [*sulkily*] You may take it to the divil if you like.

TERESA. You neednt lose your temper about it. I only thought I'd like to know. The nice fool I'd look if I went about shewing off a chain that turned out to be only brass!

o'FLAHERTY. I think you might say Thank you.

TERESA. Do you? I think you might have said something more to me than "Is that yourself?" You couldnt say less to the postman.

o'FLAHERTY [*his brow clearing*] Oh, is that whats the matter? Here! come and take the taste of the brass out of my mouth. [*He seizes her and kisses her*].

Teresa, without losing her Irish dignity, takes the kiss as appreciatively as a connoisseur might take a glass of wine, and sits down with him on the garden seat.

TERESA [*as he squeezes her waist*] Thank God the priest cant see us here!

144

o'flaherty. It's little they care for priests in France, alanna.

teresa. And what had the queen on her, Denny, when she spoke to you in the palace?

o'flaherty. She had a bonnet on without any strings to it. And she had a plakeen of embroidery down her bosom. And she had her waist where it used to be, and not where the other ladies had it. And she had little brooches in her ears, though she hadnt half the jewelry of Mrs Sullivan that keeps the popshop in Drumpogue. And she dresses her hair down over her forehead, in a fringe like. And she has an Irish look about her eyebrows. And she didnt know what to say to me, poor woman! and I didnt know what to say to her, God help me!

teresa. Youll have a pension now with the Cross, wont you, Denny?

o'flaherty. Sixpence three farthings a day.

teresa. That isnt much.

o'flaherty. I take out the rest in glory.

teresa. And if youre wounded, youll have a wound pension, wont you?

o'flaherty. I will, please God.

teresa. Youre going out again, arnt you, Denny?

o'flaherty. I cant help myself. I'd be shot for a deserter if I didnt go; and may be I'll be shot by the Boshes if I do go; so between the two of them I'm nicely fixed up.

mrs o'flaherty [calling from within the house] Tessie! Tessie darlint!

teresa [disengaging herself from his arm and rising] I'm wanted for the tea table. Youll have a pension anyhow, Denny, wont you, whether youre wounded or not?

mrs o'flaherty. Come, child, come.

teresa [impatiently] Oh, sure I'm coming. [She tries to smile at Denny, not very convincingly, and hurries into the house].

o'flaherty [alone] And if I do get a pension itself, the divil a penny of it youll ever have the spending of.

145

O'FLAHERTY V.C.

MRS O'FLAHERTY [*as she comes from the porch*] Oh, it's a shame for you to keep the girl from her juties, Dinny. You might get her into trouble.

O'FLAHERTY. Much I care whether she gets into trouble or not! I pity the man that gets her into trouble. He'll get himself into worse.

MRS O'FLAHERTY. Whats that you tell me? Have you been falling out with her, and she a girl with a fortune of ten pounds?

O'FLAHERTY. Let her keep her fortune. I wouldnt touch her with the tongs if she had thousands and millions.

MRS O'FLAHERTY. Oh fie for shame, Dinny! why would you say the like of that of a decent honest girl, and one of the Driscolls too?

O'FLAHERTY. Why wouldnt I say it? She's thinking of nothing but to get me out there again to be wounded so that she may spend my pension, bad scran to her!

MRS O'FLAHERTY. Why, whats come over you, child, at all at all?

O'FLAHERTY. Knowledge and wisdom has come over me with pain and fear and trouble. Ive been made a fool of and imposed upon all my life. I thought that covetious sthreal in there was a walking angel; and now if ever I marry at all I'll marry a Frenchwoman.

MRS O'FLAHERTY [*fiercely*] Youll not, so; and dont you dar repeat such a thing to me.

O'FLAHERTY. Wont I, faith! Ive been as good as married to a couple of them already.

MRS O'FLAHERTY. The Lord be praised, what wickedness have you been up to, you young blackguard?

O'FLAHERTY. One of them Frenchwomen would cook you a meal twice in the day and all days and every day that Sir Pearce himself might go begging through Ireland for, and never see the like of. I'll have a French wife, I tell you; and when I settle down to be a farmer I'll have a French farm, with a field as big as the continent of Europe that ten of your dirty little fields here wouldnt so much as fill the

146

ditch of.

MRS O'FLAHERTY [*furious*] Then it's a French mother you may go look for; for I'm done with you.

O'FLAHERTY. And it's no great loss youd be if it wasnt for my natural feelings for you; for it's only a silly ignorant old countrywoman you are with all your fine talk about Ireland: you that never stepped beyond the few acres of it you were born on!

MRS O'FLAHERTY [*tottering to the garden seat and shewing signs of breaking down*] Dinny darlint, why are you like this to me? Whats happened to you?

O'FLAHERTY [*gloomily*] Whats happened to everybody? thats what I want to know. Whats happened to you that I thought all the world of and was afeard of? Whats happened to Sir Pearce, that I thought was a great general, and that I now see to be no more fit to command an army than an old hen? Whats happened to Tessie, that I was mad to marry a year ago, and that I wouldnt take now with all Ireland for her fortune? I tell you the world's creation is crumbling in ruins about me; and then you come and ask whats happened to me?

MRS O'FLAHERTY [*giving way to wild grief*] Ochone! ochone! my son's turned agen me. Oh, whatll I do at all at all? Oh! oh! oh! oh!

SIR PEARCE [*running out of the house*] Whats this infernal noise? What on earth is the matter?

O'FLAHERTY. Arra hold your whisht, mother. Dont you see his honor?

MRS O'FLAHERTY. Oh, sir, I'm ruined and destroyed. Oh, wont you speak to Dinny, sir: I'm heart scalded with him. He wants to marry a Frenchwoman on me, and to go away and be a foreigner and desert his mother and betray his country. It's mad he is with the roaring of the cannons and he killing the Germans and the Germans killing him, bad cess to them! My boy is taken from me and turned agen me; and who is to take care of me in my old age after all Ive done for him, ochone! ochone!

147

o'flaherty. Hold your noise, I tell you. Who's going to leave you? I'm going to take you with me. There now: does that satisfy you?

mrs o'flaherty. Is it take me into a strange land among heathens and pagans and savages, and me not knowing a word of their language nor them of mine?

o'flaherty. A good job they dont: may be theyll think youre talking sense.

mrs o'flaherty. Ask me to die out of Ireland, is it? and the angels not to find me when they come for me!

o'flaherty. And would you ask me to live in Ireland where Ive been imposed on and kept in ignorance, and to die where the divil himself wouldnt take me as a gift, let alone the blessed angels? You can come or stay. You can take your old way or take my young way. But stick in this place I will not among a lot of good-for-nothing divils thatll not do a hand's turn but watch the grass growing and build up the stone wall where the cow walked through it. And Sir Horace Plunkett breaking his heart all the time telling them how they might put the land into decent tillage like the French and Belgians.

sir pearce. Yes: he's quite right, you know, Mrs O'Flaherty: quite right there.

mrs o'flaherty. Well, sir, please God the war will last a long time yet; and may be I'll die before it's over and the separation allowance stops.

o'flaherty. Thats all you care about. It's nothing but milch cows we men are for the women, with their separation allowances, ever since the war began, bad luck to them that made it!

teresa [coming from the porch between the General and Mrs O'Flaherty] Hannah sent me out for to tell you, sir, that the tea will be black and the cake not fit to eat with the cold if yous all dont come at wanst.

mrs o'flaherty [breaking out again] Oh, Tessie darlint, what have you been saying to Dinny at all at all? Oh! oh—

sir pearce [out of patience] You cant discuss that here.

148

We shall have Tessie beginning now.

O'FLAHERTY. Thats right, sir: drive them in.

TERESA. I havnt said a word to him. He—

SIR PEARCE. Hold your tongue; and go in and attend to your business at the tea table.

TERESA. But amment I telling your honor that I never said a word to him? He gave me a beautiful gold chain. Here it is to shew your honour thats it's no lie I'm telling you.

SIR PEARCE. Whats this, O'Flaherty? Youve been looting some unfortunate officer.

O'FLAHERTY. No sir: I stole it from him of his own accord.

MRS O'FLAHERTY. Wouldnt your honor tell him that his mother has the first call on it? What would a slip of a girl like that be doing with a gold chain round her neck?

TERESA [*venomously*] Anyhow, I have a neck to put it round and not a hank of wrinkles.

At this unfortunate remark, Mrs O'Flaherty bounds from her seat; and an appalling tempest of wordy wrath breaks out. The remonstrances and commands of the General, and the protests and menaces of O'Flaherty, only increase the hubbub. They are soon all speaking at once at the top of their voices.

MRS O'FLAHERTY [*solo*] You impudent young heifer, how dar you say such a thing to me? [*Teresa retorts furiously; the men interfere; and the solo becomes a quartet, fortissimo*]. Ive a good mind to clout your ears for you to teach you manners. Be ashamed of yourself, do; and learn to know who youre speaking to. That I maytnt sin! but I dont know what the good God was thinking about when he made the like of you. Let me not see you casting sheep's eyes at my son again. There never was an O'Flaherty yet that would demean himself by keeping company with a dirty Driscoll; and if I see you next or nigh my house I'll put you in the ditch with a flea in your ear: mind that now.

THERESA. Is it me you offer such a name to, you foulmouthed, dirty minded, lying, sloothering old sow, you? I wouldnt soil my tongue by calling you in your right name

149

and telling Sir Pearce whats the common talk of the town about you. You and your O'Flahertys! setting yourself up agen the Driscolls that would never lower themselves to be seen in conversation with you at the fair. You can keep your ugly stingy lump of a son; for what he is but a common soldier? and God help the girl that gets him, say I! So the back of my hand to you, Mrs O'Flaherty; and that the cat may tear your ugly old face!

SIR PEARCE. Silence. Tessie: did you here me ordering you to go into the house? Mrs O'Flaherty! [*Louder*] Mrs O'Flaherty!! Will you just listen to me one moment? Please. [*Furiously*] Do you hear me speaking to you, woman? Are you human beings or are you wild beasts? Stop that noise immediately: do you hear? [*Yelling*] Are you going to do what I order you, or are you not? Scandalous! Disgraceful! This comes of being too familiar with you. O'Flaherty: shove them into the house. Out with the whole damned pack of you.

O'FLAHERTY [*to the women*] Here now: none of that, none of that. Go easy, I tell you. Hold your whisht, mother, will you, or youll be sorry for it after. [*To Teresa*] Is that the way for a decent young girl to speak? [*Despairingly*] Oh, for the Lord's sake, shut up, will yous? Have yous no respect for yourselves or your betters? [*Peremptorily*] Let me have no more of it, I tell you. Och! the divil's in the whole crew of you. In with you into the house this very minute and tear one another's eyes out in the kitchen if you like. In with you.

The two men seize the two women, and push them, still violently abusing one another, into the house. Sir Pearce slams the door upon them savagely. Immediately a heavenly silence falls on the summer afternoon. The two sit down out of breath; and for a long time nothing is said. Sir Pearce sits on an iron chair. O'Flaherty sits on the garden seat. The thrush begins to sing melodiously. O'Flaherty cocks his ears, and looks up at it. A smile spreads over his troubled features. Sir Pearce, with a long sigh, takes out his pipe, and begins to fill it.

O'FLAHERTY [*idyllically*] What a discontented sort of an

animal a man is, sir! Only a month ago, I was in the quiet of the country out at the front, with not a sound except the birds and the bellow of a cow in the distance as it might be, and the shrapnel making little clouds in the heavens, and the shells whistling, and may be a yell or two when one of us was hit; and would you believe it, sir, I complained of the noise and wanted to have a peaceful hour at home. Well: them two has taught me a lesson. This morning, sir, when I was telling the boys here how I was longing to be back taking my part for king and country with the others, I was lying, as you well knew, sir. Now I can go and say it with a clear conscience. Some likes war's alarums; and some likes home life. Ive tried both, sir; and I'm all for war's alarums now. I always was a quiet lad by natural disposition.

SIR PEARCE. Strictly between ourselves, O'Flaherty, and as one soldier to another [*O'Flaherty salutes, but without stiffening*], do you think we should have got an army without conscription if domestic life had been as happy as people say it is?

O'FLAHERTY. Well, between you and me and the wall, Sir Pearce, I think the less we say about that until the war's over, the better.

He winks at the General. The General strikes a march. The thrush sings. A jay laughs. The conversation drops.

THE MUSIC-CURE

A PIECE OF UTTER NONSENSE

Written in 1913

First Performed London 1914

See Preface: Trifles and Tomfooleries (*Volume IV, page 721*)

THIS is not a serious play: it is what is called a Variety Turn for two musicians. It is written for two pianists, but can be adapted to any instruments on which the performers happen to be proficient. At its first performance by Miss Madge McIntosh and Mr William Armstrong the difficulty arose that, though Mr Armstrong was an accomplished pianist, Miss McIntosh's virtuosity was confined to the English concertina. That did just as well.

As a last desperate resort a pianola behind the scenes can be employed; but the result will lack spontaneity.

There is, however, no pressing reason why the thing should be performed at all.

THE MUSIC-CURE

LORD REGINALD FITZAMBEY, *a fashionably dressed, rather pretty young man of 22, is prostrate on a sofa in a large hotel drawing room, crying convulsively. His doctor is trying to soothe him. The doctor is about a dozen years his senior; and his ways are the ways of a still youthful man who considers himself in smart society as well as professionally attendant on it.*

The drawing room has tall central doors, at present locked. If anyone could enter under these circumstances, he would find on his left a grand piano with the keyboard end towards him, and a smaller door beyond the piano. On his right would be the window, and, further on, the sofa on which the unhappy youth is wallowing, with, close by it, the doctor's chair and a little table accommodating the doctor's hat, a plate, a medicine bottle, a half emptied glass, and a bell call.

THE DOCTOR. Come come! be a man. Now really this is silly. You mustnt give way like this. I tell you nothing's happened to you. Hang it all! it's not the end of the world if you did buy a few shares—

REGINALD [*interrupting him frantically*] I never meant any harm in buying those shares. I am ready to give them up. Oh, I never meant any harm in buying those shares. I never meant any harm in buying those shares. [*Clutching the doctor imploringly*] Wont you believe me, Doctor? I never meant any harm in buying those shares. I never—

THE DOCTOR [*extricating himself and replacing Reginald on the couch, not very gently*] Of course you didnt. I know you didnt.

REGINALD. I never—

THE DOCTOR [*desperate*] Dont go on saying that over and over again or you will drive us all as distracted as you are yourself. This is nothing but nerves. Remember that youre in a hotel. Theyll put you out if you make a row.

REGINALD [*tearfully*] But you dont understand. Oh, why wont anybody understand? I never—

THE DOCTOR [*shouting him down*] You never meant any

155

harm in buying those shares. This is the four hundredth time youve said it.

REGINALD [*wildly*] Then why do you keep asking me the same questions over and over again? It's not fair. Ive told you I never meant any harm in—

THE DOCTOR. Yes, yes, yes: I know, I know. You think you made a fool of yourself before that committee. Well, you didnt. You stood up to it for six days with the coolness of an iceberg and the cheerfulness of an idiot. Every member of it had a go at you; and everyone of them, including some of the cleverest cross-examiners in London, fell back baffled before your fatuous self-satisfaction, your impenetrable inability to see any reason why you shouldnt have bought those shares.

REGINALD. But why shouldnt I have bought them? I made no secret of it. When the Prime Minister ragged me about it I offered to sell him the shares for what I gave for them.

THE DOCTOR. Yes, after they had fallen six points. But never mind that. The point for you is that you are an undersecretary in the War Office. You knew that the army was going to be put on vegetarian diet, and that the British Maccaroni Trust shares would go up with a rush when this became public. And what did you do?

REGINALD. I did what any fellow would have done. I bought all the shares I could afford.

THE DOCTOR. You bought a great many more than you could afford.

REGINALD. But why shouldnt I? Explain it to me. I'm anxious to learn. I meant no harm. I see no harm. Why am I to be badgered because the beastly Opposition papers and all the Opposition rotters on that committee try to make party capital out of it by saying that it was disgraceful? It wasnt disgraceful: it was simple common sense. I'm not a financier; but you cant persuade me that if you happen to know that certain shares are going to rise you shouldnt buy them. It would be flying in the face of Providence not to.

156

And they wouldnt see that. They pretended not to see it. They worried me, and kept asking me the same thing over and over again, and wrote blackguardly articles about me—

THE DOCTOR. And you got the better of them all because you couldnt see their point of view. But what beats me is why you broke down afterwards.

REGINALD. Everyone was against me. I thought the committee a pack of fools; and I as good as told them so. But everyone took their part. The governor said I had disgraced the family name. My brothers said I ought to resign from my clubs. My mother said that all her hopes of marrying me to a rich woman were shattered. And I'd done nothing: absolutely n o t h i n g towhat otherchaps are doing every day.

THE DOCTOR. Well, the long and short of it is that officials mustnt gamble.

REGINALD. But I wasnt gambling. I k n e w. It isnt gambling if you know that the shares will go up. It's a cert.

THE DOCTOR. Well, all I can tell you is that if you werent a son of the Duke of Dunmow, youd have to resign; and—

REGINALD [*breaking down*] Oh, stop talking to me about it. Let me alone. I cant bear it. I never meant any harm in buying those shares. I never meant any harm—

THE DOCTOR. Sh-sh-sh-sh-sh! There: I shouldnt have started the subject again. Take some of this valerian [*he puts the glass to Reginald's lips*]. Thats right. Now youre better.

REGINALD [*exhausted but calm*] Why does valerian soothe me when it excites cats? Theres a question to reflect on! You know, they ought to have made me a philosopher.

THE DOCTOR. Philosophers are born, not made.

REGINALD. Fine old chestnut, that. Everybody's born, not made.

THE DOCTOR. Youre getting almost clever. I dont like it: youre not yourself today. I wish I could take your mind off your troubles. Suppose you try a little music.

REGINALD. I cant play. My fingers wont obey me. And I cant stand the sound of the piano. I sounded a note this morning; and it made me scream.

157

THE MUSIC-CURE

THE DOCTOR. But why not get somebody to play to you?

REGINALD. Whom could I get, even if I could bear it? You cant play.

THE DOCTOR. Well: I'm not the only person in the world.

REGINALD. If you bring anyone else in here, I shall go mad. I'll throw myself out of the window. I cant bear the idea of music. I dread it, hate it, loathe it.

THE DOCTOR. Thats very serious, you know.

REGINALD. Why is it serious?

THE DOCTOR. Well, what would become of you without your turn for music? You have absolutely no capacity in any other direction.

REGINALD. I'm in Parliament. And I'm an under-secretary.

THE DOCTOR. Thats because your father is a Duke. If you were in a Republic you wouldnt be trusted to clean boots, unless your father was a millionaire. No, Reginald: the day you give up vamping accompaniments and playing the latest ragtimes by ear, youre a lost man socially.

REGINALD [*deprecating*] Oh, I say!

THE DOCTOR [*rising*] However, perhaps it's too soon for you to try the music-cure yet. It was your mother's idea; but I'll call and tell her to wait a day or two. I think she meant to send somebody to play. I must be off now. Look in again later. Meanwhile, sleep as much as you can. Or you might read a little.

REGINALD. What can I read?

THE DOCTOR. Try the Strand Magazine.

REGINALD. But it's so frightfully intellectual. It would overtax my brain.

THE DOCTOR. Oh, well, I suppose it would. Well, sleep. Perhaps I'd better give you something to send you off [*he produces a medicine case*].

REGINALD. Whats this? Veronal?

THE DOCTOR. Dont be alarmed. Only the old-fashioned remedy: opium. Take this [*Reginald takes a pill*]: that will do the trick, I expect. If you find after half an hour that it

158

THE MUSIC-CURE

has only excited you, take another. I'll leave one for you [*he puts one on the plate, and pockets his medicine case*].

REGINALD. Better leave me a lot. I like pills.

THE DOCTOR. Thank you: I'm not treating you with a view to a coroner's inquest. You know, dont you, that opium is a poison?

REGINALD. Yes, opium. But not pills.

THE DOCTOR. Well, Heaven forbid that I, a doctor, should shake anybody's faith in pills. But I shant leave you enough to kill you. [*He puts on his hat*].

REGINALD. Youll tell them, wont you, not to let anyone in. Really and truly I shall throw myself out of the window if any stranger comes in. I should go out of my mind.

THE DOCTOR. None of us have very far to go to do that, my young friend. Ta ta, for the moment [*he makes for the central doors*].

REGINALD. You cant go out that way. I made my mother lock it and take away the key. I felt sure theyd let somebody in that way if she didnt. Youll have to go the way you came.

THE DOCTOR [*returning*] Right. Now let me see you settle down before I go. I want you to be asleep before I leave the room.

Reginald settles himself to sleep with his face to the back of the sofa. The doctor goes softly to the side door and goes out.

REGINALD [*sitting up wildly and staring affrightedly at the piano*] Doctor! Doctor! Help!!!

THE DOCTOR [*returning hastily*] What is it?

REGINALD [*after another doubtful look at the piano*] Nothing. [*He composes himself to sleep again*].

THE DOCTOR. Nothing! There must have been something or you wouldnt have yelled like that. [*Pulling Reginald over so as to see his face*] Here! what was it?

REGINALD. Well, it's gone.

THE DOCTOR. Whats gone?

REGINALD. The crocodile.

THE DOCTOR. The crocodile!

REGINALD. Yes. It laughed at me, and was going to play

159

the piano with its tail.

THE DOCTOR. Opium in small doses doesnt agree with you, my young friend. [*Taking the spare pill from the plate*] I shall have to give you a second pill.

REGINALD. But suppose two crocodiles come!

THE DOCTOR. They wont. If anything comes it will be something pretty this time. Thats how opium acts. Anyhow, youll be fast asleep in ten minutes. Here. Take it.

REGINALD [*after taking the pill*] It was awfully silly of me. But you know I really saw the thing.

THE DOCTOR. You neednt trouble about what you see with your eyes shut. [*He turns to the door*].

REGINALD. Would you mind looking under the sofa to make sure the crocodile isnt there?

THE DOCTOR. Why not look yourself? that would be more convincing.

REGINALD. I darent.

THE DOCTOR. You duffer! [*He looks*]. All serene. No crocodile. Now go bye bye. [*He goes out*].

Reginald again composes himself to sleep. Somebody unlocks the central doors. A lovely lady enters with a bouquet in her hand. She looks about her; takes a letter from wherever she carries letters; and starts on a voyage of discovery round the room, checking her observations by the contents of the letter. The piano seems specially satisfactory: she nods as she sees it. Reginald seems also to be quite expected. She does not speak to him. When she is quite satisfied that she is in the right room, she goes to the piano and tantalizes the expectant audience for about two minutes by putting down her flowers on the candle-stand; taking off her gloves and putting them with the flowers; taking off half a dozen diamond rings in the same way; sitting down to the keyboard and finding it too near to the piano, then too far, then too high, then too low: in short, exhausting all the tricks of the professional pianist before she at last strikes the keys and preludes brilliantly. At the sound, Reginald, with a scream, rolls from the sofa and writhes on the carpet in horrible contortions. She stops playing, amazed.

REGINALD. Oh! Oh! Oh! The crocodiles! Stop! Ow!

Oh! [*He looks at the piano and sees the lady*] Oh I say!

THE LADY. What on earth do you mean by making that noise when I'm playing? Have you no sense? Have you no manners?

REGINALD [*sitting on the floor*] I'm awfully sorry.

THE LADY. Sorry! Why did you do it?

REGINALD. I thought you were a crocodile.

THE LADY. What a silly thing to say! Do I look like a crocodile?

REGINALD. No.

THE LADY. Do I play like a crocodile!

REGINALD [*cautiously rising and approaching her*] Well, you know, it's so hard to know how a crocodile would play.

THE LADY. Stuff! [*She resumes her playing*].

REGINALD. Please! [*He stops her by shutting the keyboard lid*]. Who let you in?

THE LADY [*rising threateningly*] What is that to you, pray?

REGINALD [*retreating timidly*] It's my room, you know.

THE LADY. It's nothing of the sort. It's the Duchess of Dunmow's room. I know it's the right one, because she gave me the key; and it was the right key.

REGINALD. But what did she do that for? Who are you, if you dont mind my asking?

THE LADY. I do mind your asking. It's no business of yours. However, youd better know to whom you are speaking. I am Strega Thundridge. [*She pronounces it Strayga*].

REGINALD. What! The female Paderewski!

STREGA. Pardon me. I believe Mr Paderewski has been called the male Thundridge; but no gentleman would dream of repeating such offensive vulgarities. Will you be good enough to return to your sofa, and hold your tongue, or else leave the room.

REGINALD. But, you know, I am ill.

STREGA. Then go to bed, and send for a doctor. [*She sits down again to the keyboard*].

REGINALD [*falling on his knees*] You mustnt play. You really mustnt. I cant stand it. I shall simply not be myself if

THE MUSIC-CURE

you start playing.

STREGA [*raising the lid*] Then I shall start at once.

REGINALD [*running to her on his knees and snatching at her hands*] No, you shant. [*She rises indignantly. He holds on to her hands, but exclaims ecstatically*] Oh, I say, what lovely hands youve got!

STREGA. The idea! [*She hurls him to the carpet*].

REGINALD [*on the floor staring at her*] You a r e strong.

STREGA. My strength has been developed by playing left hand octave passages—like this. [*She begins playing Liszt's transcription of Schubert's Erl König*].

REGINALD [*puts his fingers in his ears, but continues to stare at her*].

STREGA [*stopping*] I really cannot play if you keep your ears stopped. It is an insult. Leave the room.

REGINALD. But I tell you it's my room.

STREGA [*rising*] Leave the room, or I will ring your bell and have you put out. [*She goes to the little table, and poises her fingers over the bell call*].

REGINALD [*rushing to her*] No no: somebody will come if you ring; and I shall go distracted if a stranger comes in. [*With a touch of her left hand she sends him reeling. He appeals to her plaintively*] Dont you see that I am ill?

STREGA. I see that you are mentally afflicted. But that doesnt matter to me. The Duchess of Dunmow has engaged me to come to this room and play for two hours. I never break an engagement, especially a two hundred and fifty guinea one. [*She turns towards the piano*].

REGINALD. But didnt she tell you anything about me?

STREGA [*turning back to him*] She said there would be a foolish young man in the room, but that I was not to mind him. She assured me you were not dangerous except to yourself [*Collaring him and holding him bent backwards over the piano*]. But I will have no nonsense about not listening. All the world listens when I play. Listen, or go.

REGINALD [*helpless*] But I shall have to sit on the stairs. I darent go into any of the rooms: I should meet people there.

162

STREGA. You will meet plenty of people on the stairs, young man. They are sitting six on each stair, not counting those who are sitting astride the banisters on the chance of hearing me play.

REGINALD. How dreadful! [*Tearfully*] Youve no right to bully me like this. I'm ill: I cant bear it. I'll throw myself out of the window.

STREGA [*releasing him*] Do. What an advertisement! It will be really kind of you. [*She goes back to the keyboard and sits down to play*].

REGINALD [*crossing to the window*] Youll be sorry you were so unfeeling when you see my mangled body. [*He opens the window; looks out; shuts it hastily, and retreats with a scream*]. Theres a crowd. I darent.

STREGA [*pleased*] Waiting to hear me play [*she preludes softly*].

REGINALD [*ravished*] Oh! I can stand that, you know.

STREGA [*ironically, still preluding*] Thank you.

REGINALD. The fact is, I can play a bit myself.

STREGA [*still preluding*] An amateur, I presume.

REGINALD. I have often been told I could make a living at it if I tried. But of course it wouldnt do for a man in my position to lower himself by becoming a professional.

STREGA [*abruptly ceasing to play*] Tactful, that, I dont think! And what do you play, may I ask?

REGINALD. Oh, all the very best music.

STREGA. For instance?

REGINALD. I wish you belonged to me.

STREGA [*rising outraged*] You young blackguard! How dare you?

REGINALD. You dont understand: it's the name of a tune. Let me play it for you. [*He sits down at the keyboard*] I dont think you believe I can play.

STREGA. Pardon me. I have heard a horse play the harmonium at a music hall. I can believe anything.

REGINALD. Aha! [*He plays*]. Do you like that?

STREGA. What is it? Is it intended for music?

163

REGINALD. Oh, you beautiful doll.

STREGA. Take that [*she knocks him sprawling over the keyboard*]! Beautiful doll indeed!

REGINALD. Oh, I say! Look here: thats the name of the tune too. You seem quite ignorant of the best music. Dont you know Rum Tum Tiddle, and Alexander's Rag Time Band, and Take me back to the Garden of Love, and Everybody likes our Mary.

STREGA. Young man: I have never even heard of these abominations. I am now going to educate you musically. I am going to play Chopin, and Brahms, and Bach, and Schumann, and—

REGINALD [*horrified*] You dont mean classical music?

STREGA. I do [*he bolts through the central doors*].

STREGA [*disgusted*] Pig! [*She sits down at the piano again*].

REGINALD [*rushing back into the room*] I forgot the people on the stairs: crowds of them. Oh, what shall I do! Oh dont, Dont, DONT play classical music to me. Say you wont. Please.

STREGA [*looks at him enigmatically and softly plays a Liebeslieder Waltz*]!!

REGINALD. Oh, I say: thats rather pretty.

STREGA. Like it?

REGINALD. Awfully. Oh, I say, you know: I really do wish you belonged to me. [*Strega suddenly plays a violent Chopin study. He goes into convulsions*]. Oh! Stop! Mercy! Help! Oh please, please!

STREGA [*pausing with her hands raised over the keyboard, ready to pounce on the chords*] Will you ever say that again?

REGINALD. Never. I beg your pardon.

STREGA [*satisfied*] Hm! [*She drops her hands in her lap*].

REGINALD [*wiping his brow*] Oh, that was fearfully classical.

STREGA. You want your back stiffened a little, my young friend. Besides, I really cannot earn two hundred and fifty guineas by playing soothing syrup to you. Now prepare for the worst. I'm going to make a man of you.

REGINALD. How?

STREGA. With Chopin's Polonaise in A Flat. Now. Imagine yourself going into battle. [*He runs away as before*]. Goose!

REGINALD [*returning as before*] The crowd is worse than ever. Have you no pity?

STREGA. Come here. Dont imagine yourself going into battle. Imagine that you have just been in a battle; and that you have saved your country by deeds of splendid bravery; and that you are going to dance with beautiful women who are proud of you. Can you imagine that?

REGINALD. Rathe-e-e-errr. Thats how I always do imagine myself.

STREGA. Right. Now listen. [*She plays the first section of the Polonaise. Reginald flinches at first, but gradually braces himself; stiffens; struts; throws up his head and slaps his chest*]. Thats better. What a hero! [*After a difficult passage*]. Takes a bit of doing, that, dearest child. [*Coming to the chords which announce the middle section*] Now for it.

REGINALD [*unable to contain himself*] Oh, this is too glorious. I must have a turn or I shall forget myself.

STREGA. Can you play this? Nothing but this. [*She plays the octave passage in the bass*].

REGINALD. Just riddle tiddle, riddle tiddle, riddle tiddle, riddle tiddle? Nothing but that?

STREGA. Very softly at first. Like the ticking of a watch. Then louder and louder, as you feel my soul swelling.

REGINALD. I understand. Just give me those chords again to buck me up to it. [*She plays the chords again. He plays the octave passages; and they play the middle section as a duet. At the repeat he cries*] Again! again!

STREGA. It's meant to be played again. Now.

They repeat it. At the end of the section she pushes him off the bench on to the floor, and goes on with the Polonaise alone.

REGINALD. Wonderful woman: I have a confession to make, a confidence to impart. Your playing draws it from me. Listen, Strega [*she plays a horrible discord*] I mean Miss

165

Thundridge.

STREGA. Thats better; but I prefer Wonderful Woman.

REGINALD. You are a wonderful woman, you know. Adored one—would you mind my taking a little valerian? I'm so excited [*he takes some*]. A—a—ah! Now I feel that I can speak. Listen to me, goddess. I am not happy. I hate my present existence. I loathe parliament. I am not fit for public affairs. I am condemned to live at home with five coarse and brutal sisters who care for nothing but Alpine climbing, and looping the loop on aeroplanes, and going on deputations, and fighting the police. Do you know what they call me?

STREGA [*playing softly*] What do they call you, dear?

REGINALD. They call me a Clinger. Well, I confess it. I am a Clinger. I am not fit to be thrown unprotected upon the world. I want to be shielded. I want a strong arm to lean on, a dauntless heart to be gathered to and cherished, a breadwinner on whose income I can live without the sordid horrors of having to make money for myself. I am a poor little thing, I know, Strega; but I could make a home for you. I have great taste in carpets and pictures. I can cook like anything. I can play quite nicely after dinner. Though you mightnt think it, I can be quite stern and strongminded with servants. I get on splendidly with children: they never talk over my head as grown-up people do. I have a real genius for home life. And I shouldnt at all mind being tyrannized over a little: in fact, I like it. It saves me the trouble of having to think what to do. Oh, Strega, dont you want a dear little domesticated husband who would have no concern but to please you, no thought outside our home, who would be unspotted and unsoiled by the rude cold world, who would never meddle in politics or annoy you by interfering with your profession? Is there any hope for me?

STREGA [*coming away from the piano*] My child: I am a hard, strong, independent, muscular woman. How can you, with your delicate soft nature, see anything to love in me? I

should hurt you, shock you, perhaps—yes: let me confess
it—I have a violent temper, and might even, in a transport
of rage, beat you.

REGINALD. Oh do, do. Dont laugh at this ridiculous confession; but ever since I was a child I have had only one
secret longing, and that was to be mercilessly beaten by a
splendid, strong, beautiful woman.

STREGA [*solemnly*] Reginald—I think your mother spoke
of you as Reginald?—

REGINALD. Rejjy.

STREGA. I too have a confession to make. I too need some
music to speak through. Will you be so good?

REGINALD. Angel. [*He rushes to the piano and plays sympathetically whilst she speaks*].

STREGA. I, too, have had my dream. It has consoled me
through the weary hours when I practised scales for eight
hours a day. It has pursued me through the applause of admiring thousands in Europe and America. It is a dream of a
timid little heart fluttering against mine, of a gentle voice to
welcome me home, of a silky moustache to kiss my weary
fingers when I return from a Titanic struggle with Tchaikovsky's Concerto in G major, of somebody utterly dependent on me, utterly devoted to me, utterly my own, living
only to be cherished and worshipped by me.

REGINALD. But you would be angry sometimes: terrible,
splendid, ruthless, violent. You would throw down the thing
you loved and trample on it as it clung to your feet.

STREGA. Yes—oh, why do you force me to confess it?—
I should beat it to a jelly, and then cast myself in transports
of remorse on its quivering frame and smother it with passionate kisses.

REGINALD [*transported*] Let it be me, let it be me.

STREGA. You dare face this terrible destiny?

REGINALD. I embrace it. I adore you. I am wholly yours.
Oh, let me cling, cling, cling.

STREGA [*embracing him fiercely*] Nothing shall tear you
from my arms now.

THE MUSIC-CURE

REGINALD. Nothing. I am provided for. Oh how happy this will make my mother!

STREGA. Sweet: name the day.

He plays a wedding march. She plays the bass.

AYOT ST LAWRENCE, 21*st January* 1914.

THE SHEWING-UP OF BLANCO POSNET

A SERMON IN CRUDE MELODRAMA

Written in 1909

First Performed Dublin 1909

THE CENSORSHIP

THIS little play is really a religious tract in dramatic form. If our silly censorship would permit its performance, it might possibly help to set right-side-up the perverted conscience and re-invigorate the starved self-respect of our considerable class of loose-lived play-goers whose point of honor is to deride all official and conventional sermons. As it is, it only gives me an opportunity of telling the story of the Select Committee of both Houses of Parliament which sat last year to inquire into the working of the censorship, against which it was alleged by myself and others that as its imbecility and mischievousness could not be fully illustrated within the limits of decorum imposed on the press, it could only be dealt with by a parliamentary body subject to no such limits.

A READABLE BLUEBOOK

Few books of the year 1909 can have been cheaper and more entertaining than the report of this Committee. Its full title is REPORT FROM THE JOINT SELECT COMMITTEE OF THE HOUSE OF LORDS AND THE HOUSE OF COMMONS ON THE STAGE PLAYS (CENSORSHIP) TOGETHER WITH THE PROCEEDINGS OF THE COMMITTEE, MINUTES OF EVIDENCE, AND APPENDICES. What the phrase "the Stage Plays" means in this title I do not know; nor does anyone else. The number of the Bluebook is 214. How interesting it is may be judged from the fact that it contains verbatim reports of long and animated interviews between the Committee and such witnesses as Mr William Archer, Mr Granville Barker, Mr J. M. Barrie, Mr Forbes Robertson, Mr Cecil Raleigh, Mr John Galsworthy, Mr Laurence Housman, Sir Herbert Beerbohm Tree, Mr W. L. Courtney, Sir William Gilbert, Mr. A. B. Walkley, Miss Lena Ashwell, Professor Gilbert Murray, Mr George Alexander, Mr George Edwardes, Mr Comyns Carr, the Speaker of the House of Commons, the Bishop of Southwark, Mr Hall Caine, Mr Israel Zangwill, Sir Squire Bancroft, Sir Arthur Pinero, and Mr Gilbert

Chesterton, not to mention myself and a number of gentlemen less well known to the general public, but important in
the world of the theatre. The publication of a book by so
many famous contributors would be beyond the means of
any commercial publishing firm. His Majesty's Stationery
Office sells it to all comers by weight at the very reasonable
price of three-and-threepence a copy.

HOW NOT TO DO IT

It was pointed out by Charles Dickens in Little Dorrit,
which remains the most accurate and penetrating study of
the genteel littleness of our class governments in the English
language, that whenever an abuse becomes oppressive
enough to persuade our party parliamentarians that something must be done, they immediately set to work to face the
situation and discover How Not To Do It. Since Dickens's
day the exposures effected by the Socialists have so shattered
the self-satisfaction of modern commercial civilization that
it is no longer difficult to convince our governments that
something must be done, even to the extent of attempts at a
reconstruction of civilization on a thoroughly uncommercial
basis. Consequently, the first part of the process described
by Dickens: that in which the reformers were snubbed by
front bench demonstrations that the administrative departments were consuming miles of red tape in the correctest
forms of activity, and that everything was for the best in the
best of all possible worlds, is out of fashion; and we are in
that other phase, familiarized by the history of the French
Revolution, in which the primary assumption is that the
country is in danger, and that the first duty of all parties,
politicians, and governments is to save it. But as the effect of
this is to give governments a great many more things to do,
it also gives a powerful stimulus to the art of How Not To
Do Them: that is to say, the art of contriving methods of
reform which will leave matters exactly as they are.

The report of the Joint Select Committee is a capital
illustration of this tendency. The case against the censorship was overwhelming; and the defence was more damag-

ing to it than no defence at all could have been. Even had this not been so, the mere caprice of opinion had turned against the institution; and a reform was expected, evidence or no evidence. Therefore the Committee was unanimous as to the necessity of reforming the censorship; only, unfortunately, the majority attached to this unanimity the usual condition that nothing should be done to disturb the existing state of things. How this was effected may be gathered from the recommendations finally agreed on, which are as follows.

1. The drama is to be set entirely free by the abolition of the existing obligation to procure a licence from the Censor before performing a play; but every theatre lease is in future to be construed as if it contained a clause giving the landlord power to break it and evict the lessee if he produces a play without first obtaining the usual licence from the Lord Chamberlain.

2. Some of the plays licensed by the Lord Chamberlain are so vicious that their present practical immunity from prosecution must be put an end to; but no manager who procures the Lord Chamberlain's licence for a play can be punished in any way for producing it, though a special tribunal may order him to discontinue the performance; and even this order must not be recorded to his disadvantage on the licence of his theatre, nor may it be given as a judicial reason for cancelling that licence.

3. Authors and managers producing plays without first obtaining the usual licence from the Lord Chamberlain shall be perfectly free to do so, and shall be at no disadvantage compared to those who follow the existing practice, except that they may be punished, have the licences of their theatres endorsed and cancelled, and have the performance stopped pending the proceedings without compensation in the event of the proceedings ending in their acquittal.

4. Authors are to be rescued from their present subjection to an irresponsible secret tribunal which can condemn their plays without giving reasons by the substitution for that tribunal of a Committee of the Privy Council, which is to be

the final authority on the fitness of a play for representation; and this Committee is to sit *in camera* if and when it pleases.

5. The power to impose a veto on the production of plays is to be abolished because it may hinder the growth of a great national drama; but the Office of Examiner of Plays shall be continued; and the Lord Chamberlain shall retain his present powers to license plays, but shall be made responsible to Parliament to the extent of making it possible to ask questions there concerning his proceedings, especially now that members have discovered a method of doing this indirectly.

And so on, and so forth. The thing is to be done; and it is not to be done. Everything is to be changed and nothing is to be changed. The problem is to be faced and the solution to be shirked. And the word of Dickens is to be justified.

THE STORY OF THE JOINT SELECT COMMITTEE

Let me now tell the story of the Committee in greater detail, partly as a contribution to history; partly because, like most true stories, it is more amusing than the official story.

All commissions of public enquiry are more or less intimidated both by the interests on which they have to sit in judgment and, when their members are party politicians, by the votes at the back of those interests; but this unfortunate Committee sat under a quite exceptional cross fire. First, there was the king. The Censor is a member of his household retinue; and as a king's retinue has to be jealously guarded to avoid curtailment of the royal state no matter what may be the function of the particular retainer threatened, nothing but an express royal intimation to the contrary, which is a constitutional impossibility, could have relieved the Committee from the fear of displeasing the king by any proposal to abolish the censorship of the Lord Chamberlain. Now all the lords on the Committee and some of the commoners could have been wiped out of society (in their sense of the word) by the slightest intimation that the king would prefer not to meet them; and this was a heavy risk to run on the chance of "a great and serious national drama" ensuing on the removal of the Lord Chamberlain's veto on Mrs Warren's Profession. Second, there was the Nonconformist conscience, holding the Liberal Government responsible for the Committee it had appointed, and holding also, to the extent of votes enough to turn the scale in some constituencies, that the theatre is the gate of hell, to be tolerated, as vice is tolerated, only because the power to suppress it could not be given to any public body without too serious an interference with certain Liberal traditions of liberty which are still useful to Nonconformists in other directions. Third, there was the commercial interest of the theatrical managers and their syndicates of backers in the City, to whom, as I shall shew later on, the censorship affords a cheap insurance of enormous value. Fourth, there was the powerful interest of the trade in intoxicating liquors, fiercely determined to resist any extension of the authority of teetotaller-led local governing bodies over theatres. Fifth, there were the playwrights, without political power, but with a very close natural monopoly of a talent not only for play-writing but for satirical polemics. And since every interest has its opposition, all these influences had created hostile bodies by the operation of the mere impulse to contradict them, always strong in English human nature.

WHY THE MANAGERS LOVE THE CENSORSHIP

The only one of these influences which seems to be generally misunderstood is that of the managers. It has been assumed repeatedly that managers and authors are affected in the same way by the censorship. When a prominent author protests against the censorship, his opinion is supposed to be balanced by that of some prominent manager who declares that the censorship is the mainstay of the theatre, and his relations with the Lord Chamberlain and the Examiner of Plays a cherished privilege and an inexhaustible joy. This error was not removed by the evidence given before the Joint Select Committee. The managers did not make their case clear there, partly because they did not understand it,

and partly because their most eminent witnesses were not
personally affected by it, and would not condescend to
plead it, feeling themselves, on the contrary, compelled by
their self-respect to admit and even emphasize the fact that
the Lord Chamberlain in the exercise of his duties as
licenser had done those things which he ought not to have
done, and left undone those things which he ought to have
done. Mr Forbes Robertson and Sir Herbert Tree, for instance, had never felt the real disadvantage of which
managers have to complain. This disadvantage was not
put directly to the Committee; and though the managers
are against me on the question of the censorship, I will now
put their case for them as they should have put it themselves, and as it can be read between the lines of their
evidence when once the reader has the clue.

The manager of a theatre is a man of business. He is not
an expert in politics, religion, art, literature, philosophy, or
law. He calls in a playwright just as he calls in a doctor, or
consults a lawyer, or engages an architect, depending on the
playwright's reputation and past achievements for a satisfactory result. A play by an unknown man may attract him
sufficiently to induce him to give that unknown man a trial;
but this does not occur often enough to be taken into account: his normal course is to resort to a well-known author
and take (mostly with misgiving) what he gets from him.
Now this does not cause any anxiety to Mr Forbes Robertson and Sir Herbert Tree, because they are only incidentally
managers and men of business: primarily they are highly
cultivated artists, quite capable of judging for themselves
anything that the most abstruse playwright is likely to put
before them. But the plain-sailing tradesman who must be
taken as the typical manager (for the west end of London is
not the whole theatrical world) is by no means equally qualified to judge whether a play is safe from prosecution or not.
He may not understand it, may not like it, may not know
what the author is driving at, may have no knowledge of the
ethical, political, and sectarian controversies which may

form the intellectual fabric of the play, and may honestly see nothing but an ordinary "character part" in a stage figure which may be a libellous and unmistakeable caricature of some eminent living person of whom he has never heard. Yet if he produces the play he is legally responsible just as if he had written it himself. Without protection he may find himself in the dock answering a charge of blasphemous libel, seditious libel, obscene libel, or all three together, not to mention the possibility of a private action for defamatory libel. His sole refuge is the opinion of the Examiner of Plays, his sole protection the licence of the Lord Chamberlain. A refusal to license does not hurt him, because he can produce another play: it is the author who suffers. The granting of the licence practically places him above the law; for though it may be legally possible to prosecute a licensed play, nobody ever dreams of doing it. The really responsible person, the Lord Chamberlain, could not be put into the dock; and the manager could not decently be convicted when he could produce in his defence a certificate from the chief officer of the King's Household that the play was a proper one.

A TWO GUINEA INSURANCE POLICY

The censorship, then, provides the manager, at the negligible premium of two guineas per play, with an effective insurance against the author getting him into trouble, and a complete relief from all conscientious responsibility for the character of the entertainment at his theatre. Under such circumstances, managers would be more than human if they did not regard the censorship as their most valuable privilege. This is the simple explanation of the rally of the managers and their Associations to the defence of the censorship, of their reiterated resolutions of confidence in the Lord Chamberlain, of their presentations of plate, and, generally, of their enthusiastic contentment with the present system, all in such startling contrast to the denunciations of the censorship by the authors. It also explains why the managerial witnesses who had least to fear from the Censor were the most reluctant in his defence, whilst those whose practice it is to strain his indulgence to the utmost were al-most rapturous in his praise. There would be absolute un-animity among the managers in favor of the censorship if they were all simply tradesmen. Even those actor-managers who made no secret before the Committee of their contempt for the present operation of the censorship, and their indig-nation at being handed over to a domestic official as casual servants of a specially disorderly kind, demanded, not the abolition of the institution, but such a reform as might make it consistent with their dignity and unobstructive to their higher artistic aims. Feeling no personal need for protec-tion against the author, they perhaps forgot the plight of many a manager to whom the modern advanced drama is so much Greek; but they did feel very strongly the need of being protected against Vigilance Societies and Munici-palities and common informers in a country where a large section of the community still believes that art of all kinds is inherently sinful.

WHY THE GOVERNMENT INTERFERED

It may now be asked how a Liberal government had been persuaded to meddle at all with a question in which so many conflicting interests were involved, and which had probably no electoral value whatever. Many simple souls believed that it was because certain severely virtuous plays by Ibsen, by M. Brieux, by Mr Granville Barker, and by me, were sup-pressed by the censorship, whilst plays of a scandalous char-acter were licensed without demur. No doubt this influenced public opinion; but those who imagine that it could influ-ence British governments little know how remote from pub-lic opinion and how full of their own little family and party affairs British governments, both Liberal and Unionist, still are. The censorship scandal had existed for years without any parliamentary action being taken in the matter, and might have existed for as many more had it not happened in 1906 that Mr Robert Vernon Harcourt entered parlia-ment as a member of the Liberal Party, of which his father had been one of the leaders during the Gladstone era. Mr

178

Harcourt was thus a young man marked out for office both by his parentage and his unquestionable social position as one of the governing class. Also, and this was much less usual, he was brilliantly clever, and was the author of a couple of plays of remarkable promise. Mr Harcourt informed his leaders that he was going to take up the subject of the censorship. The leaders, recognizing his hereditary right to a parliamentary canter of some sort as a prelude to his public career, and finding that all the clever people seemed to be agreed that the censorship was an anti-Liberal institution and an abominable nuisance to boot, indulged him by appointing a Select Committee of both Houses to investigate the subject. The then Chancellor of the Duchy of Lancaster, Mr Herbert Samuel (now Postmaster-General), who had made his way into the Cabinet twenty years ahead of the usual age, was made Chairman. Mr Robert Harcourt himself was of course a member. With him, representing the Commons, was Mr Alfred Mason, a man of letters who had won a seat in parliament as offhandedly as he has since discarded it, or as he once appeared on the stage to help me out of a difficulty in casting Arms and the Man when that piece was the newest thing in the advanced drama. There was Mr Hugh Law, an Irish member, son of an Irish Chancellor, presenting a keen and joyous front to English intellectual sloth. Above all, there was Colonel Lockwood to represent at one stroke the Opposition and the average popular man. This he did by standing up gallantly for the Censor, to whose support the Opposition was in no way committed, and by visibly defying the most cherished conventions of the average man with a bunch of carnations in his buttonhole as large as a dinner-plate, which would have made a Bunthorne blench, and which very nearly did make Mr Granville Barker (who has an antipathy to the scent of carnations) faint.

THE PEERS ON THE JOINT SELECT COMMITTEE

The House of Lords then proceeded to its selection. As fashionable drama in Paris and London concerns itself almost exclusively with adultery, the first choice fell on Lord Gorell, who had for many years presided over the Divorce Court. Lord Plymouth, who had been Chairman to the Shakespear Memorial project (now merged in the Shakespear Memorial National Theatre), was obviously marked out for selection; and it was generally expected that the Lords Lytton and Esher, who had taken a prominent part in the same movement, would have been added. This expectation was not fulfilled. Instead, Lord Willoughby de Broke, who had distinguished himself as an amateur actor, was selected along with Lord Newton, whose special qualifications for the Committee, if he had any, were unknown to the public. Finally Lord Ribblesdale, the argute son of a Scotch mother, was thrown in to make up for any shortcoming in intellectual subtlety that might arise in the case of his younger colleagues; and this completed the two teams.

THE COMMITTEE'S ATTITUDE TOWARDS THE THEATRE

In England, thanks chiefly to the censorship, the theatre is not respected. It is indulged and despised as a department of what is politely called gaiety. It is therefore not surprising that the majority of the Committee began by taking its work uppishly and carelessly. When it discovered that the contemporary drama, licensed by the Lord Chamberlain, included plays which could be described only behind closed doors, and in the discomfort which attends discussions of very nasty subjects between men of widely different ages, it calmly puts its own convenience before its public duty by ruling that there should be no discussion of particular plays, much as if a committee on temperance were to rule that drunkenness was not a proper subject of conversation among gentlemen.

A BAD BEGINNING

This was a bad beginning. Everybody knew that in England the censorship would not be crushed by the weight of the constitutional argument against it, heavy as that was, unless it were also brought home to the Committee and to the pub-

lic that it had sanctioned and protected the very worst practicable examples of the kind of play it professed to extirpate.
For it must be remembered that the other half of the practical side of the case, dealing with the merits of the plays it had
suppressed, could never secure a unanimous assent. If the
Censor had suppressed Hamlet, as he most certainly would
have done had it been submitted to him as a new play, he
would have been supported by a large body of people to
whom incest is a tabooed subject which must not be mentioned on the stage or anywhere else outside a criminal court.
Hamlet, Oedipus, and The Cenci, Mrs Warren's Profession, Brieux's Maternité, and Les Avariés, Maeterlinck's
Monna Vanna and Mr Granville Barker's Waste may or
may not be great poems, or edifying sermons, or important
documents, or charming romances: our tribal citizens know
nothing about that and do not want to know anything: all
that they do know is that incest, prostitution, abortion, contagious diseases, and nudity are improper, and that all conversations, or books, or plays in which they are discussed are
improper conversations, improper books, improper plays,
and should not be allowed. The Censor may prohibit all such
plays with complete certainty that there will be a chorus of
"Quite right too" sufficient to drown the protests of the few
who know better. The Achilles heel of the censorship is
therefore not the fine plays it has suppressed, but the abominable plays it has licensed: plays which the Committee itself
had to turn the public out of the room and close the doors
before it could discuss, and which I myself have found it impossible to expose in the press because no editor of a paper
or magazine intended for general family reading could admit into his columns the baldest narration of the stories which
the Censor has not only tolerated but expressly certified as
fitting for presentation on the stage. When the Committee
ruled out this part of the case it shook the confidence of the
authors in its impartiality and its seriousness. Of course it
was not able to enforce its ruling thoroughly. Plays which
were merely lightminded and irresponsible in their vicious-

ness were repeatedly mentioned by Mr Harcourt and others. But the really detestable plays, which would have damned the censorship beyond all apology or salvation, were never referred to; and the moment Mr Harcourt or anyone else made the Committee uncomfortable by a move in their direction, the ruling was appealed to at once, and the censorship saved.

A COMIC INTERLUDE

It was part of this nervous dislike of the unpleasant part of its business that led to the comic incident of the Committee's sudden discovery that I had insulted it, and its suspension of its investigation for the purpose of elaborately insulting me back again. Comic to the lookers-on, that is; for the majority of the Committee made no attempt to conceal the fact that they were wildly angry with me; and I, though my public experience and skill in acting enabled me to maintain an appearance of imperturbable good-humor, was equally furious. The friction began as follows.

The precedents for the conduct of the Committee were to be found in the proceedings of the Committee of 1892. That Committee, no doubt recognizing the absurdity of calling on distinguished artists to give their views before it, and then refusing to allow them to state their views except in nervous replies to such questions as it might suit members to put to them, allowed Sir Henry Irving and Sir John Hare to prepare and read written statements, and formally invited them to read them to the Committee before being questioned. I accordingly prepared such a statement. For the greater convenience of the Committee, I offered to have this statement printed at my own expense, and to supply the members with copies. The offer was accepted; and the copies supplied. I also offered to provide the Committee with copies of those plays of mine which had been refused a licence by the Lord Chamberlain. That offer also was accepted; and the books duly supplied.

AN ANTI-SHAVIAN PANIC

As far as I can guess, the next thing that happened was

that some timid or unawakened member of the Committee read my statement and was frightened or scandalized out of his wits by it. At all events it is certain that the majority of the Committee allowed themselves to be persuaded to refuse to allow any statement to be read; but to avoid the appearance of pointing this expressly at me, the form adopted was a resolution to adhere strictly to precedent, the Committee being then unaware that the precedents were on my side. Accordingly, when I appeared before the Committee, and proposed to read my statement "according to precedent," the Committee was visibly taken aback. The Chairman was bound by the letter of the decision arrived at to allow me to read my statement, since that course was according to precedent; but as this was exactly what the decision was meant to prevent, the majority of the Committee would have regarded this hoisting of them with their own petard as a breach of faith on the part of the Chairman, who, I infer, was not in agreement with the suppressive majority. There was nothing for it, after a somewhat awkward pause, but to clear me and the public out of the room and reconsider the situation *in camera*. When the doors were opened again I was informed simply that the Committee would not hear my statement. But as the Committee could not very decently refuse my evidence altogether, the Chairman, with a printed copy of my statement in his hand as "proof," was able to come to the rescue to some extent by putting to me a series of questions to which no doubt I might have replied by taking another copy out of my pocket, and quoting my statement paragraph by paragraph, as some of the later witnesses did. But as in offering the Committee my statement for burial in their bluebook I had made a considerable sacrifice, being able to secure greater publicity for it by independent publication on my own account; and as, further, the circumstances of the refusal made it offensive enough to take all heart out of the scrupulous consideration with which I had so far treated the Committee, I was not disposed to give its majority a second chance, or to lose the opportunity offered

183

me by the questions to fire an additional broadside into the censorship. I pocketed my statement, and answered the questions *vivâ voce*. At the conclusion of this, my examination-in-chief, the Committee adjourned, asking me to present myself again for (virtually) cross-examination. But this cross-examination never came off, as the sequel will shew.

A RARE AND CURIOUS FIRST EDITION

The refusal of the Committee to admit my statement had not unnaturally created the impression that it must be a scandalous document; and a lively demand for copies at once set in. And among the very first applicants were members of the majority which had carried the decision to exclude the document. They had given so little attention to the business that they did not know, or had forgotten, that they had already been supplied with copies at their own request. At all events, they came to me publicly and cleaned me out of the handful of copies I had provided for distribution to the press. And after the sitting it was intimated to me that yet more copies were desired for the use of the Committee: a demand, under the circumstances, of breath-bereaving coolness. At the same time, a brisk demand arose outside the Committee, not only among people who were anxious to read what I had to say on the subject, but among victims of the craze for collecting first editions, copies of privately circulated pamphlets, and other real or imaginary rarities. Such maniacs will cheerfully pay five guineas for any piece of discarded old rubbish of mine when they will not pay as many shillings for a clean new copy of it, because everyone else can get it for the same price too.

THE TIMES TO THE RESCUE

The day after the refusal of the Committee to face my statement, I transferred the scene of action to the columns of The Times, which did yeoman's service to the public on this, as on many other occasions, by treating the question as a public one without the least regard to the supposed susceptibilities of the Court on the one side, or the avowed prejudices of the Free Churches or the interests of the managers

or theatrical speculators on the other. The Times published
the summarized conclusions of my statement, and gave me
an opportunity of saying as much as it was then advisable to
say of what had occurred. For it must be remembered that,
however impatient and contemptuous I might feel of the intellectual cowardice shewn by the majority of the Committee
face to face with myself, it was none the less necessary to keep
up its prestige in every possible way, not only for the sake of
the dignity and importance of the matter with which it had
to deal, and in the hope that the treatment of subsequent witnesses and the final report might make amends for a feeble
beginning, but also out of respect and consideration for the
minority. For it is fair to say that the majority was never more
than a bare majority, and that the worst thing the Committee
did—the exclusion of references to particular plays—was
perpetrated in the absence of the Chairman.

I, therefore, had to treat the Committee in The Times
very much better than its majority deserved, an injustice for
which I now apologize. I did not, however, resist the temptation to hint, quite good-humoredly, that my politeness to the
Committee had cost me quite enough already, and that I was
not prepared to supply the members of the Committee, or
anyone else, with extra copies merely as collectors' curiosities.

THE COUNCIL OF TEN

Then the fat was in the fire. The majority, chaffed for its
eagerness to obtain copies of scarce pamphlets retailable at
five guineas, went dancing mad. When I presented myself,
as requested, for cross-examination, I found the doors of the
Committee room shut, and the corridors of the House of
Lords filled by a wondering crowd, to whom it had somehow leaked out that something terrible was happening inside. It could not be another licensed play too scandalous to
be discussed in public, because the Committee had decided
to discuss no more of these examples of the Censor's notions
of purifying the stage; and what else the Committee might
have to discuss that might not be heard by all the world was
not easily guessable.

THE SHEWING-UP OF BLANCO POSNET

Without suggesting that the confidence of the Committee was in any way violated by any of its members further than was absolutely necessary to clear them from suspicion of complicity in the scene which followed, I think I may venture to conjecture what was happening. It was felt by the majority, first, that it must be cleared at all costs of the imputation of having procured more than one copy each of my statement, and that one not from any interest in an undesirable document by an irreverent author, but in the reluctant discharge of its solemn public duty; second, that a terrible example must be made of me by the most crushing public snub in the power of the Committee to administer. To throw my wretched little pamphlet at my head and to kick me out of the room was the passionate impulse which prevailed in spite of all the remonstrances of the Commoners, seasoned to the give-and-take of public life, and of the single peer who kept his head. The others, for the moment, had no heads to keep. And the fashion in which they proposed to wreak their vengeance was as follows.

THE SENTENCE

I was to be admitted, as a lamb to the slaughter, and allowed to take my place as if for further examination. The Chairman was then to inform me coldly that the Committee did not desire to have anything more to say to me. The members were thereupon solemnly to hand me back the copies of my statement as so much waste paper, and I was to be suffered to slink away with what countenance I could maintain in such disgrace.

But this plan required the active co-operation of every member of the Committee; and whilst the majority regarded it as an august and impressive vindication of the majesty of parliament, the minority regarded it with equal conviction as a puerile tomfoolery, and declined altogether to act their allotted parts in it. Besides, they did not all want to part with the books. For instance, Mr Hugh Law, being an Irishman, with an Irishman's sense of how to behave like a gallant gentleman on occasion, was determined to be able to assure

me that nothing should induce him to give up my statement
or prevent him from obtaining and cherishing as many copies
as possible. (I quote this as an example to the House of Lords
of the right thing to say in such emergencies.) So the program had to be modified. The minority could not prevent the
enraged majority from refusing to examine me further; nor
could the Chairman refuse to communicate that decision to
me. Neither could the minority object to the secretary handing me back such copies as he could collect from the majority. And at that the matter was left. The doors were opened;
the audience trooped in; I was called to my place in the dock
(so to speak); and all was ready for the sacrifice.

THE EXECUTION

Alas! the majority reckoned without Colonel Lockwood.
That hardy and undaunted veteran refused to shirk his share
in the scene merely because the minority was recalcitrant
and the majority perhaps subject to stage fright. When Mr
Samuel had informed me that the Committee had no further
questions to ask me with an urbanity which gave the public
no clue as to the temper of the majority; when I had jumped
up with the proper air of relief and gratitude; when the secretary had handed me his little packet of books with an affability which effectually concealed his dramatic function as
executioner; when the audience was simply disappointed at
being baulked of the entertainment of hearing Mr Robert
Harcourt cross-examine me; in short, when the situation
was all but saved by the tact of the Chairman and secretary,
Colonel Lockwood rose, with all his carnations blazing, and
gave away the whole case by handing me, with impressive
simplicity and courtesy, his *two* copies of the precious statement. And I believe that if he had succeeded in securing ten,
he would have handed them all back to me with the most sincere conviction that every one of the ten must prove a crushing addition to the weight of my discomfiture. I still cherish
that second copy, a little blue-bound pamphlet, methodically
autographed "Lockwood B" among my most valued literary trophies.

187

THE SHEWING-UP OF BLANCO POSNET

An innocent lady told me afterwards that she never knew that I could smile so beautifully, and that she thought it shewed very good taste on my part. I was not conscious of smiling; but I should have embraced the Colonel had I dared. As it was, I turned expectantly to his colleagues, mutely inviting them to follow his example. But there was only one Colonel Lockwood on that Committee. No eye met mine except minority eyes, dancing with mischief. There was nothing more to be said. I went home to my morning's work, and returned in the afternoon to receive the apologies of the minority for the conduct of the majority, and to see Mr Granville Barker, overwhelmed by the conscience-stricken politeness of the now almost abject Committee, and by a powerful smell of carnations, heading the long list of playwrights who came there to testify against the censor-ship, and whose treatment, I am happy to say, was every-thing they could have desired.

After all, ridiculous as the scene was, Colonel Lock-wood's simplicity and courage were much more serviceable to his colleagues than their own inept *coup de théâtre* would have been if he had not spoiled it. It was plain to everyone that he had acted in entire good faith, without a thought as to these apparently insignificant little books being of any importance or having caused me or anybody else any trouble, and that he was wounded in his most sensitive spot by the construction my Times letter had put on his action. And in Colonel Lockwood's case one saw the case of his party on the Committee. They had simply been thoughtless in the matter.

I hope nobody will suppose that this in any way exoner-ates them. When people accept public service for one of the most vital duties that can arise in our society, they have no right to be thoughtless. In spite of the fun of the scene on the surface, my public sense was, and still is, very deeply offended by it. It made an end for me of the claim of the majority to be taken seriously. When the Government comes to deal with the question, as it presumably will before long, I invite it to

PREFACE

be guided by the Chairman, the minority, and by the witnesses according to their weight, and to pay no attention whatever to those recommendations which were obviously inserted solely to conciliate the majority and get the report through and the Committee done with.

My evidence will be found in the Bluebook, pp. 46–53. And here is the terrible statement which the Committee went through so much to suppress.

THE REJECTED STATEMENT
PART I
THE WITNESS'S QUALIFICATIONS

I AM by profession a playwright. I have been in practice since 1892. I am a member of the Managing Committee of the Society of Authors and of the Dramatic Sub-Committee of that body. I have written nineteen plays, some of which have been translated and performed in all European countries except Turkey, Greece, and Portugal. They have been performed extensively in America. Three of them have been refused licences by the Lord Chamberlain. In one case a licence has since been granted. The other two are still unlicensed. I have suffered both in pocket and reputation by the action of the Lord Chamberlain. In other countries I have not come into conflict with the censorship except in Austria, where the production of a comedy of mine was postponed for a year because it alluded to the part taken by Austria in the Servo-Bulgarian war. This comedy was not one of the plays suppressed in England by the Lord Chamberlain. One of the plays so suppressed was prosecuted in America by the police in consequence of an immense crowd of disorderly persons having been attracted to the first performance by the Lord Chamberlain's condemnation of it; but on appeal to a higher court it was decided that the representation was lawful and the intention innocent, since when it has been repeatedly performed.

I am not an ordinary playwright in general practice. I am a specialist in immoral and heretical plays. My reputation has been gained by my persistent struggle to force the public to reconsider its morals. In particular, I regard much current morality as to economic and sexual relations as disastrously wrong; and I regard certain doctrines of the Christian religion as understood in England today with abhorrence. I write plays with the deliberate object of converting the nation to my opinions in these matters. I have no other effectual incentive to write plays, as I am not dependent on the theatre for my livelihood. If I were prevented from pro-

190

ducing immoral and heretical plays, I should cease to write
for the theatre, and propagate my views from the platform
and through books. I mention these facts to shew that I have
a special interest in the achievement by my profession of
those rights of liberty of speech and conscience which are
matters of course in other professions. I object to censorship
not merely because the existing form of it grievously injures
and hinders me individually, but on public grounds.

THE DEFINITION OF IMMORALITY

In dealing with the question of the censorship, everything depends on the correct use of the word immorality,
and a careful discrimination between the powers of a magistrate or judge to administer a code, and those of a censor to
please himself.

Whatever is contrary to established manners and customs
is immoral. An immoral act or doctrine is not necessarily a
sinful one: on the contrary, every advance in thought and
conduct is by definition immoral until it has converted the
majority. For this reason it is of the most enormous importance that immorality should be protected jealously against
the attacks of those who have no standard except the standard
of custom, and who regard any attack on custom—that is,
on morals—as an attack on society, on religion, and on
virtue.

A censor is never intentionally a protector of immorality.
He always aims at the protection of morality. Now morality
is extremely valuable to society. It imposes conventional conduct on the great mass of persons who are incapable of original ethical judgment, and who would be quite lost if they
were not in leading-strings devised by lawgivers, philosophers, prophets, and poets for their guidance. But morality
is not dependent on censorship for protection. It is already
powerfully fortified by the magistracy and the whole body
of law. Blasphemy, indecency, libel, treason, sedition, obscenity, profanity, and all the other evils which a censorship
is supposed to avert, are punishable by the civil magistrate
with all the severity of vehement prejudice. Morality has not

only every engine that lawgivers can devise in full operation for its protection, but also that enormous weight of public opinion enforced by social ostracism which is stronger than all the statutes. A censor pretending to protect morality is like a child pushing the cushions of a railway carriage to give itself the sensation of making the train travel at sixty miles an hour. It is immorality, not morality, that needs protection: it is morality, not immorality, that needs restraint; for morality, with all the dead weight of human inertia and superstition to hang on the back of the pioneer, and all the malice of vulgarity and prejudice to threaten him, is responsible for many persecutions and many martyrdoms.

Persecutions and martyrdoms, however, are trifles compared to the mischief done by censorships in delaying the general march of enlightenment. This can be brought home to us by imagining what would have been the effect of applying to all literature the censorship we still apply to the stage. The works of Linnaeus and the evolutionists of 1790–1830, of Darwin, Wallace, Huxley, Helmholtz, Tyndall, Spencer, Carlyle, Ruskin, and Samuel Butler, would not have been published, as they were all immoral and heretical in the very highest degree, and gave pain to many worthy and pious people. They are at present condemned by the Greek and Roman Catholic censorships as unfit for general reading. A censorship of conduct would have been equally disastrous. The disloyalty of Hampden and of Washington; the revolting immorality of Luther in not only marrying when he was a priest, but actually marrying a nun; the heterodoxy of Galileo; the shocking blasphemies and sacrileges of Mahomet against the idols whom he dethroned to make way for his conception of one god; the still more startling blasphemy of Jesus when He declared God to be the son of man and Himself to be the son of God, are all examples of shocking immoralities (every immorality shocks somebody), the suppression and extinction of which would have been more disastrous than the utmost mischief that can be conceived as ensuing from the toleration of vice.

192

THE SHEWING-UP OF BLANCO POSNET

These facts, glaring as they are, are disguised by the promotion of immoralities into moralities which is constantly going on. Christianity and Mahometanism, once thought of and dealt with exactly as Anarchism is thought of and dealt with today, have become established religions; and fresh immoralities are persecuted in their name. The truth is that the vast majority of persons professing these religions have never been anything but simple moralists. The respectable Englishman who is a Christian because he was born in Clapham would be a Mahometan for the cognate reason if he had been born in Constantinople. He has never willingly tolerated immorality. He did not adopt any innovation until it had become moral; and then he adopted it, not on its merits, but solely because it had become moral. In doing so he never realized that it had ever been immoral: consequently its early struggles taught him no lesson; and he has opposed the next step in human progress as indignantly as if neither manners, customs, nor thought had ever changed since the beginning of the world. Toleration must be imposed on him as a mystic and painful duty by his spiritual and political leaders, or he will condemn the world to stagnation, which is the penalty of an inflexible morality.

WHAT TOLERATION MEANS

This must be done all the more arbitrarily because it is not possible to make the ordinary moral man understand what toleration and liberty really mean. He will accept them verbally with alacrity, even with enthusiasm, because the word toleration has been moralized by eminent Whigs; but what he means by toleration is toleration of doctrines that he considers enlightened, and, by liberty, liberty to do what he considers right: that is, he does not mean toleration or liberty at all; for there is no need to tolerate what appears enlightened or to claim liberty to do what most people consider right. Toleration and liberty have no sense or use except as toleration of opinions that are considered damnable, and liberty to do what seems wrong. Setting Englishmen free to marry their deceased wife's sisters is not tolerated by the

193

people who approve of it, but by the people who regard it as incestuous. Catholic Emancipation and the admission of Jews to parliament needed no toleration from Catholics and Jews: the toleration they needed was that of the people who regarded the one measure as a facilitation of idolatry, and the other as a condonation of the crucifixion. Clearly such toleration is not clamored for by the multitude or by the press which reflects its prejudices. It is essentially one of those abnegations of passion and prejudice which the common man submits to because uncommon men whom he respects as wiser than himself assure him that it must be so, or the higher affairs of human destiny will suffer.

Such submission is the more difficult because the arguments against tolerating immorality are the same as the arguments against tolerating murder and theft; and this is why the Censor seems to the inconsiderate as obviously desirable a functionary as the police magistrate. But there is this simple and tremendous difference between the cases: that whereas no evil can conceivably result from the total suppression of murder and theft, and all communities prosper in direct proportion to such suppression, the total suppression of immorality, especially in matters of religion and sex, would stop enlightenment, and produce what used to be called a Chinese civilization until the Chinese lately took to immoral courses by permitting railway contractors to desecrate the graves of their ancestors, and their soldiers to wear clothes which indecently revealed the fact that they had legs and waists and even posteriors. At about the same moment a few bold Englishwomen ventured on the immorality of riding astride their horses, a practice that has since established itself so successfully that before another generation has passed away there may not be a new side-saddle in England, or a woman who could use it if there was.

THE CASE FOR TOLERATION

Accordingly, there has risen among wise and far-sighted men a perception of the need for setting certain departments of human activity entirely free from legal interference. This

194

has nothing to do with any sympathy these liberators may themselves have with immoral views. A man with the strongest conviction of the Divine ordering of the universe and of the superiority of monarchy to all forms of government may nevertheless quite consistently and conscientiously be ready to lay down his life for the right of every man to advocate Atheism or Republicanism if he believes in them. An attack on morals may turn out to be the salvation of the race. A hundred years ago nobody foresaw that Tom Paine's centenary would be the subject of a laudatory special article in The Times; and only a few understood that the persecution of his works and the transportation of men for the felony of reading them was a mischievous mistake. Even less, perhaps, could they have guessed that Proudhon, who became notorious by his essay entitled "What is Property? It is Theft," would have received, on the like occasion and in the same paper, a respectful consideration which nobody would now dream of according to Lord Liverpool or Lord Brougham. Nevertheless there was a mass of evidence to shew that such a development was not only possible but fairly probable, and that the risks of suppressing liberty of propaganda were far graver than the risk of Paine's or Proudhon's writings wrecking civilization. Now there was no such evidence in favor of tolerating the cutting of throats and the robbing of tills. No case whatever can be made out for the statement that a nation cannot do without common thieves and homicidal ruffians. But an overwhelming case can be made out for the statement that no nation can prosper or even continue to exist without heretics and advocates of shockingly immoral doctrines. The Inquisition and the Star Chamber, which were nothing but censorships, made ruthless war on impiety and immorality. The result was once familiar to Englishmen, though of late years it seems to have been forgotten. It cost England a revolution to get rid of the Star Chamber. Spain did not get rid of the Inquisition, and paid for that omission by becoming a barely third-rate power politically, and intellectually no power at all, in the

THE REJECTED STATEMENT

Europe she had once dominated as the mightiest of the Christian empires.

THE LIMITS TO TOLERATION

But the large toleration these considerations dictate has limits. For example, though we tolerate, and rightly tolerate, the propaganda of Anarchism as a political theory which embraces all that is valuable in the doctrine of Laisser-Faire and the method of Free Trade as well as all that is shocking in the views of Bakounine, we clearly cannot, or at all events will not, tolerate assassination of rulers on the ground that it is "propaganda by deed" or sociological experiment. A play inciting to such an assassination cannot claim the privileges of heresy or immorality, because no case can be made out in support of assassination as an indispensable instrument of progress. Now it happens that we have in the Julius Cæsar of Shakespear a play which the Tsar of Russia or the Governor-General of India would hardly care to see performed in their capitals just now. It is an artistic treasure; but it glorifies a murder which Goethe described as the silliest crime ever committed. It may quite possibly have helped the regicides of 1649 to see themselves, as it certainly helped generations of Whig statesmen to see them, in a heroic light; and it unquestionably vindicates and ennobles a conspirator who assassinated the head of the Roman State not because he abused his position but solely because he occupied it, thus affirming the extreme republican principle that all kings, good or bad, should be killed because kingship and freedom cannot live together. Under certain circumstances this vindication and ennoblement might act as an incitement to an actual assassination as well as to Plutarchian republicanism; for it is one thing to advocate republicanism or royalism: it is quite another to make a hero of Brutus or Ravaillac, or a heroine of Charlotte Corday. Assassination is the extreme form of censorship; and it seems hard to justify an incitement to it on anti-censorial principles. The very people who would have scouted the notion of prohibiting the performances of Julius Cæsar at His Majesty's

196

Theatre in London last year, might now entertain very seriously a proposal to exclude Indians from them, and to suppress the play completely in Calcutta and Dublin; for if the assassin of Cæsar was a hero, why not the assassins of Lord Frederick Cavendish, Presidents Lincoln and McKinley, and Sir Curzon Wyllie? Here is a strong case for some constitutional means of preventing the performance of a play. True, it is an equally strong case for preventing the circulation of the Bible, which was always in the hands of our regicides; but as the Roman Catholic Church does not hesitate to accept that consequence of the censorial principle, it does not invalidate the argument.

Take another actual case. A modern comedy, Arms and The Man, though not a comedy of politics, is nevertheless so far historical that it reveals the unacknowledged fact that as the Servo-Bulgarian War of 1885 was much more than a struggle between the Servians and Bulgarians, the troops engaged were officered by two European Powers of the first magnitude. In consequence, the performance of the play was for some time forbidden in Vienna, and more recently it gave offence in Rome at a moment when popular feeling was excited as to the relations of Austria with the Balkan States. Now if a comedy so remote from political passion as Arms and The Man can, merely because it refers to political facts, become so inconvenient and inopportune that Foreign Offices take the trouble to have its production postponed, what may not be the effect of what is called a patriotic drama produced at a moment when the balance is quivering between peace and war? Is there not something to be said for a political censorship, if not for a moral one? May not those continental governments who leave the stage practically free in every other respect, but muzzle it politically, be justified by the practical exigencies of the situation?

THE DIFFERENCE BETWEEN LAW AND CENSORSHIP

The answer is that a pamphlet, a newspaper article, or a resolution moved at a political meeting can do all the mischief that a play can, and often more; yet we do not set up a permanent censorship of the press or of political meetings. Any journalist may publish an article, any demagogue may deliver a speech without giving notice to the government or obtaining its licence. The risk of such freedom is great; but as it is the price of our political liberty, we think it worth paying. We may abrogate it in emergencies by a Coercion Act, a suspension of the Habeas Corpus Act, or a proclamation of martial law, just as we stop the traffic in a street during a fire, or shoot thieves at sight if they loot after an earthquake. But when the emergency is past, liberty is restored everywhere except in the theatre. The Act of 1843 is a permanent Coercion Act for the theatre, a permanent suspension of the Habeas Corpus Act as far as plays are concerned, a permanent proclamation of martial law with a single official substituted for a court martial. It is, in fact, assumed that actors, playwrights, and theatre managers are dangerous and dissolute characters whose existence creates a chronic state of emergency, and who must be treated as earthquake looters are treated. It is not necessary now to discredit this assumption. It was broken down by the late Sir Henry Irving when he finally shamed the Government into extending to his profession the official recognition enjoyed by the other branches of fine art. To-day we have on the roll of knighthood actors, authors, and managers. The rogue and vagabond theory of the depravity of the theatre is as dead officially as it is in general society; and with it has perished the sole excuse for the Act of 1843 and for the denial to the theatre of the liberties secured, at far greater social risk, to the press and the platform.

There is no question here of giving the theatre any larger liberties than the press and the platform, or of claiming larger powers for Shakespear to eulogize Brutus than Lord Rosebery has to eulogize Cromwell. The abolition of the censorship does not involve the abolition of the magistrate and of the whole civil and criminal code. On the contrary, it would make the theatre more effectually subject to them than it is at present; for once a play now runs the gauntlet of the censorship, it is practically placed above the law. It is almost humiliating to have to demonstrate the essential difference between a censor and a magistrate or a sanitary inspector; but it is impossible to ignore the carelessness with which even distinguished critics of the theatre assume that all the arguments proper to the support of a magistracy and body of jurisprudence apply equally to a censorship.

A magistrate has laws to administer: a censor has nothing but his own opinion. A judge leaves the question of guilt to the jury: the Censor is jury and judge as well as lawgiver. A magistrate may be strongly prejudiced against an atheist or an anti-vaccinator, just as a sanitary inspector may have formed a careful opinion that drains are less healthy than cesspools; but the magistrate must allow the atheist to affirm instead of to swear, and must grant the anti-vaccinator an exemption certificate, when their demands are lawfully made; and in cities the inspector must compel the builder to make drains and must prosecute him if he makes cesspools. The law may be only the intolerance of the community; but it is a defined and limited intolerance. The limitation is sometimes carried so far that a judge cannot inflict the penalty for housebreaking on a burglar who can prove that he found the door open and therefore made only an unlawful entry. On the other hand, it is sometimes so vague, as for example in the case of the American law against obscenity, that it makes the magistrate virtually a censor. But in the main a citizen can ascertain what he may do and what he may not do; and, though no one knows better than a magistrate that a single ill-conducted family may demoralize a whole street, no magistrate can imprison or otherwise restrain its members on the ground that their immorality may corrupt their neighbors. He can prevent any citizen from carrying certain specified weapons, but not from handling pokers, table-knives, bricks or bottles of corrosive fluid, on the ground that he might use them to commit murder or inflict malicious injury. He has no general power to prevent citizens from selling unhealthy or poisonous substances, or judging for themselves what substances are unhealthy and what wholesome, what poisonous and what innocuous: what he *can* do is to prevent anybody who has not a specific qualification from selling certain specified poisons of which a schedule is kept. Nobody is forbidden to sell minerals without a licence; but everybody is forbidden to sell silver without a licence. When the law has forgotten some atrocious sin—for instance, contracting marriage whilst suffering from contagious disease—the magistrate cannot arrest or punish the wrongdoer, however he may abhor his wickedness. In short, no man is lawfully at the mercy of the magistrate's personal caprice, prejudice, ignorance, superstition, temper, stupidity, resentment, timidity, ambition, or private conviction. But a playwright's livelihood, his reputation, and his inspiration and mission are at the personal mercy of the Censor. The two do not stand, as the criminal and the judge stand, in the presence of a law that binds them both equally, and was made by neither of them, but by the deliberate collective wisdom of the community. The only law that affects them is the Act of 1843, which empowers one of them to do absolutely and finally what he likes with the other's work. And when it is remembered that the slave in this case is the man whose profession is that of Eschylus and Euripides, of Shakespear and Goethe, of Tolstoy and Ibsen, and the master the holder of a party appointment which by the nature of its duties practically excludes the possibility of its acceptance by a serious statesman or great lawyer, it will be seen that the playwrights are justified in reproaching the framers of that Act for having failed not only to appreciate the immense importance of the theatre as a most powerful instrument for teaching the nation how and what to think and feel, but even to conceive that those who make their living by the theatre are normal human beings with the common rights of English citizens. In this extremity of inconsiderateness it is not surprising that they also did not trouble themselves to study the difference between a censor and a

magistrate. And it will be found that almost all the people
who disinterestedly defend the censorship today are defending him on the assumption that there is no constitutional difference between him and any other functionary whose duty
it is to restrain crime and disorder.

One further difference remains to be noted. As a magistrate grows old his mind may change or decay; but the law
remains the same. The censorship of the theatre fluctuates
with every change in the views and character of the man who
exercises it. And what this implies can only be appreciated
by those who can imagine what the effect on the mind must
be of the duty of reading through every play that is produced
in the kingdom year in, year out.

WHY THE LORD CHAMBERLAIN?

What may be called the high political case against censorship as a principle is now complete. The pleadings are
those which have already freed books and pulpits and political platforms in England from censorship, if not from
occasional legal persecution. The stage alone remains under
a censorship of a grotesquely unsuitable kind. No play can
be performed if the Lord Chamberlain happens to disapprove of it. And the Lord Chamberlain's functions have
no sort of relationship to dramatic literature. A great judge
of literature, a far-seeing statesman, a born champion of
liberty of conscience and intellectual integrity—say a Mil-
ton, a Chesterfield, a Bentham—would be a very bad Lord
Chamberlain: so bad, in fact, that his exclusion from such a
post may be regarded as decreed by natural law. On the
other hand, a good Lord Chamberlain would be a stickler
for morals in the narrowest sense, a busy-body, a man to
whom a matter of two inches in the length of a gentleman's
sword or the absence of a feather from a lady's head-dress
would be a graver matter than the Habeas Corpus Act. The
Lord Chancellor, as Censor of the theatre, is a direct descend-
ant of the King's Master of the Revels, appointed in 1544
by Henry VIII. to keep order among the players and musicians of that day when they performed at Court. This first

appearance of the theatrical censor in politics as the whipper-in of the player, with its conception of the player as a rich man's servant hired to amuse him, and, outside his professional duties, as a gay, disorderly, anarchic spoilt child, half privileged, half outlawed, probably as much vagabond as actor, is the real foundation of the subjection of the whole profession, actors, managers, authors and all, to the despotic authority of an officer whose business it is to preserve decorum among menials. It must be remembered that it was not until a hundred years later, in the reaction against the Puritans, that a woman could appear on the English stage without being pelted off as the Italian actresses were. The theatrical profession was regarded as a shameless one; and it is only of late years that actresses have at last succeeded in living down the assumption that actress and prostitute are synonymous terms, and made good their position in respectable society. This makes the survival of the old ostracism in the Act of 1843 intolerably galling; and though it explains the apparently unaccountable absurdity of choosing as Censor of dramatic literature an official whose functions and qualifications have nothing whatever to do with literature, it also explains why the present arrangement is not only criticized as an institution, but resented as an insult.

THE DIPLOMATIC OBJECTION TO THE LORD CHAMBERLAIN

There is another reason, quite unconnected with the susceptibilities of authors, which makes it undesirable that a member of the King's Household should be responsible for the character and tendency of plays. The drama, dealing with all departments of human life, is necessarily political. Recent events have shewn—what indeed needed no demonstration—that it is impossible to prevent inferences being made, both at home and abroad, from the action of the Lord Chamberlain. The most talked-about play of the present year (1909), An Englishman's Home, has for its main interest an invasion of England by a fictitious power which is understood, as it is meant to be understood, to represent

Germany. The lesson taught by the play is the danger of
invasion and the need for every English citizen to be a
soldier. The Lord Chamberlain licensed this play, but refused to license a parody of it. Shortly afterwards he refused
to license another play in which the fear of a German invasion was ridiculed. The German press drew the inevitable
inference that the Lord Chamberlain was an anti-German
alarmist, and that his opinions were a reflection of those
prevailing in St. James's Palace. Immediately after this, the
Lord Chamberlain licensed the play. Whether the inference,
as far as the Lord Chamberlain was concerned, was justified
is of no consequence. What is important is that it was sure to
be made, justly or unjustly, and extended from the Lord
Chamberlain to the Throne.

THE OBJECTION OF COURT ETIQUET

There is another objection to the Lord Chamberlain's
censorship which affects the author's choice of subject.
Formerly very little heed was given in England to the susceptibilities of foreign courts. For instance, the notion that
the Mikado of Japan should be as sacred to the English playwright as he is to the Japanese Lord Chamberlain would
have seemed grotesque a generation ago. Now that the
maintenance of *entente cordiale* between nations is one of the
most prominent and most useful functions of the crown, the
freedom of authors to deal with political subjects, even his-
torically, is seriously threatened by the way in which the
censorship makes the King responsible for the contents of
every play. One author—the writer of these lines, in fact—
has long desired to dramatize the life of Mahomet. But the
possibility of a protest from the Turkish Ambassador—or
the fear of it—causing the Lord Chamberlain to refuse to
license such a play has prevented the play from being written.
Now, if the censorship were abolished, nobody but the
author could be held responsible for the play. The Turkish
Ambassador does not now protest against the publication of
Carlyle's essay on the prophet, or of the English translations
of the Koran in the prefaces to which Mahomet is criticized

as an impostor, or of the older books in which he is reviled as Mahound and classed with the devil himself. But if these publications had to be licensed by the Lord Chamberlain it would be impossible for the King to allow the licence to be issued, as he would thereby be made responsible for the opinions expressed. This restriction of the historical drama is an unmixed evil. Great religious leaders are more interesting and more important subjects for the dramatist than great conquerors. It is a misfortune that public opinion would not tolerate a dramatization of Mahomet in Constantinople. But to prohibit it here, where public opinion would tolerate it, is an absurdity which, if applied in all directions, would make it impossible for the Queen to receive a Turkish ambassador without veiling herself, or the Dean and Chapter of St. Paul's to display a cross on the summit of their Cathedral in a city occupied largely and influentially by Jews. Court etiquet is no doubt an excellent thing for court ceremonies; but to attempt to impose it on the drama is about as sensible as an attempt to make everybody in London wear court dress.

WHY NOT AN ENLIGHTENED CENSORSHIP

In the above cases the general question of censorship is separable from the question of the present form of it. Everyone who condemns the principle of censorship must also condemn the Lord Chamberlain's control of the drama; but those who approve of the principle do not necessarily approve of the Lord Chamberlain being the Censor *ex officio*. They may, however, be entirely opposed to popular liberties, and may conclude from what has been said, not that the stage should be made as free as the church, press, or platform, but that these institutions should be censored as strictly as the stage. It will seem obvious to them that nothing is needed to remove all objections to a censorship except the placing of its powers in better hands.

Now though the transfer of the censorship to, say, the Lord Chancellor, or the Primate, or a Cabinet Minister, would be much less humiliating to the persons immediately concerned, the inherent vices of the institution would not be appreciably less disastrous. They would even be aggravated, for reasons which do not appear on the surface, and therefore need to be followed with some attention.

It is often said that the public is the real censor. That this is to some extent true is proved by the fact that plays which are licensed and produced in London have to be expurgated for the provinces. This does not mean that the provinces are more strait-laced, but simply that in many provincial towns there is only one theatre for all classes and all tastes, whereas in London there are separate theatres for separate sections of playgoers: so that, for example, Sir Herbert Beerbohm Tree can conduct His Majesty's Theatre without the slightest regard to the tastes of the frequenters of the Gaiety Theatre; and Mr. George Edwardes can conduct the Gaiety Theatre without catering in any way for lovers of Shakespear. Thus the farcical comedy which has scandalized the critics in London by the libertinage of its jests is played to the respectable dress circle of Northampton with these same jests slurred over so as to be imperceptible by even the most prurient spectator. The public, in short, takes care that nobody shall outrage it.

But the public also takes care that nobody shall starve it, or regulate its dramatic diet as a schoolmistress regulates the reading of her pupils. Even when it wishes to be debauched, no censor can—or at least no censor does—stand out against it. If a play is irresistibly amusing, it gets licensed no matter what its moral aspect may be. A brilliant instance is the Divorçons of the late Victorien Sardou, which may not have been the naughtiest play of the 19th century, but was certainly the very naughtiest that any English manager in his senses would have ventured to produce. Nevertheless, being a very amusing play, it passed the licenser with the exception of a reference to impotence as a ground for divorce which no English actress would have ventured on in any case. Within the last few months a very amusing comedy with a strongly polygamous moral was found irresistible by the Lord Chamberlain. Plenty of fun and a happy ending will get anything licensed, because the public will have it so, and the Examiner of Plays, as the holder of the office testified before the Commission of 1892 (Report, page 330), feels with the public, and knows that his office could not survive a widespread unpopularity. In short, the support of the mob—that is, of the unreasoning, unorganized, uninstructed mass of popular sentiment—is indispensable to the censorship as it exists today in England. This is the explanation of the toleration by the Lord Chamberlain of coarse and vicious plays. It is not long since a judge before whom a licensed play came in the course of a lawsuit expressed his scandalized astonishment at the licensing of such a work. Eminent churchmen have made similar protests. In some plays the simulation of criminal assaults on the stage has been carried to a point at which a step further would have involved the interference of the police. Provided the treatment of the theme is gaily or hypocritically popular, and the ending happy, the indulgence of the Lord Chamberlain can be counted on. On the other hand, anything unpleasing and unpopular is rigorously censored. Adultery and prostitution are tolerated and even encouraged to such an extent that plays which do not deal with them are commonly said not to be plays at all. But if any of the unpleasing consequences of adultery and prostitution—for instance, an *unsuccessful* illegal operation (successful ones are tolerated) or venereal disease—are mentioned, the play is prohibited. This principle of shielding the playgoer from unpleasant reflections is carried so far that when a play was submitted for licence in which the relations of a prostitute with all the male characters in the piece was described as "immoral," the Examiner of Plays objected to that passage, though he made no objection to the relations themselves. The Lord Chamberlain dare not, in short, attempt to exclude from the stage the tragedies of murder and lust, or the farces of mendacity, adultery, and dissolute gaiety in which vulgar people delight. But when these same vulgar people are threatened with an unpopular play in which dissoluteness is shewn to be

206

no laughing matter, it is prohibited at once amid the vulgar
applause, the net result being that vice is made delightful
and virtue banned by the very institution which is supported
on the understanding that it produces exactly the opposite
result.

THE WEAKNESS OF THE
LORD CHAMBERLAIN'S DEPARTMENT

Now comes the question, Why is our censorship, armed
as it is with apparently autocratic powers, so scandalously
timid in the face of the mob? Why is it not as autocratic in
dealing with playwrights below the average as with those
above it? The answer is that its position is really a very weak
one. It has no direct coercive forces, no funds to institute
prosecutions and recover the legal penalties of defying it, no
powers of arrest or imprisonment, in short, none of the
guarantees of autocracy. What it can do is to refuse to renew
the licence of a theatre at which its orders are disobeyed.
When it happens that a theatre is about to be demolished, as
was the case recently with the Imperial Theatre after it had
passed into the hands of the Wesleyan Methodists, unlicensed plays can be performed, technically in private, but
really in full publicity, without risk. The prohibited plays of
Brieux and Ibsen have been performed in London in this
way with complete impunity. But the impunity is not confined to condemned theatres. Not long ago a West End
manager allowed a prohibited play to be performed at his
theatre, taking his chance of losing his licence in consequence. The event proved that the manager was justified in
regarding the risk as negligible; for the Lord Chamberlain's remedy—the closing of a popular and well-conducted
theatre—was far too extreme to be practicable. Unless the
play had so outraged public opinion as to make the manager
odious and provoke a clamor for his exemplary punishment,
the Lord Chamberlain could only have had his revenge at
the risk of having his powers abolished as unsupportably
tyrannical.

The Lord Chamberlain then has his powers so adjusted

that he is tyrannical just where it is important that he should be tolerant, and tolerant just where he could screw up the standard a little by being tyrannical. His plea that there are unmentionable depths to which managers and authors would descend if he did not prevent them is disproved by the plain fact that his indulgence goes as far as the police, and sometimes further than the public, will let it. If our judges had so little power there would be no law in England. If our churches had so much, there would be no theatre, no literature, no science, no art, possibly no England. The institution is at once absurdly despotic and abjectly weak.

AN ENLIGHTENED CENSORSHIP STILL WORSE THAN THE LORD CHAMBERLAIN'S

Clearly a censorship of judges, bishops, or statesmen would not be in this abject condition. It would no doubt make short work of the coarse and vicious pieces which now enjoy the protection of the Lord Chamberlain, or at least of those of them in which the vulgarity and vice are discoverable by merely reading the prompt copy. But it would certainly disappoint the main hope of its advocates: the hope that it would protect and foster the higher drama. It would do nothing of the sort. On the contrary, it would inevitably suppress it more completely than the Lord Chamberlain does, because it would understand it better. The one play of Ibsen's which is prohibited on the English stage, Ghosts, is far less subversive than A Doll's House. But the Lord Chamberlain does not meddle with such far-reaching matters as the tendency of a play. He refuses to license Ghosts exactly as he would refuse to license Hamlet if it were submitted to him as a new play. He would license even Hamlet if certain alterations were made in it. He would disallow the incestuous relationship between the King and Queen. He would probably insist on the susbtitution of some fictitious country for Denmark in deference to the near relations of our reigning house with that realm. He would certainly make it an absolute condition that the closet scene, in which a son, in an agony of shame and revulsion, reproaches his mother for

208

her relations with his uncle, should be struck out as unbearably horrifying and improper. But compliance with these conditions would satisfy him. He would raise no speculative objections to the tendency of the play.

This indifference to the larger issues of a theatrical performance could not be safely predicated of an enlightened censorship. Such a censorship might be more liberal in its toleration of matters which are only objected to on the ground that they are not usually discussed in general social conversation or in the presence of children; but it would presumably have a far deeper insight to and concern for the real ethical tendency of the play. For instance, had it been in existence during the last quarter of a century, it would have perceived that those plays of Ibsen's which have been licensed without question are fundamentally immoral to an altogether extraordinary degree. Every one of them is a deliberate act of war on society as at present constituted. Religion, marriage, ordinary respectability, are subjected to a destructive exposure and criticism which seems to mere moralists—that is, to persons of no more than average depth of mind—to be diabolical. It is no exaggeration to say that Ibsen gained his overwhelming reputation by undertaking a task of no less magnitude than changing the mind of Europe with the view of changing its morals. Now you can not license work of that sort without making yourself responsible for it. The Lord Chamberlain accepted the responsibility because he did not understand it or concern himself about it. But what really enlightened and conscientious official dare take such a responsibility? The strength of character and range of vision which made Ibsen capable of it are not to be expected from any official, however eminent. It is true that an enlightened censor might, whilst shrinking even with horror from Ibsen's views, perceive that any nation which suppressed Ibsen would presently find itself falling behind the nations which tolerated him just as Spain fell behind England; but the proper action to take on such a conviction is the abdication of censorship, not the practice of it. As long as a censor is a censor, he cannot endorse by his licence opinions which seem to him dangerously heretical.

We may, therefore, conclude that the more enlightened a censorship is, the worse it would serve us. The Lord Chamberlain, an obviously unenlightened Censor, prohibits Ghosts and licenses all the rest of Ibsen's plays. An enlightened censorship would possibly license Ghosts; but it would certainly suppress many of the other plays. It would suppress subversiveness as well as what is called bad taste. The Lord Chamberlain prohibits one play by Sophocles because, like Hamlet, it mentions the subject of incest; but an enlightened censorship might suppress all the plays of Euripides because Euripides, like Ibsen, was a revolutionary Freethinker. Under the Lord Chamberlain, we can smuggle a good deal of immoral drama and almost as much coarsely vulgar and furtively lascivious drama as we like. Under a college of cardinals, or bishops, or judges, or any other conceivable form of experts in morals, philosophy, religion, or politics, we should get little except stagnant mediocrity.

THE PRACTICAL IMPOSSIBILITIES OF CENSORSHIP

There is, besides, a crushing material difficulty in the way of an enlightened censorship. It is not too much to say that the work involved would drive a man of any intellectual rank mad. Consider, for example, the Christmas pantomimes. Imagine a judge of the High Court, or an archbishop, or a Cabinet Minister, or an eminent man of letters, earning his living by reading through the mass of trivial doggerel represented by all the pantomimes which are put into rehearsal simultaneously at the end of every year. The proposal to put such mind-destroying drudgery upon an official of the class implied by the demand for an enlightened censorship falls through the moment we realize what it implies in practice.

Another material difficulty is that no play can be judged by merely reading the dialogue. To be fully effective a cen-

sor should witness the performance. The *mise-en-scène* of a
play is as much a part of it as the words spoken on the stage.
No censor could possibly object to such a speech as "Might
I speak to you for a moment, miss?" yet that apparently
innocent phrase has often been made offensively improper
on the stage by popular low comedians, with the effect of
changing the whole character and meaning of the play as
understood by the official Examiner. In one of the plays of
the present season, the dialogue was that of a crude melodrama dealing in the most conventionally correct manner
with the fortunes of a good-hearted and virtuous girl. Its
morality was that of the Sunday school. But the principal
actress, between two speeches which contained no reference
to her action, changed her underclothing on the stage! It is
true that in this case the actress was so much better than her
part that she succeeded in turning what was meant as an
impropriety into an inoffensive stroke of realism; yet it is
none the less clear that stage business of this character, on
which there can be no check except the actual presence of a
censor in the theatre, might convert any dialogue, however
innocent, into just the sort of entertainment against which
the Censor is supposed to protect the public.

It was this practical impossibility that prevented the
London County Council from attempting to apply a censorship of the Lord Chamberlain's pattern to the London
music halls. A proposal to examine all entertainments before
permitting their performance was actually made; and it was
abandoned, not in the least as contrary to the liberty of the
stage, but because the executive problem of how to do it at
once reduced the proposal to absurdity. Even if the Council
devoted all its time to witnessing rehearsals of variety performances, and putting each item to the vote, possibly after
a prolonged discussion followed by a division, the work
would still fall into arrear. No committee could be induced
to undertake such a task. The attachment of an inspector
of morals to each music hall would have meant an appre-
ciable addition to the ratepayers' burden. In the face of such

211

difficulties the proposal melted away. Had it been pushed through, and the inspectors appointed, each of them would have become a censor, and the whole body of inspectors would have become a *police des mœurs*. Those who know the history of such police forces on the Continent will understand how impossible it would be to procure inspectors whose characters would stand the strain of their opportunities of corruption, both pecuniary and personal, at such salaries as a local authority could be persuaded to offer.

It has been suggested that the present censorship should be supplemented by a board of experts, who should deal, not with the whole mass of plays sent up for licence, but only those which the Examiner of Plays refuses to pass. As the number of plays which the Examiner refuses to pass is never great enough to occupy a Board in permanent session with regular salaries, and as casual employment is not compatible with public responsibility, this proposal would work out in practice as an addition to the duties of some existing functionary. A Secretary of State would be objectionable as likely to be biased politically. An ecclesiastical referee might be biased against the theatre altogether. A judge in chambers would be the proper authority. This plan would combine the inevitable intolerance of an enlightened censorship with the popular laxity of the Lord Chamberlain. The judge would suppress the pioneers, whilst the Examiner of Plays issued two guinea certificates for the vulgar and vicious plays. For this reason the plan would no doubt be popular; but it would be very much as a relaxation of the administration of the Public Health Acts accompanied by the cheapening of gin would be popular.

THE ARBITRATION PROPOSAL

On the occasion of a recent deputation of playwrights to the Prime Minister it was suggested that if a censorship be inevitable, provision should be made for an appeal from the Lord Chamberlain in cases of refusal of licence. The authors of this suggestion propose that the Lord Chamberlain shall choose one umpire and the author another. The two umpires shall then elect a referee, whose decision shall be final.

This proposal is not likely to be entertained by constitutional lawyers. It is a naïve offer to accept the method of arbitration in what is essentially a matter, not between one private individual or body and another, but between a public offender and the State. It will presumably be ruled out as a proposal to refer a case of manslaughter to arbitration would be ruled out. But even if it were constitutionally sound, it bears all the marks of that practical inexperience which leads men to believe that arbitration either costs nothing or is at least cheaper than law. Who is to pay for the time of the three arbitrators, presumably men of high professional standing? The author may not be able: the manager may not be willing: neither of them should be called upon to pay for a public service otherwise than by their contributions to the revenue. Clearly the State should pay. But even so, the difficulties are only beginning. A licence is seldom refused except on grounds which are controversial. The two arbitrators selected by the opposed parties to the controversy are to agree to leave the decision to a third party unanimously chosen by themselves. That is very far from being a simple solution. An attempt to shorten and simplify the passing of the Finance Bill by referring it to an arbitrator chosen unanimously by Mr Asquith and Mr Balfour might not improbably cost more and last longer than a civil war. And why should the chosen referee—if he ever succeeded in getting chosen—be assumed to be a safer authority than the Examiner of Plays? He would certainly be a less responsible one: in fact, being (however eminent) a casual person called in to settle a single case, he would be virtually irresponsible. Worse still, he would take all responsibility away from the Lord Chamberlain, who is at least an official of the King's Household and a nominee of the Government. The Lord Chamberlain, with all his shortcomings, thinks twice before he refuses a licence, knowing that his refusal is final and may promptly be made public. But if he could transfer his responsibility to an arbitrator, he would naturally do so whenever he felt the slightest misgiving, or whenever, for diplomatic reasons, the licence would come more gracefully from an authority unconnected with the court. These considerations, added to the general objection to the principle of censorship, seem sufficient to put the arbitration expedient quite out of the question.

END OF THE FIRST PART OF THE REJECTED STATEMENT

214

THE REJECTED STATEMENT
PART II
THE LICENSING OF THEATRES
THE DISTINCTION BETWEEN LICENSING AND CENSORSHIP

IT must not be concluded that the uncompromising abolition of all censorship involves the abandonment of all control and regulation of theatres. Factories are regulated in the public interest; but there is no censorship of factories. For example, many persons are sincerely convinced that cotton clothing is unhealthy; that alcoholic drinks are demoralizing; and that playing-cards are the devil's picture-books. But though the factories in which cotton, whiskey, and cards are manufactured are stringently regulated under the factory code and the Public Health and Building Acts, the inspectors appointed to carry out these Acts never go to a manufacturer and inform him that unless he manufactures woollens instead of cottons, ginger-beer instead of whiskey, Bibles instead of playing-cards, he will be forbidden to place his products on the market. In the case of premises licensed for the sale of spirits the authorities go a step further. A public-house differs from a factory in the essential particular that whereas disorder in a factory is promptly and voluntarily suppressed, because every moment of its duration involves a measurable pecuniary loss to the proprietor, disorder in a public-house may be a source of profit to the proprietor by its attraction for disorderly customers. Consequently a publican is compelled to obtain a licence to pursue his trade; and this licence lasts only a year, and need not be renewed if his house has been conducted in a disorderly manner in the meantime.

PROSTITUTION AND DRINK IN THEATRES

The theatre presents the same problem as the public-house in respect to disorder. To begin with, a theatre is actually a place licensed for the sale of spirits. The bars at a London theatre can be let without difficulty for £30 a week and upwards. And though it is clear that nobody will pay

215

from a shilling to half a guinea for access to a theatre bar
when he can obtain access to an ordinary public-house for
nothing, there is no law to prevent the theatre proprietor
from issuing free passes broadcast and recouping himself by
the profit on the sale of drink. Besides, there may be some
other attraction than the sale of drink. When this attraction
is that of the play no objection need be made. But it happens
that the auditorium of a theatre, with its brilliant lighting
and luxurious decorations, makes a very effective shelter and
background for the display of fine dresses and pretty faces.
Consequently theatres have been used for centuries in England as markets by prostitutes. From the Restoration to the
days of Macready all theatres were made use of in this way
as a matter of course; and to this, far more than to any prejudice against dramatic art, we owe the Puritan formula that
the theatre door is the gate of hell. Macready had a hard
struggle to drive the prostitutes from his theatre; and since
his time the London theatres controlled by the Lord Chamberlain have become respectable and even socially pretentious. But some of the variety theatres still derive a revenue
by selling admissions to women who do not look at the performance, and men who go to purchase or admire the
women. And in the provinces this state of things is by no
means confined to the variety theatres. The real attraction is
sometimes not the performance at all. The theatre is not
really a theatre: it is a drink shop and a prostitution market;
and the last shred of its disguise is stripped by the virtually
indiscriminate issue of free tickets to the men. Access to the
stage is also easily obtained; and the plays preferred by the
management are those in which the stage is filled with young
women who are not in any serious technical sense of the
word actresses at all. Considering that all this is now possible
at any theatre, and actually occurs at some theatres, the fact
that our best theatres are as respectable as they are is much
to their credit; but it is still an intolerable evil that respectable managers should have to fight against the free tickets
and disorderly housekeeping of unscrupulous competitors.

216

THE REJECTED STATEMENT

The dramatic author is equally injured. He finds that unless he writes plays which make suitable side-shows for drinking-bars and brothels, he may be excluded from towns where there is not room for two theatres, and where the one existing theatre is exploiting drunkenness and prostitution instead of carrying on a legitimate dramatic business. Indeed everybody connected with the theatrical profession suffers in reputation from the detestable tradition of such places, against which the censorship has proved quite useless.

Here we have a strong case for applying either the licensing system or whatever better means may be devized for securing the orderly conduct of houses of public entertainment, dramatic or other. Liberty must, no doubt, be respected in so far that no manager should have the right to refuse admission to decently dressed, sober, and well-conducted persons, whether they are prostitutes, soldiers in uniform, gentlemen not in evening dress, Indians, or what not; but when disorder is stopped, disorderly persons will either cease to come or else reform their manners. It is, however, quite arguable that the indiscriminate issue of free admissions, though an apparently innocent and good-natured, and certainly a highly popular proceeding, should expose the proprietor of the theatre to the risk of a refusal to renew his licence.

WHY THE MANAGERS DREAD LOCAL CONTROL

All this points to the transfer of the control of theatres from the Lord Chamberlain to the municipality. And this step is opposed by the long-run managers, partly because they take it for granted that municipal control must involve municipal censorship of plays, so that plays might be licensed in one town and prohibited in the next, and partly because, as they have no desire to produce plays which are in advance of public opinion, and as the Lord Chamberlain in every other respect gives more scandal by his laxity than trouble by his severity, they find in the present system a cheap and easy means of procuring a certificate which relieves them of all social responsibility, and provides them with so strong a weapon of defence in case of a prosecution that it acts in practice as a bar to any such proceedings. Above all, they know that the Examiner of Plays is free from the pressure of that large body of English public opinion already alluded to, which regards the theatre as the Prohibitionist Teetotaller regards the public-house: that is, as an abomination to be stamped out unconditionally. The managers rightly dread this pressure more than anything else; and they believe that it is so strong in local governments as to be a characteristic bias of municipal authority. In this they are no doubt mistaken. There is not a municipal authority of any importance in the country in which a proposal to stamp out the theatre, or even to treat it illiberally, would have a chance of adoption. Municipal control of the variety theatres (formerly called music halls) has been very far from illiberal, except in the one particular in which the Lord Chamberlain is equally illiberal. That particular is the assumption that a draped figure is decent and an undraped one indecent. It is useless to point to actual experience, which proves abundantly that naked or apparently naked figures, whether exhibited as living pictures, animated statuary, or in a dance, are at their best not only innocent, but refining in their effect, whereas those actresses and skirt dancers who have brought the peculiar aphrodisiac effect which is objected to to the highest pitch of efficiency wear twice as many petticoats as an ordinary lady does, and seldom exhibit more than their ankles. Unfortunately, municipal councillors persist in confusing decency with drapery; and both in London and the provinces certain positively edifying performances have been forbidden or withdrawn under pressure, and replaced by coarse and vicious ones. There is not the slightest reason to suppose that the Lord Chamberlain would have been any more tolerant; but this does not alter the fact that the municipal licensing authorities have actually used their powers to set up a censorship which is open to all the objections to censorship in general, and which, in addition, sets up the objection from which central control is free: namely, the impossibility of planning theatrical tours without the serious commercial risk of having the performance forbidden in some of the towns booked. How can this be prevented?

DESIRABLE LIMITATIONS OF LOCAL CONTROL

The problem is not a difficult one. The municipality can be limited just as the monarchy is limited. The Act transferring theatres to local control can be a charter of the liberties of the stage as well as an Act to reform administration. The power to refuse to grant or renew a licence to a theatre need not be an arbitrary one. The municipality may be required to state the ground of refusal; and certain grounds can be expressly declared as unlawful; so that it shall be possible for the manager to resort to the courts for a mandamus to compel the authority to grant a licence. It can be declared unlawful for a licensing authority to demand from the manager any disclosure of the nature of any entertainment he proposes to give, or to prevent its performance, or to refuse to renew his licence on the ground that the tendency of his entertainments is contrary to religion and morals, or that the theatre is an undesirable institution, or that there are already as many theatres as are needed, or that the theatre draws people away from the churches, chapels, mission halls, and the like in its neighborhood. The assumption should be that every citizen has a right to open and conduct a theatre, and therefore has a right to a licence unless he has forfeited that right by allowing his theatre to become a disorderly house, or failing to provide a building which complies with the regulations concerning sanitation and egress in case of fire, or being convicted of an offence against public decency. Also, the licensing powers of the authority should not be delegated to any official or committee; and the manager or lessee of the theatre should have a right to appear in person or by counsel to plead against any motion to refuse to grant or renew his licence. With these safeguards the licensing power could not be stretched to censorship.

The manager would enjoy liberty of conscience as far as the local authority is concerned; but on the least attempt on his part to keep a disorderly house under cover of opening a theatre he would risk his licence.

But the managers will not and should not be satisfied with these limits to the municipal power. If they are deprived of the protection of the Lord Chamberlain's licence, and at the same time efficiently protected against every attempt at censorship by the licensing authority, the enemies of the theatre will resort to the ordinary law, and try to get from the prejudices of a jury what they are debarred from getting from the prejudices of a County Council or City Corporation. Moral Reform Societies, "Purity" Societies, Vigilance Societies, exist in England and America for the purpose of enforcing the existing laws against obscenity, blasphemy, Sabbath-breaking, the debauchery of children, prostitution, and so forth. The paid officials of these societies, in their anxiety to produce plenty of evidence of their activity in the annual reports which go out to the subscribers, do not always discriminate between an obscene postcard and an artistic one, or to put it more exactly, between a naked figure and an indecent one. They often combine a narrow but terribly sincere sectarian bigotry with a complete ignorance of art and history. Even when they have some culture, their livelihood is at the mercy of subscribers and committee men who have none. If these officials had any power of distinguishing between art and blackguardism, between morality and virtue, between immorality and vice, between conscientious heresy and mere baseness of mind and foulness of mouth, they might be trusted by theatrical managers not to abuse the powers of the common informer. As it is, it has been found necessary, in order to enable good music to be performed on Sunday, to take away these powers in that particular, and vest them solely in the Attorney-General. This disqualification of the common informer should be extended to the initiation of all proceedings of a censorial character against theatres. Few people are aware of the monstrous laws against blasphemy which still disgrace our statute book. If any serious attempt were made to carry them out, prison accommodation would have to be provided for almost every educated person in the country, beginning with the Archbishop of Canterbury. Until some government with courage and character enough to repeal them comes into power, it is not too much to ask that such infamous powers of oppression should be kept in responsible hands and not left at the disposal of every bigot ignorant enough to be unaware of the social dangers of persecution. Besides, the common informer is not always a sincere bigot who believes he is performing an action of signal merit in silencing and ruining a heretic. He is unfortunately just as often a blackmailer, who has studied his powers as a common informer in order that he may extort money for refraining from exercising them. If the manager is to be responsible he should be made responsible to a responsible functionary. To be responsible to every fanatical ignoramus who chooses to prosecute him for exhibiting a cast of the Hermes of Praxiteles in his vestibule, or giving a performance of Measure for Measure, is mere slavery. It is made bearable at present by the protection of the Lord Chamberlain's certificate. But when that is no longer available, the common informer must be disarmed if the manager is to enjoy security.

SUMMARY

THE general case against censorship as a principle, and the particular case against the existing English censorship and against its replacement by a more enlightened one, is now complete. The following is a recapitulation of the propositions and conclusions contended for.

1. The question of censorship or no censorship is a question of high political principle and not of petty policy.

2. The toleration of heresy and shocks to morality on the stage, and even their protection against the prejudices and superstitions which necessarily enter largely into morality and public opinion, are essential to the welfare of the nation.

3. The existing censorship of the Lord Chamberlain does not only intentionally suppress heresy and challenges to morality in their serious and avowed forms, but unintentionally gives the special protection of its official license to the most extreme impropriety that the lowest section of London playgoers will tolerate in theatres especially devoted to their entertainment, licensing everything that is popular and forbidding any attempt to change public opinion or morals.

4. The Lord Chamberlain's censorship is open to the special objection that its application to political plays is taken to indicate the attitude of the Crown on questions of domestic and foreign policy, and that it imposes the limits of etiquet on the historical drama.

5. A censorship of a more enlightened and independent kind, exercised by the most eminent available authorities, would prove in practice more disastrous than the censorship of the Lord Chamberlain, because the more eminent its members were the less possible would it be for them to accept the responsibility for heresy or immorality by licensing them, and because the many heretical and immoral plays which now pass the Lord Chamberlain because he does not understand them, would be understood and suppressed by a more highly enlightened censorship.

6. A reconstructed and enlightened censorship would

be armed with summary and effective powers which would stop the evasions by which heretical and immoral plays are now performed in spite of the Lord Chamberlain; and such powers would constitute a tyranny which would ruin the theatre spiritually by driving all independent thinkers from the drama into the uncensored forms of art.

7. The work of critically examining all stage plays in their written form, and of witnessing their performance in order to see that the sense is not altered by the stage business, would, even if it were divided among so many officials as to be physically possible, be mentally impossible to persons of taste and enlightenment.

8. Regulation of theatres is an entirely different matter from censorship, inasmuch as a theatre, being not only a stage, but a place licensed for the sale of spirits, and a public resort capable of being put to disorderly use, and needing special provision for the safety of audiences in cases of fire, etc., cannot be abandoned wholly to private control, and may therefore reasonably be made subject to an annual licence like those now required before allowing premises to be used publicly for music and dancing.

9. In order to prevent the powers of the licensing authority being abused so as to constitute a virtual censorship, any Act transferring the theatres to the control of a licensing authority should be made also a charter of the rights of dramatic authors and managers by the following provisions:

A. The public prosecutor (the Attorney-General) alone should have the right to set the law in operation against the manager of a theatre or the author of a play in respect of the character of the play or entertainment.

B. No disclosure of the particulars of a theatrical entertainment shall be required before performance.

C. Licences shall not be withheld on the ground that the existence of theatres is dangerous to religion and morals, or on the ground that any entertainment given or contemplated is heretical or immoral.

D. The licensing area shall be no less than that of a

223

County Council or City Corporation, which shall not delegate its licensing powers to any minor local authority or to any official or committee; it shall decide all questions affecting the existence of a theatrical licence by vote of the entire body; managers, lessees, and proprietors of theatres shall have the right to plead, in person or by counsel, against a proposal to withhold a licence; and the licence shall not be withheld except for stated reasons, the validity of which shall be subject to the judgment of the high courts.

E. The annual licence, once granted, shall not be cancelled or suspended unless the manager has been convicted by public prosecution of an offence against the ordinary laws against disorderly housekeeping, indecency, blasphemy, etc., except in cases where some structural or sanitary defect in the building necessitates immediate action for the protection of the public against physical injury.

F. No licence shall be refused on the ground that the proximity of the theatre to a church, mission hall, school or other place of worship, edification, instruction, or entertainment (including another theatre) would draw the public away from such places into its own doors.

PREFACE RESUMED
MR GEORGE ALEXANDER'S PROTEST

ON the facts mentioned in the foregoing statement, and in my evidence before the Joint Select Committee, no controversy arose except on one point. Mr George Alexander protested vigorously and indignantly against my admission that theatres, like public-houses, need special control on the ground that they can profit by disorder, and are sometimes conducted with that end in view. Now, Mr Alexander is a famous actor-manager; and it is very difficult to persuade the public that the more famous an actor-manager is the less he is likely to know about any theatre except his own. When the Committee of 1892 reported, I was considered guilty of a perverse paradox when I said that the witness who knew least about the theatre was Henry Irving. Yet a moment's consideration would have shewn that the paradox was a platitude. For about quarter of a century Irving was confined night after night to his own theatre and his own dressing-room, never seeing a play even there because he was himself part of the play; producing the works of long-departed authors; and, to the extent to which his talent was extraordinary, necessarily making his theatre unlike any other theatre. When he went to the provinces or to America, the theatres to which he went were swept and garnished for him, and their staffs replaced—as far as he came in contact with them—by his own lieutenants. In the end, there was hardly a first-nighter in his gallery who did not know more about the London theatres and the progress of dramatic art than he; and as to the provinces, if any chief constable had told him the real history and character of many provincial theatres, he would have denounced that chief constable as an ignorant libeller of a noble profession. But the constable would have been right for all that. Now if this was true of Sir Henry Irving, who did not become a London manager until he had roughed it for years in the provinces, how much more true must it be of, say, Mr George Alexander, whose successful march through his profession has passed as far from the purlieus of our theatrical world as the king's naval career from the Isle of Dogs? The moment we come to that necessary part of the censorship question which deals with the control of theatres from the point of view of those who know how much money can be made out of them by managers who seek to make the auditorium attractive rather than the stage, you find the managers divided into two sections. The first section consists of honorable and successful managers like Mr Alexander, who know nothing of such abuses, and deny, with perfect sincerity and indignant vehemence, that they exist except, perhaps, in certain notorious variety theatres. The other is the silent section which knows better, but is very well content to be publicly defended and privately amused by Mr Alexander's innocence. To accept a West End manager as an expert in theatres because he is an actor is much as if we were to accept the organist of St Paul's Cathedral as an expert on music halls because he is a musician. The real experts are all in the conspiracy to keep the police out of the theatre. And they are so successful that even the police do not know as much as they should.

The police should have been examined by the Committee, and the whole question of the extent to which theatres are disorderly houses in disguise sifted to the bottom. For it is on this point that we discover behind the phantoms of the corrupt dramatists who are restrained by the censorship from debauching the stage, the reality of the corrupt managers and theatre proprietors who actually do debauch it without let or hindrance from the censorship. The whole case for giving control over theatres to local authorities rests on this reality.

ELIZA AND HER BATH

The persistent notion that a theatre is an Alsatia where the king's writ does not run, and where any wickedness is possible in the absence of a special tribunal and a special police, was brought out by an innocent remark made by Sir William Gilbert, who, when giving evidence before the Committee, was asked by Colonel Lockwood whether a law sufficient to restrain impropriety in books would also restrain impropriety in plays. Sir William replied: "I should say there is a very wide distinction between what is read and what is seen. In a novel one may read that 'Eliza stripped off her dressing-gown and stepped into her bath' without any harm; but I think if that were presented on the stage it would be shocking." All the stupid and inconsiderate people seized eagerly on this illustration as if it were a successful attempt to prove that without a censorship we should be unable to prevent actresses from appearing naked on the stage. As a matter of fact, if an actress could be persuaded to do such a thing (and it would be about as easy to persuade a bishop's wife to appear in church in the same condition) the police would simply arrest her on a charge of indecent exposure. The extent to which this obvious safeguard was overlooked may be taken as a measure of the thoughtlessness and frivolity of the excuses made for the censorship. It should be added that the artistic representation of a bath, with every suggestion of nakedness that the law as to decency allows, is one of the most familiar subjects of scenic art. From the Rhine maidens in Wagner's Trilogy, and the bathers in the second act of Les Huguenots, to the ballets of water nymphs in our Christmas pantomimes and at our variety theatres, the sound hygienic propaganda of the bath, and the charm of the undraped human figure, are exploited without offence on the stage to an extent never dreamt of by any novelist.

A KING'S PROCTOR

Another hare was started by Professor Gilbert Murray and Mr Laurence Housman, who, in pure kindness to the managers, asked whether it would not be possible to establish for their assistance a sort of King's Proctor to whom plays might be referred for an official legal opinion as to their compliance with the law before production. There are several objections to this proposal; and they may as well be stated in case the proposal should be revived. In the first place, no lawyer with the most elementary knowledge of the law of libel in its various applications to sedition, obscenity, and blasphemy, could answer for the consequences of producing any play whatsoever as to which the smallest question could arise in the mind of any sane person. I have been a critic and an author in active service for thirty years; and though nothing I have written has ever been prosecuted in England or made the subject of legal proceedings, yet I have never published in my life an article, a play, or a book, as to which, if I had taken legal advice, an expert could have assured me that I was proof against prosecution or against an action for damages by the persons criticized. No doubt a sensible solicitor might have advised me that the risk was no greater than all men have to take in dangerous trades; but such an opinion, though it may encourage a client, does not protect him. For example, if a publisher asks his solicitor whether he may venture on an edition of Sterne's Sentimental Journey, or a manager whether he may produce King Lear without risk of prosecution, the solicitor will advise him to go ahead. But if the solicitor or counsel consulted by him were asked for a guarantee that neither of these works was a libel, he would have to reply that he could give no such guarantee; that, on the contrary, it was his duty to warn his client that both of them are obscene libels; that King Lear, containing as it does perhaps the most appalling blasphemy that despair ever uttered, is a blasphemous libel, and that it is doubtful whether it could not be construed as a seditious libel as well. As to Ibsen's Brand (the play which made him popular with the most earnestly religious people) no sane solicitor would advise his client even to chance it except in a broadly cultivated and tolerant (or indifferent) modern city. The lighter plays would be no better off. What lawyer could accept any responsibility for the production of Sardou's Divorçons or Clyde Fitch's The Woman in the Case? Put the proposed King's Proctor in operation tomorrow; and what will be the result? The managers will find that instead of insuring them as the Lord Chamberlain does, he will warn them that every play they submit to him is vulnerable to the law, and that they must produce it not only on the ordinary risk of acting on their own responsibility, but at the very grave additional risk of doing so in the teeth of an official warning. Under such circumstances, what manager would resort a second time to the Proctor; and how would the Proctor live without fees, unless indeed the Government gave him a salary for doing nothing? The institution would not last a year, except as a job for somebody.

COUNSEL'S OPINION

The proposal is still less plausible when it is considered that at present, without any new legislation at all, any manager who is doubtful about a play can obtain the advice of his solicitor, or Counsel's opinion, if he thinks it will be of any service to him. The verdict of the proposed King's Proctor would be nothing but Counsel's opinion without the liberty of choice of Counsel, possibly cheapened, but sure to be adverse; for an official cannot give practical advice as a friend and a man of the world; he must stick to the letter of the law and take no chances. And as far as the law is concerned, journalism, literature, and the drama exist only by custom or sufferance.

WANTED: A NEW MAGNA CHARTA

This leads us to a very vital question. Is it not possible to amend the law so as to make it possible for a lawyer to advise his client that he may publish the works of Blake, Zola, and Swinburne, or produce the plays of Ibsen and Mr Granville Barker, or print ordinary criticism in his newspaper, without the possibility of finding himself in prison, or mulcted in damages and costs in consequence? No doubt it is; but only by a declaration of constitutional right to blaspheme, rebel, and deal with tabooed subjects. Such a declaration is not just now within the scope of practical politics, although we are compelled to act to a great extent as if it was actually part of the constitution. All that can be done is to take my advice and limit the necessary public control of the theatres in such a manner as to prevent its being abused as a censorship. We have ready to our hand the machinery of licensing as applied

229

to public-houses. A licensed victualler can now be assured confidently by his lawyer that a magistrate cannot refuse to renew his licence on the ground that he (the magistrate) is a teetotaller and has seen too much of the evil of drink to sanction its sale. The magistrate must give a judicial reason for his refusal, meaning really a constitutional reason; and his teetotallism is not such a reason. In the same way you can protect a theatrical manager by ruling out certain reasons as unconstitutional, as suggested in my statement. Combine this with the abolition of the common informer's power to initiate proceedings; and you will have gone as far as seems possible at present. You will have local control of the theatres for police purposes and sanitary purposes without censorship; and I do not see what more is possible until we get a formal Magna Charta declaring all the categories of libel and the blasphemy laws contrary to public liberty, and repealing and defining accordingly.

PROPOSED: A NEW STAR CHAMBER

Yet we cannot mention Magna Charta without recalling how useless such documents are to a nation which has no more political comprehension nor political virtue than King John. When Henry VII. calmly proceeded to tear up Magna Charta by establishing the Star Chamber (a criminal court consisting of a committee of the Privy Council without a jury) nobody objected until, about a century and a half later, the Star Chamber began cutting off the ears of eminent Nonconformist divines and standing them in the pillory; and then the Nonconformists, and nobody else, abolished the Star Chamber. And if anyone doubts that we are quite ready to establish the Star Chamber again, let him read the Report of the Joint Select Committee, on which I now venture to offer a few criticisms.

The report of the Committee, which will be found in the bluebook, should be read with attention and respect as far as page x, up to which point it is an able and well-written statement of the case. From page x onward, when it goes on from diagnosing the disease to prescribing the treatment, it should be read with even greater attention but with no respect whatever, as the main object of the treatment is to conciliate the How Not To Do It majority. It contains, however, one very notable proposal, the same being nothing more nor less than to revive the Star Chamber for the purpose of dealing with heretical or seditious plays and their authors, and indeed with all charges against theatrical entertainments except common police cases of indecency. The reason given is that for which the Star Chamber was created by Henry VII.: that is, the inadequacy of the ordinary law. "We consider," says the report, "that the law which prevents or punishes indecency, blasphemy and libel in printed publications [it does not, by the way, except in the crudest police cases] would not be adequate for the control of the drama." Therefor a committee of the Privy Council is to be empowered to suppress plays and punish managers and authors at its pleasure, on the motion of the Attorney-General, without a jury. The members of the Committee will, of course, be men of high standing and character: otherwise they would not be on the Privy Council. That is to say, they will have all the qualifications of Archbishop Laud.

Now I have no guarantee that any member of the majority of the Joint Select Committee ever heard of the Star Chamber or of Archbishop Laud. One of them did not know that politics meant anything more than party electioneering. Nothing is more alarming than the ignorance of our public men of the commonplaces of our history, and their consequent readiness to repeat experiments which have in the past produced national catastrophes. At all events, whether they knew what they were doing or not, there can be no question as to what they did. They proposed virtually that the Act of the Long Parliament in 1641 shall be repealed, and the Star Chamber re-established, in order that playwrights and managers may be punished for unspecified offences unknown to the law. When I say unspecified, I should say specified as follows (see page xi of the report) in the case of a play:—

(a) To be indecent.

231

(*b*) To contain offensive personalities.

(*c*) To represent on the stage in an invidious manner a living person, or any person recently dead.

(*d*) To do violence to the sentiment of religious reverence.

(*e*) To be calculated to conduce to vice or crime.

(*f*) To be calculated to impair friendly relations with any foreign power.

(*g*) To be calculated to cause a breach of the peace.

Now it is clear that there is no play yet written, or possible to be written, in this world, that might not be condemned under one or other of these heads. How any sane man, not being a professed enemy of public liberty, could put his hand to so monstrous a catalogue passes my understanding. Had a comparatively definite and innocent clause been added forbidding the affirmation or denial of the doctrine of Transubstantiation, the country would have been up in arms at once. Lord Ribblesdale made an effort to reduce the seven categories to the old formula "not to be fitting for the preservation of good manners, decorum, or the public peace"; but this proposal was not carried; whilst on Lord Gorell's motion a final widening of the net was achieved by adding the phrase "to be calculated to"; so that even if a play does not produce any of the results feared, the author can still be punished on the ground that his play is "calculated" to produce them. I have no hesitation in saying that a committee capable of such an outrageous display of thoughtlessness and historical ignorance as this paragraph of its report implies deserves to be haled before the tribunal it has itself proposed, and dealt with under a general clause levelled at conduct "calculated to" overthrow the liberties of England.

POSSIBILITIES OF THE PROPOSAL

Still, though I am certainly not willing to give Lord Gorell the chance of seeing me in the pillory with my ears cut off if I can help it, I daresay many authors would rather take their chance with a Star Chamber than with a jury, just as some soldiers would rather take their chance with a court-martial than at Quarter Sessions. For that matter, some of them would rather take their chance with the Lord Chamberlain than with either. And though this is no reason for depriving the whole body of authors of the benefit of Magna Charta, still, if the right of the proprietor of a play to refuse the good offices of the Privy Council and to perform the play until his accusers had indicted him at law, and obtained the verdict of a jury against him, were sufficiently guarded, the proposed Committee might be set up and used for certain purposes. For instance, it might be made a condition of the intervention of the Attorney-General or the Director of Public Prosecutions that he should refer an accused play to the Committee, and obtain their sanction before taking action, offering the proprietor of the play, if the Committee thought fit, an opportunity of voluntarily accepting trial by the Committee as an alternative to prosecution in the ordinary course of law. But the Committee should have no powers of punishment beyond the power (formidable enough) of suspending performances of the play. If it thought that additional punishment was called for, it could order a prosecution without allowing the proprietor or author of the play the alternative of a trial by itself. The author of the play should be made a party to all proceedings of the Committee, and have the right to defend himself in person or by counsel. This would provide a check on the Attorney-General (who might be as bigoted as any of the municipal aldermen who are so much dreaded by the actor-managers) without enabling the Committee to abuse its powers for party, class, or sectarian ends beyond that irreducible minimum of abuse which a popular jury would endorse, for which minimum there is no remedy.

But when everything is said for the Star Chamber that can be said, and every precaution taken to secure to those whom it pursues the alternative of trial by jury, the expedient still remains a very questionable one, to be endured for the sake of its protective rather than its repressive powers. It should abolish the present quaint toleration of rioting in theatres.

For example, if it is to be an offence to perform a play which
the proposed new Committee shall condemn, it should also
be made an offence to disturb a performance which the
Committee has not condemned. "Brawling" at a theatre
should be dealt with as severely as brawling in church if the
censorship is to be taken out of the hands of the public. At
present Jenny Geddes may throw her stool at the head of a
playwright who preaches unpalatable doctrine to her, or
rather, since her stool is a fixture, she may hiss and hoot and
make it impossible to proceed with the performance, even
although nobody has compelled her to come to the theatre or
suspended her liberty to stay away, and although she has no
claim on an unendowed theatre for her spiritual necessities,
as she has on her parish church. If mob censorship cannot
be trusted to keep naughty playwrights in order, still less
can it be trusted to keep the pioneers of thought in countenance; and I submit that anyone hissing a play permitted by
the new censorship should be guilty of contempt of court.

STAR CHAMBER SENTIMENTALITY

But what is most to be dreaded in a Star Chamber is not
its sternness but its sentimentality. There is no worse censorship than one which considers only the feelings of the
spectators, except perhaps one which considers the feelings
of people who do not even witness the performance. Take
the case of the Passion Play at Oberammergau. The offence
given by a representation of the Crucifixion on the stage is
not bounded by frontiers: further, it is an offence of which
the voluntary spectators are guilty no less than the actors.
If it is to be tolerated at all: if we are not to make war on the
German Empire for permitting it, nor punish the English
people who go to Bavaria to see it and thereby endow it with
English money, we may as well tolerate it in London, where
nobody need go to see it except those who are not offended
by it. When Wagner's Parsifal becomes available for representation in London, many people will be sincerely horrified
when the miracle of the Mass is simulated on the stage of
Covent Garden, and the Holy Ghost descends in the form of

a dove. But if the Committee of the Privy Council, or the Lord Chamberlain, or anyone else, were to attempt to keep Parsifal from us to spare the feelings of these people, it would not be long before even the most thoughtless champions of the censorship would see that the principle of doing nothing that could shock anybody had reduced itself to absurdity. No quarter whatever should be given to the bigotry of people so unfit for social life as to insist not only that their own prejudices and superstitions should have the fullest toleration but that everybody else should be compelled to think and act as they do. Every service in St Paul's Cathedral is an outrage to the opinions of the congregation of the Roman Catholic Cathedral of Westminster. Every Liberal meeting is a defiance and a challenge to the most cherished opinions of the Unionists. A law to compel the Roman Catholics to attend service at St Paul's, or the Liberals to attend the meetings of the Primrose League would be resented as an insufferable tyranny. But a law to shut up both St Paul's and the Westminster Cathedral, and to put down political meetings and associations because of the offence given by them to many worthy and excellent people, would be a far worse tyranny, because it would kill the religious and political life of the country outright, whereas to compel people to attend the services and meetings of their opponents would greatly enlarge their minds, and would actually be a good thing if it were enforced all round. I should not object to a law to compel everybody to read two newspapers, each violently opposed to the other in politics; but to forbid us to read newspapers at all would be to maim us mentally and cashier our country in the ranks of civilization. I deny that anybody has the right to demand more from me, over and above lawful conduct in a general sense, than liberty to stay away from the theatre in which my plays are represented. If he is unfortunate enough to have a religion so petty that it can be insulted (any man is as welcome to insult my religion, if he can, as he is to insult the universe) I claim the right to insult it to my heart's content, if I choose, provided I do not

235

compel him to come and hear me. If I think this country ought to make war on any other country, then, so long as war remains lawful, I claim full liberty to write and perform a play inciting the country to that war without interference from the ambassadors of the menaced country. I may "give pain to many worthy people, and pleasure to none," as the Censor's pet phrase puts it: I may even make Europe a cockpit and Asia a shambles: no matter: if preachers and politicians, statesmen and soldiers, may do these things—if it is right that such things should be done, then I claim my share in the right to do them. If the proposed Committee is meant to prevent me from doing these things whilst men of other professions are permitted to do them, then I protest with all my might against the formation of such a Committee. If it is to protect me, on the contrary, against the attacks that bigots and corrupt pornographers may make on me by appealing to the ignorance and prejudices of common jurors, then I welcome it; but is that really the object of its proposers? And if it is, what guarantee have I that the new tribunal will not presently resolve into a mere committee to avoid unpleasantness and keep the stage "in good taste"? It is no more possible for me to do my work honestly as a playwright without giving pain than it is for a dentist. The nation's morals are like its teeth: the more decayed they are the more it hurts to touch them. Prevent dentists and dramatists from giving pain, and not only will our morals become as carious as our teeth, but toothache and the plagues that follow neglected morality will presently cause more agony than all the dentists and dramatists at their worst have caused since the world began.

ANYTHING FOR A QUIET LIFE

Another doubt: would a Committee of the Privy Council really face the risks that must be taken by all communities as the price of our freedom to evolve? Would it not rather take the popular English view that freedom and virtue generally are sweet and desirable only when they cost nothing? Nothing worth having is to be had without risk. A mother

236

risks her child's life every time she lets it ramble through the countryside, or cross the street, or clamber over the rocks on the shore by itself. A father risks his son's morals when he gives him a latchkey. The members of the Joint Select Committee risked my producing a revolver and shooting them when they admitted me to the room without having me handcuffed. And these risks are no unreal ones. Every day some child is maimed or drowned and some young man infected with disease; and political assassinations have been appallingly frequent of late years. Railway travelling has its risks; motoring has its risks; aeroplaning has its risks; every advance we make costs us a risk of some sort. And though these are only risks to the individual, to the community they are certainties. It is not certain that I will be killed this year in a railway accident; but it is certain that somebody will. The invention of printing and the freedom of the press have brought upon us, not merely risks of their abuse, but the establishment as part of our social routine of some of the worst evils a community can suffer from. People who realize these evils shriek for the suppression of motor cars, the virtual imprisonment and enslavement of the young, the passing of Press Laws (especially in Egypt, India, and Ireland), exactly as they shriek for a censorship of the stage. The freedom of the stage will be abused just as certainly as the complaisance and innocence of the censorship is abused at present. It will also be used by writers like myself for raising very difficult and disturbing questions, social, political, and religious, at moments which may be extremely inconvenient to the government. Is it certain that a Committe of the Privy Council would stand up to all this as the price of liberty? I doubt it. If I am to be at the mercy of a nice amiable Committee of elderly gentlemen (I know all about elderly gentlemen, being one myself) whose motto is the highly popular one, "Anything for a quiet life," and who will make the inevitable abuses of freedom by our blackguards an excuse for interfering with any disquieting use of it by myself, then I shall be worse off than I am with the

THE SHEWING-UP OF BLANCO POSNET

Lord Chamberlain, whose mind is not broad enough to obstruct the whole range of thought. If it were, he would be given a more difficult post.

SHALL THE EXAMINER OF PLAYS STARVE?

And here I may be reminded that if I prefer the Lord Chamberlain I can go to the Lord Chamberlain, who is to retain all his present functions for the benefit of those who prefer to be judged by him. But I am not so sure that the Lord Chamberlain will be able to exercise those functions for long if resort to him is to be optional. Let me be kinder to him than he has been to me, and uncover for him the pitfalls which the Joint Select Committee have dug (and concealed) in his path. Consider how the voluntary system must inevitably work. The Joint Select Committee expressly urges that the Lord Chamberlain's licence must not be a bar to a prosecution. Granted that in spite of this reservation the licence would prove in future as powerful a defence as it has been in the past, yet the voluntary clause nevertheless places the manager at the mercy of any author who makes it a condition of his contract that his play shall not be submitted for licence. I should probably take that course without opposition from the manager. For the manager, knowing that three of my plays have been refused a licence, and that it would be far safer to produce a play for which no licence had been asked than one for which it had been asked and refused, would agree that it was more prudent, in my case, to avail himself of the power of dispensing with the Lord Chamberlain's licence. But now mark the consequences. The manager, having thus discovered that his best policy was to dispense with the licence in the few doubtful cases, would presently ask himself why he should spend two guineas each on licences for the many plays as to which no question could conceivably arise. What risk does any manager run in producing such works as Sweet Lavender, Peter Pan, The Silver King, or any of the 99 per cent of plays that are equally neutral on controversial questions. Does anyone seriously believe that the managers would continue to pay the Lord

238

Chamberlain two guineas a play out of mere love and loyalty, only to create an additional risk in the case of controversial plays, and to guard against risks that do not exist in the case of the great bulk of other productions? Only those would remain faithful to him who produce such plays as the Select Committee began by discussing *in camera*, and ended by refusing to discuss at all because they were too nasty. These people would still try to get a licence, and would still no doubt succeed as they do today. But could the King's Reader of Plays live on his fees from these plays alone; and if he could how long would his post survive the discredit of licensing only pornographic plays? It is clear to me that the Examiner would be starved out of existence, and the censorship perish of desuetude. Perhaps that is exactly what the Select Committee contemplated. If so, I have nothing more to say, except that I think sudden death would be more merciful.

LORD GORELL'S AWAKENING

In the meantime, conceive the situation which would arise if a licensed play were prosecuted. To make it clearer, let us imagine any other offender—say a company promoter with a fraudulent prospectus—pleading in Court that he had induced the Lord Chamberlain to issue a certificate that the prospectus contained nothing objectionable, and that on the strength of that certificate he issued it; also, that by law the Court could do nothing to him except order him to wind up this company. Some such vision as this must have come to Lord Gorell when he at last grappled seriously with the problem. Mr Harcourt seized the opportunity to make a last rally. He seconded Lord Gorell's proposal that the Committee should admit that its scheme of an optional censorship was an elaborate absurdity, and report that all censorship before production was out of the question. But it was too late: the *volte face* was too sudden and complete. It was Lord Gorell whose vote had turned the close division which took place on the question of receiving my statement. It was Lord Gorell without whose countenance and authority the farce of the books could never have been performed. Yet

239

here was Lord Gorell, after assenting to all the provisions for the optional censorship paragraph by paragraph, suddenly informing his colleagues that they had been wrong all through and that I had been right all through, and inviting them to scrap half their work and adopt my conclusion. No wonder Lord Gorell got only one vote: that of Mr Harcourt. But the incident is not the less significant. Lord Gorell carried more weight than any other member of the Committee on the legal and constitutional aspect of the question. Had he begun where he left off—had he at the outset put down his foot on the notion that an optional penal law could ever be anything but a gross contradiction in terms, that part of the Committee's proposals would never have come into existence.

JUDGES: THEIR PROFESSIONAL LIMITATIONS

I do not, however, appeal to Lord Gorell's judgment on all points. It is inevitable that a judge should be deeply impressed by his professional experience with a sense of the impotence of judges and laws and courts to deal satisfactorily with evils which are so Protean and elusive as to defy definition, and which yet seem to present quite simple problems to the common sense of men of the world. You have only to imagine the Privy Council as consisting of men of the world highly endowed with common sense, to persuade yourself that the supplementing of the law by the common sense of the Privy Council would settle the whole difficulty. But no man knows what he means by common sense, though every man can tell you that it is very uncommon, even in Privy Councils. And since every ploughman is a man of the world, it is evident that even the phrase itself does not mean what it says. As a matter of fact, it means in ordinary use simply a man who will not make himself disagreeable for the sake of a principle: just the sort of man who should never be allowed to meddle with political rights. Now to a judge a political right, that is, a dogma which is above our laws and conditions our laws, instead of being subject to them, is anarchic and abhorrent. That is why I trust Lord Gorell

240

when he is defending the integrity of the law against the proposal to make it in any sense optional, whilst I very strongly mistrust him, as I mistrust all professional judges, when political rights are in danger.

CONCLUSION

I must conclude by recommending the Government to take my advice wherever it conflicts with that of the Joint Select Committee. It is, I think, obviously more deeply considered and better informed, though I say it that should not. At all events, I have given my reasons; and at that I must leave it. As the tradition which makes Malvolio not only Master of the Revels but Master of the Mind of England, and which has come down to us from Henry VIII., is manifestly doomed to the dustbin, the sooner it goes there the better; for the democratic control which naturally succeeds it can easily be limited so as to prevent it becoming either a censorship or a tyranny. The Examiner of Plays should receive a generous pension, and be set free to practise privately as an expert adviser of theatrical managers. There is no reason why they should be deprived of the counsel they so highly value.

It only remains to say that public performances of The Shewing-up of Blanco Posnet are still prohibited in Great Britain by the Lord Chamberlain. An attempt was made to prevent even its performance in Ireland by some indiscreet Castle officials in the absence of the Lord Lieutenant. This attempt gave extraordinary publicity to the production of the play; and every possible effort was made to persuade the Irish public that the performance would be an outrage to their religion, and to provoke a repetition of the rioting that attended the first performances of Synge's Playboy of the Western World before the most sensitive and, on provocation, the most turbulent audience in the kingdom. The directors of the Irish National Theatre, Lady Gregory and Mr William Butler Yeats, rose to the occasion with inspiriting courage. I am a conciliatory person, and was willing, as I always am, to make every concession in return for having

THE SHEWING-UP OF BLANCO POSNET

my own way. But Lady Gregory and Mr Yeats not only would not yield an inch, but insisted, within the due limits of gallant warfare, on taking the field with every circumstance of defiance, and winning the battle with every trophy of victory. Their triumph was as complete as they could have desired. The performance exhausted the possibilities of success, and provoked no murmur, though it inspired several approving sermons. Later on, Lady Gregory and Mr Yeats brought the play to London and performed it under the Lord Chamberlain's nose, through the instrumentality of the Stage Society.

After this, the play was again submitted to the Lord Chamberlain. But, though beaten, he, too, understands the art of How Not To Do It. He licensed the play, but endorsed on his licence the condition that all the passages which implicated God in the history of Blanco Posnet must be omitted in representation. All the coarseness, the profligacy, the prostitution, the violence, the drinking-bar humor into which the light shines in the play are licensed, but the light itself is extinguished. I need hardly say that I have not availed myself of this licence, and do not intend to. There is enough licensed darkness in our theatres today without my adding to it.

Ayot St. Lawrence,
14th July 1910.

242

PREFACE

POSTSCRIPT.—Since the above was written the Lord Chamberlain has made an attempt to evade his responsibility and perhaps to postpone his doom by appointing an advisory committee, unknown to the law, on which he will presumably throw any odium that may attach to refusals of licences in the future. This strange and lawless body will hardly reassure our moralists, who object much more to the plays he licenses than to those he suppresses, and are therefore unmoved by his plea that his refusals are few and far between. It consists of two eminent actors (one retired), an Oxford professor of literature, and two eminent barristers. As their assembly is neither created by statute nor sanctioned by custom, it is difficult to know what to call it until it advises the Lord Chamberlain to deprive some author of his means of livelihood, when it will, I presume, become a conspiracy, and be indictable accordingly; unless, indeed, it can persuade the Courts to recognize it as a new Estate of the Realm, created by the Lord Chamberlain. This constitutional position is so questionable that I strongly advise the members to resign promptly before the Lord Chamberlain gets them into trouble.

THE SHEWING-UP OF BLANCO POSNET

A NUMBER *of women are sitting together in a big room not unlike an old English tithe barn in its timbered construction, but with windows high up next the roof. It is furnished as a courthouse, with the floor raised next the walls, and on this raised flooring a seat for the Sheriff, a rough jury box on his right, and a bar to put prisoners to on his left. In the well in the middle is a table with benches round it. A few other benches are in disorder round the room. The autumn sun is shining warmly through the windows and the open door. The women, whose dress and speech are those of pioneers of civilization in a territory of the United States of America, are seated round the table and on the benches, shucking nuts. The conversation is at its height.*

BABSY [*a bumptious young slattern, with some good looks*] I say that a man that would steal a horse would do anything.

LOTTIE [*a sentimental girl, neat and clean*] Well, I never should look at it in that way. I do think killing a man is worse any day than stealing a horse.

HANNAH [*elderly and wise*] I dont say it's right to kill a man. In a place like this, where every man has to have a revolver, and where theres so much to try people's tempers, the men get to be a deal too free with one another in the way of shooting. God knows it's hard enough to have to bring a boy into the world and nurse him up to be a man only to have him brought home to you on a shutter, perhaps for nothing, or only just to shew that the man that killed him wasnt afraid of him. But men are like children when they get a gun in their hands: theyre not content til theyve used it on somebody.

JESSIE [*a good-natured but sharp-tongued, hoity-toity young woman; Babsy's rival in good looks and her superior in tidiness*] They shoot for the love of it. Look at them at a lynching. Theyre not content to hang the man; but directly the poor creature is swung up they all shoot him full of holes, wasting their cartridges that cost solid money, and pretending they do it in horror of his wickedness, though half of them would have a rope round their own necks if all they did was known. Let alone the mess it makes.

LOTTIE. I wish we could get more civilized. I dont like all

this lynching and shooting. I dont believe any of us like it, if the truth were known.

BABSY. Our Sheriff is a real strong man. You want a strong man for a rough lot like our people here. He aint afraid to shoot and he aint afraid to hang. Lucky for us quiet ones, too.

JESSIE. Oh, dont talk to me. I know what men are. Of course he aint afraid to shoot and he aint afraid to hang. Wheres the risk in that with the law on his side and the whole crowd at his back longing for the lynching as if it was a spree? Would one of them own to it or let him own to it if they lynched the wrong man? Not them. What they call justice in this place is nothing but a breaking out of the devil thats in all of us. What I want to see is a Sheriff that aint afraid not to shoot and not to hang.

EMMA [*a sneak who sides with Babsy or Jessie, according to the fortune of war*] Well, I must say it does sicken me to see Sheriff Kemp putting down his foot, as he calls it. Why dont he put it down on his wife? She wants it worse than half the men he lynches. He and his Vigilance Committee, indeed!

BABSY [*incensed*] Oh, well! if people are going to take the part of horse-thieves against the Sheriff—?

JESSIE. Who's taking the part of horse-thieves against the Sheriff?

BABSY. You are. Waitle your own horse is stolen, and youll know better. I had an uncle that died of thirst in the sage brush because a negro stole his horse. But they caught him and burned him; and serve him right, too.

EMMA. I have known a child that was born crooked because its mother had to do a horse's work that was stolen.

BABSY. There! You hear that? I say stealing a horse is ten times worse than killing a man. And if the Vigilance Committee ever gets hold of you, youd better have killed twenty men than as much as stole a saddle or bridle, much less a horse.

Elder Daniels comes in.

ELDER DANIELS. Sorry to disturb you, ladies; but the Vigilance Committee has taken a prisoner; and they want the room to try him in.

JESSIE. But they cant try him til Sheriff Kemp comes back from the wharf.

ELDER DANIELS. Yes; but we have to keep the prisoner here til he comes.

BABSY. What do you want to put him here for? Cant you tie him up in the Sheriff's stable?

ELDER DANIELS. He has a soul to be saved, almost like the rest of us. I am bound to try to put some religion into him before he goes into his Maker's presence after the trial.

HANNAH. What has he done, Mr Daniels?

ELDER DANIELS. Stole a horse.

BABSY. And are we to be turned out of the town hall for a horse-thief? Aint a stable good enough for his religion?

ELDER DANIELS. It may be good enough for his, Babsy; but, by your leave, it is not good enough for mine. While I am Elder here, I shall umbly endeavour to keep up the dignity of Him I serve to the best of my small ability. So I must ask you to be good enough to clear out. Allow me. [*He takes the sack of husks and puts it out of the way against the panels of the jury box*].

THE WOMEN [*murmuring*] Thats always the way. Just as we'd settled down to work. What harm are we doing? Well, it is tiresome. Let them finish the job themselves. Oh dear, oh dear! We cant have a minute to ourselves. Shoving us out like that!

HANNAH. Whose horse was it, Mr Daniels?

ELDER DANIELS [*returning to move the other sack*] I am sorry to say it was the Sheriff's horse—the one he loaned to young Strapper. Strapper loaned it to me; and the thief stole it, thinking it was mine. If it had been mine, I'd have forgiven him cheerfully. I'm sure I hoped he would get away; for he had two hours start of the Vigilance Committee. But they caught him. [*He disposes of the other sack also*].

JESSIE. It cant have been much of a horse if they caught him with two hours start.

THE SHEWING-UP OF BLANCO POSNET

ELDER DANIELS [*coming back to the centre of the group*] The strange thing is that he wasnt on the horse when they took him. He was walking; and of course he denies that he ever had the horse. The Sheriff's brother wanted to tie him up and lash him til he confessed what he'd done with it; but I couldnt allow that: it's not the law.

BABSY. Law! What right has a horse-thief to any law? Law is thrown away on a brute like that.

ELDER DANIELS. Dont say that, Babsy. No man should be made to confess by cruelty until religion has been tried and failed. Please God I'll get the whereabouts of the horse from him if youll be so good as to clear out from this. [*Disturbance*]. They are bringing him in. Now ladies! please, please.

They rise reluctantly. Hannah, Jessie, and Lottie retreat to the Sheriff's bench, shepherded by Daniels; but the other women crowd forward behind Babsy and Emma to see the prisoner.

Blanco Posnet is brought in by Strapper Kemp, the Sheriff's brother, and a cross-eyed man called Squinty. Others follow. Blanco is evidently a blackguard. It would be necessary to clean him to make a close guess at his age; but he is under forty, and an upturned, red moustache, and the arrangement of his hair in a crest on his brow, proclaim the dandy in spite of his intense disreputableness. He carries his head high, and has a fairly resolute mouth, though the fire of incipient delirium tremens is in his eye.

His arms are bound with a rope with a long end, which Squinty holds. They release him when he enters; and he stretches himself and lounges across the courthouse in front of the women. Strapper and the men remain between him and the door.

BABSY [*spitting at him as he passes her*] Horse-thief! horse-thief!

OTHERS. You will hang for it; do you hear? And serve you right. Serve you right. That will teach you. I wouldnt wait to try you. Lynch him straight off, the varmint. Yes, yes. Tell the boys. Lynch him.

BLANCO [*mocking*] "Angels ever bright and fair—"

BABSY. You call me an angel, and I'll smack your dirty face for you.

248

BLANCO. "Take, oh take me to your care."

EMMA. There wont be any angels where youre going to.

OTHERS. Aha! Devils, more likely. And too good company for a horse-thief.

ALL. Horse-thief! Horse-thief! Horse-thief!

BLANCO. Do women make the law here, or men? Drive these heifers out.

THE WOMEN. Oh! [*They rush at him, vituperating, screaming passionately, tearing at him. Lottie puts her fingers in her ears and runs out. Hannah follows, shaking her head. Blanco is thrown down*]. Oh, did you hear what he called us? You foul-mouthed brute! You liar! How dare you put such a name to a decent woman? Let me get at him. You coward! Oh, he struck me: did you see that? Lynch him! Pete, will you stand by and hear me called names by a skunk like that? Burn him: burn him! Thats what I'd do with him. Aye, burn him!

THE MEN [*pulling the women away from Blanco, and getting them out partly by violence and partly by coaxing*] Here! come out of this. Let him alone. Clear the courthouse. Come on now. Out with you. Now, Sally: out you go. Let go my hair, or I'll twist your arm out. Ah, would you? Now, then: get along. You know you must go. Whats the use of scratching like that? Now, ladies, ladies, ladies. How would you like it if you were going to be hanged?

At last the women are pushed out, leaving Elder Daniels, the Sheriff's brother Strapper Kemp, and a few others with Blanco. Strapper is a lad just turning into a man: strong, selfish, sulky, and determined.

BLANCO [*sitting up and tidying himself*]—

Oh woman, in our hours of ease,

Uncertain, coy, and hard to please—

Is my face scratched? I can feel their damned claws all over me still. Am I bleeding? [*He sits on the nearest bench*].

ELDER DANIELS. Nothing to hurt. Theyve drawn a drop or two under your left eye.

STRAPPER. Lucky for you to have an eye left in your head.

BLANCO [*wiping the blood off*]—

249

When pain and anguish wring the brow,
A ministering angel thou.
Go out to them, Strapper Kemp; and tell them about your
big brother's little horse that some wicked man stole. Go and
cry in your mammy's lap.

STRAPPER [*furious*]You jounce me any more about that
horse, Blanco Posnet; and I'll—I'll—

BLANCO. Youll scratch my face, wont you? Yah! Your
brother's the Sheriff, aint he?

STRAPPER. Yes, he is. He hangs horse-thieves.

BLANCO [*with calm conviction*] He's a rotten Sheriff. Oh,
a rotten Sheriff. If he did his first duty he'd hang himself.
This is a rotten town. Your fathers came here on a false
alarm of gold-digging; and when the gold didnt pan out,
they lived by licking their young into habits of honest industry.

STRAPPER. If I hadnt promised Elder Daniels here to give
him a chance to keep you out of Hell, I'd take the job of
twisting your neck off the hands of the Vigilance Committee.

BLANCO [*with infinite scorn*] You and your rotten Elder,
and your rotten Vigilance Committee!

STRAPPER. Theyre sound enough to hang a horse-thief,
anyhow.

BLANCO. Any fool can hang the wisest man in the country.
Nothing he likes better. But you cant hang me.

STRAPPER. Cant we?

BLANCO. No, you cant. I left the town this morning before sunrise, because it's a rotten town, and I couldnt bear
to see it in the light. Your brother's horse did the same, as
any sensible horse would. Instead of going to look for the
horse, you went looking for me. That was a rotten thing to
do, because the horse belonged to your brother—or to the
man he stole it from—and I dont belong to him. Well, you
found me; but you didnt find the horse. If I had took the
horse, I'd have been on the horse. Would I have taken all
that time to get to where I did if I'd a horse to carry me?
250

THE SHEWING-UP OF BLANCO POSNET

STRAPPER. I dont believe you started not for two hours after you say you did.

BLANCO. Who cares what you believe or dont believe? Is a man worth six of you to be hanged because youve lost your big brother's horse, and youll want to kill somebody to relieve your rotten feelings when he licks you for it? Not likely. Til you can find a witness that saw me with that horse you cant touch me; and you know it.

STRAPPER. Is that the law, Elder?

ELDER DANIELS. The Sheriff knows the law. I wouldnt say for sure; but I think it would be more seemly to have a witness. Go and round one up, Strapper; and leave me here alone to wrestle with his poor blinded soul.

STRAPPER. I'll get a witness all right enough. I know the road he took; and I'll ask at every house within sight of it for a mile out. Come, boys.

Strapper goes out with the others, leaving Blanco and Elder Daniels together. Blanco rises and strolls over to the Elder, surveying him with extreme disparagement.

BLANCO. Well, brother? Well, Boozy Posnet, alias Elder Daniels? Well, thief? Well, drunkard?

ELDER DANIELS. It's no good, Blanco. Theyll never believe we're brothers.

BLANCO. Never fear. Do you suppose I want to claim you? Do you suppose I'm proud of you? Youre a rotten brother, Boozy Posnet. All you ever did when I owned you was to borrow money from me to get drunk with. Now you lend money and sell drink to other people. I was ashamed of you before; and I'm worse ashamed of you now. I wont have you for a brother. Heaven gave you to me; but I return the blessing without thanks. So be easy: I shant blab. [*He turns his back on him and sits down*].

ELDER DANIELS. I tell you they wouldnt believe you; so what does it matter to me whether you blab or not? Talk sense, Blanco: theres no time for your foolery now; for youll be a dead man an hour after the Sheriff comes back. What possessed you to steal that horse?

251

THE SHEWING-UP OF BLANCO POSNET

BLANCO I didnt steal it. I distrained on it for what you owed me. I thought it was yours. I was a fool to think that you owned anything but other people's property. You laid your hands on everything father and mother had when they died. I never asked you for a fair share. I never asked you for all the money I'd lent you from time to time. I asked you for mother's old necklace with the hair locket in it. You wouldnt give me that: you wouldnt give me anything. So as you refused me my due I took it, just to give you a lesson.

ELDER DANIELS. Why didnt you take the necklace if you must steal something? They wouldnt have hanged you for that.

BLANCO. Perhaps I'd rather be hanged for stealing a horse than let off for a damned piece of sentimentality.

ELDER DANIELS. Oh, Blanco, Blanco: spiritual pride has been your ruin. If youd only done like me, youd be a free and respectable man this day instead of laying there with a rope round your neck.

BLANCO [turning on him] Done like you! What do you mean? Drink like you, eh? Well, Ive done some of that lately. I see things.

ELDER DANIELS. Too late, Blanco: too late. [Convulsively] Oh, why didnt you drink as I used to? Why didnt you drink as I was led to by the Lord for my good, until the time came for me to give it up? It was drink that saved my character when I was a young man; and it was the want of it that spoiled yours. Tell me this. Did I ever get drunk when I was working?

BLANCO. No but then you never worked when you had money enough to get drunk.

ELDER DANIELS. That just shews the wisdom of Providence and the Lord's mercy. God fulfils himself in many ways: ways we little think of when we try to set up our own shortsighted laws against his Word. When does the Devil catch hold of a man? Not when he's working and not when he's drunk; but when he's idle and sober. Our own natures tell us to drink when we have nothing else to do. Look at you

252

and me! When we'd both earned a pocketful of money, what did we do? Went on the spree, naturally. But I was humble minded. I did as the rest did. I gave my money in at the drink-shop; and I said, "Fire me out when I have drunk it all up." Did you ever see me sober while it lasted?

BLANCO. No; and you looked so disgusting that I wonder it didnt set me against drink for the rest of my life.

ELDER DANIELS. That was your spiritual pride, Blanco. You never reflected that when I was drunk I was in a state of innocence. Temptations and bad company and evil thoughts passed by me like the summer wind as you might say: I was too drunk to notice them. When the money was gone, and they fired me out, I was fired out like gold out of the furnace, with my character unspoiled and unspotted; and when I went back to work, the work kept me steady. Can you say as much, Blanco? Did y o u r holidays leave y o u r character unspoiled? Oh, no, no. It was theatres: it was gambling: it was evil company: it was reading vain romances: it was women, Blanco, women: it was wrong thoughts and gnawing discontent. It ended in your becoming a rambler and a gambler: it is going to end this evening on the gallows tree. Oh, what a lesson against spiritual pride! Oh, what a— [*Blanco throws his hat at him*].

BLANCO. Stow it, Boozy. Sling it. Cut it. Cheese it. Shut up. "Shake not the dying sinner's sand."

ELDER DANIELS. Aye: there you go, with your scraps of lustful poetry. But you cant deny what I tell you. Why, do you think I would put my soul in peril by selling drink if I thought it did no good, as them silly temperance reformers make out, flying in the face of the natural tastes implanted in us all for a good purpose? Not if I was to starve for it to-morrow. But I know better. I tell you, Blanco, what keeps America to-day the purest of the nations is that when she's not working she's too drunk to hear the voice of the tempter.

BLANCO. Dont deceive yourself, Boozy. You sell drink because you make a bigger profit out of it than you can by selling tea. And you gave up drink yourself because when you got that fit at Edwardstown the doctor told you youd die the next time; and that frightened you off it.

ELDER DANIELS [*fervently*] Oh thank God selling drink pays me! And thank God He sent me that fit as a warning that my drinking time was past and gone, and that He needed me for another service!

BLANCO. Take care, Boozy. He hasnt finished with you yet. He always has a trick up His sleeve—

ELDER DANIELS. Oh, is that the way to speak of the ruler of the universe—the great and almighty God?

BLANCO. He's a sly one. He's a mean one. He lies low for you. He plays cat and mouse with you. He lets you run loose until you think youre shut of Him; and then, when you least expect it, He's got you.

ELDER DANIELS. Speak more respectful, Blanco—more reverent.

BLANCO [*springing up and coming at him*] Reverent! Who taught you your reverent cant? Not your Bible. It says He cometh like a thief in the night—aye, like a thief—a horse-thief—

ELDER DANIELS [*shocked*] Oh!

BLANCO [*overbearing him*] And it's true. Thats how He caught me and put my neck into the halter. To spite me because I had no use for Him—because I lived my own life in my own way, and would have no truck with His "Dont do this," and "You mustnt do that," and "Youll go to Hell if you do the other." I gave Him the go-bye and did without Him all these years. But He caught me out at last. The laugh is with Him as far as hanging me goes. [*He thrusts his hands into his pockets and lounges moodily away from Daniels, to the table, where he sits facing the jury box*].

ELDER DANIELS. Dont dare to put your theft on Him, man. It was the Devil tempted you to steal the horse.

BLANCO. Not a bit of it. Neither God nor Devil tempted me to take the horse: I took it on my own. He had a cleverer trick than that ready for me. [*He takes his hands out of his pockets and clenches his fists*]. Gosh! When I think that I might

254

have been safe and fifty miles away by now with that horse; and here I am waiting to be hung up and filled with lead! What came to me? What made me such a fool? Thats what I want to know. Thats the great secret.

ELDER DANIELS [*at the opposite side of the table*] Blanco: the great secret now is, what did you do with the horse?

BLANCO [*striking the table with his fist*] May my lips be blighted like my soul if ever I tell that to you or any mortal man! They may roast me alive or cut me to ribbons; but Strapper Kemp shall never have the laugh on me over that job. Let them hang me. Let them shoot. So long as they are shooting a man and not a snivelling skunk and softy, I can stand up to them and take all they can give me—game.

ELDER DANIELS. Dont be headstrong, Blanco. Whats the use? [*Slyly*] They might let up on you if you put Strapper in the way of getting his brother's horse back.

BLANCO. Not they. Hanging's too big a treat for them to give up a fair chance. Ive done it myself. Ive yelled with the dirtiest of them when a man no worse than myself was swung up. Ive emptied my revolver into him, and persuaded myself that he deserved it and that I was doing justice with strong stern men. Well, my turn's come now. Let the men I yelled at and shot at look up out of Hell and see the boys yelling and shooting at me as *I* swing up.

ELDER DANIELS. Well, even if you want to be hanged, is that any reason why Strapper shouldnt have his horse? I tell you I'm responsible to him for it. [*Bending over the table and coaxing him*]. Act like a brother, Blanco: tell me what you done with it.

BLANCO [*shortly, getting up and leaving the table*] Never you mind what I done with it. I was done out of it: let that be enough for you.

ELDER DANIELS [*following him*] Then why dont you put us on to the man that done you out of it?

BLANCO. Because he'd be too clever for you, just as he was too clever for me.

ELDER DANIELS. Make your mind easy about that, Blanco.

255

He wont be too clever for the boys and Sheriff Kemp if you put them on his trail.

BLANCO. Yes, he will. It wasnt a man.

ELDER DANIELS. Then what was it?

BLANCO [*pointing upward*] Him.

ELDER DANIELS. Oh what a way to utter His holy name!

BLANCO. He done me out of it. He meant to pay off old scores by bringing me here. He means to win the deal and you cant stop Him. Well, He's made a fool of me; but He cant frighten me. I'm not going to beg off. I'll fight off if I get a chance. I'll lie off if they cant get a witness against me. But back down I never will, not if all the hosts of heaven come to snivel at me in white surplices and offer me my life in exchange for an umble and a contrite heart.

ELDER DANIELS. Youre not in your right mind. Blanco. I'll tell em youre mad. I believe theyll let you off on that. [*He makes for the door*].

BLANCO [*seizing him, with horror in his eyes*] Dont go: dont leave me alone: do you hear?

ELDER DANIELS. Has your conscience brought you to this that youre afraid to be left alone in broad daylight, like a child in the dark.

BLANCO. I'm afraid of Him and His tricks. When I have you to raise the devil in me—when I have people to shew off before and keep me game, I'm all right; but Ive lost my nerve for being alone since this morning. It's when youre alone that He takes His advantage. He might turn my head again. He might send people to me—not real people perhaps. [*Shivering*] By God, I dont believe that woman and the child were real. I dont. I never noticed them til they were at my elbow.

ELDER DANIELS. What woman and what child? What are you talking about? Have you been drinking too hard?

BLANCO. Never you mind. Youve got to stay with me: thats all; or else send someone else—someone rottener than yourself to keep the devil in me. Strapper Kemp will do. Or a few of those scratching devils of women.

THE SHEWING-UP OF BLANCO POSNET

Strapper Kemp comes back.

ELDER DANIELS [*to Strapper*] He's gone off his head.

STRAPPER. Foxing, more likely. [*Going past Daniels and talking to Blanco nose to nose*]. It's no good: we hang madmen here; and a good job too!

BLANCO. I feel safe with you, Strapper. Youre one of the rottenest.

STRAPPER. You know youre done, and that you may as well be hanged for a sheep as a lamb. So talk away. Ive got my witness; and I'll trouble you not to make a move towards her when she comes in to identify you.

BLANCO [*retreating in terror*] A woman? She aint real: neither is the child.

ELDER DANIELS. He's raving about a woman and a child. I tell you he's gone off his chump.

STRAPPER [*calling to those without*] Shew the lady in there.

Feemy Evans comes in. She is a young woman of 23 or 24, with impudent manners, battered good looks, and dirty-fine dress.

ELDER DANIELS. Morning, Feemy.

FEEMY. Morning, Elder. [*She passes on and slips her arm familiarly through Strapper's*].

STRAPPER. Ever see him before, Feemy?

FEEMY. Thats the little lot that was on your horse this morning, Strapper. Not a doubt of it.

BLANCO [*implacably contemptuous*] Go home and wash yourself, you slut.

FEEMY [*reddening, and disengaging her arm from Strapper's*] I'm clean enough to hang you, anyway. [*Going over to him threateningly*]. Youre no true American man, to insult a woman like that.

BLANCO. A woman! Oh Lord! You saw me on a horse, did you?

FEEMY. Yes, I did.

BLANCO. Got up early on purpose to do it, didnt you?

FEEMY. No I didnt: I stayed up late on a spree.

BLANCO. I was on a horse, was I?

FEEMY. Yes you were; and if you deny it youre a liar.

THE SHEWING-UP OF BLANCO POSNET

BLANCO [*to Strapper*] She saw a man on a horse when she was too drunk to tell which was the man and which was the horse——

FEEMY [*breaking in*] You lie. I wasnt drunk—at least not as drunk as that.

BLANCO [*ignoring the interruption*]—and you found a man without a horse. Is a man on a horse the same as a man on foot? Yah! Take your witness away. Who's going to believe her? Throw her out on the dump. Youve got to find that horse before you get a rope round my neck. [*He turns away from her contemptuously, and sits at the table with his back to the jury box*].

FEEMY [*following him*] I'll hang you, you dirty horse-thief; or not a man in this camp will ever get a word or a look from me again. Youre just trash: thats what you are. White trash.

BLANCO. And what are you, darling? What are you? Youre a worse danger to a town like this than ten horse-thieves.

FEEMY. Mr Kemp: will you stand by and hear me insulted in that low way? [*To Blanco, spitefully*] I'll see you swung up and I'll see you cut down: I'll see you high and I'll see you low, as dangerous as I am. [*He laughs*]. Oh you neednt try to brazen it out. Youll look white enough before the boys are done with you.

BLANCO. You do me good, Feemy. Stay by me to the end, wont you? Hold my hand to the last; and I'll die game. [*He puts out his hand: she strikes savagely at it; but he withdraws it in time and laughs at her discomfiture*].

FEEMY. You—

ELDER DANIELS. Never mind him, Feemy: he's not right in his head to-day. [*She receives the assurance with contemptuous incredulity, and sits down on the step of the Sheriff's dais*].

Sheriff Kemp comes in: a stout man, with large flat ears, and a neck thicker than his head.

ELDER DANIELS. Morning, Sheriff.

258

THE SHEWING-UP OF BLANCO POSNET

THE SHERIFF. Morning, Elder. [*Passing on*]. Morning, Strapper. [*Passing on*]. Morning, Miss Evans. [*Stopping between Strapper and Blanco*]. Is this the prisoner?

BLANCO [*rising*] Thats so. Morning, Sheriff.

THE SHERIFF. Morning. You know, I suppose, that if youve stole a horse and the jury find against you, you wont have any time to settle your affairs. Consequently, if you feel guilty, youd better settle em now.

BLANCO. Affairs be damned! Ive got none.

THE SHERIFF. Well, are you in a proper state of mind? Has the Elder talked to you?

BLANCO. He has. And I say it's against the law. It's torture: thats what it is.

ELDER DANIELS. He's not accountable. He's out of his mind, Sheriff. He's not fit to go into the presence of his Maker.

THE SHERIFF. You are a merciful man, Elder; but you wont take the boys with you there. [*To Blanco*] If it comes to hanging you, youd better for your own sake be hanged in a proper state of mind than in an improper one. But it wont make any difference to us: make no mistake about that.

BLANCO. Lord keep me wicked till I die! Now Ive said my little prayer. I'm ready. Not that I'm guilty, mind you; but this is a rotten town, dead certain to do the wrong thing.

THE SHERIFF. You wont be asked to live long in it, I guess. [*To Strapper*] Got the witness all right, Strapper?

STRAPPER. Yes, got everything.

BLANCO. Except the horse.

THE SHERIFF. Whats that? Aint you got the horse?

STRAPPER. No. He traded it before we overtook him, I guess. But Feemy saw him on it.

FEEMY. She did.

STRAPPER. Shall I call in the boys?

BLANCO. Just a moment, Sheriff. A good appearance is everything in a low-class place like this. [*He takes out a pocket comb and mirror, and retires towards the dais to arrange his hair*].

259

ELDER DANIELS. Oh, think of your immortal soul, man, not of your foolish face.

BLANCO. I cant change my soul, Elder: it changes me—sometimes. Feemy: I'm too pale. Let me rub my cheek against yours, darling.

FEEMY. You lie: my color's my own, such as it is. And a pretty color youll be when youre hung white and shot red.

BLANCO. Aint she spiteful, Sheriff?

THE SHERIFF. Time's wasted on you. [To Strapper] Go and see if the boys are ready. Some of them were short of cartridges, and went down to the store to buy them. They may as well have their fun; and itll be shorter for him.

STRAPPER. Young Jack has brought a boxful up. Theyre all ready.

THE SHERIFF [going to the dais and addressing Blanco] Your place is at the bar there. Take it. [Blanco bows ironically and goes to the bar]. Miss Evans: youd best sit at the table. [She does so, at the corner nearest the bar. The Elder takes the opposite corner. The Sheriff takes his chair]. All ready, Strapper.

STRAPPER [at the door] All in to begin.

The crowd comes in and fills the court. Babsy, Jessie, and Emma come to the Sheriff's right; Hannah and Lottie to his left.

THE SHERIFF. Silence there. The Jury will take their places as usual. [They do so].

BLANCO. I challenge this jury, Sheriff.

THE FOREMAN. Do you, by Gosh?

THE SHERIFF. On what ground?

BLANCO. On the general ground that it's a rotten jury. [Laughter].

THE SHERIFF. Thats not a lawful ground of challenge.

THE FOREMAN. It's a lawful ground for me to shoot yonder skunk at sight, first time I meet him, if he survives this trial.

BLANCO. I challenge the Foreman because he's prejudiced.

THE FOREMAN. I say you lie. We mean to hang you, Blanco Posnet; but you will be hanged fair.

THE SHEWING-UP OF BLANCO POSNET

THE JURY. Hear, hear!

STRAPPER [*to the Sheriff*] George: this is rot. How can you get an unprejudiced jury if the prisoner starts by telling them theyre all rotten? If theres any prejudice against him he has himself to thank for it.

THE BOYS. Thats so. Of course he has. Insulting the court! Challenge be jiggered! Gag him.

NESTOR [*a juryman with a long white beard, drunk, the oldest man present*] Besides, Sheriff, I go so far as to say that the man that is not prejudiced against a horse-thief is not fit to sit on a jury in this town.

THE BOYS. Right. Bully for you, Nestor! Thats the straight truth. Of course he aint. Hear, hear!

THE SHERIFF. That is no doubt true, old man. Still, you must get as unprejudiced as you can. The critter has a right to his chance, such as he is. So now go right ahead. If the prisoner dont like this jury, he should have stole a horse in another town; for this is all the jury he'll get here.

THE FOREMAN. Thats so, Blanco Posnet.

THE SHERIFF [*to Blanco*] Dont you be uneasy. You will get justice here. It may be rough justice; but it is justice.

BLANCO. What is justice?

THE SHERIFF. Hanging horse-thieves is justice; so now you know. Now then: weve wasted enough time. Hustle with your witness there, will you?

BLANCO [*indignantly bringing down his fist on the bar*] Swear the jury. A rotten Sheriff you are not to know that the jury's got to be sworn.

THE FOREMAN [*galled*] Be swore for you! Not likely. What do you say, old son?

NESTOR [*deliberately and solemnly*] I say: GUILTY!!!

THE BOYS [*tumultuously rushing at Blanco*] Thats it. Guilty, guilty. Take him out and hang him. He's found guilty. Fetch a rope. Up with him. [*They are about to drag him from the bar*].

THE SHERIFF [*rising, pistol in hand*] Hands off that man. Hands off him, I say, Squinty, or I drop you, and would if

THE SHEWING-UP OF BLANCO POSNET

you were my own son. [*Dead silence*]. I'm Sheriff here; and it's for me to say when he may lawfully be hanged. [*They release him*].

BLANCO. As the actor says in the play, "a Daniel come to judgment." Rotten actor he was, too.

THE SHERIFF. Elder Daniel is come to judgment all right, my lad. Elder: the floor is yours. [*The Elder rises*]. Give your evidence. The truth and the whole truth and nothing but the truth, so help you God.

ELDER DANIELS. Sheriff: let me off this. I didnt ought to swear away this man's life. He and I are, in a manner of speaking, brothers.

THE SHERIFF. It does you credit, Elder: every man here will acknowledge it. But religion is one thing: law is another. In religion we're all brothers. In law we cut our brother off when he steals horses.

THE FOREMAN. Besides, you neednt hang him, you know. Theres plenty of willing hands to take that job off your conscience. So rip ahead, old son.

STRAPPER. Youre accountable to me for the horse until you clear yourself, Elder: remember that.

BLANCO. Out with it, you fool.

ELDER DANIELS. You might own up, Blanco, as far as my evidence goes. Everybody knows I borrowed one of the Sheriff's horses from Strapper because my own's gone lame. Everybody knows you arrived in the town yesterday and put up my house. Everybody knows that in the morning the horse was gone and you were gone.

BLANCO [*in a forensic manner*] Sheriff: the Elder, though known to you and to all here as no brother of mine and the rottenest liar in this town, is speaking the truth for the first time in his life as far as what he says about me is concerned. As to the horse, I say nothing; except that it was the rottenest horse you ever tried to sell.

THE SHERIFF. How do you know it was a rotten horse if you didnt steal it?

BLANCO. I dont know of my own knowledge. I only argue that if the horse had been worth its keep, you wouldnt have lent it to Strapper, and Strapper wouldnt have lent it to this eloquent and venerable ram. [*Suppressed laughter*]. And now I ask him this. [*To the Elder*] Did we or did we not have a quarrel last evening about a certain article that was left by my mother, and that I considered I had a right to more than you? And did you say one word to me about the horse not belonging to you?

ELDER DANIELS. Why should I? We never said a word about the horse at all. How was I to know what it was in your mind to do?

BLANCO. Bear witness all that I had a right to take a horse from him without stealing to make up for what he denied me. I am no thief. But you havnt proved yet that I took the horse. Strapper Kemp: had I the horse when you took me or had I not?

STRAPPER. No, nor you hadnt a railway train neither. But Feemy Evans saw you pass on the horse at four o'clock twenty-five miles from the spot where I took you at seven on the road to Pony Harbor. Did you walk twenty-five miles in three hours? That so, Feemy? eh?

FEEMY. Thats so. At four I saw him. [*To Blanco*] Thats done for you.

THE SHERIFF. You say you saw him on my horse?

FEEMY. I did.

BLANCO. And I ate it, I suppose, before Strapper fetched up with me. [*Suddenly and dramatically*] Sheriff: I accuse Feemy of immoral relations with Strapper.

FEEMY. Oh you liar!

BLANCO. I accuse the fair Euphemia of immoral relations with every man in this town, including yourself, Sheriff. I say this is a conspiracy to kill me between Feemy and Strapper because I wouldnt touch Feemy with a pair of tongs. I say you darent hang any white man on the word of a woman of bad character. I stand on the honor and virtue of my American manhood. I say that she's not had the oath, and that you darent for the honor of the town give her the

263

oath because her lips would blaspheme the holy Bible if they touched it. I say thats the law; and if you are a proper United States Sheriff and not a low-down lyncher, youll hold up the law and not let it be dragged in the mud by your brother's kept woman.

Great excitement among the women. The men much puzzled.

JESSIE. Thats right. She didnt ought to be let kiss the Book.

EMMA. How could the like of her tell the truth?

BABSY. It would be an insult to every respectable woman here to believe her.

FEEMY. It's easy to be respectable with nobody ever offering you a chance to be anything else.

THE WOMEN [*clamoring all together*] Shut up, you hussy. Youre a disgrace. How dare you open your lips to answer your betters? Hold your tongue and learn your place, miss. You painted slut! Whip her out of the town!

THE SHERIFF. Silence. Do you hear. Silence. [*The clamor ceases*]. Did anyone else see the prisoner with the horse?

FEEMY [*passionately*] Aint I good enough?

BABSY. No. Youre dirt: thats what you are.

FEEMY. And you—

THE SHERIFF. Silence. This trial is a man's job; and if the women forget their sex they can go out or be put out. Strapper and Miss Evans: you cant have it two ways. You can run straight, or you can run gay, so to speak; but you cant run both ways together. There is also a strong feeling among the men of this town that a line should be drawn between those that are straight wives and mothers and those that are, in the words of the Book of Books, taking the primrose path. We dont wish to be hard on any woman; and most of us have a personal regard for Miss Evans for the sake of old times; but theres no getting out of the fact that she has private reasons for wishing to oblige Strapper, and that—if she will excuse my saying so—she is not what I might call morally particular as to what she does to oblige him. Therefore I ask the prisoner not to drive us to give

264

THE SHEWING-UP OF BLANCO POSNET

Miss Evans the oath. I ask him to tell us fair and square, as a man who has but a few minutes between him and eternity, what he done with my horse.

THE BOYS. Hear, hear! Thats right. Thats fair. That does it. Now Blanco. Own up.

BLANCO. Sheriff: you touch me home. This is a rotten world; but there is still one thing in it that remains sacred even to the rottenest of us, and that is a horse.

THE BOYS. Good. Well said, Blanco. Thats straight.

BLANCO. You have a right to your horse, Sheriff; and if I could put you in the way of getting it back, I would. But if I had that horse I shouldnt be here. As I hope to be saved, Sheriff—or rather as I hope to be damned; for I have no taste for pious company and no talent for playing the harp —I know no more of that horse's whereabouts than you do yourself.

STRAPPER. Who did you trade him to?

BLANCO. I did not trade him. I got nothing for him or by him. I stand here with a rope round my neck for the want of him. When you took me, did I fight like a thief or run like a thief; and was there any sign of a horse on me or near me?

STRAPPER. You were looking at a rainbow like a damned silly fool instead of keeping your wits about you; and we stole up on you and had you tight before you could draw a bead on us.

THE SHERIFF. That dont sound like good sense. What would he look at a rainbow for?

BLANCO. I'll tell you, Sheriff. I was looking at it because there was something written on it?

SHERIFF. How do you mean written on it?

BLANCO. The words were, "Ive got the cinch on you this time, Blanco Posnet." Yes, Sheriff, I saw those words in green on the red streak of the rainbow; and as I saw them I felt Strapper's grab on my arm and Squinty's on my pistol.

THE FOREMAN. He's shammin mad: thats what he is. Aint it about time to give a verdict and have a bit of fun, Sheriff?

THE BOYS. Yes, lets have a verdict. We're wasting the whole afternoon. Cut it short.

THE SHERIFF [*making up his mind*] Swear Feemy Evans, Elder. She dont need to touch the Book. Let her say the words.

FEEMY. Worse people than me has kissed that Book. What wrong Ive done, most of you went shares in. Ive to live, havnt I? same as the rest of you. However, it makes no odds to me, I guess the truth is the truth and a lie is a lie, on the Book or off it.

BABSY. Do as youre told. Who are you, to be let talk about it?

THE SHERIFF. Silence there, I tell you. Sail ahead, Elder.

ELDER DANIELS. Feemy Evans: do you swear to tell the truth and the whole truth and nothing but the truth, so help you God.

FEEMY. I do, so help me—

SHERIFF. Thats enough. Now, on your oath, did you see the prisoner on my horse this morning on the road to Pony Harbor?

FEEMY. On my oath—[*Disturbance and crowding at the door*].

AT THE DOOR. Now then, now then! Where are you shovin to? Whats up? Order in court. Chuck him out. Silence. You cant come in here. Keep back.

Strapper rushes to the door and forces his way out.

SHERIFF [*savagely*] Whats this noise? Cant you keep quiet there? Is this a Sheriff's court or is it a saloon?

BLANCO. Dont interrupt a lady in the act of hanging a gentleman. Wheres your manners?

FEEMY. I'll hang you, Blanco Posnet. I will. I wouldnt for fifty dollars I hadnt seen you this morning. I'll teach you to be civil to me next time, for all I'm not good enough to kiss the Book.

BLANCO. Lord keep me wicked till I die! I'm game for anything while youre spitting dirt at me, Feemy.

RENEWED TUMULT AT THE DOOR. Here, whats this? Fire

266

them out. Not me. Who are you that I should get out of your way? Oh, stow it. Well, she cant come in. What woman? What horse? Whats the good of shoving like that? Who says? No! you dont say!

THE SHERIFF. Gentlemen of the Vigilance Committee: clear that doorway. Out with them in the name of the law.

STRAPPER [*without*] Hold hard, George. [*At the door*] Theyve got the horse. [*He comes in, followed by Waggoner Jo, an elderly carter, who crosses the court to the jury side. Strapper pushes his way to the Sheriff and speaks privately to him*].

THE BOYS. What! No! Got the horse! Sheriff's horse! Who took it, then? Where? Get out. Yes it is, sure. I tell you it is. It's the horse all right enough. Rot. Go and look. By Gum!

THE SHERIFF [*to Strapper*] You dont say!

STRAPPER. It's here, I tell you.

WAGGONER JO. It's here all right enough, Sheriff.

STRAPPER. And theyve got the thief too.

ELDER DANIELS. Then it aint Blanco.

STRAPPER. No: it's a woman. [*Blanco yells and covers his eyes with his hands*].

THE WHOLE CROWD. A woman!

THE SHERIFF. Well, fetch her in. [*Strapper goes out. The Sheriff continues, to Feemy*] And what do you mean, you lying jade, by putting up this story on us about Blanco?

FEEMY. I aint put up no story on you. This is a plant: you see if it isnt.

Strapper returns with a woman. Her expression of intense grief silences them as they crane over one another's heads to see her. Strapper takes her to the corner of the table. The Elder moves up to make room for her.

BLANCO [*terrified*] Sheriff: that woman aint real. You take care. That woman will make you do what you never intended. Thats the rainbow woman. Thats the woman that brought me to this.

THE SHERIFF. Shut your mouth, will you. Youve got the horrors. [*To the woman*] Now you. Who are you? and what are you doing with a horse that doesnt belong to you?

THE WOMAN. I took it to save my child's life. I thought it would get me to a doctor in time. The child was choking with croup.

BLANCO [*strangling, and trying to laugh*] A little choker: thats the word for him. His choking wasnt real: wait and see mine. [*He feels his neck with a sob*].

THE SHERIFF. Where's the child?

STRAPPER. On Pug Jackson's bench in his shed. He's makin a coffin for it.

BLANCO [*with a horrible convulsion of the throat—frantically*] Dead! The little Judas kid! The child I gave my life for! [*He breaks into hideous laughter*].

THE SHERIFF [*jarred beyond endurance by the sound*] Hold your noise, will you. Shove his neckerchief into his mouth if he dont stop. [*To the woman*] Dont you mind him, maam: he's mad with drink and devilment. I suppose theres no fake about this, Strapper. Who found her?

WAGGONER JO. I did, Sheriff. Theres no fake about it. I came on her on the track round by Red Mountain. She was settin on the ground with the dead body on her lap, stupid-like. The horse was grazin on the other side o the road.

THE SHERIFF [*puzzled*] Well, this is blamed queer. [*To the woman*] What call had you to take the horse from Elder Daniel's stable to find a doctor? Theres a doctor in the very next house.

BLANCO [*mopping his dabbled red crest and trying to be ironically gay*] Story simply wont wash, my angel. You got it from the man that stole the horse. He gave it to you because he was a softy and went to bits when you played off the sick kid on him. Well, I guess that clears me. I'm not that sort. Catch me putting my neck in a noose for anybody's kid!

THE FOREMAN. Dont you go putting her up to what to say. She said she took it.

THE WOMAN. Yes: I took it from a man that met me. I thought God sent him to me. I rode here joyfully thinking so all the time to myself. Then I noticed that the child was like

268

lead in my arms. God would never have been so cruel as to send me the horse to disappoint me like that.

BLANCO. Just what He would do.

STRAPPER. We aint got nothin to do with that. This is the man, aint he? [*pointing to Blanco*].

THE WOMAN [*pulling herself together after looking scaredly at Blanco, and then at the Sheriff and at the jury*] No.

THE FOREMAN. You lie.

THE SHERIFF. Youve got to tell us the truth. Thats the law, you know.

THE WOMAN. The man looked a bad man. He cursed me; and he cursed the child: God forgive him! But something came over him. I was desperate. I put the child in his arms; and it got its little fingers down his neck and called him Daddy and tried to kiss him; for it was not right in its head with the fever. He said it was a little Judas kid, and that it was betraying him with a kiss, and that he'd swing for it. And then he gave me the horse, and went away crying and laughing and singing dreadful dirty wicked words to hymn tunes like as if he had seven devils in him.

STRAPPER. She's lying. Give her the oath, George.

THE SHERIFF. Go easy there. Youre a smart boy, Strapper; but youre not Sheriff yet. This is my job. You just wait. I submit that we're in a difficulty here. If Blanco was the man, the lady cant, as a white woman, give him away. She oughtnt to be put in the position of having either to give him away or commit perjury. On the other hand, we dont want a horse-thief to get off through a lady's delicacy.

THE FOREMAN. No we dont; and we dont intend he shall. Not while I am foreman of this jury.

BLANCO [*with intense expression*] A rotten foreman! Oh, what a rotten foreman!

THE SHERIFF. Shut up, will you. Providence shows us a way out here. Two women saw Blanco with a horse. One has a delicacy about saying so. The other will excuse me saying that delicacy is not her strongest holt. She can give the necessary witness. Feemy Evans: youve taken the oath.

269

You saw the man that took the horse.

FEEMY. I did. And he was a low-down rotten drunken lying hound that would go further to hurt a woman any day than to help her. And if he ever did a good action it was because he was too drunk to know what he was doing. So it's no harm to hang him. She said he cursed her and went away blaspheming and singing things that were not fit for the child to hear.

BLANCO [*troubled*] I didnt mean them for the child to hear, you venomous devil.

THE SHERIFF. All thats got nothing to do with us. The question you have to answer is, was that man Blanco Posnet?

THE WOMAN. No. I say no. I swear it. Sheriff: dont hang that man: oh dont. You may hang me instead if you like: Ive nothing to live for now. You darent take her word against mine. She never had a child: I can see it in her face.

FEEMY [*stung to the quick*] I can hang him in spite of you, anyhow. Much good your child is to you now, lying there on Pug Jackson's bench!

BLANCO [*rushing at her with a shriek*] I'll twist your heart out of you for that. [*They seize him before he can reach her*].

FEEMY [*mocking him as he struggles to get at her*] Ha, ha, Blanco Posnet. You cant touch me; and I can hang you. Ha, ha! Oh, I'll do for you. I'll twist your heart and I'll twist your neck [*He is dragged back to the bar and leans on it, gasping and exhausted*]. Give me the oath again, Elder. I'll settle him. And do you [*to the woman*] take your sickly face away from in front of me.

STRAPPER. Just turn your back on her there, will you?

THE WOMAN. God knows I dont want to see her commit murder. [*She folds her shawl over her head*].

THE SHERIFF. Now, Miss Evans: cut it short. Was the prisoner the man you saw this morning or was he not? Yes or no?

FEEMY [*a little hysterically*] I'll tell you fast enough. Dont think I'm a softy.

THE SHERIFF [*losing patience*] Here: weve had enough of

this. You tell the truth, Feemy Evans; and let us have no
more of your lip. Was the prisoner the man or was he not?
On your oath?

FEEMY. On my oath and as I'm a living woman—[*flinching*] Oh God! he felt the little child's hands on his neck—I
cant [*bursting into a flood of tears and scolding at the other
woman*] It's you with your snivelling face that has put me
off it. [*Desperately*] No: it wasnt him. I only said it out of
spite because he insulted me. May I be struck dead if I ever
saw him with the horse!

Everybody draws a long breath. Dead silence.

BLANCO [*whispering at her*] Softy! Cry-baby! Landed
like me! Doing what you never intended! [*Taking up his hat
and speaking in his ordinary tone*] I presume I may go now,
Sheriff.

STRAPPER. Here, hold hard.

THE FOREMAN. Not if we know it, you dont.

THE BOYS [*barring the way to the door*] You stay where
you are. Stop a bit, stop a bit. Dont you be in such a hurry.
Dont let him go. Not much.

*Blanco stands motionless, his eye fixed, thinking hard, and
apparently deaf to what is going on.*

THE SHERIFF [*rising solemnly*] Silence there. Wait a bit.
I take it that if the Sheriff is satisfied and the owner of the
horse is satisfied, theres no more to be said. I have had to
remark on former occasions that what is wrong with this
court is that theres too many Sheriffs in it. Today there is
going to be one, and only one; and that one is your humble
servant. I call that to the notice of the Foreman of the jury,
and also to the notice of young Strapper. I am also the
owner of the horse. Does any man say I am not? [*Silence*].
Very well, then. In my opinion, to commandeer a horse for
the purpose of getting a dying child to a doctor is not stealing, provided, as in the present case, that the horse is returned safe and sound. I rule that there has been no theft.

NESTOR. That aint the law.

THE SHERIFF. I fine you a dollar for contempt of court,

and will collect it myself off you as you leave the building. And as the boys have been disappointed of their natural sport, I shall give them a little fun by standing outside the door and taking up a collection for the bereaved mother of the late kid that shewed up Blanco Posnet.

THE BOYS. A collection. Oh, I say! Calls that sport? Is this a mothers' meeting? Well, I'll be jiggered! Where does the sport come in?

THE SHERIFF [*continuing*] The sport comes in, my friends, not so much in contributing as in seeing others fork out. Thus each contributes to the general enjoyment; and all contribute to his. Blanco Posnet: you go free under the protection of the Vigilance Committee for just long enough to get you out of this town, which is not a healthy place for you. As you are in a hurry, I'll sell you the horse at a reasonable figure. Now, boys, let nobody go out till I get to the door. The court is adjourned. [*He goes out*].

STRAPPER [*to Feemy, as he goes to the door*] I'm done with you. Do you hear? I'm done with you. [*He goes out sulkily*].

FEEMY [*calling after him*] As if I cared about a stingy brat like you! Go back to the freckled maypole you left for me: youve been fretting for her long enough.

THE FOREMAN [*to Blanco, on his way out*] A man like you makes me sick. Just sick. [*Blanco makes no sign. The Foreman spits disgustedly, and follows Strapper out. The Jurymen leave the box, except Nestor, who collapses in a drunken sleep*].

BLANCO [*suddenly rushing from the bar to the table and jumping up on it*] Boys, I'm going to preach you a sermon on the moral of this day's proceedings.

THE BOYS [*crowding round him*] Yes: lets have a sermon. Go ahead, Blanco. Silence for Elder Blanco. Tune the organ Let us pray.

NESTOR [*staggering out of his sleep*] Never hold up your head in this town again. I'm done with you.

BLANCO [*pointing inexorably to Nestor*] Drunk in church. Disturbing the preacher. Hand him out.

THE BOYS [*chivying Nestor out*] Now, Nestor, outside.

Outside, Nestor. Out you go. Get your subscription ready for the Sheriff. Skiddoo, Nestor.

NESTOR. Afraid to be hanged! Afraid to be hanged! [*At the door*] Coward! [*He is thrown out*].

BLANCO. Dearly beloved brethren—

A BOY. Same to you, Blanco. [*Laughter*].

BLANCO. And many of them. Boys: this is a rotten world.

ANOTHER BOY. Lord have mercy on us, miserable sinners. [*More laughter*].

BLANCO [*forcibly*] No: thats where youre wrong. Dont flatter yourselves that youre miserable sinners. Am I a miserable sinner? No: I'm a fraud and a failure. I started in to be a bad man like the rest of you. You all started in to be bad men or you wouldnt be in this jumped-up, jerked-off, hospital-turned-out camp that calls itself a town. I took the broad path because I thought I was a man and not a snivelling canting turning-the-other-cheek apprentice angel serving his time in a vale of tears. They talked Christianity to us on Sundays; but when they really meant business they told us never to take a blow without giving it back, and to get dollars. When they talked the golden rule to me, I just looked at them as if they werent there, and spat. But when they told me to try to live my life so that I could always look my fellowman straight in the eye and tell him to go to hell, that fetched me.

THE BOYS. Quite right. Good. Bully for you, Blanco, old son. Right good sense too. Aha-a-ah!

BLANCO. Yes; but whats come of it all? Am I a real bad man? a man of game and grit? a man that does what he likes and goes over or through other people to his own gain? or am I a snivelling cry-baby that let a horse his life depended on be took from him by a woman, and then sat on the grass looking at the rainbow and let himself be took like a hare in a trap by Strapper Kemp: a lad whose back I or any grown man here could break against his knee? I'm a rottener fraud and failure than the Elder here. And youre all as rotten as me, or youd have lynched me.

273

THE SHEWING-UP OF BLANCO POSNET

A BOY. Anything to oblige you, Blanco.

ANOTHER. We can do it yet if you feel really bad about it.

BLANCO. No: the devil's gone out of you. We're all frauds. Theres none of us real good and none of us real bad.

ELDER DANIELS. There is One above, Blanco.

BLANCO. What do y o u know about Him? you that always talk as if He never did anything without asking your rotten leave first? Why did the child die? Tell me that if you can. He cant have wanted to kill the child. Why did He make me go soft on the child if He was going hard on it Himself? Why should He go hard on the innocent kid and go soft on a rotten thing like me? Why did I go soft myself? Why did the Sheriff go soft? Why did Feemy go soft? Whats this game that upsets our game? For seems to me theres two games bein played. Our game is a rotten game that makes me feel I'm dirt and that your all as rotten dirt as me. T'other game may be a silly game; but it aint rotten. When the Sheriff played it he stopped being rotten. When Feemy played it the paint nearly dropped off her face. When I played it I cursed myself for a fool; but I lost the rotten feel all the same.

ELDER DANIELS. It was the Lord speaking to your soul, Blanco.

BLANCO. Oh yes: you know all about the Lord, dont you? Youre in the Lord's confidence. He wouldnt for the world to anything to shock you, would He, Boozy dear? Yah! What about the croup? It was early days when He made the croup, I guess. It was the best He could think of then; but when it turned out wrong on His hands He made you and me to fight the croup for him. You bet He didnt make us for nothing; and He wouldnt have made us at all if He could have done His work without us. By Gum, that must be what we're for! He'd never have made us to be rotten drunken blackguards like me, and good-for-nothing rips like Feemy. He made me because He had a job for me. He let me run loose til the job was ready; and then I had to come along and do it, hanging or no hanging. And I tell you it didnt feel

274

rotten: it felt b u l l y, just bully. Anyhow, I got the rotten feel off me for a minute of my life; and I'll go through fire to get it off me again. Look here! which of you will marry Feemy Evans?

THE BOYS [*uproariously*] Who speaks first? Who'll marry Feemy? Come along, Jack. Nows your chance, Peter. Pass along a husband for Feemy. Oh my! Feemy!

FEEMY [*shortly*] Keep your tongue off me, will you?

BLANCO. Feemy was a rose of the broad path, wasnt she? You all thought her the champion bad woman of this district. Well, she's a failure as a bad woman; and I'm a failure as a bad man. So let Brother Daniels marry us to keep all the rottenness in the family. What do you say, Feemy?

FEEMY. Thank you; but when I marry I'll marry a man that could do a decent action without surprising himself out of his senses. Youre like a child with a new toy: you and your bit of human kindness!

THE WOMAN. How many would have done it with their life at stake?

FEEMY. Oh well, if youre so much taken with him, marry him yourself. Youd be what people call a good wife to him, wouldnt you?

THE WOMAN. I was a good wife to the child's father. I dont think any woman wants to be a good wife twice in her life. I want somebody to be a good husband to me now.

BLANCO. Any offer, gentlemen, on that understanding? [*The boys shake their heads*]. Oh, it's a rotten game, our game. Here's a real good woman; and she's had enough of it, finding that it only led to being put upon.

HANNAH. Well, if there was nothing wrong in the world there wouldnt be anything left for us to do, would there?

ELDER DANIELS. Be of good cheer, brothers. Seek the path.

BLANCO. No. No more paths. No more broad and narrow. No more good and bad. Theres no good and bad; but by Jiminy, gents, theres a rotten game, and theres a great game. I played the rotten game; but the great game was played on me; and now I'm for the great game every time. Amen.

275

THE SHEWING-UP OF BLANCO POSNET

Gentlemen: let us adjourn to the saloon. I stand the drinks. [*He jumps down from the table*].

THE BOYS. Right you are, Blanco. Drinks round. Come along, boys. Blanco's standing. Right along to the Elder's. Hurrah! [*They rush out, dragging the Elder with them*].

BLANCO [*to Feemy, offering his hand*] Shake, Feemy.

FEEMY. Get along, you blackguard.

BLANCO. It's come over me again, same as when the kid touched me, same as when you swore a lie to save my neck.

FEEMY. Oh well, here. [*They shake hands*].

THE ADMIRABLE BASHVILLE

or

CONSTANCY REWARDED

(BEING A NOVEL OF CASHEL BYRON'S PROFESSION
DONE INTO A STAGE PLAY IN BLANK VERSE)

See Preface: Trifles and Tomfooleries (*Volume IV, page 721*)

Written in 1901

First Performed London 1902

PREFACE

IT may be asked why I wrote The Admirable Bashville in blank verse. My answer is that the operation of the copyright law of that time (now happily superseded) left me only a week to write it in. Blank verse is so childishly easy and expeditious (hence, by the way, Shakespear's copious output), that by adopting it I was enabled to do within the week what would have cost me a month in prose.

Besides, I am fond of blank verse. Not nineteenth century blank verse, of course, nor indeed, with a very few exceptions, any post-Shakespearean blank verse. Nay, not Shakespearean blank verse itself later than the histories. I am quite sure that anyone who is to recover the charm of blank verse must go back frankly to its beginnings, and start a literary pre-Raphaelite Brotherhood. I like the melodious sing-song, the clear simple one-line and two-line sayings, and the occasional rhymed tags, like the half closes in an eighteenth century symphony, in Peele, Kyd, Greene, and the histories of Shakespear. Accordingly, I poetasted The Admirable Bashville in the primitive Elizabethan style. And lest the literary connoisseurs should declare that there was not a single correct line in all my three acts, I stole or paraphrased a few from Marlowe and Shakespear (not to mention Henry Carey); so that if any man dared quote me derisively, he should do so in peril of inadvertently lighting on a purple patch from Hamlet or Faustus.

I also endeavored in this little play to prove that I was not the heartless creature some of my critics took me for. I observed the established laws of stage popularity and probability. I simplified the character of the heroine, and summed up her sweetness in the one sacred word: Love. I gave consistency to the heroism of Cashel. I paid to Morality, in the final scene, the tribute of poetic justice. I restored to Patriotism its usual place on the stage, and gracefully acknowledged The Throne as the fountain of social honor. I paid particular attention to the construction of the play, which

279

will be found equal in this respect to the best contemporary models.

And the result was that the British playgoer, to whom Elizabethan English is a dead language, only half understood nine-tenths of the play, and applauded the other tenth (the big speeches) with a seriousness that was far funnier than any burlesque.

The play, by the way, should be performed on an Elizabethan stage, with traverses for the indoor scenes, and with only one interval after the second act.

*   *   *   *   *   *

On reading over the above after a lapse of thirty years I am not quite so sure as I was that Elizabethan English may not again become a living language to the ordinary playgoer. To people who never read anything but newspapers and popular magazines, a good deal of Shakespear's more euphuistic blank verse is hardly more intelligible than classical Greek. Even actors may be heard repeating it by rote with an air that persuades the public that they understand what they are saying; but it cannot impose any such illusion on a professionally skilled listener.

Then there are the people who do not go to Protestant churches nor read anything at all, and consequently understand no English except modern vernacular English. This class is by no means a negligible one even in the theatre; for it includes a large body of intelligent manual and open air workers and sportsmen who, though after their day's exertions they fall asleep in less than a minute if they sit down with an open book in their hands, can be kept awake and alert very effectually in the theatre by a play. Only, it must be a play in the vernacular. Otherwise it does not exist for them except as an incomprehensible bore.

There was a time when not only the theatres but the newspapers addressed themselves to the literate alone. Hunt up an old melodrama (say Sweeny Todd the Demon Barber of Fleet Street) or an old newspaper file; and you will at once see that the writers of the play and of the contemporary

280

PREFACE

leading articles, though they may have been the seediest of
Bohemians, had learnt Latin grammar and read books
written by persons similarly schooled. They had literally
the benefit of clergy, and wrote accordingly. With the advent of compulsory education sixty years ago, and the creation thereby of a class which could read and write, but had
no Latin and less Greek, newspapers and plays alike soon
came to be written by illiterate masters of the vernacular;
and I myself welcomed the change and discarded my early
very classical style for a vernacular one. Nowadays, when
I read typewritten plays by young authors, as I sometimes
have occasion to do, I find in them such illiteracies as He
exits, She exits, They exit etc. etc. Chapman, who wrote all
his stage directions in Latin, or Ben Jonson, who deplored
the slenderness of Shakespear's classical education, would
have risen up and roared for a birchrod to castigate such
execrable solecisms. By the end of the nineteenth century
the press and the theatre had lost all their Latinity; and this
was why, whenever The Admirable Bashville was performed, men of letters like Maurice Hewlett would chuckle
delightedly over it almost line by line, whilst the ordinary
playgoers would listen with a puzzled and troubled stare,
wondering what on earth it was all about and how they
ought to take it, and the unfortunate persons who had been
forced to "get up Shakespear" as part of an academic course
on English literature, sat with a scowl of malignant hatred
that poisoned the atmosphere. When Bashville was followed
by a piece in the vernacular the relief of the audience was so
great that there was always a burst of applause at the very
first sentence.

And yet, whenever the meaning of the words was clear,
the listeners shewed unmistakably that they liked hyper-
bolical rhetoric and deliberately artificial language. My
parodies of the Elizabethan mannerism, and funny echoes
of pet lines from the Elizabethan playwrights were, as such,
quite lost on them; but Ben Webster brought down the
house with Cashel Byron's declamatory repudiation of the

name of gentleman, and James Hearn's lamentation over
the tragedy of Cetewayo came off, not as a mockery, but as
genuine tragedy, which indeed it also is. It was the literary
fun that proved a mere puzzle, in spite of the acting of casts
which included such accomplished comedians as Charles
Quatermaine, William Wyes, Lennox Pawle, Henrietta
Watson, Marie Lohr, and Fanny Brough.

Another significant fact pointed in the same direction.
In no country is the worship of the old authorized version of
the Bible carried to greater lengths than in the United
States of America. To alter a single word of it was, it was
believed, to incur the curse in the last chapter of Revelations. Even in England the very timid official revision of
1885 shocked our native Fundamentalists (a ridiculous but
convenient name not then invented). Yet it was in the
United States that the ministers of religion first found
themselves compelled to produce versions in modern vernacular and journalese under stress of the flat fact that their
flocks often could not understand the old authorized version, and always found the style so artificial that though it
could produce an unintelligent reverence it brought no
intimate conviction to the reader.

Sometimes, however, the simple and direct passages
were not sentimental enough to satisfy people whose minds
were steeped in modern literary sob stuff. For instance, such
bald statements about Barabbas as that he was a robber, or
that he had killed a certain man in a sedition, quite failed to
interest anyone in him; but when Marie Corelli expanded
this concise information into a novel in her own passionate
and richly colored style it sold like hot cakes.

I must make a personal confession in this matter. Though
I was saturated with the Bible and with Shakespear before
I was ten years old, and the only grammar I ever learned
was Latin grammar, so that Elizabethan English became a
mother tongue to me, yet when I first read such vivid and
unaffected modern versions as Dr James Moffatt's New
Translation of the New Testament I at once got from them

so many lights on the Bible narratives which I had missed in the authorized version that I said to myself "Some day I will translate Hamlet into modern vernacular English." But indeed if the alienation of our young from Elizabethan English continues it will be necessary to produce revised versions not only of Shakespear but of Sir Walter Scott and even of my own early novels.

Still, a revival of Elizabethan literature may be possible. If I, as an Irish child in the eighteen-sixties, could without enforced study become so familiar with it that I had some difficulty as a journalist later on in getting rid of it, it must be possible for the same thing to occur to an English child in the nineteen-sixties. The Elizabethan style has many charms for imaginative children. It is bloody, bombastic, violent, senselessly pretentious, barbarous and childish in its humor, and full of music. In short, the taste for it, as anyone can observe at the Old Vic or the Stratford Festivals, is essentially half childish, half musical. To acquire it, all that is necessary is access to it. Now the opportunities for such access are enormously wider than they used to be. Of course as long as we persist in stuffing Shakespear and the Bible down our children's throats with threats of condign punishment if they fail to answer silly questions about them, they will continue to be loathed as they very largely are at present. But if our children, when they have been simply taught to read, have plenty of dramatically illustrated Bibles and Shakespears left in their way, with the illustrated passages printed under the pictures, it will soon be possible to find a general audience which can laugh at The Admirable Bashville as heartily as Maurice Hewlett did, and for repertory theatres to amuse themselves and their congregations with occasional performances of Carey's Chrononhotonthologos, Fielding's Tom Thumb, and even Bombastes Furioso.

I shall not here raise the question of whether such a revival is desirable. It would carry me too far and plunge me too deep for a volume of trifles and tomfooleries. But as

THE ADMIRABLE BASHVILLE

the Elizabethan style is unquestionably both musical and powerful, I may at least say that it is better to have a sense of it and a fancy for it than to have no sense of style or literary fancy at all.

THE ADMIRABLE BASHVILLE; OR,
CONSTANCY UNREWARDED

ACT I

A glade in Wiltstoken Park
Enter LYDIA

LYDIA. Ye leafy breasts and warm protecting wings
  Of mother trees that hatch our tender souls,
  And from the well of Nature in our hearts
Thaw the intolerable inch of ice
That bears the weight of all the stamping world,
Hear ye me sing to solitude that I,
Lydia Carew, the owner of these lands,
Albeit most rich, most learned, and most wise,
Am yet most lonely. What are riches worth
When wisdom with them comes to show the purse bearer
That life remains unpurchasable? Learning
Learns but one lesson: doubt! To excel all
Is to be lonely. Oh, ye busy birds,
Engrossed with real needs, ye shameless trees
With arms outspread in welcome of the sun,
Your minds, bent singly to enlarge your lives,
Have given you wings and raised your delicate heads
High heavens above us crawlers.

> [*A rook sets up a great cawing; and the other birds chatter
> loudly as a gust of wind sets the branches swaying. She
> makes as though she would shew them her sleeves.*

                                   Lo, the leaves
That hide my drooping boughs! Mock me—poor maid!—
Deride with joyous comfortable chatter
These stolen feathers. Laugh at me, the clothed one.
Laugh at the mind fed on foul air and books.
Books! Art! And Culture! Oh, I shall go mad.
Give me a mate that never heard of these,
A sylvan god, tree born in heart and sap;
Or else, eternal maidhood be my hap.

> [*Another gust of wind and bird-chatter. She sits on the mossy root
> of an oak and buries her face in her hands. Cashel Byron,*

in a white singlet and breeches, comes through the trees.

CASHEL. Whats this? Whom have we here? A woman!

LYDIA [*looking up*]   Yes.

CASHEL. You have no business here. I have. Away!

Women distract me. Hence!

LYDIA.   Bid you me hence?

I am upon mine own ground. Who are you?

I take you for a god, a sylvan god.

This place is mine: I share it with the birds,

The trees, the sylvan gods, the lovely company

Of haunted solitudes.

CASHEL.   A sylvan god!

A goat-eared image! Do your statues speak?

Walk? heave the chest with breath? or like a feather

Lift you—like this?   [*He sets her on her feet.*

LYDIA [*panting*] You take away my breath!

Youre strong. Your hands off, please. Thank you. Farewell.

CASHEL. Before you go: when shall we meet again?

LYDIA. Why should we meet again?

CASHEL.   Who knows? We shall.

That much I know by instinct. Whats your name?

LYDIA. Lydia Carew.

CASHEL.   Lydia's a pretty name.

Where do you live?

LYDIA.   I' the castle.

CASHEL [*thunderstruck*]   Do not say

You are the lady of this great domain.

LYDIA. I am.

CASHEL.   Accursed luck! I took you for

The daughter of some farmer. Well, your pardon.

I came too close: I looked too deep. Farewell.

LYDIA. I pardon that. Now tell me who you are.

CASHEL. Ask me not whence I come, nor what I am.

You are the lady of the castle. I

Have but this hard and blackened hand to live by.

LYDIA. I have felt its strength and envied you. Your
name?

286

I have told you mine.

    CASHEL.   My name is Cashel Byron.

    LYDIA. I never heard the name; and yet you utter it
As men announce a celebrated name.
Forgive my ignorance.

    CASHEL.   I bless it, Lydia.
I have forgot your other name.

    LYDIA.   Carew.
Cashel's a pretty name too.

    MELLISH [*calling through the wood*] Coo-ee! Byron!

    CASHEL. A thousand curses! Oh, I beg you, go.
This is a man you must not meet.

    MELLISH [*further off*]   Coo-ee!

    LYDIA. He's losing us. What does he in my woods?

    CASHEL. He is a part of what I am. What that is
You must not know. It would end all between us.
And yet there's no dishonor in 't: your lawyer,
Who let your lodge to me, will vouch me honest.
I am ashamed to tell you what I am—
At least, as yet. Some day, perhaps.

    MELLISH [*nearer*]   Coo-ee!

    LYDIA. His voice is nearer. Fare you well, my tenant.
When next your rent falls due, come to the castle.
Pay me in person. Sir: your most obedient.

                           [*She curtsies and goes.*

    CASHEL. Lives in this castle! Owns this park! A lady
Marry a prizefighter! Impossible.
And yet the prizefighter must marry her.

                  Enter MELLISH
Ensanguined swine, whelped by a doggish dam,
Is this thy park, that thou, with voice obscene,
Fillst it with yodeled yells, and screamst my name
For all the world to know that Cashel Byron
Is training here for combat.

    MELLISH.   Swine you me?
Ive caught you, have I? You have found a woman.
Let her shew here again, I'll set the dog on her.

I will. I say it. And my name's Bob Mellish.

CASHEL. Change thy initial and be truly hight
Hellish. As for thy dog, why dost thou keep one
And bark thyself? Begone.

MELLISH.   I'll not begone.
You shall come back with me and do your duty—
Your duty to your backers, do you hear?
You have not punched the bag this blessèd day.

CASHEL. The putrid bag engirdled by thy belt
Invites my fist.

MELLISH [*weeping*] Ingrate! O wretched lot!
Who would a trainer be? O Mellish, Mellish,
Trainer of heroes, builder-up of brawn,
Vicarious victor, thou createst champions
That quickly turn thy tyrants. But beware:
Without me thou art nothing. Disobey me,
And all thy boasted strength shall fall from thee.
With flaccid muscles and with failing breath
Facing the fist of thy more faithful foe,
I'll see thee on the grass cursing the day
Thou didst forswear thy training.

CASHEL.   Noisome quack
That canst not from thine own abhorrent visage
Take one carbuncle, thou contaminat'st
Even with thy presence my untainted blood.
Preach abstinence to rascals like thyself
Rotten with surfeiting. Leave me in peace.
This grove is sacred: thou profanest it.
Hence! I have business that concerns thee not.

MELLISH. Ay, with your woman. You will lose your fight.
Have you forgot your duty to your backers?
Oh, what a sacred thing your duty is!
What makes a man but duty? Where were we
Without our duty? Think of Nelson's words:
England expects that every man—

CASHEL.   Shall twaddle
About his duty. Mellish: at no hour
288

Can I regard thee wholly without loathing;
But when thou playst the moralist, by Heaven,
My soul flies to my fist, my fist to thee;
And never did the Cyclops' hammer fall
On Mars's armor—but enough of that.
It does remind me of my mother.

MELLISH.   Ah,
Byron, let it remind thee. Once I heard
An old song: it ran thus. [*He clears his throat*] Ahem, Ahem!
   [*Sings*]—They say there is no other
         Can take the place of mother—
I am out o' voice: forgive me; but remember:
Thy mother—were that sainted woman here—
Would say, Obey thy trainer.

CASHEL.   Now, by Heaven,
Some fate is pushing thee upon thy doom.
Canst thou not hear thy sands as they run out?
They thunder like an avalanche. Old man:
Two things I hate, my duty and my mother.
Why dost thou urge them both upon me now?
Presume not on thine age and on thy nastiness.
Vanish, and promptly.

MELLISH.   Can I leave thee here
Thus thinly clad, exposed to vernal dews?
Come back with me, my son, unto our lodge.

CASHEL. Within this breast a fire is newly lit
Whose glow shall sun the dew away, whose radiance
Shall make the orb of night hang in the heavens
Unnoticed, like a glow-worm at high noon.

MELLISH. Ah me, ah me, where wilt thou spend the night?

CASHEL. Wiltstoken's windows wandering beneath,
Wiltstoken's holy bell hearkening,
Wiltstoken's lady loving breathlessly.

MELLISH. The lady of the castle! Thou art mad.

CASHEL. Tis thou art mad to trifle in my path.
Thwart me no more. Begone.

MELLISH.   My boy, my son,

289

I'd give my heart's blood for thy happiness.
Thwart thee, my son! Ah no. I'll go with thee.
I'll brave the dews. I'll sacrifice my sleep.
I am old—no matter: ne'er shall it be said
Mellish deserted thee.

      CASHEL.   You resolute gods
That will not spare this man, upon your knees
Take the disparity twixt his age and mine.
Now from the ring to the high judgment seat
I step at your behest. Bear you me witness
This is not Victory, but Execution.

     [*He solemnly projects his fist with colossal force against the
        waistcoat of Mellish, who doubles up like a folded towel,
        and lies without sense or motion.*
And now the night is beautiful again.

        [*The castle clock strikes the hour in the distance.*
Hark! Hark! Hark! Hark! Hark! Hark! Hark! Hark!
   Hark! Hark!
It strikes in poetry. Tis ten o'clock.
Lydia: to thee!

     [*He steals off towards the castle. Mellish stirs and groans.*

London. A room in Lydia's house
Enter LYDIA *and* LUCIAN

LYDIA. Welcome, dear cousin, to my London house.
      Of late you have been chary of your visits.
            LUCIAN. I have been greatly occupied of late.
The minister to whom I act as scribe
In Downing Street was born in Birmingham,
And, like a thoroughbred commercial statesman,
Splits his infinitives, which I, poor slave,
Must reunite, though all the time my heart
Yearns for my gentle coz's company.
      LYDIA. Lucian: there is some other reason. Think!
Since England was a nation every mood
Her scribes with adverbs recklessly have split,
But thine avoidance dates from yestermonth.
      LUCIAN. There is a man I like not haunts this house.
      LYDIA. Thou speakst of Cashel Byron?
      LUCIAN.   Aye, of him.
Hast thou forgotten that eventful night
When as we gathered were at Hoskyn House
To hear a lecture by Herr Abendgasse,
He placed a single finger on my chest,
And I, ensorceled, would have sunk supine
Had not a chair received my falling form.
      LYDIA. Pooh! That was but by way of illustration.
      LUCIAN. What right had he to illustrate his point
Upon my person? Was I his assistant
That he should try experiments on me
As Simpson did on his with chloroform?
Now, by the cannon balls of Galileo
He hath unmanned me: all my nerve is gone.
This very morning my official chief,
Tapping with friendly forefinger this button,
Levelled me like a thunderstricken elm
Flat upon the Colonial Office floor.
      LYDIA. Fancies, coz.

THE ADMIRABLE BASHVILLE

LUCIAN.   Fancies! Fits! the chief said fits!
Delirium tremens! the chlorotic dance
Of Vitus! What could anyone have thought?
Your ruffian friend hath ruined me. By Heaven,
I tremble at a thumbnail. Give me drink.

LYDIA. What ho, without there! Bashville.

BASHVILLE [*without*]   Coming, madam.

Enter BASHVILLE

LYDIA. My cousin ails, Bashville. Procure some wet.

           [*Exit* BASHVILLE.

LUCIAN. Some wet!!! Where learnt you that atrocious
    word?
This is the language of a flower-girl.

LYDIA. True. It is horrible. Said I "Some wet"?
I meant, some drink. Why did I say "Some wet"?
Am I ensorceled too? "Some wet"! Fie! fie!
I feel as though some hateful thing had stained me.
Oh, Lucian, how could I have said "Some wet"?

LUCIAN. The horrid conversation of this man
Hath numbed thy once unfailing sense of fitness.

LYDIA. Nay, he speaks very well: he's literate:
Shakespear he quotes unconsciously.

LUCIAN.   And yet
Anon he talks pure pothouse.

Enter BASHVILLE

BASHVILLE.   Sir: your potion.

LUCIAN. Thanks. [*He drinks*]. I am better.

A NEWSBOY [*calling without*]   Extra special Star!
Result of the great fight! Name of the winner!

LYDIA. Who calls so loud?

BASHVILLE.   The papers, madam.

LYDIA.   Why?
Hath ought momentous happened?

BASHVILLE.   Madam: yes.

       [*He produces a newspaper.*

All England for these thrilling paragraphs
A week has waited breathless.

LYDIA. Read them us.

BASHVILLE [*reading*] "At noon today, unknown to the police,
Within a thousand miles of Wormwood Scrubbs,
Th' Australian Champion and his challenger,
The Flying Dutchman, formerly engaged
I' the mercantile marine, fought to a finish.
Lord Worthington, the well-known sporting peer,
Was early on the scene."

LYDIA. Lord Worthington!

BASHVILLE. "The bold Ned Skene revisited the ropes
To hold the bottle for his quondam novice;
Whilst in the seaman's corner were assembled
Professor Palmer and the Chelsea Snob.
Mellish, whose epigastrium has been hurt,
Tis said, by accident at Wiltstoken,
Looked none the worse in the Australian's corner.
The Flying Dutchman wore the Union Jack:
His colors freely sold amid the crowd;
But Cashel's well-known spot of white on blue—"

LYDIA. Whose, did you say?

BASHVILLE. Cashel's, my lady.

LYDIA. Lucian:
Your hand—a chair—

BASHVILLE. Madam: youre ill.

LYDIA. Proceed.
What you have read I do not understand;
Yet I will hear it through. Proceed.

LUCIAN. Proceed.

BASHVILLE. "But Cashel's well-known spot of white on blue
Was fairly rushed for. Time was called at twelve,
When, with a smile of confidence upon
His ocean-beaten mug—"

LYDIA. His mug?

LUCIAN [*explaining*] His face.

BASHVILLE [*continuing*] "The Dutchman came un-

293

THE ADMIRABLE BASHVILLE

daunted to the scratch,
But found the champion there already. Both
Most heartily shook hands, amid the cheers
Of their encouraged backers. Two to one
Was offered on the Melbourne nonpareil;
And soon, so fit the Flying Dutchman seemed,
Found takers everywhere. No time was lost
In getting to the business of the day.
The Dutchman led at once, and seemed to land
On Byron's dicebox; but the seaman's reach,
Too short for execution at long shots,
Did not get fairly home upon the ivory;
And Byron had the best of the exchange."

    LYDIA. I do not understand. What were they doing?

    LUCIAN. Fighting with naked fists.

    LYDIA.   Oh, horrible!

I'll hear no more. Or stay: how did it end?
Was Cashel hurt?

    LUCIAN [to Bashville] Skip to the final round.

    BASHVILLE. "Round Three: the rumors that had gone
      about
Of a breakdown in Byron's recent training
Seemed quite confirmed. Upon the call of time
He rose, and, looking anything but cheerful,
Proclaimed with every breath Bellows to Mend.
At this point six to one was freely offered
Upon the Dutchman; and Lord Worthington
Plunged at this figure till he stood to lose
A fortune should the Dutchman, as seemed certain,
Take down the number of the Panley boy.
The Dutchman, glutton as we know he is,
Seemed this time likely to go hungry. Cashel
Was clearly groggy as he slipped the sailor,
Who, not to be denied, followed him up,
Forcing the fighting mid tremendous cheers."

    LYDIA. Oh stop—no more—or tell the worst at once.
I'll be revenged. Bashville: call the police.

294

This brutal sailor shall be made to know
There's law in England.

LUCIAN.   Do not interrupt him:
Mine ears are thirsting. Finish, man. What next?

BASHVILLE. "Forty to one, the Dutchman's friends ex-
claimed.
Done, said Lord Worthington, who shewed himself
A sportsman every inch. Barely the bet
Was booked, when, at the reeling champion's jaw
The sailor, bent on winning out of hand,
Sent in his right. The issue seemed a cert,
When Cashel, ducking smartly to his left,
Cross-countered like a hundredweight of brick—"

LUCIAN. Death and damnation!

LYDIA.   Oh, what does it mean?

BASHVILLE. "The Dutchman went to grass, a beaten
man."

LYDIA. Hurrah! Hurrah! Hurrah! Oh, well done,
Cashel!

BASHVILLE. "A scene of indescribable excitement
Ensued; for it was now quite evident
That Byron's grogginess had all along
Been feigned to make the market for his backers.
We trust this sample of colonial smartness
Will not find imitators on this side.
The losers settled up like gentlemen;
But many felt that Byron shewed bad taste
In taking old Ned Skene upon his back,
And, with Bob Mellish tucked beneath his oxter,
Sprinting a hundred yards to show the crowd
The perfect pink of his condition"—[a knock].

LYDIA [turning pale]   Bashville,
Didst hear? A knock.

BASHVILLE.   Madam: tis Byron's knock.
Shall I admit him?

LUCIAN.   Reeking from the ring!
Oh, monstrous! Say youre out.

LYDIA.   Send him away.
I will not see the wretch. How dare he keep
Secrets from ME? I'll punish him. Pray say
I'm not at home. [*Bashville turns to go*]. Yet stay. I am afraid
He will not come again.

LUCIAN.   A consummation
Devoutly to be wished by any lady.
Pray, do you wish this man to come again?

LYDIA. No, Lucian. He hath used me very ill.
He should have told me. I will ne'er forgive him.
Say, Not at home.

BASHVILLE.   Yes, madam.   [*Exit.

LYDIA.   Stay—

LUCIAN [*stopping her*]   No, Lydia:
You shall not countermand that proper order.
Oh, would you cast the treasure of your mind,
The thousands at your bank, and, above all,
Your unassailable social position
Before this soulless mass of beef and brawn.

LYDIA. Nay, coz: youre prejudiced.

CASHEL [*without*]   Liar and slave!

LYDIA. What words were those?

LUCIAN.   The man is drunk with slaughter.

Enter BASHVILLE *running: he shuts the door and locks it.*

BASHVILLE. Save yourselves: at the staircase foot the
    champion
Sprawls on the mat, by trick of wrestler tripped;
But when he rises, woe betide us all!

LYDIA. Who bade you treat my visitor with violence?

BASHVILLE. He would not take my answer; thrust the
    door
Back in my face; gave me the lie i' th' throat;
Averred he felt your presence in his bones.
I said he should feel mine there too, and felled him;
Then fled to bar your door.

LYDIA.   O lover's instinct!
He felt my presence. Well, let him come in.

We must not fail in courage with a fighter.
Unlock the door.

LUCIAN. Stop. Like all women, Lydia,
You have the courage of immunity.
To strike you were against his code of honor;
But me, above the belt, he may perform on
T'th' height of his profession. Also Bashville.

BASHVILLE. Think not of me, sir. Let him do his worst.
Oh, if the valor of my heart could weigh
The fatal difference twixt his weight and mine,
A second battle should he do this day:
Nay, though outmatched I be, let but my mistress
Give me the word: instant I'll take him on
Here—now—at catchweight. Better bite the carpet
A man, than fly, a coward.

LUCIAN. Bravely said:
I will assist you with the poker.

LYDIA. No:
I will not have him touched. Open the door.

BASHVILLE. Destruction knocks thereat. I smile, and
open.
[*Bashville opens the door. Dead silence. Cashel enters, in
tears. A solemn pause.*
CASHEL. You know my secret?
LYDIA. Yes.
CASHEL. And thereupon
You bade your servant fling me from your door.

LYDIA. I bade my servant say I was not here.

CASHEL [*to Bashville*] Why didst thou better thy instruc-
tion, man?
Hadst thou but said, "She bade me tell thee this,"
Thoudst burst my heart. I thank thee for thy mercy.

LYDIA. Oh, Lucian, didst thou call him "drunk with
slaughter"?
Canst thou refrain from weeping at his woe?

CASHEL [*to Lucian*] The unwritten law that shields the
amateur

297

Against professional resentment, saves thee.
O coward, to traduce behind their backs
Defenceless prizefighters!

    LUCIAN.   Thou dost avow
Thou art a prizefighter.

    CASHEL.   It was my glory.
I had hoped to offer to my lady there
My belts, my championships, my heaped-up stakes,
My undefeated record; but I knew
Behind their blaze a hateful secret lurked.

    LYDIA. Another secret?

    LUCIAN.   Is there worse to come?

    CASHEL. Know ye not then my mother is an actress?

    LUCIAN. How horrible!

    LYDIA.   Nay, nay: how interesting!

    CASHEL. A thousand victories cannot wipe out
That birthstain. Oh, my speech bewrayeth it:
My earliest lesson was the player's speech
In Hamlet; and to this day I express myself
More like a mobled queen than like a man
Of flesh and blood. Well may your cousin sneer!
What's Hecuba to him or he to Hecuba?

    LUCIAN. Injurious upstart: if by Hecuba
Thou pointest darkly at my lovely cousin,
Know that she is to me, and I to her,
What never canst thou be. I do defy thee;
And maugre all the odds thy skill doth give,
Outside I will await thee.

    LYDIA.   I forbid
Expressly any such duello. Bashville:
The door. Put Mr Webber in a hansom,
And bid the driver hie to Downing Street.
No answer: tis my will. [*Exeunt* LUCIAN *and* BASHVILLE.
                    And now, farewell.
You must not come again, unless indeed
You can some day look in my eyes and say:
Lydia: my occupation's gone.

CASHEL.   Ah no:
It would remind you of my wretched mother.
O God, let me be natural a moment!
What other occupation can I try?
What would you have me be?

LYDIA.   A gentleman.

CASHEL. A gentleman! Cashel Byron, stoop
To be the thing that bets on me! the fool
I flatter at so many coins a lesson!
The screaming creature who beside the ring
Gambles with basest wretches for my blood,
And pays with money that he never earned!
Let me die broken hearted rather!

LYDIA.   But
You need not be an idle gentleman.
I call you one of Nature's gentlemen.

CASHEL. Thats the collection for the loser, Lydia.
I am not wont to need it. When your friends
Contest elections, and at foot o' th' poll
Rue their presumption, tis their wont to claim
A moral victory. In a sort they are
Nature's M.P.s. I am not yet so threadbare
As to accept these consolation stakes.

LYDIA. You are offended with me.

CASHEL.   Yes I am.
I can put up with much; but— "Nature's gentleman"!
I thank your ladyship of Lyons, but
Must beg to be excused.

LYDIA.   But surely, surely,
To be a prizefighter, and maul poor mariners
With naked knuckles, is no work for you.

CASHEL. Thou dost arraign the inattentive Fates
That weave my thread of life in ruder patterns
Than these that lie, antimacassarly,
Asprent thy drawing room. As well demand
Why I at birth chose to begin my life
A speechless babe. hairless, incontinent,

299

Hobbling upon all fours, a nurse's nuisance?
Or why I do propose to lose my strength,
To blanch my hair, to let the gums recede
Far up my yellowing teeth, and finally
Lie down and moulder in a rotten grave?
Only one thing more foolish could have been,
And that was to be born, not man, but woman.
This was thy folly, why rebuk'st thou mine?

LYDIA. These are not things of choice.

CASHEL.   And did I choose
My quick divining eye, my lightning hand,
My springing muscle and untiring heart?
Did I implant the instinct in the race
That found a use for these, and said to me,
Fight for us, and be fame and fortune thine?

LYDIA. But there are other callings in the world.

CASHEL. Go tell thy painters to turn stockbrokers,
Thy poet friends to stoop oer merchants' desks
And pen prose records of the gains of greed.
Tell bishops that religion is outworn,
And that the Pampa to the horsebreaker
Opes new careers. Bid the professor quit
His fraudulent pedantries, and do i' the world
The thing he would teach others. Then return
To me and say: Cashel: they have obeyed;
And on that pyre of sacrifice I, too,
Will throw my championship.

LYDIA.   But tis so cruel.

CASHEL. Is it so? I have hardly noticed that,
So cruel are all callings. Yet this hand,
That many a two days bruise hath ruthless given,
Hath kept no dungeon locked for twenty years,
Hath slain no sentient creature for my sport.
I am too squeamish for your dainty world,
That cowers behind the gallows and the lash,
The world that robs the poor, and with their spoil
Does what its tradesmen tell it. Oh, your ladies!

300

Sealskinned and egret-feathered; all defiance
To Nature; cowering if one say to them
"What will the servants think?" Your gentlemen!
Your tailor-tyrannized visitors of whom
Flutter of wing and singing in the wood
Make chickenbutchers. And your medicine men!
Groping for cures in the tormented entrails
Of friendly dogs. Pray have you asked all these
To change their occupations? Find you mine
So grimly crueller? I cannot breathe
An air so petty and so poisonous.
    LYDIA. But find you not their manners very nice?
    CASHEL. To me, perfection. Oh, they condescend
With a rare grace. Your duke, who condescends
Almost to the whole world, might for a Man
Pass in the eyes of those who never saw
The duke capped with a prince. See then, ye gods,
The duke turn footman, and his eager dame
Sink the great lady in the obsequious housemaid!
Oh, at such moments I could wish the Court
Had but one breadbasket, that with my fist
I could make all its windy vanity
Gasp itself out on the gravel. Fare you well.
I did not choose my calling; but at least
I can refrain from being a gentleman.
    LYDIA. You say farewell to me without a pang.
    CASHEL. My calling hath apprenticed me to pangs.
This is a rib-bender; but I can bear it.
It is a lonely thing to be a champion.
    LYDIA. It is a lonelier thing to be a woman.
    CASHEL. Be lonely then. Shall it be said of thee
That for his brawn thou misalliance mad'st
Wi' the Prince of Ruffians? Never. Go thy ways;
Or, if thou hast nostalgia of the mud,
Wed some bedoggéd wretch that on the slot
Of gilded snobbery, *ventre à terre*,
Will hunt through life with eager nose on earth

And hang thee thick with diamonds. I am rich;
But all my gold was fought for with my hands.

  LYDIA. What dost thou mean by rich?

  CASHEL.   There is a man,
Hight Paradise, vaunted unconquerable,
Hath dared to say he will be glad to hear from me.
I have replied that none can hear from me
Until a thousand solid pounds be staked.
His friends have confidently found the money.
Ere fall of leaf that money shall be mine;
And then I shall possess ten thousand pounds.
I had hoped to tempt thee with that monstrous sum.

  LYDIA. Thou silly Cashel, tis but a week's income.
I did propose to give thee three times that
For pocket money when we two were wed.

  CASHEL. Give me my hat. I have been fooling here.
Now, by the Hebrew lawgiver, I thought
That only in America such revenues
Were decent deemed. Enough. My dream is dreamed.
Your gold weighs like a mountain on my chest.
Farewell.

  LYDIA. The golden mountain shall be thine
The day thou quitst thy horrible profession.

  CASHEL. Tempt me not, woman. It is honor calls.
Slave to the Ring I rest until the face
Of Paradise be changed.

      Enter BASHVILLE

  BASHVILLE.   Madam, your carriage,
Ordered by you at two. Tis now half-past.

  CASHEL. Sdeath! is it half-past two? The king! the king!

  LYDIA. The king! What mean you?

  CASHEL.   I must meet a monarch
This very afternoon at Islington.

  LYDIA. At Islington! You must be mad.

  CASHEL.   A cab!
Go call a cab; and let a cab be called;
And let the man that calls it be thy footman.

LYDIA. You are not well. You shall not go alone.
My carriage waits. I must accompany you.
I go to find my hat.   [*Exit.*

    CASHEL.   Like Paracelsus,
Who went to find his soul. [*To Bashville*] And now, young
    man,
How comes it that a fellow of your inches,
So deft a wrestler and so bold a spirit,
Can stoop to be a flunkey? Call on me
On your next evening out. I'll make a man of you.
Surely you are ambitious and aspire—
    BASHVILLE. To be a butler and draw corks; wherefore,
By Heaven, I will draw yours.

           [*He hits Cashel on the nose, and runs out.*
    CASHEL [*thoughtfully putting the side of his forefinger to his
    nose, and studying the blood on it*] Too quick for me!
There's money in this youth.

        Re-enter LYDIA, *hatted and gloved*
    LYDIA.   O Heaven! you bleed.
    CASHEL. Lend me a key or other frigid object,
That I may put it down my back, and staunch
The welling life stream.
    LYDIA [*giving him her keys*] Oh, what h a v e you done?
    CASHEL. Flush on the boko napped your footman's left.
    LYDIA. I do not understand.
    CASHEL.   True. Pardon me.
I have received a blow upon the nose
In sport from Bashville. Next, ablution; else
I shall be total gules.   [*He hurries out.*
    LYDIA.   How well he speaks!
There is a silver trumpet in his lips
That stirs me to the finger ends. His nose
Dropt lovely color: tis a perfect blood.
I would twere mingled with mine own!
           Enter BASHVILLE
                   What now?
    BASHVILLE. Madam, the coachman can no longer wait:

The horses will take cold.

LYDIA.   I do beseech him
A moment's grace. Oh, mockery of wealth!
The third class passenger unchidden rides
Whither and when he will: obsequious trams
Await him hourly: subterranean tubes
With tireless coursers whisk him through the town;
But we, the rich, are slaves to Houyhnhnms:
We wait upon their colds, and frowst all day
Indoors, if they but cough or spurn their hay.

    BASHVILLE. Madam, an omnibus to Euston Road,
And thence t' th' Angel—

Enter CASHEL

    LYDIA.   Let us haste, my love:
The coachman is impatient.

    CASHEL.   Did he guess
He stays for Cashel Byron, he'd outwait
Pompei's sentinel. Let us away.
This day of deeds, as yet but half begun,
Must ended be in merrie Islington.

            [*Exeunt* LYDIA *and* CASHEL.

    BASHVILLE. Gods! how she hangs on's arm! I am alone.
Now let me lift the cover from my soul.
O wasted humbleness! Deluded diffidence!
How often have I said, Lie down, poor footman:
She'll never stoop to thee, rear as thou wilt
Thy powder to the sky. And now, by Heaven,
She stoops below me; condescends upon
This hero of the pothouse, whose exploits,
Writ in my character from my last place,
Would damn me into ostlerdom. And yet
Theres an eternal justice in it; for
By so much as the ne'er subduéd Indian
Excels the servile negro, doth this ruffian
Precedence take of me. "*Ich dien*." Damnation!
I serve. My motto should have been, "I scalp."
And yet I do not bear the yoke for gold.

OR, CONSTANCY UNREWARDED

Because I love her I have blacked her boots;
Because I love her I have cleaned her knives,
Doing in this the office of a boy,
Whilst, like the celebrated maid that milks
And does the meanest chares, Ive shared the passions
Of Cleopatra. It has been my pride
To give her place the greater altitude
By lowering mine, and of her dignity
To be so jealous that my cheek has flamed
Even at the thought of such a deep disgrace
As love for such a one as I would be
For such a one as she; and now! and now!
A prizefighter! O irony! O bathos!
To have made way for this! Oh, Bashville, Bashville:
Why hast thou thought so lowly of thyself,
So heavenly high of her? Let what will come,
My love must speak: twas my respect was dumb.

SCENE II

*The Agricultural Hall in Islington, crowded with spectators.
In the arena a throne, with a boxing ring before it. A
balcony above on the right, occupied by persons of fashion: among others, Lydia and Lord Worthington.
Flourish. Enter* LUCIAN *and* CETEWAYO, *with Chiefs
in attendance*

CETEWAYO. Is this the Hall of Husbandmen?
LUCIAN.   It is.
CETEWAYO. Are these anæmic dogs the English people?
LUCIAN. Mislike us not for our complexions,
The pallid liveries of the pall of smoke
Belched by the mighty chimneys of our factories,
And by the million patent kitchen ranges
Of happy English homes.
CETEWAYO.   When first I came
I deemed those chimneys the fuliginous altars
Of some infernal god. I now perceive

305

THE ADMIRABLE BASHVILLE

The English dare not look upon the sky.
They are moles and owls: they call upon the soot
To cover them.

     LUCIAN.   You cannot understand
The greatness of this people, Cetewayo.
You are a savage, reasoning like a child.
Each pallid English face conceals a brain
Whose powers are proven in the works of Newton
And in the plays of the immortal Shakespear.
There is not one of all the thousands here
But, if you placed him naked in the desert,
Would presently construct a steam engine,
And lay a cable t' th' Antipodes.

     CETEWAYO. Have I been brought a million miles by sea
To learn how men can lie! Know, Father Webber,
Men become civilized through twin diseases,
Terror and Greed to wit: these two conjoined
Become the grisly parents of Invention.
Why does the trembling white with frantic toil
Of hand and brain produce the magic gun
That slays a mile off, whilst the manly Zulu
Dares look his foe i' the face; fights foot to foot;
Lives in the present; drains the Here and Now;
Makes life a long reality, and death
A moment only; whilst your Englishman
Glares on his burning candle's winding-sheets,
Counting the steps of his approaching doom,
And in the murky corners ever sees
Two horrid shadows, Death and Poverty:
In the which anguish an unnatural edge
Comes on his frighted brain, which straight devises
Strange frauds by which to filch unearnéd gold,
Mad crafts by which to slay unfacéd foes,
Until at last his agonized desire
Makes possibility its slave. And then—
Horrible climax! All-undoing spite!—
Th' importunate clutching of the coward's hand

306

From wearied Nature Devastation's secrets
Doth wrest; when straight the brave black-livered man
Is blown explosively from off the globe;
And Death and Dread, with their white-livered slaves,
Oer-run the earth, and through their chattering teeth
Stammer the words "Survival of the Fittest."
Enough of this: I came not here to talk.
Thou sayst thou hast two white-faced ones who dare
Fight without guns, and spearless, to the death.
Let them be brought.

   LUCIAN.   They fight not to the death,
But under strictest rules: as, for example,
Half of their persons shall not be attacked;
Nor shall they suffer blows when they fall down,
Nor stroke of foot at any time. And, further,
That frequent opportunities of rest
With succor and refreshment be secured them.

   CETEWAYO. Ye gods, what cowards! Zululand, my Zulu-
land:
Personified Pusillanimity
Hath taen thee from the bravest of the brave!

   LUCIAN. Lo the rude savage whose untutored mind
Cannot perceive self-evidence, and doubts
That Brave and English mean the self-same thing!

   CETEWAYO. Well, well, produce these heroes. I surmise
They will be carried by their nurses, lest
Some barking dog or bumbling bee should scare them.

    CETEWAYO *takes his state. Enter* PARADISE

   LYDIA. What hateful wretch is this whose mighty thews
Presage destruction to his adversaries.

   LORD WORTHINGTON. Tis Paradise.

   LYDIA.   He of whom Cashel spoke?
A dreadful thought ices my heart. Oh, why
Did Cashel leave us at the door?

     Enter CASHEL

   LORD WORTHINGTON.   Behold!
The champion comes.

LYDIA.   Oh, I could kiss him now
Here, before all the world. His boxing things
Render him most attractive. But I fear
Yon villain's fists may maul him.

WORTHINGTON.   Have no fear.
Hark! the king speaks.

CETEWAYO.   Ye sons of the white queen:
Tell me your names and deeds ere ye fall to.

PARADISE. Your royal highness, you beholds a bloke
What gets his living honest by his fists.
I may not have the polish of some toffs
As I could mention on; but up to now
No man has took my number down. I scale
Close on twelve stun; my age is twenty-three;
And at Bill Richardson's Blue Anchor pub
Am to be heard of any day by such
As likes the job. I dont know, governor,
As ennythink remains for me to say.

CETEWAYO. Six wives and thirty oxen shalt thou have
If on the sand thou leave thy foeman dead.
Methinks he looks full scornfully on thee.
[*To Cashel*] Ha! dost thou not so?

CASHEL.   Sir, I do beseech you
To name the bone, or limb, or special place
Where you would have me hit him with this fist.

CETEWAYO. Thou hast a noble brow; but much I fear
Thine adversary will disfigure it.

CASHEL. There's a divinity that shapes our ends
Rough hew them how we will. Give me the gloves.

THE MASTER OF THE REVELS. Paradise, a professor. Cashel
      Byron,
Also professor. Time!   [*They spar*.

LYDIA.   Eternity
It seems to me until this fight be done.

CASHEL. Dread monarch: this is called the upper cut,
And this a hook-hit of mine own invention.
The hollow region where I plant this blow
308

Is called the mark. My left, you will observe,
I chiefly use for long shots: with my right
Aiming beside the angle of the jaw
And landing with a certain delicate screw
I without violence knock my foeman out.
Mark how he falls forward upon his face!
The rules allow ten seconds to get up;
And as the man is still quite silly, I
Might safely finish him; but my respect
For your most gracious majesty's desire
To see some further triumphs of the science
Of self-defence postpones awhile his doom.

PARADISE. How can a bloke do hisself proper justice
With pillows on his fists?

       [He tears off his gloves and attacks Cashel
         with his bare knuckles.

THE CROWD.   Unfair! The rules!

CETEWAYO. The joy of battle surges boiling up
And bids me join the mellay. Isandhlana
And Victory!   *[He falls on the bystanders.*

THE CHIEFS. Victory and Isandhlana!

   [They run amok. General panic and stampede.
     The ring is swept away.

LUCIAN. Forbear these most irregular proceedings.
Police! Police!

 [He engages Cetewayo with his umbrella. The balcony
 comes down with a crash. Screams from its occupants.
 Indescribable confusion.

CASHEL *[dragging Lydia from the struggling heap]* My
 love, my love, art hurt?

LYDIA. No, no; but save my sore oermatchéd cousin.

A POLICEMAN. Give us a lead, sir. Save the English flag.
Africa tramples on it.

CASHEL.   Africa!
Not all the continents whose mighty shoulders
The dancing diamonds of the seas bedeck
Shall trample on the blue with spots of white.

Now, Lydia, mark thy lover.   [*He charges the Zulus.*

LYDIA.   Hercules
Cannot withstand him. See: the king is down;
The tallest chief is up, heels over head,
Tossed corklike oer my Cashel's sinewy back;
And his lieutenant all deflated gasps
For breath upon the sand. The others fly.
In vain: his fist oer magic distances
Like a chameleon's tongue shoots to its mark;
And the last African upon his knees
Sues piteously for quarter. [*Rushing into Cashel's arms*]
       Oh, my hero:
Thoust saved us all this day.

CASHEL.   Twas all for thee.

CETEWAYO [*trying to rise*] Have I been struck by lightning?

LUCIAN.   Sir, your conduct
Can only be described as most ungentlemanly.

POLICEMAN. One of the prone is white.

CASHEL.   Tis Paradise.

POLICEMAN. He's choking: he has something in his
   mouth.

LYDIA [*to Cashel*] Oh Heaven! there is blood upon your
   hip.
Youre hurt.

CASHEL.   The morsel in yon wretch's mouth
Was bitten out of me.

       [*Sensation. Lydia screams and swoons in Cashel's arms.*

ACT III

Wiltstoken. A room in the Warren Lodge
Lydia at her writing-table

LYDIA. O Past and Present, how ye do conflict
    As here I sit writing my father's life!
    The autumn woodland woos me from without
With whispering of leaves and dainty airs
To leave this fruitless haunting of the past.
My father was a very learnéd man.
I sometimes think I shall oldmaided be
Ere I unlearn the things he taught to me.

Enter POLICEMAN

POLICEMAN. Asking your ladyship to pardon me
For this intrusion, might I be so bold
As ask a question of your people here
Concerning the Queen's peace?

LYDIA.   My people here
Are but a footman and a simple maid;
And both have craved a holiday to join
Some local festival. But, sir, your helmet
Proclaims the Metropolitan Police.

POLICEMAN. Madam, it does; and I may now inform you
That what you term a local festival
Is a most hideous outrage gainst the law,
Which we to quell from London have come down:
In short, a prizefight. My sole purpose here
Is to inquire whether your ladyship
Any bad characters this afternoon
Has noted in the neighborhood.

LYDIA.   No, none, sir.
I had not let my maid go forth today
Thought I the roads unsafe.

POLICEMAN.   Fear nothing, madam:
The force protects the fair. My mission here
Is to wreak ultion for the broken law.
I wish your ladyship good afternoon.

LYDIA. Good afternoon.   [*Exit* POLICEMAN.

311

A prizefight! O my heart!
Cashel: hast thou deceived me? Can it be
Thou hast backslidden to the hateful calling
I asked thee to eschew?

O wretched maid,
Why didst thou flee from London to this place
To write thy father's life, whenas in town
Thou mightst have kept a guardian eye on him—
Whats that? A flying footstep—

Enter CASHEL

CASHEL. Sanctuary!
The law is on my track. What! Lydia here!

LYDIA. Ay: Lydia here. Hast thou done murder, then,
That in so horrible a guise thou comest?

CASHEL. Murder! I would I had. Yon cannibal
Hath forty thousand lives; and I have taen
But thousands thirty-nine. I tell thee, Lydia,
On the impenetrable sarcolobe
That holds his seedling brain these fists have pounded
By Shrewsb'ry clock an hour. This bruiséd grass
And cakéd mud adhering to my form
I have acquired in rolling on the sod
Clinched in his grip. This scanty reefer coat
For decency snatched up as fast I fled
When the police arrived, belongs to Mellish.
Tis all too short; hence my display of rib
And forearm mother-naked. Be not wroth
Because I seem to wink at you: by Heaven,
Twas Paradise that plugged me in the eye
Which I perforce keep closing. Pity me,
My training wasted and my blows unpaid,
Sans stakes, sans victory, sans everything
I had hoped to win. Oh, I could sit me down
And weep for bitterness.

LYDIA. Thou wretch, begone.

CASHEL. Begone!

LYDIA. I say begone. Oh, tiger's heart

312

Wrapped in a young man's hide, canst thou not live
In love with Nature and at peace with Man?
Must thou, although thy hands were never made
To blacken other's eyes, still batter at
The image of Divinity? I loathe thee.
Hence from my house and never see me more.

    CASHEL. I go. The meanest lad on thy estate
Would not betray me thus. But tis no matter.

                          [He opens the door.

Ha! the police. I'm lost.   *[He shuts the door again.*
                 Now shalt thou see
My last fight fought. Exhausted as I am,
To capture me will cost the coppers dear.
Come one, come all!

    LYDIA.   Oh, hide thee, I implore:
I cannot see thee hunted down like this.
There is my room. Conceal thyself therein.
Quick, I command.   *[He goes into the room.*
             With horror I foresee,
Lydia, that never lied, must lie for thee.

Enter POLICEMAN, *with* PARADISE *and* MELLISH *in custody,*
    BASHVILLE, constables, and others

    POLICEMAN. Keep back your bruiséd prisoner lest he
      shock
This wellbred lady's nerves. Your pardon, maam;
But have you seen by chance the other one?
In this direction he was seen to run.

    LYDIA. A man came here anon with bloody hands
And aspect that did turn my soul to snow.

    POLICEMAN. Twas he. What said he?

    LYDIA.   Begged for sanctuary.
I bade the man begone.

    POLICEMAN.   Most properly.
Saw you which way he went?

    LYDIA.   I cannot tell.

    PARADISE. He seen me coming; and he done a bunk.

313

POLICEMAN. Peace, there. Excuse his damaged features,
 lady:
He's Paradise; and this one's Byron's trainer,
Mellish.

  MELLISH. Injurious copper, in thy teeth
I hurl the lie. I am no trainer, I.
My father, a respected missionary,
Apprenticed me at fourteen years of age
T' the poetry writing. To these woods I came
With Nature to commune. My revery
Was by a sound of blows rudely dispelled.
Mindful of what my sainted parent taught
I rushed to play the peacemaker, when lo!
These minions of the law laid hands on me.

  BASHVILLE. A lovely woman, with distracted cries,
In most resplendent fashionable frock,
Approaches like a wounded antelope.

    Enter ADELAIDE GISBORNE

  ADELAIDE. Where is my Cashel? Hath he been arrested?

  POLICEMAN. I would I had thy Cashel by the collar:
He hath escaped me.

  ADELAIDE.   Praises be for ever!

  LYDIA. Why dost thou call the missing man thy Cashel?

  ADELAIDE. He is mine only son.

  ALL.   Thy son!

  ADELAIDE.   My son.

  LYDIA. I thought his mother hardly would have known
 him,
So crushed his countenance.

  ADELAIDE.   A ribald peer,
Lord Worthington by name, this morning came
With honeyed words beseeching me to mount
His four-in-hand, and to the country hie
To see some English sport. Being by nature
Frank as a child, I fell into the snare,
But took so long to dress that the design
Failed of its full effect; for not until

314

The final round we reached the horrid scene.
Be silent all; for now I do approach
My tragedy's catastrophe. Know, then,
That Heaven did bless me with an only son,
A boy devoted to his doting mother—

POLICEMAN. Hark! did you hear an oath from yonder
room?

ADELAIDE. Respect a broken-hearted mother's grief,
And do not interrupt me in my scene.
Ten years ago my darling disappeared
(Ten dreary twelvemonths of continuous tears,
Tears that have left me prematurely aged;
For I am younger far than I appear).
Judge of my anguish when today I saw
Stripped to the waist, and fighting like a demon
With one who, whatsoe'er his humble virtues,
Was clearly not a gentleman, my son!

ALL. O strange event! O passing tearful tale!

ADELAIDE. I thank you from the bottom of my heart
For the reception you have given my woe;
And now I ask, where is my wretched son?
He must at once come home with me, and quit
A course of life that cannot be allowed.

Enter CASHEL

CASHEL. Policeman: I do yield me to the law.

LYDIA. Oh no.

ADELAIDE.   My son!

CASHEL.   My mother! Do not kiss me.
My visage is too sore.

POLICEMAN.   The lady hid him.
This is a regular plant. You cannot be
Up to that sex. [*To Cashel*] You come along with me.

LYDIA. Fear not, my Cashel: I will bail thee out.

CASHEL. Never. I do embrace my doom with joy.
With Paradise in Pentonville or Portland
I shall feel safe: there are no mothers there.

ADELAIDE. Ungracious boy—

315

CASHEL. Constable: bear me hence.

MELLISH. Oh, let me sweetest reconcilement make
By calling to thy mind that moving song:—
[*Sings*] They say there is no other—

CASHEL. Forbear at once, or the next note of music
That falls upon thine ear shall clang in thunder
From the last trumpet.

ADELAIDE. A disgraceful threat
To level at this virtuous old man.

LYDIA. Oh, Cashel, if thou scornst thy mother thus,
How wilt thou treat thy wife?

CASHEL. There spake my fate:
I knew you would say that. Oh, mothers, mothers,
Would you but let your wretched sons alone
Life were worth living! Had I any choice
In this importunate relationship?
None. And until that high auspicious day
When the millennium on an orphaned world
Shall dawn, and man upon his fellow look,
Reckless of consanguinity, my mother
And I within the self-same hemisphere
Conjointly may not dwell.

ADELAIDE. Ungentlemanly!

CASHEL. I am no gentleman. I am a criminal,
Redhanded, baseborn—

ADELAIDE. Baseborn! Who dares say it?
Thou art the son and heir of Bingley Bumpkin
FitzAlgernon de Courcy Cashel Byron,
Sieur of Park Lane and Overlord of Dorset,
Who after three months wedded happiness
Rashly fordid himself with prussic acid,
Leaving a tearstained note to testify
That having sweetly honeymooned with me,
He now could say, O Death, where is thy sting?

POLICEMAN. Sir: had I known your quality, this cop
I had averted; but it is too late.
The law's above us both.

316

OR, CONSTANCY UNREWARDED

Enter LUCIAN, *with an Order in Council*

LUCIAN.   Not so, policeman.
I bear a message from The Throne itself
Of fullest amnesty for Byron's past.
Nay, more: of Dorset deputy lieutenant
He is proclaimed. Further, it is decreed,
In memory of his glorious victory
Over our country's foes at Islington,
The flag of England shall for ever bear
On azure field twelve swanlike spots of white;
And by an exercise of feudal right
Too long disused in this anarchic age
Our sovereign doth confer on him the hand
Of Miss Carew, Wiltstoken's wealthy heiress.

                        [General acclamation.

POLICEMAN. Was anything, sir, said about me?
LUCIAN. Thy faithful services are not forgot:
In future call thyself Inspector Smith.

                        [Renewed acclamation.

POLICEMAN. I thank you, sir. I thank you, gentlemen.
LUCIAN. My former opposition, valiant champion,
Was based on the supposed discrepancy
Betwixt your rank and Lydia's. Here's my hand.
BASHVILLE. And I do here unselfishly renounce
All my pretensions to my lady's favor.   *[Sensation.*
LYDIA. What, Bashville! didst thou love me?
BASHVILLE.   Madam: yes.
Tis said: now let me leave immediately.
LYDIA. In taking, Bashville, this most tasteful course
You are but acting as a gentleman
In the like case would act. I fully grant
Your perfect right to make a declaration
Which flatters me and honors your ambition.
Prior attachment bids me firmly say
That whilst my Cashel lives, and polyandry
Rests foreign to the British social scheme,
Your love is hopeless; still, your services,

317

Made zealous by disinterested passion,
Would greatly add to my domestic comfort;
And if—

CASHEL. Excuse me. I have other views.
Ive noted in this man such aptitude
For art and exercise in his defence
That I prognosticate for him a future
More glorious than my past. Henceforth I dub him
The Admirable Bashville, Byron's Novice;
And to the utmost of my mended fortunes
Will back him gainst the world at ten stone six.

ALL. Hail, Byron's Novice, champion that shall be!

BASHVILLE. Must I renounce my lovely lady's service,
And mar the face of man?

CASHEL.   Tis Fate's decree.
For know, rash youth, that in this star crost world
Fate drives us all to find our chiefest good
In what we c a n, and not in what we w o u l d.

POLICEMAN. A post-horn—hark!

CASHEL.   What noise of wheels is this?

Lord Worthington drives upon the scene in his
four-in-hand, and descends

ADELAIDE. Perfidious peer!

LORD WORTHINGTON.   Sweet Adelaide—

ADELAIDE.   Forbear,
Audacious one: my name is Mrs Byron.

LORD WORTHINGTON. Oh, change that title for the sweeter
   one
Of Lady Worthington.

CASHEL.   Unhappy man,
You know not what you do.

LYDIA.   Nay, tis a match
Of most auspicious promise. Dear Lord Worthington,
You tear from us our mother-in-law—

CASHEL.   Ha! True.

LYDIA. —but we will make the sacrifice. She blushes:
At least she very prettily produces

Blushing's effect.

ADELAIDE.   My lord: I do accept you.

[*They embrace. Rejoicings.*

CASHEL [*aside*] It wrings my heart to see my noble backer
Lay waste his future thus. The world's a chessboard,
And we the merest pawns in fist of Fate.
[*Aloud*] And now, my friends, gentle and simple both,
Our scene draws to a close. In lawful course
As Dorset's deputy lieutenant I
Do pardon all concerned this afternoon
In the late gross and brutal exhibition
Of miscalled sport.

LYDIA [*throwing herself into his arms*] Your boats are
burnt at last.

CASHEL. This is the face that burnt a thousand boats,
And ravished Cashel Byron from the ring.
But to conclude. Let William Paradise
Devote himself to science, and acquire,
By studying the player's speech in Hamlet,
A more refined address. You, Robert Mellish,
To the Blue Anchor hostelry attend him;
Assuage his hurts, and bid Bill Richardson
Limit his access to the fatal tap.
Now mount we on my backer's four-in-hand,
And to St George's Church, whose portico
Hanover Square shuts off from Conduit Street,
Repair we all. Strike up the wedding march;
And, Mellish, let thy melodies trill forth
Broad oer the wold as fast we bowl along.
Give me the post-horn. Loose the flowing rein;
And up to London drive with might and main.

[*Exeunt.*

ANDROCLES AND THE LION

A FABLE PLAY

Written in 1912

First Performed London 1913

PREFACE ON THE PROSPECTS OF
CHRISTIANITY
WHY NOT GIVE CHRISTIANITY A TRIAL?

THE question seems a hopeless one after 2000 years of resolute adherence to the old cry of "Not this man, but Barabbas." Yet it is beginning to look as if Barabbas was a failure, in spite of his strong right hand, his victories, his empires, his millions of money, and his moralities and churches and political constitutions. "This man" has not been a failure yet; for nobody has ever been sane enough to try his way. But he has had one quaint triumph. Barabbas has stolen his name and taken his cross as a standard. There is a sort of compliment in that. There is even a sort of loyalty in it, like that of the brigand who breaks every law and yet claims to be a patriotic subject of the king who makes them. We have always had a curious feeling that though we crucified Christ on a stick, he somehow managed to get hold of the right end of it, and that if we were better men we might try his plan. There have been one or two grotesque attempts at it by inadequate people, such as the Kingdom of God in Munster, which was ended by a crucifixion so much more atrocious than the one on Calvary that the bishop who took the part of Annas went home and died of horror. But responsible people have never made such attempts. The moneyed, respectable, capable world has been steadily anti-Christian and Barabbasque since the crucifixion; and the specific doctrine of Jesus has not in all that time been put into political or general social practice. I am no more a Christian than Pilate was, or you, gentle reader; and yet, like Pilate, I greatly prefer Jesus to Annas and Caiaphas; and I am ready to admit that after contemplating the world and human nature for nearly sixty years, I see no way out of the world's misery but the way which would have been found by Christ's will if he had undertaken the work of a modern practical statesman.

Pray do not at this early point lose patience with me and shut the book. I assure you I am as sceptical and scientific

323

and modern a thinker as you will find anywhere. I grant you I know a great deal more about economics and politics than Jesus did, and can do things he could not do. I am by all Barabbasque standards a person of much better character and standing, and greater practical sense. I have no sympathy with vagabonds and talkers who try to reform society by taking men away from their regular productive work and making vagabonds and talkers of them too; and if I had been Pilate I should have recognized as plainly as he the necessity for suppressing attacks on the existing social order, however corrupt that order might be, by people with no knowledge of government and no power to construct political machinery to carry out their views, acting on the very dangerous delusion that the end of the world was at hand. I make no defence of such Christians as Savonarola and John of Leyden: they were scuttling the ship before they had learned how to build a raft; and it became necessary to throw them overboard to save the crew. I say this to set myself right with respectable society; but I must still insist that if Jesus could have worked out the practical problems of a Communist constitution, an admitted obligation to deal with crime without revenge or punishment, and a full assumption by humanity of divine responsibilities, he would have conferred an incalculable benefit on mankind, because these distinctive demands of his are now turning out to be good sense and sound economics.

I say distinctive, because his common humanity and his subjection to time and space (that is, to the Syrian life of his period) involved his belief in many things, true and false, that in no way distinguish him from other Syrians of that time. But such common beliefs do not constitute specific Christianity any more than wearing a beard, working in a carpenter's shop, or believing that the earth is flat and that the stars could drop on it from heaven like hailstones. Christianity interests practical statesmen now because of the doctrines that distinguished Christ from the Jews and the Barabbasques generally, including ourselves.

324

PREFACE
WHY JESUS MORE THAN ANOTHER?

I do not imply, however, that these doctrines were peculiar to Christ. A doctrine peculiar to one man would be only a craze, unless its comprehension depended on a development of human faculty so rare that only one exceptionally gifted man possessed it. But even in this case it would be useless, because incapable of spreading. Christianity is a step in moral evolution which is independent of any individual preacher. If Jesus had never existed (and that he ever existed in any other sense than that in which Shakespear's Hamlet existed has been vigorously questioned) Tolstoy would have thought and taught and quarrelled with the Greek Church all the same. Their creed has been fragmentarily practised to a considerable extent in spite of the fact that the laws of all countries treat it, in effect, as criminal. Many of its advocates have been militant atheists. But for some reason the imagination of white mankind has picked out Jesus of Nazareth as *the* Christ, and attributed all the Christian doctrines to him; and as it is the doctrine and not the man that matters, and, as, besides, one symbol is as good as another provided everyone attaches the same meaning to it, I raise, for the moment, no question as to how far the gospels are original, and how far they consist of Greek and Chinese interpolations. The record that Jesus said certain things is not invalidated by a demonstration that Confucius said them before him. Those who claim a literal divine paternity for him cannot be silenced by the discovery that the same claim was made for Alexander and Augustus. And I am not just now concerned with the credibility of the gospels as records of fact; for I am not acting as a detective, but turning our modern lights on to certain ideas and doctrines in them which disentangle themselves from the rest because they are flatly contrary to common practice, common sense, and common belief, and yet have, in the teeth of dogged incredulity and recalcitrance, produced an irresistible impression that Christ, though rejected by his posterity as an unpractical dreamer, and executed by his con-

325

temporaries as a dangerous anarchist and blasphemous madman, was greater than his judges.

WAS JESUS A COWARD?

I know quite well that this impression of superiority is not produced on everyone, even of those who profess extreme susceptibility to it. Setting aside the huge mass of inculcated Christ-worship which has no real significance because it has no intelligence, there is, among people who are really free to think for themselves on the subject, a great deal of hearty dislike of Jesus and of contempt for his failure to save himself and overcome his enemies by personal bravery and cunning as Mahomet did. I have heard this feeling expressed far more impatiently by persons brought up in England as Christians than by Mahometans, who are, like their prophet, very civil to Jesus, and allow him a place in their esteem and veneration at least as high as we accord to John the Baptist. But this British bulldog contempt is founded on a complete misconception of his reasons for submitting voluntarily to an ordeal of torment and death. The modern Secularist is often so determined to regard Jesus as a man like himself and nothing more, that he slips unconsciously into the error of assuming that Jesus shared that view. But it is quite clear from the New Testament writers (the chief authorities for believing that Jesus ever existed) that Jesus at the time of his death believed himself to be the Christ, a divine personage. It is therefore absurd to criticize his conduct before Pilate as if he were Colonel Roosevelt or Admiral von Tirpitz or even Mahomet. Whether you accept his belief in his divinity as fully as Simon Peter did, or reject it as a delusion which led him to submit to torture and sacrifice his life without resistance in the conviction that he would presently rise again in glory, you are equally bound to admit that, far from behaving like a coward or a sheep, he shewed considerable physical fortitude in going through a cruel ordeal against which he could have defended himself as effectually as he cleared the money-changers out of the temple. "Gentle Jesus, meek and mild"

326

is a snivelling modern invention, with no warrant in the gospels. St Matthew would as soon have thought of applying such adjectives to Judas Maccabeus as to Jesus; and even St Luke, who makes Jesus polite and gracious, does not make him meek. The picture of him as an English curate of the farcical comedy type, too meek to fight a policeman, and everybody's butt, may be useful in the nursery to soften children; but that such a figure could ever have become a centre of the world's attention is too absurd for discussion: grown men and women may speak kindly of a harmless creature who utters amiable sentiments and is a helpless nincompoop when he is called on to defend them; but they will not follow him, nor do what he tells them, because they do not wish to share his defeat and disgrace.

WAS JESUS A MARTYR?

It is important therefore that we should clear our minds of the notion that Jesus died, as some of us are in the habit of declaring, for his social and political opinions. There have been many martyrs to those opinions; but he was not one of them, nor, as his words shew, did he see any more sense in martyrdom than Galileo did. He was executed by the Jews for the blasphemy of claiming to be a God; and Pilate, to whom this was a mere piece of superstitious nonsense, let them execute him as the cheapest way of keeping them quiet, on the formal plea that he had committed treason against Rome by saying that he was the King of the Jews. He was not falsely accused, nor denied full opportunities of defending himself. The proceedings were quite straightforward and regular; and Pilate, to whom the appeal lay, favored him and despised his judges, and was evidently willing enough to be conciliated. But instead of denying the charge, Jesus repeated the offence. He knew what he was doing: he had alienated numbers of his own disciples and been stoned in the streets for doing it before. He was not lying: he believed literally what he said. The horror of the High Priest was perfectly natural: he was a Primate confronted with a heterodox street preacher uttering what seemed to him an appalling and impudent blasphemy. The fact that the blasphemy was to Jesus a simple statement of fact, and that it has since been accepted as such by all western nations, does not invalidate the proceedings, nor give us the right to regard Annas and Caiaphas as worse men than the Archbishop of Canterbury and the Head Master of Eton. If Jesus had been indicted in a modern court, he would have been examined by two doctors; found to be obsessed by a delusion; declared incapable of pleading; and sent to an asylum: that is the whole difference. But please note that when a man is charged before a modern tribunal (to take a case that happened the other day) of having asserted and maintained that he was an officer returned from the front to receive the Victoria Cross at the hands of the King, although he was in fact a mechanic, nobody thinks of treating him as afflicted with a delusion. He is punished for false pretences, because his assertion is credible and therefore misleading. Just so, the claim to divinity made by Jesus was to the High Priest, who looked forward to the coming of a Messiah, one that might conceivably have been true, and might therefore have misled the people in a very dangerous way. That was why he treated Jesus as an impostor and a blasphemer where we should have treated him as a madman.

THE GOSPELS WITHOUT PREJUDICE

All this will become clear if we read the gospels without prejudice. When I was young it was impossible to read them without fantastic confusion of thought. The confusion was so utterly confounded that it was called the proper spirit to read the Bible in. Jesus was a baby; and he was older than creation. He was a man who could be persecuted, stoned, scourged, and killed; and he was a god, immortal and all-powerful, able to raise the dead and call millions of angels to his aid. It was a sin to doubt either view of him: that is, it was a sin to reason about him; and the end was that you did not reason about him, and read about him only when you were compelled. When you heard the gospel

328

stories read in church, or learnt them from painters and poets, you came out with an impression of their contents that would have astonished a Chinaman who had read the story without prepossession. Even sceptics who were specially on their guard, put the Bible in the dock, and read the gospels with the object of detecting discrepancies in the four narratives to shew that the writers were as subject to error as the writers of yesterday's newspaper.

All this has changed greatly within two generations. Today the Bible is so little read that the language of the Authorized Version is rapidly becoming obsolete; so that even in the United States, where the old tradition of the verbal infallibility of "the book of books" lingers more strongly than anywhere else except perhaps in Ulster, retranslations into modern English have been introduced perforce to save its bare intelligibility. It is quite easy today to find cultivated persons who have never read the New Testament, and on whom therefore it is possible to try the experiment of asking them to read the gospels and state what they have gathered as to the history and views and character of Christ.

THE GOSPELS NOW UNINTELLIGIBLE TO NOVICES

But it will not do to read the gospels with a mind furnished only for the reception of, say, a biography of Goethe. You will not make sense of them, nor even be able without impatient weariness to persevere in the task of going steadily through them, unless you know something of the history of the human imagination as applied to religion. Not long ago I asked a writer of distinguished intellectual competence whether he had made a study of the gospels since his childhood. His reply was that he had lately tried, but "found it all such nonsense that I could not stick it." As I do not want to send anyone to the gospels with this result, I had better here give a brief exposition of how much of the history of religion is needed to make the gospels and the conduct and ultimate fate of Jesus intelligible and interesting.

329

WORLDLINESS OF THE MAJORITY

The first common mistake to get rid of is that mankind consists of a great mass of religious people and a few eccentric atheists. It consists of a huge mass of worldly people, and a small percentage of persons deeply interested in religion and concerned about their own souls and other people's; and this section consists mostly of those who are passionately affirming the established religion and those who are passionately attacking it, the genuine philosophers being very few. Thus you never have a nation of millions of Wesleys and one Tom Paine. You have a million Mr Worldly Wisemans, one Wesley, with his small congregation, and one Tom Paine, with *his* smaller congregation. The passionately religious are a people apart; and if they were not hopelessly outnumbered by the worldly, they would turn the world upside down, as St Paul was reproached, quite justly, for wanting to do. Few people can number among their personal acquaintances a single atheist or a single Plymouth Brother. Unless a religious turn in ourselves has led us to seek the little Societies to which these rare birds belong, we pass our lives among people who, whatever creeds they may repeat, and in whatever temples they may avouch their respectability and wear their Sunday clothes, have robust consciences, and hunger and thirst, not for righteousness, but for rich feeding and comfort and social position and attractive mates and ease and pleasure and respect and consideration: in short, for love and money. To these people one morality is as good as another provided they are used to it and can put up with its restrictions without unhappiness; and in the maintenance of this morality they will fight and punish and coerce without scruple. They may not be the salt of the earth, these Philistines; but they are the substance of civilization; and they save society from ruin by criminals and conquerors as well as by Savonarolas and Knipperdollings. And as they know, very sensibly, that a little religion is good for children and serves morality, keeping the poor in goodhumor or in awe by promising rewards

in heaven or threatening torments in hell, they encourage
the religious people up to a certain point: for instance, if
Savonarola only tells the ladies of Florence that they ought
to tear off their jewels and finery and sacrifice them to God,
they offer him a cardinal's hat, and praise him as a saint;
but if he induces them to actually do it, they burn him as a
public nuisance.

RELIGION OF THE MINORITY.
SALVATIONISM

The religion of the tolerated religious minority has
always been essentially the same religion: that is why its
changes of name and form have made so little difference.
That is why, also, a nation so civilized as the English can
convert negroes to their faith with great ease, but cannot
convert Mahometans or Jews. The negro finds in civilized
Salvationism an unspeakably more comforting version of
his crude creed; but neither Saracen nor Jew sees any advantage in it over his own version. The Crusader was surprised to find the Saracen quite as religious and moral as
himself, and rather more than less civilized. The Latin
Christian has nothing to offer the Greek Christian that
Greek Christianity has not already provided. They are all,
at root, Salvationists.

Let us trace this religion of Salvation from its beginnings. So many things that man does not himself contrive
or desire are always happening: death, plagues, tempests,
blights, floods, sunrise and sunset, growths and harvests
and decay, and Kant's two wonders of the starry heavens
above us and the moral law within us, that we conclude that
somebody must be doing it all, or that somebody is doing
the good and somebody else doing the evil, or that armies of
invisible persons, beneficent and malevolent, are doing it;
hence you postulate gods and devils, angels and demons.
You propitiate these powers with presents, called sacrifices,
and flatteries, called praises. Then the Kantian moral law
within you makes you conceive your god as a judge; and
straightway you try to corrupt him, also with presents and

331

flatteries. This seems shocking to us; but our objection to it is quite a recent development: no longer ago than Shakespear's time it was thought quite natural that litigants should give presents to human judges; and the buying off of divine wrath by actual money payments to priests, or, in the reformed churches which discountenance this, by subscriptions to charities and church building and the like, is still in full swing. Its practical disadvantage is that though it makes matters very easy for the rich, it cuts off the poor from all hope of divine favor. And this quickens the moral criticism of the poor to such an extent, that they soon find the moral law within them revolting against the idea of buying off the deity with gold and gifts, though they are still quite ready to buy him off with the paper money of praise and professions of repentance. Accordingly, you will find that though a religion may last unchanged for many centuries in primitive communities where the conditions of life leave no room for poverty and riches, and the process of propitiating the supernatural powers is as well within the means of the least of the members as within those of the headman, yet when commercial civilization arrives, and capitalism divides the people into a few rich and a great many so poor that they can barely live, a movement for religious reform will arise among the poor, and will be essentially a movement for cheap or entirely gratuitous salvation.

To understand what the poor mean by propitiation, we must examine for a moment what they mean by justice.

THE DIFFERENCE BEWEEN ATONEMENT AND PUNISHMENT

The primitive idea of justice is partly legalized revenge and partly expiation by sacrifice. It works out from both sides in the notion that two blacks make a white, and that when a wrong has been done, it should be paid for by an equivalent suffering. It seems to the Philistine majority a matter of course that this compensating suffering should be inflicted on the wrongdoer for the sake of its deterrent effect on other would-be wrongdoers; but a moment's reflection will shew that this utilitarian application corrupts the whole transaction. For example, the shedding of innocent blood cannot be balanced by the shedding of guilty blood. Sacrificing a criminal to propitiate God for the murder of one of his righteous servants is like sacrificing a mangy sheep or an ox with the rinderpest: it calls down divine wrath instead of appeasing it. In doing it we offer God as a sacrifice the gratification of our own revenge and the protection of our own lives without cost to ourselves; and cost to ourselves is the essence of sacrifice and expiation. However much the Philistines have succeeded in confusing these things in practice, they are to the Salvationist sense distinct and even contrary. The Baronet's cousin in Dickens's novel, who, perplexed by the failure of the police to discover the murderer of the baronet's solicitor, said "Far better hang wrong fellow than no fellow," was not only expressing a very common sentiment, but trembling on the brink of the rarer Salvationist opinion that it is much better to hang the wrong fellow: that, in fact, the wrong fellow is the right fellow to hang.

The point is a cardinal one, because until we grasp it not only does historical Christianity remain unintelligible to us, but those who do not care a rap about historical Christianity may be led into the mistake of supposing that if we discard revenge, and treat murderers exactly as God treated Cain: that is, exempt them from punishment by putting a brand on them as unworthy to be sacrificed, and let them face the world as best they can with that brand on them, we should get rid both of punishment and sacrifice. It would not at all follow: on the contrary, the feeling that there must be an expiation of the murder might quite possibly lead to our putting some innocent person—the more innocent the better—to a cruel death to balance the account with divine justice.

SALVATION AT FIRST A CLASS PRIVILEGE; AND THE REMEDY

Thus, even when the poor decide that the method of

purchasing salvation by offering rams and goats or bringing gold to the altar must be wrong because they cannot afford it, we still do not feel "saved" without a sacrifice and a victim. In vain do we try to substitute mystical rites that cost nothing, such as circumcision, or, as a substitute for that, baptism. Our sense of justice still demands an expiation, a sacrifice, a sufferer for our sins. And this leaves the poor man still in his old difficulty; for if it was impossible for him to procure rams and goats and shekels, how much more impossible is it for him to find a neighbor who will voluntarily suffer for his sins: one who will say cheerfully "You have committed a murder. Well, never mind: I am willing to be hanged for it in your stead"?

Our imagination must come to our rescue. Why not, instead of driving ourselves to despair by insisting on a separate atonement by a separate redeemer for every sin, have one great atonement and one great redeemer to compound for the sins of the world once for all? Nothing easier, nothing cheaper. The yoke is easy, the burden light. All you have to do when the redeemer is once found (or invented by the imagination) is to believe in the efficacy of the transaction, and you are saved. The rams and goats cease to bleed; the altars which ask for expensive gifts and continually renewed sacrifices are torn down; and the Church of the single redeemer and the single atonement rises on the ruins of the old temples, and becomes a single Church of the Christ.

RETROSPECTIVE ATONEMENT; AND THE EXPECTATION OF THE REDEEMER

But this does not happen at once. Between the old costly religion of the rich and the new gratuitous religion of the poor there comes an interregnum in which the redeemer, though conceived by the human imagination, is not yet found. He is awaited and expected under the names of the Christ, the Messiah, Baldur the Beautiful, or what not; but he has not yet come. Yet the sinners are not therefore in despair. It is true that they cannot say, as we say, "The

PREFACE

Christ has come, and has redeemed us"; but they can say "The Christ will come, and will redeem us," which, as the atonement is conceived as retrospective, is equally consoling. There are periods when nations are seething with this expectation and crying aloud with prophecy of the Redeemer through their poets. To feel that atmosphere we have only to take up the Bible and read Isaiah at one end of such a period and Luke and John at the other.

COMPLETION OF THE SCHEME BY LUTHER AND CALVIN

We now see our religion as a quaint but quite intelligible evolution from crude attempts to propitiate the destructive forces of Nature among savages to a subtle theology with a costly ritual of sacrifice possible only to the rich as a luxury, and finally to the religion of Luther and Calvin. And it must be said for the earlier forms that they involved very real sacrifices. The sacrifice was not always vicarious, and is not yet universally so. In India men pay with their own skins, torturing themselves hideously to attain holiness. In the west, saints amazed the world with their austerities and self-scourgings and confessions and vigils. But Luther delivered us from all that. His reformation was a triumph of imagination and a triumph of cheapness. It brought you complete salvation and asked you for nothing but faith. Luther did not know what he was doing in the scientific sociological way in which we know it; but his instinct served him better than knowledge could have done; for it was instinct rather than theological casuistry that made him hold so resolutely to Justification by Faith as the trump card by which he should beat the Pope, or, as he would have put it, the sign in which he should conquer. He may be said to have abolished the charge for admission to heaven. Paul had advocated this; but Luther and Calvin did it.

JOHN BARLEYCORN

There is yet another page in the history of religion which must be conned and digested before the career of Jesus can be fully understood. People who can read long books will

335

find it in Frazer's Golden Bough. Simpler folk will find it
in the peasant's song of John Barleycorn, now made access-
ible to our drawing room amateurs in the admirable collec-
tions of Somersetshire Folk Songs by Mr Cecil Sharp.
From Frazer's *magnum opus* you will learn how the same
primitive logic which makes the Englishman believe today
that by eating a beefsteak he can acquire the strength and
courage of the bull, and to hold that belief in the face of
the most ignominious defeats by vegetarian wrestlers and
racers and bicyclists, led the first men who conceived God
as capable of incarnation to believe that they could acquire
a spark of his divinity by eating his flesh and drinking his
blood. And from the song of John Barleycorn you may learn
how the miracle of the seed, the growth, and the harvest,
still the most wonderful of all the miracles and as inexplic-
able as ever, taught the primitive husbandman, and, as we
must now affirm, taught him quite rightly, that God is in the
seed, and that God is immortal. And thus it became the test
of Godhead that nothing that you could do to it could kill it,
and that when you buried it, it would rise again in renewed
life and beauty and give mankind eternal life on condition
that it was eaten and drunk, and again slain and buried, to
rise again for ever and ever. You may, and indeed must, use
John Barleycorn "right barbarouslee," cutting him "off at
knee" with your scythes, scourging him with your flails,
burying him in the earth; and he will not resist you nor reproach you, but will rise again in golden beauty amidst a
great burst of sunshine and bird music, and save you and
renew your life. And from the interweaving of these two
traditions with the craving for the Redeemer, you at last get
the conviction that when the Redeemer comes he will be
immortal; he will give us his body to eat and his blood to
drink; and he will prove his divinity by suffering a barbarous
death without resistance or reproach, and rise from the dead
and return to the earth in glory as the giver of life eternal.

LOOKING FOR THE END OF THE WORLD

Yet another persistent belief has beset the imagination
336

of the religious ever since religion spread among the poor, or, rather, ever since commercial civilization produced a hopelessly poor class cut off from enjoyment in this world. That belief is that the end of this world is at hand, and that it will presently pass away and be replaced by a kingdom of happiness, justice, and bliss in which the rich and the oppressors and the unjust shall have no share. We are all familiar with this expectation: many of us cherish some pious relative who sees in every great calamity a sign of the approaching end. Warning pamphlets are in constant circulation: advertisements are put in the papers and paid for by those who are convinced, and who are horrified at the indifference of the irreligious to the approaching doom. And revivalist preachers, now as in the days of John the Baptist, seldom fail to warn their flocks to watch and pray, as the great day will steal upon them like a thief in the night, and cannot be long deferred in a world so wicked. This belief also associates itself with Barleycorn's second coming; so that the two events become identified at last.

There is the other and more artificial side of this belief, on which it is an inculcated dread. The ruler who appeals to the prospect of heaven to console the poor and keep them from insurrection also curbs the vicious by threatening them with hell. In the Koran we find Mahomet driven more and more to this expedient of government; and experience confirms his evident belief that it is impossible to govern without it in certain phases of civilization. We shall see later on that it gives a powerful attraction to the belief in a Redeemer, since it adds to remorse of conscience, which hardened men bear very lightly, a definite dread of hideous and eternal torture.

THE HONOR OF DIVINE PARENTAGE

One more tradition must be noted. The consummation of praise for a king is to declare that he is the son of no earthly father, but of a god. His mother goes into the temple of Apollo, and Apollo comes to her in the shape of a serpent, or the like. The Roman emperors, following the example of

337

Augustus, claimed the title of God. Illogically, such divine
kings insist a good deal on their royal human ancestors.
Alexander, claiming to be the son of Apollo, is equally determined to be the son of Philip. As the gospels stand, St Mat-
hew and St Luke give genealogies (the two are different)
establishing the descent of Jesus through Joseph from the
royal house of David, and yet declare that not Joseph but the
Holy Ghost was the father of Jesus. It is therefore now held
that the story of the Holy Ghost is a later interpolation borrowed from the Greek and Roman imperial tradition. But
experience shews that simultaneous faith in the descent from
David and the conception by the Holy Ghost is possible.
Such double beliefs are entertained by the human mind without uneasiness or consciousness of the contradiction involved. Many instances might be given: a familiar one to
my generation being that of the Tichborne claimant, whose
attempt to pass himself off as a baronet was supported by an
association of laborers on the ground that the Tichborne
family, in resisting it, were trying to do a laborer out of his
rights. It is quite possible that Matthew and Luke may have
been unconscious of the contradiction: indeed the interpolation theory does not remove the difficulty, as the interpola-
tors themselves must have been unconscious of it. A better
ground for suspecting interpolation is that St Paul knew nothing of the divine birth, and taught that Jesus came into
the world at his birth as the son of Joseph, but rose from the
dead after three days as the son of God. Here again, few
notice the discrepancy: the three views are accepted simultaneously without intellectual discomfort. We can provisionally entertain half a dozen contradictory versions of
an event if we feel either that it does not greatly matter, or
that there is a category attainable in which the contradic-
tions are reconciled.

But that is not the present point. All that need be noted
here is that the legend of divine birth was sure to be attached
sooner or later to very eminent persons in Roman imperial
times, and that modern theologians, far from discrediting it,

have very logically affirmed the miraculous conception not only of Jesus but of his mother.

With no more scholarly equipment than a knowledge of these habits of the human imagination, anyone may now read the four gospels without bewilderment, and without the contemptuous incredulity which spoils the temper of many modern atheists, or the senseless credulity which sometimes makes pious people force us to shove them aside in emergencies as impracticable lunatics when they ask us to meet violence and injustice with dumb submission in the belief that the strange demeanor of Jesus before Pilate was meant as an example of normal human conduct. Let us admit that without the proper clues the gospels are, to a modern educated person, nonsensical and incredible, whilst the apostles are unreadable. But with the clues, they are fairly plain sailing. Jesus becomes an intelligible and consistent person. His reasons for going "like a lamb to the slaughter" instead of saving himself as Mahomet did, become quite clear. The narrative becomes as credible as any other historical narrative of its period.

MATTHEW
THE ANNUNCIATION:
THE MASSACRE: THE FLIGHT

Let us begin with the gospel of Matthew, bearing in mind that it does not profess to be the evidence of an eyewitness. It is a chronicle, founded, like other chronicles, on such evidence and records as the chronicler could get hold of. The only one of the evangelists who professes to give first-hand evidence as an eyewitness naturally takes care to say so; and the fact that Matthew makes no such pretension, and writes throughout as a chronicler, makes it clear that he is telling the story of Jesus as Holinshed told the story of Macbeth, except that, for a reason to be given later on, he must have collected his material and completed his book within the lifetime of persons contemporary with Jesus. Allowance must also be made for the fact that the gospel is

339

written in the Greek language, whilst the first-hand traditions and the actual utterances of Jesus must have been in Aramic, the dialect of Palestine. These distinctions are important, as you will find if you read Holinshed or Froissart and then read Benvenuto Cellini. You do not blame Holinshed or Froissart for believing and repeating the things they had read or been told, though you cannot always believe these things yourself. But when Cellini tells you that he saw this or did that, and you find it impossible to believe him, you lose patience with him, and are disposed to doubt everything in his autobiography. Do not forget, then, that Matthew is Holinshed and not Benvenuto. The very first pages of his narrative will put your attitude to the test.

Matthew tells us that the mother of Jesus was betrothed to a man of royal pedigree named Joseph, who was rich enough to live in a house in Bethlehem to which kings could bring gifts of gold without provoking any comment. An angel announces to Joseph that Jesus is the son of the Holy Ghost, and that he must not accuse her of infidelity because of her bearing a son of which he is not the father; but this episode disappears from the subsequent narrative: there is no record of its having been told to Jesus, nor any indication of his having any knowledge of it. The narrative, in fact, proceeds in all respects as if the annunciation formed no part of it.

Herod the Tetrarch, believing that a child has been born who will destroy him, orders all the male children to be slaughtered; and Jesus escapes by the flight of his parents into Egypt, whence they return to Nazareth when the danger is over. Here it is necessary to anticipate a little by saying that none of the other evangelists accepts this story, as none of them except John, who throws over Matthew altogether, shares his craze for treating history and biography as mere records of the fulfilment of ancient Jewish prophecies. This craze no doubt led him to seek for some legend bearing out Hosea's "Out of Egypt have I called my son," and Jeremiah's Rachel weeping for her children: in fact, he says so.

PREFACE

Nothing that interests us nowadays turns on the credibility of the massacre of the innocents and the flight into Egypt. We may forget them, and proceed to the important part of the narrative, which skips at once to the manhood of Jesus.

JOHN THE BAPTIST

At this moment, a Salvationist prophet named John is stirring the people very strongly. John has declared that the rite of circumcision is insufficient as a dedication of the individual to God, and has substituted the rite of baptism. To us, who are accustomed to baptism as a matter of course, and to whom circumcision is a rather ridiculous foreign practice of no consequence, the sensational effect of such a heresy as this on the Jews is not apparent: it seems to us as natural that John should have baptized people as that the rector of our village should do so. But, as St Paul found to his cost later on, the discarding of circumcision for baptism was to the Jews as startling a heresy as the discarding of transubstantiation in the Mass was to the Catholics of the XVI century.

JESUS JOINS THE BAPTISTS

Jesus entered as a man of thirty (Luke says) into the religious life of his time by going to John the Baptist and demanding baptism from him, much as certain well-to-do young gentlemen forty years ago "joined the Socialists." As far as established Jewry was concerned, he burnt his boats by this action, and cut himself off from the routine of wealth, respectability, and orthodoxy. He then began preaching John's gospel, which, apart from the heresy of baptism, the value of which lay in its bringing the Gentiles (that is, the uncircumcised) within the pale of salvation, was a call to the people to repent of their sins, as the kingdom of heaven was at hand. Luke adds that he also preached the communism of charity; told the surveyors of taxes not to over-assess the taxpayers; and advised soldiers to be content with their wages and not to be violent or lay false accusations. There is no record of John going beyond this.

341

ANDROCLES AND THE LION
THE SAVAGE JOHN AND THE
CIVILIZED JESUS

Jesus went beyond it very rapidly, according to Matthew. Though, like John, he became an itinerant preacher, he departed widely from John's manner of life. John went into the wilderness, not into the synagogues; and his baptismal font was the river Jordan. He was an ascetic, clothed in skins and living on locusts and wild honey, practising a savage austerity. He courted martyrdom, and met it at the hands of Herod. Jesus saw no merit either in asceticism or martyrdom. In contrast to John he was essentially a highly-civilized, cultivated person. According to Luke, he pointed out the contrast himself, chaffing the Jews for complaining that John must be possessed by the devil because he was a teetotaller and vegetarian, whilst, because Jesus was neither one nor the other, they reviled him as a gluttonous man and a winebibber, the friend of the officials and their mistresses. He told straitlaced disciples that they would have trouble enough from other people without making any for themselves, and that they should avoid martyrdom and enjoy themselves whilst they had the chance. "When they persecute you in this city," he says, "flee into the next." He preaches in the synagogues and in the open air indifferently, just as they come. He repeatedly says, "I desire mercy and not sacrifice," meaning evidently to clear himself of the inveterate superstition that suffering is gratifying to God. "Be not, as the Pharisees, of a sad countenance," he says. He is convivial, feasting with Roman officials and sinners. He is careless of his person, and is remonstrated with for not washing his hands before sitting down to table. The followers of John the Baptist, who fast, and who expect to find the Christians greater ascetics than themselves, are disappointed at finding that Jesus and his twelve friends do not fast; and Jesus tells them that they should rejoice in him instead of being melancholy. He is jocular, and tells them they will all have as much fasting as they want soon enough, whether they like it or not. He is not afraid of disease, and dines with

342

a leper. A woman, apparently to protect him against infection, pours a costly unguent on his head, and is rebuked because what it cost might have been given to the poor. He poohpoohs that lowspirited view, and says, as he said when he was reproached for not fasting, that the poor are always there to be helped, but that he is not there to be anointed always, implying that you should never lose a chance of being happy when there is so much misery in the world. He breaks the Sabbath; is impatient of conventionality when it is uncomfortable or obstructive; and outrages the feelings of the Jews by breaches of it. He is apt to accuse people who feel that way of hypocrisy. Like the late Samuel Butler, he regards disease as a department of sin, and on curing a lame man, says "Thy sins are forgiven" instead of "Arise and walk," subsequently maintaining, when the Scribes reproach him for assuming power to forgive sin as well as to cure disease, that the two come to the same thing. He has no modest affectations, and claims to be greater than Solomon or Jonah. When reproached, as Bunyan was, for resorting to the art of fiction when teaching in parables, he justifies himself on the ground that art is the only way in which the people can be taught. He is, in short, what we should call an artist and a Bohemian in his manner of life.

JESUS NOT A PROSELYTIST

A point of considerable practical importance today is that he expressly repudiates the idea that forms of religion, once rooted, can be weeded out and replanted with the flowers of a foreign faith. "If you try to root up the tares you will root up the wheat as well." Our proselytizing missionary enterprises are thus flatly contrary to his advice; and their results appear to bear him out in his view that if you convert a man brought up in another creed, you inevitably demoralize him. He acts on this view himself, and does not convert his disciples from Judaism to Christianity. To this day a Christian would be in religion a Jew initiated by baptism instead of circumcision, and accepting Jesus as the Messiah, and his teachings as of higher authority than those

343

of Moses, but for the action of the Jewish priests, who, to save Jewry from being submerged in the rising flood of Christianity after the capture of Jerusalem and the destruction of the Temple, set up what was practically a new religious order, with new Scriptures and elaborate new observances, and to their list of the accursed added one Jeschu, a bastard magician, whose comic rogueries brought him to a bad end like Punch or Til Eulenspiegel: an invention which cost them dear when the Christians got the upper hand of them politically. The Jew as Jesus, himself a Jew, knew him, never dreamt of such things, and could follow Jesus without ceasing to be a Jew.

THE TEACHINGS OF JESUS

So much for his personal life and temperament. His public career as a popular preacher carries him equally far beyond John the Baptist. He lays no stress on baptism or vows, and preaches conduct incessantly. He advocates communism, the widening of the private family with its cramping ties into the great family of mankind under the fatherhood of God, the abandonment of revenge and punishment, the counteracting of evil by good instead of by a hostile evil, and an organic conception of society in which you are not an independent individual but a member of society, your neighbor being another member, and each of you members one of another, as two fingers on a hand, the obvious conclusion being that unless you love your neighbor as yourself and he reciprocates you will both be the worse for it. He conveys all this with extraordinary charm, and entertains his hearers with fables (parables) to illustrate them. He has no synagogue or regular congregation, but travels from place to place with twelve men whom he has called from their work as he passed, and who have abandoned it to follow him.

THE MIRACLES

He has certain abnormal powers by which he can perform miracles. He is ashamed of these powers, but, being extremely compassionate, cannot refuse to exercise them when afflicted people beg him to cure them, when multitudes of people are hungry, and when his disciples are terrified by storms on the lakes. He asks for no reward, but begs the people not to mention these powers of his. There are two obvious reasons for his dislike of being known as a worker of miracles. One is the natural objection of all men who possess such powers, but have far more important business in the world than to exhibit them, to be regarded primarily as charlatans, besides being pestered to give exhibitions to satisfy curiosity. The other is that his view of the effect of miracles upon his mission is exactly that taken later on by Rousseau. He perceives that they will discredit him and divert attention from his doctrine by raising an entirely irrelevant issue between his disciples and his opponents.

Possibly my readers may not have studied Rousseau's Letters Written From The Mountain, which may be regarded as the classic work on miracles as credentials of divine mission. Rousseau shews, as Jesus foresaw, that the miracles are the main obstacle to the acceptance of Christianity, because their incredibility (if they were not incredible they would not be miracles) makes people sceptical as to the whole narrative, credible enough in the main, in which they occur, and suspicious of the doctrine with which they are thus associated. "Get rid of the miracles," said Rousseau, "and the whole world will fall at the feet of Jesus Christ." He points out that miracles offered as evidence of divinity, and failing to convince, make divinity ridiculous. He says, in effect, there is nothing in making a lame man walk: thousands of lame men have been cured and have walked without any miracle. Bring me a man with only one leg and make another grow instantaneously on him before my eyes, and I will be really impressed; but mere cures of ailments that have often been cured before are quite useless as evidence of anything else than desire to help and power to cure.

Jesus, according to Matthew, agreed so entirely with Rousseau, and felt the danger so strongly, that when people who were not ill or in trouble came to him and asked him to exercise his powers as a sign of his mission, he was irritated

345

beyond measure, and refused with an indignation which
they, not seeing Rousseau's point, must have thought very
unreasonable. To be called "an evil and adulterous generation" merely for asking a miracle worker to give an exhibition of his powers, is rather a startling experience. Mahomet,
by the way, also lost his temper when people asked him to
perform miracles. But Mahomet expressly disclaimed any
unusual powers; whereas it is clear from Matthew's story
that Jesus (unfortunately for himself, as he thought) had
some powers of healing. It is also obvious that the exercise
of such powers would give rise to wild tales of magical feats
which would expose their hero to condemnation as an impostor among people whose good opinion was of great consequence to the movement started by his mission.

But the deepest annoyance arising from the miracles
would be the irrelevance of the issue raised by them. Jesus's
teaching has nothing to do with miracles. If his mission had
been simply to demonstrate a new method of restoring lost
eyesight, the miracle of curing the blind would have been
entirely relevant. But to say "You should love your enemies;
and to convince you of this I will now proceed to cure this
gentleman of cataract" would have been, to a man of Jesus's
intelligence, the proposition of an idiot. If it could be proved
today that not one of the miracles of Jesus actually occurred,
that proof would not invalidate a single one of his didactic
utterances; and conversely, if it could be proved that not
only did the miracles actually occur, but that he had wrought
a thousand other miracles a thousand times more wonderful, not a jot of weight would be added to his doctrine. And
yet the intellectual energy of sceptics and divines has been
wasted for generations in arguing about the miracles on the
assumption that Christianity is at stake in the controversy
as to whether the stories of Matthew are false or true. According to Matthew himself, Jesus must have known this
only too well; for wherever he went he was assailed with a
clamor for miracles, though his doctrine created bewilderment.

346

So much for the miracles! Matthew tells us further, that Jesus declared that his doctrines would be attacked by Church and State, and that the common multitude were the salt of the earth and the light of the world. His disciples, in their relations with the political and ecclesiastical organizations, would be as sheep among wolves.

MATTHEW IMPUTES BIGOTRY TO JESUS

Matthew, like most biographers, strives to identify the opinions and prejudices of his hero with his own. Although he describes Jesus as tolerant even to carelessness, he draws the line at the Gentile, and represents Jesus as a bigoted Jew who regards his mission as addressed exclusively to "the lost sheep of the house of Israel." When a woman of Canaan begged Jesus to cure her daughter, he first refused to speak to her, and then told her brutally that "It is not meet to take the children's bread and cast it to the dogs." But when the woman said, "Truth, Lord; yet the dogs eat of the crumbs which fall from their master's table," she melted the Jew out of him and made Christ a Christian. To the woman whom he had just called a dog he said, "O woman, great is thy faith: be it unto thee even as thou wilt." This is somehow one of the most touching stories in the gospel; perhaps because the woman rebukes the prophet by a touch of his own finest quality. It is certainly out of character; but as the sins of good men are always out of character, it is not safe to reject the story as invented in the interest of Matthew's determination that Jesus shall have nothing to do with the Gentiles. At all events, there the story is; and it is by no means the only instance in which Matthew reports Jesus, in spite of the charm of his preaching, as extremely uncivil in private intercourse.

THE GREAT CHANGE

So far the history is that of a man sane and interesting apart from his special gifts as orator, healer, and prophet. But a startling change occurs. One day, after the disciples have discouraged him for a long time by their misunderstandings of his mission, and their speculations as to whether he is one of the old prophets come again, and if so, which, his disciple Peter suddenly solves the problem by exclaiming, "Thou art the Christ, the son of the living God." At this Jesus is extraordinarily pleased and excited. He declares that Peter has had a revelation straight from God. He makes a pun on Peter's name, and declares him the founder of his Church. And he accepts his destiny as a god by announcing that he will be killed when he goes to Jerusalem; for if he is really the Christ, it is a necessary part of his legendary destiny that he shall be slain. Peter, not understanding this, rebukes him for what seems mere craven melancholy; and Jesus turns fiercely on him and cries, "Get thee behind me, Satan."

Jesus now becomes obsessed with a conviction of his divinity, and talks about it continually to his disciples, though he forbids them to mention it to others. They begin to dispute among themselves as to the position they shall occupy in heaven when his kingdom is established. He rebukes them strenuously for this, and repeats his teaching that greatness means service and not domination; but he himself, always instinctively somewhat haughty, now becomes arrogant, dictatorial, and even abusive, never replying to his critics without an insulting epithet, and even cursing a fig-tree which disappoints him when he goes to it for fruit. He assumes all the traditions of the folk-lore gods, and announces that, like John Barleycorn, he will be barbarously slain and buried, but will rise from the earth and return to life. He attaches to himself the immemorial tribal ceremony of eating the god, by blessing bread and wine and handing them to his disciples with the words "This is my body: this is my blood." He forgets his own teaching and threatens eternal fire and eternal punishment. He announces, in addition to his Barleycorn resurrection, that he will come to the world a second time in glory and establish his kingdom on earth. He fears that this may lead to the appearance of impostors claiming to be himself, and declares explicitly and repeatedly that no matter what wonders these impostors

348

may perform, his own coming will be unmistakable, as the stars will fall from heaven, and trumpets be blown by angels. Further he declares that this will take place during the lifetime of persons then present.

JERUSALEM AND THE MYSTICAL SACRIFICE

In this new frame of mind he at last enters Jerusalem amid great popular curiosity; drives the moneychangers and sacrifice sellers out of the temple in a riot; refuses to interest himself in the beauties and wonders of the temple building on the ground that presently not a stone of it shall be left on another; reviles the high priests and elders in intolerable terms; and is arrested by night in a garden to avoid a popular disturbance. He makes no resistance, being persuaded that it is part of his destiny as a god to be murdered and to rise again. One of his followers shews fight, and cuts off the ear of one of his captors. Jesus rebukes him, but does not attempt to heal the wound, though he declares that if he wished to resist he could easily summon twelve million angels to his aid. He is taken before the high priest and by him handed over to the Roman governor, who is puzzled by his silent refusal to defend himself in any way, or to contradict his accusers or their witnesses, Pilate having naturally no idea that the prisoner conceives himself as going through an inevitable process of torment, death, and burial as a prelude to resurrection. Before the high priest he has also been silent except that when the priest asks him is he the Christ, the Son of God, he replies that they shall all see the Son of Man sitting at the right hand of power, and coming on the clouds of heaven. He maintains this attitude with frightful fortitude whilst they scourge him, mock him, torment him, and finally crucify him between two thieves. His prolonged agony of thirst and pain on the cross at last breaks his spirit, and he dies with a cry of "My God: why hast Thou forsaken me?"

NOT THIS MAN BUT BARABBAS

Meanwhile he has been definitely rejected by the people as well as by the priests. Pilate, pitying him, and unable to

349

make out exactly what he has done (the blasphemy that has horrified the high priest does not move the Roman), tries to get him off by reminding the people that they have, by custom, the right to have a prisoner released at that time, and suggests that he should release Jesus. But they insist on his releasing a prisoner named Barabbas instead, and on having Jesus crucified. Matthew gives no clue to the popularity of Barabbas, describing him simply as "a notable prisoner." The later gospels make it clear, very significantly, that his offence was sedition and insurrection; that he was an advocate of physical force; and that he had killed his man. The choice of Barabbas thus appears as a popular choice of the militant advocate of physical force as against the unresisting advocate of mercy.

THE RESURRECTION

Matthew then tells how after three days an angel opened the family vault of one Joseph, a rich man of Arimathea, who had buried Jesus in it, whereupon Jesus rose and returned from Jerusalem to Galilee and resumed his preaching with his disciples, assuring them that he would now be with them to the end of the world.

At that point the narrative abruptly stops. The story has no ending.

DATE OF MATTHEW'S NARRATIVE

One effect of the promise of Jesus to come again in glory during the lifetime of some of his hearers is to date the gospel without the aid of any scholarship. It must have been written during the lifetime of Jesus's contemporaries: that is, whilst it was still possible for the promise of his Second Coming to be fulfilled. The death of the last person who had been alive when Jesus said "There be some of them that stand here that shall in no wise taste death til they see the Son of Man coming in his kingdom" destroyed the last possibility of the promised Second Coming, and bore out the incredulity of Pilate and the Jews. And as Matthew writes as one believing in that Second Coming, and in fact left his story unfinished to be ended by it, he must have produced his gospel within

350

PREFACE

a lifetime of the crucifixion. Also, he must have believed that reading books would be one of the pleasures of the kingdom of heaven on earth.

CLASS TYPE OF MATTHEW'S JESUS

One more circumstance must be noted as gathered from Matthew. Though he begins his story in such a way as to suggest that Jesus belonged to the privileged classes, he mentions later on that when Jesus attempted to preach in his own country, and had no success there, the people said, "Is not this the carpenter's son?" But Jesus's manner throughout is that of an aristocrat, or at the very least the son of a rich bourgeois, and by no means a lowly-minded one at that. We must be careful therefore to conceive Joseph, not as a modern proletarian carpenter working for weekly wages, but as a master craftsman of royal descent. John the Baptist may have been a Keir Hardie; but the Jesus of Matthew is of the Ruskin-Morris class.

This haughty characterization is so marked that if we had no other documents concerning Jesus than the gospel of Matthew, we should not feel as we do about him. We should have been much less loth to say, "There is a man here who was sane until Peter hailed him as the Christ, and who then became a monomaniac." We should have pointed out that his delusion is a very common delusion among the insane, and that such insanity is quite consistent with the retention of the argumentative cunning and penetration which Jesus displayed in Jerusalem after his delusion had taken complete hold of him. We should feel horrified at the scourging and mocking and crucifixion just as we should if Ruskin had been treated in that way when he also went mad, instead of being cared for as an invalid. And we should have had no clear perception of any special significance in his way of calling the Son of God the Son of Man. We should have noticed that he was a Communist; that he regarded much of what we call law and order as machinery for robbing the poor under legal forms; that he thought domestic ties a snare for the soul; that he agreed with the proverb "The

351

nearer the Church, the farther from God"; that he saw very plainly that the masters of the community should be its servants and not its oppressors and parasites; and that though he did not tell us not to fight our enemies, he did tell us to love them, and warned us that they who draw the sword shall perish by the sword. All this shews a great power of seeing through vulgar illusions, and a capacity for a higher morality than has yet been established in any civilized community; but it does not place Jesus above Confucius or Plato, not to mention more modern philosophers and moralists.

MARK

THE WOMEN DISCIPLES AND THE ASCENSION

Let us see whether we can get anything more out of Mark, whose gospel, by the way, is supposed to be older than Matthew's. Mark is brief; and it does not take long to discover that he adds nothing to Matthew except the ending of the story by Christ's ascension into heaven, and the news that many women had come with Jesus to Jerusalem, including Mary Magdalene, out of whom he had cast seven devils. On the other hand Mark says nothing about the birth of Jesus, and does not touch his career until his adult baptism by John. He apparently regards Jesus as a native of Nazareth, as John does, and not of Bethlehem, as Matthew and Luke do, Bethlehem being the city of David, from whom Jesus is said by Matthew and Luke to be descended. He describes John's doctrine as "Baptism of repentance unto remission of sins": that is, a form of Salvationism. He tells us that Jesus went into the synagogues and taught, not as the Scribes but as one having authority: that is, we infer, he preaches his own doctrine as an original moralist instead of repeating what the books say. He describes the miracle of Jesus reaching the boat by walking across the sea, but says nothing about Peter trying to do the same. Mark sees what he relates more vividly than Matthew, and gives touches of detail that bring the event more clearly before the reader. He says, for instance, that when Jesus walked on the waves

352

to the boat, he was passing it by when the disciples called out to him. He seems to feel that Jesus's treatment of the woman of Canaan requires some apology, and therefore says that she was a Greek of Syrophenician race, which probably excused any incivility to her in Mark's eyes. He represents the father of the boy whom Jesus cured of epilepsy after the transfiguration as a sceptic who says "Lord, I believe: help thou mine unbelief." He tells the story of the widow's mite, omitted by Matthew. He explains that Barabbas was "lying bound with them that made insurrection, men who in the insurrection had committed murder." Joseph of Arimathea, who buried Jesus in his own tomb, and who is described by Matthew as a disciple, is described by Mark as "one who also himself was looking for the kingdom of God," which suggests that he was an independent seeker. Mark earns our gratitude by making no mention of the old prophecies, and thereby not only saves time, but avoids the absurd implication that Christ was merely going through a predetermined ritual, like the works of a clock, instead of living. Finally Mark reports Christ as saying, after his resurrection, that those who believe in him will be saved and those who do not, damned; but it is impossible to discover whether he means anything by a state of damnation beyond a state of error. The paleographers regard this passage as tacked on by a later scribe.

On the whole Mark leaves the modern reader where Matthew left him.

LUKE

LUKE THE LITERARY ARTIST

When we come to Luke, we come to a later story-teller, and one with a stronger natural gift for his art. Before you have read twenty lines of Luke's gospel you are aware that you have passed from the chronicler writing for the sake of recording important facts, to the artist, telling the story for the sake of telling it. At the very outset he achieves the most charming idyll in the Bible: the story of Mary crowded out of the inn into the stable and laying her newly-born son in the manger, and of the shepherds abiding in the field keeping watch over their flocks by night, and how the angel of the Lord came upon them, and the glory of the Lord shone around them, and suddenly there was with the angel a multitude of the heavenly host. These shepherds go to the stable and take the place of the kings in Matthew's chronicle. So completely has this story conquered and fascinated our imagination that most of us suppose all the gospels to contain it; but it is Luke's story and his alone: none of the others have the smallest hint of it.

THE CHARM OF LUKE'S NARRATIVE

Luke gives the charm of sentimental romance to every incident. The Annunciation, as described by Matthew, is made to Joseph, and is simply a warning to him not to divorce his wife for misconduct. In Luke's gospel it is made to Mary herself, at much greater length, with a sense of the ecstasy of the bride of the Holy Ghost. Jesus is refined and softened almost out of recognition: the stern peremptory disciple of John the Baptist, who never addresses a Pharisee or a Scribe without an insulting epithet, becomes a considerate, gentle, sociable, almost urbane person; and the Chauvinist Jew becomes a pro-Gentile who is thrown out of the synagogue in his own town for reminding the congregation that the prophets had sometimes preferred Gentiles to Jews. In fact they try to throw him down from a sort of Tarpeian rock which they use for executions; but he makes his way through them and escapes: the only suggestion of a feat of arms on his part in the gospels. There is not a word of the Syrophenician woman. At the end he is calmly superior to his sufferings; delivers an address on his way to execution with unruffled composure; does not despair on the cross; and dies with perfect dignity, commending his spirit to God, after praying for the forgiveness of his persecutors on the ground that "They know not what they do." According to Matthew, it is part of the bitterness of his death that even the thieves who are crucified with him revile him. According to Luke, only one of them does this; and he

354

PREFACE

is rebuked by the other, who begs Jesus to remember him when he comes into his kingdom. To which Jesus replies, "This day shalt thou be with me in Paradise," implying that he will spend the three days of his death there. In short, every device is used to get rid of the ruthless horror of the Matthew chronicle, and to relieve the strain of the Passion by touching episodes, and by representing Christ as superior to human suffering. It is Luke's Jesus who has won our hearts.

THE TOUCH OF PARISIAN ROMANCE

Luke's romantic shrinking from unpleasantness, and his sentimentality, are illustrated by his version of the woman with the ointment. Matthew and Mark describe it as taking place in the house of Simon the Leper, where it is objected to as a waste of money. In Luke's version the leper becomes a rich Pharisee; the woman becomes a Dame aux Camellias; and nothing is said about money and the poor. The woman washes the feet of Jesus with her tears and dries them with her hair; and he is reproached for suffering a sinful woman to touch him. It is almost an adaptation of the unromantic Matthew to the Parisian stage. There is a distinct attempt to increase the feminine interest all through. The slight lead given by Mark is taken up and developed. More is said about Jesus's mother and her feelings. Christ's following of women, just mentioned by Mark to account for their presence at his tomb, is introduced earlier; and some of the women are named; so that we are introduced to Joanna the wife of Chuza, Herod's steward, and Susanna. There is the quaint little domestic episode between Mary and Martha. There is the parable of the Prodigal Son, appealing to the indulgence romance has always shewn to Charles Surface and Des Grieux. Women follow Jesus to the cross; and he makes them a speech beginning "Daughters of Jerusalem." Slight as these changes may seem, they make a great change in the atmosphere. The Christ of Matthew could never have become what is vulgarly called a woman's hero (though the truth is that the popular demand for sentiment, as far as it is

not simply human, is more manly than womanly); but the
Christ of Luke has made possible those pictures which now
hang in many ladies' chambers, in which Jesus is represented
exactly as he is represented in the Lourdes cinematograph,
by a handsome actor. The only touch of realism which Luke
does not instinctively suppress for the sake of producing
this kind of amenity is the reproach addressed to Jesus for
sitting down to table without washing his hands; and that is
retained because an interesting discourse hangs on it.

WAITING FOR THE MESSIAH

Another new feature in Luke's story is that it begins in
a world in which everyone is expecting the advent of the
Christ. In Matthew and Mark, Jesus comes into a normal
Philistine world like our own of today. Not until the Baptist
foretells that one greater than himself shall come after him
does the old Jewish hope of a Messiah begin to stir again;
and as Jesus begins as a disciple of John, and is baptized by
him, nobody connects him with that hope until Peter has
the sudden inspiration which produces so startling an effect
on Jesus. But in Luke's gospel men's minds, and especially
women's minds, are full of eager expectation of a Christ not
only before the birth of Jesus, but before the birth of John
the Baptist, the event with which Luke begins his story.
Whilst Jesus and John are still in their mothers' wombs,
John leaps at the approach of Jesus when the two mothers
visit one another. At the circumcision of Jesus pious men
and women hail the infant as the Christ.

The Baptist himself is not convinced; for at quite a late
period in his former disciple's career he sends two young
men to ask Jesus is he really the Christ. This is noteworthy
because Jesus immediately gives them a deliberate exhibition of miracles, and bids them tell John what they have
seen, and ask him what he thinks *now*. This is in complete
contradiction to what I have called the Rousseau view of
miracles as inferred from Matthew. Luke shews all a ro-
mancer's thoughtlessness about miracles: he regards them
as "signs": that is, as proofs of the divinity of the person

performing them, and not merely of thaumaturgic powers. He revels in miracles just as he revels in parables: they make such capital stories. He cannot allow the calling of Peter, James, and John from their boats to pass without a comic miraculous overdraft of fishes, with the net sinking the boats and provoking Peter to exclaim, "Depart from me; for I am a sinful man, O Lord," which should probably be translated, "I want no more of your miracles: natural fishing is good enough for my boats."

There are some other novelties in Luke's version. Pilate sends Jesus to Herod, who happens to be in Jerusalem just then, because Herod had expressed some curiosity about him; but nothing comes of it: the prisoner will not speak to him. When Jesus is ill received in a Samaritan village James and John propose to call down fire from heaven and destroy it; and Jesus replies that he is come not to destroy lives but to save them. The bias of Jesus against lawyers is emphasized, and also his resolution not to admit that he is more bound to his relatives than to strangers. He snubs a woman who blesses his mother. As this is contrary to the traditions of sentimental romance, Luke would presumably have avoided it had he not become persuaded that the brotherhood of Man and the Fatherhood of God are superior even to sentimental considerations. The story of the lawyer asking what are the two chief commandments is changed by making Jesus put the question to the lawyer instead of answering it.

As to doctrine, Luke is only clear when his feelings are touched. His logic is weak; for some of the sayings of Jesus are pieced together wrongly, as anyone who has read them in the right order and context in Matthew will discover at once. He does not make anything new out of Christ's mission, and, like the other evangelists, thinks that the whole point of it is that Jesus was the long expected Christ, and that he will presently come back to earth and establish his kingdom, having duly died and risen again after three days. Yet Luke not only records the teaching as to communism and the discarding of hate, which have, of course, nothing to do with the Second Coming, but quotes one very remarkable saying which is not compatible with it, which is, that people must not go about asking where the kingdom of heaven is, and saying "Lo, here!" and "Lo, there!" because the kingdom of heaven is within them. But Luke has no sense that this belongs to a quite different order of thought to his Christianity, and retains undisturbed his view of the kingdom as a locality as definite as Jerusalem or Madagascar.

JOHN
A NEW STORY AND A NEW CHARACTER

The gospel of John is a surprise after the others. Matthew, Mark and Luke describe the same events in the same order (the variations in Luke are negligible), and their gospels are therefore called the synoptic gospels. They tell substantially the same story of a wandering preacher who at the end of his life came to Jerusalem. John describes a preacher who spent practically his whole adult life in the capital, with occasional visits to the provinces. His circumstantial account of the calling of Peter and the sons of Zebedee is quite different from the others; and he says nothing about their being fishermen. He says expressly that Jesus, though baptized by John, did not himself practise baptism, and that his disciples did. Christ's agonized appeal against his doom in the garden of Gethsemane becomes a cold-blooded suggestion made in the temple at a much earlier period. Jesus argues much more; complains a good deal of the unreasonableness and dislike with which he is met; is by no means silent before Caiaphas and Pilate; lays much greater stress on his resurrection and on the eating of his body (losing all his disciples except the twelve in consequence); says many apparently contradictory and nonsensical things to which no ordinary reader can now find any clue; and gives the impression of an educated, not to say sophisticated mystic, different both in character and schooling from the simple and downright preacher of Matthew and Mark, and the urbane easyminded charmer of Luke. Indeed, the Jews say of him

"How knoweth this man letters, having never learnt?"

JOHN THE IMMORTAL EYE-WITNESS

John, moreover, claims to be not only a chronicler but a witness. He declares that he is "the disciple whom Jesus loved," and that he actually leaned on the bosom of Jesus at the last supper and asked in a whisper which of them it was that should betray him. Jesus whispered that he would give a sop to the traitor, and thereupon handed one to Judas, who ate it and immediately became possessed by the devil. This is more natural than the other accounts, in which Jesus openly indicates Judas without eliciting any protest or exciting any comment. It also implies that Jesus deliberately bewitched Judas in order to bring about his own betrayal. Later on John claims that Jesus said to Peter "If I will that John tarry til I come, what is that to thee?" and John, with a rather obvious mock modesty, adds that he must not claim to be immortal, as the disciples concluded; for Christ did not use that expression, but merely remarked "If I will that he tarry til I come." No other evangelist claims personal intimacy with Christ, or even pretends to be his contemporary (there is no ground for identifying Matthew the publican with Matthew the Evangelist); and John is the only evangelist whose account of Christ's career and character is hopelessly irreconcilable with Matthew's. He is almost as bad as Matthew, by the way, in his repeated explanations of Christ's actions as having no other purpose than to fulfill the old prophecies. The impression is more unpleasant, because, as John, unlike Matthew, is educated, subtle, and obsessed with artificial intellectual mystifications, the discovery that he is stupid or superficial in so simple a matter strikes one with distrust and dislike, in spite of his great literary charm, a good example of which is his transfiguration of the harsh episode of the Syrophenician woman into the pleasant story of the woman of Samaria. This perhaps is why his claim to be John the disciple, or to be a contemporary of Christ or even of any survivor of Christ's generation, has been disputed, and finally, it seems, disallowed. But I repeat, I take

359

no note here of the disputes of experts as to the date of the
gospels, not because I am not acquainted with them, but
because, as the earliest codices are Greek manuscripts of the
fourth century A. D., and the Syrian ones are translations
from the Greek, the paleographic expert has no difficulty in
arriving at whatever conclusion happens to suit his beliefs
or disbeliefs; and he never succeeds in convincing the other
experts except when they believe or disbelieve exactly as he
does. Hence I conclude that the dates of the original narratives cannot be ascertained, and that we must make the best
of the evangelists' own accounts of themselves. There is, as
we have seen, a very marked difference between them, leaving no doubt that we are dealing with four authors of well-
marked diversity; but they all end in an attitude of expect-
ancy of the Second Coming which they agree in declaring
Jesus to have positively and unequivocally promised within
the lifetime of his contemporaries. Any believer compiling
a gospel after the last of these contemporaries had passed
away, would either reject and omit the tradition of that promise on the ground that since it was not fulfilled, and could
never now be fulfilled, it could not have been made, or else
have had to confess to the Jews, who were the keenest critics
of the Christians, that Jesus was either an impostor or the
victim of a delusion. Now all the evangelists except Matthew
expressly declare themselves to be believers; and Matthew's
narrative is obviously not that of a sceptic. I therefore assume
as a matter of common sense that, interpolations apart, the
gospels are derived from narratives written in the first century A. D. I include John, because though it may be claimed
that he hedged his position by claiming that Christ, who
specially loved him, endowed him with a miraculous life
until the Second Coming, the conclusion being that John is
alive at this moment, I cannot believe that a literary forger
could hope to save the situation by so outrageous a pretension. Also, John's narrative is in many passages nearer to the
realities of public life than the simple chronicle of Matthew
or the sentimental romance of Luke. This may be because

John was obviously more a man of the world than the others, and knew, as mere chroniclers and romancers never know, what actually happens away from books and desks. But it may also be because he saw and heard what happened instead of collecting traditions about it. The paleographers and daters of first quotations may say what they please: John's claim to give evidence as an eyewitness whilst the others are only compiling history is supported by a certain verisimilitude which appeals to me as one who has preached a new doctrine and argued about it, as well as written stories. This verisimilitude may be dramatic art backed by knowledge of public life; but even at that we must not forget that the best dramatic art is the operation of a divinatory instinct for truth. Be that as it may, John was certainly not the man to believe in the Second Coming and yet give a date for it after that date had passed. There is really no escape from the conclusion that the originals of all the gospels date from the period within which there was still a possibility of the Second Coming occurring at the promised time.

THE PECULIAR THEOLOGY OF JESUS

In spite of the suspicions roused by John's idiosyncrasies, his narrative is of enormous importance to those who go to the gospels for a credible modern religion. For it is John who adds to the other records such sayings as that "I and my father are one"; that "God is a spirit"; that the aim of Jesus is not only that the people should have life, but that they should have it "more abundantly" (a distinction much needed by people who think a man is either alive or dead, and never consider the important question how much alive he is); and that men should bear in mind what they were told in the 82nd Psalm: that they are gods, and are responsible for the doing of the mercy and justice of God. The Jews stoned him for saying these things, and, when he remonstrated with them for stupidly stoning one who had done nothing to them but good works, replied "For a good work we stone thee not; but for blasphemy, because that thou, being a man, makest thyself God." He insists (refer-

361

ring to the 82nd Psalm) that if it is part of their own religion
that they are gods on the assurance of God himself, it cannot
be blasphemy for him, whom the Father sanctified and sent
into the world, to say "I am the son of God." But they will
not have this at any price; and he has to escape from their
fury. Here the point is obscured by the distinction made by
Jesus between himself and other men. He says, in effect, "If
you are gods, then, *à fortiori*, I am a god." John makes him
say this, just as he makes him say "I am the light of the
world." But Matthew makes him say to the people "Ye are
the light of the world." John has no grip of the significance
of these scraps which he has picked up: he is far more interested in a notion of his own that men can escape death
and do even more extraordinary things than Christ himself:
in fact, he actually represents Jesus as promising this explicitly, and is finally led into the audacious hint that he,
John, is himself immortal in the flesh. Still, he does not miss
the significant sayings altogether. However inconsistent
they may be with the doctrine he is consciously driving at,
they appeal to some sub-intellectual instinct in him that
makes him stick them in, like a child sticking tinsel stars
on the robe of a toy angel.

John does not mention the ascension; and the end of his
narrative leaves Christ restored to life, and appearing from
time to time among his disciples. It is on one of these occasions that John describes the miraculous draught of fishes
which Luke places at the other end of Christ's career, at the
call of the sons of Zebedee.

JOHN AGREED AS TO THE TRIAL AND CRUCIFIXION

Although John, following his practice of shewing Jesus's
skill as a debater, makes him play a less passive part at his
trial, he still gives substantially the same account of it as all
the rest. And the question that would occur to any modern
reader never occurs to him, any more than it occurred to
Matthew, Mark, or Luke. That question is, Why on earth
did not Jesus defend himself, and make the people rescue

him from the High Priest? He was so popular that they were unable to prevent him driving the moneychangers out of the temple, or to arrest him for it. When they did arrest him afterwards, they had to do it at night in a garden. He could have argued with them as he had often done in the temple, and justified himself both to the Jewish law and to Caesar. And he had physical force at his command to back up his arguments: all that was needed was a speech to rally his followers; and he was not gagged. The reply of the evangelists would have been that all these inquiries are idle, because if Jesus had wished to escape, he could have saved himself all that trouble by doing what John describes him as doing: that is, casting his captors to the earth by an exertion of his miraculous power. If you asked John why he let them get up again and torment and execute him, John would have replied that it was part of the destiny of God to be slain and buried and to rise again, and that to have avoided this destiny would have been to repudiate his Godhead. And that is the only apparent explanation. Whether you believe with the evangelists that Christ could have rescued himself by a miracle, or, as a modern Secularist, point out that he could have defended himself effectually, the fact remains that according to all the narratives he did not do so. He had to die like a god, not to save himself "like one of the princes."[1] The consensus on this point is important, because it proves the absolute sincerity of Jesus's declaration that he was a god. No impostor would have accepted such dreadful consequences without an effort to save himself. No impostor would have been nerved to endure them by the conviction that he would rise from the grave and live again after three

---

[1] Jesus himself had referred to that psalm (LXXXII) in which men who have judged unjustly and accepted the persons of the wicked (including by anticipation practically all the white inhabitants of the British Isles and the North American continent, to mention no other places) are condemned in the words, "I have said, ye are gods; and all of ye are children of the Most High; but ye shall die like men, and fall like one of the princes."

days. If we accept the story at all, we must believe this, and believe also that his promise to return in glory and establish his kingdom on earth within the lifetime of men then living, was one which he believed that he could, and indeed must fulfil. Two evangelists declare that in his last agony he despaired, and reproached God for forsaking him. The other two represent him as dying in unshaken conviction and charity with the simple remark that the ordeal was finished. But all four testify that his faith was not deceived, and that he actually rose again after three days. And I think it unreasonable to doubt that all four wrote their narratives in full faith that the other promise would be fulfilled too, and that they themselves might live to witness the Second Coming.

CREDIBILITY OF THE GOSPELS

It will be noted by the older among my readers, who are sure to be obsessed more or less by elderly wrangles as to whether the gospels are credible as matter-of-fact narratives, that I have hardly raised this question, and have accepted the credible and incredible with equal complacency. I have done this because credibility is a subjective condition, as the evolution of religious belief clearly shews. Belief is not dependent on evidence and reason. There is as much evidence that the miracles occurred as that the battle of Waterloo occurred, or that a large body of Russian troops passed through England in 1914 to take part in the war on the western front. The reasons for believing in the murder of Pompey are the same as the reasons for believing in the raising of Lazarus. Both have been believed and doubted by men of equal intelligence. Miracles, in the sense of phenomena we cannot explain, surround us on every hand: life itself is the miracle of miracles. Miracles in the sense of events that violate the normal course of our experience are vouched for every day: the flourishing Church of Christ Scientist is founded on a multitude of such miracles. Nobody believes all the miracles: everybody believes some of them. I cannot tell why men who will not believe that Jesus ever existed yet believe firmly that Shakespear was Bacon. I can-

364

not tell why people who believe that angels appeared and fought on our side at the battle of Mons, and who believe that miracles occur quite frequently at Lourdes, nevertheless boggle at the miracle of the liquefaction of the blood of St Januarius, and reject it as a trick of priestcraft. I cannot tell why people who will not believe Matthew's story of three kings bringing costly gifts to the cradle of Jesus, believe Luke's story of the shepherds and the stable. I cannot tell why people, brought up to believe the Bible in the old literal way as an infallible record and revelation, and rejecting that view later on, begin by rejecting the Old Testament, and give up the belief in a brimstone hell before they give up (if they ever do) the belief in a heaven of harps, crowns, and thrones. I cannot tell why people who will not believe in baptism on any terms believe in vaccination with the cruel fanaticism of inquisitors. I am convinced that if a dozen sceptics were to draw up in parallel columns a list of the events narrated in the gospels which they consider credible and incredible respectively, their lists would be different in several particulars. Belief is literally a matter of taste.

FASHIONS IN BELIEF

Now matters of taste are mostly also matters of fashion. We are conscious of a difference between medieval fashions in belief and modern fashions. For instance, though we are more credulous than men were in the Middle Ages, and entertain such crowds of fortune-tellers, magicians, miracle workers, agents of communication with the dead, discoverers of the elixir of life, transmuters of metals, and healers of all sorts, as the Middle Ages never dreamed of as possible, yet we will not take our miracles in the form that convinced the Middle Ages. Arithmetical numbers appealed to the Middle Ages just as they do to us, because they are difficult to deal with, and because the greatest masters of numbers, the Newtons and Leibnitzes, rank among the greatest men. But there are fashions in numbers too. The Middle Ages took a fancy to some familiar number like seven; and because it was an odd number, and the world was made in seven days, and there are seven stars in Charles's Wain, and for a dozen other reasons, they were ready to believe anything that had a seven or a seven times seven in it. Seven deadly sins, seven swords of sorrow in the heart of the Virgin, seven champions of Christendom, seemed obvious and reasonable things to believe in simply because they were seven. To us, on the contrary, the number seven is the stamp of superstition. We will believe in nothing less than millions. A medieval doctor gained his patient's confidence by telling him that his vitals were being devoured by seven worms. Such a diagnosis would ruin a modern physician. The modern physician tells his patient that he is ill because every drop of his blood is swarming with a million microbes; and the patient believes him abjectly and instantly. Had a bishop told William the Conqueror that the sun was seventy-seven miles distant from the earth, William would have believed him not only out of respect for the Church, but because he would have felt that seventy-seven miles was the proper distance. The Kaiser, knowing just as little about it as the Conqueror, would send that bishop to an asylum. Yet he (I presume) unhesitatingly accepts the estimate of ninety-two and nine-tenths millions of miles, or whatever the latest big figure may be.

CREDIBILITY AND TRUTH

And here I must remind you that our credulity is not to be measured by the truth of the things we believe. When men believed that the earth was flat, they were not credulous: they were using their common sense, and, if asked to prove that the earth was flat, would have said simply, "Look at it." Those who refuse to believe that it is round are exercising a wholesome scepticism. The modern man who believes that the earth is round is grossly credulous. Flat Earth men drive him to fury by confuting him with the greatest ease when he tries to argue about it. Confront him with a theory that the earth is cylindrical, or annular, or hour-glass shaped, and he is lost. The thing he believes may be true, but that is not why he believes it: he believes it because in some mysterious way it appeals to his imagination. If you ask him why

366

he believes that the sun is ninety-odd million miles off, either he will have to confess that he doesnt know, or he will say that Newton proved it. But he has not read the treatise in which Newton proved it, and does not even know that it was written in Latin. If you press an Ulster Protestant as to why he regards Newton as an infallible authority, and St Thomas Aquinas or the Pope as superstitious liars whom, after his death, he will have the pleasure of watching from his place in heaven whilst they roast in eternal flame, or if you ask me why I take into serious consideration Colonel Sir Almroth Wright's estimates of the number of streptococci contained in a given volume of serum whilst I can only laugh at the earlier estimates of the number of angels that can be accommodated on the point of a needle, no reasonable reply is possible except that somehow sevens and angels are out of fashion, and billions and streptococci are all the rage. I simply cannot tell you why Bacon, Montaigne, and Cervantes had a quite different fashion of credulity and incredulity from the Venerable Bede and Piers Plowman and the divine doctors of the Aquinas-Aristotle school, who were certainly no stupider, and had the same facts before them. Still less can I explain why, if we assume that these leaders of thought had all reasoned out their beliefs, their authority seemed conclusive to one generation and blasphemous to another, neither generation having followed the reasoning or gone into the facts of the matter for itself at all.

It is therefore idle to begin disputing with the reader as to what he should believe in the gospels and what he should disbelieve. He will believe what he can, and disbelieve what he must. If he draws any lines at all, they will be quite arbitrary ones. St John tells us that when Jesus explicitly claimed divine honors by the sacrament of his body and blood, so many of his disciples left him that their number was reduced to twelve. Many modern readers will not hold out so long: they will give in at the first miracle. Others will discriminate. They will accept the healing miracles, and reject the feeding of the multitude. To some the walking on

367

the water will be a legendary exaggeration of a swim, ending in an ordinary rescue of Peter; and the raising of Lazarus will be only a similar glorification of a commonplace feat of artificial respiration, whilst others will scoff at it as a planned imposture in which Lazarus acted as a confederate. Between the rejection of the stories as wholly fabulous and the acceptance of them as the evangelists themselves mean them to be accepted, there will be many shades of belief and disbelief, of sympathy and derision. It is not a question of being a Christian or not. A Mahometan Arab will accept literally and without question parts of the narrative which an English Archbishop has to reject or explain away; and many Theosophists and lovers of the wisdom of India, who never enter a Christian Church except as sightseers, will revel in parts of John's gospel which mean nothing to a pious matter-of-fact Bradford manufacturer. Every reader takes from the Bible what he can get. In submitting a précis of the gospel narratives I have not implied any estimate either of their credibility or of their truth. I have simply informed him or reminded him, as the case may be, of what those narratives tell us about their hero.

CHRISTIAN ICONOLATRY AND THE PERIL OF THE ICONOCLAST

I must now abandon this attitude, and make a serious draft on the reader's attention by facing the question whether, if and when the medieval and Methodist will-to-believe the Salvationist and miraculous side of the gospel narratives fails us, as it plainly has failed the leaders of modern thought, there will be anything left of the mission of Jesus: whether, in short, we may not throw the gospels into the waste-paper basket, or put them away on the fiction shelf of our libraries. I venture to reply that we shall be, on the contrary, in the position of the man in Bunyan's riddle who found that "the more he threw away, the more he had." We get rid, to begin with, of the idolatrous or iconographic worship of Christ. By this I mean literally that worship which is given to pictures and statues of him, and to finished and unalterable stories about him. The test of the prevalence of this is that if you speak or write of Jesus as a real live person, or even as a still active God, such wor-- shippers are more horrified than Don Juan was when the statue stepped from its pedestal and came to supper with him. You may deny the divinity of Jesus; you may doubt whether he ever existed; you may reject Christianity for Judaism, Mahometanism, Shintoism, or Fire Worship; and the iconolaters, placidly contemptuous, will only classify you as a freethinker or a heathen. But if you venture to wonder how Christ would have looked if he had shaved and had his hair cut, or what size in shoes he took, or whether he swore when he stood on a nail in the carpenter's shop, or could not button his robe when he was in a hurry, or whether he laughed over the repartees by which he baffled the priests when they tried to trap him into sedition and blasphemy, or even if you tell any part of his story in the vivid terms of modern colloquial slang, you will produce an extraordinary dismay and horror among the iconolaters. You will have made the picture come out of its frame, the statue descend from its pedestal, the story become real, with all the incalculable consequences that may flow from this terrifying miracle. It is at such moments that you realize that the iconolaters have never for a moment conceived Christ as a real person who meant what he said, as a fact, as a force like electricity, only needing the invention of suitable political machinery to be applied to the affairs of mankind with revolutionary effect.

Thus it is not disbelief that is dangerous in our society: it is belief. The moment it strikes you (as it may any day) that Christ is not the lifeless harmless image he has hitherto been to you, but a rallying centre for revolutionary influences which all established States and Churches fight, you must look to yourselves; for you have brought the image to life; and the mob may not be able to bear that horror.

THE ALTERNATIVE TO BARABBAS
But mobs must be faced if civilization is to be saved. It

did not need the present war to shew that neither the iconographic Christ nor the Christ of St Paul has succeeded in
effecting the salvation of human society. Whilst I write, the
Turks are said to be massacring the Armenian Christians
on an unprecedented scale; but Europe is not in a position
to remonstrate; for her Christians are slaying one another
by every device which civilization has put within their
reach as busily as they are slaying the Turks. Barabbas is
triumphant everywhere; and the final use he makes of his
triumph is to lead us all to suicide with heroic gestures and
resounding lies. Now those who, like myself, see the Barabbasque social organization as a failure, and are convinced
that the Life Force (or whatever you choose to call it) cannot be finally beaten by any failure, and will even supersede
humanity by evolving a higher species if we cannot master
the problems raised by the multiplication of our own numbers, have always known that Jesus had a real message, and
have felt the fascination of his character and doctrine. Not
that we should nowadays dream of claiming any supernatural authority for him, much less the technical authority
which attaches to an educated modern philosopher and
jurist. But when, having entirely got rid of Salvationist
Christianity, and even contracted a prejudice against Jesus
on the score of his involuntary connection with it, we engage
on a purely scientific study of economics, criminology, and
biology, and find that our practical conclusions are virtually
those of Jesus, we are distinctly pleased and encouraged to
find that we were doing him an injustice, and that the nim-
bus that surrounds his head in the pictures may be interpreted some day as a light of science rather than a declaration of sentiment or a label of idolatry.

The doctrines in which Jesus is thus confirmed are,
roughly, the following:

1. The kingdom of heaven is within you. You are the
son of God; and God is the son of man. God is a spirit, to
be worshipped in spirit and in truth, and not an elderly
gentleman to be bribed and begged from. We are members

370

one of another; so that you cannot injure or help your neighbor without injuring or helping yourself. God is your father: you are here to do God's work; and you and your father are one.

2. Get rid of property by throwing it into the common stock. Dissociate your work entirely from money payments. If you let a child starve you are letting God starve. Get rid of all anxiety about tomorrow's dinner and clothes, because you cannot serve two masters: God and Mammon.

3. Get rid of judges and punishment and revenge. Love your neighbor as yourself, he being a part of yourself. And love your enemies: they are your neighbors.

4. Get rid of your family entanglements. Every mother you meet is as much your mother as the woman who bore you. Every man you meet is as much your brother as the man she bore after you. Dont waste your time at family funerals grieving for your relatives: attend to life, not to death: there are as good fish in the sea as ever came out of it, and better. In the kingdom of heaven, which, as aforesaid, is within you, there is no marriage nor giving in marriage, because you cannot devote your life to two divinities: God and the person you are married to.

Now these are very interesting propositions; and they become more interesting every day, as experience and science drive us more and more to consider them favorably. In considering them, we shall waste our time unless we give them a reasonable construction. We must assume that the man who saw his way through such a mass of popular passion and illusion as stands between us and a sense of the value of such teaching was quite aware of all the objections that occur to an average stockbroker in the first five minutes. It is true that the world is governed to a considerable extent by the considerations that occur to stockbrokers in the first five minutes; but as the result is that the world is so badly governed that those who know the truth can hardly bear to live in it, an objection from an average stockbroker constitutes in itself a *prima facie* case for any social reform.

ANDROCLES AND THE LION
THE REDUCTION TO MODERN PRACTICE OF CHRISTIANITY

All the same, we must reduce the ethical counsels and proposals of Jesus to modern practice if they are to be of any use to us. If we ask our stockbroker to act simply as Jesus advised his disciples to act, he will reply, very justly, "You are advising me to become a tramp." If we urge a rich man to sell all that he has and give it to the poor, he will inform us that such an operation is impossible. If he sells his shares and his lands, their purchaser will continue all those activities which oppress the poor. If all the rich men take the advice simultaneously the shares will fall to zero and the lands be unsaleable. If one man sells out and throws the money into the slums, the only result will be to add himself and his dependents to the list of the poor, and to do no good to the poor beyond giving a chance few of them a drunken spree. We must therefore bear in mind that whereas, in the time of Jesus, and in the ages which grew darker and darker after his death until the darkness, after a brief false dawn in the Reformation and the Renascence, culminated in the commercial night of the nineteenth century, it was believed that you could not make men good by Act of Parliament, we now know that you cannot make them good in any other way, and that a man who is better than his fellows is a nuisance. The rich man must sell up not only himself but his whole class; and that can be done only through the Chancellor of the Exchequer. The disciple cannot have his bread without money until there is bread for everybody without money; and that requires an elaborate municipal organization of the food supply, rate supported. Being members one of another means One Man One Vote, and One Woman One Vote, and universal suffrage and equal incomes and all sorts of modern political measures. Even in Syria in the time of Jesus his teachings could not possibly have been realized by a series of independent explosions of personal righteousness on the part of the separate units of the population. Jerusalem could not have done what even a

372

village community cannot do, and what Robinson Crusoe himself could not have done if his conscience, and the stern compulsion of Nature, had not imposed a common rule on the half dozen Robinson Crusoes who struggled within him for not wholly compatible satisfactions. And what cannot be done in Jerusalem or Juan Fernandez cannot be done in London, New York, Paris, and Berlin.

In short, Christianity, good or bad, right or wrong, must perforce be left out of the question in human affairs until it is made practically applicable to them by complicated political devices; and to pretend that a field preacher under the governorship of Pontius Pilate, or even Pontius Pilate himself in council with all the wisdom of Rome, could have worked out applications of Christianity or any other system of morals for the twentieth century, is to shelve the subject much more effectually than Nero and all its other persecutors ever succeeded in doing. Personal righteousness, and the view that you cannot make people moral by Act of Parliament, is, in fact, the favorite defensive resort of the people who, consciously or subconsciously, are quite determined not to have their property meddled with by Jesus or any other reformer.

MODERN COMMUNISM

Now let us see what modern experience and sociology have to say to the suggestion of Jesus that you should get rid of your property by throwing it into the common stock. One can hear the Pharisees of Jerusalem and Chorazin and Bethsaida saying, "My good fellow, if you were to divide up the wealth of Judea equally today, before the end of the year you would have rich and poor, poverty and affluence, just as you have today; for there will always be the idle and the industrious, the thrifty and the wasteful, the drunken and the sober; and, as you yourself have very justly observed, the poor we shall have always with us." And we can hear the reply, "Woe unto you, liars and hypocrites; for ye have this very day divided up the wealth of the country yourselves, as must be done every day (for man liveth not otherwise than

373

from hand to mouth, nor can fish and eggs endure for ever);
and ye have divided it unjustly; also ye have said that my
reproach to you for having the poor always with you was
a law unto you that this evil should persist and stink in the
nostrils of God to all eternity; wherefore I think that
Lazarus will yet see you beside Dives in hell." Modern
Capitalism has made short work of the primitive pleas for
inequality. The Pharisees themselves have organized communism in capital. Joint stock is the order of the day. An
attempt to return to individual properties as the basis of
our production would smash civilization more completely
than ten revolutions. You cannot get the fields tilled today
until the farmer becomes a co-operator. Take the shareholder to his railway, and ask him to point out to you the
particular length of rail, the particular seat in the railway
carriage, the particular lever in the engine that is his very
own and nobody elses; and he will shun you as a madman,
very wisely. And if, like Ananias and Sapphira, you try to
hold back your little shop or what not from the common
stock, represented by the Trust, or Combine, or Kartel,
the Trust will presently freeze you out and rope you in
and finally strike you dead industrially as thoroughly as
St Peter himself. There is no longer any practical question
open as to Communism in production: the struggle today
is over the distribution of the product: that is, over the
daily dividing-up which is the first necessity of organized
society.

REDISTRIBUTION

Now it needs no Christ to convince anybody today that
our system of distribution is wildly and monstrously wrong.
We have million-dollar babies side by side with paupers
worn out by a long life of unremitted drudgery. One person
in every five dies in a workhouse, a public hospital, or a
madhouse. In cities like London the proportion is very
nearly one in two. Naturally so outrageous a distribution
has to be effected by violence pure and simple. If you demur, you are sold up. If you resist the selling up you are

bludgeoned and imprisoned, the process being euphemistic-
ally called the maintenance of law and order. Iniquity can
go no further. By this time nobody who knows the figures
of the distribution defends them. The most bigoted British
Conservative hesitates to say that his king should be much
poorer than Mr Rockefeller, or to proclaim the moral superiority of prostitution to needlework on the ground that it
pays better. The need for a drastic redistribution of income
in all civilized countries is now as obvious and as generally
admitted as the need for sanitation.

SHALL HE WHO MAKES, OWN?

It is when we come to the question of the proportions in
which we are to redistribute that controversy begins. We
are bewildered by an absurdly unpractical notion that in
some way a man's income should be given to him, not to
enable him to live, but as a sort of Sunday School Prize
for good behavior. And this folly is complicated by a less
ridiculous but quite as unpractical belief that it is possible
to assign to each person the exact portion of the national income that he or she has produced. To a child it seems that
the blacksmith has made a horse-shoe, and that therefore
the horse-shoe is his. But the blacksmith knows that the
horse-shoe does not belong solely to him, but to his landlord, to the rate collector and taxgatherer, to the men from
whom he bought the iron and anvil and the coals, leaving
only a scrap of its value for himself; and this scrap he has to
exchange with the butcher and baker and the clothier for
the things that he really appropriates as living tissue or its
wrappings, paying for all of them more than their cost; for
these fellow traders of his have also their landlords and
moneylenders to satisfy. If, then, such simple and direct
village examples of apparent individual production turn out
on a moment's examination to be the products of an elaborate social organization, what is to be said of such products
as dreadnoughts, factory-made pins and needles, and steel
pens? If God takes the dreadnought in one hand and a steel
pen in the other, and asks Job who made them, and to whom

375

they should belong by maker's right, Job must scratch his
puzzled head with a potsherd and be dumb, unless indeed it
strikes him that God is the ultimate maker, and that all we
have a right to do with the product is to feed his lambs.

LABOR TIME

So maker's right as an alternative to taking the advice of
Jesus would not work. In practice nothing was possible in
that direction but to pay a worker by labor time: so much an
hour or day or week or year. But how much? When that
question came up, the only answer was "as little as he can be
starved into accepting," with the ridiculous results already
mentioned, and the additional anomaly that the largest share
went to the people who did not work at all, and the least to
those who worked hardest. In England nine-tenths of the
wealth goes into the pockets of one-tenth of the population.

THE DREAM OF DISTRIBUTION
ACCORDING TO MERIT

Against this comes the protest of the Sunday School
theorists "Why not distribute according to merit?" Here
one imagines Jesus, whose smile has been broadening down
the ages as attempt after attempt to escape from his teaching
has led to deeper and deeper disaster, laughing outright.
Was ever so idiotic a project mooted as the estimation of
virtue in money? The London School of Economics is, we
must suppose, to set examination papers with such questions as, "Taking the money value of the virtues of Jesus as
100, and of Judas Iscariot as zero, give the correct figures
for, respectively, Pontius Pilate, the proprietor of the Gadarene swine, the widow who put her mite in the poor-box, Mr
Horatio Bottomley, Shakespear, Mr Jack Johnson, Sir Isaac
Newton, Palestrina, Offenbach, Sir Thomas Lipton, Mr
Paul Cinquevalli, your family doctor, Florence Nightingale,
Mrs Siddons, your charwoman, the Archbishop of Canterbury, and the common hangman." Or "The late Mr Barney
Barnato received as his lawful income three thousand times
as much money as an English agricultural laborer of good
general character. Name the principal virtues in which Mr

Barnato exceeded the laborer three thousandfold; and give in figures the loss sustained by civilization when Mr Barnato was driven to despair and suicide by the reduction of his multiple to one thousand." The Sunday School idea, with its principle "to each the income he deserves," is really too silly for discussion. Hamlet disposed of it three hundred years ago. "Use every man after his deserts, and who shall scape whipping?" Jesus remains unshaken as the practical man; and we stand exposed as the fools, the blunderers, the unpractical visionaries. The moment you try to reduce the Sunday School idea to figures you find that it brings you back to the hopeless plan of paying for a man's time; and your examination paper will read "The time of Jesus was worth nothing (he complained that the foxes had holes and the birds of the air nests whilst he had not a place to lay his head). Dr Crippen's time was worth, say, three hundred and fifty pounds a year. Criticize this arrangement; and, if you dispute its justice, state in pounds, dollars, france and marks, what their relative time wages ought to have been." Your answer may be that the question is in extremely bad taste and that you decline to answer it. But you cannot object to being asked how many minutes of a bookmaker's time are worth two hours of an astronomer's?

VITAL DISTRIBUTION

In the end you are forced to ask the question you should have asked at the beginning. What do you give a man an income for? Obviously to keep him alive. Since it is evident that the first condition on which he can be kept alive without enslaving somebody else is that he shall produce an equivalent for what it costs to keep him alive, we may quite rationally compel him to abstain from idling by whatever means we employ to compel him to abstain from murder, arson, forgery, or any other crime. The one supremely foolish thing to do with him is to do nothing: that is, to be as idle, lazy, and heartless in dealing with him as he is in dealing with us. Even if we provided work for him instead of basing, as we do, our whole industrial system on successive com-

377

petitive waves of overwork with their ensuing troughs of unemployment, we should still sternly deny him the alternative of not doing it; for the result must be that he will become poor and make his children poor if he has any; and poor people are cancers in the commonwealth, costing far more than if they were handsomely pensioned off as incurables. Jesus had more sense than to propose anything of the sort. He said to his disciples, in effect, "Do your work for love; and let the other people lodge and feed and clothe you for love." Or, as we should put it nowadays, "for nothing." All human experience and all natural uncommercialized human aspiration point to this as the right path. The Greeks said, "First secure an independent income; and then practise virtue." We all strive towards an independent income. We all know as well as Jesus did that if we have to take thought for the morrow as to whether there shall be anything to eat or drink it will be impossible for us to think of nobler things, or live a higher life than that of a mole, whose life is from beginning to end a frenzied pursuit of food. Until the community is organized in such a way that the fear of bodily want is forgotten as completely as the fear of wolves already is in civilized capitals, we shall never have a decent social life. Indeed the whole attraction of our present arrangement lies in the fact that it does relieve a handful of us from this fear; but as the relief is effected stupidly and wickedly by making the favored handful parasitic on the rest, they are smitten with the degeneracy which seems to be the inevitable biological penalty of complete parasitism. They corrupt culture and statecraft instead of contributing to them, their excessive leisure being as mischievous as the excessive toil of the laborers. Anyhow, the moral is clear. The two main problems of organized society: how to produce subsistence enough for all its members, and how to prevent the theft of that subsistence by idlers, should be carefully dissociated; for the triumphant solution of the first by our inventors and chemists has been offset by the disastrous failure of our rulers to solve the

other. Optimism on this point is only wilful blindness: we
all have the hard fact of the failure before us. The only
people who cling to the lazy delusion that it is possible to
find a just distribution that will work automatically are
those who postulate some revolutionary change like land
nationalization, which by itself would obviously only force
into greater urgency the problem of how to distribute the
product of the land among all the individuals in the community.

EQUAL DISTRIBUTION

When that problem is at last faced, the question of the
proportion in which the national income shall be distributed
can have only one answer. All our shares must be equal. It
has always been so: it always will be so. It is true that the
incomes of robbers vary considerably from individual to
individual; and the variation is reflected in the incomes of
their parasites. The commercialization of certain exceptional talents has also produced exceptional incomes, direct
and derivative. Persons who live on rent of land and capital
are economically, though not legally, in the category of
robbers, and have grotesquely different incomes. But in the
huge mass of mankind variation of income from individual
to individual is unknown, because it is ridiculously impracticable. As a device for persuading a carpenter that a judge
is a creature of superior nature to himself, to be deferred and
submitted to even to the death, we may give a carpenter a
hundred pounds a year and a judge five thousand; but the
wage for one carpenter is the wage for all the carpenters: the
salary for one judge is the salary for all the judges.

THE CAPTAIN AND THE CABIN BOY

Nothing, therefore, is really in question, or ever has
been, but the differences between class incomes. Already
there is economic equality between captains, and economic
equality between cabin boys. What is at issue still is whether
there shall be economic equality between captains and cabin
boys. What would Jesus have said? Presumably he would
have said that if your only object is to produce a captain and

379

a cabin boy for the purpose of transferring you from Liverpool to New York, or to manœuvre a fleet and carry powder from the magazine to the gun, then you need give no more than a shilling to the cabin boy for every pound you give to the more expensively trained captain. But if in addition to this you desire to allow the two human souls which are inseparable from the captain and the cabin boy, and which alone differentiate them from the donkey-engine, to develop all their possibilities, then you may find the cabin boy costing rather more than the captain, because cabin boy's work does not do so much for the soul as captain's work. Consequently you will have to give him at least as much as the captain unless you definitely wish him to be a lower creature, in which case the sooner you are hanged as an abortionist the better. That is the fundamental argument.

THE POLITICAL AND BIOLOGICAL OBJECTIONS TO INEQUALITY

But there are other reasons for objecting to class stratification of income which have heaped themselves up since the time of Jesus. In politics it defeats every form of government except that of a necessarily corrupt oligarchy. Democracy in the most democratic modern republics: France and the United States for example, is an imposture and a delusion. It reduces justice and law to a farce: law becomes merely an instrument for keeping the poor in subjection; and accused workmen are tried, not by a jury of their peers, but by conspiracies of their exploiters. The press is the press of the rich and the curse of the poor: it becomes dangerous to teach men to read. The priest becomes the mere complement of the policeman in the machinery by which the countryhouse oppresses the village. Worst of all, marriage becomes a class affair: the infinite variety of choice which nature offers to the young in search of a mate is narrowed to a handful of persons of similar income; and beauty and health become the dreams of artists and the advertisements of quacks instead of the normal conditions of life. Society is not only divided but actually destroyed in all directions

380

by inequality of income between classes: such stability as it has is due to the huge blocks of people between whom there is equality of income.

JESUS AS ECONOMIST

It seems therefore that we must begin by holding the right to an income as sacred and equal, just as we now begin by holding the right to life as sacred and equal. Indeed the one right is only a restatement of the other. To hang me for cutting a dock laborer's throat after making much of me for leaving him to starve when I do not happen to have a ship for him to unload is idiotic; for as he does far less mischief with his throat cut than when he is starving, a rational society would esteem the cutthroat more highly than the capitalist. The thing has become so obvious, and the evil so unendurable, that if our attempt at civilization is not to perish like all the previous ones, we shall have to organize our society in such a way as to be able to say to every person in the land, "Take no thought, saying What shall we eat? or What shall we drink? or Wherewithal shall we be clothed?" We shall then no longer have a race of men whose hearts are in their pockets and safes and at their bankers. As Jesus said, where your treasure is, there will your heart be also. That was why he recommended that money should cease to be a treasure, and that we should take steps to make ourselves utterly reckless of it, setting our minds free for higher uses. In other words, that we should all be gentlemen and take care of our country because our country takes care of us, instead of the commercialized cads we are, doing everything and anything for money, and selling our souls and bodies by the pound and the inch after wasting half the day haggling over the price. Decidedly, whether you think Jesus was God or not, you must admit that he was a first-rate political economist.

JESUS AS BIOLOGIST

He was also, as we now see, a first-rate biologist. It took a century and a half of evolutionary preachers, from Buffon and Goethe to Butler and Bergson, to convince us that we

381

and our father are one; that as the kingdom of heaven is within us we need not go about looking for it and crying Lo here! and Lo there!; that God is not a picture of a pompous person in white robes in the family Bible, but a spirit; that it is through this spirit that we evolve towards greater abundance of life; that we are the lamps in which the light of the world burns: that, in short, we are gods though we die like men. All that is today sound biology and psychology; and the efforts of Natural Selectionists like Weismann to reduce evolution to mere automatism have not touched the doctrine of Jesus, though they have made short work of the theologians who conceived God as a magnate keeping men and angels as Lord Rothschild keeps buffaloes and emus at Tring.

MONEY THE MIDWIFE OF SCIENTIFIC COMMUNISM

It may be asked here by some simple-minded reader why we should not resort to crude Communism as the disciples were told to do. This would be quite practicable in a village where production was limited to the supply of the primitive wants which nature imposes on all human beings alike. We know that people need bread and boots without waiting for them to come and ask for these things and offer to pay for them. But when civilization advances to the point at which articles are produced that no man absolutely needs and that only some men fancy or can use, it is necessary that individuals should be able to have things made to their order and at their own cost. It is safe to provide bread for everybody because everybody wants and eats bread; but it would be absurd to provide microscopes and trombones, pet snakes and polo mallets, alembics and test tubes for everybody, as nine-tenths of them would be wasted; and the nine-tenths of the population who do not use such things would object to their being provided at all. We have in the invaluable instrument called money a means of enabling every individual to order and pay for the particular things he desires over and above the things he must consume in order to re-
382

main alive, plus the things the State insists on his having
and using whether he wants to or not: for example, clothes,
sanitary arrangements, armies and navies.|In large com-
munities, where even the most eccentric demands for manufactured articles average themselves out until they can be
foreseen within a negligible margin of error, direct communism (Take what you want without payment, as the
people do in Morris's News From Nowhere) will, after a
little experience, be found not only practicable but highly
economical to an extent that now seems impossible. The
sportsmen, the musicians, the physicists, the biologists will
get their apparatus for the asking as easily as their bread, or,
as at present, their paving, street lighting, and bridges; and
the deaf man will not object to contribute to communal
flutes when the musician has to contribute to communal ear
trumpets. There are cases (for example, radium) in which
the demand may be limited to the merest handful of laboratory workers, and in which nevertheless the whole community must pay because the price is beyond the means of
any individual worker. But even when the utmost allowance
is made for extensions of communism that now seem fabulous, there will still remain for a long time to come regions of
supply and demand in which men will need and use money
or individual credit, and for which, therefore, they must
have individual incomes. Foreign travel is an obvious instance. We are so far from even national communism still,
that we shall probably have considerable developments of
local communism before it becomes possible for a Man-
chester man to go up to London for a day without taking
any money with him. The modern practical form of the
communism of Jesus is therefore, for the present, equal distribution of the surplus of the national income that is not
absorbed by simple communism.

JUDGE NOT

In dealing with crime and the family, modern thought
and experience have thrown no fresh light on the views of
Jesus. When Swift had occasion to illustrate the corruption

of our civilization by making a catalogue of the types of scoundrels it produces, he always gave judges a conspicuous place alongside of them they judged. And he seems to have done this not as a restatement of the doctrine of Jesus, but as the outcome of his own observation and judgment. One of Mr Gilbert Chesterton's stories has for its hero a judge who, whilst trying a criminal case, is so overwhelmed by the absurdity of his position and the wickedness of the things it forces him to do, that he throws off the ermine there and then, and goes out into the world to live the life of an honest man instead of that of a cruel idol. There has also been a propaganda of a soulless stupidity called Determinism, representing man as a dead object driven hither and thither by his environment, antecedents, circumstances, and so forth, which nevertheless does remind us that there are limits to the number of cubits an individual can add to his stature morally or physically, and that it is silly as well as cruel to torment a man five feet high for not being able to pluck fruit that is within the reach of men of average height. I have known a case of an unfortunate child being beaten for not being able to tell the time after receiving an elaborate explanation of the figures on a clock dial, the fact being that she was short-sighted and could not see them. This is a typical illustration of the absurdities and cruelties into which we are led by the counter-stupidity to Determinism: the doctrine of Free Will. The notion that people can be good if they like, and that you should give them a powerful additional motive for goodness by tormenting them when they do evil, would soon reduce itself to absurdity if its application were not kept within the limits which nature sets to the self-control of most of us. Nobody supposes that a man with no ear for music or no mathematical faculty could be compelled on pain of death, however cruelly inflicted, to hum all the themes of Beethoven's symphonies or to complete Newton's work on fluxions.

LIMITS TO FREE WILL

Consequently such of our laws as are not merely the

intimidations by which tyrannies are maintained under pretext of law, can be obeyed through the exercise of a quite common degree of reasoning power and self-control. Most men and women can endure the ordinary annoyances and disappointments of life without committing murderous assaults. They conclude therefore that any person can refrain from such assaults if he or she chooses to, and proceed to reinforce self-control by threats of severe punishment. But in this they are mistaken. There are people, some of them possessing considerable powers of mind and body, who can no more restrain the fury into which a trifling mishap throws them than a dog can restrain himself from snapping if he is suddenly and painfully pinched. People fling knives and lighted paraffin lamps at one another in a dispute over a dinner-table. Men who have suffered several long sentences of penal servitude for murderous assaults will, the very day after they are released, seize their wives and cast them under drays at an irritating word. We have not only people who cannot resist an opportunity of stealing for the sake of satisfying their wants, but even people who have a specific mania for stealing, and do it when they are in no need of the things they steal. Burglary fascinates some men as sailoring fascinates some boys. Among respectable people how many are there who can be restrained by the warnings of their doctors and the lessons of experience from eating and drinking more than is good for them? It is true that between self-controlled people and ungovernable people there is a narrow margin of moral malingerers who can be made to behave themselves by the fear of consequences; but it is not worth while maintaining an abominable system of malicious, deliberate, costly and degrading ill-treatment of criminals for the sake of these marginal cases. For practical dealing with crime, Determinism or Predestination is quite a good working rule. People without self-control enough for social purposes may be killed, or may be kept in asylums with a view to studying their condition and ascertaining whether it is curable. To torture them and give ourselves virtuous

385

airs at their expense is ridiculous and barbarous; and the desire to do it is vindictive and cruel. And though vindictiveness and cruelty are at least human qualities when they are frankly proclaimed and indulged, they are loathsome when they assume the robes of Justice. Which, I take it, is why Shakespear's Isabella gave such a dressing-down to Judge Angelo, and why Swift reserved the hottest corner of his hell for judges. Also, of course, why Jesus said "Judge not that ye be not judged" and "If any man hear my words and believe not, I judge him not" because "he hath one that judgeth him": namely, the Father who is one with him.

When we are robbed we generally appeal to the criminal law, not considering that if the criminal law were effective we should not have been robbed. That convicts us of vengeance.

I need not elaborate the argument further. I have dealt with it sufficiently elsewhere. I have only to point out that we have been judging and punishing ever since Jesus told us not to; and I defy anyone to make out a convincing case for believing that the world has been any better than it would have been if there had never been a judge, a prison, or a gallows in it all that time. We have simply added the misery of punishment to the misery of crime, and the cruelty of the judge to the cruelty of the criminal. We have taken the bad man, and made him worse by torture and degradation, incidentally making ourselves worse in the process. It does not seem very sensible, does it? It would have been far easier to kill him as kindly as possible, or to label him and leave him to his conscience, or to treat him as an invalid or a lunatic is now treated (it is only of late years, by the way, that madmen have been delivered from the whip, the chain, and the cage); and this, I presume, is the form in which the teaching of Jesus could have been put into practice.

JESUS ON MARRIAGE AND THE FAMILY

When we come to marriage and the family, we find Jesus making the same objection to that individual appropriation of human beings which is the essence of matrimony as to

386

the individual appropriation of wealth. A married man, he said, will try to please his wife, and a married woman to please her husband, instead of doing the work of God. This is another version of "Where your treasure is, there will your heart be also." Eighteen hundred years later we find a very different person from Jesus, Talleyrand to wit, saying the same thing. A married man with a family, said Talleyrand, will do anything for money. Now this, though not a scientifically precise statement, is true enough to be a moral objection to marriage. As long as a man has a right to risk his life or his livelihood for his ideas he needs only courage and conviction to make his integrity unassailable. But he forfeits that right when he marries. It took a revolution to rescue Wagner from his Court appointment at Dresden; and his wife never forgave him for being glad and feeling free when he lost it and threw her back into poverty. Millet might have gone on painting potboiling nudes to the end of his life if his wife had not been of a heroic turn herself. Women, for the sake of their children and parents, submit to slaveries and prostitutions that no unattached woman would endure.

This was the beginning and the end of the objection of Jesus to marriage and family ties, and the explanation of his conception of heaven as a place where there should be neither marrying nor giving in marriage. Now there is no reason to suppose that when he said this he did not mean it. He did not, as St Paul did afterwards in his name, propose celibacy as a rule of life; for he was not a fool, nor, when he denounced marriage, had he yet come to believe, as St Paul did, that the end of the world was at hand and there was therefore no more need to replenish the earth. He must have meant that the race should be continued without dividing with women and men the allegiance the individual owes to God within him. This raises the practical problem of how we are to secure the spiritual freedom and integrity of the priest and the nun without their barrenness and uncompleted experience. Luther the priest did not solve the problem by marrying a nun: he only testified in the most convincing and practical way to the fact that celibacy was a worse failure than marriage.

WHY JESUS DID NOT MARRY

To all appearance the problem oppresses only a few exceptional people. Thoroughly conventional women married to thoroughly conventional men should not be conscious of any restriction: the chain not only leaves them free to do whatever they want to do, but greatly facilitates their doing it. To them an attack on marriage is not a blow struck in defence of their freedom but at their rights and privileges. One would expect that they would not only demur vehemently to the teachings of Jesus in this matter, but object strongly to his not having been a married man himself. Even those who regard him as a god descended from his throne in heaven to take on humanity for a time might reasonably declare that the assumption of humanity must have been incomplete at its most vital point if he were a celibate. But the facts are flatly contrary. The mere thought of Jesus as a married man is felt to be blasphemous by the most conventional believers; and even those of us to whom Jesus is no supernatural personage, but a prophet only as Mahomet was a prophet, feel that there was something more dignified in the bachelordom of Jesus than in the spectacle of Mahomet lying distracted on the floor of his harem whilst his wives stormed and squabbled and henpecked round him. We are not surprised that when Jesus called the sons of Zebedee to follow him, he did not call their father, and that the disciples, like Jesus himself, were all men without family entanglements. It is evident from his impatience when people excused themselves from following him because of their family funerals, or when they assumed that his first duty was to his mother, that he had found family ties and domestic affections in his way at every turn, and had become persuaded at last that no man could follow his inner light until he was free from their compulsion. The absence of any protest against this tempts us to

388

declare that on this question of marriage there are no conventional people; and that everyone of us is at heart a good Christian sexually.

INCONSISTENCY OF THE SEX INSTINCT

But the question is not so simple as that. Sex is an exceedingly subtle and complicated instinct; and the mass of mankind neither know nor care much about freedom of conscience, which is what Jesus was thinking about, and are concerned almost to obsession with sex, as to which Jesus said nothing. In our sexual natures we are torn by an irresistible attraction and an overwhelming repugnance and disgust. We have two tyrannous physical passions: concupiscence and chastity. We become mad in pursuit of sex: we become equally mad in the persecution of that pursuit. Unless we gratify our desire the race is lost: unless we restrain it we destroy ourselves. We are thus led to devise marriage institutions which will at the same time secure opportunities for the gratification of sex and raise up innumerable obstacles to it; which will sanctify it and brand it as infamous; which will identify it with virtue and with sin simultaneously. Obviously it is useless to look for any consistency in such institutions; and it is only by continual reform and readjustment, and by a considerable elasticity in their enforcement, that a tolerable result can be arrived at. I need not repeat here the long and elaborate examination of them that I prefixed to my play entitled Getting Married. Here I am concerned only with the views of Jesus on the question; and it is necessary, in order to understand the attitude of the world towards them, that we should not attribute the general approval of the decision of Jesus to remain unmarried as an endorsement of his views. We are simply in a state of confusion on the subject; but it is part of the confusion that we should conclude that Jesus was a celibate, and shrink even from the idea that his birth was a natural one, yet cling with ferocity to the sacredness of the institution which provides a refuge from celibacy.

FOR BETTER FOR WORSE

Jesus, however, did not express a complicated view of marriage. His objection to it was quite simple, as we have seen. He perceived that nobody could live the higher life unless money and sexual love were obtainable without sacrificing it; and he saw that the effect of marriage as it existed among the Jews (and as it still exists among ourselves) was to make the couples sacrifice every higher consideration until they had fed and pleased one another. The worst of it is that this dangerous preposterousness in marriage, instead of improving as the general conduct of married couples improves, becomes much worse. The selfish man to whom his wife is nothing but a slave, the selfish woman to whom her husband is nothing but a scapegoat and a breadwinner, are not held back from spiritual or any other adventures by fear of their effect on the welfare of their mates. Their wives do not make recreants and cowards of them: their husbands do not chain them to the cradle and the cooking range when their feet should be beautiful on the mountains. It is precisely as people become more kindly, more conscientious, more ready to shoulder the heavier part of the burden (which means that the strong shall give way to the weak and the slow hold back the swift), that marriage becomes an intolerable obstacle to individual evolution. And that is why the revolt against marriage of which Jesus was an exponent always recurs when civilization raises the standard of marital duty and affection, and at the same time produces a greater need for individual freedom in pursuit of a higher evolution.

THE REMEDY

This, fortunately, is only one side of marriage; and the question arises, can it not be eliminated? The reply is reassuring: of course it can. There is no mortal reason in the nature of things why a married couple should be economically dependent on one another. The Communism advocated by Jesus, which we have seen to be entirely practicable, and indeed inevitable if our civilization is to be saved from collapse, gets rid of that difficulty completely. And with the

economic dependence will go the force of the outrageous
claims that derive their real sanction from the economic
pressure behind them. When a man allows his wife to turn
him from the best work he is capable of doing, and to sell
his soul at the highest commercial prices obtainable; when
he allows her to entangle him in a social routine that is weari-
some and debilitating to him, or tie him to her apron strings
when he needs that occasional solitude which is one of the
most sacred of human rights, he does so because he has no
right to impose eccentric standards of expenditure and un-
social habits on her, and because these conditions have produced by their pressure so general a custom of chaining
wedded couples to one another that married people are
coarsely derided when their partners break the chain. And
when a woman is condemned by her parents to wait in
genteel idleness and uselessness for a husband when all her
healthy social instincts call her to acquire a profession and
work, it is again her economic dependence on them that
makes their tyranny effective.

THE CASE FOR MARRIAGE

Thus, though it would be too much to say that everything that is obnoxious in marriage and family life will be
cured by Communism, yet it can be said that it will cure
what Jesus objected to in these institutions. He made no
comprehensive study of them: he only expressed his own
grievance with an overwhelming sense that it is a grievance
so deep that all the considerations on the other side are as
dust in the balance. Obviously there are such considerations,
and very weighty ones too. When Talleyrand said that a
married man with a family is capable of anything, he meant
anything evil; but an optimist may declare, with equal half
truth, that a married man is capable of anything good; that
marriage turns vagabonds into steady citizens; and that
men and women will, for love of their mates and children,
practise virtues that unattached individuals are incapable
of. It is true that too much of this domestic virtue is self-
denial, which is not a virtue at all; but then the following

of the inner light at all costs is largely self-indulgence, which is just as suicidal, just as weak, just as cowardly as self-denial. Ibsen, who takes us into the matter far more resolutely than Jesus, is unable to find any golden rule: both Brand and Peer Gynt come to a bad end; and though Brand does not do as much mischief as Peer, the mischief he does do is of extraordinary intensity.

CELIBACY NO REMEDY

We must, I think, regard the protest of Jesus against marriage and family ties as the claim of a particular kind of individual to be free from them because they hamper his own work intolerably. When he said that if we are to follow him in the sense of taking up his work we must give up our family ties, he was simply stating a fact; and to this day the Roman Catholic priest, the Buddhist lama, and the fakirs of all the eastern denominations accept the saying. It is also accepted by the physically enterprising, the explorers, the restlessly energetic of all kinds: in short, by the adventurous. The greatest sacrifice in marriage is the sacrifice of the adventurous attitude towards life: the being settled. Those who are born tired may crave for settlement; but to fresher and stronger spirits it is a form of suicide.

Now to say of any institution that it is incompatible with both the contemplative and adventurous life is to disgrace it so vitally that all the moralizings of all the Deans and Chapters cannot reconcile our souls to its slavery. The unmarried Jesus and the unmarried Beethoven, the unmarried Joan of Arc, Clare, Teresa, Florence Nightingale seem as they should be; and the saying that there is always something ridiculous about a married philosopher becomes inevitable. And yet the celibate is still more ridiculous than the married man: the priest, in accepting the alternative of celibacy, disables himself; and the best priests are those who have been men of this world before they became men of the world to come. But as the taking of vows does not annul an existing marriage, and a married man cannot become a priest, we are again confronted with the absurdity that the best priest is a reformed rake. Thus does marriage, itself intolerable, thrust us upon intolerable alternatives. The practical solution is to make the individual economically independent of marriage and the family, and to make marriage as easily dissoluble as any other partnership: in other words, to accept the conclusions to which experience is slowly driving both our sociologists and our legislators. This will not instantly cure all the evils of marriage, nor root up at one stroke its detestable tradition of property in human bodies. But it will leave Nature free to effect a cure; and in free soil the root may wither and perish.

This disposes of all the opinions and teachings of Jesus which are still matters of controversy. They are all in line with the best modern thought. He told us what we have to do; and we have had to find the way to do it. Most of us are still, as most were in his own time, extremely recalcitrant, and are being forced along that way by painful pressure of circumstances, protesting at every step that nothing will induce us to go; that it is a ridiculous way, a disgraceful way, a socialistic way, an atheistic way, an immoral way, and that the vanguard ought to be ashamed of themselves and must be made to turn back at once. But they find that they have to follow the vanguard all the same if their lives are to be worth living.

AFTER THE CRUCIFIXION

Let us now return to the New Testament narrative; for what happened after the disappearance of Jesus is instructive. Unfortunately, the crucifixion was a complete political success. I remember that when I described it in these terms once before, I greatly shocked a most respectable newspaper in my native town, the Dublin Daily Express, because my journalistic phrase shewed that I was treating it as an ordinary event like Home Rule or the Insurance Act: that is (though this did not occur to the editor), as a real event which had really happened, instead of a portion of the Church service. I can only repeat, assuming as I am that it *was* a real event and did actually happen, that it was as complete a success as any in history. Christianity as a specific doctrine was slain with Jesus, suddenly and utterly. He was hardly cold in his grave, or high in his heaven (as you please), before the apostles dragged the tradition of him down to the level of the thing it has remained ever since. And that thing the intelligent heathen may study, if they would be instructed in it by modern books, in Samuel Butler's novel, The Way of All Flesh.

THE VINDICTIVE MIRACLES AND THE STONING OF STEPHEN

Take, for example, the miracles. Of Jesus alone of all the Christian miracle workers there is no record, except in certain gospels that all men reject, of a malicious or destructive miracle. A barren fig-tree was the only victim of his anger. Every one of his miracles on sentient subjects was an act of kindness. John declares that he healed the wound of the man whose ear was cut off (by Peter, John says) at the arrest in the garden. One of the first things the apostles did with their miraculous power was to strike dead a wretched man and his wife who had defrauded them by holding back some money from the common stock. They struck people blind or dead without remorse, judging because they had been judged. They healed the sick and raised the dead apparently in a spirit of pure display and advertisement. Their doctrine did not contain a ray of that light which reveals Jesus as one of the redeemers of men from folly and error. They cancelled him, and went back straight to John the Baptist and his formula of securing remission of sins by repentance and the rite of baptism (being born again of water and the spirit). Peter's first harangue softens us by the human touch of its exordium, which was a quaint assurance to his hearers that they must believe him to be sober because it was too early in the day to get drunk; but of Jesus he had nothing to say except that he was the Christ foretold by the prophets as coming from the seed of David, and that they must believe this and be baptized. To this the other apostles added incessant denunciations of the Jews for having crucified him, and threats of the destruction that would overtake them if they did not repent: that is, if they did not join the sect which the apostles were now forming. A quite intolerable young speaker named Stephen delivered an oration to the council, in which he first inflicted on them a tedious sketch of the history of Israel, with which they were presumably as well acquainted as he, and then reviled them in the most insulting terms as "stiffnecked and uncircumcized." Finally, after boring and annoying them to the utmost bearable extremity, he looked up and declared that he saw the heavens open, and Christ standing on the right hand of God. This was too much: they threw him out of the city and stoned him to death. It was a severe way of suppressing a tactless and conceited bore; but it was pardonable and human in comparison to the slaughter of poor Ananias and Sapphira.

PAUL

Suddenly a man of genius, Paul, violently anti-Christian, enters on the scene, holding the clothes of the men who are stoning Stephen. He persecutes the Christians with great vigor, a sport which he combines with the business of a tentmaker. This temperamental hatred of Jesus, whom he has never seen, is a pathological symptom of that particular sort of conscience and nervous constitution which brings its victims under the tyranny of two delirious terrors: the terror of sin and the terror of death, which may be called also the terror of sex and the terror of life. Now Jesus, with his healthy conscience on his higher plane, was free from these terrors. He consorted freely with sinners, and was never concerned for a moment, as far as we know, about whether his conduct was sinful or not; so that he has forced us to accept him as the man without sin. Even if we reckon his last days as the days of his delusion, he none the less gave a fairly convincing exhibition of superiority to the fear of death. This must have both fascinated and horrified Paul, or Saul, as he was first called. The horror accounts for his fierce persecution of the Christians. The fascination accounts for the strangest of his fancies: the fancy for attaching the name of Jesus Christ to the great idea which flashed upon him on the road to Damascus, the idea that he could not only make a religion of his two terrors, but that the movement started by Jesus offered him the nucleus for his new Church. It was a monstrous idea; and the shock of it, as he afterwards declared, struck him blind for days. He heard Jesus calling to him from the clouds, "Why persecute me?" His natural hatred of the teacher for whom Sin and Death had no terrors turned into a wild personal worship of him which has the ghastliness of a beautiful thing seen in a false light.

The chronicler of the Acts of the Apostles sees nothing of the significance of this. The great danger of conversion in all ages has been that when the religion of the high mind is offered to the lower mind, the lower mind, feeling its fascination without understanding it, and being incapable of rising to it, drags it down to its level by degrading it. Years ago I said that the conversion of a savage to Christianity is the conversion of Christianity to savagery. The conversion of Paul was no conversion at all: it was Paul who converted the religion that had raised one man above sin and death into a religion that delivered millions of men so completely into their dominion that their own common nature became a horror to them, and the religious life became a denial of life. Paul had no intention of surrendering either his Judaism or his Roman citizenship to the new moral world (as Robert Owen called it) of Communism and Jesuism. Just as in our own time Karl Marx, not content to take political economy as he found it, insisted on rebuilding it from the bottom upwards in his own way, and thereby gave a new lease of life to the errors it was just outgrowing, so Paul reconstructed the old Salvationism from which Jesus had vainly tried to redeem him, and produced a fantastic theology which is still the most amazing thing of the kind known to us. Being intellectually an inveterate Roman Rationalist, always discarding the irrational real thing for the unreal but ratiocinable postulate, he began by discarding Man as he is, and substituted a postulate which he called Adam. And when he was asked, as he surely must have been in a world not wholly mad, what had become of the natural man, he replied "Adam *is* the natural man." This was confusing to simpletons, because according to tradition Adam was certainly the name of the natural man as created in the garden of Eden. It was as if a preacher of our own time had described as typically British Frankenstein's monster, and called him Smith, and somebody, on demanding what about the man in the street, had been told "Smith *is* the man in the street." The thing happens often enough; for indeed the world is full of these Adams and Smiths and men in the street and average sensual men and economic men and womanly women and what not, all of them imaginary Atlases carrying imaginary worlds on their unsubstantial shoulders.

The Eden story provided Adam with a sin: the "original sin" for which we are all damned. Baldly stated, this seems ridiculous; nevertheless it corresponds to something actually existent not only in Paul's consciousness but in our own. The original sin was not the eating of the forbidden fruit, but the consciousness of sin which the fruit produced. The moment Adam and Eve tasted the apple they found themselves ashamed of their sexual relation, which until then had seemed quite innocent to them; and there is no getting over the hard fact that this shame, or state of sin, has persisted to this day, and is one of the strongest of our instincts. Thus Paul's postulate of Adam as the natural man was pragmatically true: it worked. But the weakness of Pragmatism is that most theories will work if you put your back into making them work, provided they have some point of contact with human nature. Hedonism will pass the pragmatic test as well as Stoicism. Up to a certain point every social principle that is not absolutely idiotic works: Autocracy works in Russia and Democracy in America; Atheism works in France, Polytheism in India, Monotheism throughout Islam, and Pragmatism, or No-ism, in England. Paul's fantastic conception of the damned Adam, represented by Bunyan as a pilgrim with a great burden of sins on his back, corresponded to the fundamental condition of evolution, which is, that life, including human life, is continually evolving, and must therefore be continually ashamed of itself and its present and past. Bunyan's pilgrim wants to get rid of his bundle of sins; but he also wants to reach "yonder shining light"; and when at last his bundle falls off him into the sepulchre of Christ, his pilgrimage is still unfinished and his hardest trials still ahead of him. His conscience remains uneasy; "original sin" still torments him; and his adventure with Giant Despair, who throws him into the dungeon of Doubting Castle, from which he escapes by the use of a skeleton key, is more terrible than any he met whilst the bundle was still on his back. Thus Bunyan's allegory of human nature breaks through the Pauline theology at a hundred points. His theological allegory, The Holy War, with its troops of Election Doubters, and its cavalry of "those that rode Reformadoes," is, as a whole, absurd, impossible, and, except in passages where the artistic old Adam momentarily got the better of the Salvationist theologian, hardly readable.

Paul's theory of original sin was to some extent idiosyncratic. He tells us definitely that he finds himself quite well able to avoid the sinfulness of sex by practising celibacy; but he recognizes, rather contemptuously, that in this respect he is not as other men are, and says that they had better marry than burn, thus admitting that though marriage may lead to placing the desire to please wife or husband before the desire to please God, yet preoccupation with unsatisfied desire may be even more ungodly than preoccupation with domestic affection. This view of the case inevitably led him to insist that a wife should be rather a slave than a partner, her real function being, not to engage a man's love and loyalty, but on the contrary to release them for God by relieving the man of all preoccupation with sex just as in her capacity of housekeeper and cook she relieves his preoccupation with hunger by the simple expedient of satisfying his appetite. This slavery also justifies itself pragmatically by working effectively; but it has made Paul the eternal enemy of Woman. Incidentally it has led to many foolish surmises about Paul's personal character and circumstances, by people so enslaved by sex that a celibate appears to them a sort of monster. They forget that not only whole priesthoods, official and unofficial, from Paul to Carlyle and Ruskin, have defied the tyranny of sex, but immense numbers of ordinary citizens of both sexes have, either voluntarily or under pressure of circumstances easily surmountable, saved their energies for less primitive activities.

Howbeit, Paul succeeded in stealing the image of Christ crucified for the figure-head of his Salvationist vessel, with its Adam posing as the natural man, its doctrine of original sin, and its damnation avoidable only by faith in the sacrifice of the cross. In fact, no sooner had Jesus knocked over the dragon of superstition than Paul boldly set it on its legs again in the name of Jesus.

THE CONFUSION OF CHRISTENDOM

Now it is evident that two religions having such contrary effects on mankind should not be confused as they are under a common name. There is not one word of Pauline Christianity in the characteristic utterances of Jesus. When Saul watched the clothes of the men who stoned Stephen, he was not acting upon beliefs which Paul renounced. There is no record of Christ's having ever said to any man: "Go and sin as much as you like: you can put it all on me." He said "Sin no more," and insisted that he was putting up the standard of conduct, not debasing it, and that the righteousness of the Christian must exceed that of the Scribe and Pharisee. The notion that he was shedding his blood in order that every petty cheat and adulterator and libertine might wallow in it and come out whiter than snow, cannot be imputed to him on his own authority. "I come as an infallible patent medicine for bad consciences" is not one of the sayings in the gospels. If Jesus could have been consulted on Bunyan's allegory as to that business of the burden of sin dropping from the pilgrim's back when he caught sight of the cross, we must infer from his teaching that he would have told Bunyan in forcible terms that he had never made a greater mistake in his life, and that the business of a Christ was to make self-satisfied sinners feel the burden of their sins and stop committing them instead of assuring them that they could not help it, as it was all Adam's fault, but that it did not matter as long as they were credulous and friendly about himself. Even when he believed himself to be a god, he did not regard himself as a scapegoat. He was to take away the sins of the world by good government, by justice and mercy, by setting the welfare of little children above the pride of princes, by casting all the quackeries and idolatries which now usurp and malversate the power of God into what our local authorities quaintly call the dust destructor, and by riding on the clouds of heaven in glory instead of in a thousand-guinea motor car. That was delirious, if you like; but it was the delirium of a free soul, not of a shamebound one like Paul's. There has really never been a more monstrous imposition perpetrated than the imposition of the limitations of Paul's soul upon the soul of Jesus.

THE SECRET OF PAUL'S SUCCESS

Paul must soon have found that his followers had gained peace of mind and victory over death and sin at the cost of all moral responsibility; for he did his best to reintroduce it by making good conduct the test of sincere belief, and insisting that sincere belief was necessary to salvation. But as his system was rooted in the plain fact that as what he called sin includes sex and is therefore an ineradicable part of human nature (why else should Christ have had to atone for the sin of all future generations?) it was impossible for him to declare that sin, even in its wickedest extremity, could forfeit the sinner's salvation if he repented and believed. And to this day Pauline Christianity is, and owes its enormous vogue to being, a premium on sin. Its consequences have had to be held in check by the worldlywise majority

400

through a violently anti-Christian system of criminal law and stern morality. But of course the main restraint is human nature, which has good impulses as well as bad ones, and refrains from theft and murder and cruelty, even when it is taught that it can commit them all at the expense of Christ and go happily to heaven afterwards, simply because it does not always want to murder or rob or torture.

It is now easy to understand why the Christianity of Jesus failed completely to establish itself politically and socially, and was easily suppressed by the police and the Church, whilst Paulinism overran the whole western civilized world, which was at that time the Roman Empire, and was adopted by it as its official faith, the old avenging gods falling helplessly before the new Redeemer. It still retains, as we may see in Africa, its power of bringing to simple people a message of hope and consolation that no other religion offers. But this enchantment is produced by its spurious association with the personal charm of Jesus, and exists only for untrained minds. In the hands of a logical Frenchman like Calvin, pushing it to its utmost conclusions, and devising "institutes" for hardheaded adult Scots and literal Swiss, it becomes the most infernal of fatalisms; and the lives of civilized children are blighted by its logic whilst negro piccaninnies are rejoicing in its legends.

PAUL'S QUALITIES

Paul, however, did not get his great reputation by mere imposition and reaction. It is only in comparison with Jesus (to whom many prefer him) that he appears common and conceited. Though in The Acts he is only a vulgar revivalist, he comes out in his own epistles as a genuine poet, though by flashes only. He is no more a Christian than Jesus was a Baptist: he is a disciple of Jesus only as Jesus was a disciple of John. He does nothing that Jesus would have done, and says nothing that Jesus would have said, though much, like the famous ode to charity, that he would have admired. He is more Jewish than the Jews, more Roman than the Romans, proud both ways, full of startling confessions and self-reve-

lations that would not surprise us if they were slipped into
the pages of Nietzsche, tormented by an intellectual conscience that demanded an argued case even at the cost of
sophistry, with all sorts of fine qualities and occasional illu-
minations, but always hopelessly in the toils of Sin, Death,
and Logic, which had no power over Jesus. As we have seen,
it was by introducing this bondage and terror of his into the
Christian doctrine that he adapted it to the Church and
State systems which Jesus transcended, and made it practicable by destroying the specifically Jesuist side of it. He
would have been quite in his place in any modern Protestant
State; and he, not Jesus, is the true head and founder of our
Reformed Church, as Peter is of the Roman Church. The
followers of Paul and Peter made Christendom, whilst the
Nazarenes were wiped out.

THE ACTS OF THE APOSTLES

Here we may return to the narrative called The Acts of
the Apostles, which we left at the point where the stoning
of Stephen was followed by the introduction of Paul. The
author of The Acts, though a good story-teller, like Luke,
was (herein also like Luke) much weaker in power of thought
than in imaginative literary art. Hence we find Luke
credited with the authorship of The Acts by people who like
stories and have no aptitude for theology, whilst the book itself is denounced as spurious by Pauline theologians because
Paul, and indeed all the apostles, are represented in it as very
commonplace revivalists, interesting us by their adventures
more than by any qualities of mind or character. Indeed, but
for the epistles, we should have a very poor opinion of the
apostles. Paul in particular is described as setting a fashion
which has remained in continual use to this day. Whenever
he addresses an audience, he dwells with great zest on his
misdeeds before his pseudo conversion, with the effect of
throwing into stronger relief his present state of blessed-
ness; and he tells the story of that conversion over and over
again, ending with exhortations to the hearers to come and
be saved, and threats of the wrath that will overtake them if

they refuse. At any revival meeting today the same thing may be heard, followed by the same conversions. This is natural enough; but it is totally unlike the preaching of Jesus, who never talked about his personal history, and never "worked up" an audience to hysteria. It aims at a purely nervous effect; it brings no enlightenment; the most ignorant man has only to become intoxicated with his own vanity, and mistake his self-satisfaction for the Holy Ghost, to become qualified as an apostle; and it has absolutely nothing to do with the characteristic doctrines of Jesus. The Holy Ghost may be at work all round producing wonders of art and science, and strengthening men to endure all sorts of martyrdoms for the enlargement of knowledge, and the enrichment and intensification of life ("that ye may have life more abundantly"); but the apostles, as described in The Acts, take no part in the struggle except as persecutors and revilers. To this day, when their successors get the upper hand, as in Geneva (Knox's "perfect city of Christ") and in Scotland and Ulster, every spiritual activity but moneymaking and churchgoing is stamped out; heretics are ruthlessly persecuted; and such pleasures as money can purchase are suppressed so that its possessors are compelled to go on making money because there is nothing else to do. And the compensation for all this privation is partly an insane conceit of being the elect of God, with a reserved seat in heaven, and partly, since even the most infatuated idiot cannot spend his life admiring himself, the less innocent excitement of punishing other people for not admiring him, and the nosing out of the sins of the people who, being intelligent enough to be incapable of mere dull self-righteousness, and highly susceptible to the beauty and interest of the real workings of the Holy Ghost, try to live more rational and abundant lives. The abominable amusement of terrifying children with threats of hell is another of these diversions, and perhaps the vilest and most mischievous of them. The net result is that the imitators of the apostles, whether they are called Holy Willies or Stigginses in derision, or,

403

in admiration, Puritans or saints, are, outside their own congregations, and to a considerable extent inside them, heartily detested. Now nobody detests Jesus, though many who have been tormented in their childhood in his name include him in their general loathing of everything connected with the word religion; whilst others, who know him only by misrepresentation as a sentimental pacifist and an ascetic, include him in their general dislike of that type of character. In the same way a student who has had to "get up" Shakespear as a college subject may hate Shakespear; and people who dislike the theatre may include Molière in that dislike without ever having read a line of his or witnessed one of his plays; but nobody with any knowledge of Shakespear or Molière could possibly detest them, or read without pity and horror a description of their being insulted, tortured, and killed. And the same is true of Jesus. But it requires the most strenuous effort of conscience to refrain from crying "Serve him right" when we read of the stoning of Stephen; and nobody has ever cared twopence about the martyrdom of Peter: many better men have died worse deaths: for example, honest Hugh Latimer, who was burned by us, was worth fifty Stephens and a dozen Peters. One feels at last that when Jesus called Peter from his boat, he spoiled an honest fisherman, and made nothing better out of the wreck than a salvation monger.

THE CONTROVERSIES ON BAPTISM AND TRANSUBSTANTIATION

Meanwhile the inevitable effect of dropping the peculiar doctrines of Jesus and going back to John the Baptist, was to make it much easier to convert Gentiles than Jews; and it was by following the line of least resistance that Paul became the apostle to the Gentiles. The Jews had their own rite of initiation: the rite of circumcision; and they were fiercely jealous for it, because it marked them as the chosen people of God, and set them apart from the Gentiles, who were simply the uncircumcized. When Paul, finding that baptism made way faster among the Gentiles than among the Jews, as it enabled them to plead that they too were sanctified by a rite of later and higher authority than the Mosaic rite, he was compelled to admit that circumcision did not matter; and this, to the Jews, was an intolerable blasphemy. To Gentiles like ourselves, a good deal of the Epistle to the Romans is now tedious to unreadableness because it consists of a hopeless attempt by Paul to evade the conclusion that if a man were baptized it did not matter a rap whether he was circumcized or not. Paul claims circumcision as an excellent thing in its way for a Jew; but if it has no efficacy towards salvation, and if salvation is the one thing needful—and Paul was committed to both propositions—his pleas in mitigation only made the Jews more determined to stone him.

Thus from the very beginning of apostolic Christianity, it was hampered by a dispute as to whether salvation was to be attained by a surgical operation or by a sprinkling of water: mere rites on which Jesus would not have wasted twenty words. Later on, when the new sect conquered the Gentile west, where the dispute had no practical application, the other ceremony—that of eating the god—produced a still more disastrous dispute, in which a difference of belief, not as to the obligation to perform the ceremony, but as to whether it was a symbolic or a real ingestion of divine substance, produced persecution, slaughter, hatred, and everything that Jesus loathed, on a monstrous scale.

But long before that, the superstitions which had fastened on the new faith made trouble. The parthenogenetic birth of Christ, simple enough at first as a popular miracle, was not left so simple by the theologians. They began to ask of what substance Christ was made in the womb of the virgin. When the Trinity was added to the faith the question arose, was the virgin the mother of God or only the mother of Jesus? Arian schisms and Nestorian schisms arose on these questions; and the leaders of the resultant agitations rancorously deposed one another and excommunicated one another according to their luck in enlisting the

405

emperors on their side. In the IV century they began to burn
one another for differences of opinion in such matters. In
the VIII century Charlemagne made Christianity compulsory by killing those who refused to embrace it; and though
this made an end of the voluntary character of conversion,
Charlemagne may claim to be the first Christian who put
men to death for any point of doctrine that really mattered.
From his time onward the history of Christian controversy
reeks with blood and fire, torture and warfare. The Crusades,
the persecutions in Albi and elsewhere, the Inquisition, the
"wars of religion" which followed the Reformation, all presented themselves as Christian phenomena; but who can
doubt that they would have been repudiated with horror by
Jesus? Our own notion that the massacre of St Bartholo-
mew's was an outrage on Christianity, whilst the campaigns
of Gustavus Adolphus, and even of Frederick the Great,
were a defence of it, is as absurd as the opposite notion that
Frederick was Antichrist and Torquemada and Ignatius
Loyola men after the very heart of Jesus. Neither they nor
their exploits had anything to do with him. It is probable
that Archbishop Laud and John Wesley died equally persuaded that he in whose name they had made themselves
famous on earth would receive them in Heaven with open
arms. George Fox the Quaker would have had ten times their
chance; and yet Fox made rather a miserable business of life.
    Nevertheless all these perversions of the doctrine of
Jesus derived their moral force from his credit, and so had
to keep his gospel alive. When the Protestants translated
the Bible into the vernacular and let it loose among the
people, they did an extremely dangerous thing, as the mischief which followed proves; but they incidentally let loose
the sayings of Jesus in open competition with the sayings of
Paul and Koheleth and David and Solomon and the authors
of Job and the Pentateuch; and, as we have seen, Jesus seems
to be the winning name. The glaring contradiction between
his teaching and the practice of all the States and all the
Churches is no longer hidden. And it may be that though

nineteen centuries have passed since Jesus was born (the date of his birth is now quaintly given as 7 B.C., though some contend for 100 B.C.), and though his Church has not yet been founded nor his political system tried, the bankruptcy of all the other systems when audited by our vital statistics, which give us a final test for all political systems, is driving us hard into accepting him, not as a scapegoat, but as one who was much less of a fool in practical matters than we have hitherto all thought him.

THE ALTERNATIVE CHRISTS

Let us now clear up the situation a little. The New Testament tells two stories for two different sorts of readers. One is the old story of the achievement of our salvation by the sacrifice and atonement of a divine personage who was barbarously slain and rose again on the third day: the story as it was accepted by the apostles. And in this story the political, economic, and moral views of the Christ have no importance: the atonement is everything; and we are saved by our faith in it, and not by works or opinions (other than that particular opinion) bearing on practical affairs.

The other is the story of a prophet who, after expressing several very interesting opinions as to practical conduct, both personal and political, which are now of pressing importance, and instructing his disciples to carry them out in their daily life, lost his head; believed himself to be a crude legendary form of god; and under that delusion courted and suffered a cruel execution in the belief that he would rise from the dead and come in glory to reign over a regenerated world. In this form, the political, economic, and moral opinions of Jesus, as guides to conduct, are interesting and important: the rest is mere psychopathy and superstition. The accounts of the resurrection, the parthenogenetic birth, and the more incredible miracles are rejected as inventions; and such episodes as the conversation with the devil are classed with similar conversations recorded of St Dunstan, Luther, Bunyan, Swedenborg, and Blake.

CREDULITY NO CRITERION
This arbitrary acceptance and rejection of parts of the gospel is not peculiar to the Secularist view. We have seen Luke and John reject Matthew's story of the massacre of the innocents and the flight into Egypt without ceremony. The notion that Matthew's manuscript is a literal and infallible record of facts, not subject to the errors that beset all earthly chroniclers, would have made John stare, being as it is a comparatively modern fancy of intellectually untrained people who keep the Bible on the same shelf with Napoleon's Book of Fate, Old Moore's Almanack, and handbooks of therapeutic herbalism. You may be a fanatical Salvationist and reject more miracle stories than Huxley did; and you may utterly repudiate Jesus as the Savior and yet cite him as a historical witness to the possession by men of the most marvellous thaumaturgical powers. "Christ Scientist" and Jesus the Mahatma are preached by people whom Peter would have struck dead as worse infidels than Simon Magus; and the Atonement is preached by Baptist and Congregationalist ministers whose views of the miracles are those of Ingersoll and Bradlaugh. Luther, who made a clean sweep of all the saints with their million miracles, and reduced the Blessed Virgin herself to the status of an idol, concentrated Salvationism to a point at which the most execrable murderer who believes in it when the rope is round his neck, flies straight to the arms of Jesus, whilst Tom Paine and Shelley fall into the bottomless pit to burn there to all eternity. And sceptical physicists like Sir William Crookes demonstrate by laboratory experiments that "mediums" like Dunglas Home can make the pointer of a spring-balance go round without touching the weight suspended from it.

BELIEF IN PERSONAL IMMORTALITY NO CRITERION
Nor is belief in individual immortality any criterion. Theosophists, rejecting vicarious atonement so sternly that they insist that the smallest of our sins brings its Karma, also

insist on individual immortality and metempsychosis in order to provide an unlimited field for Karma to be worked out by the unredeemed sinner. The belief in the prolongation of individual life beyond the grave is far more real and vivid among table-rapping Spiritualists than among conventional Christians. The notion that those who reject the Christian (or any other) scheme of salvation by atonement must reject also belief in personal immortality and in miracles is as baseless as the notion that if a man is an atheist he will steal your watch.

I could multiply these instances to weariness. The main difference that set Gladstone and Huxley by the ears is not one between belief in supernatural persons or miraculous events and the sternest view of such belief as a breach of intellectual integrity: it is the difference between belief in the efficacy of the crucifixion as an infallible cure for guilt, and a congenital incapacity for believing this, or (the same thing) desiring to believe it.

THE SECULAR VIEW NATURAL, NOT RATIONAL, THEREFORE INEVITABLE

It must therefore be taken as a flat fundamental modern fact, whether we like it or not, that whilst many of us cannot believe that Jesus got his curious grip of our souls by mere sentimentality, neither can we believe that he was John Barleycorn. The more our reason and study lead us to believe that Jesus was talking the most penetrating good sense when he preached Communism; when he declared that the reality behind the popular belief in God was a creative spirit in ourselves called by him the Heavenly Father and by us Evolution, Élan Vital, Life Force and other names; when he protested against the claims of marriage and the family to appropriate that high part of our energy that was meant for the service of his Father, the more impossible it becomes for us to believe that he was talking equally good sense when he so suddenly announced that he was himself a visible concrete God; that his flesh and blood were miraculous food for us; that he must be tortured and slain in the traditional manner and would rise from the dead after three days; and that at his Second Coming the stars would fall from heaven and he become king of an earthly paradise. But it is easy and reasonable to believe that an overwrought preacher at last went mad as Swift and Ruskin and Nietzsche went mad. Every asylum has in it a patient suffering from the delusion that he is a god, yet otherwise sane enough. These patients do not nowadays declare that they will be barbarously slain and will rise from the dead, because they have lost that tradition of the destiny of godhead; but they claim everything appertaining to divinity that is within their knowledge.

Thus the gospels as memoirs and suggestive statements of sociological and biological doctrine, highly relevant to modern civilization, though ending in the history of a psychopathic delusion, are quite credible, intelligible, and interesting to modern thinkers. In any other light they are neither credible, intelligible, nor interesting except to people upon whom the delusion imposes.

"THE HIGHER CRITICISM"

Historical research and paleographic criticism will no doubt continue their demonstrations that the New Testament, like the Old, seldom tells a single story or expounds a single doctrine, and gives us often an accretion and conglomeration of widely discrete and even unrelated traditions and doctrines. But these disintegrations, though technically interesting to scholars, and gratifying or exasperating, as the case may be, to people who are merely defending or attacking the paper fortifications of the infallibility of the Bible, have hardly anything to do with the purpose of these pages. I have mentioned the fact that most of the authorities are now agreed (for the moment) that the date of the birth of Jesus may be placed at about 7 B.C.; but they do not therefore date their letters 1923, nor, I presume, do they expect me to do so. What I am engaged in is a criticism (in the Kantian sense) of an established body of belief which has become an actual part of the mental fabric of my readers; and I should be the most exasperating of triflers and pedants if

410

PREFACE

I were to digress into a criticism of some other belief or no-
belief which my readers might conceivably profess if they
were erudite Scriptural paleographers and historians, in
which case, by the way, they would have to change their
views so frequently that the gospel they received in their
childhood would dominate them after all by its superior per-
sistency. The chaos of mere facts in which the Sermon on the
Mount and the Ode to Charity suggest nothing but disputes as to whether they are interpolations or not, in which
Jesus becomes nothing but a name suspected of belonging
to ten different prophets or executed persons, in which Paul
is only the man who could not possibly have written the
epistles attributed to him, in which Chinese sages, Greek
philosophers, Latin authors, and writers of ancient anony-
mous inscriptions are thrown at our heads as the sources of
this or that scrap of the Bible, is neither a religion nor a criticism of religion: one does not offer the fact that a good deal
of the medieval building in Peterborough Cathedral was
found to be flagrant jerry-building as a criticism of the
Dean's sermons. For good or evil, we have made a synthesis
out of the literature we call the Bible; and though the discovery that there is a good deal of jerry-building in the Bible
is interesting in its way, because everything about the Bible
is interesting, it does not alter the synthesis very materially
even for the paleographers, and does not alter it at all for
those who know no more about modern paleography than
Archbishop Ussher did. I have therefore indicated little
more of the discoveries than Archbishop Ussher might have
guessed for himself if he had read the Bible without pre-
possessions.

For the rest, I have taken the synthesis as it really lives
and works in men. After all, a synthesis is what you want: it
is the case you have to judge brought to an apprehensible
issue for you. Even if you have little more respect for synthetic biography than for synthetic rubber, synthetic milk,
and the still unachieved synthetic protoplasm which is to
enable us to make different sorts of men as a pastrycook

411

makes different sorts of tarts, the practical issue still lies as plainly before you as before the most credulous votaries of what pontificates as the Higher Criticism.

THE PERILS CF SALVATIONISM

The secular view of Jesus is powerfully reinforced by the increase in our day of the number of people who have had the means of educating and training themselves to the point at which they are not afraid to look facts in the face, even such terrifying facts as sin and death. The result is greater sternness in modern thought. The conviction is spreading that to encourage a man to believe that though his sins be as scarlet he can be made whiter than snow by an easy exercise of self-conceit, is to encourage him to be a rascal. It did not work so badly when you could also conscientiously assure him that if he let himself be caught napping in the matter of faith by death, a red-hot hell would roast him alive to all eternity. In those days a sudden death —the most enviable of all deaths—was regarded as the most frightful calamity. It was classed with plague, pestilence, and famine, battle and murder, in our prayers. But belief in that hell is fast vanishing. All the leaders of thought have lost it; and even for the rank and file it has fled to those parts of Ireland and Scotland which are still in the seventeenth century. Even there, it is tacitly reserved for the other fellow.

THE IMPORTANCE OF HELL IN THE SALVATION SCHEME

The seriousness of throwing over hell whilst still clinging to the Atonement is obvious. If there is no punishment for sin there can be no self-forgiveness for it. If Christ paid our score, and if there is no hell and therefore no chance of our getting into trouble by forgetting the obligation, then we can be as wicked as we like with impunity inside the secular law, even from self-reproach, which becomes mere ingratitude to the Savior. On the other hand, if Christ did not pay our score, it still stands against us; and such debts make us extremely uncomfortable. The drive of evolution,

412

which we call conscience and honor, seizes on such slips, and shames us to the dust for being so low in the scale as to be capable of them. The "saved" thief experiences an ecstatic happiness which can never come to the honest atheist: he is tempted to steal again to repeat the glorious sensation. But if the atheist steals he has no such happiness. He is a thief and knows that he is a thief. Nothing can rub that off him. He may try to soothe his shame by some sort of restitution or equivalent act of benevolence; but that does not alter the fact that he did steal; and his conscience will not be easy until he has conquered his will to steal and changed himself into an honest man by developing that divine spark within him which Jesus insisted on as the everyday reality of what the atheist denies.

Now though the state of the believers in the Atonement may thus be the happier, it is most certainly not more desirable from the point of view of the community. The fact that a believer is happier than a sceptic is no more to the point than the fact that a drunken man is happier than a sober one. The happiness of credulity is a cheap and dangerous quality of happiness, and by no means a necessity of life. Whether Socrates got as much happiness out of life as Wesley is an unanswerable question; but a nation of Socrateses would be much safer and happier than a nation of Wesleys; and its individuals would be higher in the evolutionary scale. At all events it is in the Socratic man and not in the Wesleyan that our hope lies now.

THE RIGHT TO REFUSE ATONEMENT

Consequently, even if it were mentally possible for all of us to believe in the Atonement, we should have to cry off it, as we evidently have a right to do. Every man to whom salvation is offered has an inalienable natural right to say "No, thank you: I prefer to retain my full moral responsibility: it is not good for me to be able to load a scapegoat with my sins: I should be less careful how I committed them if I knew they would cost me nothing." Then, too, there is the attitude of Ibsen: that iron moralist to whom the whole scheme of salvation was only an ignoble attempt to cheat God; to get into heaven without paying the price. To be let off, to beg for and accept eternal life as a present instead of earning it, would be mean enough even if we accepted the contempt of the Power on whose pity we were trading; but to bargain for a crown of glory as well! that was too much for Ibsen: it provoked him to exclaim, "Your God is an old man whom you cheat," and to lash the deadened conscience of the nineteenth century back to life with a whip of scorpions.

THE TEACHING OF CHRISTIANITY

And there I must leave the matter to such choice as your nature allows you. The honest teacher who has to make known to a novice the facts about Christianity cannot in any essential regard, I think, put the facts otherwise than as I have put them. If children are to be delivered from the proselytizing atheist on the one hand, and the proselytizing nun in the convent school on the other, with all the other proselytizers that lie between them, they must not be burdened with idle controversies as to whether there was ever such a person as Jesus or not. When Hume said that Joshua's campaigns were impossible, Whately did not wrangle about it: he proved, on the same lines, that the campaigns of Napoleon were impossible. Only fictitious characters will stand Hume's sort of examination: nothing will ever make Edward the Confessor and St Louis as real to us as Don Quixote and Mr Pickwick. We must cut the controversy short by declaring that there is the same evidence for the existence of Jesus as for that of any other person of his time; and the fact that you may not believe everything Matthew tells you no more disproves the existence of Jesus than the fact that you do not believe everything Macaulay tells you disproves the existence of William III. The gospel narratives in the main give you a biography which is quite credible and accountable on purely secular grounds when you have trimmed off everything that Hume or Grimm or Rousseau or Huxley or any modern bishop could reject as fanci-

414

ful. Without going further than this, you can become a
follower of Jesus just as you can become a follower of Confucius or Lao Tse, and may therefore call yourself a Jesuist,
or even a Christian, if you hold, as the strictest Secularist
quite legitimately may, that all prophets are inspired, and
all men with a mission, Christs.

The teacher of Christianity has then to make known to
the child, first the song of John Barleycorn, with the fields
and seasons as witness to its eternal truth. Then, as the
child's mind matures, it can learn, as historical and psycho-
logical phenomena, the tradition of the scapegoat, the Redeemer, the Atonement, the Resurrection, the Second Coming, and how, in a world saturated with this tradition, Jesus
has been largely accepted as the long expected and often
prophesied Redeemer, the Messiah, *the* Christ. It is open to
the child also to accept him. If the child is built like Gladstone, he will accept Jesus as his Savior, and Peter and John
the Baptist as the Savior's revealer and forerunner respectively. If he is built like Huxley, he will take the secular
view, in spite of all that a pious family can do to prevent
him. The important thing now is that the Gladstones and
Huxleys should no longer waste their time irrelevantly and
ridiculously wrangling about the Gadarene swine, and that
they should make up their minds as to the soundness of the
secular doctrines of Jesus; for it is about these that they
may come to blows in our own time.

CHRISTIANITY AND THE EMPIRE

Finally, let us ask why it is that the old superstitions
have so suddenly lost countenance that although, to the
utter disgrace of the nation's leaders and rulers, the laws by
which persecutors can destroy or gag all freedom of thought
and speech in these matters are still unrepealed and ready to
the hand of our bigots and fanatics (quite recently a respectable shopkeeper was convicted of "blasphemy" for saying
that if a modern girl accounted for an illicit pregnancy by
saying she had conceived of the Holy Ghost, we should
know what to think: a remark which would never have

occurred to him had he been properly taught how the story was grafted on the gospel), yet somehow they are used only against poor men, and that only in a half-hearted way. When we consider that from the time when the first scholar ventured to whisper as a professional secret that the Pentateuch could not possibly have been written by Moses to the time within my own recollection when Bishop Colenso, for saying the same thing openly, was inhibited from preaching and actually excommunicated, eight centuries elapsed (the point at issue, though technically interesting to paleographers and historians, having no more bearing on human welfare than the controversy as to whether uncial or cursive is the older form of writing); yet now, within fifty years of Colenso's heresy, there is not a Churchman of any authority living, or an educated layman, who could without ridicule declare that Moses wrote the Pentateuch as Pascal wrote his Thoughts or D'Aubigny his History of the Reformation, or that St Jerome wrote the passage about the three witnesses in the Vulgate, or that there are less than three different accounts of the creation jumbled together in the book of Genesis. Now the maddest Progressive will hardly contend that our growth in wisdom and liberality has been greater in the last half century than in the sixteen half centuries preceding: indeed it would be easier to sustain the thesis that the last fifty years have witnessed a distinct reaction from Victorian Liberalism to Collectivism which has perceptibly strengthened the State Churches. Yet the fact remains that whereas Byron's Cain, published a century ago, is a leading case on the point that there is no copyright in a blasphemous book, the Salvation Army might now include it among its publications without shocking anyone.

I suggest that the causes which have produced this sudden clearing of the air include the transformation of many modern States, notably the old self-contained French Republic and the tight little Island of Britain, into empires which overflow the frontiers of all the Churches. In India, for example, there are less than four million Christians out of a population of three hundred and sixteen and a half millions. The King of England is the defender of the faith; but what faith is now *the* faith? The inhabitants of this island would, within the memory of persons still living, have claimed that their faith is surely *the* faith of God, and that all others are heathen. But we islanders are only forty-five millions; and if we count ourselves all as Christians, there are still seventy-seven and a quarter million Mahometans in the Empire. Add to these the Hindoos and Buddhists, Sikhs and Jains, whom I was taught in my childhood, by way of religious instruction, to regard as gross idolaters consigned to eternal perdition, but whose faith I can now be punished for disparaging by a provocative word, and you have a total of over three hundred and forty-two and a quarter million heretics to swamp our forty-five million Britons, of whom, by the way, only six thousand call themselves distinctively "disciples of Christ," the rest being members of the Church of England and other denominations whose discipleship is less emphatically affirmed. In short, the Englishman of today, instead of being, like the forefathers whose ideas he clings to, a subject of a State practically wholly Christian, is now crowded, and indeed considerably overcrowded, into a corner of an Empire in which the Christians are a mere eleven per cent of the population; so that the Nonconformist who allows his umbrella stand to be sold up rather than pay rates towards the support of a Church of England school, finds himself paying taxes not only to endow the Church of Rome in Malta, but to send Christians to prison for the blasphemy of offering Bibles for sale in the streets of Khartoum.

Turn to France, a country ten times more insular in its preoccupation with its own language, its own history, its own character, than we, who have always been explorers and colonizers and grumblers. This once self-centred nation is forty millions strong. The total population of the French Republic is about one hundred and fourteen millions. The French are not in our hopeless Christian minority of eleven per cent; but they are in a minority of thirty-five per cent, which is fairly conclusive. And, being a more logical people than we, they have officially abandoned Christianity and declared that the French State has no specific religion.

Neither has the British State, though it does not say so. No doubt there are many innocent people in England who take Charlemagne's view, and would, as a matter of course, offer our eighty-nine per cent of "pagans, I regret to say" the alternative of death or Christianity but for a vague impression that these lost ones are all being converted gradually by the missionaries. But no statesman can entertain such ludicrously parochial delusions. No English king or French president can possibly govern on the assumption that the theology of Peter and Paul, Luther and Calvin, has any objective validity, or that the Christ is more than the Buddha or Jehovah more than Krishna, or Jesus more or less human than Mahomet or Zoroaster or Confucius. He is actually compelled, in so far as he makes laws against blasphemy at all, to treat all the religions, including Christianity, as blasphemous when paraded before people who are not accustomed to them and do not want them. And even that is a concession to a mischievous intolerance which an empire should use its control of education to eradicate.

On the other hand, Governments cannot really divest themselves of religion, or even of dogma. When Jesus said that people should not only live but live more abundantly, he was dogmatizing; and many Pessimist sages, including Shakespear, whose hero begged his friend to refrain from suicide in the words "Absent thee from felicity awhile," would say dogmatizing very perniciously. Indeed many preachers and saints declare, some of them in the name of Jesus himself, that this world is a vale of tears, and that our lives had better be passed in sorrow and even in torment, as a preparation for a better life to come. Make these sad people comfortable; and they baffle you by putting on hair shirts.

None the less, Governments must proceed on dogmatic assumptions, whether they call them dogmas or not; and they must clearly be assumptions common enough to stamp those who reject them as eccentrics or lunatics. And the greater and more heterogeneous the population the commoner the assumptions must be. A Trappist monastery can be conducted on assumptions which would in twenty-four hours provoke the village at its gates to insurrection. That is because the monastery selects its people; and if a Trappist does not like it he can leave it. But a subject of the British Empire or the French Republic is not selected; and if he does not like it he must lump it; for emigration is practicable only within narrow limits, and seldom provides an effective remedy, all civilizations being now much alike.

To anyone capable of comprehending government at all it must be evident without argument that the set of fundamental assumptions drawn up in the thirty-nine articles or in the Westminster Confession are wildly impossible as political constitutions for modern empires. A personal profession of them by any person disposed to take such professions seriously would practically disqualify him for high imperial office. A Calvinist Viceroy of India and a Particular Baptist Secretary of State for Foreign Affairs would wreck the empire. The Stuarts wrecked even the tight little island which was the nucleus of the empire by their Scottish logic and theological dogma; and it may be sustained very plausibly that the alleged aptitude of the English for self-government, which is contradicted by every chapter of their history, is really only an incurable inaptitude for theology, and indeed for co-ordinated thought in any direction, which makes them equally impatient of systematic despotism and systematic good government: their history being that of a badly governed and accidentally free people (comparatively). Thus our success in colonizing, as far as it has not been produced by exterminating the natives, has been due to our indifference to the salvation of our subjects. Ireland is the exception which proves the rule; for Ireland, the standing instance of the inability of the English to colonize without extermination of natives, is also the one country

419

under British rule in which the conquerors and colonizers proceeded on the assumption that their business was to establish Protestantism as well as to make money and thereby secure at least the lives of the unfortunate inhabitants out of whose labor it could be made. At this moment Ulster is refusing to accept fellow-citizenship with the other Irish provinces because the south believes in St Peter and Bossuet, and the north in St Paul and Calvin. Imagine the effect of trying to govern India or Egypt from Belfast or from the Vatican!

The position is perhaps graver for France than for England, because the sixty-five per cent of French subjects who are neither French nor Christian nor Modernist includes some thirty millions of negroes who are susceptible, and indeed highly susceptible, of conversion to those salvationist forms of pseudo-Christianity which have produced all the persecutions and religious wars of the last fifteen hundred years. When the late explorer Sir Henry Stanley told me of the emotional grip which Christianity had over the Baganda tribes, and read me their letters, which were exactly like medieval letters in their literal faith and ever-present piety, I said "Can these men handle a rifle?" To which Stanley replied with some scorn "Of course they can, as well as any white man." Now at this moment (1915) a vast European war is being waged, in which the French are using Senegalese soldiers. I ask the French Government, which, like our own Government, is deliberately leaving the religious instruction of these negroes in the hands of missions of Petrine Catholics and Pauline Calvinists, whether they have considered the possibility of a new series of crusades, by ardent African Salvationists, to rescue Paris from the grip of the modern scientific "infidel," and to raise the cry of "Back to the Apostles: back to Charlemagne!"

We are more fortunate in that an overwhelming majority of our subjects are Hindoos, Mahometans, and Buddhists: that is, they have, as a prophylactic against salvationist Christianity, highly civilized religions of their own. Mahometanism, which Napoleon at the end of his career classed as perhaps the best popular religion for modern political use, might in some respects have arisen as a reformed Christianity if Mahomet had had to deal with a population of seventeenth-century Christians instead of Arabs who worshipped stones. As it is, men do not reject Mahomet for Calvin; and to offer a Hindoo so crude a theology as ours in exchange for his own, or our Jewish canonical literature as an improvement on Hindoo scripture, is to offer old lamps for older ones in a market where the oldest lamps, like old furniture in England, are the most highly valued.

Yet, I repeat, government is impossible without a religion: that is, without a body of common assumptions. The open mind never acts: when we have done our utmost to arrive at a reasonable conclusion, we still, when we can reason and investigate no more, must close our minds for the moment with a snap, and act dogmatically on our conclusions. The man who waits to make an entirely reasonable will dies intestate. A man so reasonable as to have an open mind about theft and murder, or about the need for food and reproduction, might just as well be a fool and a scoundrel for any use he could be as a legislator or a State official. The modern pseudo-democratic statesman, who says that he is only in power to carry out the will of the people, and moves only as the cat jumps, is clearly a political and intellectual brigand. The rule of the negative man who has no convictions means in practice the rule of the positive mob. Freedom of conscience as Cromwell used the phrase is an excellent thing; nevertheless if any man had proposed to give effect to freedom of conscience as to cannibalism in England, Cromwell would have laid him by the heels almost as promptly as he would have laid a Roman Catholic, though in Fiji at the same moment he would have supported heartily the freedom of conscience of a vegetarian who disparaged the sacred diet of Long Pig.

Here then comes in the importance of the repudiation by Jesus of proselytism. His rule "Dont pull up the tares: sow

421

the wheat: if you try to pull up the tares you will pull up the wheat with it" is the only possible rule for a statesman governing a modern empire, or a voter supporting such a statesman. There is nothing in the teaching of Jesus that cannot be assented to by a Brahman, a Mahometan, a Buddhist or a Jew, without any question of their conversion to Christianity. In some ways it is easier to reconcile a Mahometan to Jesus than a British parson, because the idea of a professional priest is unfamiliar and even monstrous to a Mahometan (the tourist who persists in asking who is the dean of St Sophia puzzles beyond words the sacristan who lends him a huge pair of slippers); and Jesus never suggested that his disciples should separate themselves from the laity: he picked them up by the wayside, where any man or woman might follow him. For priests he had not a civil word; and they shewed their sense of his hostility by getting him killed as soon as possible. He was, in short, a thoroughgoing anti-Clerical. And though, as we have seen, it is only by political means that his doctrine can be put into practice, he not only never suggested a sectarian theocracy as a form of government, and would certainly have prophesied the downfall of the late President Kruger if he had survived to his time, but, when challenged, he refused to teach his disciples not to pay tribute to Caesar, admitting that Caesar, who presumably had the kingdom of heaven within him as much as any disciple, had his place in the scheme of things. Indeed the apostles made this an excuse for carrying subservience to the State to a pitch of idolatry that ended in the theory of the divine right of kings, and provoked men to cut kings' heads off to restore some sense of proportion in the matter. Jesus certainly did not consider the overthrow of the Roman empire or the substitution of a new ecclesiastical organization for the Jewish Church or for the priesthood of the Roman gods as part of his program. He said that God was better than Mammon; but he never said that Tweedledum was better than Tweedledee; and that is why it is now possible for British citizens and statesmen to follow Jesus,

422

though they cannot possibly follow either Tweedledum or Tweedledee without bringing the empire down with a crash on their heads. And at that I must leave it.

LONDON, *December* 1915.

PROGRAM NOTE

When the play was first produced, a small souvenir book-let, included in the program, contained the following note:

The version of the old story of Androcles and the Lion to be played to-night at the St. James's Theatre is not hampered by a pedantic retention of the details as given by Aulus Gellius. His Androcles was called Androclus, and Androclus was neither a Greek nor a tailor nor a Christian, but a Roman slave who ran away from the cruelties of his master and was later on captured and condemned to be devoured by wild beasts in the arena. But it happened that during his flight he had taken refuge in a cave: and into this cave came a lion who had a thorn in his paw which Androclus extracted. It was to this very lion that Androclus was afterwards thrown in the arena: and the lion, instead of eating him, caressed him. The story figured in natural histories like those of Aelian and was found to please children, in whose story books it has appeared ever since. Nobody believes it; though everybody believes much more improbable stories. It would be incredible of some lions just as the action of Androclus would be incredible of some men. But there are lions and lions, just as there are men and men. The author of the present version has petted a full-grown lion and had his advances received with much more cordiality than he could expect from most St. Bernard dogs. He conceives the lion of Androclus to have been just such a fearless and amiable creature. He conceives Androclus as having that fellow feeling for animals which it becomes the most highly evolved of animals to have (Man is your real king of beasts) and which enables some men to handle bees without being stung and snakes without being bitten. Given such a pair, there is nothing incredible in the story except the theatrical coincidence of the meeting of the two in the arena. Such coincidences are privileged on the stage, and are the special delight of this particular author. And really, when one considers how many men met lions in the arena from first to last, it is not too much to ask you to believe that just for once they turned out to be old friends.

If the author is asked why he has made Androcles a Christian, he can only ask why not. St. Francis preached to the birds as to his 'little brothers'; and St. Francis was a Christian. St. Anthony preached to the fishes, who probably understood at least as much of his sermon as a modern fashionable congregation would have done; and St. Anthony was a Christian. Depend on it, Androcles had that root of the religious matter in him which made all religions free to him except the religion of hunting and killing. That is, the religion of the English country house.

But the twentieth-century Christian need not regard the Christianity of the early Christian martyrs as having much to do with his safe and eminently respectable Sunday profession of faith. Christians in those days were neither safe nor respectable. What is more, some of the most eminent Christians were by no means fond of the average Christians of their time. The author once asked an old Owenite Socialist why he had given up Socialism. He replied that after preaching it for some years he had noticed that it seemed to have a very bad effect on the moral character of those who gave themselves up to its propaganda. The same may be said of all persecuted creeds. A doctrine may be true and important, and its persecutors may be altogether in the wrong; but this makes the position of the man who is persecuted for propagating it all the more morbid. One sane man in a lunatic asylum can no more keep his normal health and temper than one lunatic in a *conseil de prudhommes*. Add to this consideration the fact that all movements which attack the existing state of society attract both the people who are not good enough for the world and the people for whom the world is not good enough; so that the saint is always embarrassed by finding that the dynamiter and the assassin, the thief and the libertine, make common cause with him; and you will not be sur-

PROGRAM NOTE

prised to learn, if you do not know it already, that early Christians like Saint Augustine have a good many stories to tell of Christians who thoroughly deserved their evil reputation. The character of Spintho in the present play is by no means a malicious invention of the author's. Indeed had he gone on to exhibit Spintho as having taken the precaution to marry an orthodox Roman in order to shirk the Christian obligation to practise Communism, and as ostentatiously giving the lady black eyes to show how his conjugal duties revolted his ascetic nature, there would have been warrant for that, too, and worse, in the records of the Fathers of the Church.

In representing a Roman centurion and a Roman captain (a pure invention) as corresponding to a British sergeant and a British company officer, some violence may or may not have been done to the petty accuracies of military history. Centurions were much chaffed in Rome as being mostly thick-booted vulgar persons, whacking their man with vinewood cudgels, and out of place in refined society; and the nearest thing to a modern captain as far as rank was concerned was probably not much more of a patrician. The patrician soldier was not a professional soldier: he commanded armies or adorned Senates or governed Provinces as part of the natural pursuits of a patrician. But the relation of patrician officer to plebeian routineer existed as it exists to-day; and whether my captain should have been called something else, or my Centurion a Decurion, does not trouble me any more than the old controversy as to whether the audience turned their thumbs up or down when they wanted a defeated gladiator slain.

In short, if you demand my authorities for this and that, I must reply that only those who have never hunted up the authorities as I have believe that there is any authority who is not contradicted flatly by some other authority. Marshal Junot, reproached for having no respect for ancestry, said that he was an ancestor himself. In the

427

PROGRAM NOTE

same spirit I point out that the authorities on the story of Androcles and on the history of the early Christian martyrs are the people who have written about them; and now that I, too, have written about them, I take my place as the latest authority on the subject, and ask you to respect me accordingly.

ANDROCLES AND THE LION

PROLOGUE

OVERTURE: forest sounds, roaring of lions, Christian hymn faintly.

A jungle path. A lion's roar, a melancholy suffering roar, comes from the jungle. It is repeated nearer. The lion limps from the jungle on three legs, holding up his right forepaw, in which a huge thorn sticks. He sits down and contemplates it. He licks it. He shakes it. He tries to extract it by scraping it along the ground, and hurts himself worse. He roars piteously. He licks it again. Tears drop from his eyes. He limps painfully off the path and lies down under the trees, exhausted with pain. Heaving a long sigh, like wind in a trombone, he goes to sleep.

Androcles and his wife Megaera come along the path. He is a small, thin, ridiculous little man who might be any age from thirty to fifty-five. He has sandy hair, watery compassionate blue eyes, sensitive nostrils, and a very presentable forehead; but his good points go no further: his arms and legs and back, though wiry of their kind, look shrivelled and starved. He carries a big bundle, is very poorly clad, and seems tired and hungry.

His wife is a rather handsome pampered slattern, well fed and in the prime of life. She has nothing to carry, and has a stout stick to help her along.

MEGAERA [*suddenly throwing down her stick*] I wont go another step.

ANDROCLES [*pleading wearily*] Oh, not again, dear. Whats the good of stopping every two miles and saying you wont go another step? We must get on to the next village before night. There are wild beasts in this wood: lions, they say.

MEGAERA. I dont believe a word of it. You are always threatening me with wild beasts to make me walk the very soul out of my body when I can hardly drag one foot before another. We havnt seen a single lion yet.

ANDROCLES. Well, dear, do you want to see one?

MEGAERA [*tearing the bundle from his back*] You cruel brute, you dont care how tired I am, or what becomes of me [*she throws the bundle on the ground*]: always thinking of yourself. Self! self! self! always yourself! [*She sits down on the bundle*].

ANDROCLES [*sitting down sadly on the ground with his elbows on his knees and his head in his hands*] We all have to think of ourselves occasionally, dear.

MEGAERA. A man ought to think of his wife sometimes.

ANDROCLES. He cant always help it, dear. You make me think of you a good deal. Not that I blame you.

MEGAERA. Blame me! I should think not indeed. Is it my fault that I'm married to you?

ANDROCLES. No, dear: that is my fault.

MEGAERA. Thats a nice thing to say to me. Arnt you happy with me?

ANDROCLES. I dont complain, my love.

MEGAERA. You ought to be ashamed of yourself.

ANDROCLES. I am, my dear.

MEGAERA. Youre not: you glory in it.

ANDROCLES. In what, darling?

MEGAERA. In everything. In making me a slave, and making yourself a laughing-stock. It's not fair. You get me the name of being a shrew with your meek ways, always talking as if butter wouldnt melt in your mouth. And just because I look a big strong woman, and because I'm goodhearted and a bit hasty, and because youre always driving me to do things I'm sorry for afterwards, people say "Poor man: what a life his wife leads him!" Oh, if they only knew! And you think I dont know. But I do, I do, [*screaming*] I do.

ANDROCLES. Yes, my dear: I know you do.

MEGAERA. Then why dont you treat me properly and be a good husband to me?

ANDROCLES. What can I do, my dear?

MEGAERA. What can you do! You can return to your duty, and come back to your home and your friends, and sacrifice to the gods as all respectable people do, instead of having us hunted out of house and home for being dirty disreputable blaspheming atheists.

ANDROCLES. I'm not an atheist, dear: I am a Christian.

MEGAERA. Well, isnt that the same thing, only ten times worse? Everybody knows that the Christians are the very lowest of the low.

ANDROCLES. Just like us, dear.

MEGAERA. Speak for yourself. Dont you dare to compare me to common people. My father owned his own public-house; and sorrowful was the day for me when you first came drinking in our bar.

ANDROCLES. I confess I was addicted to it, dear. But I gave it up when I became a Christian.

MEGAERA. Youd much better have remained a drunkard. I can forgive a man being addicted to drink: it's only natural; and I dont deny I like a drop myself sometimes. What I cant stand is your being addicted to Christianity. And whats worse again, your being addicted to animals. How is any woman to keep her house clean when you bring in every stray cat and lost cur and lame duck in the whole country-side? You took the bread out of my mouth to feed them: you know you did: dont attempt to deny it.

ANDROCLES. Only when they were hungry and you were getting too stout, dearie.

MEGAERA. Yes: insult me, do. [Rising] Oh! I wont bear it another moment. You used to sit and talk to those dumb brute beasts for hours, when you hadnt a word for me.

ANDROCLES. They never answered back, darling. [He rises and again shoulders the bundle].

MEGAERA. Well, if youre fonder of animals than of your own wife, you can live with them here in the jungle. Ive had enough of them and enough of you. I'm going back. I'm going home.

ANDROCLES [barring the way back] No, dearie: dont take on like that. We cant go back. Weve sold everything: we should starve; and I should be sent to Rome and thrown to the lions—

MEGAERA. Serve you right! I wish the lions joy of you. [Screaming] Are you going to get out of my way and let me go home?

431

ANDROCLES. No, dear—

MEGAERA. Then I'll make my way through the forest; and when I'm eaten by the wild beasts youll know what a wife youve lost. [*She dashes into the jungle and nearly falls over the sleeping lion*]. Oh! Oh! Andy! Andy! [*She totters back and collapses into the arms of Androcles, who, crushed by her weight, falls on his bundle*].

ANDROCLES [*extracting himself from beneath her and slapping her hands in great anxiety*] What is it, my precious, my pet? Whats the matter? [*He raises her head. Speechless with terror, she points in the direction of the sleeping lion. He steals cautiously towards the spot indicated by Megaera. She rises with an effort and totters after him*].

MEGAERA. No, Andy: youll be killed. Come back.

The lion utters a long snoring sigh. Androcles sees the lion, and recoils fainting into the arms of Megaera, who falls back on the bundle. They roll apart and lie staring in terror at one another. The lion is heard groaning heavily in the jungle.

ANDROCLES [*whispering*] Did you see? A lion.

MEGAERA [*despairing*] The gods have sent him to punish us because youre a Christian. Take me away, Andy. Save me.

ANDROCLES [*rising*] Meggy: theres one chance for you. Itll take him pretty nigh twenty minutes to eat me (I'm rather stringy and tough) and you can escape in less time than that.

MEGAERA. Oh, dont talk about eating. [*The lion rises with a great groan and limps towards them*]. Oh! [*She faints*].

ANDROCLES [*quaking, but keeping between the lion and Megaera*] Dont you come near my wife, do you hear? [*The lion groans. Androcles can hardly stand for trembling*]. Meggy: run. Run for your life. If I take my eye off him, it's all up. [*The lion holds up his wounded paw and flaps it piteously before Androcles*]. Oh, he's lame, poor old chap! He's got a thorn in his paw. A frightfully big thorn. [*Full of sympathy*] Oh, poor old man! Did um get an awful thorn into um's tootsums wootsums? Has it made um too sick to eat a nice little Christian man for um's breakfast? Oh, a nice little Christian

432

man will get um's thorn out for um; and then um shall eat the nice Christian man and the nice Christian man's nice big tender wifey pifey. [*The lion responds by moans of self-pity*]. Yes, yes, yes, yes, yes. Now, now [*taking the paw in his hand*], um is not to bite and not to scratch, not even if it hurts a very very little. Now make velvet paws. Thats right. [*He pulls gingerly at the thorn. The lion, with an angry yell of pain, jerks back his paw so abruptly that Androcles is thrown on his back*]. Steadeee! Oh, did the nasty cruel little Christian man hurt the sore paw? [*The lion moans assentingly but apologetically*]. Well, one more little pull and it will be all over. Just one little, little, leetle pull; and then um will live happily ever after. [*He gives the thorn another pull. The lion roars and snaps his jaws with a terrifying clash*]. Oh, mustnt frighten um's good kind doctor, um's affectionate nursey. That didnt hurt at all: not a bit. Just one more. Just to shew how the brave big lion can bear pain, not like the little crybaby Christian man. Oopsh! [*The thorn comes out. The lion yells with pain, and shakes his paw wildly*]. Thats it! [*Holding up the thorn*]. Now it's out. Now lick um's paw to take away the nasty inflammation. See? [*He licks his own hand. The lion nods intelligently and licks his paw industriously*]. Clever little liony-piony! Understands um's dear old friend Andy Wandy. [*The lion licks his face*]. Yes, kissums Andy Wandy. [*The lion, wagging his tail violently, rises on his hind legs, and embraces Androcles, who makes a wry face and cries*] Velvet paws! Velvet paws! [*The lion draws in his claws*]. Thats right. [*He embraces the lion, who finally takes the end of his tail in one paw, places that tight round Androcles' waist, resting it on his hip. Androcles takes the other paw in his hand, stretches out his arm, and the two waltz rapturously round and round and finally away through the jungle*].

MEGAERA [*who has revived during the waltz*] Oh, you coward, you havnt danced with me for years; and now you go off dancing with a great brute beast that you havnt known for ten minutes and that wants to eat your own wife. Coward! Coward! Coward! [*She rushes off after them into the jungle*].

ACT I

EVENING. *The end of three converging roads to Rome. Three triumphal arches span them where they debouch on a square at the gate of the city. Looking north through the arches one can see the campagna threaded by the three long dusty tracks. On the east and west sides of the square are long stone benches. An old beggar sits on the east side, his bowl at his feet.*

Through the eastern arch a squad of Roman soldiers tramps along escorting a batch of Christian prisoners of both sexes and all ages, among them one Lavinia, a good-looking resolute young woman, apparently of higher social standing than her fellow-prisoners. A centurion, carrying his vinewood cudgel, trudges alongside the squad, on its right, in command of it. All are tired and dusty; but the soldiers are dogged and indifferent, the Christians lighthearted and determined to treat their hardships as a joke and encourage one another.

A bugle is heard far behind on the road, where the rest of the cohort is following.

CENTURION [*stopping*] Halt! Orders from the Captain. [*They halt and wait*]. Now then, you Christians, none of your larks. The Captain's coming. Mind you behave yourselves. No singing. Look respectful. Look serious, if youre capable of it. See that big building over there! Thats the Coliseum. Thats where youll be thrown to the lions or set to fight the gladiators presently. Think of that; and itll help you to behave properly before the Captain. [*The Captain arrives*]. Attention! Salute! [*The soldiers salute*].

A CHRISTIAN [*cheerfully*] God bless you, Captain!

THE CENTURION [*scandalized*] Silence!

The Captain, a patrician, handsome, about thirty-five, very cold and distinguished, very superior and authoritative, steps up on a stone seat at the west side of the square, behind the centurion, so as to dominate the others more effectually.

THE CAPTAIN. Centurion.

THE CENTURION [*standing at attention and saluting*] Sir?

THE CAPTAIN [*speaking stiffly and officially*] You will re-

434

mind your men, Centurion, that we are now entering Rome. You will instruct them that once inside the gates of Rome they are in the presence of the Emperor. You will make them understand that the lax discipline of the march cannot be permitted here. You will instruct them to shave every day, not every week. You will impress on them particularly that there must be an end to the profanity and blasphemy of singing Christian hymns on the march. I have to reprimand you, Centurion, for not only allowing this, but actually doing it yourself.

THE CENTURION [*apologetic*] The men march better, Captain.

THE CAPTAIN. No doubt. For that reason an exception is made in the case of the march called Onward Christian Soldiers. This may be sung, except when marching through the forum or within hearing of the Emperor's palace; but the words must be altered to "Throw them to the Lions."

The Christians burst into shrieks of uncontrollable laughter, to the great scandal of the Centurion.

CENTURION. Silence! Silen-n-n-n-nce! Wheres your behavior? Is that the way to listen to an officer? [*To the Captain*] Thats what we have to put up with from these Christians every day, sir. Theyre always laughing and joking something scandalous. Theyve no religion: thats how it is.

LAVINIA. But I think the Captain meant us to laugh, Centurion. It was so funny.

CENTURION. Youll find out how funny it is when youre thrown to the lions tomorrow. [*To the Captain, who looks displeased*] Beg pardon, Sir. [*To the Christians*] Silennnnce!

THE CAPTAIN. You are to instruct your men that all intimacy with Christian prisoners must now cease. The men have fallen into habits of dependence upon the prisoners, especially the female prisoners, for cooking, repairs to uniforms, writing letters, and advice in their private affairs. In a Roman soldier such dependence is inadmissible. Let me see no more of it whilst we are in the city. Further, your orders are that in addressing Christian prisoners, the man-

435

ners and tone of your men must express abhorrence and contempt. Any shortcoming in this respect will be regarded as a breach of discipline. [*He turns to the prisoners*] Prisoners.

CENTURION [*fiercely*] Prisonerrrrrs! Tention! Silence!

THE CAPTAIN. I call your attention, prisoners, to the fact that you may be called on to appear in the Imperial Circus at any time from tomorrow onwards according to the requirements of the managers. I may inform you that as there is a shortage of Christians just now, you may expect to be called on very soon.

LAVINIA. What will they do to us, Captain?

CENTURION. Silence!

THE CAPTAIN. The women will be conducted into the arena with the wild beasts of the Imperial Menagerie, and will suffer the consequences. The men, if of an age to bear arms, will be given weapons to defend themselves, if they choose, against the Imperial Gladiators.

LAVINIA. Captain: is there no hope that this cruel persecution—

CENTURION [*shocked*] Silence! Hold your tongue, there. Persecution, indeed!

THE CAPTAIN [*unmoved and somewhat sardonic*] Persecution is not a term applicable to the acts of the Emperor. The Emperor is the Defender of the Faith. In throwing you to the lions he will be upholding the interests of religion in Rome. If you were to throw him to the lions, that would no doubt be persecution.

The Christians again laugh heartily.

CENTURION [*horrified*] Silence, I tell you! Keep silence there. Did anyone ever hear the like of this?

LAVINIA. Captain: there will be nobody to appreciate your jokes when we are gone.

THE CAPTAIN [*unshaken in his official delivery*] I call the attention of the female prisoner Lavinia to the fact that as the Emperor is a divine personage, her imputation of cruelty is not only treason, but sacrilege. I point out to her further that there is no foundation for the charge, as the Emperor

436

does not desire that any prisoner should suffer; nor can any
Christian be harmed save through his or her own obstinacy.
All that is necessary is to sacrifice to the gods: a simple and
convenient ceremony effected by dropping a pinch of incense on the altar, after which the prisoner is at once set free.
Under such circumstances you have only your own perverse folly to blame if you suffer. I suggest to you that if you
cannot burn a morsel of incense as a matter of conviction,
you might at least do so as a matter of good taste, to avoid
shocking the religious convictions of your fellow citizens. I
am aware that these considerations do not weigh with Christians; but it is my duty to call your attention to them in order
that you may have no ground for complaining of your treatment, or of accusing the Emperor of cruelty when he is shewing you the most signal clemency. Looked at from this point
of view, every Christian who has perished in the arena has
really committed suicide.

LAVINIA. Captain: your jokes are too grim. Do not think
it is easy for us to die. Our faith makes life far stronger and
more wonderful in us than when we walked in darkness and
had nothing to live for. Death is harder for us than for you:
the martyr's agony is as bitter as his triumph is glorious.

THE CAPTAIN [*rather troubled, addressing her personally and
gravely*] A martyr, Lavinia, is a fool. Your death will prove
nothing.

LAVINIA. Then why kill me?

THE CAPTAIN. I mean that truth, if there be any truth,
needs no martyrs.

LAVINIA. No; but my faith, like your sword, needs testing.
Can you test your sword except by staking your life on it?

THE CAPTAIN [*suddenly resuming his official tone*] I call the
attention of the female prisoner to the fact that Christians
are not allowed to draw the Emperor's officers into arguments and put questions to them for which the military
regulations provide no answer. [*The Christians titter*].

LAVINIA. Captain: how c a n you?

THE CAPTAIN. I call the female prisoner's attention speci-

437

ally to the fact that four comfortable homes have been offered her by officers of this regiment, of which she can have her choice the moment she chooses to sacrifice as all wellbred Roman ladies do. I have no more to say to the prisoners.

CENTURION. Dismiss! But stay where you are.

THE CAPTAIN. Centurion: you will remain here with your men in charge of the prisoners until the arrival of three Christian prisoners in the custody of a cohort of the tenth legion. Among these prisoners you will particularly identify an armorer named Ferrovius, of dangerous character and great personal strength, and a Greek tailor reputed to be a sorcerer, by name Androcles. You will add the three to your charge here and march them all to the Coliseum, where you will deliver them into the custody of the master of the gladiators and take his receipt, countersigned by the keeper of the beasts and the acting manager. You understand your instructions?

CENTURION. Yes, sir.

THE CAPTAIN. Dismiss. [*He throws off his air of parade, and descends from his perch. The Centurion seats himself on it and prepares for a nap, whilst his men stand at ease. The Christians sit down on the west side of the square, glad to rest. Lavinia alone remains standing to speak to the Captain*].

LAVINIA. Captain: is this man who is to join us the famous Ferrovius, who has made such wonderful conversions in the northern cities?

THE CAPTAIN. Yes. We are warned that he has the strength of an elephant and the temper of a mad bull. Also that he is stark mad. Not a model Christian, it would seem.

LAVINIA. You need not fear him if he is a Christian, Captain.

THE CAPTAIN [*coldly*] I shall not fear him in any case, Lavinia.

LAVINIA [*her eyes dancing*] How brave of you, Captain!

THE CAPTAIN. You are right: it was a silly thing to say. [*In a lower tone, humane and urgent*] Lavinia: do Christians know how to love?

438

LAVINIA [*composedly*] Yes, Captain: they love even their enemies.

THE CAPTAIN. Is that easy?

LAVINIA. Very easy, Captain, when their enemies are as handsome as you.

THE CAPTAIN. Lavinia: you are laughing at me.

LAVINIA. At you, Captain! Impossible.

THE CAPTAIN. Then you are flirting with me, which is worse. Dont be foolish.

LAVINIA. But such a very handsome captain.

THE CAPTAIN. Incorrigible! [*Urgently*] Listen to me. The men in that audience tomorrow will be the vilest of voluptuaries: men in whom the only passion excited by a beautiful woman is a lust to see her tortured and torn shrieking limb from limb. It is a crime to gratify that passion. It is offering yourself for violation by the whole rabble of the streets and the riff-raff of the court at the same time. Why will you not choose rather a kindly love and an honorable alliance?

LAVINIA. They cannot violate my soul. I alone can do that by sacrificing to false gods.

THE CAPTAIN. Sacrifice then to the true God. What does his name matter? We call him Jupiter. The Greeks call him Zeus. Call him what you will as you drop the incense on the altar flame: He will understand.

LAVINIA. No. I couldnt. That is the strange thing, Captain, that a little pinch of incense should make all that difference. Religion is such a great thing that when I meet really religious people we are friends at once, no matter what name we give to the divine will that made us and moves us. Oh, do you think that I, a woman, would quarrel with you for sacrificing to a woman god like Diana, if Diana meant to you what Christ means to me? No: we should kneel side by side before her altar like two children. But when men who believe neither in my god nor in their own—men who do not know the meaning of the word religion—when these men drag me to the foot of an iron statue that has become the symbol of the terror and darkness through which they walk,

439

of their cruelty and greed, of their hatred of God and their oppression of man—when they ask me to pledge my soul before the people that this hideous idol is God, and that all this wickedness and falsehood is divine truth, I cannot do it, not if they could put a thousand cruel deaths on me. I tell you, it is physically impossible. Listen, Captain: did you ever try to catch a mouse in your hand? Once there was a dear little mouse that used to come out and play on my table as I was reading. I wanted to take him in my hand and caress him; and sometimes he got among my books so that he could not escape me when I stretched out my hand. And I did stretch out my hand; but it always came back in spite of me. I was not afraid of him in my heart; but my hand refused: it is not in the nature of my hand to touch a mouse. Well, Captain, if I took a pinch of incense in my hand and stretched it out over the altar fire, my hand would come back. My body would be true to my faith even if you could corrupt my mind. And all the time I should believe more in Diana than my persecutors have ever believed in anything. Can you understand that?

THE CAPTAIN [*simply*] Yes: I understand that. But my hand would not come back. The hand that holds the sword has been trained not to come back from anything but victory.

LAVINIA. Not even from death?

THE CAPTAIN. Least of all from death.

LAVINIA. Then I must not come back from death either. A woman has to be braver than a soldier.

THE CAPTAIN. Prouder, you mean.

LAVINIA [*startled*] Prouder! You call our courage pride!

THE CAPTAIN. There is no such thing as courage: there is only pride. You Christians are the proudest devils on earth.

LAVINIA [*hurt*] Pray God then my pride may never become a false pride. [*She turns away as if she did not wish to continue the conversation, but softens and says to him with a smile*] Thank you for trying to save me.

THE CAPTAIN. I knew it was no use; but one tries in spite of one's knowledge.

LAVINIA. Something stirs, even in the iron breast of a Roman soldier?

THE CAPTAIN. It will soon be iron again. I have seen many women die, and forgotten them in a week.

LAVINIA. Remember me for a fortnight, handsome Captain. I shall be watching you, perhaps.

THE CAPTAIN. From the skies? Do not deceive yourself, Lavinia. There is no future for you beyond the grave.

LAVINIA. What does that matter? Do you think I am only running away from the terrors of life into the comfort of heaven? If there were no future, or if the future were one of torment, I should have to go just the same. The hand of God is upon me.

THE CAPTAIN. Yes: when all is said, we are both patricians, Lavinia, and must die for our beliefs. Farewell. [*He offers her his hand. She takes it and presses it. He walks away, trim and calm. She looks after him for a moment, and cries a little as he disappears through the eastern arch. A trumpet-call is heard from the road through the western arch*].

CENTURION [*waking up and rising*] Cohort of the tenth with prisoners. Two file out with me to receive them. [*He goes out through the western arch, followed by four soldiers in two files*].

Lentulus and Metellus come into the square from the west side with a little retinue of servants. Both are young courtiers, dressed in the extremity of fashion. Lentulus is slender, fairhaired, epicene. Metellus is manly, compactly built, olive skinned, not a talker.

LENTULUS. Christians, by Jove! Lets chaff them.

METELLUS. Awful brutes. If you knew as much about them as I do you wouldnt want to chaff them. Leave them to the lions.

LENTULUS [*indicating Lavinia, who is still looking towards the arches after the Captain*] That woman's got a figure. [*He walks past her, staring at her invitingly; but she is preoccupied and is not conscious of him*]. Do you turn the other cheek when they kiss you?

LAVINIA [*starting*] What?

LENTULUS. Do you turn the other cheek when they kiss you, fascinating Christian?

LAVINIA. Dont be foolish. [*To Metellus, who has remained on her right, so that she is between them*] Please dont let your friend behave like a cad before the soldiers. How are they to respect and obey patricians if they see them behaving like street boys? [*Sharply to Lentulus*] Pull yourself together, man. Hold your head up. Keep the corners of your mouth firm; and treat me respectfully. What do you take me for?

LENTULUS [*irresolutely*] Look here, you know: I—you— I—

LAVINIA. Stuff! Go about your business. [*She turns decisively away and sits down with her comrades, leaving him disconcerted*].

METELLUS. You didnt get much out of that. I told you they were brutes.

LENTULUS. Plucky little filly! I suppose she thinks I care. [*With an air of indifference he strolls with Metellus to the east side of the square, where they stand watching the return of the Centurion through the western arch with his men, escorting three prisoners: Ferrovius, Androcles, and Spintho. Ferrovius is a powerful, choleric man in the prime of life, with large nostrils, staring eyes, and a thick neck: a man whose sensibilities are keen and violent to the verge of madness. Spintho is a debauchee, the wreck of a good-looking man gone hopelessly to the bad. Androcles is overwhelmed with grief, and is restraining his tears with great difficulty*].

THE CENTURION [*to Lavinia*] Here are some pals for you. This little bit is Ferrovius that you talk so much about. [*Ferrovius turns on him threateningly. The Centurion holds up his left forefinger in admonition*]. Now remember that youre a Christian, and that youve got to return good for evil. [*Ferrovius controls himself convulsively; moves away from temptation to the east side near Lentulus; clasps his hands in silent prayer; and throws himself on his knees*]. Thats the way to manage them, eh! This fine fellow [*indicating Androcles, who*

comes to his left, and makes Lavinia a heart-broken salutation]
is a sorcerer. A Greek tailor, he is. A real sorcerer, too: no
mistake about it. The tenth marches with a leopard at the
head of the column. He made a pet of the leopard; and now
he's crying at being parted from it. [*Androcles sniffs lament-
ably*]. Aint you, old chap? Well, cheer up, we march with a
Billy goat [*Androcles brightens up*] thats killed two leopards
and ate a turkey-cock. You can have him for a pet if you like.
[*Androcles, quite consoled, goes past the Centurion to Lavinia,
and sits down contentedly on the ground on her left*]. This dirty
dog [*collaring Spintho*] is a real Christian. He mobs the
temples, he does [*at each accusation he gives the neck of
Spintho's tunic a twist*]; he goes smashing things mad drunk,
he does; he steals the gold vessels, he does; he assaults the
priestesses, he does—yah! [*He flings Spintho into the middle
of the group of prisoners*]. Youre the sort that makes duty a
pleasure, you are.

SPINTHO [*gasping*] Thats it: strangle me. Kick me. Beat
me. Revile me. Our Lord was beaten and reviled. Thats my
way to heaven. Every martyr goes to heaven, no matter what
he's done. That is so, isnt it, brother?

CENTURION. Well, if youre going to heaven, *I* dont want
to go there. I wouldnt be seen with you.

LENTULUS. Haw! Good! [*Indicating the kneeling Ferrovius*]. Is this one of the turn-the-other-cheek gentlemen,
Centurion?

CENTURION. Yes, sir. Lucky for you too, sir, if you want
to take any liberties with him.

LENTULUS [*to Ferrovius*] You turn the other cheek when
youre struck, I'm told.

FERROVIUS [*slowly turning his great eyes on him*] Yes, by
the grace of God, I do, now.

LENTULUS. Not that youre a coward, of course; but out
of pure piety.

FERROVIUS. I fear God more than man; at least I try to.

LENTULUS. Lets see. [*He strikes him on the cheek. Androcles
makes a wild movement to rise and interfere; but Lavinia holds*

443

him down, watching Ferrovius intently. Ferrovius, without flinching, turns the other cheek. Lentulus, rather out of countenance, titters foolishly, and strikes him again feebly]. You know, I should feel ashamed if I let myself be struck like that, and took it lying down. But then I'm not a Christian: I'm a man. *[Ferrovius rises impressively and towers over him. Lentulus becomes white with terror; and a shade of green flickers in his cheek for a moment].*

FERROVIUS *[with the calm of a steam hammer]* I have not always been faithful. The first man who struck me as you have just struck me was a stronger man than you: he hit me harder than I expected. I was tempted and fell; and it was then that I first tasted bitter shame. I never had a happy moment after that until I had knelt and asked his forgiveness by his bedside in the hospital. *[Putting his hands on Lentulus's shoulders with paternal weight].* But now I have learnt to resist with a strength that is not my own. I am not ashamed now, nor angry.

LENTULUS *[uneasily]* Er—good evening. *[He tries to move away].*

FERROVIUS *[gripping his shoulders]* Oh, do not harden your heart, young man. Come: try for yourself whether our way is not better than yours. I will now strike you on one cheek; and you will turn the other and learn how much better you will feel than if you gave way to the promptings of anger.*[He holds him with one hand and clenches the other fist].*

LENTULUS. Centurion: I call on you to protect me.

CENTURION. You asked for it, sir. It's no business of ours. Youve had two whacks at him. Better pay him a trifle and square it that way.

LENTULUS. Yes, of course. *[To Ferrovius]* It was only a bit of fun, I assure you: I meant no harm. Here. *[He proffers a gold coin].*

FERROVIUS *[taking it and throwing it to the old beggar, who snatches it up eagerly, and hobbles off to spend it]* Give all thou hast to the poor. Come, friend: courage! I may hurt your

444

body for a moment; but your soul will rejoice in the victory of the spirit over the flesh. [*He prepares to strike*].

ANDROCLES. Easy, Ferrovius, easy: you broke the last man's jaw.

Lentulus, with a moan of terror, attempts to fly; but Ferrovius holds him ruthlessly.

FERROVIUS. Yes; but I saved his soul. What matters a broken jaw?

LENTULUS. Dont touch me, do you hear? The law—

FERROVIUS. The law will throw me to the lions tomorrow: what worse could it do were I to slay you? Pray for strength; and it shall be given to you.

LENTULUS. Let me go. Your religion forbids you to strike me.

FERROVIUS. On the contrary, it commands me to strike you. How can you turn the other cheek, if you are not first struck on the one cheek?

LENTULUS [*almost in tears*] But I'm convinced already that what you said is quite right. I apologize for striking you.

FERROVIUS [*greatly pleased*] My son: have I softened your heart? Has the good seed fallen in a fruitful place? Are your feet turning towards a better path?

LENTULUS [*abjectly*] Yes, yes. Theres a great deal in what you say.

FERROVIUS [*radiant*] Join us. Come to the lions. Come to suffering and death.

LENTULUS [*falling on his knees and bursting into tears*] Oh, help me. Mother! mother!

FERROVIUS. These tears will water your soul and make it bring forth good fruit, my son. God has greatly blessed my efforts at conversion. Shall I tell you a miracle—yes, a miracle—wrought by me in Cappadocia? A young man—just such a one as you, with golden hair like yours—scoffed at and struck me as you scoffed at and struck me. I sat up all night with that youth wrestling for his soul; and in the morning not only was he a Christian, but his hair was as white as snow. [*Lentulus falls in a dead faint*]. There, there:

445

take him away. The spirit has overwrought him, poor lad. Carry him gently to his house; and leave the rest to heaven.

CENTURION. Take him home. [*The servants, intimidated, hastily carry him out. Metellus is about to follow when Ferrovius lays his hand on his shoulder*].

FERROVIUS. You are his friend, young man. You will see that he is taken safely home.

METELLUS [*with awestruck civility*] Certainly, sir. I shall do whatever you think best. Most happy to have made your acquaintance, I'm sure. You may depend on me. Good evening, sir.

FERROVIUS [*with unction*] The blessing of heaven upon you and him.

Metellus follows Lentulus. The Centurion returns to his seat to resume his interrupted nap. The deepest awe has settled on the spectators. Ferrovius, with a long sigh of happiness, goes to Lavinia, and offers her his hand.

LAVINIA [*taking it*] So that is how you convert people, Ferrovius.

FERROVIUS. Yes: there has been a blessing on my work in spite of my unworthiness and my backslidings—all through my wicked, devilish temper. This man—

ANDROCLES [*hastily*] Dont slap me on the back, brother. She knows you mean me.

FERROVIUS. How I wish I were weak like our brother here! for then I should perhaps be meek and gentle like him. And yet there seems to be a special providence that makes my trials less than his. I hear tales of the crowd scoffing and casting stones and reviling the brethren; but when I come, all this stops: my influence calms the passions of the mob: they listen to me in silence; and infidels are often converted by a straight heart-to-heart talk with me. Every day I feel happier, more confident. Every day lightens the load of the great terror.

LAVINIA. The great terror? What is that?

Ferrovius shakes his head and does not answer. He sits down beside her on her left, and buries his face in his hands in gloomy

446

meditation.

ANDROCLES. Well, you see, sister, he's never quite sure of himself. Suppose at the last moment in the arena, with the gladiators there to fight him, one of them was to say anything to annoy him, he might forget himself and lay that gladiator out.

LAVINIA. That would be splendid.

FERROVIUS [*springing up in horror*] What!

ANDROCLES. Oh, sister!

FERROVIUS. Splendid to betray my master, like Peter! Splendid to act like any common blackguard in the day of my proving! Woman: you are no Christian. [*He moves away from her to the middle of the square, as if her neighborhood contaminated him*].

LAVINIA [*laughing*] You know, Ferrovius, I am not always a Christian. I dont think anybody is. There are moments when I forget all about it, and something comes out quite naturally, as it did then.

SPINTHO. What does it matter? If you die in the arena, youll be a martyr; and all martyrs go to heaven, no matter what they have done. Thats so, isnt it, Ferrovius?

FERROVIUS. Yes: that is so, if we are faithful to the end.

LAVINIA. I'm not so sure.

SPINTHO. Dont say that. Thats blasphemy. Dont say that, I tell you. We shall be saved, no matter WHAT we do.

LAVINIA. Perhaps you men will all go into heaven bravely and in triumph, with your heads erect and golden trumpets sounding for you. But I am sure I shall only be allowed to squeeze myself in through a little crack in the gate after a great deal of begging. I am not good always: I have moments only.

SPINTHO. Youre talking nonsense, woman. I tell you, martyrdom pays all scores.

ANDROCLES. Well, let us hope so, brother, for your sake. Youve had a gay time, havnt you? with your raids on the temples. I cant help thinking that heaven will be very dull for a man of your temperament. [*Spintho snarls*]. Dont be

447

angry: I say it only to console you in case you should die in your bed tonight in the natural way. Theres a lot of plague about.

SPINTHO [*rising and running about in abject terror*] I never thought of that. Oh Lord, spare me to be martyred. Oh, what a thought to put into the mind of a brother! Oh, let me be martyred today, now. I shall die in the night and go to hell. Youre a sorcerer: youve put death into my mind. Oh, curse you, curse you! [*He tries to seize Androcles by the throat*].

FERROVIUS [*holding him in a grasp of iron*] Whats this, brother? Anger! Violence! Raising your hand to a brother Christian!

SPINTHO. It's easy for you. Youre strong. Your nerves are all right. But I'm full of disease. [*Ferrovius takes his hand from him with instinctive disgust*]. Ive drunk all my nerves away. I shall have the horrors all night.

ANDROCLES [*sympathetic*] Oh, dont take on so, brother. We're all sinners.

SPINTHO [*snivelling, trying to feel consoled*] Yes: I daresay if the truth were known, youre all as bad as I am.

LAVINIA [*contemptuously*] Does that comfort you ?

FERROVIUS [*sternly*] Pray, man, pray.

SPINTHO. Whats the good of praying? If we're martyred we shall go to heaven, shant we, whether we pray or not?

FERROVIUS. Whats that? Not pray! [*Seizing him again*] Pray this instant, you dog, you rotten hound, you slimy snake, you beastly goat, or—

SPINTHO. Yes: beat me: kick me. I forgive you: mind that.

FERROVIUS [*spurning him with loathing*] Yah! [*Spintho reels away and falls in front of Ferrovius*].

ANDROCLES [*reaching out and catching the skirt of Ferrovius's tunic*] Dear brother: if you wouldnt mind—just for my sake—

FERROVIUS. Well?

ANDROCLES. Dont call him by the names of the animals. Weve no right to. Ive had such friends in dogs. A pet snake

448

is the best of company. I was nursed on goat's milk. Is it fair to them to call the like of him a dog or a snake or a goat?

FERROVIUS. I only meant that they have no souls.

ANDROCLES [*anxiously protesting*] Oh, believe me, they have. Just the same as you and me. I really dont think I could consent to go to heaven if I thought there were to be no animals there. Think of what they suffer here.

FERROVIUS. Thats true. Yes: that is just. They will have their share in heaven.

SPINTHO [*who has picked himself up and is sneaking past Ferrovius on his left, sneers derisively*]!!

FERROVIUS [*turning on him fiercely*] Whats that you say?

SPINTHO [*cowering*] Nothing.

FERROVIUS [*clenching his fist*] Do animals go to heaven or not?

SPINTHO. I never said they didnt.

FERROVIUS [*implacable*] Do they or do they not?

SPINTHO. They do: they do. [*Scrambling out of Ferrovius's reach*]. Oh, curse you for frightening me!

A bugle call is heard.

CENTURION [*waking up*] Tention! Form as before. Now then, prisoners: up with you and trot along spry. [*The soldiers fall in. The Christians rise*].

A man with an ox goad comes running through the central arch.

THE OX DRIVER. Here, you soldiers! clear out of the way for the Emperor.

THE CENTURION. Emperor! Wheres the Emperor? You aint the Emperor, are you?

THE OX DRIVER. It's the menagerie service. My team of oxen is drawing the new lion to the Coliseum. You clear the road.

CENTURION. What! Go in after you in your dust, with half the town at the heels of you and your lion! Not likely. We go first.

THE OX DRIVER. The menagerie service is the Emperor's personal retinue. You clear out, I tell you.

449

ANDROCLES AND THE LION

CENTURION. You tell me, do you? Well, I'll tell you something. If the lion is menagerie service, the lion's dinner is menagerie service too. This [*pointing to the Christians*] is the lion's dinner. So back with you to your bullocks double quick; and learn your place. March. [*The soldiers start*]. Now then, you Christians: step out there.

LAVINIA [*marching*] Come along, the rest of the dinner. I shall be the olives and anchovies.

ANOTHER CHRISTIAN [*laughing*] I shall be the soup.

ANOTHER. I shall be the fish.

ANOTHER. Ferrovius shall be the roast boar.

FERROVIUS [*heavily*] I see the joke. Yes, yes: I shall be the roast boar. Ha! ha! [*He laughs conscientiously and marches out with them*].

ANDROCLES [*following*] I shall be the mince pie. [*Each announcement is received with a louder laugh by all the rest as the joke catches on*].

CENTURION [*scandalized*] Silence! Have some sense of your situation. Is this the way for martyrs to behave? [*To Spintho, who is quaking and loitering*] I know what youll be at that dinner. Youll be the emetic. [*He shoves him rudely along*].

SPINTHO. It's too dreadful: I'm not fit to die.

CENTURION. Fitter than you are to live, you swine.

They pass from the square westward. The oxen, drawing a waggon with a great wooden cage and the lion in it, arrive through the central arch.

450

ACT II

BEHIND the Emperor's box at the Coliseum, where the performers assemble before entering the arena. In the middle a wide passage leading to the arena descends from the floor level under the imperial box. On both sides of this passage steps ascend to a landing at the back entrance to the box. The landing forms a bridge across the passage. At the entrance to the passage are two bronze mirrors, one on each side.

On the west side of this passage, on the right hand of anyone coming from the box and standing on the bridge, the martyrs are sitting on the steps. Lavinia is seated half-way up, thoughtful, trying to look death in the face. On her left Androcles consoles himself by nursing a cat. Ferrovius stands behind them, his eyes blazing, his figure stiff with intense resolution. At the foot of the steps crouches Spintho, with his head clutched in his hands, full of horror at the approach of martyrdom.

On the east side of the passage the gladiators are standing and sitting at ease, waiting, like the Christians, for their turn in the arena. One (Retiarius) is a nearly naked man with a net and a trident. Another (Secutor) is in armor with a sword. He carries a helmet with a barred visor. The editor of the gladiators sits on a chair a little apart from them.

The Call Boy enters from the passage.

THE CALL BOY. Number six. Retiarius versus Secutor.

The gladiator with the net picks it up. The gladiator with the helmet puts it on; and the two go into the arena, the net thrower taking out a little brush and arranging his hair as he goes, the other tightening his straps and shaking his shoulders loose. Both look at themselves in the mirrors before they enter the passage.

LAVINIA. Will they really kill one another?

SPINTHO. Yes, if the people turn down their thumbs.

THE EDITOR. You know nothing about it. The people indeed! Do you suppose we would kill a man worth perhaps fifty talents to please the riffraff? I should like to catch any of my men at it.

SPINTHO. I thought—

451

THE EDITOR [*contemptuously*] You thought! Who cares what you think? Youll be killed all right enough.

SPINTHO [*groans and again hides his face*]!!!!

LAVINIA. Then is nobody ever killed except us poor Christians?

THE EDITOR. If the vestal virgins turn down their thumbs, thats another matter. Theyre ladies of rank.

LAVINIA. Does the Emperor ever interfere?

THE EDITOR. Oh, yes: he turns his thumb up fast enough if the vestal virgins want to have one of his pet fighting men killed.

ANDROCLES. But dont they ever just only pretend to kill one another? Why shouldnt you pretend to die, and get dragged out as if you were dead; and then get up and go home, like an actor?

THE EDITOR. See here: you want to know too much. There will be no pretending about the new lion: let that be enough for you. He's hungry.

SPINTHO [*groaning with horror*] Oh, Lord! cant you stop talking about it? Isnt it bad enough for us without that?

ANDROCLES. I'm glad he's hungry. Not that I want him to suffer, poor chap! but then he'll enjoy eating me so much more. Theres a cheerful side to everything.

THE EDITOR [*rising and striding over to Androcles*] Here: dont you be obstinate. Come with me and drop the pinch of incense on the altar. Thats all you need do to be let off.

ANDROCLES. No: thank you very much indeed; but I really mustnt.

THE EDITOR. What! Not to save your life?

ANDROCLES. I'd rather not. I couldnt sacrifice to Diana: she's a huntress, you know, and kills things.

THE EDITOR. That dont matter. You can choose your own altar. Sacrifice to Jupiter: he likes animals: he turns himself into an animal when he goes off duty.

ANDROCLES. No: it's very kind of you; but I feel I cant save myself that way.

THE EDITOR. But I dont ask you to do it to save yourself:

I ask you to do it to oblige me personally.

ANDROCLES [*scrambling up in the greatest agitation*] Oh, please dont say that. This is dreadful. You mean so kindly by me that it seems quite horrible to disoblige you. If you could arrange for me to sacrifice when theres nobody looking, I shouldnt mind. But I must go into the arena with the rest. My honor, you know.

THE EDITOR. Honor! The honor of a tailor?

ANDROCLES [*apologetically*] Well, perhaps honor is too strong an expression. Still, you know, I couldnt allow the tailors to get a bad name through me.

THE EDITOR. How much will you remember of all that when you smell the beast's breath and see his jaws opening to tear out your throat?

SPINTHO [*rising with a yell of terror*] I cant bear it. Wheres the altar? I'll sacrifice.

FERROVIUS. Dog of an apostate. Iscariot!

SPINTHO. I'll repent afterwards. I fully mean to die in the arena: I'll die a martyr and go to heaven; but not this time, not now, not until my nerves are better. Besides, I'm too young: I want to have just one more good time. [*The gladiators laugh at him*]. Oh, will no one tell me where the altar is? [*He dashes into the passage and vanishes*].

ANDROCLES [*to the Editor, pointing after Spintho*] Brother: I cant do that, not even to oblige you. Dont ask me.

THE EDITOR. Well, if youre determined to die, I cant help you. But I wouldnt be put off by a swine like that.

FERROVIUS. Peace, peace: tempt him not. Get thee behind him, Satan.

THE EDITOR [*flushing with rage*] For two pins I'd take a turn in the arena myself today, and pay you out for daring to talk to me like that.

Ferrovius springs forward.

LAVINIA [*rising quickly and interposing*] Brother, brother: you forget.

FERROVIUS [*curbing himself by a mighty effort*] Oh, my temper, my wicked temper! [*To the Editor, as Lavinia sits*

453

down again, reassured] Forgive me, brother. My heart was full of wrath: I should have been thinking of your dear precious soul.

THE EDITOR. Yah! [*He turns his back on Ferrovius contemptuously, and goes back to his seat*].

FERROVIUS [*continuing*] And I forgot it all: I thought of nothing but offering to fight you with one hand tied behind me.

THE EDITOR [*turning pugnaciously*] What!

FERROVIUS [*on the border line between zeal and ferocity*] Oh, dont give way to pride and wrath, brother. I could do it so easily. I could—

They are separated by the Menagerie Keeper, who rushes in from the passage, furious.

THE KEEPER. Heres a nice business! Who let that Christian out of here down to the dens when we were changing the lion into the cage next the arena?

THE EDITOR. Nobody let him. He let himself.

THE KEEPER. Well, the lion's ate him.

Consternation. The Christians rise, greatly agitated. The gladiators sit callously, but are highly amused. All speak or cry out or laugh at once. Tumult.

LAVINIA. Oh, poor wretch! FERROVIUS. The apostate has perished. Praise be to God's justice! ANDROCLES. The poor beast was starving. It couldnt help itself. THE CHRISTIANS. What! Ate him! How frightful! How terrible! Without a moment to repent! God be merciful to him, a sinner! Oh, I cant bear to think of it! In the midst of his sin! Horrible, horrible! THE EDITOR. Serve the rotter right! THE GLADIATORS. Just walked into it, he did. He's martyred all right enough. Good old lion! Old Jock doesnt like that: look at his face. Devil a better! The Emperor will laugh when he hears of it. I cant help smiling. Ha ha ha!!!!!

THE KEEPER. Now his appetite's taken off, he wont as much as look at another Christian for a week.

ANDROCLES. Couldnt you have saved him, brother?

THE KEEPER. Saved him! Saved him from a lion that I'd

454

just got mad with hunger! a wild one that came out of the forest not four weeks ago! He bolted him before you could say Balbus.

LAVINIA [*sitting down again*] Poor Spintho! And it wont even count as martyrdom!

THE KEEPER. Serve him right! What call had he to walk down the throat of one of my lions before he was asked?

ANDROCLES. Perhaps the lion wont eat me now.

THE KEEPER. Yes: thats just like a Christian: think only of yourself! What am *I* to do? What am I to say to the Emperor when he sees one of my lions coming into the arena half asleep?

THE EDITOR. Say nothing. Give your old lion some bitters and a morsel of fried fish to wake up his appetite. [*Laughter*].

THE KEEPER. Yes: it's easy for you to talk; but—

THE EDITOR [*scrambling to his feet*] Sh! Attention there! The Emperor. [*The Keeper bolts precipitately into the passage. The gladiators rise smartly and form into line*].

The Emperor enters on the Christians' side, conversing with Metellus, and followed by his suite.

THE GLADIATORS. Hail, Caesar! those about to die salute thee.

CAESAR. Good morrow, friends.

Metellus shakes hands with the Editor, who accepts his condescension with bluff respect.

LAVINIA. Blessing, Caesar, and forgiveness!

CAESAR [*turning in some surprise at the salutation*] There is no forgiveness for Christianity.

LAVINIA. I did not mean that, Caesar. I mean that we forgive you.

METELLUS. An inconceivable liberty! Do you not know, woman, that the Emperor can do no wrong and therefore cannot be forgiven?

LAVINIA. I expect the Emperor knows better. Anyhow, we forgive him.

THE CHRISTIANS. Amen!

CAESAR. Metellus: you see now the disadvantage of too

455

much severity. These people have no hope; therefore they have nothing to restrain them from saying what they like to me. They are almost as impertinent as the gladiators. Which is the Greek sorcerer?

ANDROCLES [*humbly touching his forelock*] Me, your Worship.

CAESAR. My Worship! Good! A new title. Well: what miracles can you perform?

ANDROCLES. I can cure warts by rubbing them with my tailor's chalk; and I can live with my wife without beating her.

CAESAR. Is that all?

ANDROCLES. You dont know her, Caesar, or you wouldnt say that.

CAESAR. Ah, well, my friend, we shall no doubt contrive a happy release for you. Which is Ferrovius?

FERROVIUS. I am he.

CAESAR. They tell me you can fight.

FERROVIUS. It is easy to fight. *I* can die, Caesar.

CAESAR. That is still easier, is it not?

FERROVIUS. Not to me, Caesar. Death comes hard to my flesh; and fighting comes very easily to my spirit [*beating his breast and lamenting*] Oh, sinner that I am! [*He throws himself down on the steps, deeply discouraged*].

CAESAR. Metellus: I should like to have this man in the Pretorian Guard.

METELLUS. *I* should not, Caesar. He looks a spoilsport. There are men in whose presence it is impossible to have any fun: men who are a sort of walking conscience. He would make us all uncomfortable.

CAESAR. For that reason, perhaps, it might be well to have him. An Emperor can hardly have too many consciences. [*To Ferrovius*] Listen, Ferrovius. [*Ferrovius shakes his head and will not look up*]. You and your friends shall not be outnumbered today in the arena. You shall have arms; and there will be no more than one gladiator to each Christian. If you come out of the arena alive, I will consider favorably any request of yours, and give you a place in the Pretorian Guard. Even if the request be that no questions be asked about your faith I shall perhaps not refuse it.

FERROVIUS. I will not fight. I will die. Better stand with the archangels than with the Pretorian Guard.

CAESAR. I cannot believe that the archangels—whoever they may be—would not prefer to be recruited from the Pretorian Guard. However, as you please. Come: let us see the show.

As the Court ascends the steps, Secutor and Retiarius return from the arena through the passage: Secutor covered with dust and very angry: Retiarius grinning.

SECUTOR. Ha, the Emperor. Now we shall see. Caesar: I ask you whether it is fair for the Retiarius, instead of making a fair throw of his net at me, to swish it along the ground and throw the dust in my eyes, and then catch me when I'm blinded. If the vestals had not turned up their thumbs I should have been a dead man.

CAESAR [*halting on the stair*] There is nothing in the rules against it.

SECUTOR [*indignantly*] Caesar: is it a dirty trick or is it not?

CAESAR. It is a dusty one, my friend. [*Obsequious laughter*]. Be on your guard next time.

SECUTOR. Let him be on his guard. Next time I'll throw my sword at his heels and strangle him with his own net before he can hop off. [*To the Retiarius*] You see if I dont. [*He goes out past the gladiators, sulky and furious*].

CAESAR [*to the chuckling Retiarius*]. These tricks are not wise, my friend. The audience likes to see a dead man in all his beauty and splendor. If you smudge his face and spoil his armor they will shew their displeasure by not letting you kill him. And when your turn comes, they will remember it against you and turn their thumbs down.

THE RETIARIUS. Perhaps that is why I did it, Caesar. He bet me ten sesterces that he would vanquish me. If I had had to kill him I should not have had the money.

457

CAESAR [*indulgent, laughing*] You rogues: there is no end to your tricks. I'll dismiss you all and have elephants to fight. T h e y fight fairly. [*He goes up to his box, and knocks at it. It is opened from within by the Captain, who stands as on parade to let him pass*].

The Call Boy comes from the passage, followed by three attendants carrying respectively a bundle of swords, some helmets, and some breastplates and pieces of armor which they throw down in a heap.

THE CALL BOY. By your leave, Caesar. Number eleven! Gladiators and Christians!

Ferrovius springs up, ready for martyrdom. The other Christians take the summons as best they can, some joyful and brave, some patient and dignified, some tearful and helpless, some embracing one another with emotion. The Call Boy goes back into the passage.

CAESAR [*turning at the door of the box*] The hour has come, Ferrovius. I shall go into my box and see you killed, since you scorn the Pretorian Guard. [*He goes into the box. The Captain shuts the door, remaining inside with the Emperor. Metellus and the rest of the suite disperse to their seats. The Christians, led by Ferrovius, move towards the passage*].

LAVINIA [*to Ferrovius*] Farewell.

THE EDITOR. Steady there. You Christians have got to fight. Here! arm yourselves.

FERROVIUS [*picking up a sword*] I'll die sword in hand to shew people that I could fight if it were my Master's will, and that I could kill the man who kills me if I chose.

THE EDITOR. Put on that armor.

FERROVIUS. No armor.

THE EDITOR [*bullying him*] Do what youre told. Put on that armor.

FERROVIUS [*gripping the sword and looking dangerous*] I said, No armor.

THE EDITOR. And what am I to say when I am accused of sending a naked man in to fight my men in armor?

FERROVIUS. Say your prayers, brother; and have no fear

of the princes of this world.

THE EDITOR. Tsha! You obstinate fool! [*He bites his lips irresolutely, not knowing exactly what to do*].

ANDROCLES [*to Ferrovius*] Farewell, brother, till we meet in the sweet by-and-by.

THE EDITOR [*to Androcles*] You are going too. Take a sword there; and put on any armor you can find to fit you.

ANDROCLES. No, really: I cant fight: I never could: I cant bring myself to dislike anyone enough. I'm to be thrown to the lions with the lady.

THE EDITOR. Then get out of the way and hold your noise. [*Androcles steps aside with cheerful docility*]. Now then! Are you all ready there?

A trumpet is heard from the arena.

FERROVIUS [*starting convulsively*] Heaven give me strength!

THE EDITOR. Aha! That frightens you, does it?

FERROVIUS. Man: there is no terror like the terror of that sound to me. When I hear a trumpet or a drum or the clash of steel or the hum of the catapult as the great stone flies, fire runs through my veins: I feel my blood surge up hot behind my eyes: I must charge: I must strike: I must conquer: Caesar himself will not be safe in his imperial seat if once that spirit gets loose in me. Oh, brothers, pray! exhort me! remind me that if I raise my sword my honor falls and my Master is crucified afresh.

ANDROCLES. Just keep thinking how cruelly you might hurt the poor gladiators.

FERROVIUS. It does not hurt a man to kill him.

LAVINIA. Nothing but faith can save you.

FERROVIUS. Faith! Which faith? There are two faiths. There is our faith. And there is the warrior's faith, the faith in fighting, the faith that sees God in the sword. How if that faith should overwhelm me?

LAVINIA. You will find your real faith in the hour of trial.

FERROVIUS. That is what I fear. I know that I am a fighter. How can I feel sure that I am a Christian?

ANDROCLES. Throw away the sword, brother.

FERROVIUS. I cannot. It cleaves to my hand. I could as easily throw a woman I loved from my arms. [*Starting*] Who spoke that blasphemy? Not I.

LAVINIA. I cant help you, friend. I cant tell you not to save your own life. Something wilful in me wants to see you fight your way into heaven.

FERROVIUS. Ha!

ANDROCLES. But if you are going to give up our faith, brother, why not do it without hurting anybody? Dont fight them. Burn the incense.

FERROVIUS. Burn the incense! Never.

LAVINIA. This is only pride, Ferrovius.

FERROVIUS. Only pride! What is nobler than pride? [*Conscience stricken*] Oh, I'm steeped in sin. I'm proud of my pride.

LAVINIA. They say we Christians are the proudest devils on earth—that only the weak are meek. Oh, I am worse than you. I ought to send you to death; and I am tempting you.

ANDROCLES. Brother, brother: let them rage and kill: let us be brave and suffer. You must go as a lamb to the slaughter.

FERROVIUS. Aye, aye: that is right. Not as a lamb is slain by the butcher; but as a butcher might let himself be slain by a [*looking at the Editor*] by a silly ram whose head he could fetch off in one twist.

Before the Editor can retort, the Call Boy rushes up through the passage, and the Captain comes from the Emperor's box and descends the steps.

THE CALL BOY. In with you: into the arena. The stage is waiting.

THE CAPTAIN. The Emperor is waiting. [*To the Editor*] What are you dreaming of, man? Send your men in at once.

THE EDITOR. Yes, sir: it's these Christians hanging back.

FERROVIUS [*in a voice of thunder*] Liar!

THE EDITOR [*not heeding him*] March. [*The gladiators told off to fight with the Christians march down the passage*] Follow

460

up there, you.

THE CHRISTIAN MEN AND WOMEN [*as they part*] Be steadfast, brother. Farewell. Hold up the faith, brother. Farewell. Go to glory, dearest. Farewell. Remember: we are praying for you. Farewell. Be strong, brother. Farewell. Dont forget that the divine love and our love surround you. Farewell. Nothing can hurt you: remember that, brother. Farewell. Eternal glory, dearest. Farewell.

THE EDITOR [*out of patience*] Shove them in, there.

The remaining gladiators and the Call Boy make a movement towards them.

FERROVIUS [*interposing*] Touch them, dogs; and we die here, and cheat the heathen of their spectacle. [*To his fellow Christians*] Brothers: the great moment has come. That passage is your hill to Calvary. Mount it bravely, but meekly; and remember! not a word of reproach, not a blow nor a struggle. Go. [*They go out through the passage. He turns to Lavinia*] Farewell.

LAVINIA. You forget: I must follow before you are cold.

FERROVIUS. It is true. Do not envy me because I pass before you to glory. [*He goes through the passage*].

THE EDITOR [*to the Call Boy*] Sickening work, this. Why cant they all be thrown to the lions? It's not a man's job. [*He throws himself moodily into his chair*].

The remaining gladiators go back to their former places indifferently. The Call Boy shrugs his shoulders and squats down at the entrance to the passage, near the Editor.

Lavinia and the Christian women sit down again, wrung with grief, some weeping silently, some praying, some calm and steadfast. Androcles sits down at Lavinia's feet. The Captain stands on the stairs, watching her curiously

ANDROCLES. I'm glad I havnt to fight. That would really be an awful martyrdom. I am lucky.

LAVINIA [*looking at him with a pang of remorse*] Androcles: burn the incense: youll be forgiven. Let my death atone for both. I feel as if I were killing you.

ANDROCLES. Dont think of me, sister. Think of yourself.

That will keep your heart up.

The Captain laughs sardonically.

LAVINIA [*startled: she had forgotten his presence*] Are you there, handsome Captain? Have you come to see me die?

THE CAPTAIN [*coming to her side*] I am on duty with the Emperor, Lavinia.

LAVINIA. Is it part of your duty to laugh at us?

THE CAPTAIN. No: that is part of my private pleasure. Your friend here is a humorist. I laughed at his telling you to think of yourself to keep up your heart. *I* say, think of yourself and burn the incense.

LAVINIA. He is not a humorist: he was right. You ought to know that, Captain: you have been face to face with death.

THE CAPTAIN. Not with certain death, Lavinia. Only death in battle, which spares more men than death in bed. What you are facing is certain death. You have nothing left now but your faith in this craze of yours: this Christianity. Are your Christian fairy stories any truer than our stories about Jupiter and Diana, in which, I may tell you, I believe no more than the Emperor does, or any educated man in Rome?

LAVINIA. Captain: all that seems nothing to me now. I'll not say that death is a terrible thing; but I will say that it is so real a thing that when it comes close, all the imaginary things—all the stories, as you call them—fade into mere dreams beside that inexorable reality. I know now that I am not dying for stories or dreams. Did you hear of the dreadful thing that happened here while we were waiting?

THE CAPTAIN. I heard that one of your fellows bolted, and ran right into the jaws of the lion. I laughed. I still laugh.

LAVINIA. Then you dont understand what that meant?

THE CAPTAIN. It meant that the lion had a cur for his breakfast.

LAVINIA. It meant more than that, Captain. It meant that a man cannot die for a story and a dream. None of us believed the stories and the dreams more devoutly than poor Spintho; but he could not face the great reality. What he

462

would have called my faith has been oozing away minute by minute whilst Ive been sitting here, with death coming nearer and nearer, with reality become realler and realler, with stories and dreams fading away into nothing.

THE CAPTAIN. Are you then going to die for nothing?

LAVINIA. Yes: that is the wonderful thing. It is since all the stories and dreams have gone that I have now no doubt at all that I must die for something greater than dreams or stories.

THE CAPTAIN. But for what?

LAVINIA. I dont know. If it were for anything small enough to know, it would be too small to die for. I think I'm going to die for God. Nothing else is real enough to die for.

THE CAPTAIN. What is God?

LAVINIA. When we know that, Captain, we shall be gods ourselves.

THE CAPTAIN. Lavinia: come down to earth. Burn the incense and marry me.

LAVINIA. Handsome Captain: would you marry me if I hauled down the flag in the day of battle and burnt the incense? Sons take after their mothers, you know. Do you want your son to be a coward?

THE CAPTAIN [*strongly moved*] By great Diana, I think I would strangle you if you gave in now.

LAVINIA [*putting her hand on the head of Androcles*] The hand of God is on us three, Captain.

THE CAPTAIN. What nonsense it all is! And what a monstrous thing that you should die for such nonsense, and that I should look on helplessly when my whole soul cries out against it! Die then if you must; but at least I can cut the Emperor's throat and then my own when I see your blood.

The Emperor throws open the door of his box angrily, and appears in wrath on the threshold. The Editor, the Call Boy, and the gladiators spring to their feet.

THE EMPEROR. The Christians will not fight; and your curs cannot get their blood up to attack them. It's all that fellow with the blazing eyes. Send for the whip. [*The Call*

Boy rushes out on the east side for the whip]. If that will not move them, bring the hot irons. The man is like a mountain. [*He returns angrily into the box and slams the door*].

The Call Boy returns with a man in a hideous Etruscan mask, carrying a whip. They both rush down the passage into the arena.

LAVINIA [*rising*] Oh, that is unworthy. Can they not kill him without dishonoring him?

ANDROCLES [*scrambling to his feet and running into the middle of the space between the staircases*] It's dreadful. Now *I* want to fight. I cant bear the sight of a whip. The only time I ever hit a man was when he lashed an old horse with a whip. It was terrible: I danced on his face when he was on the ground. He mustnt strike Ferrovius: I'll go into the arena and kill him first. [*He makes a wild dash into the passage. As he does so a great clamor is heard from the arena, ending in wild applause. The gladiators listen and look inquiringly at one another*].

THE EDITOR. Whats up now?

LAVINIA [*to the Captain*] What has happened, do you think?

THE CAPTAIN. What can happen? They are killing them, I suppose.

ANDROCLES [*running in through the passage, screaming with horror and hiding his eyes*]!!!

LAVINIA. Androcles, Androcles: whats the matter?

ANDROCLES. Oh dont ask me, dont ask me. Something too dreadful. Oh! [*He crouches by her and hides his face in her robe, sobbing*].

THE CALL BOY [*rushing through from the passage as before*] Ropes and hooks there! Ropes and hooks!

THE EDITOR. Well, need you excite yourself about it? [*Another burst of applause*].

Two slaves in Etruscan masks, with ropes and drag hooks, hurry in.

ONE OF THE SLAVES. How many dead?

THE CALL BOY. Six. [*The slave blows a whistle twice; and four more masked slaves rush through into the arena with the same apparatus*] And the basket. Bring the baskets [*The slave whistles three times, and runs through the passage with his companion*].

THE CAPTAIN. Who are the baskets for?

THE CALL BOY. For the whip. He's in pieces. Theyre all in pieces, more or less. [*Lavinia hides her face*].

Two more masked slaves come in with a basket and follow the others into the arena, as the Call Boy turns to the gladiators and exclaims, exhausted] Boys: he's killed the lot.

THE EMPEROR [*again bursting from his box, this time in an ecstasy of delight*] Where is he? Magnificent! He shall have a laurel crown.

Ferrovius, madly waving his bloodstained sword, rushes through the passage in despair, followed by his co-religionists, and by the menagerie keeper, who goes to the gladiators. The gladiators draw their swords nervously].

FERROVIUS. Lost! lost for ever! I have betrayed my Master. Cut off this right hand: it has offended. Ye have swords, my brethren: strike.

LAVINIA. No, no. What have you done, Ferrovius?

FERROVIUS. I know not; but there was blood behind my eyes; and theres blood on my sword. What does that mean?

THE EMPEROR [*enthusiastically, on the landing outside his box*] What does it mean? It means that you are the greatest man in Rome. It means that you shall have a laurel crown of gold. Superb fighter: I could almost yield you my throne. It is a record for my reign: I shall live in history. Once, in Domitian's time, a Gaul slew three men in the arena and gained his freedom. But when before has one naked man slain six armed men of the bravest and best? The persecution shall cease: if Christians can fight like this, I shall have none but Christians to fight for me. [*To the Gladiators*] You are ordered to become Christians, you there: do you hear?

RETIARIUS. It is all one to us, Caesar. Had I been there with my net, the story would have been different.

THE CAPTAIN [*suddenly seizing Lavinia by the wrist and dragging her up the steps to the Emperor*] Caesar: this woman is the sister of Ferrovius. If she is thrown to the lions he will fret. He will lose weight; get out of condition—

465

THE EMPEROR. The lions? Nonsense! [*To Lavinia*] Madam: I am proud to have the honor of making your acquaintance. Your brother is the glory of Rome.

LAVINIA. But my friends here. Must they die?

THE EMPEROR. Die! Certainly not. There has never been the slightest idea of harming them. Ladies and gentlemen: you are all free. Pray go into the front of the house and enjoy the spectacle to which your brother has so splendidly contributed. Captain: oblige me by conducting them to the seats reserved for my personal friends.

THE MENAGERIE KEEPER. Caesar: I must have one Christian for the lion. The people have been promised it; and they will tear the decorations to bits if they are disappointed.

THE EMPEROR. True, true: we must have somebody for the new lion.

FERROVIUS. Throw me to him. Let the apostate perish.

THE EMPEROR. No, no: you would tear him in pieces, my friend; and we cannot afford to throw away lions as if they were mere slaves. But we must have somebody. This is really extremely awkward.

THE MENAGERIE KEEPER. Why not that little Greek chap? He's not a Christian: he's a sorcerer.

THE EMPEROR. The very thing: he will do very well.

THE CALL BOY [*issuing from the passage*] Number twelve. The Christian for the new lion.

ANDROCLES [*rising, and pulling himself sadly together*] Well, it was to be, after all.

LAVINIA. I'll go in his place, Caesar. Ask the Captain whether they do not like best to see a woman torn to pieces. He told me so yesterday.

THE EMPEROR. There is something in that: there is certainly something in that—if only I could feel sure that your brother would not fret.

ANDROCLES. No: I should never have another happy hour. No: on the faith of a Christian and the honor of a tailor, I accept the lot that has fallen on me. If my wife turns up, give her my love and say that my wish was that she should be

ANDROCLES AND THE LION

happy with her next, poor fellow! Caesar: go to your box and see how a tailor can die. Make way for number twelve there. [*He marches out along the passage*].

The vast audience in the amphitheatre now sees the Emperor re-enter his box and take his place as Androcles, desperately frightened, but still marching with piteous devotion, emerges from the other end of the passage, and finds himself at the focus of thousands of eager eyes. The lion's cage, with a heavy portcullis grating, is on his left. The Emperor gives a signal. A gong sounds. Androcles shivers at the sound; then falls on his knees and prays. The grating rises with a clash. The lion bounds into the arena. He rushes round frisking in his freedom. He sees Androcles. He stops; rises stiffly by straightening his legs; stretches out his nose forward and his tail in a horizontal line behind, like a pointer, and utters an appalling roar. Androcles crouches and hides his face in his hands. The lion gathers himself for a spring, swishing his tail to and fro through the dust in an ecstasy of anticipation. Androcles throws up his hands in supplication to heaven. The lion checks at the sight of Androcles's face. He then steals towards him; smells him; arches his back; purrs like a motor car; finally rubs himself against Androcles, knocking him over. Androcles, supporting himself on his wrist, looks affrightedly at the lion. The lion limps on three paws, holding up the other as if it was wounded. A flash of recognition lights up the face of Androcles. He flaps his hand as if it had a thorn in it, and pretends to pull the thorn out and to hurt himself. The lion nods repeatedly. Androcles holds out his hands to the lion, who gives him both paws, which he shakes with enthusiasm. They embrace rapturously, finally waltz round the arena amid a sudden burst of deafening applause, and out through the passage, the Emperor watching them in breathless astonishment until they disappear, when he rushes from his box and descends the steps in frantic excitement.

THE EMPEROR. My friends, an incredible! an amazing thing! has happened. I can no longer doubt the truth of Christianity. [*The Christians press to him joyfully*]. This Christian sorcerer—[*with a yell, he breaks off as he sees Androcles and the lion emerge from the passage, waltzing. He bolts wildly up the steps into his box, and slams the door. All, Christians and gladiators alike, fly for their lives, the gladiators bolting into the arena, the others in all directions. The place is emptied with magical suddenness*].

ANDROCLES [*naïvely*] Now I wonder why they all run away from us like that. [*The lion, combining a series of yawns, purrs, and roars, achieves something very like a laugh.*]

THE EMPEROR [*standing on a chair inside his box and looking over the wall*] Sorcerer: I command you to put that lion to death instantly. It is guilty of high treason. Your conduct is most disgra—[*the lion charges at him up the stairs*] Help! [*He disappears. The lion rears against the box; looks over the partition at him; and roars. The Emperor darts out through the door and down to Androcles, pursued by the lion.*]

ANDROCLES. Dont run away, sir: he cant help springing if you run. [*He seizes the Emperor and gets between him and the lion, who stops at once*]. Dont be afraid of him.

THE EMPEROR. I am n o t afraid of him. [*The lion crouches, growling. The Emperor clutches Androcles*]. Keep between us.

ANDROCLES. Never be afraid of animals, your worship: thats the great secret. He'll be as gentle as a lamb when he knows that you are his friend. Stand quite still; and smile; and let him smell you all over just to reassure him; for, you see, he's afraid of you; and he must examine you thoroughly before he gives you his confidence. [*To the lion*] Come now, Tommy; and speak nicely to the Emperor, the great good Emperor who has power to have all our heads cut off if we dont behave very very respectfully to him.

The lion utters a fearful roar. The Emperor dashes madly up the steps, across the landing, and down again on the other side, with the lion in hot pursuit. Androcles rushes after the lion; overtakes him as he is descending; and throws himself on his back, trying to use his toes as a brake. Before he can stop him the lion gets hold of the trailing end of the Emperor's robe.

ANDROCLES. Oh bad wicked Tommy, to chase the Emperor like that! Let go the Emperor's robe at once, sir: wheres your manners? [*The lion growls and worries the robe*].

Dont pull it away from him, your worship. He's only playing. Now I shall be really angry with you, Tommy, if you
dont let go. [*The lion growls again*]. I'll tell you what it is,
sir: he thinks you and I are not friends.

THE EMPEROR [*trying to undo the clasp of his brooch*] Friends!
You infernal scoundrel [*the lion growls*]—dont let him go.
Curse this brooch! I cant get it loose.

ANDROCLES. We mustnt let him lash himself into a rage.
You must shew him that you are my particular friend—if
you will have the condescension. [*He seizes the Emperor's
hands and shakes them cordially*]. Look, Tommy: the nice
Emperor is the dearest friend Andy Wandy has in the whole
world: he loves him like a brother.

THE EMPEROR. You little brute, you damned filthy little
dog of a Greek tailor: I'll have you burnt alive for daring to
touch the divine person of the Emperor. [*The lion growls*].

ANDROCLES. Oh dont talk like that, sir. He understands
every word you say: all animals do: they take it from the
tone of your voice. [*The lion growls and lashes his tail*]. I
think he's going to spring at your worship. If you wouldn'
mind saying something affectionate. [*The lion roars*].

THE EMPEROR [*shaking Androcles's hands frantically*] My
dearest Mr Androcles, my sweetest friend, my long lost
brother, come to my arms. [*He embraces Androcles*]. Oh,
what an abominable smell of garlic!

*The lion lets go the robe and rolls over on his back, clasping
his forepaws over one another coquettishly above his nose.*

ANDROCLES. There! You see, your worship, a child might
play with him now. See! [*He tickles the lion's belly. The lion
wriggles ecstatically*]. Come and pet him.

THE EMPEROR. I must conquer these unkingly terrors.
Mind you dont go away from him, though. [*He pats the
lion's chest*].

ANDROCLES. Oh, sir, how few men would have the courage
to do that!

THE EMPEROR. Yes: it takes a bit of nerve. Let us have the
Court in and frighten them. Is he safe, do you think?

ANDROCLES. Quite safe now, sir.

THE EMPEROR [*majestically*] What ho, there! All who are within hearing, return without fear. Caesar has tamed the lion. [*All the fugitives steal cautiously in. The menagerie keeper comes from the passage with other keepers armed with iron bars and tridents*]. Take those things away. I have subdued the beast. [*He places his foot on it*].

FERROVIUS [*timidly approaching the Emperor and looking down with awe on the lion*] It is strange that I, who fear no man, should fear a lion.

THE CAPTAIN. Every man fears something, Ferrovius.

THE EMPEROR. How about the Pretorian Guard now?

FERROVIUS. In my youth I worshipped Mars, the God of War. I turned from him to serve the Christian god; but to-day the Christian god forsook me; and Mars overcame me and took back his own. The Christian god is not yet. He will come when Mars and I are dust; but meanwhile I must serve the gods that are, not the God that will be. Until then I accept service in the Guard, Caesar.

THE EMPEROR. Very wisely said. All really sensible men agree that the prudent course is to be neither bigoted in our attachment to the old nor rash and unpractical in keeping an open mind for the new, but to make the best of both dispensations.

THE CAPTAIN. What do you say, Lavinia? Will you too be prudent?

LAVINIA [*on the stairs*] No: I'll strive for the coming of the God who is not yet.

THE CAPTAIN. May I come and argue with you occasionally?

LAVINIA. Yes, handsome Captain: you may. [*He kisses her hand*].

THE EMPEROR. And now, my friends, though I do not, as you see, fear this lion, yet the strain of his presence is considerable; for none of us can feel quite sure what he will do next.

THE MENAGERIE KEEPER. Caesar: give us this Greek sor-

cerer to be a slave in the menagerie. He has a way with the
beasts.

ANDROCLES [*distressed*] Not if they are in cages. They
should not be kept in cages. They must be all let out.

THE EMPEROR. I give this sorcerer to be a slave to the first
man who lays hands on him. [*The menagerie keepers and the
gladiators rush for Androcles. The lion starts up and faces them.
They surge back*]. You see how magnanimous we Romans
are, Androcles. We suffer you to go in peace.

ANDROCLES. I thank your worship. I thank you all, ladies
and gentlemen. Come, Tommy. Whilst we stand together,
no cage for you: no slavery for me. [*He goes out with the lion,
everybody crowding away to give him as wide a berth as possible*].

* * * * * *

In this play I have presented one of the Roman persecutions of the early Christians, not as the conflict of a false
theology with a true, but as what all such persecutions essentially are: an attempt to suppress a propaganda that seemed
to threaten the interests involved in the established law and
order, organized and maintained in the name of religion and
justice by politicians who are pure opportunist Have-and-
Holders. People who are shewn by their inner light the possibility of a better world based on the demand of the spirit
for a nobler and more abundant life, not for themselves at
the expense of others, but for everybody, are naturally
dreaded and therefore hated by the Have-and-Holders, who
keep always in reserve two sure weapons against them. The
first is a persecution effected by the provocation, organization, and arming of that herd instinct which makes men
abhor all departures from custom, and, by the most cruel
punishments and the wildest calumnies, force eccentric
people to behave and profess exactly as other people do. The
second is by leading the herd to war, which immediately and
infallibly makes them forget everything, even their most
cherished and hard won public liberties and private interests,
in the irresistible surge of their pugnacity and the tense preoccupation of their terror.

471

ANDROCLES AND THE LION

There is no reason to believe that there was anything more in the Roman persecutions than this. The attitude of the Roman Emperor and the officers of his staff towards the opinions at issue were much the same as those of a modern British Home Secretary towards members of the lower middle classes when some pious policeman charges them with Bad Taste, technically called blasphemy: Bad Taste being a violation of Good Taste, which in such matters practically means Hypocrisy. The Home Secretary and the judges who try the case are usually far more sceptical and blasphemous than the poor men whom they persecute; and their professions of horror at the blunt utterance of their own opinions are revolting to those behind the scenes who have any genuine religious sensibility; but the thing is done because the governing classes, provided only the law against blasphemy is not applied to themselves, strongly approve of such persecution because it enables them to represent their own privileges as part of the religion of the country.

Therefore my martyrs are the martyrs of all time, and my persecutors the persecutors of all time. My Emperor, who has no sense of the value of common people's lives, and amuses himself with killing as carelessly as with sparing, is the sort of monster you can make of any silly-clever gentleman by idolizing him. We are still so easily imposed on by such idols that one of the leading pastors of the Free Churches in London denounced my play on the ground that my persecuting Emperor is a very fine fellow, and the persecuted Christians ridiculous. From which I conclude that a popular pulpit may be as perilous to a man's soul as an imperial throne.

All my articulate Christians, the reader will notice, have different enthusiasms, which they accept as the same religion only because it involves them in a common opposition to the official religion and consequently in a common doom. Androcles is a humanitarian naturalist, whose views surprise everybody. Lavinia, a clever and fearless freethinker, shocks the Pauline Ferrovius, who is comparatively stupid and

472

conscience ridden. Spintho, the blackguardly debauchee, is presented as one of the typical Christians of that period on the authority of St Augustine, who seems to have come to the conclusion at one period of his development that most Christians were what we call wrong uns. No doubt he was to some extent right: I have had occasion often to point out that revolutionary movements attract those who are not good enough for established institutions as well as those who are too good for them.

But the most striking aspect of the play at this moment is the terrible topicality given it by the war. We were at peace when I pointed out, by the mouth of Ferrovius, the path of an honest man who finds out, when the trumpet sounds, that he cannot follow Jesus. Many years earlier, in The Devil's Disciple, I touched the same theme even more definitely, and shewed the minister throwing off his black coat for ever when he discovered, amid the thunder of the captains and the shouting, that he was a born fighter. Great numbers of our clergy have found themselves of late in the position of Ferrovius and Anthony Anderson. They have discovered that they hate not only their enemies but everyone who does not share their hatred, and that they want to fight and to force other people to fight. They have turned their churches into recruiting stations and their vestries into munition workshops. But it has never occurred to them to take off their black coats and say quite simply, "I find in the hour of trial that the Sermon on the Mount is tosh, and that I am not a Christian. I apologize for all the unpatriotic nonsense I have been preaching all these years. Have the goodness to give me a revolver and a commission in a regiment which has for its chaplain a priest of the god Mars: *my* God." Not a bit of it. They have stuck to their livings and served Mars in the name of Christ, to the scandal of all religious mankind. When the Archbishop of York behaved like a gentleman and the Head Master of Eton preached a Christian sermon, and were reviled by the rabble, the Martian parsons encouraged the rabble. For this they made no apo-

473

logies or excuses, good or bad. They simply indulged their passions, just as they had always indulged their class prejudices and commercial interests, without troubling themselves for a moment as to whether they were Christians or not. They did not protest even when a body calling itself the Anti-German League (not having noticed, apparently, that it had been anticipated by the British Empire, the French Republic, and the Kingdoms of Italy, Japan, and Serbia) actually succeeded in closing a church at Forest Hill in which God was worshipped in the German language. One would have supposed that this grotesque outrage on the commonest decencies of religion would have provoked a remonstrance from even the worldliest bench of bishops. But no: apparently it seemed to the bishops as natural that the House of God should be looted when He allowed German to be spoken in it as that a baker's shop with a German name over the door should be pillaged. Their verdict was, in effect, "Serve God right, for creating the Germans!" The incident would have been impossible in a country where the Church was as powerful as the Church of England, had it had at the same time a spark of catholic as distinguished from tribal religion in it. As it is, the thing occurred; and as far as I have observed, the only people who gasped were the Freethinkers.

Thus we see that even among men who make a profession of religion the great majority are as Martian as the majority of their congregations. The average clergyman is an official who makes his living by christening babies, marrying adults, conducting a ritual, and making the best he can (when he has any conscience about it) of a certain routine of school superintendence, district visiting, and organization of almsgiving, which does not necessarily touch Christianity at any point except the point of the tongue. The exceptional or religious clergyman may be an ardent Pauline salvationist, in which case his more cultivated parishioners dislike him, and say that he ought to have joined the Methodists. Or he may be an artist expressing religious emotion without in-

474

tellectual definition by means of poetry, music, vestments, and architecture, also producing religious ecstasy by physical expedients, such as fasts and vigils, in which case he is denounced as a Ritualist. Or he may be either a Unitarian Deist like Voltaire or Tom Paine, or the more modern sort of Anglican Theosophist to whom the Holy Ghost is the Élan Vital of Bergson, and the Father and Son are an expression of the fact that our functions and aspects are manifold, and that we are all sons and all either potential or actual parents, in which case he is strongly suspected by the straiter Salvationists of being little better than an Atheist. All these varieties, you see, excite remark. They may be very popular with their congregations; but they are regarded by the average man as the freaks of the Church. The Church, like the society of which it is an organ, is balanced and steadied by the great central Philistine mass above whom theology looms as a highly spoken of and doubtless most important thing, like Greek Tragedy, or classical music, or the higher mathematics, but who are very glad when church is over and they can go home to lunch or dinner, having in fact, for all practical purposes, no reasoned convictions at all, and being equally ready to persecute a poor Freethinker for saying that St James was not infallible, and to send one of the Peculiar People to prison for being so very peculiar as to take St James seriously.

In short, a Christian martyr was thrown to the lions not because he was a Christian, but because he was a crank: that is, an unusual sort of person. And multitudes of people, quite as civilized and amiable as we, crowded to see the lions eat him just as they now crowd the lion-house in the Zoo at feeding-time, not because they really cared twopence about Diana or Christ, or could have given you any intelligent or correct account of the things Diana and Christ stood against one another for, but simply because they wanted to see a curious and exciting spectacle. You, dear reader, have probably run to see a fire; and if somebody came in now and told you that a lion was chasing a man down the street you would rush to the window. And if anyone were to say that you were as cruel as the people who let the lion loose on the man, you would be justly indignant. Now that we may no longer see a man hanged, we assemble outside the jail to see the black flag run up. That is our duller method of enjoying ourselves in the old Roman spirit. And if the Government decided to throw persons of unpopular or eccentric views to the lions in the Albert Hall or the Earl's Court stadium tomorrow, can you doubt that all the seats would be crammed, mostly by people who could not give you the most superficial account of the views in question. Much less unlikely things have happened. It is true that if such a revival does take place soon, the martyrs will not be members of heretical religious sects: they will be Peculiars, Anti-Vivisectionists, Flat-Earth men, scoffers at the laboratories, or infidels who refuse to kneel down when a procession of doctors goes by. But the lions will hurt them just as much, and the spectators will enjoy themselves just as much, as the Roman lions and spectators used to do.

It was currently reported in the Berlin newspapers that when Androcles was first performed in Berlin, the Crown Prince rose and left the house, unable to endure the (I hope) very clear and fair exposition of autocratic Imperialism given by the Roman captain to his Christian prisoners. No English Imperialist was intelligent and earnest enough to do the same in London. If the report is correct, I confirm the logic of the Crown Prince, and am glad to find myself so well understood. But I can assure him that the Empire which served for my model when I wrote Androcles was, as he is now finding to his cost, much nearer my home than the German one.

ON THE ROCKS

(A POLITICAL COMEDY)

Written in 1933

First Performed London 1933

PREFACE
EXTERMINATION

IN this play a reference is made by a Chief of Police to the political necessity for killing people: a necessity so distressing to the statesmen and so terrifying to the common citizen that nobody except myself (as far as I know) has ventured to examine it directly on its own merits, although every Government is obliged to practise it on a scale varying from the execution of a single murderer to the slaughter of millions of quite innocent persons. Whilst assenting to these proceedings, and even acclaiming and celebrating them, we dare not tell ourselves what we are doing or why we are doing it; and so we call it justice or capital punishment or our duty to king and country or any other convenient verbal whitewash for what we instinctively recoil from as from a dirty job. These childish evasions are revolting. We must strip off the whitewash and find out what is really beneath it. Extermination must be put on a scientific basis if it is ever to be carried out humanely and apologetically as well as thoroughly.

KILLING AS A POLITICAL FUNCTION

That killing is a necessity is beyond question by any thoughtful person. Unless rabbits and deer and rats and foxes are killed, or "kept down" as we put it, mankind must perish; and that section of mankind which lives in the country and is directly and personally engaged in the struggle with Nature for a living has no sentimental doubts that they must be killed. As to tigers and poisonous snakes, their incompatibility with human civilization is unquestioned. This does not excuse the use of cruel steel traps, agonizing poisons, or packs of hounds as methods of extermination. Killing can be cruelly or kindly done; and the deliberate choice of cruel ways, and their organization as popular pleasures, is sinful; but the sin is in the cruelty and the enjoyment of it, not in the killing.

479

ON THE ROCKS
THE SACREDNESS OF HUMAN LIFE

In law we draw a line between the killing of human animals and non-human ones, setting the latter apart as brutes. This was founded on a general belief that humans have immortal souls and brutes none. Nowadays more and more people are refusing to make this distinction. They may believe in The Life Everlasting and The Life to Come; but they make no distinction between Man and Brute, because some of them believe that brutes have souls, whilst other refuse to believe that the physical materializations and personifications of The Life Everlasting are themselves everlasting. In either case the mystic distinction between Man and Brute vanishes; and the murderer pleading that though a rabbit should be killed for being mischievous he himself should be spared because he has an immortal soul and a rabbit has none is as hopelessly out of date as a gentleman duellist pleading his clergy. When the necessity for killing a dangerous human being arises, as it still does daily, the only distinction we make between a man and a snared rabbit is that we very quaintly provide the man with a minister or religion to explain to him that we are not killing him at all, but only expediting his transfer to an eternity of bliss.

The political necessity for killing him is precisely like that for killing the cobra or the tiger: he is so ferocious or unscrupulous that if his neighbors do not kill him he will kill or ruin his neighbor; so that there is nothing for it but to disable him once for all by making an end of him, or else waste the lives of useful and harmless people in seeing that he does no mischief, and caging him cruelly like a lion in a show.

Here somebody is sure to interject that there is the alternative of teaching him better manners; but I am not here dealing with such cases: the real necessity arises only in dealing with untameable persons who are constitutionally unable to restrain their violent or acquisitive impulses, and have no compunction about sacrificing others to their own immediate convenience. To punish such persons is ridiculous: we might as reasonably punish a tile for flying off a roof in a storm and knocking a clergyman on the head. But to kill them is quite reasonable and very necessary.

PRESENT EXTERMINATIONS

All this so far is mere elementary criminology, already dealt with very fully by me in my Essay on Prisons, which I recommend to those readers who may feel impelled to ramble away at this point into the prosings about Deterrence beloved by our Prison commissioners and judges. It disposes of the dogma of the unconditional sacredness of human life, or any other incarnation of life; but it covers only a corner of the field opened up by modern powers of extermination. In Germany it is suggested that the Nordic race should exterminate the Latin race. As both these lingual stocks are hopelessly interbred by this time, such a sacrifice to ethnological sciolism is not practicable; but its discussion familiarizes the idea and clears the way for practicable suggestions. The extermination of whole races and classes has been not only advocated but actually attempted. The extirpation of the Jew as such figured for a few mad moments in the program of the Nazi party in Germany. The extermination of the peasant is in active progress in Russia, where the extermination of the class of ladies and gentlemen of so-called independent means has already been accomplished; and an attempt to exterminate the old Conservative professional class and the kulak or prosperous farmer class has been checked only by the discovery that they cannot as yet be done without. Outside Russia the extermination of Communists is widely advocated; and there is a movement in the British Empire and the United States for the extermination of Fascists. In India the impulse of Moslems and Hindus to exterminate one another is complicated by the impulse of the British Empire to exterminate both when they happen to be militant Nationalists.

ON THE ROCKS
PREVIOUS ATTEMPTS MISS THE POINT

The novelty and significance of these instances consists in the equal status of the parties. The extermination of what the exterminators call inferior races is as old as history. "Stone dead hath no fellow" said Cromwell when he tried to exterminate the Irish. "The only good nigger is a dead nigger" say the Americans of the Ku-Klux temperament. "Hates any man the thing he would not kill?" sail Shylock naïvely. But we white men, as we absurdly call ourselves in spite of the testimony of our looking glasses, regard all differently colored folk as inferior species. Ladies and gentlemen class rebellious laborers with vermin. The Dominicans, the watchdogs of God, regarded the Albigenses as the enemies of God, just as Torquemada regarded the Jews as the murderers of God. All that is an old story: what we are confronted with now is a growing perception that if we desire a certain type of civilization and culture we must exterminate the sort of people who do not fit into it. There is a difference between the shooting at sight of aboriginal natives in the back blocks of Australia and the massacres of aristocrats in the terror which followed the foreign attacks on the French Revolution. The Australian gunman pots the aboriginal natives to satisfy his personal antipathy to a black man with uncut hair. But nobody in the French Republic had this feeling about Lavoisier, nor can any German Nazi have felt that way about Einstein. Yet Lavoisier was guillotined; and Einstein has had to fly for his life from Germany. It was silly to say that the Republic had no use for chemists; and no Nazi has stultified his party to the extent of saying that the new National Socialist Fascist State in Germany has no use for mathematician-physicists. The proposition is that aristocrats (Lavoisier's class) and Jews (Einstein's race) are unfit to enjoy the privilege of living in a modern society founded on definite principles of social welfare as distinguished from the old promiscuous aggregations

482

crudely policed by chiefs who had no notion of social criticism and no time to invent it.

KING CHARLES'S HEAD

It was, by the way, the English Revolution which introduced the category of Malignant or Man of Blood, and killed the King as an affirmation that even kings must not survive if they are malignant. This was much more advanced than the execution in the following century of Louis XVI as an ordinary traitor, or of the Tsar in our own time to prevent his being captured by the Tchekoslovakian contingent and used as a standard to rally the royalist reaction. Charles affirmed a divine personal right to govern as against the parliament and would keep no bargain with it. Parliament denied his right, and set up against it a divine right of election winners to govern. They fought it out; and the victorious election winners exterminated the king, very logically. Finding that their authority still needed a royal disguise they drove a hard bargain for a crown with his son, and, after ejecting the next king who broke it, a still harder one with his Dutch grandson before they allowed the title of king, with nine tenths of the meaning knocked out of it, to be used as a matter of convenience again in England. Nobody had a word to say against Charles's private character. It was solely for incompatibility of politics that he was eliminated, or "liquidated" as we say now. There was a real novelty in the transaction. The Church had for centuries before compelled the secular State to liquidate heretics; and the slaughter of rebels who tried to substitute one dynasty for another, or to seize the throne for themselves, was common routine. But Charles was neither a heretic nor a rebel. He was the assertor of a divine right to govern without winning elections; and because that right could not co-exist with the supremacy of a much richer and more powerful plutocracy off went his head.

Charles was only the first victim. After Culloden the

defeated Highland chiefs and their clansmen were butchered like sheep on the field. Had they been merely prisoners of war, this would have been murder. But as they were also Incompatibles with British civilization, it was only liquidation.

RIGHT TO EXTERMINATE CONFERRED BY PRIVATE PROPERTY

Having disposed of the divine right of kings the political liquidators turned their attention slowly to its derivatory the divine right of landlords, which had gradually disguised itself as private property in land. For when a tract of land becomes the private property of an individual who has to depend on it for his subsistence, the relation between him and the inhabitants of that tract becomes an economic one; and if they become economically superfluous or wasteful, he must exterminate them. This is continually happening wherever private property in land exists. If I possess land and find it profitable to grow wheat on it, I need many agricultural laborers to enable me to do it; and I tolerate their existence accordingly. If I presently find that it is more profitable to cover my land with sheep and sell their wool, I have to tolerate the existence of the sheep; but I no longer need tolerate the existence of the laborers; so I drive them off my land, which is my legal method of extermination, retaining only a few to act as shepherds. Later on I find that it is more profitable to cover my land with wild deer, and collect money from gentlemen and ladies who enjoy shooting them. I then exterminate my shepherds and keep only a few gamekeepers. But I may do much better by letting my land to industrialists for the erection of factories. They exterminate the sheep and the deer; but they need far more men than I needed even when I grew wheat. The driven-offs crowd into the factories and multiply like rabbits; and for the moment population grows instead of diminishing. But soon machines come along and make millions of proletarians economically superfluous. The factory owner ac-

cordingly sacks them, which is his legal method of extermination. During these developments the exterminated,
or, as we call them, the evicted and sacked, try to avoid
starvation partly by emigration, but mostly by offering
themselves for all sorts of employment as soldiers, servants, prostitutes, police officers, scavengers, and operators
of the immense machinery of amusement and protection
for the idle rich classes created by the private property system. By organization in trade unions, municipal and parliamentary Labor Parties, and the like, and maintaining
a sort of continual civil war consisting of strikes and riots,
they extort from the proprietors enough to reduce the rate
of extermination (shewn by the actuarial expectation of
life of the unpropertied) for periods described as progressive, until the proprietors, by engaging in suicidal wars,
are forced to intensify their economies, and the rate of
extermination rises again.

DISGUISES UNDER WHICH PRIVATE EXTERMINATION OPERATES

Note that during all this the Registrar General's returns do not give us the deaths of the exterminated as
such, because the exterminated do not starve as lost travellers starve in the desert. Their starvation is more or less
protracted; and when the final catastrophe arrives, it is
disguised under an imposing array of doctors' names for
moribundity. The victims die mostly in their first year,
and subsequently at all ages short of the age at which
properly nourished people die. Sometimes they are starved
into attaining an age at which people with well filled pockets eat themselves to death. Either way and all ways the
extermination is a real and permanent feature of private
property civilization, though it is never mentioned as such,
and ladies and gentlemen are carefully educated to be unconscious of its existence and to talk nonsense about its
facts when they are too obvious or become too scandalous
to be ignored, when they often advocate emigration or
Birth Control or war as remedies. And against the facts

there is a chronic humanitarian revolt expressing itself
either underground or overground in revolutionary movements; making our political constitutions very unstable;
and imposing an habitual disingenuousness on conservative statesmen.

PRIVATE POWERS OF LIFE AND DEATH

Now the central fact of all these facts is that the private proprietors have irresponsible powers of life and
death in the State. Such powers may be tolerated as long
as the Government is in effect a committee of private proprietors; yet if such a committee be widened into or superseded by a Government acting in the interest of the
whole people, that Government will not suffer any private class to hold the lives of the citizens at its mercy and
thereby become their real masters. A popular Government, before it fully grasps the situation, usually begins
by attempting to redistribute property in such a manner
as to make everyone a petty proprietor, as in the French
Revolution. But when the impossibility of doing this (except in the special case of agricultural land) becomes apparent, and the question is probed to the bottom by unpropertied political philosophers like Proudhon and Marx,
private property is sooner or later excommunicated and
abolished; and what was formerly called "real property"
is replaced by ordinary personal property and common
property administered by the State.

All modern progressive and revolutionary movements
are at bottom attacks on private property. A Chancellor of
the Exchequer apologizing for an increase in the surtax,
a Fascist dictator organizing a Corporate State, a Soviet
Commissar ejecting a kulak and adding his acres to a collective farm, are all running the same race, though all of
them except the Commissar may be extremely reluctant
to win it. For in the long run the power to exterminate is
too grave to be left in any hands but those of a thoroughly
Communist Government responsible to the whole community. The landlord with his writ of ejectment and the
486

employer with his sack, must finally go the way of the
nobleman with his sword and his benefit of clergy, and of
Hannibal Chollop with his bowie knife and pistol.

Let us then assume that private property, already
maimed by factory legislation, surtax, and a good deal of
petty persecution in England, and in Russia tolerated only
provisionally as a disgraceful necessity pending its complete extirpation, is finally discarded by civilized communities, and the duty of maintaining it at all costs replaced
by the duty of giving effect to the dogma that every able-
bodied and ableminded and ablesouled person has an absolute right to an equal share in the national dividend.
Would the practice of extermination thereupon disappear?
I suggest that, on the contrary, it might continue much
more openly and intelligently and scientifically than at
present, because the humanitarian revolt against it would
probably become a humanitarian support of it; and there
would be an end of the hypocrisy, the venal special pleading, and the concealment or ignoring of facts which are
imposed on us at present because extermination for the
benefit of a handful of private persons against the interests
of the race is permitted and practised. The old doctrine of
the sacredness of human life, which in our idiot asylums
at Darenth and elsewhere still terrifies us into wasting the
lives of capable people in preserving the lives of monsters,
was a crude expedient for beginning civilization. At present we discard it in dealing with murderers, heretics, traitors, and (in Scotland) vitriol throwers, who can be legally killed. A runaway convict can also be summarily
shot by a warder to save the trouble of pursuing and re-
capturing him; and although the convict is not under capital sentence and the case is therefore clearly one of wilful murder, coroners' juries persist in treating it as a
harmless and necessary incident in prison routine.

Unfortunately the whole question is bedevilled by our
anti-Christian vice of punishment, expiation, sacrfice, and
all the cognate tribal superstitions which are hammered

487

into us in our childhood by barbarous scripturists, irascible or sadist parents, and a hideous criminal code. When the horrors of anarchy force us to set up laws that forbid us to fight and torture one another for sport, we still snatch at every excuse for declaring individuals outside the protection of law and torturing them to our hearts content.

CRUELTY'S EXCUSES

There have been summits of civilization at which heretics like Socrates, who was killed because he was wiser than his neighbors, have not been tortured, but ordered to kill themselves in the most painless manner known to their judges. But from that summit there was a speedy relapse into our present savagery. For Wallace, whom the Scots adored as a patriot and the English executed as a traitor, the most cruel and obscene method of killing that the human imagination could conceive at its vilest was specially invented to punish him for being a traitor (or "larn him to be a toad"); and this sentence has been passed, though not carried out, within the memory of persons now living. John of Leyden, for being a Communist, was tortured so frightfully before being hung up in a cage on the church tower to starve to death in sight of all the citizens and their little children, that the bishop who was officially obliged to witness it died of horror. Joan of Arc, for wearing men's clothes and being a Protestant and a witch, was burnt alive, after a proposal to torture her had been barely defeated. The people who saw her burnt were quite accustomed to such spectacles, and regarded them as holiday attractions. A woman's sex was made an excuse for burning her instead of more mercifully hanging her. Male criminals were broken on the wheel: that is, battered to death with iron bars, until well into the nineteenth century. This was a public spectacle; and the prolongation of the victim's suffering was so elaborately studied and arranged that Cartouche, one of the kings of scoundrelism, was bribed to betray his accomplices by the promise that he should be killed by the sixth blow of the bar. The wheel and the stake have lately gone out of use; but the Sadist mania for flogging seems ineradicable; for after a partially successful attempt to discard it in Victorian times it has revived again with redoubled ferocity: quite recently a criminal was sentenced to a flogging and ten years penal servitude; and although the victim escaped his punishment and gave a sensational advertisement to its savagery by committing suicide, nobody protested, though thirty years ago there would have been a strenuous outcry against it, raised by the old Humanitarian League, and voiced in Parliament by the Irish Nationalists. Alas! the first thing the Irish did when they at last enjoyed self-government was to get rid of these sentimental Nationalists and put flogging on their statute book in a series of Coercion Acts that would have horrified Dublin Castle. In a really civilized state flogging would cease because it would be impossible to induce any decent citizen to flog another. Among us a perfectly respectable official will do it for half a crown, and probably enjoy the job.

LEADING CASE OF JESUS CHRIST

I dislike cruelty, even cruelty to other people, and should therefore like to see all cruel people exterminated. But I should recoil with horror from a proposal to punish them. Let me illustrate my attitude by a very famous, indeed far too famous, example of the popular conception of criminal law as a means of delivering up victims to the normal popular lust for cruelty which has been mortified by the restraint imposed on it by civilization. Take the case of the extermination of Jesus Christ. No doubt there was a strong case for it. Jesus was from the point of view of the High Priest a heretic and an impostor. From the point of view of the merchants he was a rioter and a Communist. From the Roman Imperialist point of view he was a traitor. From the commonsense point of view he was a dangerous madman. From the snobbish point of view, always a very influential one, he was a penniless vagrant. From the police point of view he was an obstructor of

489

thoroughfares, a beggar, an associate of prostitutes, an apologist of sinners, and a disparager of judges; and his daily companions were tramps whom he had seduced into vagabondage from their regular trades. From the point of view of the pious he was a Sabbath breaker, a denier of the efficacy of circumcision and the advocate of a strange rite of baptism, a gluttonous man and a winebibber. He was abhorrent to the medical profession as an unqualified practitioner who healed people by quackery and charged nothing for the treatment. He was not anti-Christ: nobody had heard of such a power of darkness then; but he was startlingly anti-Moses. He was against the priests, against the judiciary, against the military, against the city (he declared that it was impossible for a rich man to enter the kingdom of heaven), against all the interests, classes, principalities and powers, inviting everybody to abandon all these and follow him. By every argument, legal, political, religious, customary, and polite, he was the most complete enemy of the society of his time ever brought to the bar. He was guilty on every count of the indictment, and on many more that his accusers had not the wit to frame. If he was innocent then the whole world was guilty. To acquit him was to throw over civilization and all its institutions. History has borne out the case against him; for no State has ever constituted itself on his principles or made it possible to live according to his commandments: those States who have taken his name have taken it as an alias to enable them to persecute his followers more plausibly.

It is not surprising that under these circumstances, and in the absence of any defence, the Jerusalem community and the Roman government decided to exterminate Jesus. They had just as much right to do so as to exterminate the two thieves who perished with him. But there was neither right nor reason in torturing him. He was entitled to the painless death of Socrates. We may charitably suppose that if the death could have been arranged privately be-

490

tween Pilate and Caiaphas Jesus would have been dispatched as quickly and suddenly as John the Baptist. But the mob wanted the horrible fun of seeing somebody crucified: an abominably cruel method of execution. Pilate only made matters worse by trying to appease them by having Jesus flogged. The soldiers, too, had to have their bit of sport, to crown him with thorns and, when they buffeted him, challenge him ironically to guess which of them had struck the blow.

"CROSSTIANITY"

All this was cruelty for its own sake, for the pleasure of it. And the fun did not stop there. Such was and is the attraction of these atrocities that the spectacle of them has been reproduced in pictures and waxworks and exhibited in churches ever since as an aid to piety. The chief instrument of torture is the subject of a special Adoration. Little models of it in gold and ivory are worn as personal ornaments; and big reproductions in wood and marble are set up in sacred places and on graves. Contrasting the case with that of Socrates, one is forced to the conclusion that if Jesus had been humanely exterminated his memory would have lost ninetynine per cent of its attraction for posterity. Those who were specially susceptible to his morbid attraction were not satisfied with symbolic crosses which hurt nobody. They soon got busy with "acts of faith" which consisted of great public shows at which Jews and Protestants or Catholics, and anyone else who could be caught out on a point of doctrine, were burnt alive. Cruelty is so infectious that the very compassion it rouses is infuriated to take revenge by still viler cruelties.

The tragedy of this—or, if you will, the comedy—is that it was his clearness of vision on this very point that set Jesus so high above his persecutors. He taught that two blacks do not make a white; that evil should not be countered by worse evil but by good; that revenge and punishment only duplicate wrong; that we should conceive God, not as an irascible and vindictive tyrant but as an affectionate father. No doubt many private amiabilities have been inspired by this teaching; but politically it has received no more quarter than Pilate gave it. To all Governments it has remained paradoxical and impracticable. A typical acknowledgment of it was the hanging of a crucifix above the seat of the judge who was sentencing evildoers to be broken on the wheel.

CHRISTIANITY AND THE SIXTH COMMANDMENT

Now it is not enough to satirize this. We must examine why it occurred. It is not enough to protest that evildoers must not be paid in their own coin by treating them as cruelly as they have treated others. We still have to stop the mischief they do. What is to be done with them? It is easy to suggest that they should be reformed by gentleness and shamed by non-resistance. By all means, if they respond to that treatment. But if gentleness fails to reform them and non-resistance encourages them to further aggression, what then? A month spent in a Tolstoyan community will convince anybody of the soundness of the nearest police inspector's belief that every normal human group contains not only a percentage of saints but also a percentage of irreclaimable scoundrels and good-for-nought who will wreck any community unless they are expensively restrained or cheaply exterminated. Our Mosaic system of vindictive punishment, politely called "retributory" by Prison Commissioners, disposes of them temporarily; but it wastes the lives of honest citizens in guarding them; sets a horrible example of cruelty and malicious injury; costs a good deal of money that might be better spent; and, after all, sooner or later lets the scoundrel loose again to recommence his depredations. It would be much more sensible and less cruel to treat him as we treat mad dogs or adders, without malice or cruelty, and without reference to catalogues of particular crimes. The notion that persons should be safe from extermination as long as they do not commit wilful murder, or levy war against

492

the Crown, or kidnap, or throw vitriol, is not only to limit social responsibility unnecessarily, and to privilege the large range of intolerable misconduct that lies outside them, but to divert attention from the essential justification for extermination, which is always incorrigible social incompatibility and nothing else.

THE RUSSIAN EXPERIMENT

The only country which has yet awakened to this extension of social responsibility is Russia. When the Soviet Government undertook to change over from Capitalism to Communism it found itself without any instruments for the maintenance of order except a list of crimes and punishments administered through a ritual of criminal law. And in the list of crimes the very worst offences against Communist society had no place: on the contrary they were highly honored and rewarded. As our English doggerel runs, the courts could punish a man for stealing the goose from off the common, but not the man who stole the common from the goose. The idler, that common enemy of mankind who robs everybody all the time, though he is so carefully protected from having his own pocket picked, incurred no penalty, and had actually passed the most severe laws against any interference with his idling. It was the business of the Soviet to make all business public business and all persons public servants; but the view of the ordinary Russian citizen was that a post in a public service was an exceptional stroke of good luck for the holder because it was a sinecure carrying with it the privilege of treating the public insolently and extorting bribes from it. For example, when the Russian railways were communized, some of the local stationmasters interpreted the change as meaning that they might now be as lazy and careless as they pleased, whereas in fact it was of life-or-death importance that they should redouble their activity and strain every nerve to make the service efficient. The unfortunate Commissar who was Minister of Transport found himself obliged to put a pistol in his pocket and

493

with his own hand shoot stationmasters who had thrown his telegrams into the dustbin instead of attending to them, so that he might the more impressively ask the rest of the staff whether they yet grasped the fact that orders are meant to be executed.

INADEQUACY OF PENAL CODES

Now being Minister of Transport, or Minister of any other public service, is a whole time job: it cannot be permanently combined with that of amateur executioner, carrying with it the reputation in all the capitalist papers of the west of being a ferocious and coldblooded murderer. And no conceivable extension of the criminal code nor of the service disciplines, with their lists of specific offences and specific penalties, could have provided for instant exemplary exterminations of this kind, any more than for the growing urgency of how to dispose of people who would not or could not fit themselves into the new order of things by conforming to its new morality. It would have been easy to specify certain offences and certain penalties in the old fashion: as, for instance, if you hoard money you will be shot: if you speculate in the difference in purchasing power of the rouble in Moscow and Berlin you will be shot; if you buy at the Co-operative to sell at the private trader's shop you will be shot, if you take bribes you will be shot; if you falsify farm or factory balance sheets you will be shot; if you exploit labor you will be shot; and it will be useless to plead that you have been brought up to regard these as normal business activities, and that the whole of respectable society outside Russia agrees with you. But the most elaborate code of this sort would still have left unspecified a hundred ways in which wreckers of Communism could have side-tracked it without ever having to face the essential questions: are you pulling your weight in the social boat? are you giving more trouble than you are worth? have you earned the privilege of living in a civilized community? That is why

494

the Russians were forced to set up an Inquisition or Star
Chamber, called at first the Cheka and now the Gay Pay
Oo (Ogpu), to go into these questions and "liquidate"
persons who could not answer them satisfactorily. The security against the abuse of this power of life and death was
that the Cheka had no interest in liquidating anybody who
could be made publicly useful, all its interests being in the
opposite direction.

LIMITED LIABILITY IN MORALS

Such a novelty is extremely terrifying to us, who are
still working on a system of limited liability in morals.
Our "free" British citizens can ascertain exactly what they
may do and what they may not do if they are to keep out
of the hands of the police. Our financiers know that they
must not forge share certificates nor overstate their assets
in the balance sheets they send to their shareholders. But
provided they observe a few conditions of this kind they
are free to enter upon a series of quite legitimate but not
the less nefarious operations. For example, making a corner in wheat or copper or any other cornerable commodity
and forcing up prices so as to make enormous private fortunes for themselves, or making mischief between nations
through the Press to stimulate the private trade in armaments. Such limited liability no longer exists in Russia,
and is not likely to exist in the future in any highly civilized state. It may be quite impossible to convict a fore-
staller or regrator under a criminal code of having taken
a single illegal step, but quite easy to convince any reasonable body of judges that he is what the people call "a
wrong one." In Russia such a conviction would lead to his
disappearance and the receipt by his family of a letter to
say that they need not wait up for him, as he would not
return home any more.[1] In our country he would enjoy

[1] Note, however, that a sentence of extermination should never be so
certain as to make it worth the delinquent's while to avoid arrest by murdering his or her pursuers.

his gains in high honor and personal security, and thank his stars that he lived in a free country and not in Communist Russia.

But as the new tribunal has been forced on Russia by pressure of circumstances and not planned and thought out at leisure, the two institutions, the Ogpu and the ordinary police administering the criminal code, work side by side, with the odd result that the surest way to escape the Ogpu is to commit an ordinary crime and take refuge in the arms of the police and the magistrate, who cannot exterminate you because capital punishment has been abolished in Russia (liquidation by the Ogpu is not punishment: it is only "weeding the garden"); and the sentence of imprisonment, though it may seem severe to us in view of the cruelty of our treatment of criminals, will be carried out with comparative leniency, and probably, if the culprit behaves well, be remitted after a while. As four years imprisonment is considered enough for any reasonable sort of murder, a cornerer who finds himself in imminent danger of detection and liquidation by the Ogpu would be well advised to lose his temper and murder his mother-in-law, thereby securing a lease of life for at least four years.

Sooner or later this situation will have to be thoroughly studied and thought out to its logical conclusion in all civilized countries. The lists of crimes and penalties will obsolesce like the doctors' lists of diseases and medicines; and it will become possible to be a judge without ceasing to be a Christian. And extermination, my present subject, will become a humane science instead of the miserable mixture of piracy, cruelty, vengeance, race conceit, and superstition it now is.

NATURAL LIMIT TO EXTERMINATION

Fortunately the more frankly and realistically it is faced the more it detaches itself from the associations with crude slaughter which now make it terrible. When Charlemagne founded the Holy Roman Empire (as far as anyone can be said to have founded it) he postulated that all

its subjects must be Catholic Christians, and made an ama-
teurish attempt to secure this condition of social stability
by killing everyone who fell into his power and refused to
be baptized. But he cannot ever have got very far with it,
because there is one sort of bird you must not kill on any
pretext whatever: namely, the goose that lays the golden
eggs. In Russia the Soviet Government began by a Char-
lemagnesque attempt to exterminate the bourgeoisie by
classing them as intelligentsia, restricting their rations,
and putting their children at the foot of the overcrowded
educational list. They also proscribed the kulak, the able,
hardheaded, hardfisted farmer who was richer than his
neighbors and liked to see them poorer than himself. Him
they rudely took by the shoulders and threw destitute into
the lane. There were plausible reasons for this beginning
of selection in population; for the moral outlook of the
bourgeoisie and the kulaks was dangerously anti-social.
But the results were disastrous. The bourgeoisie contained
the professional class and the organizing business class.
Without professional men and business organizers nothing
could be done in the industries; and the hope that picked
members of the proletariat could take up professional and
organizing work on the strength of their native talent in
sufficient numbers was crushingly disappointed. When the
kulak was thrown out of his farm, and his farming ability
paralyzed, food ran short. Very soon the kulak had to be
thrown back into his farm and told to carry on until his
hour had come; and a pleasant convention was established
whereby all educated persons, however obviously ladies or
gentlemen, who were willing to assure the authorities that
their fathers had "worked on the land with their hands"
were accepted as genuine proletarians, and transferred
from the infamous category of intelligentsia to the honorable one of "the intellectual proletariat." Even Lenin and
his colleagues, all ultra-bourgeois (otherwise they would
never have so absurdly overestimated the intellectual resources of the proletariat and been so contemptuous of the

pretension of their own class to be indispensable), allowed their parents to be described as hornyhanded cultivators of the soil. The pretence has now become a standing joke; but you will still come up against it if you accuse any Russian of being a lady or gentleman.

INCOMPATIBILITY OF PEASANTRY WITH MODERN CIVILIZATION

These, however, are merely expedients of transition. The Russian proletariat is now growing its own professional and organizing class; and the ex-bourgeois is dying out, after seeing his children receive a sound Communist education and being lectured by them on his oldfashioned prejudices. And the planners of the Soviet State have no time to bother about moribund questions; for they are confronted with the new and overwhelming necessity for exterminating the peasants, who still exist in formidable numbers. The notion that a civilized State can be made out of any sort of human material is one of our old Radical delusions. As to building Communism with such trash as the Capitalist system produces it is out of the question. For a Communist Utopia we need a population of Utopians; and Utopians do not grow wild on the bushes nor are they to be picked up in the slums: they have to be cultivated very carefully and expensively. Peasants will not do; yet without the peasants the Communists could never have captured the Russian Revolution. Nominally it was the Soviets of peasants and soldiers who backed Lenin and saved Communism when all Western Europe set on him like a pack of hounds on a fox. But as all the soldiers were peasants, and all the peasants hungry for property, the military element only added to the peasants' cry of Give us land, the soldiers' cry of Give us peace. Lenin said, in effect, Take the land; and if feudally minded persons obstruct you, exterminate them; but do not burn their houses, as you will need them to live in. And it was the resultant legions of petty landed proprietors that made Lenin's position impregnable, and provided Trotsky and

498

Stalin with the Red soldiers who defeated the counter-revolutionists of 1918. For the counter-revolution, in which we, to our eternal shame, took part (England sets the example of revolution and then attacks all other countries which presume to follow it), meant bringing the old landlords back; and the peasant fought against that as the mercenaries and conscripts of the Capitalist armies would not fight in favor of it.

A PEASANT VICTORY IS A VICTORY FOR PRIVATE PROPERTY

So far so good for Lenin; but the war against the counter-revolutionists, when it ended in victory for the peasant proprietor, was really a victory for private property, and was therefore succeeded by a fiercer struggle between the fanatically Communist Government and the fiercely individualist peasant proprietor, who wanted the produce of his plot for himself, and had no notion of pooling it with anybody, least of all with the urban proletarians who seemed like another species to him. Left to themselves the moujiks would have reproduced Capitalist civilization at its American worst in ten years. Thus the most urgent task before the victorious Communist Government was the extermination of the moujik; and yet the moujik, being still the goose that laid the golden eggs, could not be exterminated summarily without incidentally exterminating the whole Russian nation.

The way out of this deadlock was obvious enough, though very expensive and tedious. You can exterminate any human class not only by summary violence but by bringing up its children to be different. In the case of the Russian peasantry the father lives in a lousy kennel, at no man's call but his own, and extracts a subsistence by primitive methods from a strip of land on which a tractor could hardly turn even if he could afford such a luxury, but which is his very own. His book is a book of Nature, from which all wisdom can be gathered by those who have been taught to read it by due practice on printed books; but he

499

has not been so practised, and for cultural purposes has to be classed as ignorant, though he knows things that university professors do not know. He is brutalized by excessive muscular labor; he is dirty; his freedom from civilized control leaves him so unprotected from the tyranny of Nature that it becomes evident to his children that the highly regulated people in the nearest collectivist farm, where thousands of acres are cultivated by dozens of tractors, and nobody can put his foot on one of the acres or his hand on one of the tractors and say "This is my own to do what I like with," are better fed and housed, nicer, and much more leisured, and consequently free, than he ever is.

PREVENTIVE EXTERMINATION: ITS DIFFICULTIES

In short, you exterminate the peasant by bringing up his children to be scientifically mechanized farmers and to live a collegiate life in cultivated society. It sounds simple; but the process requires better planning than is always forthcoming (with local famines and revolts as the penalty); for while the grass grows the steed starves; and when education means not only schools and teachers, but giant collective farms equipped with the most advanced agricultural machinery, which means also gigantic engineering works for the production of the machinery, you may easily find that you have spent too much on these forms of capitalization and are running short of immediately consumable goods, presenting the spectacle of the nation with the highest level of general culture running short of boots and tightening its belt for lack of sufficient food.

I must not suggest that this has occurred all over Russia; for I saw no underfed people there; and the children were remarkably plump. And I cannot trust the reports; for I have no sooner read in The Times a letter from Mr Kerensky assuring me that in the Ukraine the starving people are eating one another, than M. Herriot, the eminent French statesman, goes to Russia and insists on visiting the Ukraine so that he may have ocular proof of the alleged cannibalism, but can find no trace of it. Still, between satiety and starvation mitigated by cannibalism there are many degrees of shortages; and it is no secret that the struggle of the Russian Government to provide more collective farms and more giant factories to provide agricultural machinery for them has to be carried on against a constant clamor from the workers for new boots and clothes, and more varied food and more of it: in short, less sacrifice of the present to the future. As Stalin said quaintly "They will be demanding silver watches next." The constant correction of the inevitable swerves towards one extreme or the other, analogous to the control of the Bank rate by the Bank of England (only enormously more laborious), strains all the wit and industry of the Russian rulers; and occasional sideslips must be inevitable during these years when the ablest and oldest Communists are still learners.

TEMPERAMENTAL DIFFICULTIES

Even when the extinction of the bourgeoisie and the kulaks and the old aristocracy is complete, and the Russian population consists of citizens educated as Communists, there will still be questions to settle which are at bottom questions as to the sort of civilization that is desirable; and this involves a decision as to the sort of people that are desirable and undesirable. Some of us, believing that a more primitive life than ours would be happier and better, advocate "a return to nature." Others dream of a much more mechanized, specialized, and complicated life. Some of us value machinery because it makes a shorter working day possible for us: others value it because it enriches us by increasing the product per hour. Some of us would like to take things easy and retire at 60: others would like to work their utmost and retire at 40. Some of us will say Let us be content with £200 a year: others No: let us live at the rate of £20,000 a year and strain every faculty to earn it. Some of us want a minimum of necessary work and a maximum of liberty to think and discover and experiment in the extension of science and art, philosophy and religion, sport and exploration: others, caring for none of these things, and desiring nothing more than to be saved the trouble of thinking and to be told what to do at every turn, would prefer thoughtless and comfortable tutelage and routine, not knowing what to do with themselves when at liberty. A life filled with scientific curiosity would be hell for the people who would not cross the street to find out whether the earth is flat or round; and a person with no ear for music would strenuously object to work for the support of municipal bands, whilst people of Shakespear's tastes would agitate for the extermination of the unmusical.

IMPORTANCE OF LAZINESS FOR FALLOWING

Some of these differences could be settled on give-and-take lines. The division of society into classes with different tastes and capacities—different natures, as folks call it—would not shake social stability provided everyone had an equal share of the national dividend. It is not true that it takes all sorts to make a world; for there are some sorts that would destroy any world very soon if they were suffered to live and have their way; but it is true that in the generations of men continuous high cultivation is not expedient: there must be fallows, or at least light croppings, between the intense cultivations; for we cannot expect the very energetic and vital Napoleon to be the son of an equally energetic father or the father of an equally vital son. Nobody has yet calculated how many lazy ancestors it takes to produce an indefatigable prodigy; but it is certain that dynasties of geniuses do not occur, and that this is the decisive objection to hereditary rulers (though not, let me hasten to add, to hereditary figure heads). There is a large field for toleration here: the clever people must suffer fools gladly, and the easygoing ones find out how to keep the energetic ones busy. There may be as good biological

PREFACE

reasons for the existence of the workshy as of the work-mad. Even one and the same person may have spells of intense activity and slackness varying from weeks to years.

STANDARD RELIGION INDISPENSABLE

Nevertheless there will be conflicts to the death in the creation of artificial humanity. There is nothing that can be changed more completely than human nature when the job is taken in hand early enough. Such artificial products as our agricultural laborers and urban mechanics, our country gentlemen and city plutocrats, though they are from the same human stock, are so different that they cannot live together without great discomfort, and are practically not intermarriageable. It is possible to get rid of their social incompatibility by giving them all the same education and income, and ranking them all in the same class. For example, Lord Lonsdale is not in the least socially incompatible with Dean Inge, though a really critical naturalist would as soon class Shetland ponies with zebras as lump these two gentlemen under the same heading. But the question remains, what is this same education to be? The training of the scholar and the sportsman may split and diverge as they adolesce; but they must start from a common training and a common morality as children. And when the state has to prescribe a uniform moral curriculum the variety of our temperaments makes it impossible to please everybody. The Quaker and the Ritualist, the Fundamentalist and the Freethinker, the Vegetarian and the flesh eater, the missionary and the cannibal, the humanitarian and the sportsman-hunter, the military terrorist and the Christian, will not agree as to the faiths and habits to be inculcated upon the children of the community in order that they may be good citizens. Each temperament will demand the extermination of the other through the schools and nurseries, and the establishment of its temperamental faith and habits as standard in these factories of future citizens. All will agree to exterminate illiteracy by compulsory reading, writing, and arithmetic:

indeed they have already done so. But all will not agree on a standard religion. Yet a standard religion is indispensable, however completely it may shed the old theologies. Every attempt to banish religion from the schools proves that in this respect Nature abhors a vacuum, and that the community must make up its mind, or have its mind made up for it by its official thinkers, as to what its children are to be taught to believe and how they should be trained to behave. Compromise is ruled out by the nature of the case. What compromise is possible between myself, for instance, who believe in the religion of Creative Evolution, the economics of Socialism, and a diet from which the dead bodies of men, fish, fowls, and animals are rigidly excluded, and my Fundamentalist neighbors who believe that all Evolutionists go to hell; that children languish and die without beefsteaks; and that without private property civilization must perish? We cannot exterminate one another at present; but the time cannot be very far off when the education authorities will have to consider which set of beliefs is the better qualification for citizenship in Utopia.

ECLECTIC RELIGIONS

They will probably pigeon-hole both, and proceed eclectically to compile several creeds suitable to the several capacities and ages of the children. For there is clearly no sense in offering the religion of a mature and scholarly philosopher to a child of five, nor attempting to bring the cosmogonies of Dante and Aquinas, Hegel and Marx, within the comprehension of a village dunce. Nurses rule their little charges by threatening them with bogies in whose existence no nurse believes, exactly as Mahomet ruled his Arabs by promises of a paradise and threats of a hell the details of which he must have known to be his own invention even if he did believe generally in a post mortem life of rewards and punishments for conduct in this world. Therefore I do not suggest that the education authorities in Utopia will seek for absolute truth in order to inculcate it though the heavens fall. Nor do I advise a return to Queen Elizabeth's plan of 39 Articles to please everybody by alternately affirming and denying all the disputed beliefs. The likeliest outcome is an elaborate creed of useful illusions, to be discarded bit by bit as the child is promoted from standard to standard or form to form, except such of them as adults may be allowed to comfort themselves with for the sake of the docility they produce.

There would be nothing new in this: it is what our authorities do at present, except that they do it unsystematically and unconsciously, being mostly more or less duped themselves by the illusions. Unfortunately they allow the illusions to fall behind the times and become incredible, at which point they become exceedingly dangerous; for when people are brought up on creeds which they cannot believe, they are left with no creeds at all, and are apt to buy pistols and take to banditry bag snatching and racketeering when employment fails and they find themselves short of money. It is the importance of keeping our inculcated illusions up to date that throws our higher professional classes into wild alarm when the individual liberty of thought, speech, and conscience which they think they possess (this is one of their inculcated illusions) is threatened by the dictatorships which are springing up all over the world as our pseudo-democratic parliamentary institutions reduce themselves more and more disastrously to absurdity.

IMPORTANCE OF FREE THOUGHT

Let me try to straighten this out for them. It was very generally believed as lately as in Victorian times that religious education consisted in imparting to children certain eternal, final, and absolute truths. I, for instance, being the son of an Irish Protestant gentleman, found myself, at the dawn of my infant conscience, absolutely convinced that all Roman Catholics go to hell when they die, a conviction which involved not only a belief in the existence of hell but a whole series of implications as to the nature and character of God. Now that I am older I cannot regard this as anything more than a provisional hypothesis which, on consideration, I must definitely reject. As the more pious of my uncles would have put it, I have lost my religious faith and am in peril of damnation as an Apostate. But I do not present my creed of Creative Evolution as anything more than another provisional hypothesis. It differs from the old Dublin brimstone creed solely in its greater credibility: that is, its more exact conformity to the facts alleged by our scientific workers, who have somehow won that faith in their infallibility formerly enjoyed by our priests. No future education authority, unless it is as badly educated as our present ones, will imagine that it has any final and eternal truths to inculcate: it can only select the most useful working hypotheses and inculcate them very much as it inculcates standard behavior throughout that vast field of civilized conduct in which it does not matter in the least how people act in particular situations provided they all act in the same way, as in the rule of the road. All the provisional hypotheses may be illusions; but if they conduce to beneficial conduct they must be inculcated and acted on by Governments until better ones arrive.

TOLERATION MOSTLY ILLUSORY

But, cry the professors, are the hypotheses never to be questioned? Is disillusion to be punished as a crime? That will always depend a good deal on circumstances. One of the best religious brains in England has said that the war of 1914–18 was foolish and unnecessary; and nobody now dreams of prosecuting him; but he would not have been allowed to go through the trenches from platoon to platoon saying so just before zero hour, with or without the addition "Sirs, ye are brethren: why do ye wrong one to another?" I have no illusion of being free to say and write what I please. I went round the world lately preaching that if Russia were thrust back from Communism into competitive Capitalism, and China developed into a predatory Capitalist State, either independently or as part of a Japanese Asiatic hegemony, all the western States would have to quintuple their armies and lie awake at nights in continual dread of hostile aeroplanes, the obvious moral being that whether we choose Communism for ourselves or not, it is our clear interest, even from the point of view of our crudest and oldest militarist diplomacy, to do everything in our power to sustain Communism in Russia and extend it in China, where at present provinces containing at the least of many conflicting estimates eighteen millions of people, have adopted it. Now I was not physically prevented from saying this, nor from writing and printing it. But in a western world suffering badly from Marxphobia, and frantically making itself worse like a shrew in a bad temper, I could not get a single newspaper to take up my point or report my utterance. When I say anything silly, or am reported as saying anything reactionary, it runs like wildfire through the Press of the whole world. When I say anything that could break the carefully inculcated popular faith in Capitalism the silence is so profound as to be almost audible. I do not complain, because I do not share the professorial illusion that there is any more freedom for disillusionists in the British Empire and the United States of North America than in Italy, Germany, and Russia. I have seen too many newspapers suppressed and editors swept away, not only in Ireland and India but in London in my time, to be taken in by Tennyson's notion that we live in a land where a man can say the thing he will. There is no such country. But this is no excuse for the extravagances of censorship indulged in by jejune governments of revolutionists, and by Churches who imagine they possess the eternal truth about everything, to say nothing of hereditary autocrats who conceive that they are so by divine right. Our papers are silent about the suppression of liberty in Imperialist Japan, though in Japan it is a crime to have "dangerous thoughts." In my native Ireland, now nominally a Free State, one of my books is on the index; and I have no doubt all the rest will follow as soon as the clerical censorship discovers their existence. In Austria my chronicle play St Joan had to be altered to please Catholic authorities who know much less about Catholicism than I do. In America books which can be bought anywhere in Europe are forbidden. The concentration of British and American attention on the intolerances of Fascism and Communism creates an illusion that they do not exist elsewhere; but they exist everywhere, and must be met, not with ridiculous hotheaded attacks on Germany, Italy, and Russia, but by a restatement of the case for Toleration in general.

LEADING CASES: SOCRATES AND JESUS

It is a historical misfortune that the most world-famous victims of persecution made no valid defence. Socrates and Jesus are the most talked of in Christian countries. Socrates at his trial was in full possession of his faculties, and was allowed to say everything he had to say in his defence; but instead of defending his right to criticize he infuriated his accusers by launching at them a damning contrast between their infamous corruption and mendacity and his own upright disinterestedness and blameless record as citizen and soldier. Jesus made no defence at all. He did not regard himself as a prisoner being tried for a vulgar offence and using all his wit to escape condemnation. He believed that he was going through a sacrificial rite in which he should be slain, after which he should rise from the dead and come again in glory to establish his kingdom on earth for ever. It does not matter to our present purpose whether this was the delusion of a madman or a hard and holy fact: in either case the question of toleration was not at issue for him; therefore he did not raise it.

THE CASE OF GALILEO

In the epoch which Jesus inaugurated, or at least in which his name was habitually taken in vain, we have Joan of Arc and John of Leyden, Giordano Bruno and Galileo,

PREFACE

Servetus and John Hus and the heroes of Foxe's Book of
Martyrs standing out in our imagination from thousands
of forgotten martyrdoms. Galileo is a favored subject with
our scientists; but they miss the point because they think
that the question at issue at his trial was whether the earth
went round the sun or was the stationary centre round
which the sun circled. Now that was not the issue. Taken
by itself it was a mere question of physical fact without
any moral significance, and therefore no concern of the
Church. As Galileo was not burnt and certainly not ab-
horred, it is quite credible that both his immediate judges
and the Pope believed with at least half their minds that
he was right about the earth and the sun. But what they
had to consider was whether the Christian religion, on
which to the best of their belief not only the civilization of
the world but its salvation depended, and which had accepted the Hebrew scriptures and the Greek testament as
inspired revelations, could stand the shock of the discovery
that many of its tales, from the tactics of Joshua in the
battle of Gibeon to the Ascension, must have been written
by somebody who did not know what the physical universe
was really like. I am quite familiar with the pre-Galileo
universe of the Bible and St Augustine. As a child I
thought of the earth as being an immense ground floor
with a star studded ceiling which was the floor of heaven,
and a basement which was hell. That Jesus should be
taken up into the clouds as the shortest way to heaven
seemed as natural to me as that, at the Opera, Mephi-
stopheles should come up from hell through a trap in the
floor. But if instead of telling me that Jesus was taken up
into the clouds and that the disciples saw him no more,
which still makes me feel quite holy, you tell me that he
went up like a balloon into the stratosphere, I do not feel
holy: I laugh obstreperously. The exalting vision has suddenly become a ribald joke. That is what the Church
feared; and that is what has actually happened. Is it any
wonder that the Pope told Galileo that he really must keep

509

his discoveries to himself, and that Galileo consented to deny them? Possibly it was the Pope who, to console him, whispered "E pur se muove."

FIGMENT OF THE SELFREGARDING ACTION

St Joan did not claim toleration: she was so far from believing in it that she wanted to lead a crusade of extermination against the Husites, though she was burnt for sharing their heresy. That is how all the martyrs have missed the point of their defence. They all claimed to possess absolute truth as against the error of their persecutors, and would have considered it their duty to persecute for its sake if they had had the power. Real toleration: the toleration of error and falsehood, never occurred to them as a principle possible for any sane government. And so they have left us no model defence. And there is no modern treatise known to me which quite supplies this need. Stuart Mill's Essay on Liberty satisfied the nineteenth century, and was my own first textbook on the subject; but its conclusion that selfregarding actions should not be interfered with by the authorities carries very little weight for Socialists who perceive that in a complex modern civilization there are no purely selfregarding actions in the controversial sphere. The color of a man's braces or a woman's garters may concern the wearers alone; but people have never been burnt for wearing black underclothes instead of white; and the notion that preaching a sermon or publishing a pamphlet can be classed as a selfregarding action is manifestly absurd. All great Art and Literature is propaganda. Most certainly the heresies of Galileo were not selfregarding actions: his feat of setting the earth rolling was as startling as Joshua's feat of making the sun stand still. The Church's mistake was not in interfering with his liberty, but in imagining that the secret of the earth's motion could be kept, and fearing that religion could not stand the shock of its disclosure, or a thousand such. It was idiotic to try to adapt Nature to the Church instead of continually adapting the Church to

Nature by changing its teaching on physical matters with every advance made in our knowledge of Nature. In treating the legend of Joshua's victory as a religious truth instead of insisting that it did not make the smallest difference to religion whether Joshua was any more real than Jack the Giant Killer, and that Galileo might play skittles with the whole solar system without moving the Eternal Throne and the Papal Chair which was its visible tangible symbol on earth a single inch, it lost a great opportunity, as it has since lost many others, leaving itself open to the reproach of stupidity in not understanding Galileo's argument, of pride in not having humility enough to admit that it had been wrong in its astronomy, and of feebleness of faith and confusion of the temporal with the spiritual as aforesaid, laying itself open to much damaging Protestant and scientific disparagement, both mostly open to precisely the same reproaches.

INCOMPLETENESS OF THE GREAT TRIALS

No doubt Galileo missed the real point at issue as completely as Socrates or Jesus. For this we need not blame him: he was a physicist and not a politician; and to him the only questions at issue were whether the earth moved or not, and whether a ten pound cannon ball would fall twice as fast as a five pound one or only just as fast and no faster. But Socrates was by vocation and habit a solver of problems of conduct, both personal and political; and Jesus, who had spent his life in propounding the most staggering paradoxes on the same subject, not by any means always in the abstract, but as personal directions to his followers, must, if he had any sense of moral responsibility, have been challenged by his own conscience again and again as to whether he had any right to set men on a path which was likely to lead the best of them to the cross and the worst of them to the moral destruction described by St Augustine. No man could expressly admit that his word would bring not peace but a sword without having satisfied himself that he was justified in doing so. He must have been told as frequently as I have been told that he was giving pain to many worthy people; and even with the fullest allowance for the strain of impishness with which the Life Force endows those of us who are destined by it to *épater le bourgeois,* he cannot have believed that the mere satisfaction of this Punchesque *Schadenfreude* could justify him in hurting anyone's feelings. What, then, would have been his defence if, at his trial, he had been his old self, defending himself as an accused man threatened with a horrible penalty, instead of a god going through an inevitable ordeal as a prelude to the establishment of his kingdom on earth?

A MODERN PASSION PLAY IMPOSSIBLE

The question is of such importance at the present crisis, when the kingdoms are breaking up, and upstart rulers are sowing their wild oats by such grotesque persecutions that Galileo's great successor Einstein is a plundered fugitive from officially threatened extermination, that I must endeavor to dramatize the trial of Jesus as it might have proceeded had it taken place before Peter uttered his momentous exclamation "Thou art the Christ." I have been asked repeatedly to dramatize the Gospel story, mostly by admirers of my dramatization of the trial of St Joan. But the trial of a dumb prisoner, at which the judge who puts the crucial question to him remains unanswered, cannot be dramatized unless the judge is to be the hero of the play. Now Pilate, though perhaps a trifle above the average of colonial governors, is not a heroic figure. Joan tackled her judges valiantly and wittily: her trial was a drama ready made, only needing to be brought within theatrical limits of time and space to be a thrilling play. But Jesus would not defend himself. It was not that he had not a word to say for himself, nor that he was denied the opportunity of saying it. He was not only allowed but challenged to defend himself. He was an experienced public speaker, able to hold multitudes with his oratory, happy and ready in debate and repartee, full of

512

the illustrative hypothetical cases beloved of lawyers (called parables in the Gospels), and never at a loss when plied with questions. If ever there was a full dress debate for the forensic championship to be looked forward to with excited confidence by the disciples of the challenged expert it was this trial of Christ. Yet their champion put up no fight: he went like a lamb to the slaughter, dumb. Such a spectacle is disappointing on the stage, which is the one thing that a drama must not be; and when the disappointment is followed by scourging and crucifixion it is unbearable: not even the genius of our Poet Laureate, with all the magic of Canterbury Cathedral for scenery, can redeem it except for people who enjoy horror and catastrophe for their own sake and have no intellectual expectations to be disappointed.

DIFFERENCE BETWEEN READER AND SPECTATOR

It may be asked why the incident of the trial and execution must fail on the stage, seeing that the gospel narrative is so pathetic, and so many of us have read it without disappointment. The answer is very simple: we have read it in childhood; and children go on from horror to horror breathlessly, knowing nothing of the constitutional questions at issue. Some of them remain in this condition of intellectual innocence to the end of their lives, whilst the cleverer ones seldom reconsider the impressions they have received as little children. Most Christians, I suspect, are afraid to think about it critically at all, having been taught to consider criticism blasphemous when applied to Bible stories. Besides, there are a thousand things that will pass in a well told story that will not bear being brought to actuality on the stage. The evangelists can switch off our attention from Jesus to Peter hearing the cock crow (or the bugle blow) or to Pilate chaffering with the crowd about Barabbas; but on the stage the dumb figure cannot be got rid of: it is to him that we look for a speech that will take us up to heaven, and not to the weeping of

Peter and the bawling of the mob, which become unbearable interruptions instead of skilful diversions.

For my part, when I read the story over again as an adult and as a professional critic to boot, I felt the disappointment so keenly that I have been ever since in the condition of the musician who, when he had gone to bed, heard somebody play an unresolved discord, and could not go to sleep until he had risen to play the resolution on his piano. What follows is my attempt to resolve Pilate's discord. I begin with the narrative of St John, the only one of the four which represents Jesus as saying anything more than any crazy person might in the same circumstances.

PILATE. Are you the king of the Jews?

JESUS. Do you really want to know? or have those people outside put it into your head to ask me?

PILATE. Am I a Jew, that I should trouble myself about you? Your own people and their priests have brought you to me for judgment. What have you done?

JESUS. My kingdom is not of this world: if it were, my followers would have fought the police and rescued me. But that sort of thing does not happen in my kingdom.

PILATE. Then you are a king?

JESUS. You say so. I came into this world and was born a common man for no other purpose than to reveal the truth. And everyone capable of receiving the truth recognizes it in my voice.

PILATE. What is truth?

JESUS. You are the first person I have met intelligent enough to ask me that question.

PILATE. Come on! no flattery. I am a Roman, and no doubt seem exceptionally intelligent to a Jew. You Jews are always talking about truth and righteousness and justice: you feed on words when you are tired of making money, or too poor to have anything else to feed on. They want me to nail you up on a cross; but as I do not yet see

514

what particular harm you have done I prefer to nail you down to an argument. Fine words butter no parsnips in Rome. You say your vocation is to reveal the truth. I take your word for it; but I ask you what is truth?

JESUS. It is that which a man must tell even if he be stoned or crucified for telling it. I am not offering you the truth at a price for my own profit: I am offering it freely to you for your salvation at the peril of my own life. Would I do that if I were not driven by God to do it against all the protests of my shrinking flesh?

PILATE. You Jews are a simple folk. You have found only one god. We Romans have found many; and one of them is a God of Lies. Even you Jews have to admit a Father of Lies whom you call the devil, deceiving yourselves with words as usual. But he is a very potent god, is he not? And as he delights not only in lies but in all other mischief such as stonings and crucifixions of innocent men, how am I to judge whether it is he who is driving you to sacrifice yourself for a lie, or Minerva driving you to be sacrificed for the truth? I ask you again, what is truth?

JESUS. It is what you know by your experience to be true or feel in your soul must be true.

PILATE. You mean that truth is a correspondence between word and fact. It is true that I am sitting in this chair; but I am not the truth and the chair is not the truth: we are only the facts. My perception that I am sitting here may be only a dream; therefore my perception is not the truth.

JESUS. You say well. The truth is the truth and nothing else. That is your answer.

PILATE. Aye; but how far is it discoverable? We agree that it is true that I am sitting in this chair because our senses tell us so; and two men are not likely to be dreaming the same dream at the same moment. But when I rise from my chair this truth is no longer true. Truth is of the present, not of the future. Your hopes for the future are not the truth. Even in the present your opinions are not the truth. It is true that I sit in this chair. But is it true that it is better for your people that I should sit in this chair and impose on them the peace of Rome than that they should be left to slaughter oneanother in their own native savagery, as they are now clamoring to me to slaughter you?

JESUS. There is the peace of God that is beyond our understanding; and that peace shall prevail over the peace of Rome when God's hour strikes.

PILATE. Very pretty, my friend; but the hour of the gods is now and always; and all the world knows what the peace of your Jewish God means. Have I not read it in the campaigns of Joshua? We Romans have purchased the *pax Romana* with our blood; and we prefer it as a plain understandable thing which keeps men's knives off one-another's throats to your peace which is beyond understanding because it slaughters man, woman and child in the name of your God. But that is only our opinion. It is not yours. Therefore it is not necessarily the truth. I must act on it, because a governor must act on something: he cannot loaf round the roads and talk beautifully as you do. If you were a responsible governor instead of a poetic vagrant, you would soon discover that my choice must lie, not between truth and falsehood, neither of which I can ever ascertain, but between reasonable and well informed opinion and sentimental and ill informed impulse.

JESUS. Nevertheless, opinion is a dead thing and impulse a live thing. You cannot impose on me with your reasonable and well informed opinion. If it is your will to crucify me, I can find you a dozen reasons for doing so; and your police can supply you with a hundred facts to support the reasons. If it is your will to spare me I can find you just as many reasons for that; and my disciples will supply you with more facts than you have time or patience to listen to. That is why your lawyers can plead as well for one side as another, and can therefore plead without dishonor for the side that pays them, like the hackney chari-

516

oteer who will drive you north as readily as south for the same fare.

PILATE. You are cleverer than I thought; and you are right. There is my will; and there is the will of Cæsar to which my will must give way; and there is above Cæsar the will of the gods. But these wills are in continual conflict with oneanother; therefore they are not truth: for truth is one, and cannot conflict with itself. There are conflicting opinions and conflicting wills; but there is no truth except the momentary truth that I am sitting in this chair. Yet you tell me that you are here to bear witness to the truth! You, a vagrant, a talker, who have never had to pass a sentence nor levy a tax nor issue an edict! What have you to say that I should not have the presumption scourged out of you by my executioners?

JESUS. Scourging is not a cure for presumption, nor is it justice, though you will perhaps call it so in your report to Cæsar: it is cruelty; and that cruelty is wicked and horrible because it is the weapon with which the sons of Satan slay the sons of God is part of the eternal truth you seek.

PILATE. Leave out cruelty: all government is cruel; for nothing is so cruel as impunity. A salutary severity—

JESUS. Oh please! You must excuse me, noble Governor; but I am so made by God that official phrases make me violently sick. Salutary severity is ipecacuanha to me. I have spoken to you as one man to another, in living words. Do not be so ungrateful as to answer me in dead ones.

PILATE. In the mouth of a Roman words mean something: in the mouth of a Jew they are a cheap substitute for strong drink. If we allowed you you would fill the whole world with your scriptures and psalms and talmuds; and the history of mankind would become a tale of fine words and villainous deeds.

JESUS. Yet the word came fire, before it was made flesh. The word was the beginning. The word was with God before he made us. Nay, the word was God.

517

PILATE. And what may all that mean, pray?

JESUS. The difference between man and Roman is but a word; but it makes all the difference. The difference between Roman and Jew is only a word.

PILATE. It is a fact.

JESUS. A fact that was first a thought; for a thought is the substance of a word. I am no mere chance pile of flesh and bone: if I were only that, I should fall into corruption and dust before your eyes. I am the embodiment of a thought of God: I am the Word made flesh: that is what holds me together standing before you in the image of God.

PILATE. That is well argued; but what is sauce for the goose is sauce for the gander; and it seems to me that if you are the Word made flesh so also am I.

JESUS. Have I not said so again and again? Have they not stoned me in the streets for saying it? Have I not sent my apostles to proclaim this great news to the Gentiles and to the very ends of the world? The Word is God. And God is within you. It was when I said this that the Jews —my own people—began picking up stones. But why should you, the Gentile, reproach me for it?

PILATE. I have not reproached you for it. I pointed it out to you.

JESUS. Forgive me. I am so accustomed to be contradicted—

PILATE. Just so. There are many sorts of words; and they are all made flesh sooner or later. Go among my soldiers and you will hear many filthy words and witness many cruel and hateful deeds that began as thoughts. I do not allow those words to be spoken in my presence. I punish those deeds as crimes. Your truth, as you call it, can be nothing but the thoughts for which you have found words which will take effect in deeds if I set you loose to scatter your words broadcast among the people. Your own people who bring you to me tell me that your thoughts are abominable and your words blasphemous. How am I to refute them? How am I to distinguish between the blasphemies of my soldiers reported to me by my centurions and your blasphemies reported to me by your High Priest?

JESUS. Woe betide you and the world if you do not distinguish!

PILATE. So you think. I am not frightened. Why do you think so?

JESUS. I do not think: I know. I have it from God.

PILATE. I have the same sort of knowledge from several gods.

JESUS. In so far as you know the truth you have it from my God, who is your heavenly father and mine. He has many names and his nature is manifold. Call him what you will: he is still Our Father. Does a father tell his children lies?

PILATE. Yet: many lies. You have an earthly father and an earthly mother. Did they tell you what you are preaching?

JESUS. Alas! no.

PILATE. Then you are defying your father and mother. You are defying your Church. You are breaking your God's commandments, and claiming a right to do so. You are pleading for the poor, and declaring that it is easier for a camel to pass through the eye of a needle than for a rich man to enter your God's paradise. Yet you have feasted at the tables of the rich, and encouraged harlots to spend on perfume for your feet money that might have been given to the poor, thereby so disgusting your treasurer that he has betrayed you to the High Priest for a handful of silver. Well, feast as much as you please: I do not blame you for refusing to play the fakir and make yourself a walking exhibition of silly austerities; but I must draw the line at your making a riot in the temple and throwing the gold of the moneychangers to be scrambled for by your partizans. I have a law to administer. The law forbids obscenity, sedition, and blasphemy. You are accused of sedition and blasphemy. You do not deny them:

519

you only talk about the truth, which turns out to be nothing but what you like to believe. Your blasphemy is nothing to me: the whole Jewish religion is blasphemy from beginning to end from my Roman point of view; but it means a great deal to the High Priest; and I cannot keep order in Jewry except by dealing with Jewish fools according to Jewish folly. But sedition concerns me and my office very closely; and when you undertook to supersede the Roman Empire by a kingdom in which you and not Cæsar are to occupy the throne, you were guilty of the uttermost sedition. I am loth to have you crucified; for though you are only a Jew, and a half baked young one at that, yet I perceive that you are in your Jewish way a man of quality; and it makes me uneasy to throw a man of quality to the mob, even if his quality be only a Jewish quality. For I am a patrician and therefore myself a man of quality; and hawks should not pick out hawks' eyes. I am actually condescending to parley with you at this length in the merciful hope of finding an excuse for tolerating your blasphemy and sedition. In defence you offer me nothing but an empty phrase about the truth. I am sincere in wishing to spare you; for if I do not release you I shall have to release that blackguard Barabbas, who has gone further than you and killed somebody, whereas I understand that you have only raised a Jew from the dead. So for the last time set your wits to work, and find me a sound reason for letting a seditious blasphemer go free.

JESUS. I do not ask you to set me free; nor would I accept my life at the price of Barabbas's death even if I believed that you could countermand the ordeal to which I am predestined. Yet for the satisfaction of your longing for the truth I will tell you that the answer to your demand is your own argument that neither you nor the prisoner whom you judge can prove that he is in the right; therefore you must not judge me lest you be yourself judged. Without sedition and blasphemy the world would stand still and the Kingdom of God never be a stage nearer.

PREFACE

The Roman Empire began with a wolf suckling two human infants. If these infants had not been wiser than their fostermother your empire would be a pack of wolves. It is by children who are wiser than their fathers, subjects who are wiser than their emperors, beggars and vagrants who are wiser than their priests, that men rise from being beasts of prey to believing in me and being saved.

PILATE. What do you mean by believing in you?

JESUS. Seeing the world as I do. What else could it mean?

PILATE. And you are the Christ, the Messiah, eh?

JESUS. Were I Satan, my argument would still hold.

PILATE. And I am to spare and encourage every heretic, every rebel, every lawbreaker, every rapscallion lest he should turn out to be wiser than all the generations who made the Roman law and built up the Roman Empire on it?

JESUS. By their fruits ye shall know them. Beware how you kill a thought that is new to you. For that thought may be the foundation of the kingdom of God on earth.

PILATE. It may also be the ruin of all kingdoms, all law, and all human society. It may be the thought of the beast of prey striving to return.

JESUS. The beast of prey is not striving to return: the kingdom of God is striving to come. The empire that looks back in terror shall give way to the kingdom that looks forward with hope. Terror drives men mad: hope and faith give them divine wisdom. The men whom you fill with fear will stick at no evil and perish in their sin: the men whom I fill with faith shall inherit the earth. I say to you Cast out fear. Speak no more vain things to me about the greatness of Rome. The greatness of Rome, as you call it, is nothing but fear: fear of the past and fear of the future, fear of the poor, fear of the rich, fear of the High Priests, fear of the Jews and Greeks who are learned, fear of the Gauls and Goths and Huns who are barbarians, fear of the Carthage you destroyed to save you from your

fear of it and new fear worse than ever, fear of imperial
Cæsar, the idol you have yourself created, and fear of me,
the penniless vagrant, buffeted and mocked, fear of everything except the rule of God: faith in nothing but blood
and iron and gold. You, standing for Rome, are the universal coward: I, standing for the kingdom of God, have
braved everything, lost everything, and won an eternal
crown.

PILATE. You have won a crown of thorns; and you
shall wear it on the cross. You are a more dangerous fellow than I thought. For your blasphemy against the god
of the high priests I care nothing: you may trample their
religion into hell for all I care; but you have blasphemed
against Cæsar and against the Empire; and you mean it,
and have the power to turn men's hearts against it as you
have half turned mine. Therefore I must make an end of
you whilst there is still some law left in the world.

JESUS. Law is blind without counsel. The counsel men
agree with is vain: it is only the echo of their own voices.
A million echoes will not help you to rule righteously.
But he who does not fear you and shews you the other
side is a pearl of the greatest price. Slay me and you go
blind to your damnation. The greatest of God's names is
Counsellor; and when your Empire is dust and your name
a byword among the nations the temples of the living God
shall still ring with his praise as Wonderful! Counsellor!
the Everlasting Father, the Prince of Peace.

THE SACREDNESS OF CRITICISM

And so the last word remains with Christ and Han-
del; and this must stand as the best defence of Tolerance
until a better man than I makes a better job of it.

Put shortly and undramatically the case is that a civilization cannot progress without criticism, and must therefore, to save itself from stagnation and putrefaction, declare impunity for criticism. This means impunity not
only for propositions which, however novel, seem interesting, statesmanlike, and respectable, but for propositions

that shock the uncritical as obscene, seditious, blasphemous, heretical, and revolutionary. That sound Catholic institution, the Devil's Advocate, must be privileged as possibly the Herald of the World to Come. The difficulty is to distinguish between the critic and the criminal or lunatic, between liberty of precept and liberty of example. It may be vitally necessary to allow a person to advocate Nudism; but it may not be expedient to allow that person to walk along Piccadilly stark naked. Karl Marx writing the death warrant of private property in the reading room of the British Museum was sacred; but if Karl Marx had sent the rent of his villa in Maitland Park to the Chancellor of the Exchequer, and shot the landlord's agents when they came to distrain on his furniture or execute a writ of ejectment, he could hardly have escaped hanging by pleading his right to criticize. Not until the criticism changes the law can the magistrate allow the critic to give effect to it. We are so dangerously uneducated in citizenship that most of us assume that we have an unlimited right to change our conduct the moment we have changed our minds. People who have a vague notion that Socialism is a state of society in which everyone gives away everything he possesses to everybody else occasionally reproach me because I, being a Socialist, do not immediately beggar myself in this fashion. People who imagined, more specifically, that a Socialist could not consistently keep a motor car, almost succeeded in making a public question of the possession of such a vehicle by a Prime Minister who at that time professed Socialism. But even if these idiots had really understood what they were talking about, they would have been wrong in supposing that a hostile critic of the existing social order either could or should behave as if he were living in his own particular Utopia. He may, at most, be a little eccentric at the cost of being indulged as slightly cracked.

On the other hand the Government, too, has not only a right but a duty of criticism. If it is to abandon once for

523

all its savage superstition that whoever breaks the law is fair game for the torturers, and that the wrong wrought by the evildoer can be expiated and undone by a worse wrong done to him by judges and priests: if it is to substitute the doctrine of Jesus that punishment is only a senseless attempt to make a white out of two blacks, and to abolish the monstrous list of crimes and punishments by which these superstitions have been reduced to practise for routine officials, then there must be a stupendous extension of governmental criticism; for every crime will raise the essential critical question whether the criminal is fit to live at all, and if so whether he is fit to live under more or less tutelage and discipline like a soldier, or at normal liberty under an obligation to make good the damage he has cost.

For such functions as these we shall need critics educated otherwise than our judges of today; but the same may be said of all whose public functions transcend the application of a routine.

I have no doubt that the eradication of malice, vindictiveness, and Sadist libido on these terms from the personal contacts of citizens with their rulers, far from having a reassuring effect, is likely to be rather terrifying at first, as all people with any tenderness of conscience will feel the deepest misgivings as to whether they are really worth keeping alive in a highly civilized community; but that will wear off as standards of worth get established and known by practice. In the meantime the terror will act as a sort of social conscience which is dangerously lacking at present, and which none of our model educational establishments ever dreams of inculcating.

Ayot St Lawrence,
22nd October, 1933.

ON THE ROCKS

ACT I

THE Cabinet Room in number ten Downing Street, Westminster, the official residence of the British Prime Minister. The illustrious holder of that office, Sir Arthur Chavender, is reading the Times on the hearth under the portrait of Walpole. The fireplace wall is covered with bookshelves; but one bit of it, on Walpole's right, is a masked door, painted with sham books and shelves, leading to the Minister's private apartments; and in the end of the same wall, on Walpole's left, is a door leading to the office of Sir Arthur's private secretary Miss Hilda Hanways. The main door is in the side wall on Walpole's right. In the opposite wall on his left are the spacious windows. Everything is on an imposing scale, including an oblong table across the middle of the room, with fourteen leather upholstered chairs, six at each side and one at each end, pushed in all along it. The presidential chair is the central one next the cold fireplace (it is mid-July); and there is a telephone and a switchboard on the table within reach of it. Sir Arthur has pulled it round and is making himself comfortable in it as he reads. At the end of the table nearest the window a silver tray, with coffee and milk for one person, indicates Sir Arthur's unofficial seat. In the corner farthest from Walpole, on his right, is a writing bureau and chair for the secretary. In the corresponding corner on his left, an armchair. There is a bluebook lying, neglected and dusty, on a half empty shelf of the bookcase within reach of the Prime Minister's seat.

Sir Arthur can hardly be much less than fifty; but his natural buoyancy makes him look younger. He has an orator's voice of pleasant tone; and his manners are very genial. In oldish clothes he has the proper aristocratic air of being carelessly but well dressed, an easy feat for him, as he is so trimly built that any clothes would look well cut on him. On the whole, a very engaging personality.

ON THE ROCKS

*He reads The Times until his secretary hurries in
from her office, with her notebook and a sheaf of letters in
her hand. Her age is unknown; but she is made up to pass
as reasonably young and attractive. She looks capable; but
she does not carry the burden of State affairs as easily as
the Prime Minister. Both are worried; but with a difference. She is worried not only by an excess of business but
a sense of responsibility. He is equally worried by the excess of business; but in him enjoyment of his position leaves
no doubt in his mind as to his own entire adequacy to it.*

HILDA. I hear you have been asking for me, Sir Arthur.
I'm so sorry to be late; but really the streets are becoming
quite impassable with the crowds of unemployed. I took a
taxi; but it was no use: we were blocked by a procession;
and I had to get out and push my way through. [*She goes
to her bureau*].

SIR ARTHUR. [*rising*] What on earth good do they
think they can do themselves by crowding aimlessly about
Westminster and the public offices?

HILDA. Thank Goodness the police wont let them into
Downing Street. [*She sits down*]. They would be all over
the doorstep.

SIR ARTHUR. It's all so foolish—so ignorant, poor
chaps! [*He throws The Times on the table and moves to
the end chair, where his coffee is*]. They think because I'm
Prime Minister I'm Divine Providence and can find jobs
for them before trade revives. [*He sits down and fidgets
with his papers*].

HILDA. Trafalgar Square's full. The Horse Guards
parade is full. The Mall is full all the way down to Marl-
borough House and Buckingham Palace.

SIR ARTHUR. They have no right to be there. Trafalgar
Square is not a public place: it belongs to the Commissioner
of Woods and Forests. The Horse Guards parade is reserved for the military. The Mall is a thoroughfare: anyone stopping there is guilty of obstruction. What are the
police thinking of? Why don't they clear them out?

526

HILDA. I asked the policeman who got me through to the gates why they didnt. He said "We're only too glad to have them where they cant break any windows, and where the mounted men can have a fair whack at the Hooligan Fringe when they get too obstreperous."

SIR ARTHUR. Hooligan Fringe! He got that out of the papers. It only encourages them to write them up like that.

HILDA. Sir Broadfoot Basham has come over from Scotland Yard. He is talking to Lady Chavender.

SIR ARTHUR [*rising and making for the telephone*] Yes: I telephoned for him. He really must do something to stop these meetings. It was a mistake to make a man with a name like that Chief Commissioner of Police. People think him a trampling, bashing, brutal terrorist no matter how considerately the police behave. What we need is a thoroughly popular figure. [*He takes up the telephone*] Ask Sir Broadfoot Basham to come up.

HILDA. I dont think any chief of police could be popular at present. Every day they are bludgeoning deputations of the unemployed. [*She sits down and busies herself with letters*].

SIR ARTHUR. Poor devils! I hate that part of the business. But what are the police to do? We cant have the sittings of the local authorities threatened by deputations. Deputations are frightful nuisances even in the quietest times; but just now they are a public danger.

The Chief Commissioner of Police enters by the main door. A capable looking man from the military point of view. He is a gentleman: and his manners are fairly pleasant; but they are not in the least conciliatory.

Hilda rises and pulls out a chair for him at the end of the table nearest to her and farthest from Sir Arthur; then returns to her work at her desk. Sir Arthur comes round to his side of the table.

SIR ARTHUR. Morning, Basham. Sit down. I'm devilishly busy; but you are always welcome to your ten minutes.

BASHAM [*coolly, sitting down*] Thank you. You sent for me. [*Anxiously*] Anything new?

SIR ARTHUR. These street corner meetings are going beyond all bounds.

BASHAM [*relieved*] What harm do they do? Crowds are dangerous when theyve nothing to listen to or look at. The meetings keep them amused. They save us trouble.

SIR ARTHUR. Thats all very well for you, Basham; but think of the trouble they make for me! Remember: this is a National Government, not a party one. I am up against my Conservative colleagues all the time; and they cant swallow the rank sedition that goes on every day at these meetings. Sir Dexter Rightside—you know what a regular old Diehard he is—heard a speaker say that if the police used tear gas the unemployed would give old Dexy something to cry for without any tear gas. That has brought matters to a head in the Cabinet. We shall make an Order in Council to enable you to put a stop to all street meetings and speeches.

BASHAM [*unimpressed—slowly*] If you dont mind, P.M., I had rather you didn't do that.

SIR ARTHUR. Why not?

BASHAM. Crowd psychology.

SIR ARTHUR. Nonsense! Really, Basham, if you are going to come this metaphysical rot over me I shall begin to wonder whether your appointment wasnt a mistake.

BASHAM. Of course it was a mistake. Dealing with the unemployed is not a soldier's job; and I was a soldier. If you want these crowds settled on soldierly lines, say so; and give me half a dozen machine guns. The streets will be clear before twelve o'clock.

SIR ARTHUR. Man: have you considered the effect on the bye-elections?

BASHAM. A soldier has nothing to do with elections. You shew me a crowd and tell me to disperse it. All youll hear is a noise like a watchman's rattle. Quite simple.

528

SIR ARTHUR. Far too simple. You soldiers never understand the difficulties a statesman has to contend with.

BASHAM. Well, whats your alternative?

SIR ARTHUR. I have told you. Arrest the sedition mongers. That will shut old Dexy's mouth.

BASHAM. So that Satan may find mischief still for idle hands to do. No, P.M.: the right alternative is mine: keep the crowd amused. You ought to know that, I think, better than most men.

SIR ARTHUR. I! What do you mean?

BASHAM. The point is to prevent the crowd doing anything, isnt it?

SIR ARTHUR. Anything mischievous: I suppose so. But—

BASHAM. An English crowd will never do anything, mischievous or the reverse, while it is listening to speeches. And the fellows who make the speeches can be depended on never to do anything else. In the first place, they dont know how. In the second, they are afraid. I am instructing my agents to press all the talking societies, the Ethical Societies, the Socialist societies, the Communists, the Fascists, the Anarchists, the Syndicalists, the official Labor Party, the Independent Labor Party, the Salvation Army, the Church Army and the Atheists, to send their best tub-thumpers into the streets to seize the opportunity.

SIR ARTHUR. What opportunity?

BASHAM. They dont know. Neither do I. It's only a phrase that means nothing: just what they are sure to rise at. I must keep Trafalgar Square going night and day. A few Labor M.P.s would help. You have a rare lot of gasbags under your thumb in the House. If you could send half a dozen of them down to the Yard, I could plant them where they would be really useful.

SIR ARTHUR [incensed] Basham: I must tell you that we are quite determined to put a stop to this modern fashion of speaking disrespectfully of the House of Commons. If it goes too far we shall not hesitate to bring prominent offenders to the bar of the House, no matter what their position is.

BASHAM. Arthur: as responsible head of the police, I am up against the facts all day and every day; and one of the facts is that nowadays nobody outside the party cliques cares a brass button for the House of Commons. [*Rising*] You will do what I ask you as to letting the speaking go on, wont you?

SIR ARTHUR. Well, I—er—

BASHAM. Unless you are game to try the machine guns.

SIR ARTHUR. Oh do drop that, Basham [*he returns to his chair and sits moodily*].

BASHAM. Righto! We'll let them talk. Thanks ever so much. Sorry to have taken up so much of your time: I know it's priceless. [*He hurries to the door; then hesitates and adds*] By the way, I know it's asking a lot; but if you could give us a turn in Trafalgar Square yourself—some Sunday afternoon would be best—it—

SIR ARTHUR [*springing up, thoroughly roused*] I!!!!

BASHAM [*hurriedly*] No: of course you couldnt. Only, it would do such a lot of good—keep the crowd quiet talking about it for a fortnight. However, of course it's impossible: say no more: so long. [*He goes out*].

SIR ARTHUR [*collapsing into his chair*] Well, really! Basham's losing his head. I wonder what he meant by saying that I ought to know better than most men. What ought I to know better than most men?

HILDA. I think he meant that you are such a wonderful speaker you ought to know what a magical effect a fine speech has on a crowd.

SIR ARTHUR [*musing*] Do you know, I am not at all sure that there is not something in his idea of my making a speech in Trafalgar Square. I have not done such a thing for many many years; but I have stood between the lions in my time; and I believe that if I were to tackle the unemployed face to face, and explain to them that I intend to call a conference in March next on the prospects of a

530

revival of trade, it would have a wonderfully soothing effect.

HILDA. But it's impossible. You have a conference every month until November. And think of the time taken by the travelling! One in Paris! Two in Geneva! One in Japan! You cant possibly do it: you will break down.

SIR ARTHUR. And shall I be any better at home here leading the House? sitting up all night in bad air listening to fools insulting me? I tell you I should have been dead long ago but for the relief of these conferences: the journeys and the change. And I look forward to Japan. I shall be able to pick up some nice old bric-a-brac there.

HILDA. Oh well! You know best.

SIR ARTHUR [*energetically*] And now to work. Work! work! work! [*He rises and paces the floor in front of the table*]. I want you to take down some notes for my speech this afternoon at the Church House. The Archbishop tells me that the Anglo-Catholics are going mad on what they call Christian Communism, and that I must head them off.

HILDA. There are those old notes on the economic difficulties of Socialism that you used at the British Association last year.

SIR ARTHUR. No: these parsons know too much about that. Besides, this is not the time to talk about economic difficulties: we're up to the neck in them. The Archbishop says "Avoid figures; and stick to the fact that Socialism would break up the family." I believe he is right: a bit of sentiment about the family always goes down well. Just jot this down for me. [*Dictating*] Family. Foundation of civilization. Foundation of the empire.

HILDA. Will there be any Hindus or Mahometans present?

SIR ARTHUR. No. No polygamists at the Church House. Besides, everybody knows that The Family means the British family. By the way, I can make a point of that. Put down in a separate line, in red capitals, "One man one wife." Let me see now: can I work that up? "One child

531

one father." How would that do?

HILDA. I think it would be safer to say "One child one mother."

SIR ARTHUR. No: that might get a laugh—the wrong sort of laugh. I'd better not risk it. Strike it out. A laugh in the wrong place in the Church House would be the very devil. Where did you get that necklace? it's rather pretty. I havnt seen it before.

HILDA. Ive worn it every day for two months. [*Striking out the "one child" note*] Yes?

SIR ARTHUR. Then—er—what subject are we on? [*Testily*] I wish you wouldnt interrupt me: I had the whole speech in my head beautifully; and now it's gone.

HILDA. Sorry. The family.

SIR ARTHUR. The family? Whose family? What family? The Holy Family? The Royal Family? The Swiss Family Robinson? Do be a little more explicit, Miss Hanways.

HILDA [*gently insistent*] Not any particular family. THE family. Socialism breaking up the family. For the Church House speech this afternoon.

SIR ARTHUR. Yes yes yes, of course. I was in the House yesterday until three in the morning; and my brains are just so much tripe.

HILDA. Why did you sit up? The business didnt matter.

SIR ARTHUR [*scandalized*] Not matter! You really must not say these things, Miss Hanways. A full dress debate on whether Jameson or Thompson was right about what Johnson said in the Cabinet!

HILDA. Ten years ago.

SIR ARTHUR. What does that matter? The real question: the question whether Jameson or Thompson is a liar, is a vital question of the first importance.

HILDA. But theyre both liars.

SIR ARTHUR. Of course they are: but the division might have affected their inclusion in the next Cabinet. The whole House rose at it. Look at the papers this morning!

532

Full of it.

HILDA. And three lines about the unemployed, though I was twenty minutes late trying to shove my way through them. Really, Sir Arthur, you should have come home to bed. You will kill yourself if you try to get through your work and attend so many debates as well: you will indeed.

SIR ARTHUR. Miss Hanways: I wish I could persuade you to remember occasionally that I happen to be the leader of the House of Commons.

HILDA. Oh, what is the use of leading the House if it never goes anywhere? It just breaks my heart to see the state you come home in. You are good for nothing next morning.

SIR ARTHUR [*yelling at her*] Dont remind me of it: do you think I dont know? My brain is overworked: my mental grasp is stretched and strained to breaking point. I shall go mad. [*Pulling himself together*] However, it's no use grousing about it: I shall have a night off going to Geneva, and a week-end at Chequers. But it is hard to govern a country and do fifty thousand other things every day that might just as well be done by the Beadle of Burlington Arcade. Well, well, we mustnt waste time. Work! work! work! [*He returns to his chair and sits down resolutely*]. Get along with it. What were we talking about?

HILDA. The family.

SIR ARTHUR [*grasping his temples distractedly*] Oh dear! Has Lady Chavender's sister-in-law been making a fuss again?

HILDA. No, no. The family. Not any real family. THE family. Socialism breaking up the family. Your speech this afternoon at the Church House.

SIR ARTHUR. Ah, of course, I am going dotty. Thirty years in Parliament and ten on the Front Bench would drive any man dotty. I have only one set of brains and I need ten. I—

HILDA [*urgently*] We must get on with the notes for your speech, Sir Arthur. The morning has half gone al-

533

ready; and weve done nothing.

SIR ARTHUR [*again infuriated*] How can the busiest man in England find time to do anything? It is you who have wasted the morning interrupting me with your silly remarks about your necklace. What do I care about your necklace?

HILDA. You gave it to me, Sir Arthur.

SIR ARTHUR. Did I? Ha ha ha! Yes: I believe I did. I bought it in Venice. But come along now. What about that speech?

HILDA. Yes. The family. It was about the family.

SIR ARTHUR. Well, I know that: I have not yet become a complete idiot. You keep saying the family, the family, the family.

HILDA. Socialism and the family. How Socialism will break up the family.

SIR ARTHUR. Who says Socialism will break up the family? Dont be a fool.

HILDA. The Archbishop wants you to say it. At the Church House.

SIR ARTHUR. Decidedly I am going mad.

HILDA. No: you are only tired. You were getting along all right. One man one wife: that is where you stopped.

SIR ARTHUR. One man one wife is one wife too many, if she has a lot of brothers who cant get on with the women they marry. Has it occurred to you, Miss Hanways, that the prospect of Socialism destroying the family may not be altogether unattractive?

HILDA [*despairingly*] Oh, Sir Arthur, we must get on with the notes: we really must. I have all the letters to do yet. Do try to pick up the thread. The family the foundation of the empire. The foundation of Christianity. Of civilization. Of human society.

SIR ARTHUR. Thats enough about the foundation: it wont bear any more. I must have another word to work up. Let me see. I have it. Nationalization of women.

HILDA [*remonstrating*] Oh, Sir Arthur!

534

SIR ARTHUR. Whats the matter now?

HILDA. Such bunk!

SIR ARTHUR. Miss Hanways: when a statesman is not talking bunk he is making trouble for himself; and Goodness knows I have trouble enough without making any more. Put this down. [*He rises and takes his platform attitude at the end of the table*]. "No, your Grace, my lords and gentlemen. Nationalize the land if you will; nationalize our industries if we must; nationalize education, housing, science, art, the theatre, the opera, even the cinema; but spare our women."

HILDA [*having taken it down*] Is that the finish?

SIR ARTHUR [*abandoning the attitude and pacing about*] No: write in red capitals under it "Rock of Ages."

HILDA. I think Rock of Ages will be rather a shock unless in connexion with something very sincere. May I suggest "The Church's One Foundation"?

SIR ARTHUR. Yes. Much better. Thank you. The family the Church's one foundation. Splendid.

Miss Flavia Chavender, 19, *bursts violently into the room through the masked door and dashes to her father.*

FLAVIA. Papa: I will not stand Mamma any longer. She interferes with me in every possible way out of sheer dislike of me. I refuse to live in this house with her a moment longer.

Lady Chavender follows her in, speaking as she enters, and comes between the Prime Minister and his assailant.

LADY CHAVENDER. I knew you were coming here to make a scene and disturb your father, though he has had hardly six hours sleep this week, and was up all night. I am so sorry, Arthur: she is uncontrollable.

David Chavender, 18, *slight, refined, rather small for his age, charges in to the table.*

DAVID [*in a childish falsetto*] Look here, Mamma. Cant you let Flavia alone? I wont stand by and see her nagged at and treated like a child of six. Nag! nag! nag! everything she does.

535

LADY CHAVENDER. Nag!! I control myself to the limit of human endurance with you all. But Flavia makes a study of annoying me.

FLAVIA. It's not true: I have considered you and given up all the things I wanted for you until I have no individuality left. If I take up a book you want me to read something else. If I want to see anybody you want me to see somebody else. If I choose the color of my own dress you want something different and dowdy. I cant sit right nor stand right nor do my hair right nor dress myself right: my life here is a hell.

LADY CHAVENDER. Flavia!!

FLAVIA [*passionately*] Yes, hell.

DAVID. Quite true. [*Fortissimo*] Hell.

LADY CHAVENDER [*quietly*] Miss Hanways: would you mind——

HILDA. Yes, Lady Chavender [*she rises to go*].

FLAVIA. You neednt go, Hilda. You know what I have to endure.

DAVID. Damn all this paralyzing delicacy! Damn it!

LADY CHAVENDER. Arthur——

SIR ARTHUR [*patting her*] Never mind, dear. They must be let talk. [*He returns placidly to his chair*]. It's just like the House of Commons, except that the speeches are shorter.

FLAVIA. Oh, it's no use trying to make papa listen to anything. [*She throws herself despairingly into Basham's chair and writhes*].

DAVID [*approaching Sir Arthur with dignity*] I really think, father, you might for once in a way take some slight interest in the family.

SIR ARTHUR. My dear boy, at this very moment I am making notes for a speech on the family. Ask Miss Hanways.

HILDA. Yes, Mr Chavender: Sir Arthur is to speak this afternoon on the disintegrating effect of Socialism on family life.

FLAVIA [*irrestible amusement struggling with hysterics and getting the better of them*] Ha ha! Ha ha ha!

DAVID [*retreating*] Ha ha! Haw! Thats the best—ha ha ha!

SIR ARTHUR. I dont see the joke. Why this hilarity?

DAVID. Treat the House to a brief description of this family; and you will get the laugh of your life.

FLAVIA. Damn the family!

LADY CHAVENDER. Flavia!

FLAVIA [*bouncing up*] Yes: there you go. I mustnt say damn. I mustnt say anything I feel and think, only what you feel and think. Thats family life. Scold, scold, scold!

DAVID. Squabble, squabble, squabble!

FLAVIA. Look at the unbearable way you treat me! Look at the unbearable way you treat Papa!

SIR ARTHUR [*rising in flaming wrath*] How dare you? Silence. Leave the room.

After a moment of awestruck silence Flavia, rather dazed by the avalanche she has brought down on herself, looks at her father in a lost way; then bursts into tears and runs out through the masked door.

SIR ARTHUR [*quietly*] Youd better go too, my boy.

David, also somewhat dazed, shrugs his shoulders and goes out. Sir Arthur looks at Hilda. She hurries out almost on tiptoe.

SIR ARTHUR [*taking his wife in his arms affectionately*] Treat me badly! You!! I could have killed her, poor little devil.

He sits down; and she passes behind him and takes the nearest chair on his right.

She is a nice woman, and goodlooking; but she is bored; and her habitual manner is one of apology for being not only unable to take an interest in people, but even to pretend that she does.

LADY CHAVENDER. It serves us right, dear, for letting them bring themselves up in the post-war fashion instead of teaching them to be ladies and gentlemen. Besides,

537

Flavia was right. I do treat you abominably. And you are so good!

SIR ARTHUR. Nonsense! Such a horrid wicked thing to say. Dont you know, my love, that you are the best of wives? the very best as well as the very dearest?

LADY CHAVENDER. You are certainly the best of husbands, Arthur. You are best of everything. I dont wonder at the country adoring you. But Flavia was quite right. It is the first time I have ever known her to be right about anything. I am a bad wife and a bad mother. I dislike my daughter and treat her badly. I like you very much; and I treat you abominably.

SIR ARTHUR. No; no.

LADY CHAVENDER. Yes, yes. I suppose it's something wrong in my constitution. I was not born for wifing and mothering. And yet I am very very fond of you, as you know. But I have a grudge against your career.

SIR ARTHUR. My career! [*Complacently*] Well, theres not much wrong with that, is there? Of course I know it keeps me too much away from home. That gives you a sort of grudge against it. All the wives of successful men are a bit like that. But it's better to see too little of a husband than too much of him, isnt it?

LADY CHAVENDER. I am so glad that you really feel successful.

SIR ARTHUR. Well, it may sound conceited and all that; but after all a man cant be Prime Minister and go about with a modest cough pretending to be a nobody. Facts are facts; and the facts in my case are that I have climbed to the top of the tree; I am happy in my work; and—

LADY CHAVENDER. Your what?

SIR ARTHUR. You are getting frightfully deaf, dear. I said "my work."

LADY CHAVENDER. You call it work?

SIR ARTHUR. Brain work, dear, brain work. Do you really suppose that governing the country is not work, but

538

a sort of gentlemanly diversion?

LADY CHAVENDER. But you dont govern the country, Arthur. The country isnt governed: it just slummocks along anyhow.

SIR ARTHUR. I have to govern within democratic limits. I cannot go faster than our voters will let me.

LADY CHAVENDER. Oh, your voters! What do they know about government? Football, prizefighting, war: that is what they like. And they like war because it isnt real to them: it's only a cinema show. War is real to me; and I hate it, as every woman to whom it is real hates it. But to you it is only part of your game: one of the regular moves of the Foreign Office and the War Office.

SIR ARTHUR. My dear, I hate war as much as you do. It makes a Prime Minister's job easy because it brings every dog to heel; but it produces coalitions; and I believe in party government.

LADY CHAVENDER [*rising*] Oh, it's no use talking to you, Arthur. [*She comes behind him and plants her hands on his shoulders*]. You are a dear and a duck and a darling; but you live in fairyland and I live in the hard wicked world. Thats why I cant be a good wife and take an interest in your career.

SIR ARTHUR. Stuff! Politics are not a woman's business: thats all it means. Thank God I have not a political wife. Look at Higginbotham! He was just ripe for the Cabinet when his wife went into Parliament and made money by journalism. That was the end of him.

LADY CHAVENDER. And I married a man with a hopelessly parliamentary mind; and that was the end of me.

SIR ARTHUR. Yes, yes, my petums. I know that you have sacrificed yourself to keeping my house and sewing on my buttons; and I am not ungrateful. I am sometimes remorseful; but I love it. And now you must run away, I am very very very busy this morning.

LADY CHAVENDER. Yes, yes, very very busy doing nothing. And it wears you out far more than if your mind

539

had something sensible to work on! Youll have a nervous breakdown if you go on like this. Promise me that you will see the lady I spoke to you about—if you wont see a proper doctor.

SIR ARTHUR. But you told me this woman is a doctor! [*He rises and breaks away from her*]. Once for all, I wont see any doctor. I'm old enough to do my own doctoring; and I'm not going to pay any doctor, male or female, three guineas to tell me what I know perfectly well already: that my brain's overworked and I must take a fortnight off on the links, or go for a sea voyage.

LADY CHAVENDER. She charges twenty guineas, Arthur.

SIR ARTHUR [*shaken*] Oh! Does she? What for?

LADY CHAVENDER. Twenty guineas for the diagnosis and twelve guineas a week at her sanatorium in the Welsh mountains, where she wants to keep you under observation for six weeks. That would really rest you; and I think you would find her a rather interesting and attractive woman.

SIR ARTHUR. Has she a good cook?

LADY CHAVENDER. I dont think that matters.

SIR ARTHUR. Not matter!

LADY CHAVENDER. No. She makes her patients fast.

SIR ARTHUR. Tell her I'm not a Mahatma. If I pay twelve guineas a week I shall expect three meals a day for it.

LADY CHAVENDER. Then you will see her?

SIR ARTHUR. Certainly not, if I have to pay twenty guineas for it.

LADY CHAVENDER. No, no. Only a social call, not a professional visit. Just to amuse you, and gratify her curiosity. She wants to meet you.

SIR ARTHUR. Very well, dear, very well, very well. This woman has got round you, I see. Well, she shant get round me; but to please you I'll have a look at her. And now you really must run away. I have a frightful mass of work to get through this morning.

LADY CHAVENDER. Thank you, darling. [*She kisses*
540

him] May I tell Flavia she is forgiven?

SIR ARTHUR. Yes. But I havnt really forgiven her. I'll never forgive her.

LADY CHAVENDER [*smiling*] Dearest. [*She kisses his fingers and goes out, giving him a parting smile as she goes through the masked door*].

Sir Arthur, left alone, looks inspired and triumphant. He addresses an imaginary assembly.

SIR ARTHUR. "My lords and gentlemen: you are not theorists. You are not rhapsodists. You are no longer young"—no, damn it, old Middlesex wont like that. "We have all been young. We have seen visions and dreamt dreams. We have cherished hopes and striven towards ideals. We have aspired to things that have not been realized. But we are now settled experienced men, family men. We are husbands and fathers. Yes, my lords and gentlemen: husbands and fathers. And I venture to claim your unanimous consent when I affirm that we have found something in these realities that was missing in the ideals. I thank you for that burst of applause: which I well know is no mere tribute to my poor eloquence, but the spontaneous and irresistible recognition of the great natural truth that our friends the Socialists have left out of their fancy pictures of a mass society in which regulation is to take the place of emotion and economics of honest human passion." Whew! that took a long breath. "They never will, gentlemen, I say they never will. They will NOT [*he smites the table and pauses, glaring round at his imaginary hearers*]. I see that we are of one mind, my lords and gentlemen. I need not labor the point." Then labor it for the next ten minutes. That will do. That will do. [*He sits down; rings the telephone bell; and seizes the milk jug, which he empties at a single draught*].

Hilda appears at the main door.

HILDA. Did you say you would receive a deputation from the Isle of Cats this morning? I have no note of it.

SIR ARTHUR. Oh, confound it, I believe I did. I totally

541

forgot it.

HILDA. Theyve come.

SIR ARTHUR. Bother them!

HILDA. By all means. But how am I to get rid of them? What am I to say?

SIR ARTHUR [*resignedly*] Oh, I suppose I must see them. Why do I do these foolish things? Tell Burton to shew them in.

HILDA. Burton is in his shirt sleeves doing something to the refrigerator. I'd better introduce them.

SIR ARTHUR. Oh, bundle them in anyhow. And tell them I am frightfully busy.

She goes out, closing the door softly behind her. He pushes away the breakfast tray and covers it with The Times, which he opens out to its fullest extent for that purpose. Then he collects his papers into the vacant space, and takes up a big blue one, in the study of which he immerses himself profoundly.

HILDA [*flinging the door open*] The worshipful the Mayor of the Isle of Cats.

The Mayor, thick and elderly, enters, a little shyly, followed by (a) an unladylike but brilliant and very confident young woman in smart factory-made clothes after the latest Parisian models, (b) a powerfully built loud voiced young man fresh from Oxford University, defying convention in corduroys, pullover, and unshaven black beard, (c) a thin, undersized lower middle class young man in an alderman's gown, evidently with a good conceit of himself, and (d) a sunny comfortable old chap in his Sunday best, who might be anything from a working man with a very sedentary job (say a watchman) to a city missionary of humble extraction. He is aggressively modest, or pretends to be, and comes in last with a disarming smile rather as a poor follower of the deputation than as presuming to form part of it. They group themselves at the door behind the Mayor, who is wearing his chain of office.

542

SIR ARTHUR [*starting from his preoccupation with important State documents, and advancing past the fireplace to greet the Mayor with charming affability*] What! My old friend Tom Humphries! How have you been all these years? Sit down. [*They shake hands, whilst Hilda deftly pulls out a chair from the end of the table nearest the door*].

The Mayor sits down, rather overwhelmed by the cordiality of his reception.

SIR ARTHUR [*continuing*] Well, well! fancy your being Mayor of—of—

HILDA [*prompting*] The Isle of Cats.

THE YOUNG WOMAN [*brightly, helping her out*] Down the river, Sir Arthur. Twenty minutes from your door by Underground.

THE OXFORD YOUTH [*discordantly*] Oh, he knows as well as you do, Aloysia. [*He advances offensively on Sir Arthur, who declines the proximity by retreating a step or two somewhat haughtily*]. Stow all this fo bunnum business, Chavender.

SIR ARTHUR. This what??

OXFORD YOUTH. Oh, chuck it. You know French as well as I do.

SIR ARTHUR. Oh, faux bonhomme, of course, yes. [*Looking him up and down*]. I see by your costume that you represent the upper classes in the Isle of Cats.

OXFORD YOUTH. There are no upper classes in the Isle of Cats.

SIR ARTHUR. In that case, since it is agreed that there is to be no fo bunnum nonsense between us, may I ask what the dickens you are doing here?

OXFORD YOUTH. I am not here to bandy personalities. Whatever the accident of birth and the humbug of rank may have made me I am here as a delegate from the Borough Council and an elected representative of the riverside proletariat.

SIR ARTHUR [*suddenly pulling out a chair from the*

middle of the table—peremptorily] Sit down. Dont break the chair. [*The Youth scowls at him and flings himself into the chair like a falling tree*]. You are all most welcome. Perhaps, Tom, you will introduce your young friends.

THE MAYOR [*introducing*] Alderwoman Aloysia Brollikins.

SIR ARTHUR [*effusively shaking her hand*] How do you do, Miss Brollikins? [*He pulls out a chair for her on the Oxford Youth's right*].

ALOYSIA. Nicely, thank you. Pleased to meet you, Sir Arthur. [*She sits*].

THE MAYOR. Alderman Blee.

SIR ARTHUR [*with flattering gravity, pressing his hand*] Ah, we have all heard of you, Mr Blee. Will you sit here? [*He indicates the presidential chair on the Oxford Youth's left*].

BLEE. Thank you. I do my best. [*He sits*].

THE MAYOR. Viscount Barking.

SIR ARTHUR [*triumphantly*] Ah! I thought so. A red Communist: what!

OXFORD YOUTH. Red as blood. Same red as the people's.

SIR ARTHUR. How did you get the blue out of it? The Barkings came over with the Conqueror.

OXFORD YOUTH [*rising*] Look here. The unemployed are starving. Is this a time for persiflage?

SIR ARTHUR. Camouflage, my lad, camouflage. Do you expect me to take you seriously in that get-up?

OXFORD YOUTH [*hotly*] I shall wear what I damn well please. I—

ALOYSIA. Shut up, Toffy. You promised to behave yourself. Sit down; and lets get to business.

BARKING [*subsides into his chair with a grunt of disgust*]!

SIR ARTHUR [*looking rather doubtfully at the old man, who is still standing*] Is this gentleman a member of your deputation?

THE MAYOR. Mr Hipney. Old and tried friend of the working class.

OXFORD YOUTH. Old Hipney. Why dont you call him by the name the East End knows him by? Old Hipney. Good old Hipney.

OLD HIPNEY [*slipping noiselessly into the secretary's chair at the bureau*] Dont mind me, Sir Arthur. I dont matter.

SIR ARTHUR. At such a crisis as the present, Mr Hipney, every public-spirited man matters. Delighted to meet you. [*He returns to his own chair and surveys them now that they are all seated, whilst Hilda slips discreetly out into her office*]. And now, what can I do for you, Miss Brollikins? What can I do for you, gentlemen?

THE MAYOR [*slowly*] Well, Sir Arthur, as far as I can make it out the difficulty seems to be that you cant do anything. But something's got to be done.

SIR ARTHUR [*stiffening suddenly*] May I ask why, if everything that is possible has already been done?

THE MAYOR. Well, the unemployed are—well, unemployed, you know.

SIR ARTHUR. We have provided for the unemployed. That provision has cost us great sacrifices; but we have made the sacrifices without complaining.

THE OXFORD YOUTH [*scornfully*] Sacrifices! What sacrifices? Are you starving? Have you pawned your overcoat? Are you sleeping ten in a room?

SIR ARTHUR. The noble lord enquires—

OXFORD YOUTH [*furiously*] Dont noble lord me: you are only doing it to rattle me. Well, you cant rattle me. But it makes me sick to see you rolling in luxury and think of what these poor chaps and their women folk are suffering.

SIR ARTHUR. I am not rolling, Toffy—I think that is what Miss Brollikins called you. [*To Aloysia*] Toffy is a diminutive of Toff, is it not, Miss Brollikins?

545

OXFORD YOUTH. Yah! Now you have something silly to talk about, youre happy. But I know what would make you sit up and do something.

SIR ARTHUR. Indeed? Thats interesting. May I ask what?

OXFORD YOUTH. Break your bloody windows.

THE MAYOR. Order! order!

ALOYSIA. Come, Toffy! you promised not to use any of your West End language here. You know we dont like it.

SIR ARTHUR. Thats right, Miss Brollikins: snub him. He is disgracing his class. As a humble representative of that class I apologize for him to the Isle of Cats. I apologize for his dress, for his manners, for his language. He must shock you every time he opens his mouth.

BLEE. We working folks know too much of bad language and bad manners to see any fun in them or think they can do any good.

THE MAYOR. Thats right.

ALOYSIA. We are as tired of bad manners as Toffy is tired of good manners. We brought Toffy here, Sir Arthur, because we knew he'd speak to you as a dock laborer would speak to you if his good manners would let him. And he's right, you know. He's rude; but he's right.

OXFORD YOUTH. Yours devotedly, Brolly. And what has his Right Honorable nibs to say to that?

SIR ARTHUR [*concentrating himself on his adversary in the House of Commons manner*] I will tell the noble lord what I have to say. He may marshal his friends the unemployed and break every window in the West End, beginning with every pane of glass in this house. What will he gain by it? Next day a score or so of his followers will be in prison with their heads broken. A few ignorant and cowardly people who have still any money to spare will send it to the funds for the relief of distress, imagining that they are ransoming their riches. You, ladies and gentlemen, will have to put your hands in your pockets to support the wives and children of the men in prison, and to pay cheap lawyers to put up perfectly useless defences for them in the police courts. And then, I suppose, the noble lord will boast that he has made me do something at last. What can I do? Do you suppose that I care less about the sufferings of the poor than you? Do you suppose I would not revive trade and put an end to it all tomorrow if I could? But I am like yourself: I am in the grip of economic forces that are beyond human control. What mortal men could do this Government has done. We have saved the people from starvation by stretching unemployment benefit to the utmost limit of our national resources. We—

OXFORD YOUTH. You have cut it down to fifteen bob a week and shoved every man you could off it with your beastly means test.

SIR ARTHUR [*fiercely*] What do you propose? Will you take my place and put the dole up to five pounds a week without any means test?

THE MAYOR. Order! order! Why are we here? We are here because we are all sick of arguing and talking, and we want something doing. And here we are arguing and talking just as if it was an all night sitting of the Borough Council about an item of three-and-six for refreshments. If you, Sir Arthur, tell us that you cant find work for our people we are only wasting your time and our own, sitting here.

He rises. The rest, except Hipney, follow his example. Sir Arthur is only too glad to rise too.

SIR ARTHUR. At least I hope I have convinced you about the windows, Mr Mayor.

THE MAYOR. We needed no convincing. More crockery than windows will have to be broken if you gentlemen can do nothing to get us out of our present mess. But some people will say that a few thousands more to the relief funds is better than nothing. And some of the unemployed are glaziers.

SIR ARTHUR. Let us close our little talk on a more

547

hopeful note. I assure you it has been intensely interesting to me; and I may tell you that signs of a revival of trade are not wholly wanting. Some of the best informed city authorities are of opinion that this year will see the end of the crisis. Some of them even hold that trade is already reviving. By the last returns the export of Spanish onions has again reached the 1913 level.

OXFORD YOUTH. Holy Jerusalem! Spanish onions! Come on, Brolly. [*He goes out*].

THE MAYOR. Weve got nothing out of this. We dont run to Spanish in the Isle. [*Resignedly*] Good morning. [*He goes out*].

SIR ARTHUR [*winningly*] And do you, Miss Brollikins, feel that you have got nothing?

ALOYSIA. I feel what they feel. And I dont believe you feel anything at all. [*She goes out, followed by Blee*].

BLEE [*turning at the door*] The Mayor's wrong. Weve got something all right.

SIR ARTHUR [*brightening*] Indeed? What is it?

BLEE [*with intense contempt*] Your measure. [*He goes out*].

The Prime Minister, nettled by this gibe, resumes his seat angrily and pushes the bluebook out of his way. Then he notices that old Hipney has not budged from his seat at the secretary's bureau.

SIR ARTHUR. The deputation has withdrawn, Mr Hipney.

HIPNEY [*rising and coming to a chair at Sir Arthur's elbow, in which he makes himself comfortable with a disarmingly pleasant air of beginning the business instead of ending it*] Yes: now we can talk a bit. I been at this game now for fifty year.

SIR ARTHUR [*interested in spite of himself*] What game? Deputations?

HIPNEY. Unemployed deputations. This is my twelfth.

SIR ARTHUR. As many as that! But these crises dont come oftener than every ten years, do they?

HIPNEY. Not what you would call a crisis, perhaps. But unemployment is chronic.

SIR ARTHUR. It always blows over, doesnt it? Trade revives.

HIPNEY. It used to. We was the workshop of the world then. But you gentlemen went out of the workshop business to make a war. And while that was going on our customers had to find out how to make things for themselves. Now we shall have to be their customers when weve any money to buy with.

SIR ARTHUR. No doubt that has occurred to some extent; but there is still an immense fringe of the human race growing up to a sense of the necessity for British goods.

HIPNEY. All goods is alike to that lot provided theyre the cheapest. They tell me the Italians are tapping their volcanoes for cheap power. We dont seem able to tap nothing. The east is chock full of volcanoes: they think no more of an earthquake there than you would of a deputation. A Chinese coolie can live on a penny a day. What can we do against labor at a penny a day and power for next to nothing out of the burning bowels of the earth?

SIR ARTHUR. Too true, Mr Hipney. Our workers must make sacrifices.

HIPNEY. They will if you drive em to it, Srarthur. But it's you theyll sacrifice.

SIR ARTHUR. Oh come, Mr. Hipney! you are a man of sense and experience. What good would it do them to sacrifice me?

HIPNEY. Not a bit in the world, sir. But that wont stop them. Look at yourself. Look at your conferences! Look at your debates! They dont do no good. But you keep on holding them. It's a sort of satisfaction to you when you feel helpless. Well, sir, if you come to helplessness there isnt on God's earth a creature more helpless than what our factories and machines have made of an English working man when nobody will give him a job and pay him to

549

do it. And when he gets it what does he understand of it? Just nothing. Where did the material that he does his little bit of a job on come from? He dont know. What will happen to it when it goes out of the factory after he and his like have all done their little bits of jobs on it? He dont know. Where could he buy it if it stopped coming to him? He dont know. Where could he sell it if it was left on his hands? He dont know. He dont know nothing of the business that his life depends on. Turn a cat loose and itll feed itself. Turn an English working man loose and he'll starve. You have to buy him off with a scrap of dole to prevent his saying "Well, if I'm to die I may as well have the satisfaction of seeing you die first."

SIR ARTHUR. But—I really must press the point—what good will that do him?

HIPNEY. What good does backing horses do him? What good does drinking do him? What good does going to political meetings do him? What good does going to church do him? Not a scrap. But he keeps on doing them all the same.

SIR ARTHUR. But surely you recognize, Mr Hipney, that all this is thoroughly wrong—wrong in feeling—contrary to English instincts—out of character, if I may put it that way.

HIPNEY. Well, Srarthur, whatever's wrong you and your like have taken on yourselves the job of setting it right. I havnt: I'm only a poor man: a nobody, as you might say.

SIR ARTHUR. I have not taken anything on myself, Mr Hipney. I have chosen a parliamentary career, and found it, let me tell you, a very arduous and trying one: I might almost say a heartbreaking one. I have just had to promise my wife to see a doctor for brain fag. But that does not mean that I have taken it on myself to bring about the millennium.

HIPNEY [*soothingly*] Just so, Srarthur: just so. It tries you and worries you, and breaks your heart and does

550

no good; but you keep on doing it. Theyve often wanted me to go into Parliament. And I could win the seat. Put up old Hipney for the Isle of Cats and your best man wouldnt have a chance against him. But not me: I know too much. It would be the end of me, as it's been the end of all the Labor men that have done it. The Cabinet is full of Labor men that started as red-hot Socialists; and what change has it made except that theyre in and out at Bucknam Palace like peers of the realm?

SIR ARTHUR. You ought to be in Parliament, Mr Hipney. You have the making of a first-rate debater in you.

HIPNEY. Psha! An old street corner speaker like me can debate the heads off you parliamentary gentlemen. You stick your thumbs in your waistcoat holes and wait half an hour between every sentence to think of what to say next; and you call that debating. If I did that in the Isle not a man would stop to listen to me. Mind you, I know you mean it as a compliment that I'd make a good parliamentary debater. I appreciate it. But people dont look to Parliament for talk nowadays: that game is up. Not like it was in old Gladstone's time, eh?

SIR ARTHUR. Parliament, Mr Hipney, is what the people of England have made it. For good or evil we have committed ourselves to democracy. I am here because the people have sent me here.

HIPNEY. Just so. Thats all the use they could make of the vote when they got it. Their hopes was in you; and your hopes is in Spanish onions. What a world it is, aint it, Srarthur?

SIR ARTHUR. We must educate our voters, Mr Hipney. Education will teach them to understand.

HIPNEY. Dont deceive yourself, Srarthur: you cant teach people anything they dont want to know. Old Dr Marx—Karl Marx they call him now—my father knew him well—thought that when he'd explained the Capitalist System to the working classes of Europe theyd unite and overthrow it. Fifty years after he founded his Red

551

International the working classes of Europe rose up and shot one another down and blew one another to bits, and turned millions and millions of their infant children out to starve in the snow or steal and beg in the sunshine, as if Dr Marx had never been born. And theyd do it again tomorrow if they was set on to do it. Why did you set them on? All they wanted was to be given their job, and fed and made comfortable according to their notion of comfort. If youd done that for them you wouldnt be having all this trouble. But you werent equal to it; and now the fat's in the fire.

SIR ARTHUR. But the Government is not responsible for that. The Government cannot compel traders to buy goods that they cannot sell. The Government cannot compel manufacturers to produce goods that the traders will not buy. Without demand there can be no supply.

HIPNEY. Theres a powerful demand just now, if demand is what you are looking for.

SIR ARTHUR. Can you point out exactly where, Mr Hipney?

HIPNEY. In our children's bellies, Srarthur. And in our own.

SIR ARTHUR. That is not an effective demand, Mr Hipney. I wish I had time to explain to you the inexorable laws of political economy. I—

HIPNEY [interrupting him confidentially] No use, Srarthur. That game is up. That stuff you learnt at college, that gave you such confidence in yourself, wont go down with my lot.

SIR ARTHUR [smiling] What is the use of saying that economic science and natural laws wont go down, Mr Hipney? You might as well say that the cold of winter wont go down.

HIPNEY. You see, you havnt read Karl Marx, have you?

SIR ARTHUR. Mr Hipney, when the Astronomer Royal tells me that it is twelve o'clock by Greenwich time I do not ask him whether he has read the nonsense of the latest flat earth man. I have something better to do with my time than to read the ravings of a half-educated German Communist. I am sorry you have wasted your own time reading such stuff.

HIPNEY. Me read Marx! Bless you, Srarthur, I am like you: I talk about the old doctor without ever having read a word of him. But I know what that man did for them as did read him.

SIR ARTHUR. Turned their heads, eh?

HIPNEY. Just that, Srarthur. Turned their heads. Turned them right round the other way to yours. I dont know whether what Marx said was right or wrong, because I dont know what he said. But I know that he puts into every man and woman that does read him a conceit that they know all about political economy and can look down on the stuff you were taught at college as ignorant old-fashioned trash. Look at that girl Aloysia Brollikins! Her father was a basket maker in Spitalfields. She's full of Marx. And as to examinations and scholarships and certificates and gold medals and the like, she's won enough of them to last your whole family for two generations. She can win them in her sleep. Look at Blee! His father was a cooper. But he managed to go through Ruskin College. You start him paying out Marx, and proving by the materialist theory of history that Capitalism is bound to develop into Communism, and that whoever doesnt know it is an ignorant nobody or a half-educated college fool; and youll realize that your college conceit is up against a Marxist conceit that beats anything you ever felt for cocksureness and despising the people that havnt got it. Look across Europe if you dont believe me. It was that conceit, sir, that nerved them Russians to go through with their Communism in 1917.

SIR ARTHUR. I must read Marx, Mr Hipney. I knew I had to deal with a sentimental revolt against unemployment. I had no idea that it had academic pretensions.

553

HIPNEY. Lord bless you, Srarthur, the Labor movement is rotten with book learning; and your people dont seem ever to read anything. When did an undersecretary ever sit up half the night after a hard day's work to read Karl Marx or anyone else? No fear. Your hearts are not in your education; but our young people lift themselves out of the gutter with it. Thats how you can shoot and you can ride and you can play golf; and some of you can talk the hind leg off a donkey; but when it comes to book learning Aloysia and Blee can wipe the floor with you.

SIR ARTHUR. I find it hard to believe that the Mayor ever burnt the midnight oil reading Marx.

HIPNEY. No more he didnt. But he has to pretend to, same as your people have to pretend to understand the gold standard.

SIR ARTHUR [*laughing frankly*] You have us there, Mr Hipney. I can make neither head nor tail of it; and I dont pretend to.

HIPNEY. Did you know the Mayor well, Srarthur? You called him your old friend Tom.

SIR ARTHUR. He took the chair for me once at an election meeting. He has an artificial tooth that looks as if it were made of zinc. I remembered him by that. [*Genially —rising*]. What humbugs we Prime Ministers have to be, Mr Hipney! You know: dont you? [*He offers his hand to signify that the conversation is over*].

MR HIPNEY [*rising and taking it rather pityingly*] Bless your innocence, Srarthur, you dont know what humbug is yet. Wait til youre a Labor leader. [*He winks at his host and makes for the door*].

SIR ARTHUR. Ha ha! Ha ha ha! Goodbye, Mr Hipney: goodbye. Very good of you to have given me so much of your time.

HIPNEY. Youre welcome to it, Srarthur. Goodbye. [*He goes out*].

Sir Arthur presses a button to summon Hilda. Then he looks at his watch, and whistles, startled to find how

*late it is. Hilda comes in quickly through the masked
door.*

SIR ARTHUR. Do you know how late it is? To work!
Work! work! work! Come along.

HILDA. I am afraid you cant do any work before you
start for the Church House lunch. The whole morning is
gone with those people from the Isle of Cats.

SIR ARTHUR. But I have mountains of work to get
through. With one thing and another I havnt been able to
do a thing for the last three weeks; and it accumulates
and accumulates. It will crush me if I dont clear it off
before it becomes impossible.

HILDA. But I keep telling you, Sir Arthur, that if you
will talk to everybody for half an hour instead of letting
me get rid of them for you in two minutes, what can you
expect? You say you havnt attended to anything for three
weeks; but really you havnt attended to anything since
the session began. I hate to say anything; but really, when
those Isle of Cats people took themselves off your hands
almost providentially, to let that ridiculous old man talk
to you for an hour—! [*She sits down angrily*].

SIR ARTHUR. Nonsense! he didnt stay two minutes;
and I got a lot out of him. What about the letters this
morning?

HILDA. I have dealt with them: you neednt bother.
There are two or three important ones that you ought to
answer: I have put them aside for you when you have
time.

*Flavia and David dash into the room through the
masked door even more excited and obstreperous than before, Flavia to her father's right, David to his left.*

FLAVIA. Papa: weve been to a meeting of the unemployed with Aloysia and Toffy.

DAVID. Such a lark!

FLAVIA. We saw a police charge. David was arrested.

SIR ARTHUR. Do you mean to say that you went with
those people who were here?

555

FLAVIA. Yes: theyve come back to lunch with us.

SIR ARTHUR. To lunch!!!

DAVID. Yes. I say: Aloysia's a marvellous girl.

SIR ARTHUR [*determinedly*] I dont mind the girl; but if that young whelp is coming to lunch here he must and shall change his clothes.

DAVID. He's gone home to change and shave: he's dotty on Flavia.

SIR ARTHUR. Why am I afflicted with such children? Tell me at once what you have been doing. What happened?

DAVID. The police brought the Chancellor of the Exchequer to make a speech to the unemployed to quiet them. The first thing we heard him say was "Gentlemen: be patient. I promise you you will soon see the one thing that can revive our industries and save our beloved country: a rise in prices." The mob just gave one howl and went for him. Then the police drew their batons and charged.

FLAVIA. Davy couldnt stand the way the people were knocked about. He screamed to them to stand. The inspector collared him.

SIR ARTHUR. Of course he did. Quite right. Such folly! [*To David*] How do you come to be here if you were arrested? Who bailed you?

DAVID. I asked the inspector who in hell he thought he was talking to. Then Flavia cut in and told him who we were and that old Basham was like a father to us. All he said was "You go home, sir; and take your sister with you. This is no place for you." So as I was rather in a funk by that time we collected Aloysia and Toffy and bunked for home.

SIR ARTHUR. I have a great mind to have that inspector severely reprimanded for letting you go. Three months would have done you a lot of good. Go back to the drawing room, both of you, and entertain your new friends. You know you are not allowed to come in here when I am at work. Be off with you. [*He goes back to his seat*].

FLAVIA. Well, what are we to do? Mamma sends us in on purpose to interrupt you when she thinks you have done enough.

DAVID. She says it's all we're good for.

SIR ARTHUR. A Prime Minister should have no children. Will you get out, both of you; or must I ring for Burton to throw you out?

FLAVIA. Mamma says you are to lunch, Hilda. She wants another woman to make up the party.

HILDA. Oh dear! [*rising*] You must excuse me, Sir Arthur: I must telephone to put off some people who were coming to lunch with me at The Apple Cart. And I must change my frock.

FLAVIA [*squabbling*] You neednt dress up for Brollikins, need you?

DAVID. You let Aloysia alone. You dont want Hilda to dress up for Barking, I suppose.

SIR ARTHUR [*out of patience*] Get out. Do you hear? Get out, the lot of you.

HILDA. Do come, Miss Chavender. Your father is very busy.

SIR ARTHUR [*furious*] Get OUT.

They retreat precipitately through the masked door. Sir Arthur, left alone, rests his wearied head on the table between his arms.

SIR ARTHUR. At last, a moment's peace.

The word rouses the orator in him. He raises his head and repeats it interrogatively; then tries its effect sweetly and solemnly again and again.

SIR ARTHUR. Peace? . . . Peace. Peace. Peace. Peace. Peace. [*Now perfectly in tune*] "Yes, your Grace, my lords and gentlemen, my clerical friends. We need peace. We English are still what we were when time-honored Lancaster described us as 'This happy breed of men.' We are above all a domestic nation. On occasion we can be as terrible in war as we have always been wise and moderate

557

in counsel. But here, in this Church House, under the banner of the Prince of Peace, we know that the heart of England is the English home. Not the battlefield but the fireside—yes, your Grace, yes, my lords and gentlemen, yes, my clerical friends, the fire—"

He starts violently as his eye, sweeping round the imaginary assembly, lights on a woman in grey robes contemplating him gravely and pityingly. She has stolen in noiselessly through the masked door.

SIR ARTHUR. Ffffff!!! Who is that? Who are you? Oh, I beg your pardon. You gave me such a— Whew!! [*He sinks back into his chair*] I didnt know there was anyone in the room.

The lady neither moves nor speaks. She looks at him with deepening pity. He looks at her, still badly scared. He rubs his eyes; shakes himself; looks again.

SIR ARTHUR. Excuse me; but are you real?

THE LADY. Yes.

SIR ARTHUR. I wish youd do something real. Wont you sit down?

THE LADY. Thank you. [*She sits down, very uncannily as it seems to him, in Basham's chair*].

SIR ARTHUR. Will you be sogood as to introduce yourself? Who are you?

THE LADY. A messenger.

SIR ARTHUR. Please do not be enigmatic. My nerves are all in rags. I did not see you come in. You appeared there suddenly looking like a messenger of death. And now you tell me you are a messenger.

THE LADY. Yes: a messenger of death.

SIR ARTHUR. I thought so. [*With sudden misgiving*] You mean my death, I hope. Not my wife nor any of the children?

THE LADY [*smiling kindly*] No. Your death.

SIR ARTHUR [*relieved*] Well, thats all right.

THE LADY. You are going to die.

ON THE ROCKS

SIR ARTHUR. So are we all. The only question is, how soon?

THE LADY. Too soon. You are half dead already. You have been dying a long time.

SIR ARTHUR: Well, I knew I was overworking: burning the candle at both ends: killing myself. It doesnt matter. I have made my will. Everything is provided for: my wife will be comfortably off; and the children will have as much as is good for them.

THE LADY. You are resigned?

SIR ARTHUR. No; but I cannot help myself.

THE LADY. Perhaps I can help you. I am not only a messenger. I am a healer.

SIR ARTHUR. A what?

THE LADY. A healer. One who heals the sick. One who holds off death until he is welcome in his proper time.

SIR ARTHUR. You cannot help me. I am caught in the wheels of a merciless political machine. The political machine will not stop for you. It has ground many men to pieces before their time; and it will grind me.

THE LADY. My business is with life and death, not with political machinery.

SIR ARTHUR. In that case I am afraid you can be of no use to me; so will you think it very uncivil of me if I go on with my work?

THE LADY. Shall I vanish?

SIR ARTHUR. Not unless you have something else to do. As you are a ghost, and therefore not in time but in eternity, another ten minutes or so wont cost you anything. Somehow, your presence is helping me. A presence is a wonderful thing. Would you mind sitting there and reading The Times while I work?

THE LADY. I never read the newspapers. I read men and women. I will sit here and read you. Or will that make you self-conscious?

SIR ARTHUR. My dear ghost, a public man is so accus-

559

tomed to people staring at him that he very soon has no self to be conscious of. You wont upset me in the least. You may even throw in a round of applause occasionally; so that I may find out the effective bits to work up.

THE LADY. Go on. I will wait as long as you like.

SIR ARTHUR. Thank you. Now let me see where I was when you appeared. [*He takes up a scrap of paper on which he has made a memorandum*]. Ah yes: Ive got it. Peace. Yes: peace. [*Trying to make out a word*] Ence— ence—what? Oh, ensue! Of course: a good word. "My friends, lay and clerical, we must ensue peace. Yes, ensue peace. Peace. Disarmament." A burst of Pacifist applause there, perhaps. "Who says that we need a hundred battle-ships, gentlemen? Christian brotherhood is a safer defence than a thousand battleships. You have my pledge that the Government will be quite content with—with—" oh, well, my secretary will fill that in with whatever number of ships the Japanese are standing out for. By the way, do you think battleships are any real use know? Kenworthy says theyre not: and he was in the navy. It would be such a tremendous score for us at Geneva if we offered to scrap all our battleships. We could make up for them in aero-planes and submarines. I should like to have the opinion of an impartial and disinterested ghost.

THE LADY. As I listen to you I seem to hear a ghost preparing a speech for his fellow ghosts, ghosts from a long dead past. To me it means nothing, because I am a ghost from the future.

SIR ARTHUR. Thats a curious idea. Of course if there are ghosts from the past there must be ghosts from the future.

THE LADY. Yes: women and men who are ahead of their time. They alone can lead the present into the future. They are ghosts from the future. The ghosts from the past are those who are behind the times, and can only drag the present back.

SIR ARTHUR. What an excellent definition of a Con-
560

servative! Thank Heaven I am a Liberal!

THE LADY. You mean that you make speeches about Progress and Liberty instead of about King and Country.

SIR ARTHUR. Of course I make speeches: that is the business of a politician. Dont you like speeches?

THE LADY. On the Great Day of Judgment the speech-makers will stand with the seducers and the ravishers, with the traffickers in maddening drugs, with those who make men drunk and rob them, who entice children and violate them.

SIR ARTHUR. What nonsense! Our sermons and speeches are the glories of our literature, and the inspired voices of our religion, our patriotism, and—of course—our politics.

THE LADY. Sermons and speeches are not religion, not patriotism, not politics: they are only the gibbering of ghosts from the past. You are a ghost from a very dead past. Why do you not die your bodily death? Is it fair for a ghost to go about with a live body?

SIR ARTHUR. This is too personal. I am afraid I cannot get on with my speech while you are there ordering my funeral. Oblige me by vanishing. Go. Disappear. Shoo!

THE LADY. I cannot vanish. [*Merrily changing her attitude*]. Shall we stop playing at ghosts, and accept one another for convenience sake as real people?

SIR ARTHUR [*shaking off his dreaminess*] Yes, lets. [*He rises and comes to her*]. We have been talking nonsense. [*He pulls out a chair. They sit close together*]. You had me half hypnotized. But first, shake hands. I want to feel that you are real.

He offers his right hand. She seizes both his hands and holds them vigorously, looking straight into his eyes.

SIR ARTHUR [*brightening*] Well, I dont know whether this is real or not; but it's electric, and very soothing and jolly. Ah-a-a-ah! [*A deep sighing breath*]. And now, my dear lady, will you be good enough to tell me who the

561

devil you are?

THE LADY [*releasing him*] Only your wife's lady doctor. Did she not tell you to expect me?

SIR ARTHUR. Of course, of course. How stupid of me! Yes,yes,yes,yes,yes, to be sure. And now I am going to be frank with you. I dont believe in doctors. Neither does my wife; but her faith in quacks is unlimited. And as I am on the verge of a nervous breakdown, she is planting every possible variety of quack on me—you will excuse the expression?—

THE LADY. I excuse everything from my patients. Go on.

SIR ARTHUR. Well, I receive them all as I am receiving you, just to gratify her, or rather to prevent her from making my life miserable. They all say the same obvious thing; and they are none of them of the slightest use. You are going to say it all over again. Can you forgive me for saying flatly that I will not pay you twenty guineas for saying it: not if you said it twenty times over?

THE LADY. Not even if I shew you how to cure yourself? The twenty guineas is an important part of the cure. It will make you take it seriously.

SIR ARTHUR. I know perfectly well how to cure myself. The cure is as simple as a b c. I am Prime Minister of Great Britain. That is, I am an overworked, overworried, overstrained, overburdened, overdriven man, suffering from late hours, irregular snatched meals, no time for digestion nor for enough sleep, and having to keep my mind at full stretch all the time struggling with problems that are no longer national problems but world problems. In short, I am suffering acutely from brain fag.

THE LADY. And the cure?

SIR ARTHUR. A fortnight's golf: thats the cure. I know it all by heart. So suppose we drop it, and part friends. You see, I am really frightfully busy.

THE LADY. That is not my diagnosis. [*She rises*]. Goodbye.

SIR ARTHUR [*alarmed*] Diagnosis! Have you been diagnosing me? Do you mean that there is something else the matter with me?

THE LADY. Not something else. Something different.

SIR ARTHUR. Sit down, pray: I can spare another two minutes. Whats wrong?

THE LADY [*resuming her seat*] You are dying of an acute want of mental exercise.

SIR ARTHUR [*unable to believe his ears*] Of—of—of WHAT, did you say?

THE LADY. You are suffering from that very common English complaint, an underworked brain. To put it in one word, a bad case of frivolity, possibly incurable.

SIR ARTHUR. Frivolity! Did I understand you to say that frivolity is a common English failing?

THE LADY. Yes. Terribly common. Almost a national characteristic.

SIR ARTHUR. Do you realize that you are utterly mad?

THE LADY. Is it you or I who have piloted England on to the rocks?

SIR ARTHUR. Come come! No politics. What do you prescribe for me?

THE LADY. I take my patients into my retreat in the Welsh mountains, formerly a monastery, now much stricter and perfectly sanitary. No newspapers, no letters, no idle ladies. No books except in the afternoon as a rest from thinking.

SIR ARTHUR. How can you think without books?

THE LADY. How can you have thoughts of your own when you are reading other people's thoughts?

SIR ARTHUR [*groaning*] Oh, do talk sense. What about golf?

THE LADY. Games are for people who can neither read nor think. Men trifle with their business and their politics; but they never trifle with their games. Golf gives them at least a weekend of earnest concentration. It brings truth home to them. They cannot pretend that they have won

563

when they have lost, nor that they made a magnificent drive when they foozled it. The Englishman is at his best on the links, and at his worst in the Cabinet. But what your country needs is not your body but your mind. And I solemnly warn you that unless you exercise your mind you will lose it. A brain underexercised is far more injurious to health than an underexercised body. You know how men become bone lazy for want of bodily exercise. Well, they become brain lazy for want of mental exercise; and if nature meant them to be thinkers the results are disastrous. All sorts of bodily diseases are produced by half used minds; for it is the mind that makes the body: that is my secret, and the secret of all the true healers. I am sorry you will not allow me to take you a little on the way back to health with me. Good morning. [*She rises*].

SIR ARTHUR. Must you go?

THE LADY. Well, you are so busy—

SIR ARTHUR [*rising*] Ah yes: I forgot. I am frightfully busy. Still, if you could spare another minute—

THE LADY. If you wish. [*She sits down*].

SIR ARTHUR [*sitting down*] You see, what makes your diagnosis so pricelessly funny to me is that as a matter of fact my life has been a completely intellectual life, and my training the finest intellectual training in the world. First rate preparatory school. Harrow. Oxford. Parliament. An Undersecretaryship. The Cabinet. Finally the Leadership of the House as Prime Minister. Intellect, intellect, all the time.

THE LADY. At Harrow you wrote Latin verses, did you not?

SIR ARTHUR. Yes, of course.

THE LADY. Do you write any now?

SIR ARTHUR. No, of course not. You dont understand. We learnt to write Latin verses not because the verses are any good—after all, it's only a trick of stringing old tags together—but because it's such a splendid training for the mind.

564

ON THE ROCKS

THE LADY. Have all the boys who made Latin verses at Harrow splendidly trained minds?

SIR ARTHUR. Yes. I unhesitatingly say yes. I dont mean, of course, that they are all geniuses; but if you go into the best society you will see that their minds are far superior to those of persons who have had no classical training.

THE LADY. You mean that they can all be trusted to say the same thing in the same way when they discuss public affairs.

SIR ARTHUR. Precisely. They are an educated class, you see.

THE LADY [*coldly, rising*] Yes: I see. I have really nothing more to say, Sir Arthur. [*She takes a card from her bag and puts it on the table*] That is the address of my retreat in Wales.

SIR ARTHUR [*rising, rather disappointed at having produced no effect*] But surely you cannot deny that a man is the better for having been put through the mill of our great educational system.

THE LADY. If a man is born with a hopelessly bad set of teeth I think it is better for him, and kinder to him, to pull them all out and replace them with a good set of artificial teeth. If some of your political colleagues had not been provided with artificial political minds in the manner you describe they would have been left without any political minds at all. But in that case they would not have meddled in politics; and that, I think, would have been a public advantage. May I reserve a bedroom and a private study for you?

SIR ARTHUR. Pooh! I am not going to your retreat.

THE LADY [*steadfastly*] I think you are.

SIR ARTHUR. I give you up. You are factproof. I am lazy; I am idle; and I am breaking down from overwork. How logical!

THE LADY. All the idlest and laziest of my patients slave from morning to midnight trifling and tittle-tattling about great things. To a retreat, Sir Arthur: get thee to a retreat. I am never mistaken in my diagnosis. I shall telephone to ask whether my number one suite, with private bath and meditation parlor, is vacant.

SIR ARTHUR. No: I wont be rushed. Do you hear? I wont be rushed. [*She is quite unshaken and he proceeds, much less resolutely*] Of course I shall have to go somewhere for a rest; and if you could really recommend it as a bracing place—

THE LADY. Bracing? What for?

SIR ARTHUR. Well, bracing, you know. Bracing.

THE LADY. Curious, how idle people are always clamoring to be braced! Like trousers.

SIR ARTHUR. Idle people! How you stick to your point! And what a humbug you are! Dont think you can impose on me with your meditation parlor and your dignified airs: I do that sort of thing myself occasionally; and you know it's no use giving tracts to a missionary. But I feel somehow that you are good for me. You are a dear delightful bighearted wrongheaded half-educated crazyboots; but a woman may be all that and yet have the right instinct as to how to flirt intellectually with a tired thinker. Will you promise to talk to me if I come?

THE LADY. I will even let you talk to me. I guarantee that in a fortnight you will begin to think before you talk. Your dead mind will come to life. I shall make a man of you. Goodbye. [*She goes out quickly through the main door*].

SIR ARTHUR [*calling after her gaily*] Ha ha! Incorrigible, incorrigible. [*He takes her card from the table, and contemplates it*]. Oh! I forgot to ask her how much a week she wants for that meditation parlor. [*He looks tragic*].

HILDA [*emerging from her office*] Anything the matter, Sir Arthur?

SIR ARTHUR. I am going into a retreat. Because my brain is underworked. Do you grasp that idea? Have you ever heard of a retreat for the mentally underworked?

HILDA. There is a very nice one at Sevenoaks that my aunt was sent to. But that is for inebriates.

SIR ARTHUR. The one I'm going to is for the mentally underworked, the thoughtless and brainless, the inveterately lazy and frivolous. Yes: the frivolous: your ears do not deceive you.

HILDA [*going to her desk*] Oh, well, theyll amuse you: you always get on well with people of that sort. Shall I pack your usual holiday books? some detective stories and Wordsworth?

SIR ARTHUR. No. You will procure all the books you can find by a revolutionary German Jew named Harry Marks—

HILDA. Dont you mean Karl Marx?

SIR ARTHUR. Thats the man. Karl Marx. Get me every blessed book by Karl Marx that you can find translated into English; and have them packed for the retreat.

HILDA. There are much newer books by Marxists: Lenin and Trotsky and Stalin and people like that.

SIR ARTHUR. Get them all. Pack the lot. By George, I'll teach Alderwoman Aloysia Brollikins to give herself airs. I'll teach her and her rabble of half-baked half-educated intellectual beggars-on-horseback that any Oxford man can beat them at their own silly game. I'll just turn Karl Marx inside-out for them. [*The household gong sounds*]. Lunch! Come on: that woman's given me an appetite. [*He goes out impetuously through the masked door*].

HILDA [*rushing after him*] No, no, Sir Arthur: the Church House! the Church House! youve forgotten that you have to lunch at [*her voice is lost in the distance*].

ACT II

THE *same scene on the* 10th *November at* 9.30 *in the morning. There is a generous fire in the grate; and the visitors wear winter clothes. Basham is on the hearthrug, warming his back and reading* The Daily Herald.

BASHAM [*amazed by what he reads*] Gosh! [*He reads further*] Wh-e-e-ew!! [*He reads still further*] Well I'll be dashed!!!

Hilda enters through the main door, and announces an explosive elderly gentleman, evidently a person of consequence, who follows her.

HILDA. Sir Dexter Rightside.

SIR DEXTER [*joining Basham on the hearth*] Ah! That you, Basham? Have you come to arrest him?

BASHAM. You may well ask. He isnt up yet. Miss Hanways: is there any sign of his getting a move on?

HILDA [*much worried*] Lady Chavender wont allow him to be disturbed. She says his speech last night at the Guildhall banquet quite tired him out. People have been ringing up and calling all the morning; but she just puts her back to his door and says that anyone who makes noise enough to waken him leaves her service that minute.

SIR DEXTER. Nonsense! He must see me. Does Lady Chavender suppose that a Prime Minister can stand the country on its head without a word of warning to his colleagues and then go to bed as if he was tired out by a day's fishing?

HILDA [*desperate*] Well, what can *I* do, Sir Dexter? [*She goes to her bureau*].

SIR DEXTER. Basham: go and break open his bedroom door.

BASHAM. I cant. I'm a policeman: I mustnt do it without a warrant. Go and do it yourself.

SIR DEXTER. I have a devilish good mind to. Can you conceive anything more monstrous, Basham? [*He sits down in the chair next the end chair*]. But I said that this

568

would happen. I said so. When we made this damned coalition that they call a National Government I was entitled to the Prime Ministership. I was the Leader of the Conservative Party. I had an enormous majority in the country: the election proved that we could have done quite well without Chavender. But I had to give way. He humbugged us. He pretended that without his old guard of Liberals and his ragtag and bobtail of Labor men and Socialists and lawyers and journalists-on-the-make and used-up trade union secretaries, and all the rest of the democratic dregs of human society, we couldnt be sure of a majority. His golden voice was to do the trick. He was the popular man, the safe man: I was the unpopular Die Hard who couldnt be trusted to keep my temper. So I stood down. I sacrificed myself. I took the Foreign Secretaryship. Well, what price your safe man now? How do you like your Bolshy Premier? Who was right? the funkers and compromisers or the old Die Hard?

BASHAM. It's amazing. I could have sworn that if there was a safe man in England that could be trusted to talk and say nothing, to thump the table and do nothing, Arthur Chavender was that man. Whats happened to him? What does it mean? Did he go mad at the sanatorium, do you think? Or was he mad before that woman took him there?

SIR DEXTER. Mad! Not a bit of it. But you had better look up that woman's record: there may be money from Moscow behind this.

BASHAM. Arthur take money! Thats going too far.

SIR DEXTER. The woman took the money. It would be waste of money to bribe Chavender: you could always trust him to say whatever he thought would please his audience without being paid for it: damned mountebank.

BASHAM. But he didnt try to please his audience at the Guildhall. They wanted some of his best soothing syrup about law and order after the attack on the Lord Mayor's Show in the afternoon by the unemployed; but according

569

to The Daily Herald here he gave them a dose of boiling Socialism instead.

SIR DEXTER [*nervously*] By the way, Basham, I hope you have the unemployed well in hand today.

BASHAM. Quiet as lambs. Theyre all reading the papers. New editions every half-hour. Like 1914 over again.

Sir Arthur's voice is heard, singing scales. Hilda looks in.

HILDA. I think I hear Sir Arthur singing. He must have got up.

SIR DEXTER. Singing! Is this a moment for minstrelsy?

HILDA. He always sings scales after his bath [*she vanishes*].

After a final burst of solfeggi the masked door is opened vigorously and Chavender enters beaming.

SIR ARTHUR. Ah, here you are, Dexy [*he proffers his hand*].

SIR DEXTER [*like a baited bull*] Dont attempt to shake hands with me. Dont dare call me Dexy.

SIR ARTHUR. What on earth's the matter? Got out at the wrong side of the bed this morning, eh? Frightfully sorry to have kept you waiting, Basham. Whats wrong with the Foreign Secretary this time?

SIR DEXTER. This time! What do you mean by this time?

SIR ARTHUR. Well theres nothing very novel about your turning up before breakfast in a blazing rage, is there? What is it, Basham?

BASHAM. Oh come, P.M.! If you were too drunk last night at the Guildhall to know what you were saying, youd better read the papers [*he offers his paper*].

SIR ARTHUR [*keeping his hands behind his back to warm them*] I remember perfectly well what I said last night. And I drank nothing but barley water.

BASHAM [*insisting*] But look at it, man. [*Quoting the headlines*] New program for winter session. Nationalization of ground rents. Nationalization of banks. Nationalization of collieries. Nationalization of transport.

SIR DEXTER [*moaning*] Nationalization of women. Why omit it? Why omit it?

BASHAM. No: nothing about women. Municipalization of urban land and the building trade, and consequent extinction of rates.

SIR DEXTER. Apostate!

BASHAM. No: nothing about the Church. Abolition of tariffs and substitution of total prohibition of private foreign trade in protected industries. State imports only, to be sold at State regulated prices.

SIR DEXTER. Rot! Incomprehensible and unheard-of rot.

BASHAM. Compulsory public service for all, irrespective of income, as in war time.

SIR DEXTER. Slavery. Call it by its proper name. Slavery.

BASHAM. Restoration of agriculture. Collective farming. Nationalization of fertilizer industries. Nitrogen from the air. Power from the tides. Britain self-supporting and blockade proof.

SIR DEXTER. Madness. Ruin to our foreign trade.

BASHAM. Ruthless extinction of parasitism.

SIR DEXTER. You dont even know the present law. You have the Verminous Persons Act. What more do you want?

BASHAM. Doubling of the surtax on unearned incomes.

SIR DEXTER. Yes: take our last penny! And when the little that the present ruinous taxation has left us is gone; when we have closed our accounts with the last tradesman and turned the last servant into the streets, where are they to find employment? Who is to pay their wages? What is to become of religion when nobody can afford pewrents or a penny to put in the plate? Even sport will not be safe: our breed of horses will be doomed; our packs of hounds sold or slaughtered; and our masters of hounds will be caddies on motor bicycles. That is to be England's future!

SIR ARTHUR. But is that all the papers have reported?

ON THE ROCKS

SIR DEXTER. All!!!

BASHAM. Oh come! All! Isnt that about enough?

SIR ARTHUR. But have they said nothing about our promise to restore the cuts made in the pay of the army and navy and police?

SIR DEXTER. Our promise! Whose promise?

BASHAM [*interested*] What was that you said? Are you going to put my men's wages up to the old figure?

SIR ARTHUR. We shall give you another five thousand men; pay the old wages with a rise of ten per cent; and double your salary.

BASHAM. Whew! That alters the case a bit.

SIR DEXTER [*rising*] Basham: you are not going to allow yourself to be corrupted like this! Are you such a dupe as to imagine that free Englishmen will tolerate such a monstrous waste of public money?

BASHAM. If I have another five thousand men and a rise on the old wages, I'll answer for the free Englishmen. If they dont like it they can lump it.

SIR DEXTER. You really believe he can keep all the monstrous promises he has made?

BASHAM. No: of course he cant. But he can keep this one. He can raise the pay of the ranks and double my salary; and that is all that concerns me. I'm a policeman, not a politician.

SIR DEXTER. Youre a mercenary gangster and a damned fool: thats what you are. [*He flings himself into the end chair*].

BASHAM [*calmly*] You seem ruffled, Sir Dexter.

Before Sir Dexter can reply, Hilda returns and announces a new visitor.

HILDA. Admiral Sir Bemrose Hotspot. [*She goes out*].

Sir Bemrose is a halfwitted admiral but the half that has not been sacrificed to his profession is sound and vigorous.

SIR BEMROSE [*in the breeziest spirits*] Morning, Dexy. Morning, Basham [*Slapping Sir Arthur on the back*]

572

Splendid, Arthur! Never heard you in better form. Thats the stuff to give em. [*They shake hands cordially*].

SIR DEXTER [*sobered by his astonishment*] Rosy: have you gone mad too? Have you forgotten that you are a Conservative, and that it was as a Conservative that you were made First Lord of the Admiralty, at my personal suggestion and insistence, in this so-called National Government, which now, thank Heaven, wont last one day after the next meeting of Parliament?

SIR BEMROSE. Wont it, by Jove! It's safe for the next five years. What the country wants is straight orders, discipline, character, pluck, a big navy, justice for the British sailor, no sham disarmaments, and absolute command of the sea. If that isnt Conservatism what is Conservatism? But mind, Arthur, I must have twelve new aeroplane-carrying battleships. I have my eye on Japan. And theres America. And, of course, Russia.

SIR ARTHUR. You shall have them, Rosy. Twentyfour if you say the word.

SIR BEMROSE. Good! Then I'll answer for the House of Commons.

SIR DEXTER. Dont be silly. What can you do with the House of Commons, except empty it whenever you get up to speak?

SIR BEMROSE. I leave the speaking to Arthur: it's his job, not mine. But if there is any further attempt to starve the navy it can give you a little surprise at Westminster. How will you feel when you see a submarine come to the surface off the terrace, and the commander sends in word that he gives you just five minutes before he torpedoes the whole damned Front Bench?

SIR DEXTER. You are talking ridiculous nonsense. Do you suppose for a moment that the navy would be allowed to interfere in politics?

SIR BEMROSE. Who's to stop it? Where would Lenin and Stalin and Trotsky and all that Bolshy lot have been without the Baltic fleet and the Kronstadt sailors? Do you

573

suppose the British navy, with its discipline and its respectable Conservative commanders, couldnt do what these Communist scoundrels did?

SIR DEXTER. How long would the British navy survive the abolition of property in this country? tell me that.

SIR BEMROSE. Dont talk to the navy about property. We dont live by property: we live by service. [*He takes the chair next to the presidential one, and pursues his personal grievance angrily*]. You and your confounded property owners grudge us a clerk's salary for commanding a battleship, and then dock a quarter off it for income tax. We cant set foot on shore without being rented and rated until we can hardly afford to educate our children. Thanks to Arthur, you are pledged now to give us our pay honestly free of income tax and make these lazy idle lubbers of landlords sweat for it. I call that the essence of Conservatism. Thats the way to dish these Labor chaps and Red flaggers and all the rest of the scum you have been pandering to ever since you gave them the vote. Give them whats good for them; and put their ballot papers behind the fire: thats what this country needs.

SIR ARTHUR. You see, Dexy: we have the navy and the police on our side.

SIR DEXTER. May I ask who are "we"?

SIR ARTHUR. Why, the National Government, of course. You and I, Dexy: you and I.

SIR DEXTER. It makes me sick to hear you couple my name with yours. It always did.

HILDA [*announcing*] The President of the Board of Trade. Mr. Glenmorison.

Glenmorison is an easy mannered Scottish gentleman, distinctly the youngest of the party.

SIR ARTHUR. Hallo, Sandy. Sit down. Lets all sit down and have it out.

They settle themselves at the table with their backs to the fire, Sir Arthur in the middle, Glenmorison on his left, Sir Bemrose on his right, and Sir Dexter and Basham right and left respectively.

GLENMORISON. Well, Sir Arthur, when you were letting yourself go so recklessly you might have said a word about Home Rule for Scotland. We may as well be hanged for a sheep as for a lamb.

SIR DEXTER. We! we! we! Who are we? If you mean the Cabinet, it is not responsible for the Prime Minister's frantic proceedings. He acted without consulting us. Do you suppose that if I had heard a word of this outburst of Bolshevism I should have consented to it?

SIR ARTHUR. That was why I didnt consult you.

SIR DEXTER. Psha!

SIR ARTHUR. The responsibility is mine and mine alone.

SIR BEMROSE. Not at all. I claim my share, Arthur. You got the part about the navy from me.

GLENMORISON. Same here, Sir Dexter. I claim at least two items.

SIR DEXTER. Much good may they do you. Arthur's seat is safe: anybody named Chavender can get in unopposed in his constituency because his cunning old father-in-law has every voter in the place bribed up to the neck. But your majority at the last election was seventeen: there were three recounts. Your seat's gone, anyhow.

GLENMORISON. On the contrary, Sir Dexter, it's safe for the first time in the history of Scotland.

SIR DEXTER. Safe! How? You will get the boot as a crazy Bolshevik unless you come out with me and repudiate Chavender promptly and decisively.

GLENMORISON. Oh, I'm afraid I cant do that, Sir Dexter. You see, the balance is held in my constituency by the tradesmen and shopkeepers. Their great grievance is the heavy rates. And though they are all doing middling well they think they could do better if they could raise enough capital to extend their businesses a bit. But the financiers and promoters wont look at small businesses. They are thinking in millions while my people are thinking in thousands, and mostly in only four figures at that. It's easy

575

enough to get a couple of hundred thousand pounds if you are willing to call it a quarter of a million and pay interest on that sum. But what good is that to a man in the High Street in my constituency who wants from five to twenty thousand to extend his little business?

SIR DEXTER. Nonsense! The bank will give him an overdraft if his credit is good.

GLENMORISON. Yes; and call it in at the next slump and panic on the Stock Exchange. I can shew you have a dozen men who were forced into bankruptcy in the last panic, though they were as solvent as you or I. But Sir Arthur's proposal of panic-proof national and municipal banks, as ready and eager to find five thousand for the five thousand man as the financiers are to find a million on condition that enough of it sticks to their own fingers, is just the thing for my people. I darent say a word against it. It's an inspiration as far as my constituents are concerned. Theyre a canny lot, my people: theyd vote for the devil if he'd promise to abolish the rates and open a municipal bank. My majority fell to seventeen last time because I went to them with empty hands and a bellyful of advice to economize and make sacrifices. This bank nationalization is good business for them: theyll just jump at it.

SIR DEXTER. In short, you will make Utopian promises that you know very well will never be carried out.

GLENMORISON. You made a lot of Utopian promises, Sir Dexter, when you formed this National Government. Instead of carrying them out you told the voters to tighten their belts and save the Bank of England. They tightened their belts; and now the Bank of England is paying twelve and sixpence in the pound. Still, I admit, you pulled down my Liberal majority over my Conservative opponent from four thousand to seventeen. Ive got to pull that up again. I say nothing about the rest of the program; but I represent the small man; and on this bank business I am with Sir Arthur all the time.

HILDA [*announcing*] Sir Jafna Pandranath. [*She with-*
576

draws].

This announcement creates a marked sensation. All five gentlemen rise as if to receive a royal personage. Sir Jafna is an elderly Cingalese plutocrat, small and slender to the verge of emaciation, elegantly dressed, but otherwise evidently too much occupied and worried by making money to get any fun out of spending it. One guesses that he must make a great deal of it; for the reverence with which he is received by the five Britons, compared with their unceremonious handling of one another, is almost sycophantic.

SIR JAFNA. Hallo! Am I breaking into a Cabinet meeting?

SIR ARTHUR. No: not a bit. Only a few friendly callers. Pray sit down.

SIR DEXTER [*offering the end chair to the visitor*] You are welcome, Sir Jafna: most welcome. You represent money; and money brings fools to their senses.

SIR JAFNA. Money! Not at all. I am a poor man. I never know from one moment to another whether I am worth thirteen millions or only three. [*He sits down. They all sit down*].

SIR BEMROSE. I happen to know, Sir Jafna, that your enterprises stand at twenty millions today at the very least.

GLENMORISON. Fifty.

SIR JAFNA. How do you know? How do you know? The way I am plundered at every turn! [*To Sir Dexter*] Your people take the shirt off my back.

SIR DEXTER. My people! What on earth do you mean?

SIR JAFNA. Your land monopolists. Your blackmailers. Your robber barons. Look at my Blayport Docks reconstruction scheme! Am I a public benefactor or am I not? Have I not enough to live on and die on without troubling myself about Blayport? Shall I be any the happier when it has ten square miles of docks instead of a tuppeny-hapeny fishing harbor? What have I to gain except the satisfaction of seeing a big publicly useful thing well done,

577

and the knowledge that without me it could not be done? Shall I not be half ruined if it fails?

SIR BEMROSE. Well, whats wrong with it, old chap?

SIR JAFNA. Rosy: you make me puke. What is wrong with it is that the owners of all the miles of land that are indispensable to my scheme, and that without it would not be worth fifteen pounds an acre, are opening their mouths so wide that they will grab sixty per cent of the profit without lifting a finger except to pocket the wealth that I shall create. I live, I work, I plan, I shatter my health and risk all I possess only to enrich these parasites, these vampires, these vermin in the commonwealth. [*Shrieking*] Yes: vermin! [*Subsiding*] You were quite right at the Guildhall last night, Arthur: you must nationalize the land and put a stop to this shameless exploitation of the financiers and entrepreneurs by a useless, idle, and predatory landed class.

SIR ARTHUR [*chuckling*] Magnificent! I have the support of the City.

SIR JAFNA. To the last vote, to the last penny. These pirates think nothing of extorting a million an acre for land in the city. A man cannot have an address in London for his letters until he has agreed to pay them from five hundred to a thousand a year. He cant even die without paying them for a grave to lie in. Make them disgorge, Arthur. Skin them alive. Tax them twenty shillings in the pound. Make them earn their own living, damn them. [*He wipes his brow and adds, rather hysterically*] Excuse me, boys; but if you saw the Blayport estimates—! [*he can no more*].

SIR DEXTER. May I ask you to address yourself to this question not as an emotional oriental [*Sir Jafna chokes convulsively*] but as a sane man of business. If you destroy the incomes of our landed gentry where will you find the capital that exists solely through their prudent saving—their abstinence?

SIR JAFNA. Bah pooh! Pooh bah! I will find it where

578

they find it, in the product of the labor I employ. At present I have to pay exorbitant and unnecessary wages. Why? Because out of those wages the laborer has to pay half or quarter as rent to the landlord. The laborer is ignorant: he thinks he is robbed by the landlord; but the robbed victim is me—ME! Get rid of the landlord and I shall have all the capital he now steals. In addition I shall have cheap labor. That is not oriental emotion: it is British commonsense. I am with you, Arthur, to the last drop of my oriental blood. Nationalized land: compulsory labor: abolition of rates: strikes made criminal: I heartily endorse them all in the name of Capital and private enterprise. I say nothing about the rest of your program, Arthur; but on these points no true Liberal can question your magnificent statesmanship.

SIR ARTHUR [*delighted*] You hear that, Dexy. Put that in your pipe and smoke it.

HILDA [*announcing*] His Grace the Duke of Domesday. [*She goes out*].

An elderly delicately built aristocrat comes in. Well preserved, but nearer 70 *than* 60.

THE DUKE [*surprised to see so many people*] Do I intrude, Arthur? I thought you were disengaged.

SIR ARTHUR. Not at all. Only a talk over last night. Make yourself at home.

SIR DEXTER. You come in the nick of time. Sir Jafna here has just been qualifying you as a bloodsucker, a pirate, a parasite, a robber baron and finally as vermin. Vermin! How do you like it?

THE DUKE [*calmly taking the end chair nearest the window, on Basham's left*] I wonder why the epithet robber is applied only to barons. You never hear of robber dukes; yet my people have done plenty of robbery in their time. [*With a sigh of regret*] Ah, thats all over now. The robbers have become the robbed. I wish you would create some intermediate class of honest folk. I dislike your calling me vermin, Arthur.

579

ON THE ROCKS

SIR ARTHUR. I didnt. It was Jafna.

THE DUKE. Ungrateful Jafna! He is buying up my Blayport estate for next to nothing.

SIR JAFNA. Next to nothing! Holy Brahma!

THE DUKE [*continuing*] He will make millions out of it. After paying off the mortgages I shall get three and a half per cent on what is left to me out of the beggarly price he offers; and on that three and a half I shall be income-taxed and surtaxed. Jafna's grandsons will go to Eton. Mine will go to a Polytechnic.

SIR BEMROSE. Send them to Dartmouth, old chap. Theres a career for them in the navy now that Arthur is at the helm.

SIR DEXTER. A lieutenant's pay and pension for the future Duke of Domesday! Thats the proposition, is it?

THE DUKE. He will be lucky to have any pay at all. But I shall support you in any case, Arthur. You have at last publicly admitted that the death duties are unsound in principle, and promised to abolish them. That will save us from utter extinction in three generations; and the landed classes are with you to the last man for it. Accept the humble gratitude of a pauperized duke.

SIR DEXTER. And the rest of the program. Do you swallow that too?

THE DUKE. I doubt if the rest of the program will come off. Besides, I dont pretend to understand it. By the way, Sir Jafna, I wish you would take Domesday Towers off my hands for a while. I cant afford to live in it. I cant afford even to keep it dusted. You can have it for a hundred a year.

SIR JAFNA. Too far from town.

THE DUKE. Not by aeroplane. Do think it over.

Sir Jafna shrugs his shoulders and intimates that it is hopeless. The Duke resigns himself to the expected.

SIR ARTHUR. Dexy: you are in a minority of one. The landlords are on my side. The capitalists, big and little, are on my side. The fighting services are on my side. The

580

police are on my side. If you leave us you go out into the wilderness alone. What have you to say?

SIR DEXTER. I have to say that you are a parcel of blind fools. You are trying to scuttle the ship on the chance of each of you grabbing a share of the insurance money. But the Country will deal with you. The Country does not want change. The Country never has wanted change. The Country never will want change. And because I will resist change while I have breath in my body I shall not be alone in England. You have all deserted me and betrayed your party; but I warn you that though I am utterly alone in this room . . .

HILDA [*reappearing*] The deputation, Sir Arthur. Theyve come back. [*She vanishes*].

The deputation enters. Hipney is not with them. Barking, shaved, brilliantly dressed, and quite transfigured, is jubilant. Aloysia glows indignation. Blee and the Mayor, doggedly wearing their hats and overcoats, are gloomy, angry, and resolute. They group themselves just inside the door, glowering at the Prime Minister and his colleagues.

SIR ARTHUR [*beaming*] Gentlemen: a Labor deputation from the Isle of Cats. The one element that was lacking in our councils. You have heard the voice of the peerage, of the city, of the King's forces. You will now hear the voice of the proletariat. Sit down, ladies and gentlemen.

THE MAYOR [*rudely*] Who are you calling the proletariat? Do you take us for Communists? [*He remains standing*].

ALOYSIA. What you are going to hear, Sir Arthur, is the voice of Labor. [*She remains standing*].

BLEE. The verdict of democracy. [*He remains standing*].

EARL OF BARKING. The bleating of a bloody lot of fools. I am with you, Chavender. [*He detaches himself from the group and flings himself into Hilda's chair with intense disgust*].

SIR ARTHUR [*surprised*] Am I to understand that your colleagues are against me?

THE MAYOR. Of course we're against you. Do you expect me to go back to my people and tell them they should vote for compulsory labor and doing away with strikes?

BLEE. Arnt the workers enslaved enough already without your depriving them of that last scrap of their liberty? the only weapon they have against the capitalists?

SIR ARTHUR. My dear Mr Mayor, what is the right to strike? The right to starve on your enemy's doorstep and set the whole public against you. Which of you starves first when it comes to the point?

THE MAYOR. I am not going to argue. You can beat me at that. But if you think that the British workingman will listen to compulsory labor and putting down strikes you dont know the world youre living in; and thats all about it.

SIR ARTHUR. But we need not compel the workers to work: they are working already. We shall compel the idlers. Not only your idlers but our idlers: all the idle young gentlemen who do nothing but waste their own time and your labor.

BLEE. We know. Keep all the soft jobs for your lot and the hard ones for us. Do you take us for fools?

BARKING. He does. And you are fools.

SIR ARTHUR. I am glad to have your lordship's support.

ALOYSIA. Support your grandparents! He wants to marry your daughter.

BARKING [*springing up*] Oh! You can hit below the belt, Aloysia. But as a matter of fact, I do want to marry your daughter, Chavender.

SIR ARTHUR. Hardly the moment to go into that now, is it?

BARKING. It was Aloysia and not I who let the cat out of the bag. Being a cat herself she had a fellow-feeling for the animal. [*He resumes his seat*].

BLEE. Youre an aristocrat, young-fellow-me-lad. I always said that when things got serious youd turn on us and side with your own.

BARKING. Rot! Youre always bragging that you are descended from the Blee of Blayport, whoever he may have been. I shouldnt have tuppence in my pocket if my grandfather hadnt made a fortune in pork pies and bought my father's Norman title for his daughter with it. The blue blood is in your skimpy little veins: the proletarian red's in mine.

ALOYSIA. Youve too much money, Toffy.

BARKING. I havnt had all the pluck taken out of me by poverty, like you chaps. And what good will it do me to have a lot of money when I have to work like anyone else?

SIR DEXTER. Why should a man work like anyone else if he has money?

BARKING. My brother had heaps of money; but he had to go into the trenches and fight like anyone else in the war. Thats how I came into the property.

BLEE. So we're all to be slaves for the sake of setting a few loafers to work. The workers will die sooner than put up with it. I want my liberty—

BARKING. Liberty to work fourteen hours a day and bring up three children on thirtyfour shillings a week, like your brother the shopman. To hell with your filthy liberty!

BLEE [*hotly*] I—

THE MAYOR. Order! order! Dont argue with him, Blee. No good ever comes of arguing with college men. I'm not arguing with Sir Arthur: I'm telling him. The long and the short of it is that if he dont withdraw that silly new program he'll lose every vote in the Isle of Cats. And what the Isle of Cats thinks today, all England thinks tomorrow.

SIR JAFNA. May I speak to this gentleman? Will you

introduce me, Arthur?

SIR ARTHUR [*introducing*] Sir Jafna Pandranath. The Mayor of the Isle of Cats.

SIR JAFNA. You have heard of me, Mr Mayor. You know that I am a man who knows what he is talking about. Well, I tell you that the fundamental question is not the Labor question but the Land Question.

THE MAYOR. Yes: we all know that.

SIR JAFNA. Then you will vote for Sir Arthur because he will nationalize the land for you.

BLEE [*scornfully*] Yes, with compensation! Take the land with one hand and give back its cash value to the landlords with the other! Not likely. I ask again, do you take us for fools?

SIR ARTHUR [*introducing*] Mr Alderman Blee.

THE DUKE. Enchanted. I happen to be a landlord—a duke, in fact—and I can assure you, Mr Alderman, that as the compensation will come out of my own pocket and that of my unfortunate fellow landlords in the form of income tax, surtax, and estate duties—what you call death duties —you will get all your cash back and the land as well.

THE MAYOR. Blee: I tell you, dont argue. Stick to your point. No compensation.

BLEE. Not a penny, by God.

THE DUKE. You believe in God, Mr Alderman. I am charmed to hear it.

Here the Duke is astonished to find Aloysia towering over him and pointing an accusing finger at him. At the moment of his introduction of himself as a duke, her eyes lighted up; and she has moved menacingly across the hearth towards him until she is now standing behind the vacant chair between him and Basham.

ALOYSIA. Have you ever heard of the Domesday clearances?

THE DUKE. Clearances? Which clearances do you refer to? The latest cleared me out of Domesday Towers. I can no longer afford to live there.

584

ALOYSIA. Dont prevaricate. You know very well what I mean. It is written in blood and tears on the pages of working class history.

SIR ARTHUR [*introducing*] Alderwoman Aloysia Brollikins. The Duke of Domesday.

THE DUKE [*rising courteously*] Wont you sit down?

ALOYSIA [*sternly*] You shall not put me out by these tricks and ceremonies. My Lord Duke: I would rather touch the hand of the most degraded criminal in London than touch yours.

THE DUKE [*collapsing into his chair*] Great heavens! Why?

ALOYSIA. Do you forget how your family drove a whole countryside of honest hardworking Scotch crofters into the sea, and turned their little farms into deer forests because you could get more shooting rents out of them in that way? Do you forget that women in childbirth were carried out by your bailiffs to die by the roadside because they clung to their ancient homesteads and ignored your infamous notices to quit? Would it surprise you to learn that I am only one of thousands of young women who have read the hideous story of this monstrous orgy of housebreaking and murder, and sworn to ourselves that never, if we can help it, will it again be possible for one wicked rich man to say to a whole population "Get off the earth."

SIR JAFNA. Admirable! What did I tell you? Hear hear!

ALOYSIA. I thank you, Sir Jafna, for shewing this man that even hardened capitalist millionaires shudder when that story is told. You will not find it in your school histories; but in the new histories, the histories of the proletariat, it has been written, not by the venal academic triflers you call historians, but by the prophets of the new order: the men in whom the word is like a burning fire shut up in their bones so that they are weary of forbearing and must speak.

585

THE MAYOR. Aye: in the Bible, that is.

ALOYSIA. The Domesday Clearances filled your pockets with gold to console you for the horror and remorse of your dreams; but the vengeance they cried to God for in vain is upon you now that Labor is coming to its own; and it is your turn now to get off the earth.

BLEE. And in the face of all this, you come whining for compensation! Compensation!! Compensation from us to you! From the oppressed to the oppressor! What a mockery!

ALOYSIA. It is from you that we shall exact compensation: aye, to the uttermost farthing. You are conspiring here with these capitalist bloodsuckers to rob us again of the value of what you have already stolen—to make us give you gilt edged securities in exchange for the land that no longer brings you in shooting rents; and you think we cannot see through the plot. But in vain is the net spread in sight of the bird. We shall expose you. We shall tell the story of the Domesday Clearances until the country rings with it if you dare to lift your dishonored head again in English politics. Your demand for compensation is dismissed, turned down: we spit it back in your face. The crofters whom you drove from their country to perish in a foreign land would turn in their graves at the chink of a single penny of public money in your hungry pocket. [*She tears out a chair from under the table and flops into it, panting with oratorical emotion*].

BLEE	Good for you, Brolly!
SIR JAFNA	[*enthused*] Hear hear! [*They ham-*
SIR BEMROSE	*mer on the table with their knuck-*
GLENMORISON	*les*].

THE DUKE [*very appreciative*] What a magnificent speech, Miss Brollikins! I really must insist on your shaking hands with me before we part.

ALOYSIA. Never. How dare you ask me? [*She sweeps away from him and sits down in the opposite chair at the other side of the table*].

586

THE DUKE [*taking the armchair*] May I not have the privilege of telling my grandchildren how I once met and shook hands with the greatest orator of my time? I assure you all these shocking things happened before I was born.

BLEE [*bawling at him*] Yes; but you still pocket the shooting rents.

THE DUKE [*brusquely*] Of course I do: and so would you too if you were in my place. [*Tenderly, to Aloysia*] I assure you, Miss Brollikins, the people make much more money out of my shooting tenants than they could as crofters: they would not go back to croftering for worlds. Wont you let bygones be bygones—except when you are exercising your wonderful gift of eloquence on the platform? Think of what your ancestors were doing in those ruthless old days!

BARKING. Grabbing all they could get, like yours or mine. Whats the good of tubthumping at these johnnies, Brolly? Theyve been doing it themselves all their lives. Cant you see that compensation makes them share the loss fairly between them?

SIR BEMROSE. It's no use. These damned Liberals cant understand anything but virtuous indignation.

THE MAYOR. Who are you calling a Liberal? I represent the Labor Party.

SIR BEMROSE. Youre a No Compensation man, arnt you?

THE MAYOR. Of course I am.

SIR BEMROSE. Then youre a Liberal.

THE MAYOR. Call me what you like. I'm not arguing. I'm telling you that the Labor Party of the Isle of Cats puts down its foot and says No Compensation. Is that plain?

SIR DEXTER. I am glad we have arrived at the same conclusion from our opposite points of view, Mr Mayor. The Party I represent, the Conservative Party, will withdraw from the Coalition if there is the slightest wobbling on this point. We shall defend our property—and yours:

yours, Mr Mayor, to the last drop of our blood.

BASHAM [*incisively re-entering the conversation; they had forgotten him, and now turn to him in some surprise*] Our blood, you mean, dont you?

SIR DEXTER [*puzzled*] Whose blood?

BASHAM. The police's blood. You landed gentlemen never do a thing yourselves: you only call us in. I have twenty thousand constables, all full of blood, to shed it in defence of whatever the Government may decide to be your property. If Sir Arthur carries his point theyll shed it for land nationalization. If you carry yours theyll stand by your rent collectors as usual.

BLEE. The police come from the ranks of labor: dont forget that.

BASHAM. Thats not how they look at it, Blee. They feel that theyve escaped from the ranks of labor; and theyre proud of it. They have a status which they feel to be a part of the status of the Duke here.

THE DUKE. I suppose that is why they are always so civil to me.

BASHAM. In short, Mister Blee, the police are what you Socialists call class-conscious. You will find that out if you are foolish enough to fall out with them.

BLEE. Who cut their pay? Tell me that.

SIR ARTHUR. I shall restore the cuts, Mr Alderman, with a premium.

THE MAYOR. There! Now you see what comes of arguing, Blee. It only gives him his chance.

ALOYSIA. You need not warn us, Sir Broadfoot Basham, D.S.O., K.C.M.G., O.B.E. In the Class War your myrmidons will be well paid.

THE DUKE. Myrmidons!

ALOYSIA. We know too well what we have to expect from your Janissaries.

BLEE. Your bludgeoning Bashi-Bazouks.

ALOYSIA. The Class War is in fact. We face it. What

we want we shall have to take; and we know it. The good
of the community is nothing to you: you care only for surplus value. You will never give up your privileges voluntarily. History teaches us that: the history you never
read.

THE DUKE. I assure you, my dear Héloïse—

ALOYSIA. Héloïse! Who are you calling Héloïse?

THE DUKE. Pardon. I could not resist the French form
of your charming name.

ALOYSIA [*interjects*] The cheek!

THE DUKE [*continuing*] I was merely going to point
out, as between one student of history and another, that in
the French Revolution it was the nobility who voluntarily
abolished all their own privileges at a single sitting, on the
sentimental principles they had acquired from reading the
works of Karl Marx's revolutionary predecessor Rousseau.
That bit of history is repeating itself today. Here is Sir
Arthur offering us a program of what seems to me to be
first rate Platonic Communism. I, a Conservative Duke,
embrace it. Sir Jafna Pandranath here, a Liberal capitalist
whose billions shame my poverty, embraces it. The Navy
embraces it with the sturdy arms of Sir Bemrose Hotspot.
The police are enthusiastic. The Army will be with Sir
Arthur to the last man. He has the whole propertied class
on his side. But the proletariat rises against him and spews
out his Socialism through the eloquent lips of its Aloysia.
I recall the warning my dear old father gave me when I
was five years old. Chained dogs are the fiercest guardians
of property; and those who attempt to unchain them are
the first to be bitten.

ALOYSIA. Your Grace calls us dogs. We shall not forget
that.

THE DUKE. I have found no friends better than faithful
dogs, Miss Brollikins. But of course I spoke figuratively. I
should not dream of calling you a dog.

ALOYSIA. No. As I am a female dog I suppose you will

call me something shorter when my back is turned.

THE DUKE. Oh! Think of the names you have called me!

THE MAYOR. Well, if you will argue, Alderwoman Brollikins, there's no use my staying here. I wish I could stop your mouth as easy as I can stop my ears. Sir Arthur: youve planked down your program and weve planked down our answer. Either you drop compulsory labor and drop compensation or never shew your face in the Isle of Cats again. [*He goes out resolutely*].

BLEE. Take this from me. I am no Communist: I am a respectable Labor man, as law abiding as any man here. I am what none of you has mentioned yet: a democrat. I am just as much against Cabinet dictatorship as individual dictatorship. What I want done is the will of the people. I am for the referendum. I am for the initiative. When a majority of the people are in favor of a measure then I am for that measure.

SIR BEMROSE. Rot! The majority is never in favor of any measure. They dont know what a measure is. What they want is their orders, and as much comfort as they are accustomed to. The lower deck doesnt want to give orders, it looks to the bridge for them. If I asked my men to do my job theyd chuck me overboard; and serve me jolly well right! You just know nothing about it, because youve never had to command; and you havnt sense enough to obey and be thankful to those who have saved you the trouble of thinking for yourself and keeping you off the rocks.

BLEE. You havnt kept us off the rocks. We're on the rocks, the whole lot of us. So long, Rosy. [*He goes out*].

BARKING. Silly swine! When they are offered what they want they wont have it just because you fellows want it too. They think there must be a catch in it somewhere.

THE DUKE. There generally is. That is how you feel, Miss Brollikins, isnt it?

ALOYSIA. You dont know how I feel; and you never will. We are going to save ourselves and not be saved by you and your class. And I prefer Sir Dexter Rightside's downright outspoken opposition to your silly-clever cynicism and your sickening compliments.

THE DUKE. It is only in middle class books, Miss Brollikins, that noblemen are always cynical and insincere. I find you a most brilliant and delightful woman. May I not tell you so? And WHAT a speaker! Will you spend a quiet week-end with me in some out-of-the-way place in the country, and let me try to convince you that a duke is a human being like yourself?

ALOYSIA [*rearing*] Are you trying to seduce me?

THE DUKE. That would be exquisite, Miss Brollikins; but I am an old and very poor man. You are young, beautiful, and probably opulent. Can you find anything seductive about me?

ALOYSIA. Yes. Youre a duke. And you have the charm of a majestic ruin, if you understand me.

BARKING [*rising*] Come on out of this, Brolly: youre only making a fool of yourself listening to that old bird buttering you up. You just dont know when to go.

ALOYSIA [*moving to the hearthrug, behind Sir Arthur*] You can go if you like. I have some business with Sir Arthur that doesnt concern you. Get out.

SIR ARTHUR. Some business with me! Public business?

ALOYSIA. Not exactly.

SIR ARTHUR. Oh! Private business?

ALOYSIA. I dont care who knows it. But perhaps you would.

BARKING. She means to marry your son David. One below the belt for you, Brolly. Ha ha! Ha ha ha ha ha! [*He goes out roaring with laughter*].

SIR ARTHUR [*after a moment of shock*] I congratulate David, Miss Brollikins. Have you arranged the date?

ALOYSIA. I havent mentioned it to him yet. I hope all you gentlemen will remember that I was not the one that blurted this out: it was your noble viscount. However, now it's out, I stand by it: David is a good boy; and his class is

591

not his fault. Goodbye all. [*She goes to the door*].

THE DUKE [*rising*] And that week-end, Miss Brollikins? Or has David cut me out?

ALOYSIA. Right you are, Your Grace! I will call for you at Domesday House on Friday at half past four. As I shall bring a few friends we shall hire an omnibus from the London Transport; so you neednt trouble about a car. You wont mind my publishing an account of what happens as a special interview: you know that we Labor intelligentsia have to live by our brains. Au revoir. [*She goes out*].

THE DUKE. There is a frightful unexpectedness about these people. Where on earth shall I borrow the money to pay for the omnibus and entertain them all? [*He goes back to his chair at the end of the table and sits down*].

BASHAM. Your share will only be a few shillings, Duke; and she will reckon on having to pay for you. What girl in her class wouldnt foot the bill if she had a duke to walk out with?

THE DUKE. You reassure me, Sir Broadfoot. Thank you.

SIR DEXTER [*triumphant*] Well, Chavender? What have you to say now? When these people came in I was saying that though I was alone in this room, the people of England were on my side and always would be when it came to the point. Was I right or wrong?

SIR BEMROSE. We never meant to desert you, Dexy. You mustnt think that.

SIR ARTHUR. As you have no more intention of consulting the people of England than I have, the situation is unaltered.

SIR DEXTER. Then you have! What do you mean? Do you think you can govern in this country without the consent of the English people?

SIR ARTHUR. No country has ever been governed by the consent of the people, because the people object to be governed at all. Even you, who ought to know better, are always complaining of the income tax.

592

ON THE ROCKS

THE DUKE. But five shillings in the pound, Arthur! Five shillings in the pound!!

SIR DEXTER. Never mind my income tax. If what you said just now means anything it means that you are going to play fast and loose with democracy: that is, you think you are going to do something that both the people and the governing class of this country are determined you shall not do. The Conservative Party, which is ten times more really democratic than you Liberals have ever been, will carry the people with it against you. How do you propose to get over that? What are you banking on? Put your cards on the table if you really have any.

SIR ARTHUR. Well, here is my ace of trumps. The people of this country, and of all the European countries, and of America, are at present sick of being told that, thanks to democracy, they are the real government of the country. They know very well that they dont govern and cant govern and know nothing about Government except that it always supports profiteering, and doesnt really respect anything else, no matter what party flag it waves. They are sick of twaddle about liberty when they have no liberty. They are sick of idling and loafing about on doles when they are not drudging for wages too beggarly to pay the rents of anything better than overcrowded one-room tenements. They are sick of me and sick of you and sick of the whole lot of us. They want to see something done that will give them decent employment. They want to eat and drink the wheat and coffee that the profiteers are burning because they cant sell it at a profit. They want to hang people who burn good food when people are going hungry. They cant set matters right themselves; so they want rulers who will discipline them and make them do it instead of making them do the other thing. They are ready to go mad with enthusiasm for any man strong enough to make them do anything, even if it is only Jew baiting, provided it's something tyrannical, something coercive, something that we all pretend no Englishman would submit to, though

593

weve known ever since we gave them the vote that theyd submit to anything.

SIR DEXTER [*impatiently*] Yes, yes: we know the cant of all the tuppeny-hapeny dictators who think themselves Mussolinis. Come down to tin tacks. How are you going to get it through Parliament?

SIR ARTHUR. I am not going to get it through Parliament: I am going to prorogue Parliament and then do it. When it is done I shall call a meeting of Parliament to pass an Act of Indemnity for all my proceedings.

SIR DEXTER. You cannot prorogue Parliament. Only the King can prorogue Parliament.

SIR ARTHUR. Precisely. Kings always have prorogued Parliament and governed without them until money ran short.

GLENMORISON. But, man alive, it is not His Majesty alone that you have to consider. The law courts will not enforce your decisions if they are illegal. The civil servants will sabotage you even if they dont flatly disobey you.

SIR ARTHUR. We shall sidetrack them quite easily by setting up new tribunals and special commissions manned by officials we can depend on.

SIR DEXTER. That was how Cromwell cut off King Charles's head. His commissioners found out afterwards that they were doing it with ropes round their rascally necks.

SIR ARTHUR. A rope round a statesman's neck is the only constitutional safeguard that really safeguards. But never fear the rope. As long as we give the people an honest good time we can do just what seems good to us. The proof of the pudding will be in the eating. That will be really responsible government at last.

SIR DEXTER. So that is your game, is it? Has it occurred to you that two can play at it? What can you do that I cannot do if you drive me to it: tell me that.

SIR ARTHUR. Nothing, if you are willing to take on my job. Are you?

SIR DEXTER. The job of ruining the country and destroying the empire? My job is to prevent you from doing that. And I will prevent you.

SIR ARTHUR. Your job is to prevent me or anybody else from doing anything. Your job is to prevent the world from moving. Well, it is moving; and if you dont get out of the way something will break; and it wont be the world.

SIR DEXTER. Nothing has broken so far except the heads of the unemployed when they are encouraged by your seditious rot to rebel against the laws of nature. England is not breaking. She stands foursquare where she always stood and always will stand: the strongest and greatest land, and the birthplace of the noblest imperial race, that ever God created.

SIR ARTHUR. Loud and prolonged cheering. Come! let us both stop tub thumping and talk business. The real master of the situation is Basham here, with his fifteen thousand police.

BASHAM. Twenty thousand.

SIR ARTHUR. Well, twenty thousand. They dont stop functioning when Parliament is prorogued, do they?

BASHAM. No. At Scotland Yard we look to the Home Secretary as far as we look to anybody.

SIR ARTHUR. I can make myself Home Secretary. So that will be all right.

SIR DEXTER. Will it, by George? If you and Basham dare to try your twenty thousand police on me, do you know what I will do?

SIR ARTHUR. What?

SIR DEXTER. I will put fifty thousand patriotic young Londoners into Union Jack shirts. You say they want discipline and action. They shall have them. They shall have machine guns and automatic pistols and tear gas bombs. My Party has the money. My Party has the newspapers. My Party has the flag, the traditions, the glory that is England, the pluck, the breed, the fighting spirit. One of us is worth ten of your half starved guttersnipes and their

595

leaders that never could afford more than a shilling for a dinner until they voted themselves four hundred a year out of our pockets.

SIR BEMROSE [*carried away*] Thats the stuff, Dexy. Now you are talking, by Jiminy.

BASHAM [*taking command of the discussion coolly*] You are all talking through your hats. The police can do nothing unless the people are on the side of the police. The police cant be everywhere: there arnt enough of them. As long as the people will call the police when anything goes wrong, and stop the runaway criminal and give evidence against him, then twenty thousand constables can keep eight million citizens in order. But if the citizens regard the policeman as their enemy—if the man who snipes a police-man in the back is not given in charge by the bystanders—if he is helped to get away—if the police cannot get a single citizen to go into the box and witness against him, where are you then? You have to double your force because the police must patrol in pairs: otherwise the men will be afraid to patrol at all. Your twenty thousand have to be reinforced up to forty thousand for their own protection; but that doesnt protect you. You would have to put two policemen standing over every able-bodied man and woman in the town to see that they behaved themselves as you want them to behave. You would need not thousands of constables but millions.

SIR DEXTER. My Union Jack men would keep order, or theyd know the reason why.

BASHAM. And who would keep them in order, I should like to know: silly amateurs. And let me remind you of one thing. It seems easy to buy a lot of black shirts, or brown shirts, or red shirts, and give one to every hooligan who is out for any sort of mischief and every suburban out-of-work who fancies himself a patriot. But dont forget that the colored shirt is a uniform.

GLENMORISON. What harm is there in that? It enables a man to recognize his friends.

596

BASHAM. Yes; but it marks him out as an enemy in uniform; and to kill an enemy in uniform at sight is not murder: it's legitimate warfare.

SIR DEXTER. Monstrous! I should give no quarter to such an outrageous piece of sophistry.

BASHAM. In war you have to give quarter because you have to ask for it as often as to give it. It's easy to sit here and think of exterminating your opponents. But a war of extermination is a massacre. How long do you think a massacre would last in England today? Just as long as it takes a drunken man to get sick and sober.

GLENMORISON. Easy, Sir Broadfoot, easy, easy. Who is talking of extermination? I dont think you will ever induce respectable Britons to wear red-white-and-blue shirts; but surely you can have volunteers, special constables, auxiliary forces—

BASHAM [*flinching violently*] Auxiliary forces! I was in command of them in Ireland when you tried that game on the Irish, who were only a little handful of peasants in their cabbage patch. I have seen these things. I have done them. I know all about it: you know nothing about it. It means extermination; and when it comes to the point you cant go through with it. I couldnt. I resigned. You couldnt: you had to back down. And I tell you, Dexy, if you try any colored shirt hooliganism on me, I'll back the P.M. and shew you what Scotland Yard can do when it's put to it.

SIR DEXTER. Traitor!

BASHAM. Liar! Now weve called one another names how much farther has it got us?

GLENMORISON. Easy, easy: dont let us quarrel. I must support the Prime Minister, Sir Dexter, to secure my seat in Parliament. But I am a Liberal, and, as such, bound by Liberal principles. Whatever we do must be done through Parliament if I am to be a party to it. I am all for the new program; but we must draw up a parliamentary timetable for it. To carry out the program will involve the introduc-

597

tion of at least twelve bills. They are highly controversial bills: everyone of them will be resisted and obstructed to the very last clause. You may have to go to the country on several of them. The committee stages will last for weeks and weeks, no matter how hard you work the guillotine: there will be thousands of amendments. Then, when you have got through what is left of your Bill and carried it, the House of Lords will turn it down; and you will have to wait two years and go through the whole job again before you can get your Bill on the statute book as an Act of Parliament. This program is not a matter of today or tomorrow. I calculate that at the very least it will take fifty years to get it through.

SIR ARTHUR. And you think the world will wait for that, Sandy?

GLENMORISON [*naïvely*] What else can it do?

SIR ARTHUR. It wont wait. Unless we can find a shorter way, the program will be fought out in the streets.

SIR DEXTER. And you think that in the streets you will win? You think the mob will be on your side? "Ye are many: they are few" eh? The Class War! Well, you will find out your mistake.

SIR ARTHUR. I dont believe in the Class War any more than you do, Dexy. I know that half the working class is slaving away to pile up riches, only to be smoked out like a hive of bees and plundered of everything but a bare living by our class. But what is the other half doing? Living on the plunder at second hand. Plundering the plunderers. As fast as we fill our pockets with rent and interest and profits theyre emptied again by West End tradesmen and hotel keepers, fashionable doctors and lawyers and parsons and fiddlers and portrait painters and all sorts, to say nothing of huntsmen and stablemen and gardeners, valets and gamekeepers and jockeys, butlers and housekeepers and ladies' maids and scullery maids and deuce knows who not.

THE DUKE. How true, Arthur! how profoundly true! I am with you there to the last drop of my blood.

598

ON THE ROCKS

SIR ARTHUR. Well, these parasites will fight for the rights of property as they would fight for their own skins. Can you get a Labor member into Parliament in the places where they are in a majority? No: there is no class war: the working class is hopelessly divided against itself. But I will tell you what there is. There is the gulf between Dexy's view of the world and mine. There is the eternal war between those who are in the world for what they can get out of it and those who are in the world to make it a better place for everybody to live in.

SIR DEXTER [*rising*] I will not sit here listening to this disgusting ungentlemanly nonsense. Chavender: the coalition is dissolved. I resign. I shall take with me three quarters of the Cabinet. I shall expose the shamelessly corrupt motives of those who have supported you here today. Basham: you will get the sack the day after the King sends for me. Domesday: you have gone gaga: go home to bed and drivel where your dotage can do no harm. Rosy: you are a damned fool; and you ought to know it by this time. Pandranath: you are only a silly nigger pretending to be an English gentleman: you are found out. Good afternoon, gentlemen.

He goes out, leaving an atmosphere of awe behind him, in which the Indian is choking with indignation, and for the moment inarticulate.

SIR BEMROSE. This is awful. We cannot do without him.

SIR JAFNA [*finding his tongue*] I am despised. I am called nigger by this dirty faced barbarian whose forefathers were naked savages worshipping acorns and mistletoe in the woods whilst my people were spreading the highest enlightenment yet reached by the human race from the temples of Brahma the thousandfold who is all the gods in one. This primitive savages dares to accuse me of imitating him: me, with the blood in my veins of conquerors who have swept through continents vaster than a million dogholes like this island of yours. They founded a civilization compared to which your little kingdom is no better than a concentration camp. What you have of religion came from the east; yet no Hindu, no Parsee, no Jain, would stoop to its crudities. Is there a mirror here? Look at your faces and look at the faces of my people in Ceylon, the cradle of the human race. There you see Man as he came from the hand of God, who has left on every feature the unmistakeable stamp of the great original creative artist. There you see Woman with eyes in her head that mirror the universe instead of little peepholes filled with faded pebbles. Set those features, those eyes, those burning colors beside the miserable smudged lumps of half baked dough, the cheap commercial copies of a far away gallery of masterpieces that you call western humanity, and tell me, if you dare, that you are the original and I the imitation. Do you not fear the lightning? the earthquake? the vengeance of Vishnu? You call me nigger, sneering at my color because you have none. The jackdaw has lost his tail and would persuade the world that his defect is a quality. You have all cringed to me, not for my greater nearness to God, but for my money and my power of making money and ever more money. But today your hatred, your envy, your insolence has betrayed itself. I am nigger. I am bad imitation of that eater of unclean foods, never sufficiently washed in his person or his garments, a British islander. I will no longer bear it. The veil of your hypocrisy is rent by your own mouths: I should dishonor my country and my race by remaining here where both have been insulted. Until now I have supported the connection between India and England because I knew that in the course of nature and by the justice of Brahma it must end in India ruling England just as I, by my wealth and my brains, govern this roomful of needy imbeciles. But I now cast you off. I return to India to detach it wholly from England, and leave you to perish in your ignorance, your vain conceit, and your abominable manners. Good morning, gentlemen. To hell with the lot of you. [*He goes out and slams the door*].

SIR ARTHUR. That one word nigger will cost us India.

How could Dexy be such a fool as to let it slip!

SIR BEMROSE [*very serious—rising solemnly*] Arthur: I feel I cannot overlook a speech like that. After all, we are white men.

SIR ARTHUR. You are not, Rosy, I assure you. You are walnut color, with a touch of claret on the nose. Glenmorison is the color of his native oatmeal: not a touch of white on him. The fairest man present is the Duke. He's as yellow as a Malayan headhunter. The Chinese call us Pinks. They flatter us.

SIR BEMROSE. I must tell you, Arthur, that frivolity on a vital point like this is in very bad taste. And you know very well that the country cannot do without Dexy. Dexy was at school with me before I went to Dartmouth. To desert him would be for me not only an act of political bad faith but of personal bad feeling. I must go and see him at once. [*He goes very sadly to the door*].

SIR ARTHUR. Make my apologies to Sir Jafna if you overtake him. How are we to hold the empire together if we insult a man who represents nearly seventy per cent of its population?

SIR BEMROSE. I dont agree with you, Arthur. It is for Pandy to apologize. Dexy really shares the premiership with you; and if a Conservative Prime Minister of England may not take down a heathen native when he forgets himself there is an end of British supremacy.

SIR ARTHUR. For Heaven's sake dont call him a native. You are a native.

SIR BEMROSE [*very solemnly*] Of Kent, Arthur: of Kent. Not of Ceylon. [*He goes out*].

GLENMORISON. I think I'd better clear out too. I can make allowances for Sir Dexter: he is an Englishman, and has not been trained to use his mind like us in Scotland. But that is just what gives him such a hold on the Country. We must face it: he's indispensable. I'll just go and assure him that we have no intention of breaking with him. Ta ta. Good morning, Duke. [*He goes out*].

ON THE ROCKS

SIR ARTHUR [*rising and strolling round to the other side of the table like a cleaned-out gambler*] That finishes me, I'm afraid.

He throws himself into the middle chair. Basham rises moodily and goes to the window to contemplate the street. The Duke comes sympathetically to Sir Arthur and sits down beside him.

THE DUKE. Oh Arthur, my dear Arthur, why didnt you play golf on your holiday instead of thinking? Didnt you know that English politics wont bear thinking about? Didnt you know that as a nation we have lost the trick of thinking? Hadnt you noticed that though in our great British Constitution there is a department for everything else in the world almost—for agriculture and health and fisheries, for home affairs and foreign affairs and education, for the exchequer and the Treasury and even the Chiltern Hundreds and the Duchy of Lancaster—we have no department for thinking? The Russians have a special Cabinet for it; and it has knocked the whole place to pieces. Where should you and I be in Russia today? [*He resumes his seat with a hopeless shrug*].

SIR ARTHUR. In our proper place, the dustbin. Yet they got their ideas from us. Karl Marx thought it all out in Bloomsbury. Lenin learnt his lesson in Holford Square, Islington. Why can we never think out anything, nor learn any lessons? I see what has to be done now; but I dont feel that I am the man to do it.

THE DUKE. Of course not. Not a gentleman's job.

SIR ARTHUR. It might be a duke's job, though. Why not have a try at it?

THE DUKE. For three reasons, Arthur. First, I'm not built that way. Second, I'm so accustomed as a duke to be treated with the utmost deference that I simply dont know how to assert myself and bully people. Third, I'm so horribly hard up for pocket money without knowing how to do without it that Ive lost all my self-respect. This job needs a man with nothing to lose, plenty of hard driving courage, and a complete incapacity for seeing any side of a question but his own. A mere hereditary duke would be no use. When Domesday Towers is sold to an American I shall have no family seat left, and must fall back on my political seat, which is at present on the fence. From that eminence I shall encourage the dictator when he arrives as far as I can without committing myself dangerously. Sorry I can be of no use to you, my dear Arthur.

SIR ARTHUR. What about you, Basham? You are a man of action.

BASHAM. I have a jolly good mind to go to the King and make him take the bit between his teeth and arrest the lot of you.

SIR ARTHUR. Do, Basham, do. You couldnt make a worse hash of things than we have.

THE DUKE. Theres nothing to prevent you. Look at Kemal Pasha! Look at Mussolini! Look at Hitler! Look at De Valera! Look at Franklin Roosevelt!

BASHAM. If only I had ambition enough I'd think very seriously over it. As it is, I'll go back quietly to Scotland Yard. [*He is going out when he is confronted in the doorway by Hipney*] Hallo! What the devil are you doing here?

SIR ARTHUR. I am afraid you are late, Mr Hipney. The deputation has been here. They have all gone.

HIPNEY [*seating himself beside Sir Arthur with his usual calm*] I came with them, Srarthur. I been listening on the quiet as you might say. I just came in to tell you not to mind that parliamentary lot. Theyre all the same, west end or east end, parkside or riverside. Theyll never do anything. They dont want to do anything.

BASHAM [*sitting down again in Hilda's chair*] Hipney: I may as well tell you that I have had my eye on you for some time. Take care I have no objection to your calling yourself a revolutionary Socialist: they all do that. But I suspect you of really meaning business.

HIPNEY. I do, Sir Broadfoot: I do. And if Srarthur

603

means business, then let him come out of Parliament and keep out. It will take the life out of him and leave him a walking talking shell of a man with nothing inside. The only man that ever had a proper understanding of Parliament was old Guy Fawkes.

SIR ARTHUR. But even if he had blown that Parliament up, they would just have elected another.

HIPNEY. Yes; but it was a sort of gesture as you might say. Symbolic, I call it. Mark my words: some day there will be a statue to old Guy in Westminster on the site of the present House of Commons.

THE DUKE. Democracy, Arthur, democracy. This is what it ends in.

SIR ARTHUR [*introducing*] His Grace the Duke of Domesday, Mr Hipney.

HIPNEY. Bless you, I know his Grace. About town, as you might say, though weve never been introduced.

THE DUKE. Very much honored, Mr Hipney.

HIPNEY. No great honor, your Grace. But old Hipney can tell you something about Democracy at first hand. Democracy was a great thing when I was young and we had no votes. We talked about public opinion and what the British people would stand and what they wouldnt stand. And it had weight, I tell you, sir: it held Governments in check: it frightened the stoutest of the tyrants and the bosses and the police: it brought a real reverence into the voices of great orators like Bright and Gladstone. But that was when it was a dream and a vision, a hope and a faith and a promise. It lasted until they dragged it down to earth, as you might say, and made it a reality by giving everybody votes. The moment they gave the working men votes they found that theyd stand anything. They gave votes to the women and found they were worse than the men; for men would vote for men—the wrong men, but men all the same—but the women wouldnt even vote for women. Since then politics have been a laughing stock. Parliamentary leaders say one thing on Monday and just

604

the opposite on Wednesday; and nobody notices any difference. They put down the people in Egypt, in Ireland, and in India with fire and sword, with floggings and hangings, burning the houses over their heads and bombing their little stores for the winter out of existence; and at the next election theyd be sent back to Parliament by working class constituencies as if they were plaster saints, while men and women like me, that had spent their lives in the service of the people, were booted out at the polls like convicted criminals. It wasnt that the poor silly sheep did it on purpose. They didnt notice: they didnt remember: they couldnt understand: they were taken in by any nonsense they heard at the meetings or read in the morning paper. You could stampede them by crying out that the Russians were coming, or rally them by promising them to hang the Kaiser, or Lord knows what silliness that shouldnt have imposed on a child of four. That was the end of democracy for me; though there was no man alive that had hoped as much from it, nor spoke deeper from his heart about all the good things that would happen when the people came to their own and had votes like the gentry. Adult suffrage: that was what was to save us all. My God! It delivered us into the hands of our spoilers and oppressors, bound hand and foot by our own folly and ignorance. It took the heart out of old Hipney; and now I'm for any Napoleon or Mussolini or Lenin or Chavender that has the stuff in him to take both the people and the spoilers and oppressors by the scruffs of their silly necks and just sling them into the way they should go with as many kicks as may be needful to make a thorough job of it.

BASHAM. A dictator: eh? Thats what you want.

HIPNEY. Better one dictator standing up responsible before the world for the good and evil he does than a dirty little dictator in every street responsible to nobody, to turn you out of your house if you dont pay him for the right to exist on the earth, or to fire you out of your job if you stand up to him as a man and an equal. You cant frighten

605

me with a word like dictator. Me and my like has been dictated to all our lives by swine that have nothing but a snout for money, and think the world is coming to an end if anybody but themselves is given the power to do anything.

SIR ARTHUR. Steady, Mr Hipney, steady! Dont empty the baby out with the bath. If the people are to have no voice in the government and no choice of who is to govern them, it will be bad for the people.

HIPNEY. Let em have a voice. Let em have a choice. Theyve neither at present. But let it be a voice to squeal with when theyre hurt, and not to pretend they know more than God Almighty does. Give em a choice between qualified men: there's always more than one pebble on the beach; but let them be qualified men and not windbags and movie stars and soldiers and rich swankers and lawyers on the make. How are they to tell the difference between any cheap Jack and Solomon or Moses? The Jews didnt elect Moses: he just told them what to do and they did it. Look at the way they went wrong the minute his back was turned! If you want to be a leader of the people, Srarthur, youve got to elect yourself by giving us a lead. Old Hipney will follow anyone that will give him a good lead; and to blazes with your elections and your Constitution and your Democracy and all the rest of it!

THE DUKE. The police wont let him, Mr Hipney.

BASHAM [*rising and planting himself between Hipney and Sir Arthur*] Ha ha ha! Dont be too sure of that. I might come down on your side, Arthur, if I spotted you as a winner. Meanwhile, Hipney, I have my eye on you as a dangerous character.

SIR ARTHUR. And on me?

BASHAM. You dont matter: he does. If the proletariat comes to the top things will be more comfortable for Hipney; but they wont be more comfortable for you. His heart is in the revolution: you have only your head in it. Your wife wouldnt like it: his would, if he has one.

606

HIPNEY. Not me. I'm under no woman's thumb. She's dead; and the children are grown up and off my hands. I'm free at last to put my neck in a noose if I like.

BASHAM. I wonder should I find any bombs in your house if I searched it.

HIPNEY. You would if you put them there first, Sir Broadfoot. What good would a police chief be if he couldnt find anything he wanted to find?

BASHAM. Thats a suggestion, Hipney, certainly. Isnt it rather rash of you to put it into my head?

HIPNEY. There's plenty to put it into your head if I didnt. You could do it if you liked; and you know it, Sir Broadfoot. But perhaps your conscience wouldnt let you.

BASHAM. Perhaps.

HIPNEY [*rising with a chuckle*] Aha! [*Impressively*] You take it from me, you three gentlemen: all this country or any country has to stand between it and blue hell is the consciences of them that are capable of governing it.

THE DUKE [*rising*] Mr Hipney: I find myself in complete agreement with you. Will you lunch with me at the Carlton?

HIPNEY. No: them big clubs is too promiscuous for the like of you and me. You come and lunch with me: I know a nice little place where the cooking's good and the company really select. You wont regret it: come along. Morning, Srarthur. Morning, Boss. [*He goes out, greatly pleased*].

SIR ARTHUR AND BASHAM [*simultaneously*] Morning. Morning.

THE DUKE. You would never have got rid of him, Arthur, if I hadn't made that move. Goodbye. Goodbye, Sir Broadfoot. [*He goes to the door*].

BASHAM. Goodbye. I wish you joy of your host.

THE DUKE. You dont appreciate him. He is absolutely unique.

BASHAM. In what way, pray?

THE DUKE. He is the only politician I ever met who had learnt anything from experience [*he goes out*].

607

BASHAM [*making for the door*] Well, I must be off to the Yard. The unemployed are going to have a general election to amuse them. I suppose youll be off to your constituency right away.

SIR ARTHUR [*rising*] No. I am not going to stand.

BASHAM [*returning to him in amazement*] Not stand! What do you mean? You cant chalk up a program like that and then run away.

SIR ARTHUR. I am through with parliament. It has wasted enough of my life.

BASHAM. Dont tell me you are going to take your politics into the street. You will only get your head broken.

SIR ARTHUR. Never fear: your fellows wont break my head: they have too much respect for an ex-Prime Minister. But I am not going into the streets. I am not a man of action, only a talker. Until the men of action clear out the talkers we who have social consciences are at the mercy of those who have none; and that, as old Hipney says, is blue hell. Can you find a better name for it?

BASHAM. Blackguardocracy, I should call it.

SIR ARTHUR. Do you believe in it? I dont.

BASHAM. It works all right up to a point. Dont run your head against it until the men of action get you past that point. Bye bye.

SIR ARTHUR. Bye bye. I wont.

Basham goes out through the main door. Sir Arthur drops into his chair again and looks rather sick, with his elbows on his knees and his temples on his fists. Barking and Miss Brollikins break into the room simultaneously by the private door, struggling for precedence, Sir Arthur straightens up wearily.

BARKING. I was here first. You get out and wait for your turn.

ALOYSIA. Ladies first, if you please. Sir Arthur——

BARKING [*barring her way with an arm of iron*] Ladies be damned! youre no lady. [*He comes past the table to Sir Arthur's right*]. Sir Arthur: I have proposed for the hand

608

of your daughter Flavia; and all I can get out of her is that she is not a gold digger, and wouldnt be seen at a wedding with a lousy viscount. She wants to marry a poor man. I said I'd go over her head straight to you. You cant let her miss so good a match. Exert your authority. Make her marry me.

SIR ARTHUR. Certainly. I'll order her to marry you if you think that will get you any further. Go and tell her so, like a good boy. I'm busy.

BARKING. Righto! [*he dashes out through the masked door*].

SIR ARTHUR. Sit down, Miss Brollikins. [*She comes round to Hipney's chair; and Sir Arthur takes the Duke's chair*]. Have you consulted David?

ALOYSIA [*sitting down rather forlornly*] Of course I have. But he's obstinate. He wont look at it the right way.

SIR ARTHUR. Did he object? He should have jumped at it.

ALOYSIA. Its very nice of you to say so if you really mean it, Sir Arthur. But he has no sense. He objects to my name. He says it's ridiculous.

SIR ARTHUR. But your marriage will change it.

ALOYSIA. Yes; but he says it would be in The Times in the births marriages and deaths: Chavender and Brollikins. My name's not good enough for him. You should have heard what he said about it.

SIR ARTHUR. I hope he did not use the adjective his sister applied to poor young Barking's title.

ALOYSIA. Yes he did. The language you West End people use! I'm sure I dont know where you pick it up.

SIR ARTHUR. It doesnt mean anything, Miss Brollikins. You mustnt mind.

ALOYSIA. Would you mind calling me Aloysia, Sir Arthur? You can call me Brolly if you like; but I prefer Aloysia.

SIR ARTHUR. Certainly, Aloysia.

ALOYSIA. Thank you. I wish I could get rid of Brollikins. I'd never stoop to be ashamed of my name; but I cant deny there's something funny about it. I'm not to blame for that, am I?

SIR ARTHUR. But you can get rid of it quite easily. You can take a new name: any name you like, by deed poll. It costs only ten pounds; and David would have to pay it if it was on his account you changed. What about Bolingbroke [*he pronounces it Bullingbrook*]? Bolingbroke would be rather a nice name for The Times; and you wouldnt have to change your initials. No bother about your clothes at the laundry, for instance.

ALOYSIA. Thank you, Sir Arthur: thats a practical suggestion. At any rate it will shut David up if he talks about my name again.

SIR ARTHUR. Well, now you can run off and marry him.

ALOYSIA. But thats not all, Sir Arthur. He's such a queer boy. He says he's never loved anyone but his sister, and that he hates his mother.

SIR ARTHUR. He had no right to tell you that he hates his mother, because as a matter of fact he doesnt. Young people nowadays read books about psycho-analysis and get their heads filled with nonsense.

ALOYSIA. Of course I know all about psycho-analysis. I explained to him that he was in love with his mother and was jealous of you. The Edipus complex, you know.

SIR ARTHUR. And what did he say to that?

ALOYSIA. He told me to go to Jericho. But I shall teach him manners.

SIR ARTHUR. Do, Aloysia. Did he make any further objection?

ALOYSIA. Well, he says his people couldnt stand my relatives.

SIR ARTHUR. Tut! the young snob! Still, snobbery is a very real thing: he made a point there, Aloysia. How did you meet it?

ALOYSIA. I said my people couldnt stand his relatives;

and no more they could. I said I wasnt asking him to marry my relatives; nor was I proposing to marry his.

SIR ARTHUR. And what did he say to that?

ALOYSIA. He told me to go to hell. He's like that, you know.

SIR ARTHUR. Yes, a hasty boy.

ALOYSIA. He is, just that. But I shall cure him of it.

SIR ARTHUR [*gravely*] Take care, Aloysia. All young women begin by believing they can change and reform the men they marry. They cant. If you marry David he will remain David and nobody else til death do you part. If he tells you to go to hell today instead of trying to argue with you, he will do the same on the morning of your silver wedding.

ALOYSIA [*grimly*] We shall see.

SIR ARTHUR. May I ask whether this match is your idea or David's? So far I do not gather that he has expressed any strong feeling of—of—shall I say devotion?—to you.

ALOYSIA. We have discussed all that.

SIR ARTHUR. Satisfactorily?

ALOYSIA. I suppose so. You see, Sir Arthur, I am not like David. I am a reading thinking modern woman; and I know how to look at these things objectively and scientifically. You know the way you meet thousands of people and they mean nothing to you sexually: you wouldnt touch one of them with a barge pole. Then all of a sudden you pick out one, and feel sexy all over. If he's not nice you feel ashamed of yourself and run away. But if he is nice you say "Thats the man for me." You have had that experience yourself, havnt you?

SIR ARTHUR. Quite. The moment I saw Lady Chavender I said "Thats the woman for me."

ALOYSIA. Well, the moment I laid eyes on David I went all over like that. You cant deny that he is a nice boy in spite of his awful language. So I said—

SIR ARTHUR. "David's the man for me"?

ALOYSIA. No. I said "Evolution is telling me to marry

611

this youth." That feeling is the only guide I have to the evolutionary appetite.

SIR ARTHUR. The what??

ALOYSIA. The evolutionary appetite. The thing that wants to develop the race. If I marry David we shall develop the race. And thats the great thing in marriage, isnt it?

SIR ARTHUR. My dear Aloysia, the evolutionary appetite may be a guide to developing the race; but it doesnt care a rap for domestic happiness. I have known the most remarkable children come of the most dreadfully unsuitable and unhappy marriages.

ALOYSIA. We have to take our chance of that, Sir Arthur. Marriage is a lottery. I think I can make David as happy as anybody ever is in this—

SIR ARTHUR. In this wicked world. Ah yes. Well, I wont press that.

ALOYSIA. I was about to say "in the capitalist phase of social development." I dont talk like your grandmother, if you will excuse me saying so.

SIR ARTHUR. I beg your pardon. I suppose I do. Have you explained this evolutionary view of the situation to David?

ALOYSIA. Of course I have. I dont treat him as a child.

SIR ARTHUR. And what did he say?

ALOYSIA. He told me to go and— Oh, I really cannot repeat what he told me to go and do. But you see how familiar we are together. I couldnt bear his being distant with me. He talks just as if we were married already.

SIR ARTHUR. Quite. But does he feel about you as you feel about him? Has he picked you out from among the thousand ladies to whom he is indifferent? To use your own expression, does he come all over like that in your presence?

ALOYSIA. He does when I get hold of him. He needs educating in these matters. I have to awaken David. But he's coming along nicely.

SIR ARTHUR. Well, if it must be it must be. I shall not withhold my blessing. That is all I can say. [*He rises: she does the same and prepares to go*]. You see, Aloysia, the effete society in which I move is based on the understanding that we shall all speak and behave in the manner in which we are expected to behave. We are helpless when this understanding is violated. We dont know what to say or what to do. Well, you have violated it recklessly. What you have said has been unexpected to the last possible degree—

ALOYSIA. It has been true.

SIR ARTHUR. That is the climax of unexpectedness in polite society. Therefore I am at a loss. Apparently my son was not at a loss. He knows how to deal with you: I do not. I must really refer you back to him for further consideration and report.

They are about to shake hands when Lady Chavender comes in through the masked door.

LADY CHAVENDER. Still here, Miss Brollikins! I thought you had gone. [*She comes past the table to Sir Arthur's right*].

SIR ARTHUR. She wants to marry David, my dear.

LADY CHAVENDER [*calmly*] Very naturally. I think if I were in Miss Brollikins' position I should want to marry David.

ALOYSIA. I know your class point of view, Lady Chavender. You think it would be a big catch for me and a come-down for him.

LADY CHAVENDER. We both know that point of view, Miss Brollikins; but it is you, not I, that have mentioned it. Wont you sit down? [*She sits down herself in the nearest chair*].

ALOYSIA [*murmurs*] I was just going. [*She resumes her seat*].

Sir Arthur also sits.

LADY CHAVENDER. I daresay a match with you might be a very good thing for David. You seem to have all the

613

qualities in which he is deficient. And he has been declaring for some months past that if he ever marries he will marry a factory girl.

ALOYSIA. Well, I have been a factory girl. I started as a school teacher; but when they cut my salary I went into the factory. I organized the girls there, and became a trade union secretary. Wherever I went I rose because I couldnt keep down. But I am proletarian, bone and blood, if thats what David wants.

LADY CHAVENDER. Nobody is that in England, Miss Brollikins. We have never had a noble caste: our younger sons have always been commoners.

SIR ARTHUR. Yes, Aloysia: all British blood is blue.

ALOYSIA. Well, call it what you like. All I say is that I belong to the common working people and am proud of it; and that is what David wants, isnt it?

LADY CHAVENDER. What I said was that he wants to marry a factory girl. But I do not know what his attitude will be when a factory girl wants to marry him. Have you proposed to him?

SIR ARTHUR. Yes. He told her to go to hell.

LADY CHAVENDER. David has rather a habit of telling people to go to hell when he is too lazy to think of anything better to say. Miss Brollikins is a resolute and successful young woman. David is an irresolute and unsuccessful young man. If she has made up her mind to marry him she will probably succeed. She will have to support him; but I daresay she can do that as easily as she can support herself.

ALOYSIA. I shall expect him to work for his living.

LADY CHAVENDER. Marriage seldom fulfils all our expectations. You dont know David yet.

ALOYSIA. I will find him a job and see that he does it. I will interest him in it.

SIR ARTHUR. Splendid!

ALOYSIA [*puzzled*] But I cant make out you two. You havnt flared up as I thought you might; but are you for

614

me or against me?

LADY CHAVENDER. Miss Brollikins: I am sorry; but there are two things that I cannot bring myself to take the smallest interest in: parliamentry affairs and love affairs. They both bore me to distraction.

ALOYSIA [*to Sir Arthur*] Well, dont you take an interest in David?

SIR ARTHUR. David is at the age at which young men have to break loose from their fathers. They are very sensitive about being interfered with at that age. He would regard my taking an interest in him as parental tyranny. Therefore I am particularly careful not to take any interest in him.

ALOYSIA [*rising*] Well, you preach at me because my conversation is unexpected; but you two are the most unexpected lot I have ever been up against. What am I to understand? Will you play fair and let David take his own way?

SIR ARTHUR [*rising*] We will even let him take your way if he wishes, Aloysia.

LADY CHAVENDER [*rising*] You may leave me out of the question, Miss Brollikins. It is not my business, but my son's. I am neither his enemy nor yours.

ALOYSIA [*perplexed*] But do you think I ought to marry him?

LADY CHAVENDER. Nobody ought to marry anybody, Aloysia. But they do.

ALOYSIA. Well, thank you for calling me Aloysia, anyhow. It's about all the satisfaction I have got here.

She is about to go when David breaks in obstreperously through the masked door, and strides between the table and the window to Aloysia's left.

DAVID. Look here, Aloysia. What are you up to here? If you think you can get round me by getting round my parents, youre very much mistaken. My parents dont care a damn what I do as long as I take myself off their hands. And I wont be interfered with. Do you hear? I wont be interfered with.

ALOYSIA. Your parents are too good for you, you uncivilized lout. Youve put me right off it by talking that way in front of your mother. If I was your mother I'd smack some manners into you.

DAVID [*appalled and imploring*] Aloysia! [*He tries to take her in his arms*].

ALOYSIA. Take your dirty hands off me [*she flings him off*]. It's off, I tell you, off. Goodbye all. [*She storms out through the main door*].

DAVID [*in loud lament to his mother*] Youve ruined my whole life. [*He goes in pursuit, crying*] Aloysia, Aloysia, wait a moment. [*With anguished intensity*] Aloysia. [*His cries recede in the distance*].

LADY CHAVENDER } *simultaneously* { He might do worse.
SIR ARTHUR } { He might do worse.

LADY CHAVENDER. I beg your pardon. What did you say?

SIR ARTHUR. I said he might do worse.

LADY CHAVENDER. That is what I said. David is overbred: he is so fine-drawn that he is good for nothing; and he is not strong enough physically. Our breed needs to be crossed with the gutter or the soil once in every three or four generations. Uncle Theodore married his cook on principle; and his wife was my favorite aunt. Brollikins may give me goose flesh occasionally; but she wont bore me as a lady daughter-in-law would. I shall be always wondering what she will say or do next. If she were a lady I'd always know. I am so tired of wellbred people, and party politics, and the London season, and all the rest of it.

SIR ARTHUR. I sometimes think you are the only really revolutionary revolutionist I have ever met.

LADY CHAVENDER. Oh, lots of us are like that. We were born into good society; and we are through with it: we have no illusions about it, even if we are fit for nothing better. I dont mind Brollikins one bit.

616

SIR ARTHUR. What about Barking?

LADY CHAVENDER. I—

Barking enters through the masked door, jubilant. He comes between the pair as they rise, and claps them both on the shoulders right and left simultaneously. They flinch violently, and stare at him in outraged amazement.

BARKING. Good news, old dears! It's all right about Flavia. We may put up the banns. Hooray! [*He rubs hands gleefully*].

SIR ARTHUR. May I ask how you have got over her craze for marrying a poor man?

BARKING. Oh, that was a girlish illusion. You see, she had a glimpse today, at the unemployed meeting, of what poor men are really like. They were awfully nice to her. That did the trick. You see, what she craved for before was their rough manners, their violence, their brutality and filthy language, their savage treatment of their women folk. That was her ideal of a delightful husband. She found today that the working man doesnt realize it. I do. I am a real he-man. I called her the foulest names until she gave in. She's a dear. We shall be perfectly happy. Good old mother-in-law. [*He kisses Lady Chavender, who is too astounded to resist or speak*]. Tootle loo, Chavender. [*He slaps him on the shoulder*]. I am off to buy her a lot of presents. [*He dashes out through the main door*].

SIR ARTHUR. So thats that.

LADY CHAVENDER. The brute! How dare he kiss me? [*She rubs the place with her handkerchief*].

SIR ARTHUR. Do you realize that we two are free at last? Free, dearest: think of that! No more children. Free to give up living in a big house and to spend the remainder of our lives as we please. A cottage near a good golf links seems to be indicated. What would you like?

LADY CHAVENDER. But your political career? Are you really going to give up that?

SIR ARTHUR. It has given me up, dearest. Arnt you glad?

617

ON THE ROCKS

LADY CHAVENDER. Arthur: I cant bear this.

SIR ARTHUR. Cant bear what?

LADY CHAVENDER. To see you discouraged. You have never been discouraged before: you have always been so buoyant. If this new departure is to do nothing for you but take away your courage and high spirits and selfconfidence, then in Heaven's name go back to your old way of life. I will put up with anything rather than see you unhappy. That sort of unhappiness kills; and if you die I'll die too. [*She throws herself into a chair and hides her face on the table*].

SIR ARTHUR. Dont fuss, dearest: I'm not unhappy. I am enjoying the enormous freedom of having found myself out and got myself off my mind. That looks like despair; but it is really the beginning of hope, and the end of hypocrisy. Do you think I didnt know, in the days of my great speeches and my roaring popularity, that I was only whitewashing the slums? I did it very well—I dont care who hears me say so—and there is always a sort of artistic satisfaction in doing a thing very well, whether it's getting a big Bill through the House, or carrying a big meeting off its feet, or winning a golf championship. It was all very jolly; and I'm still a little proud of it. But even if I had not had you here to remind me that it was all hot air, I couldnt help knowing as well as any of those damned Socialists that though the West End of London was chockful of money and nice people all calling one another by their Christian names, the lives of the millions of people whose labor was keeping the whole show going were not worth living. I knew it quite well; but I was able to put it out of my mind because I thought it couldnt be helped and I was doing the best that could be done. I know better now: I know that it can be helped, and how it can be helped. And rather than go back to the old whitewashing job, I'd seize you tight round the waist and make a hole in the river with you.

LADY CHAVENDER [*rising*] Then why, dearest love,

618

dont you—

SIR ARTHUR. Why dont I lead the revolt against it all? Because I'm not the man for the job, darling; and nobody knows that better than you. And I shall hate the man who will carry it through for his cruelty and the desolation he will bring on us and our like.

Shouting, as of an excited mob suddenly surging into the street; and a sound of breaking glass and police whistling.

LADY CHAVENDER. What on earth is that?

Hilda comes from her office and runs to the window.

LADY CHAVENDER [*joining her*] What is going on, Hilda?

HILDA. The unemployed have broken into Downing Street; and theyre breaking the windows of the Colonial Office. They think this side is only private houses.

SIR ARTHUR [*going to see*] Yes: they always break the wrong windows, poor devils!

HILDA. Oh! here come the mounted police.

SIR ARTHUR. Theyve splendid horses, those fellows.

HILDA. The people are all running away. And they cant get out: theyre in a cul-de-sac. Oh, why dont they make a stand, the cowards?

LADY CHAVENDER. Indeed I hope they wont. What are you thinking of, Hilda?

SIR ARTHUR. Men are like that, Hilda. They always run away when they have no discipline and no leader.

HILDA. Well, but cant the police let them run away without breaking their heads? Oh look: that policeman has just clubbed a quite old man.

SIR ARTHUR. Come away: it's not a nice sight. [*He draws her away, placing himself between her and the window*].

HILDA. It's all right when you only read about it in the papers; but when you actually see it you want to throw stones at the police.

Defiant singing through the tumult.

619

ON THE ROCKS

LADY CHAVENDER [*looking out*] Someone has opened the side gate and let them through into the Horse Guards Parade. They are trying to sing.

SIR ARTHUR. What are they singing? The Red Flag?

LADY CHAVENDER. No. I dont know the tune. I caught the first two words. "England, arise."

HILDA [*suddenly hysterical*] Oh, my God! I will go out and join them [*she rushes out through the main door*].

LADY CHAVENDER. Hilda! Hilda!

SIR ARTHUR. Never mind, dear: the police all know her: she'll come to no harm. She'll be back for tea. But what she felt just now other girls and boys may feel tomorrow. And just suppose—!

LADY CHAVENDER. What?

SIR ARTHUR. Suppose England really did arise!

Unemployed England, however, can do nothing but continue to sing, as best it can to a percussion accompaniment of baton thwacks, Edward Carpenter's verses

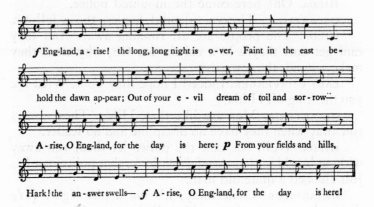

ƒ Eng-land, a - rise! the long, long night is o - ver, Faint in the east be-hold the dawn ap-pear; Out of your e - vil dream of toil and sor-row— A - rise, O Eng-land, for the day is here; ρ From your fields and hills, Hark! the an - swer swells— ƒ A - rise, O Eng-land, for the day is here!

GENEVA

A FANCIED PAGE OF HISTORY
(ANOTHER POLITICAL EXTRAVAGANZA)

Written in 1938

First Performed Malvern 1938

PREFACE

WHEN I had lived for 58 years free from the fear that war could come to my doorstep, the thing occurred. And when the war to end war had come to a glorious victory, it occurred again, worse than ever. I have now lived through two "world wars" without missing a meal or a night's sleep in my bed, though they have come near enough to shatter my windows, break in my door, and wreck my grandfather clock, keeping me for nine years of my life subject to a continual apprehension of a direct hit next time blowing me and my household to bits.

I cannot pretend that this troubled me much: people build houses and live on the slopes of Etna and Vesuvius and at the foot of Stromobli as cheerfully as on Primrose Hill. I was too old to be conscribed for military service; and the mathematical probabilities were enormously against a bomb coming my way; for at the worst of the bombardments only from ten to fifteen inhabitants of these islands were killed by air raids every day; and a dozen or so out of fortyfive millions is not very terrifying even when each of us knows that he or she is as likely as not to be one of the dozen. The risk of being run over by a motor bus, which townsmen run daily, is greater.

HOODWINKED HEROISM

It was this improbability which made pre-atomic air raiding futile as a means of intimidating a nation, and enabled the government of the raided nation to prevent the news of the damage reaching beyond its immediate neighborhood. One night early in the resumed war I saw, from a distance of 30 miles, London burning for three hours. Next morning I read in the newspapers that a bomb had fallen on the windowsill of a city office, and been extinguished before it exploded. Returning to London later on I found that half the ancient city had been levelled to the ground, leaving only St Paul's and a few church towers standing. The wireless news never went beyond

623

"some damage and a few casualties in Southern England" when in fact leading cities and seaports had been extensively wrecked. All threatening news was mentioned only in secret sessions of parliament, hidden under heavy penalties until after the victory. In 1941, after the Dunkirk rout, our position was described by the Prime Minister to the House of Commons in secret session as so desperate that if the enemy had taken advantage of it we should have been helplessly defeated; and it is now the fashion to descant dithyrambically on the steadfast heroism with which the nation faced this terrible emergency. As a matter of fact the nation knew nothing about it. Had we been told, the Germans would have overheard and rushed the threatened invasion they were bluffed into abandoning. Far from realizing our deadly peril, we were exulting in the triumph of our Air Force in "the Battle of Britain" and in an incident in South America in which three British warships drove one German one into the river Plate. Rather than be interned with his crew the German captain put to sea again against hopeless odds; scuttled his ship; and committed suicide. The British newspapers raved about this for weeks as a naval victory greater than Salamis, Lepanto, and Trafalgar rolled into one.

Later on our flight from Tobruk to the border of Egypt did not disturb us at home: it was reported as a trifling setback, whilst trumpery captures of lorries or motor bicycles by British patrols figured as victories. After major engagements German losses were given in figures: Allies' losses were not given at all, the impression left being that the Allies had killed or taken prisoner tens of thousands of Axis troops without suffering any casualties worth mentioning. Only by listening to the German broadcasts, similarly cooked, could the real facts and fortunes of the war be estimated. Of course the truth leaked out months later; but it produced only a fresh orgy of bragging about our heroic fortitude in the face of the deadly peril we knew nothing of.

All this was necessary and inevitable. It was dangerous to tell the truth about anything, even about the weather. The signposts on the roads had to be taken down and hidden lest they should help an invader to find his way. It was a crime to give an address with a date, or to scatter a few crumbs for the birds. And it was an act of heroic patriotism to drop a bomb weighing ten thousand pounds on dwellings full of women and children, or on crowded railway trains. Our bombing of foreign cities not only in Germany but in countries which we claimed to be "liberating" became so frightful that at last the word had to be given to two of our best broadcasters of war reports to excuse them on the ground that by shortening the war they were saving the lives of thousands of British soldiers.

Meanwhile nobody noticed how completely war, as an institution, had reduced itself to absurdity. When Germany annexed Poland in 1939, half of it was snatched out of her jaws by Soviet Russia. The British Commonwealth, having bound itself to maintain inviolate the frontiers of Poland as they were left after the fighting of 1914–18 with a Polish corridor cut right through Prussia to the Baltic, was committed to declare war on Germany and Russia simultaneously. But the British people and their rulers were in no mood to black out their windows and recommence the Four Years War in defence of this distant and foreign corridor. Being, as usual, unprepared for war, we tried to appease Germany and yet keep the peace with Soviet Russia.

ENGLAND FRIGHTENED AND GREAT

Nations should always be prepared for war, just as people with any property to leave should always have made their wills. But as most of them never do make their wills, and the rest seldom keep them revised and up to date, States, however militarist, are never fully prepared for war. England will do nothing outside her routine until she is thoroughly frightened; but when England is frightened England is capable of anything. Philip II of Spain frightened her. Louis XIV of France frightened her. Napoleon frightened her. Wilhelm II of the German Reich frightened her. But instead of frightening the wits out of her they frightened the wits into her. She woke up and smashed them all. In vain did the Kaiser sing *Deutschland über Alles,* and Hitler claim that his people were the Herrenvolk created by God to rule the earth. The English were equally convinced that when Britain first at Heaven's command arose from out the azure main she was destined to rule the waves, and make the earth her footstool. This is so natural to Englishmen that they are unconscious of it, just as they cannot taste water because it is always in their mouths. Long before England first sang Rule Britannia at Cliveden she had annihilated Philip's Invincible Armada to the music of the winds and waves, and, after being defeated again and again by General Luxemburg, made hay of the French armies at Blenheim, Ramilies, and Malplaquet to the senseless gibberish of Lillibullero-bullenalah. She not only took on Hitler singlehanded without a word to the League of Nations nor to anyone else, but outfought him, outbragged him, outbullied him, outwitted him in every trick and turn of warfare, and finally extinguished him and hanged his accomplices.

ENGLAND SECURE AND LAZY

The drawback to England's capacity for doing impossible things when in danger is her incapacity for doing possible things (except repeating what was done last time) in security. The prefabrication in England of harbors for France and planting them there as part of the baggage of the allied invading armies, was a feat which still seems incredible even now that it has actually been achieved; yet during the 20 years armistice England could not bridge the Severn below Gloucester, harness the Pentland tides, nor tap the volcanic fires of the earth's boiling core, much less mechanize the coalmines or even design an alphabet capable of saving billionsworth of British time, ink, and paper, by spelling English speech sounds unequivocally and economically. The moment the Cease Fire is sounded England forgets all the lessons of the war and proves the truth of Dr Inge's old comment on the Anglo-Irish situation as illustrating the difficulty of driving in double harness people who remember nothing with people who forget nothing. Still, as forgetful people who act in the present can master vindictive people who only brood on the past there is much to be said for England's full share of human thoughtlessness. It is sometimes better not to think at all than to think intensely and think wrong.

Statesmen who know no past history are dangerous because contemporary history cannot be ascertained. No epoch is intelligible until it is completed and can be seen in the distance as a whole, like a mountain. The victorious combatants in the battle of Hastings did not know that they were inaugurating feudalism for four centuries, nor the Red Roses on Bosworth Field and the Ironsides at Naseby know that they were exchanging it for Whig plutocracy. Historians and newspaper editors can see revolutions three centuries off but not three years off, much less three hours. Had Marx and Engels been contemporaries of Shakespear they could not have written the Communist Manifesto, and would probably have taken a hand, as Shakespear did, in the enclosure of common lands as a step forward in civilization.

HISTORY STOPS YESTERDAY: STATECRAFT WORKS BLINDFOLD

This is why history in our schools stops far short of the present moment, and why statesmen, though they can learn the lessons of history from books, must grope their way through daily emergencies within the limits of their ignorance as best they can. If their vision is vulgar and vindictive the guesses they make may be worse than the war. That vision has not widened nor that ability grown of late. But the perils of the situation have increased enormously. Men are what they were; but war has become many times more destructive, not of men, who can be re-

627

placed, but of the plant of civilization, the houses and factories, the railways and airways, the orchards and furrowed fields, and the spare subsistence which we call capital, without which civilized mankind would perish. Even the replacement of the slain is threatened because the latest bombs are no respecters of sex; and where there are no women there will soon be no warriors. In some of the air raids, more women were killed than men. The turning point of the war was the siege of Stalingrad, written up by the newspapers more dithyrambically than any siege in history since the siege of Troy. But when the Greeks captured Troy they had the city for their pains as well as the glory. When the Red Army triumphed at Stalingrad they had nothing but festering corpses to bury, heaps of rubble to clear away, and a host of prisoners to feed. Meanwhile the British and American armies were "liberating" French cities, Dutch cities, Belgian cities, Italian cities: that is, they were destroying them exactly as they were destroying German cities, and having to house and feed their surviving inhabitants after wrecking their water mains, electric power stations, and railway communications. From the national point of view this was conquest, glory, patriotism, bravery, all claiming to be necessary for security. From the European wider angle it was folly and devilment, savagery and suicide. The ready money collected for it (wars cannot be fought on credit) was called Savings: a barefaced wicked lie. All the belligerents have been bled white, and will find, when they claim their "savings" back from their governments, that their Chancellors of the Exchequer will reply, like the juvenile spendthrift exhorted to pay his debts by Richelieu in Lytton's play, "Willingly, your Eminence: where shall I borrow the money?"; for not a farthing of it (say 12 millions shot away every day for six years) remains; and all of it that achieved its purpose of ruin has imposed on us the added burden of repairing what we have destroyed.

So much for England frightened into fighting. The

question now is has war become frightful enough to frighten her out of it? In the last months the bombs launched by young British warriors from airplanes at the risk of their lives grew to such prodigious weight and destructiveness that they wrecked not merely houses but whole streets, and scattered blazing phosphorus and magnesium on such a scale that the victims, chiefly women with children who could not escape by flight as a few of the men did, were stifled by having nothing to breathe but white hot air, and then burnt to cinders and buried under the piles of rubble that had been their houses. We rained these monster bombs on Germany until the destruction of their railways and munition factories made retaliation in kind impossible. Our flame throwing from tanks finished the fugitives.

WE SPLIT THE ATOM

But the resources of decivilization were not exhausted. When we were exulting in our demolition of cities like Cologne and Hamburg we were very considerably frightened by the descent on London of new projectiles, unmanned yet aimed and guided, which demolished not only streets but districts. And when we and our allies "liberated" German-occupied territory (blowing its cities to smithereens largely in the process) we discovered that the manufacture of these new horrors had been planned for on such a scale that but for their capture in time the tables might have been turned on us with a vengeance.

But we had another card up our sleeve: this time a trump so diabolical that when we played it the war, which still lingered in Japan, was brought to an abrupt stop by an Anglo-American contrivance which may conceivably transform the globe into a cloud of flaming gas in which no form of life known to us could survive for a moment. That such explosions have visibly occurred on other stars (called novas) is vouched for by our astronomers, who have seen them with their naked eyes and studied their photographs and spectrographs for years past. When Eng-

land and the United States of North America got ahead
of Germany and Japan with this terrific weapon all their
opponents at once surrendered at discretion.

AN AMORAL VICTORY

This time there could be no sustainable pretence of a
moral victory, though plenty were made as usual; for
nothing yet discovered has cured mankind of lying and
boasting. It was what Wellington called Waterloo, a very
near thing; for had the Germans not concentrated on the
jet propulsion of pilotless aeroplanes instead of on the
atomic bomb, they might have contrived it before us and
made themselves masters of the situation if not of the
world. They may yet cheapen and improve on it. Or they
may discover a gas lighter than air, deadly but not destructive. And then where shall we be? Ethical victories endure.
Discoveries cannot be guaranteed for five minutes.

Still, though the victory was not a triumph of Christianity it was a triumph of Science. American and British scientists, given *carte blanche* in the matter of expense, had
concentrated on a romantic and desperate search for a
means of harnessing the mysterious forces that mould and
hold atoms into metals, minerals, and finally into such
miracles as human geniuses, taking some grains of metal
and a few salts purchasable at the nearest oil-shop and
fashioning with them the head of Shakespear, to say nothing of my own. It is already known that the energy that
makes uranium out of molecules, escapes by slow radiation
and both kills and cures living organisms, leaving behind
it not radium but lead. If this disintegration could be
speeded up to instaneousness it would make a heat so prodigious that a couple of morsels of uranium dropped from
a plane and timed to collide and disentegrate above a city
could convert that city and its inhabitants into a heap of
flaming gas in a fraction of a second. The experiment was
tried on two Japanese cities. Four square miles of them
vanished before the experimenters could say Jack Robinson.

There is no getting away from the fact that if another

world war be waged with this new weapon there may be an end of our civilization and its massed populations. Even for those philosophers who are of opinion that this would not be any great loss there is a further possibility. An atomic bomb attached to a parachute and exploded in the air would devastate only as many square miles as it was meant to; but if it hung fire and exploded in the earth it might start a continuous process of disintegration in which our planet would become a *nova* to astronomers on Mars, blazing up and dimming out, leaving nothing of it and of us in the sky but a gaseous nebula.

It seems that if "the sport of kings" is to continue it must be fought under Queensberry rules classing atomic bombs with blows below the belt, and barring them. But it was the British refusal to bar aerial bombardment that made the air battles of the world war lawful; and these air battles had already reduced war to economic absurdity before the atomic bomb came into action. War had become logical: enemies were massacred or transported: wayleave was abolished. Thus the victors were left with the terror of their own discovery, and the vanquished with the hope that they may soon discover for themselves how to disintegrate uranium or perhaps some other element with ten times its energy. And two of the great allies, England and America, flatly refuse to share the secret of the new bomb with Russia, the third. Villages in India are still wiped out to "larn" their mostly harmless inhabitants not to snipe at British soldiers. The alarm is general: the cry of all hands, the triumphant even more than the subjugated, is that there must be an end of war. But all the other cries are as warlike as ever. The victorious Allies agree in demanding that Germans and Japanese must be treated as Catholic Ireland was treated by England in the seventeenth century.

Some of them are now consoling themselves with the hope that the atomic bomb has made war impossible. That hope has often been entertained before. Colonel Robinson, in *The Nineteenth Century And After*, has given a list of

631

previous discoveries, dating back to B.C., which have developed the technique of killing from the single combats of the Trojan war, fought man to man, to artillery operations and air raids in which the combatants are hundreds of miles apart on the ground or thousands of feet up in the air dropping bombs and flying away at a speed of ten miles per second, never seeing one another nor the mischief they do. At every development it is complained that war is no longer justifiable as a test of heroic personal qualities, and demonstrated that it has become too ruinous to be tolerated as an institution. War and imperialist diplomacy persist none the less.

CIVILIZATION'S WILL TO LIVE ALWAYS DEFEATED BY DEMOCRACY

Mankind, though pugnacious, yet has an instinct which checks it on the brink of selfdestruction. We are still too close to the time when men had to fight with wild beasts for their lives and with one another for their possessions, and when women had to choose fighters for their mates to protect them from robbery and rapine at their work as mothers, nurses, cooks, and kitchen gardeners. There are still places in the world where after tribal battles the victors eat the vanquished and the women share the feast with the warriors. In others foreign explorers, visitors, and passengers are killed as strangers. The veneer of civilization which distinguishes Europeans from these tribesmen and their wives is dangerously thin. Even English ladies and gentlemen "go Fantee" occasionally. Christmas cards will not prevent them from using atomic bombs if they are again frightened and provoked. But the magnitude of the new peril rouses that other instinct, stronger finally than pugnacity, that the race must not perish. This does not mean that civilization cannot perish. Civilizations have never finally survived: they have perished over and over again because they failed to make themseles worth their cost to the masses whom they enslaved. Even at home they could not master the art of governing millions of people for the common good in spite of people's inveterate objection to be governed at all. Law has been popularly known only as oppression and taxation, and politics as a clamor for less government and more liberty. That citizens get better value for the rates and taxes they pay than for most other items in their expenditure never occurs to them. They will pay a third of their weekly earnings or more to an idle landlord as if that were a law of nature; but a collection from them by the rate collector they resent as sheer robbery: the truth being precisely the reverse. They see nothing extravagant in basing democracy on an assumption that every adult native is either a Marcus Aurelius or a combination of Saint Teresa and Queen Elizabeth Tudor, supremely competent to choose any tinker tailor soldier sailor or any goodlooking well dressed female to rule over them. This insane prescription for perfect democracy of course makes democracy impossible and the adventures of Cromwell, Napoleon, Hitler, and the innumerable conquistadores and upstart presidents of South American history inevitable. There never has been and never will be a government which is both plebiscitary and democratic, because the plebs do not want to be governed, and the plutocrats who humbug them, though they are so far democratic that they must for their own sakes keep their slaves alive and efficient, use their powers to increase their revenues and suppress resistance to their appropriation of all products and services in excess of this minimum. Substitute a plebeian government, and it can only carry on to the same point with the same political machinery, except that the plunder goes to the Trade Unions instead of to the plutocrats. This may be a considerable advance; but when the plebeian government attempts to re-organize production collectively so as to increase the product and bring the highest culture within the reach of all who are capable of it, and make the necessary basic material prosperity general and equal, the dread and hatred of government as such, calling itself Liberty and Democracy, reasserts itself and

stops the way. Only when a war makes collective organization compulsory on pain of slaughter, subjugation, and
nowadays extinction by bombs, jet propelled or atomic, is
any substantial advance made or men of action tolerated as
Prime Ministers. The first four years of world war forced
us to choose a man of action as leader; but when the
armistice came we got rid of him and had a succession of
premiers who could be trusted to do nothing revolutionary.
Our ideal was "a commonplace type with a stick and a pipe
and a half bred black and tan." Even Franklin Roosevelt
won his first presidential election more by a photograph
of himself in the act of petting a baby than by his political
program, which few understood: indeed he only half
understood it himself. When Mr Winston Churchill, as a
man of action, had to be substituted for the *fainéants* when
the war was resumed, his big cigars and the genial romantic
oratory in which he glorified the war maintained his popularity until the war was over and he opened the General
Election campaign by announcing a domestic policy which
was a hundred years out of fashion, and promised nothing
to a war weary proletariat eager for a Utopia in which there
should be no military controls and a New World inaugurated in which everybody was to be both employed and
liberated.

Mr Churchill at once shared the fate of Lloyd George;
and the Utopians carried the day triumphantly. But the
New World proved the same as the old one, with the same
fundamental resistance to change of habits and the same
dread of government interference surviving in the adult
voter like the child's dread of a policeman.

It may be asked how it is that social changes do actually
take place under these circumstances. The reply is that
other circumstances create such emergencies, dangers, and
hardships, that the very people who dread Government
action are the first to run to the Government for a remedy,
crying that "something must be done." And so civilization,
though dangerously slowed down, forces its way piecemeal

in spite of stagnant ignorance and selfishness.

Besides, there are always ancient constitutions and creeds to be reckoned with; and these are not the work of adult suffrage, but inheritances from feudal and ecclesiastical systems which had to provide law and order during the intervals between dominating personalities, when ordinary governments had to mark time by doing what was done last time until the next big boss came along and became a popular idol, worshipped at the polls by 99 per cent majorities.

All the evidence available so far is to the effect that since the dawn of history there has been no change in the natural political capacity of the human species. The comedies of Aristophanes and the Bible are at hand to convince anyone who doubts this. But this does not mean that enlightenment is impossible. Without it our attempts at democracy will wreck our civilization as they have wrecked all the earlier civilizations we know of. The ancient empires were not destroyed by foreign barbarians. They assimilated them easily. They destroyed themselves: their collapse was the work of their own well meaning native barbarians. Yet these barbarians, like our own at present, included a percentage of thinkers who had their imaginations obsessed by Utopias in which perfectly wise governments were to make everybody prosperous and happy. Their old men saw visions and their young men dreamed dreams just as they do now. But they were not all such fools as to believe that their visions and dreams could be realized by Tom, Dick, and Harriet voting for Titus Oates, Lord George Gordon, Horatio Bottomley, Napoleon, or Hitler. My experience as an enlightener, which is considerable, is that what is wrong with the average citizen is not altogether deficient political capacity. It is largely ignorance of facts, creating a vacuum into which all sorts of romantic antiquarian junk and cast-off primitive religion rushes. I have to enlighten sects describing themselves as Conservatives, Socialists, Protestants, Catholics, Communists, Fascists, Fabians,

Friends (Quakers), Ritualists, all bearing labels which none of them can define, and which indicate tenets which none of them accept as practical rules of life and many of them repudiate with abhorrence when they are presented without their labels. I was baptized as a member of the then established Protestant Episcopal Church in Ireland. My religious education left me convinced that I was entitled to call myself a Protestant because I believed that Catholics were an inferior species who would all go to hell when they died; and I daresay the Roman Catholic children with whom I was forbidden to play believed that the same eternity of torment awaited me in spite of Pope Pius the Ninth's humane instruction to them to absolve me on the plea of invincible ignorance. We were both taught to worship "a tenth rate tribal deity" of the most vindictive, jealous, and ruthless pugnacity, equally with his Christlike son. Just so today Conservatives know nothing of the Tory creed, but are convinced that the rulers of Russia are bloodstained tyrants, robbers and murderers, and their subjects slaves without rights or liberties. All good Russians believe equally that the capitalist rulers of the Western plutocracies are ruthless despots out for nothing but exploiting labor in pursuit of surplus value, as Marx called rent, interest, and profit. They group themselves in political parties and clubs in which none of them knows what he or she is talking about. Some of them have Utopian aspirations, and have read the prophets and sages, from Moses to Marx, and from Plato to Ruskin and Inge; but a question as to a point of existing law or the function of a County Council strikes them dumb. They are more dangerous than simpletons and illiterates because on the strength of their irrelevant schooling they believe themselves politically educated, and are accepted as authorities on political subjects accordingly.

Now this political ignorance and delusion is curable by simple instruction as to the facts without any increase of political capacity. I am ending as a sage with a very scrappy and partial knowledge of the world. I do not see why I should not have begun with if it I had been told it all to begin with: I was more capable of it then than I am now in my dotage. When I am not writing plays as a more or less inspired artist I write political schoolbooks in which I say nothing of the principles of Socialism or any other Ism (I disposed of all that long ago), and try to open my readers' eyes to the political facts under which they live. I cannot change their minds; but I can increase their knowledge. A little knowledge is a dangerous thing; but we must take that risk because a little is as much as our biggest heads can hold; and a citizen who knows that the earth is round and older than six thousand years is less dangerous than one of equal capacity who believes it is a flat groundfloor between a first floor heaven and a basement hell.

INCOMPETENT GOVERNMENTS ARE THE CRUELLIST

The need for confining authority to the instructed and capable has been demonstrated by terrible lessons daily for years past. As I write, dockfulls of German prisoners of war, male and female, are being tried on charges of hideous cruelties perpetrated by them at concentration camps. The witnesses describe the horrors of life and death in them; and the newspapers class the accused as fiends and monsters. But they also publish photographs of them in which they appear as ordinary human beings who could be paralleled from any crowd or army.

These Germans had to live in the camps with their prisoners. It must have been very uncomfortable and dangerous for them. But they had been placed in authority and management, and had to organize the feeding, lodging, and sanitation of more and more thousands of prisoners and refugees thrust upon them by the central government. And as they were responsible for the custody of their prisoners they had to be armed to the teeth and their prisoners completely disarmed. Only eminent leadership, experience, and organizing talent could deal with such a situation.

637

GENEVA

Well, they simply lacked these qualities. They were not fiends in human form; but they did not know what to do with the thousands thrown on their care. There was some food; but they could not distribute it except as rations among themselves. They could do nothing with their prisoners but overcrowd them within any four walls that were left standing, lock them in, and leave them almost starving to die of typhus. When further overcrowding became physically impossible they could do nothing with their unwalled prisoners but kill them and burn the corpses they could not bury. And even this they could not organize frankly and competently: they had to make their victims die of illusage instead of by military law. Under such circumstances any miscellaneous collection of irresistibly armed men would be demoralized; and the natural percentage of callous toughs among them would wallow in cruelty and in the exercise of irresponsible authority for its own sake. Man beating is better sport than bear baiting or cock fighting or even child beating, of which some sensational English cases were in the papers at home at the time. Had there been efficient handling of the situation by the authorities (assuming this to have been possible) none of these atrocities would have occurred. They occur in every war when the troops get out of hand.

HITLER

The German government was rotten at the centre as well as at the periphery. The Hohenzollern monarchy in Germany, with an enormous military prestige based on its crushing defeat of the Bonapartist French Army in 1871 (I was fifteen at the time, and remember it quite well) was swept away in 1918 by the French Republic. The rule of the monarch was succeeded by the rule of anybody chosen by everybody, supposed, as usual, to secure the greatest common measure of welfare, which is the object of democracy, but which really means that a political career is open to any adventurer. It happened that in Munich in 1930 there was a young man named Hitler who had served
638

in the Four Years War. Having no special military talent he had achieved no more as a soldier than the Iron Cross and the rank of corporal. He was poor and what we call no class, being a Bohemian with artistic tastes but neither training nor talent enough to succeed as an artist, and was thus hung up between the bourgeoisie for which he had no income and the working class for which he had no craft. But he had a voice and could talk, and soon became a beer cellar orator who could hold his audience. He joined a cellar debating society (like our old Coger's Hall) and thereby brought its numbers up to seven. His speeches soon attracted considerable reinforcements and established him as a leading spirit. Much of what he spouted was true. As a soldier he had learnt that disciplined men can make short work of mobs; that party parliaments on the British model neither could nor would abolish the poverty that was so bitter to him; that the Treaty of Versailles under which Germany, defeated and subjected far beyond the last penny she could spare, could be torn up clause by clause by anyone with a big enough army to intimidate the plunderers; and that Europe was dominated economically by a plutocracy of financiers who had got the whip hand even of the employers. So far he was on solid ground, with unquestionable facts to support him. But he mixed the facts up with fancies such as that all plutocrats are Jews; that the Jews are an accursed race who should be exterminated as such; that the Germans are a chosen race divinely destined to rule the world; and that all she needs to establish her rule is an irresistible army. These delusions were highly flattering to Hans, Fritz, and Gretchen at large as well as to the beer drinkers in the cellar; and when an attempt was made to silence the new Hitlerites by hired gangsters, Hitler organized a bodyguard for himself so effectively that the opposition was soon sprawling in the street.

With this stock in trade Hitler found himself a born leader, and, like Jack Cade, Wat Tyler, Essex under Elizabeth Tudor, Emmet under Dublin Castle, and Louis Napoleon under the Second Republic, imagined he had only to appear in the streets with a flag to be acclaimed and followed by the whole population. He tried the experiment with a general from the Four Years War at his side and such converts to his vogue and eloquence as his beer cellar orations had made. With this nucleus he marched through the streets. A rabble gathered and followed to see the fun, as rabbles always will in cities. In London I have seen thousands of citizens rushing to see why the others were rushing, and to find out why. It looked like a revolutionary *émeute*. On one occasion it was a runaway cow. On another it was Mary Pickford, "World's Sweetheart" of the old silent films, driving to her hotel in a taxi.

For a moment Hitler may have fancied that a success like that of Mussolini's march to Rome (he went by train) was within his grasp. He had the immediate precedent of Kurt Eisner's successful *Putsch* to encourage him. But Eisner was not resisted. When Hitler and his crowd came face to face with the Government troops they did not receive him as the grognards of the Bourbon army received Napoleon on his return from Elba. They opened fire on him. His rabble melted and fled. He and General Ludendorff had to throw themselves flat on the pavement to avoid the bullets. He was imprisoned for eight months for his escapade, not having frightened the Government enough to be considered worth killing as Cade, Tyler, and Essex were killed. In prison, he and his companion-secretary Hess, wrote a book entitled *Mein Kampf* (My Struggle, My Program, My Views or what you please).

Like Louis Napoleon he had now learnt his lesson: namely, that *Putsches* are a last desperate method, not a first one, and that adventurers must come to terms with the captains of finance and industry, the bankers, and the Conservatives who really control the nations wherever the people choose what rulers they please, before he can hope to be accepted by them as a figure head. Hitler had sufficient histrionic magnetism to strike this bargain even to the extent of being made perpetual chancellor of the German Realm with more than royal honors, though his whole stock-in-trade was a brazen voice and a doctrine made up of scraps of Socialism, mortal hatred of the Jews, and complete contempt for pseudo-democratic parliamentary mobocracy.

PSEUDO MESSIAH AND MADMAN

So far he was the creature and tool of the plutocracy. But the plutocracy had made a bad bargain. The moment it made Hitler a figure head, popular idolatry made a prophet and a hero of him, and gave him a real personal power far in excess of that enjoyed by any commercial magnate. He massacred all his political rivals not only with impunity but with full parliamentary approval. Like St Peter on a famous earlier occasion the German people cried "Thou art the Christ", with the same result. Power and worship turned Hitler's head; and the national benefactor who began by abolishing unemployment, tearing up the Treaty of Versailles, and restoring the selfrespect of sixty millions of his fellow countrymen, became the mad Messiah who, as lord of a Chosen Race, was destined to establish the Kingdom of God on earth—a German kingdom of a German God—by military conquest of the rest of mankind. Encouraged by spineless attempts to appease him he attacked Russia, calculating that as a crusader against Soviet Communism he would finally be joined by the whole Capitalist West.

But the Capitalist West was much too shortsighted and jealous to do anything so intelligent. It shook hands with Stalin and stabbed Hitler in the back. He put up a tremendous fight, backed by his fellow adventurers in Italy and Spain; but, being neither a Julius Cæsar nor a Mahomet, he failed to make his initial conquests welcome and permanent by improving the condition of the inhabitants. On the contrary he made his name execrated wherever he conquered. The near West rose up against him, and was joined by the mighty far West of America. After twelve years of killing other people he had to kill himself, and leave his accomplices to be hanged.

The moral for conquerors of empires is that if they substitute savagery for civilization they are doomed. If they substitute civilization for savagery they make good, and establish a legitimate title to the territories they invade. When Mussolini invaded Abyssinia and made it possible for a stranger to travel there without being killed by the native Danakils he was rendering the same service to the world as we had in rendering by the same methods (including poison gas) in the north west provinces of India, and had already completed in Australia, New Zealand, and the Scottish Highlands. It was not for us to throw stones at Musso, and childishly refuse to call his puppet king Emperor. But we did throw stones, and made no protest when his star was eclipsed and he was scandalously lynched in Milan. The Italians had had enough of him; for he, too, was neither a Cæsar nor a Mahomet.

Contemplating the careers of these two poor devils one cannot help asking was their momentary grandeur worth while? I pointed out once that the career of Bourrienne, Napoleon's valet-secretary for a while, was far longer, more fortunate, easier and more comfortable in every common-sense way, than that of Napoleon, who, with an interval of one year, was Emperor for fourteen years. Mussolini kept going for more than twenty. So did Louis Napoleon, backed by popular idolization of his uncle, who had become a national hero, as Hitler will become in Germany presently. Whether these adventurers would have been happier in obscurity hardly matters; for they were kept too busy to bother themselves about happiness; and the extent to which they enjoyed their activities and authority and deification is unknown. They were finally scrapped as failures and nuisances, though they all began by effecting some obvious reforms over which party parliaments had been boggling for centuries. Such successes as they had were reactions from the failures of the futile parliamentary talking shops, which were themselves reactions from the bankruptcies of incompetent monarchs, both mobs and monarchs being products of political idolatry and ignorance. The wider the suffrage, the greater the confusion. "Swings to the Left" followed by "swings to the Right" kept the newspapers and the political windbags amused and hopeful. We are still humbugging ourselves into the belief that the swings to the Left are democratic and those to the Right imperial. They are only swings from failure to failure to secure substantial democracy, which means impartial government for the good of the governed by qualified rulers. Popular anarchism defeats them all.

Upstart dictators and legitimate monarchs have not all been personal failures. From Pisistratus to Porfirio, Ataturk, and Stalin, able despots have made good by doing things better and much more promptly than parliaments. They have kept their heads and known their limitations. Ordinary mortals like Nero, Paul of Russia, our James the Second, Riza Khan in Iran, and some of the small fry of degenerate hereditary tribal chiefs like Theebaw in Burma have gone crazy and become worse nuisances than mad dogs. Lord Acton's dictum that power corrupts gives no idea of the extent to which flattery, deference, power, and apparently unlimited money, can upset and demoralize simpletons who in their proper places are good fellows enough. To them the exercise of authority is not a heavy and responsible job which strains their mental capacity and industry to the utmost, but a delightful sport to be indulged for its own sake, and asserted and reasserted by cruelty and monstrosity.

DEMOCRACY MISUNDERSTOOD

Democracy and equality, without which no State can achieve the maximum of beneficence and stability, are still frightfully misunderstood and confused. Popular logic about them is, like most human logic, mere association of ideas, or, to call it by the new name invented by its monstrous product Pavlov, conditional reflex. Government of

the people for the people, which is democracy, is supposed
to be achievable through government by the people in the
form of adult suffrage, which is finally so destructive of
democracy that it ends in a reaction into despot-idolatry.
Equality is supposed to mean similarity of political talent,
which varies as much as musical or mathematical or military capacity from individual to individual, from William
Rufus to Charles II, from Nero to Marcus Aurelius, from
Monmouth and Prince Charlie to Alexander and Napoleon. Genuine democracy requires that the people shall
choose their rulers, and, if they will, change them at sufficient intervals; but the choice must be limited to the public
spirited and politically talented, of whom Nature always
provides not only the necessary percentage, but superfluity
enough to give the people a choice. Equality, which in practice means intermarriageability, is based on the hard facts
that the greatest genius costs no more to feed and clothe
and lodge than the narrowest minded duffer, and at a pinch
can do with less, and that the most limited craftsman or
laborer who can do nothing without direction from a
thinker, is, if worth employing at all, as necessary and important socially as the ablest director. Equality between
them is either equality of income and of income only or
an obvious lie.

Equality of income is practicable enough: any sporting
peer with his mind bounded by the racecourse can dine on
equal terms with an astronomer whose mental domain is
the universe. Their children are intermarriageable without
misalliance. But when we face the democratic task of forming panels of the persons eligible for choice as qualified
rulers we find first that none of our tests are trustworthy or
sufficient, and finally that we have no qualified rulers at
all, only bosses. The rule of vast commonwealths is beyond
the political capacity of mankind at its ablest. Our Solons,
Cæsars and Washingtons, Lenins, Stalins and Nightingales,
may be better than their best competitors; but they die in
their childhood as far as statesmanship is concerned, playing

PREFACE

golf and tennis and bridge, smoking tobacco and drinking
alcohol as part of their daily diet, hunting, shooting, cours-
ing, reading tales of murder and adultery and police news,
wearing fantastic collars and cuffs, with the women on
high heels staining their nails, daubing their lips, painting
their faces: in short, doing all sorts of things that are child's
play and not the exercises or recreations of statesmen and
senators. Even when they have read Plato, the Gospels,
and Karl Marx, and to that extent know what they have to
do, they do not know how to do it, and stick in the old
grooves for want of the new political technique which is
evolving under pressure of circumstances in Russia. Their
attempts at education and schooling end generally in boy
farms and concentration camps with flogging blocks, from
which the prisoners when they adolesce emerge as trained
and prejudiced barbarians with a hatred of learning and
discipline, and a dense ignorance of what life is to nine
tenths of their compatriots.

"GREAT MEN"

Here and there, however, cases of extraordinary faculty
shew what mankind is capable of within its existing framework. In mathematics we have not only Newtons and
Einsteins, but obscure illiterate "lightning calculators," to
whom the answers to arithmetical and chronological problems that would cost me a long process of cyphering (if I
could solve them at all) are instantly obvious. In grammar
and scripture I am practically never at a loss; but I have
never invented a machine, though I am built like engineers
who, though they are never at a loss with machinery, are
yet so unable to put descriptions of their inventions into
words that they have to be helped out by patent agents of
no more than common literary ability. Mozart, able in his
infancy to do anything he pleased in music, from the
simplest sonata to the most elaborate symphony or from
the subtlest comic or tragic opera to fugal settings of the
Mass, resembled millions of Austrians who could not to
save their lives hum a line of *Deutschland über Alles* nor

645

compose a bar of music playable by one finger, much less concerted for 30 different orchestral instruments. In philosophy we spot Descartes and Kant, Swift and Schopenhauer, Butler and Bergson, Richard Wagner and Karl Marx, Blake and Shelley, Ruskin and Morris, with dozens of uncrucified Jesuses and saintly women in every generation, look like vindictive retaliators, pugnacious sportsmen, and devout believers in ancient tribal idols. The geniuses themselves are steeped in vulgar superstitions and prejudices: Bunyan and Newton astound us not only by their specific talents but by their credulity and Bible fetichism. We prate gravely of their achievements and faculties as attainments of mankind, as if every Italian were Michael Angelo and Raphael and Dante and Galileo rolled into one, every German a Goethe, and every Englishman a compound of Shakespear and Eddington. Of this folly we have had more than enough. The apparent freaks of nature called Great Men mark not human attainment but human possibility and hope. They prove that though we in the mass are only child Yahoos it is possible for creatures built exactly like us, bred from our unions and developed from our seeds, to reach the heights of these towering heads. For the moment, however, when we are not violently persecuting them we are like Goldsmith's villagers, wondering how their little heads can carry all they know and ranking them as passing rich on four hundred pounds a year when they are lucky enough to get paid for their work instead of persecuted.

WE CAN AND MUST LIVE LONGER

Considering now that I have lived fourteen years longer than twice as long as Mozart or Mendelssohn, and that within my experience men and women, especially women, are younger at fifty than they were at thirty in the middle of the nineteenth century, it is impossible to resist at least a strong suspicion that the term of human life cannot be fixed at seventy years or indeed fixed at all. If we master the art of living instead of digging our graves with our teeth as we do at present we may conceivably reach a point at

646

which the sole cause of death will be the fatal accident which is statistically inevitable if we live long enough. In short, it is not proved that there is such a thing as natural death: it is life that is natural and infinite.

How long, then, would it take us to mature into competent rulers of great modern States instead of, as at present, trying vainly to govern empires with the capacity of village headmen. In my Methuselah cycle I put it at three hundred years: a century of childhood and adolescence, a century of administration, and a century of oracular senatorism.

But nobody can foresee what periods my imaginary senators will represent. The pace of evolutionary development is not constant: the baby in the womb recapitulates within a few months an evolution which our biologists assure us took millions of years to acquire. The old axiom that Nature never jumps has given way to a doubt whether Nature is not an incorrigible kangaroo. What is certain is that new faculties, however long they may be dreamt of and desired, come at last suddenly and miraculously like the balancing of the bicyclist, the skater, and the acrobat. The development of homo sapiens into a competent political animal may occur in the same way.

THE NEXT DISCOVERY

Meanwhile here we are, with our incompetence armed with atomic bombs. Now power civilizes and develops mankind, though not without having first been abused to the point of wiping out entire civilizations. If the atomic bomb wipes out ours we shall just have to begin again. We may agree on paper not to use it as it is too dangerous and destructive; but tomorrow may see the discovery of that poisonous gas lighter than air and capable before it evaporates through the stratosphere of killing all the inhabitants of a city without damaging its buildings or sewers or water supplies or railways or electric plants. Victory might then win cities if it could repopulate them soon enough, whereas atomic bombing leaves nothing for anyone, victor or vanquished. It is conceivable even that the next great invention may create an overwhelming interest in pacific civilization and wipe out war. You never can tell.

Ayot Saint Lawrence
1945

PROGRAM NOTE

The following note was printed in the program of the first production of the play in London:

Geneva is a title that speaks for itself. The critics are sure to complain that I have not solved all the burning political problems of the present and future in it, and restored peace to Europe and Asia. They always do. I am flattered by the implied attribution to me of Omniscience and Omnipotence; but I am also infuriated by the unreasonableness of the demand. I am neither Omniscient nor Omnipotent; and the utmost I or any other playwright can do is to extract comedy and tragedy from the existing situation and wait to see what will become of it.

Unfortunately, nobody seems to know what the existing situation is. For instance, how many people have heard of the Intellectual Co-operation Committee? It will probably be dismissed by the critics as an overstrained fiction. It is nothing of the sort. The League of Nations had not been long in existence when a Frenchman, perceiving that without intellectual co-operation the League could do nothing but practise the old diplomacy, founded the Committee in Paris. Everyone was delighted; and the most eminent intellects in the world gave their names as intellectual co-operators. The Frenchman gave a million francs to endow the Committee; but as the French franc had dropped to twopence (having been largely borrowed at tenpence) the Committee was stony-broke at the end of a month. It still survived in a little office somewhere (I have invented one in Geneva for it in the play) and even did and does some clerical work in listing universities, learned societies, and the like; but intellectually it sank into a profound catalepsy.

When Romain Rolland, with the late Henri Barbusse and their friends tried from time to time to organize some international movement on the extreme Left, and invited me, as they always did, to join them, I asked them why

649

they did not operate through the I.C. Committee of the League, which was sleeping ready to their hands. The suggestion struck them dumb.

At last the Committee, which occasionally woke up in the person of Gilbert Murray, asked me to correspond with the League. This very nearly struck me dumb; for what on earth was I to correspond about?

Now Gilbert Murray has a strong sense of humour and believes in telepathy. He practises it too. And so it came about that I found it growing on me that there was some fun to be got on the stage out of the Committee.

That was how the play began. How it will finish—for in the theatre it only stops: it does not finish—nobody knows. I call your attention, however, to one novelty. Instead of making the worst of all the dictators, which only drives them out of the League, I have made the best of them, and may even challenge them to live up to their portraits if they can. I hope they will like it. Also I hope that you will.

GENEVA

ACT I

A MAY morning in Geneva, in a meagrely equipped office with secondhand furniture, much the worse for wear, consisting of a dingy writing table with an old typewriter on it in the middle of the room, a revolving chair for the typist, an old press which has not been painted or varnished for many years, and three chairs for visitors against the wall near the door. The stove, an undecorated iron one of the plainest sort, designed rather for central heating in a cellar than for an inhabited apartment, is to the typist's right, the press facing it at the opposite side on the typist's left. The door is beside the press. The window is behind the typist.

A young Englishwoman is seated in the revolving chair. From the state of the table she seems to have been working at the compilation of a card index, as there are cards scattered about, and an open case to put them in, also a pile of foolscap from which she has been copying the card inscriptions. But at present she is not at work. She is smoking and reading an illustrated magazine with her heels on the table. A thermos flask, a cup and saucer, and a packet of cigarettes are beside her on a sliding shelf drawn out from the table. She is a self-satisfied young person, fairly attractive and well aware of it. Her dress, though smartly cut, is factory made; and her speech and manners are London suburban.

Somebody knocks at the door. She hastily takes her heels off the table; jumps up; throws her cigarette into the stove; snatches the things off the sliding shelf and hides them in the press; finally resumes her seat and looks as busy as possible.

THE TYPIST [calling] Entrez, s'il vous plaît.

A middle-aged gentleman of distinguished appearance, with a blond beard and moustache, top hatted, frock coated, and gloved, comes in. He contemplates the room and the young woman with evident surprise.

651

HE. Pardon, mademoiselle: I seek the office of the International Committee for Intellectual Co-operation.

SHE. Yes: thats quite all right. Take a seat, please.

HE [*hesitating*] Thank you; but my business is of great importance: I must see your chief. This is not the head office, is it?

SHE. No: the head office is in Paris. This is all there is here. Not much of a place, is it?

HE. Well, I must confess that after visiting the magnificent palace of the International Labor Office and the new quarters of the Secretariat, I expected to find the Committee for Intellectual Co-operation lodged in some imposingly monumental structure.

SHE. Oh, isn't it scandalous? I wish youd write to the papers about it. Do please sit down.

HE. Thank you. [*He is about to take one of the chairs from the wall*].

SHE. No, not that one: one of its legs isnt safe: it's there only for show. Will you please take the other?

HE. Can the Committee not afford you a new chair?

SHE. It cant afford anything. The intellectual budget is the interest on two million paper francs that one is glad to get threepence for: they used to be tuppence. So here I am in one rotten little room on the third floor of a tumbledown old house full of rats. And as to my salary I should be ashamed to name it. A Church charity would be ashamed to pay it.

HE. I am utterly astounded. [*He takes a sound chair from the wall; places it near the office table; and sits down*]. The intellectual co-operation of sixty nations must be a very extensive business. How can it possibly be conducted in this bare little place?

SHE. Oh, I conduct it all right. It's never in a hurry, you know.

HE. But really—pardon me if I am taking too much of your time—

SHE. Oh, thats quite all right. I'm only too glad to have

652

a bit of chat with somebody. Nobody ever comes in here: people dont seem to know that the Committee exists.

HE. Do you mean that you have nothing to do?

SHE. Oh no. I tell you I have to do all the intellectual co-operation. I have to do it singlehanded too: I havnt even an office boy to help me. And theres no end to the work. If it werent, as I say, that theres no hurry about it, I should never get through it. Just look here at this nice little job theyve given me! A card index of all the universities with the names and addresses of their bursars and their vice chancellors. And there is a correspondence about the protection of professional titles that takes up half my time.

HE. And do they call that intellectual co-operation?

SHE. Well, what else would you call it?

HE. It is mere compilation. How are the intellectual giants who form your committee bringing the enormous dynamic force of their brains, their prestige, their authority, to bear on the destinies of the nations? What are they doing to correct the mistakes of our ignorant politicians?

SHE. Well, we have their names on our notepaper, you know. What more can they do? You cant expect them to sit in this little hole talking to people. I have never seen one of them.

HE. So they leave it all to you?

SHE. Oh, I wouldnt say all. Theres the head office in Paris, you know, and some offices in other countries. I suppose they do their bit; and anyhow we all do a lot of writing to oneanother. But I must say it's as dull as ditchwater. When I took the job I thought it was going to be interesting, and that I'd see all the great men. I am ambitious, you know: I won a London County Council scholarship. I wanted a job that would draw out my faculties, if you understand me. But theres nothing to do here that any common typist couldnt do. And nobody ever comes near the place. Oh, it is dull.

HE. Shall I give you an interesting job, mademoiselle? One that would get you appreciated and perhaps a little

653

talked about?

SHE. I'll just jump at it—if it is all right.

HE. How all right?

SHE. Morally, you know. No hanky panky. I am respectable; and I mean to keep respectable.

HE. I pledge you my word that my intentions are completely honorable.

SHE. Well, what about the pay? And how long will the job last? The work here may be dull; and the pay is just short of starvation; but I have the appointment for 25 years certain; and I darent give it up for anything chancy. You dont know what it is to be out of a job.

HE. I shall not ask you to give up your post here. On the contrary, it is essential that you should keep it. But I think I can make it more interesting for you. And I should of course make you a suitable present if at any time you found that your emoluments here were insufficient.

SHE. They are. But I mustnt take bribes, you know.

HE. You need not. Any friendly service I may be able to render will be entirely independent of your official work here.

SHE. Look here: I dont half like this. Whats the game?

THE JEW. I must begin by explaining that I am a Jew.

SHE. I dont believe you. You dont look like one.

THE JEW. I am not a primitive Hittite. You cannot draw my nose in profile by simply writing down the number six. My hair is not black, nor do I wear it in excessively oiled ringlets. I have all the marks of a German blond. German is my native language: in fact I am in every sense a German. But I worship in the synagogue; and when I worship I put my hat on, whereas a German takes it off. On this ground they class me as a non-Aryan, which is nonsense, as there is no such thing as an Aryan.

SHE. I'm so glad to hear you say that. The Germans here say that I am an Aryan; but I tell them I am nothing of the kind: I'm an Englishwoman. Not a common Englishwoman, of course: I'm a Camberwell woman; and

654

though the west end may turn up its nose at Camberwell, Camberwell is better than Peckham any day in the week.

THE JEW. No doubt. I have not been there.

SHE. I never could abide Peckham people. They are disliked everywhere. It's instinctive, somehow. Havnt you noticed it?

THE JEW. All peoples are disliked in the lump. The English are disliked: the Germans are disliked: the French are disliked. The Protestants are disliked; and all their hundreds of sects dislike oneanother. So are the Catholics, the Jesuits, the Freemasons. You tell me that the inhabitants of Peckham are disliked: no doubt they deserve it.

SHE. They do.

THE JEW. Some of the greatest men have disliked the human race. But for Noah, its Creator would have drowned it. Can we deny that He had good reasons for disliking it? Can I deny that there are good reasons for disliking Jews? On the contrary, I dislike most of them myself.

SHE. Oh, dont say that. Ive known lots of quite nice Jews. What I say is why pick on the Jews, as if they were any worse than other people?

THE JEW. That is precisely my business here today. I find you most intelligent—most sympathetic.

SHE. Come now! none of that. Whats the game?

THE JEW. I have been assaulted, plundered, and driven from my native soil by its responsible ruler. I, as a ruined individual, can do nothing. But the League of Nations can act through its Committee for Intellectual Co-operation. The Committee can act through the permanent court of International Justice at the Hague, which is also an organ of the League. My business here is to ask the Committee to apply to the court for a warrant against the responsible ruler. I charge him with assault and battery, burglary—

SHE. Burglary! Did they break into your house?

THE JEW. I cannot speak of it. Everything I treasured. Wrecked! Smashed! Defiled! Never will I forgive: never can I forget.

SHE. But why didnt you call the police?

THE JEW. Mademoiselle: the police did it. The Government did it. The Dictator who controls the police is responsible before Europe! before civilization! I look to the League of Nations for redress. It alone can call unrighteous rulers to account. The initiative must be taken by its Committee for Intellectual Co-operation: that is, for the moment, by you, mademoiselle.

SHE. But what can I do? I cant go out and collar your unrighteous ruler.

THE JEW. No, mademoiselle. What you must do is to write to the International Court, calling on it to issue a warrant for the arrest of my oppressor on a charge of attempting to exterminate a section of the human race.

SHE. Well, it seems like taking a lot on myself, doesnt it?

THE JEW. Not at all. You will be acting, not for yourself, but for the intellect of Europe. I assure you it is the correct course.

SHE. But I'm not sure that I know how to write a letter with all those police court things in it.

THE JEW. It is quite simple. But if you will allow me I will draft the letter for you.

SHE. Oh I say, Mister Jew, I dont like this.

THE JEW. Then write the letter yourself. I am sure you will do it perfectly. It will be an opportunity for you to shew the Committee what you are made of.

SHE. Well, look here. I have a particular friend, an American journalist. Would you mind if I shewed him your draft before I send it off?

THE JEW. An American journalist! Excellent, excellent. By all means submit my draft to him and ask him to correct it if necessary. My English is German English, and may leave something to be desired.

SHE. Yes: thatll be splendid. Thank you ever so much.

THE JEW. Not at all. [*Rising*] I will bring the draft in the course of the afternoon. Au revoir, then.

SHE. Au revoir.

They shake hands cordially. Meanwhile the door is opened by an obstinate-looking middle-aged man of respectable but not aristocratic appearance, speaking English like a shopkeeper from the provinces, or perhaps, by emigration, the dominions.

NEWCOMER. Can I see the boss, miss?

SHE [*with haughty nonchalance in a would-be distinguished accent startlingly unlike her unaffected deference to the gentlemanlike Jew*] I am sorry. Our chiefs are scattered over Europe, very eminent persons, you know. Can I do anything?

NEWCOMER [*looking at the Jewish gentleman*] I'm afraid I'm interrupting.

THE JEW. Not at all: my business is finished. [*Clicking his heels and bowing*] Until the afternoon, mademoiselle. Monsieur— [*He bows to the newcomer, and goes out*].

SHE. You can sit down.

NEWCOMER. I will keep you only a minute, miss. [*He sits and takes out some notes he has made*].

SHE. Be as quick as you can, please. I am busy this morning.

NEWCOMER. Yes: you have the brainwork of the world on your shoulders here. When any of the nations goes off the rails, this is the place to have it put back. Thats so, isnt it?

SHE [*with aplomb*] Undoubtedly.

NEWCOMER. Well, it's like this. In my country weve had an election. We thought it lay between our usual people: the National Party and the Labor Party; but it was won by an upstart kind of chap who called himself a Business Democrat. He got a clear majority over the Nationals and the Labor Party; so it was up to him to form a Government. And what do you suppose the fellow did when he became Prime Minister?

SHE [*bored*] Cant imagine, I'm sure.

NEWCOMER. He said he had been returned to power as

657

a business democrat, and that the business part of it meant that he was not to waste time, but to get the nation's work done as quickly as possible.

SHE. Quite, quite. Nothing to complain of in that, is there?

NEWCOMER. Wait. I'm going to astonish you. He said the country had decided by its democratic vote that it should be governed by him and his party for the next five years, and that no opposition could be tolerated. He said the defeated minority must step down and out instead of staying there to obstruct and delay and annoy him. Of course the Opposition werent going to stand that: they refused to leave the Chamber. So he adjourned the House until next day; and when the Opposition turned up the police wouldnt let them in. Most of them couldnt get as far as the doors, because the Prime Minister had organized a body of young men called the Clean Shirts, to help the police.

SHE. Well?

NEWCOMER. Well!!!! Is that all you have to say to me?

SHE. What do you expect me to say? It seems all right to me. It's what any man of business would do. Wouldnt you?

NEWCOMER. Of course I should do it in business; but this is politics.

SHE. Well! arnt politics business?

NEWCOMER. Of course theyre not. Just the opposite. You know that, dont you?

SHE. Oh, quite, quite.

NEWCOMER. What I say is, business methods are business methods; and parliamentary methods are parliamentary methods.

SHE [*brightly*] "And never the twain shall meet," as Kipling puts it.

NEWCOMER. No: I dont hold with Kipling. Too imperialist for me. I'm a democrat.

SHE. But not a business democrat, if I follow you.

658

NEWCOMER. No, no: not a business democrat. A proper democrat. I'm all for the rights of minorities.

SHE. But I always thought that democracy meant the right of the majority to have its way.

NEWCOMER. Oh no: that would be the end of all liberty. You have nothing to say against liberty, I hope.

SHE. I have nothing to say against anything. I am not here to discuss politics with everyone who walks into my office. What do you want?

NEWCOMER. Well, heres a Prime Minister committing high treason and rebellion and breach of privilege; levying armed forces against the Crown; violating the constitution; setting up a dictatorship and obstructing the lawful ingress of duly elected members to the legislative Chamber. Whats to be done with him?

SHE. Quite simple. I shall apply to the International Court at the Hague for a warrant for his arrest on all those charges. You can look in at the end of the week, when the answer from the Hague will have arrived. You will supply me with the man's name and the particulars—

NEWCOMER [*putting his notes on the table before her*] Here they are, miss. By Gosh, thats a splendid idea.

SHE. Thank you. That is all. Good morning.

NEWCOMER [*rising and going to the door*] Well, you know how to do business here: theres no mistake about that. Good morning, miss.

As he is going out the door opens in his face; and a widow comes in: a Creole lady of about forty, with the remains of a gorgeous and opulent southern beauty. Her imposing style and dress at once reduce the young lady of the office to nervous abjection.

THE WIDOW. Are you the president of the Intellectual Co-operation Committee of the League of Nations?

NEWCOMER. No, maam. This lady will do all you require [*he goes out*].

THE WIDOW. Am I to take that seriously? My business is important. I came here to place it before a body of persons of European distinction. I am not prepared to discuss it with an irresponsible young woman.

SHE. I am afraid I dont look the part, do I? I am only the staff, so to speak. Still, anything I can do I shall be most happy.

THE WIDOW. But where are your chiefs?

SHE. Ah, there you have me. They live all over the world, as you might say.

THE WIDOW. But do they not come here to attend to their business?

SHE. Well, you see, there is really nothing for them to attend to. It's only intellectual business, you know.

THE WIDOW. But do they not take part in the Assembly of the League?

SHE. Some of them have been, once. Nobody ever goes to the Assembly twice if they can help it.

THE WIDOW. But I must see somebody—somebody of importance.

SHE. Well, I'm sorry. Theres nobody but me. I can do whatever is necessary. Did you by any chance want a warrant from the International Court at the Hague?

THE WIDOW. Yes: that is exactly what I do want. A death warrant.

SHE. A what?!!

THE WIDOW. A death warrant. I will sit down, if you will allow me.

SHE. Oh please—

THE WIDOW [*sitting down*] Do you see that? [*She takes an automatic pistol from her bag, and throws it on the table*].

SHE. Oh, thats not allowed in Geneva. Put it up quick. Somebody might come in.

THE WIDOW [*replacing the pistol in her bag*] This is the most absurd place. In my country everybody carries a gun.

SHE. What country, may I ask?

THE WIDOW. The Republic of the Earthly Paradise.

SHE. My mother has a school prize called The Earthly Paradise. What a coincidence!

THE WIDOW. Then you know that the Earthly Paradise is one of the leading States in the world in culture and purity of race, and that its capital contained more than two thousand white inhabitants before the last revolution. There must be still at least fifteen hundred left.

SHE. But is it a member of the League?

THE WIDOW. Of course it is. And allow me to remind you that by its veto it can put a stop to all action by the League until its affairs are properly attended to.

SHE. Can it? I didnt know that. Of course I shall be only too pleased to apply for a warrant; but I'd rather not call it a death warrant. Death warrant sounds a bit thick, if you understand me. All you need do is to give me a list of the charges you make against—well, against whoever it is.

THE WIDOW. Simply one charge of the wilful murder of my late husband by the President of the Earthly Paradise.

SHE. Surely if a president kills anyone it's an execution; but if anyone kills a president it's an assassination.

THE WIDOW. And is not that just the state of things the League of Nations is here to put a stop to?

SHE. Oh, dont ask me. All I know about the League is that it pays my salary. Just give me the gentleman's name and who he murdered. Murder stories are thrillingly interesting.

THE WIDOW. You would not think so if you lived in a country where there is at least one murder in every family.

SHE. What an awful place! Is it as barbarous as that?

THE WIDOW. Barbarous! Certainly not. The Earthly Paradise is the most civilized country in the world. Its constitution is absolutely democratic: every president must swear to observe it in every particular. The Church is abolished: no moral authority is recognized except that of the people's will. The president and parliament are elected

661

by adult suffrage every two years. So are all the judges and all the officials, even the road sweepers. All these reforms, which have made The Earthly Paradise the most advanced member of the League of Nations, were introduced by my late husband the sixth president. He observed the constitution strictly. The elections were conducted with absolute integrity. The ballot was secret. The people felt free for the first time in their lives. Immediately after the elections the budget was passed providing for two years. My husband then prorogued the Parliament until the end of that period, and governed the country according to his own ideas whilst the people enjoyed themselves and made money in their own ways without any political disturbances or arguments. He was re-elected three times, and is now known in the Paradise as the father of his country.

SHE. But you said he was murdered, and that the president murdered him. How could that be if he was the president? He couldnt murder himself.

THE WIDOW. Unhappily he had certain weaknesses. He was an affectionate husband: I may even say an uxorious one; but he was very far from being faithful to me. When he abolished the Church he would have abolished marriage also if public opinion would have stood for it. And he was much too indulgent to his enemies. Naturally, whenever he won an election his opponent raised an army and attempted a revolution; for we are a high spirited race and do not submit to the insult of defeat at the polls. But my husband was a military genius. He had no difficulty in putting down these revolutions; but instead of having his opponent shot in the proper and customary way, he pardoned him and challenged him to try again as often as he pleased. I urged him again and again not to trifle with his own safety in this way. Useless: he would not listen to me. At last I found out the reason. He was carrying on an intrigue with his opponent's wife, my best friend. I had to shoot her—shoot her dead—my dearest friend [*she is overcome with emotion*].

662

SHE. Oh, you shouldnt have done that. That was going a little too far, wasnt it?

THE WIDOW. Public opinion obliged me to do it as a self-respecting wife and mother. God knows I did not want to do it: I loved her: I would have let her have ten husbands if I had had them to give. But what can you do against the etiquette of your class? My brothers had to fight duels and kill their best friends because it was etiquette.

SHE. But where were the police? Werent you tried for it?

THE WIDOW. Of course I was tried for it; but I pleaded the unwritten law and was acquitted. Unfortunately the scandal destroyed my husband's popularity. He was defeated at the next election by the man he had so foolishly spared. Instead of raising an army to avenge this outrage, my husband, crushed by the loss of his mistress, just moped at home until they came and shot him. They had come to shoot me; and [*with a fresh burst of tears*] I wish to Heaven they had; but I was out at the time; so they thought they might as well shoot my husband as there was nobody else to shoot.

SHE. What a dreadful thing for you!

THE WIDOW. Not at all. It served him right, absolutely. He never spoke to me after I had to kill the woman we both loved more than we loved oneanother. I believe he would have been only too glad if they had shot me; and I dont blame him. What is the use of the League of Nations if it cannot put a stop to such horrors?

SHE. Well, it's not the League's business, is it?

THE WIDOW. Not the League's business! Do you realize, young woman, that if the League does not bring the murderer of my husband to justice my son will be obliged to take up a blood feud and shoot the murderer with his own hands, though they were at the same school and are devoted to oneanother? It is against Nature, against God: if your committee does not stop it I will shoot every member of it, and you too. [*She rises*]. Excuse me. I can bear

663

no more of this: I shall faint unless I get into the fresh air. [*She takes papers and a card from her bag and throws them on the table*]. There are the particulars. This is my card. Good morning. [*She goes as abruptly as she came in*].

SHE [*rising*] Good—

But the widow has gone and the young office lady, greatly upset, drops back into her seat with a prolonged Well!!!!!

A smart young American gentleman looks in.

THE GENTLEMAN. Say, baby: who is the old girl in the mantilla? Carmen's grandmother, eh? [*He sits on the table edge, facing her, on her right*].

SHE. A murderess. Her dearest friend. She had to. Horrible. Theyve shot her husband. She says she will shoot me unless the League stops it.

HE. Grand! Fine!

SHE. Is that all you care? Well, look at my morning's work! Persecutions, revolutions, murders, all sorts. The office has been full of people all the morning. We shant have it all to ourselves any more.

HE. No, baby; but I shall have some dough to spend. I have been kicking my heels here for months faking news for my people when there was no news. And here you hand me a mouthful. What a scoop for me, honey! You are a peach. [*He kisses her*].

Someone knocks at the door.

SHE. Shsh! Someone knocking.

They separate hastily, he going to the stove and she composing herself in her chair.

HE. Come in! Entrez! Herein!

A gaitered English bishop enters. He is old, soft, gentle and rather infirm.

THE BISHOP. Excuse me; but does anyone here speak English?

HE [*putting on all the style he is capable of*] My native language, my lord. Also this lady's. [*Exchange of bows*]. Will you take a pew, my lord?

664

BISHOP [*sitting*] Thank you. Your stairs are somewhat trying to me: I am not so young as I was; and they tell me I must be careful not to overstrain my heart. The journey to Geneva is a terrible one for a man of my years. Nothing but the gravest emergency could have forced me to undertake it.

HE. Is the emergency one in which we can have the honor of assisting you, my lord?

BISHOP. Your advice would be invaluable to me; for I really dont know what to do or where to go here. I am met with indifference—with apathy—when I reveal a state of things that threatens the very existence of civilized society, of religion, of the family, of the purity of womanhood, and even, they tell me, of our commercial prosperity. Are people mad? Dont they know? Dont they care?

HE. My! my! my! [*He takes a chair to the end of the table nearest the stove*] Pray be seated, my lord. What has happened?

BISHOP [*sinking into the chair*] Sir: they are actually preaching Communism in my diocese. Communism!!! My butler, who has been in the palace for forty years, a most devoted and respectable man, tells me that my footman— I am the only bishop in England who can afford to keep a footman now—that my footman is a cell.

HE. A sell? You mean that he has disappointed you?

BISHOP. No: not that sort of cell. C.E. double L. A communist cell. Like a bee in a hive. Planted on me by the Communists to make their dreadful propaganda in my household! And my grandson at Oxford has joined a Communist club. The Union—the Oxford Union—has raised the red flag. It is dreadful. And my granddaughter a nudist! I was graciously allowed to introduce my daughters to good Queen Victoria. If she could see my granddaughter she would call the police. Is it any wonder that I have a weak heart? Shock after shock. My own footman, son of the most respectable parents, and actually an Anglo-Catholic!

665

HE. I can hardly believe it, my lord. What times we are living in!

SHE [*with her most official air*] Surely this is a case for the International Court at the Hague, my lord.

BISHOP. Yes, yes. An invaluable suggestion. The Court must stop the Bolshies from disseminating their horrible doctrines in England. It is in the treaties.

He is interrupted by the entrance of a very smart Russian gentleman, whom he receives with pleased recognition.

BISHOP [*rising*] Ah, my dear sir, we meet again. [*To the others*] I had the pleasure of making this gentleman's acquaintance last night at my hotel. His interest in the Church of England kept us up talking long after my usual hour for retirement. [*Shaking his hand warmly*] How do you do, my dear friend? how do you do?

RUSSIAN. Quite well, thank you, my lord. Am I interrupting your business?

BISHOP. No no no no: I beg you to remain. You will help: you will sympathize.

RUSSIAN. You are very kind, my lord: I am quite at your service.

BISHOP [*murmuring gratefully as he resumes his seat*] Thank you. Thank you.

RUSSIAN. Let me introduce myself. I am Commissar Posky of the Sovnarkom and Politbureau, Soviet delegate to the League Council.

BISHOP [*aghast, staggering to his feet*] You are a Bolshevik!

COMMISSAR. Assuredly.

The Bishop faints. General concern. The men rush to him.

COMMISSAR. Do not lift him yet. He will recover best as he is.

SHE. I have some iced lemonade in my thermos. Shall I give him some?

BISHOP [*supine*] Where am I? Has anything happened?

666

GENEVA

HE. You are in the office of the Intellectual Co-operation Committee in Geneva. You have had a slight heart attack.

COMMISSAR. Lie still, comrade. You will be quite yourself presently.

BISHOP [*sitting up*] It is not my heart. [*To the Commissar*] It is moral shock. You presented yourself to me yesterday as a cultivated and humane gentleman, interested in the Church of England. And now it turns out that you are a Bolshie. What right had you to practise such a cruel imposture on me? [*He rises: the Commissar helps him*] No: I can rise without assistance, thank you. [*He attempts to do so, but collapses into the arms of the Commissar*].

COMMISSAR. Steady, comrade.

BISHOP [*regaining his seat with the Commissar's assistance*] Again I must thank you. But I shudder at the touch of your bloodstained hands.

COMMISSAR. My hands are not bloodstained, comrade. I have not imposed on you. You have not quite recovered yet, I think. I am your friend of last night. Dont you recognize me?

BISHOP. A Bolshie! If I had known, sir, I should have repudiated your advances with abhorrence.

HE [*again posting himself at the stove*] Russia is a member of the League, my lord. This gentleman's standing here is the same as that of the British Foreign Secretary.

BISHOP [*intensely*] Never. Never.

SHE [*airily*] And what can we do for you, Mr Posky? I'm sorry I cant offer you a chair. That one isnt safe.

COMMISSAR. Pray dont mention it. My business will take only a moment. As you know, the Soviet Government has gone as far as possible in agreeing not to countenance or subsidize any propaganda of Communism which takes the form of a political conspiracy to overthrow the British National Government.

BISHOP. And in violation of that agreement you have corrupted my footman and changed him from an honest

667

and respectable young Englishman into a Cell.

COMMISSAR. Have we? I know nothing of your footman. If he is intelligent enough to become a Communist,
as so many famous Englishmen did long before the Russian
revolution, we cannot prevent him. But we do not employ
him as our agent nor support him financially in any way.

HE. But what, then, is your difficulty, Comrade Posky?

COMMISSAR. We have just discovered that there is a
most dangerous organization at work in Russia, financed
from the British Isles, having for its object the overthrow
of the Soviet system and the substitution of the Church of
England and the British Constitution.

BISHOP. And why not, sir? Why not? Could any object
be more desirable, more natural? Would you in your blind
hatred of British institutions and of all liberty of thought
and speech, make it a crime to advocate a system which is
universally admitted to be the best and freest in the
world?

COMMISSAR. We do not think so. And as the obligation
to refrain from this sort of propaganda is reciprocal, you
are bound by it just as we are.

HE. But what is this seditious organization you have
just discovered?

COMMISSAR. It is called the Society for the Propagation
of the Gospel in Foreign Parts. It has agents everywhere.
They call themselves missionaries.

BISHOP. I cannot bear this: the man is insane. I sub-
scribe to the Society almost beyond my means. It is a body
of the highest respectability and piety.

COMMISSAR. You are misinformed: its doctrines are of
the most subversive kind. They are penetrated to my own
household. My wife is a busy professional woman, and my
time is taken up altogether by public work. We are absolutely dependent for our domestic work on our housekeeper Feodorovna Ballyboushka. We were ideally happy
with this excellent woman for years. In her youth she was
a udarnik, what you call a shock worker.

BISHOP. You are all shock workers in Russia now. You have seen the effect on me?

COMMISSAR. That was in the early days of the revolution, when she was young and ardent. Now she is elderly; and her retirement into domestic service suits her years and her helpful and affectionate temperament. Two months ago an extraordinary change came over her. She refused to do any work that was not immediately necessary, on the ground that the end of the world is at hand. She declared that she was in a condition which she described as "saved," and interrupted my work continually with attempts to save me. She had long fits of crying because she could not bear the thought of my wife spending eternity in hell. She accused the Soviets of being the hornets prophesied in the Book of Revelation. We were about to have her certified as insane—most reluctantly; for we loved our dear Ballyboushka—when we discovered that she had been hypnotized by this illegal Society. I warned our Secret Police, formerly known to you as the Gay Pay Ooh. They followed up the clue and arrested four missionaries.

BISHOP. And shot them. Christian martyrs! All who fall into the hands of the terrible Gay Pay Ooh are shot at once, without trial, without the ministrations of the Church. But I will have a memorial service said for them. To that extent at last I can defeat your Godless tyranny.

COMMISSAR. You are quite mistaken: they have not been shot. They will be sent back to England: that is all.

BISHOP [*passionately*] What right had you to arrest them? How dare you arrest Englishmen? How dare you persecute religion?

COMMISSAR. They have been very patiently examined by our official psychologists, who report that they can discover nothing that could reasonably be called religion in their minds. They are obsessed with tribal superstitions of the most barbarous kind. They believe in human sacrifices, in what they call the remission of sins by the shedding of blood. No man's life would be safe in Russia if such doctrines were propagated there.

BISHOP. But you dont understand. Oh, what dreadful ignorance!

COMMISSAR. Let us pass on to another point. Our police have found a secret document of your State Church, called the Thirty-nine Articles.

BISHOP. Secret! It is in the Prayer Book!

COMMISSAR. It is not read in church. That fact speaks for itself. Our police have found most of the articles incomprehensible; but there is one, the eighteenth, which declares that all Russians are to be held accursed. How would you like it if our chief cultural institution, endowed by our government, the Komintern, were to send its agents into England to teach that every Englishman is to be held accursed?

BISHOP. But surely, surely, you would not compare the Komintern to the Church of England!!

COMMISSAR. Comrade Bishop: the Komintern is the State Church in Russia exactly as the Church of England is the State Church in Britain.

The Bishop slides to the floor in another faint.

SHE. Oh! He's gone off again. Shall I get my thermos?

HE. I should break things to him more gently, Mr Posky. People die of shock. He maynt recover next time. In fact, he maynt recover this time.

COMMISSAR. What am I to do? I have said nothing that could possibly shock any educated reasonable person; but this man does not seem to know what sort of world he is living in.

SHE. He's an English bishop, you know.

COMMISSAR. Well? Is he not a rational human being?

SHE. Oh no: nothing as common as that. I tell you he's a bishop.

BISHOP. Where am I? Why am I lying on the floor? What has happened?

HE. You are in the Intellectual Co-operation Bureau in Geneva; and you have just been told that the Russian

GENEVA

Komintern is analogous to the Church of England.

BISHOP [*springing to his feet unaided, his eyes blazing*] I still have life enough left in me to deny it. Karl Marx—Antichrist—said that the sweet and ennobling consolations of our faith are opium given to the poor to enable them to endure the hardships of that state of life to which it has pleased God to call them. Does your Komintern teach that blasphemy or does it not?

COMMISSAR. Impossible. There are no poor in Russia.

BISHOP. Oh! [*he drops dead*].

HE [*feeling his pulse*] I am afraid you have shocked him once too often, Comrade. His pulse has stopped. He is dead.

POSKY. Was he ever alive? To me he was incredible.

SHE. I suppose my thermos is of no use now. Shall I ring up a doctor?

HE. I think you had better ring up the police. But I say, Mr Posky, what a scoop!

COMMISSAR. A scoop? I do not understand. What is a scoop?

HE. Read all the European papers tomorrow and youll see.

ACT II

OFFICE of the secretary of the League of Nations. Except for the small writing table at which the secretary is seated there is no office furniture. The walls are covered with engraved prints or enlarged photographs of kings, presidents, and dictators, mostly in military uniforms. Above these bellicose pictures the cornice is decorated with a row of plaster doves in low relief. There is one large picture in oils, representing a lifesize Peace, with tiny figures, also in military uniforms, kneeling round her feet and bowing their heads piously beneath the wreath which she offers them. This picture faces the secretary from the other side of the room as he sits at his table with his back to the window presenting his left profile to anyone entering from the door, which is in the middle of the wall between them. A suite of half a dozen chairs is ranged round the walls, except one, which stands near the writing table for the convenience of people interviewing the secretary.

He is a disillusioned official with a habit of dogged patience acquired in the course of interviews with distinguished statesmen of different nations, all in a condition of invincible ignorance as to the spirit of Geneva and the constitution of the League of Nations, and each with a national axe to grind. On this occasion he is rather exceptionally careworn. One pities him, as he is of a refined type, and, one guesses, began as a Genevan idealist. Age fifty or thereabouts.

There is a telephone on the table which he is at present using.

THE SECRETARY. Yes: send her up instantly. Remind me of her name. What?! ... Ammonia? Nonsense! that cant be her name. Spell it ... V E? ... Oh, *B* E. Do you mean to say that her name is Begonia? Begonia Brown? ... Farcical.

He replaces the receiver as Begonia enters. She is the Intellectual Co-operation typist. She is in walking dress, *cheap, but very smart.*

THE SECRETARY. Miss Brown?

BEGONIA [*with her best smile*] Yes.

THE SECRETARY. Sit down.

BEGONIA [*complying*] Kew [*short for Thank you*].

THE SECRETARY [*gravely*] You have heard the news, no doubt?

BEGONIA. Oh yes. Jack Palamedes has won the dancing tournament. I had ten francs on him; and I have won a hundred. Had you anything on?

THE SECRETARY [*still more gravely*] I am afraid you will think me very ignorant, Miss Brown; but I have never heard of Mr Palamedes.

BEGONIA. Fancy that! He's the talk of Geneva, I assure you.

THE SECRETARY. There are other items of news, Miss Brown. Germany has withdrawn from the League.

BEGONIA. And a good riddance, if you ask me. My father lost a lot of money through the war. Otherwise— you wont mind my telling you—youd never have got me slaving at a typewriter here for my living.

THE SECRETARY. No doubt. A further item is that the British Empire has declared war on Russia.

BEGONIA. Well, what could you expect us to do with those awful Bolshies? We should have done it long ago. But thank goodness we're safe in Geneva, you and I.

THE SECRETARY. We are safe enough everywhere, so far. The war is one of sanctions only.

BEGONIA. More shame for us, say I. I should give those Bolshies the bayonet: thats the way to talk to scum of that sort. I cant contain myself when I think of all the murder and slavery of them Soviets—[*correcting herself*] those Soviets.

THE SECRETARY. In consequence Japan has declared war on Russia and is therefore in military alliance with Britain. And the result of that is that Australia, New Zealand and Canada have repudiated the war and formed

673

an anti-Japanese alliance with the United States under the title of the New British Federation. South Africa may join them at any moment.

BEGONIA [*flushing with indignation*] Do you mean that theyve broken up our dear Empire?

THE SECRETARY. They have said nothing about that.

BEGONIA. Oh, then thats quite all right. You know, when I was at school I was chosen five times to recite on Empire Day; and in my very first year, when I was the smallest child there, I presented the bouquet to King George's sister, who came to our prize giving. Say a word against the Empire, and you have finished with Begonia Brown.

THE SECRETARY. Then you went to school, did you?

BEGONIA. Well, of course: what do you take me for? I went to school for seven years and never missed a single day. I got fourteen prizes for regular attendance.

THE SECRETARY. Good God!

BEGONIA. What did you say?

THE SECRETARY. Nothing. I was about to tell you what has happened in Quetzalcopolis, the chief seaport of the Earthly Paradise.

BEGONIA. I know. In Central America, isnt it?

THE SECRETARY. Yes. The mob there has attacked the British Consulate, and torn down the British flag.

BEGONIA [*rising in a fury*] Insulted the British flag!!!

THE SECRETARY. They have also burnt down three convents and two churches.

BEGONIA. Thats nothing: theyre only Catholic churches. But do you mean to say that they have dared to touch the British flag?

THE SECRETARY. They have. Fortunately it was after hours and the staff had gone home. Otherwise they would assuredly have been massacred.

BEGONIA. Dirty swine! I hope the British fleet will not leave a stone standing or a nigger alive in their beastly seaport. Thatll teach them.

674

THE SECRETARY. There is only one other trifle of news. The little Dominion of Jacksonsland has declared itself an independent republic.

BEGONIA. It ought to be ashamed of itself. Republics are a low lot. But dont you be anxious about that: the republicans will soon be kicked out. The people may be misled for a while; but they always come back to king and country.

THE SECRETARY. And now, Miss Brown, I must ask you whether you fully realize that all this is your doing?

BEGONIA. Mine!

THE SECRETARY. Yours and nobody else's. In every one of these cases, it was your hand that started the series of political convulsions which may end in the destruction of civilization.

BEGONIA [*flattered*] Really? How?

THE SECRETARY. Those letters that you sent to the Court of International Justice at the Hague—

BEGONIA. Oh, of course. Yes. Fancy that!

THE SECRETARY. But did you not know what you were doing? You conducted the correspondence with very remarkable ability—more, I confess, than I should have given you credit for. Do you mean to tell me that you did not foresee the consequences of your action? That you did not even read the newspapers to see what was happening?

BEGONIA. I dont read political news: it's so dry. However, I seem to be having a big success; and I wont pretend I am not gratified.

THE SECRETARY. Unfortunately the Powers do not consider it a success. They are blaming me for it.

BEGONIA. Oh, if there is any blame I am ready to take it all on myself.

THE SECRETARY. That is very magnanimous of you, Miss Brown.

BEGONIA. Not so magnanimous either: thank you all the same. I tell you I back the Empire; and the Empire will back me. So dont be uneasy.

675

THE SECRETARY. You are very possibly right. And now may I ask you a personal question? How did you become interested in the League of Nations? How did you get this post of yours, which has placed the world's destiny so unexpectedly in your hands?

BEGONIA. Was I interested in the League? Let me see. You know that there is a Society called the League of Nations Union, dont you?

THE SECRETARY. I do. I shudder whenever I think of it.

BEGONIA. Oh, theres no harm in it. I'd never heard of it until last year, when they opened a branch in Camberwell with a whist drive. A friend gave me a ticket for it. It was opened by the Conservative candidate: an innocent young lad rolling in money. He saw that I was a cut above the other girls there, and picked me for his partner when he had to dance. I told him I'd won a County Council scholarship and was educated and knew shorthand and a bit of French and all that, and that I was looking out for a job. His people fixed me up for Geneva all right. A perfect gentleman I must say: never asked so much as a kiss. I was disappointed.

THE SECRETARY. Disappointed at his not kissing you?

BEGONIA. Oh no: there were plenty of kisses going from better looking chaps. But he was a bit of a sucker; and I thought he had intentions; and of course he would have been a jolly good catch for me. But when his people got wind of it they packed him off for a tour round the Empire, and got me this job here—to keep me out of his way, I suppose. Anyhow here I am, you see.

THE SECRETARY. Were you examined as to your knowledge and understanding of the Covenant of the League, and its constitution?

BEGONIA. No. They didnt need to examine me to find out that I was educated. I had lots of prizes and certificates; and there was my L.C.C. scholarship. You see, I have such a good memory: examinations are no trouble to me. Theres a book in the office about the League. I tried to read it; but it was such dry stuff I went to sleep over it.

THE SECRETARY [*rising*] Well, Miss Brown, I am glad to have made your acquaintance, and delighted to learn that though you have produced a first class political crisis, including what promises to be a world war, and made an amazing change in the constitution of the British Empire all in the course of a single morning's work, you are still in high spirits and in fact rather proud of yourself.

BEGONIA [*she has also risen*] Oh, I am not a bit proud; and I'm quite used to being a success. You know, although I was always at the top of my class at school, I never pretended to be clever. Silly clever, I call it. At first I was frightened of the girls that went in for being clever and having original ideas and all that sort of crankiness. But I beat them easily in the examinations; and they never got anywhere. That gave me confidence. Wherever I go I always find that lots of people think as I do. The best sort of people always do: the real ladies and gentlemen, you know. The others are oddities and outsiders. If you want to know what real English public opinion is, keep your eye on me. I'm not a bit afraid of war: remember that England has never lost a battle, and that it does no harm to remind the foreigners of it when they get out of hand. Good morning. So pleased to have met you.

They shake hands; and he goes to the door and opens it for her. She goes out much pleased with herself.

THE SECRETARY [*ruminating dazedly*] And thats England! [*The telephone rings. He returns to the table to attend to it*]. Yes? . . . Which Foreign Secretary? Every hole and corner in the Empire has its own Foreign Secretary now. Do you mean the British Foreign Secretary, Sir Orpheus Midlander? . . . Well, why didnt you say so? Shew him up at once.

Sir Orpheus comes in. He is a very welldressed gentle-

man of fifty or thereabouts, genial in manner, quickwitted in conversation altogether a pleasant and popular personality.

THE SECRETARY. Do sit down. I cant say how I feel about your being dragged here all the way from London in Derby week.

SIR O. [*sitting*] Well, my friend, it's you who have dragged me. And I hope you wont mind my asking you what on earth you think you have been doing? What induced you to do it?

THE SECRETARY. I didnt do it. It was done by the Committee for Intellectual Co-operation.

SIR O. The what??! I never heard of such a body.

THE SECRETARY. Neither did I until this business was sprung on me. Nobody ever heard of it. But I find now that it is part of the League, and that its members are tremendous swells with European reputations. Theyve all published translations from the Greek or discovered new planets or something of that sort.

SIR O. Ah yes: outside politics: I see. But we cant have literary people interfering in foreign affairs. And they must have held meetings before taking such an outrageous step as this. Why were we not told? We'd have squashed them at once.

THE SECRETARY. They are quite innocent: they know no more about it than I did. The whole thing was done by a young woman named Begonia Brown.

SIR O. Begonia Brown! But this is appalling. I shall be personally compromised.

THE SECRETARY. You! How?

SIR O. This woman—it must be the same woman; for there cant be another female with such a name in the world —she's engaged to my nephew.

THE SECRETARY. She told me about it. But I had no idea the man was your nephew. I see how awkward it is for you. Did you ever talk to her about it?

SIR O. I! I never set eyes on her in my life. I remember

678

her ridiculous name: thats all.

THE SECRETARY. Were you in the habit of discussing foreign affairs with your nephew?

SIR O. With Benjy! You might as well discuss Einstein's general theory of relativity with a blue behinded ape. I havnt exchanged twenty words with the boy since I tipped him when he was going from Eton to Oxford.

THE SECRETARY. Then I cant understand it. Her correspondence with the Hague Court has been conducted with remarkable ability and in first-rate style. The woman herself is quite incapable of it. There must be somebody behind her. Can it be your nephew?

SIR O. If, as you say, the work shews political ability and presentable style, you may accept my assurance that Sue's boy has nothing to do with it. Besides, he is at present in Singapore, where the native dancing girls are irresistible.

The telephone rings.

THE SECRETARY. Excuse me. Yes? . . . Hold on a moment. [*To Sir O.*] The Senior Judge of the Court of International Justice at the Hague is downstairs. Hadnt you better see him?

SIR O. By all means. Most opportune.

THE SECRETARY [*into the telephone*] Send him up.

SIR O. Have you had any correspondence about this business?

THE SECRETARY. Correspondence!!! I havnt read one tenth of it. The Abyssinian war was a holiday job in comparison. Weve never had anything like it before.

The Senior Judge enters. He is a Dutchman, much younger than a British judge: under forty, in fact, but very grave and every inch a judge.

THE SECRETARY. I am desolate at having brought your honor all the way from the Hague. A word from you would have brought me there and saved you the trouble. Have you met the British Foreign Secretary, Sir Orpheus Midlander?

JUDGE. I have not had that pleasure. How do you do,

679

Sir Midlander?

SIR O. How do you do?

They shake hands whilst the Secretary places a chair for the judge in the middle of the room, between his table and Sir Orpheus. They all sit down.

JUDGE. I thought it best to come. The extraordinary feature of this affair is that I have communicated with all the members of the Intellectual Committee; and every one of them denies any knowledge of it. Most of them did not know that they are members.

SIR O. Do you mean to say that it is all a hoax?

JUDGE. It may be that someone was hoaxing the Court. But now that the applications for warrants have been made public, the Court must take them seriously. Otherwise it would cut a ridiculous figure in the eyes of Europe.

SIR O. But surely such a procedure was never contemplated when the Powers joined the League?

JUDGE. I do not think anything was contemplated when the Powers joined the League. They signed the Covenant without reading it, to oblige President Wilson. The United States then refused to sign it to disoblige President Wilson, also without reading it. Since then the Powers have behaved in every respect as if the League did not exist, except when they could use it for their own purposes.

SIR O. [*naïvely*] But how else could they use it?

JUDGE. They could use it to maintain justice and order between the nations.

SIR O. There is nothing we desire more. The British Empire stands for justice and order. But I must tell you that the British Foreign Office would take a very grave view of any attempt on the part of the Court to do anything without consulting us. I need not remind you that without us you have no powers. You have no police to execute your warrants. You cant put the Powers in the dock: you havnt got a dock.

JUDGE. We have a court room at the Hague which can

680

easily be provided with a dock if you consider such a construction necessary, which I do not. We have employees to whom we can assign police duties to any necessary extent.

SIR O. Pooh! You cant be serious. You have no jurisdiction.

JUDGE. You mean that our jurisdiction is undefined. That means that our jurisdiction is what we choose to make it. You are familiar with what you call judgemade law in England. Well, Sir Midlander, the judges of the Court of International Justice are not nonentities. We have waited a long time for a case to set us in motion. You have provided us with four cases; and you may depend on us to make the most of them. They will affirm our existence, which is hardly known yet. They will exercise our power, which is hardly felt yet. All we needed was a *cause célèbre;* and Miss Begonia Brown has found several for us very opportunely.

SIR O. My dear sir: Miss Brown is a nobody.

JUDGE. Unless the highest court can be set in motion by the humblest individual justice is a mockery.

SIR O. Of course I agree with that—in principle. Still, you know, there are people you can take into court and people you cant. Your experience at the bar—

JUDGE [*interrupting him sharply*] I have had no experience at the bar. Please remember that you are not now in England, where judges are only worn-out barristers, most of whom have forgotten any sense of law they may ever have acquired.

SIR O. How very odd! I own I was surprised to find the judicial bench represented by so young a man; and I am afraid I must add that I prefer our British system. We should have had no trouble with a British judge.

JUDGE. Why should you have any trouble with me? I am simply a Judge, first and last. To me it is a continual trouble and scandal that modern statesmen are slipping back, one after another, from the reign of law based on the eternal principle of justice, to the maintenance of governments set up by successful demagogues or victorious soldiers, each of whom has his proscription list of enemies whom he imprisons, exiles, or murders at his pleasure until he is himself overcome by an abler rival and duly proscribed, imprisoned, exiled or assassinated in his turn. Such a state of things is abhorrent to me. I have spent years in trying to devise some judicial procedure by which these lawbreakers can be brought to justice. Well, the Intellectual Co-operation Committee—of the existence of which I must confess I was entirely ignorant—has found the procedure; and the Court will back it up to the utmost of its powers.

SIR O. I am afraid you are a bit of an idealist.

JUDGE. Necessarily. Justice is an ideal; and I am a judge. What, may I ask, are you?

SIR O. I! Oh, only a much harassed Foreign Secretary. You see, my young friend—if you will allow me to call you so—justice, as you say, is an ideal, and a very fine ideal too; but what I have to deal with is Power; and Power is often a devilishly ugly thing. If any of these demagogue dictators issues a warrant for your arrest or even an order for your execution, you will be arrested and shot the moment you set foot in their country. You may even be kidnapped and carried there: remember Napoleon and the Duc d'Enghien. But if you issue a warrant or pronounce a sentence against one of them Europe will just laugh at you, because you have no power. It will be as futile as a decree of excommunication.

JUDGE. Would you like to be excommunicated?

SIR O. Hardly a serious question, is it?

JUDGE. Very serious.

SIR O. My dear sir, it couldnt happen.

JUDGE. Pardon me: it could.

SIR O. [obstinately] Pardon me: it couldnt. Look at the thing practically. To begin with I am not a Roman Catholic. I am a member of the Church of England; and down at my place in the country the Church living is in my gift.

Without my subscription the churchwardens could not make both ends meet. The rector has no society except what he gets in my house.

JUDGE. The rector is a freeholder. If you are a notoriously evil liver, he can refuse to admit you to Communion.

SIR O. But I am not a notoriously evil liver. If the rector suggested such a thing I should have him out of his rectory and in a lunatic asylum before the end of the week.

JUDGE. Suppose the rector were prepared to risk that! Suppose the war of 1914 were renewed, and you were responsible for sending the young men of your country to drop bombs on the capital cities of Europe! Suppose your rector, as a Christian priest, took the view that you were in a condition of mortal sin and refused you Communion! Suppose, if you wish, that you had him locked up as a lunatic! Would you like it?

SIR O. Suppose the villagers burnt down his rectory and ducked him in the horse pond to teach him a little British patriotism! How would he like it?

JUDGE. Martyrdom has its attractions for some natures. But my question was not whether he would like it, but whether you would like it.

SIR O. I should treat it with contempt.

JUDGE. No doubt; but would you like it?

SIR O. Oh, come! Really! Really!

JUDGE. Believe me, Sir Midlander, you would not like it. And if the International Court, moved by the Committee for Intellectual Co-operation, were to deliver an adverse judgment on you, you would not like it. The man whom the Hague condemns will be an uncomfortable man. The State which it finds to be in the wrong will be an uncomfortable State.

SIR O. But you cant enforce anything. You have no sanctions.

JUDGE. What, exactly, do you mean by sanctions, Sir Midlander?

SIR O. I mean what everybody means. Sanctions, you

683

know. That is plain English. Oil, for instance.

JUDGE. Castor oil?

SIR O. No no: motor oil. The stuff you run your aeroplanes on.

JUDGE. Motor oil is a sanction when you withhold it. Castor oil is a sanction when you administer it. Is there any other difference?

SIR O. [*smiling*] Well, that has never occurred to me before; but now you mention it there is certainly an analogy. But in England the castor oil business is just one of those things that are not done. Castor oil is indecent. Motor oil is all right.

JUDGE. Well, you need not fear that the Hague will resort to any other sanction than the sacredness of justice. It will affirm this sacredness and make the necessary applications. It is the business of a judge to see that there is no wrong without a remedy. Your Committee for Intellectual Co-operation has been appealed to by four persons who have suffered grievous wrongs. It has very properly referred them to the International Court. As president of that court it is my business to find a remedy for their wrongs; and I shall do so to the best of my ability even if my decisions should form the beginning of a new code of international law and be quite unprecedented.

SIR O. But, my dear sir, what practical steps do you propose to take? What steps can you take?

JUDGE. I have already taken them. I have fixed a day for the trial of the cases, and summoned the plaintiffs and defendants to attend the court.

THE SECRETARY. But the defendants are the responsible heads of sovereign States. Do you suppose for a moment that they will obey your summons?

JUDGE. We shall see. That, in fact, is the object of my experiment. We shall see. [*He rises*] And now I must ask you to excuse me. Sir Midlander: our interview has been most instructive to me as to the attitude of your country. Mr Secretary: you are very good to have spared me so

684

much of your valuable time. Good afternoon, gentlemen.
[*He goes out.*]

SIR O. What are we to do with men like that?

THE SECRETARY. What are they going to do with us?
That is the question we have to face now.

SIR O. Pooh! They cant do anything, you know, except
make speeches and write articles. They are free to do that
in England. British liberty is a most useful safety valve.

THE SECRETARY. I was on his honor's side myself once,
until my official experience here taught me how hopeless
it is to knock supernationalism—

SIR O. Super what? Did you say supernaturalism?

THE SECRETARY. No. Supernationalism.

SIR O. Oh, I see. Internationalism.

THE SECRETARY. No. Internationalism is nonsense.
Pushing all the nations into Geneva is like throwing all the
fishes into the same pond: they just begin eating oneanother. We need something higher than nationalism: a
genuine political and social catholicism. How are you to
get that from these patriots, with their national anthems
and flags and dreams of war and conquest rubbed into them
from their childhood? The organization of nations is the
organization of world war. If two men want to fight how do
you prevent them? By keeping them apart, not by bringing
them together. When the nations kept apart war was an
occasional and exceptional thing: now the League hangs
over Europe like a perpetual warcloud.

SIR O. Well, dont throw it at my head as if I disagreed
with you.

THE SECRETARY. I beg your pardon. I am worried by
this crisis. Let us talk business. What are we to do with
Begonia Brown?

SIR O. Do with her! Squash her, impudent little slut.
She is nobody: she doesnt matter.

*The conversation is abruptly broken by the irruption of
Begonia herself in a state of ungovernable excitement.*

BEGONIA. Have you heard the news? [*Seeing Sir*

Orpheus] Oh, I beg your pardon: I didnt know you were engaged.

THE SECRETARY. This is Sir Orpheus Midlander, the British Foreign Secretary, Miss Brown.

BEGONIA. Oh, most pleased to meet you, Sir Orpheus. I know your nephew. We are quite dear friends [*she shakes Sir O.'s hand effusively*]. Have you heard the news? Lord Middlesex is dead.

SIR O. Indeed? Let me see. Middlesex? I dont attach any significance to the news. He must have been a back-woodsman. Remind me about him.

BEGONIA. His son is Lord Newcross.

SIR O. Oh! Then Newcross goes to the Lords to succeed his father. That means a by-election in Camberwell.

BEGONIA. Yes; and the Conservatives want me to stand.

BOTH GENTLEMEN. What!!!

BEGONIA. Dont you think I ought to? I have been a lot in the papers lately. It's six hundred a year for me if I get in. I shall be the patriotic candidate; and the Labor vote will be a split vote; for the Communists are putting up a candidate against the Labor man; and the Liberals are contesting the seat as well. It will be just a walk-over for me.

SIR O. But my nephew is the Government candidate. Has he not told you so?

BEGONIA. Oh, thats quite all right. He has withdrawn and proposed me. He'll pay my election expenses.

SIR O. I thought he was in Singapore.

BEGONIA. So he is. It's all been done by cable. Ive just this minute heard it. You see, dear Billikins is not very bright; and he'd better not be here to muddle everything up. [*She sits*].

SIR O. But will his committee accept you?

BEGONIA. Only too glad to get a candidate that will do them credit. You see, no matter how carefully they coached Bill for the public meetings he made the most awful exhibition of himself. And he knew it, poor lamb, and would never have gone in for it if his mother hadnt made him.

686

SIR O. And do you think you will be able to make a better impression at the meetings? You are not a politician, are you?

BEGONIA. The same as anybody else, I suppose. I shall pick up all the politics I need when I get into the House; and I shall get into the House because there are lots of people in Camberwell who think as I do. You bet I shall romp in at the head of the poll. I am quite excited about it. [*To the Secretary*] You were so kind to me just now that I thought you had a right to know before anyone else. [*To Sir O.*] And it's splendid news for the Government, isnt it, Sir Orpheus?

SIR O. Thrilling, Miss Brown.

BEGONIA. Oh, do call me Begonia. We're as good as related, arnt we?

SIR O. I am afraid so.

BEGONIA. I am sure to get in, arnt I?

SIR O. If your three opponents are foolish enough to go to the poll, it's a cert.

BEGONIA. Yes: isnt it? I wonder would you mind lending me my fare to London. I dont like taking money off Billikins. I will pay you when my ship comes home: the six hundred a year, you know.

SIR O. Will a five pound note be any use [*he produces one*]?

BEGONIA [*taking it*] Thanks ever so much: itll just see me through. And now I must toddle off to my little constituency. I have barely time to pack for the night train. Goodbye, Mr Secretary [*They shake hands*]; and [*to Sir O. effusively*] thanks ever so much, and au revoir. [*She goes out*].

THE SECRETARY. What an amazing young woman! You really think she will get in?

SIR O. Of course she will. She has courage, sincerity, good looks, and big publicity as the Geneva heroine. Everything that our voters love.

THE SECRETARY. But she hasnt a political idea in her

head.

SIR O. She need not have. The Whips will pilot her through the division lobby until she knows the way. She need not know anything else.

THE SECRETARY. But she is a complete ignoramus. She will give herself away every time she opens her mouth.

SIR O. Not at all. She will say pluckily and sincerely just what she feels and thinks. You heard her say that there are lots of people in Camberwell who feel and think as she does. Well, the House of Commons is exactly like Camberwell in that respect.

THE SECRETARY. But can you contemplate such a state of things without dismay?

SIR O. Of course I can. I contemplated my nephew's candidature without dismay.

THE SECRETARY. The world is mad. Quite mad.

SIR O. Pooh! you need a cup of tea. Nothing wrong with the world: nothing whatever.

THE SECRETARY [*resignedly sitting down and speaking into the telephone*] Tea for two, please.

ACT III

AFTERNOON *in the lounge of a fashionable restaurant overlooking the Lake of Geneva. Three tea tables, with two chairs at each, are in view. There is a writing table against the wall. The Secretary is seated at the centre table, reading a magazine. The American journalist comes in flourishing a cablegram.*

THE JOURNALIST. Heard the news, boss?

THE SECRETARY. What news? Anything fresh from the Hague?

THE JOURNALIST. Yes. The International Court has abolished Intellectual Co-operation [*he seats himself at the next table on the Secretary's left*].

THE SECRETARY. What!

THE JOURNALIST. They have had enough of it. The Court also finds the big Powers guilty of flagrant contempt of the League Covenant.

THE SECRETARY. So they are, of course. But the League was doing as well as could be expected until Dame Begonia took a hand in it. By the way, have you heard the latest about her?

THE JOURNALIST. No. She has dropped me completely since she became a Dame of the British Empire.

THE SECRETARY. Well, at a fashion demonstration in the Albert Hall, some blackshirt thought it would be a good joke to pretend to forget her name and call her Mongolia Muggins. Sixteen newspapers quoted this; and Begonia took an action against every one of them. They settled with her for three hundred apiece. Begonia must have netted at least four thousand.

THE JOURNALIST. And to think I might have married that girl if only I had had the foresight to push myself on her!

THE SECRETARY. Ah! A great opportunity missed: she would have made a most comfortable wife. Pleasant-looking, good-natured, able to see everything within six inches of her nose and nothing beyond. A domestic paragon: a

689

political idiot. In short, an ideal wife.

The widow enters on the arm of Sir Orpheus Mid-lander. She still carries her handbag, heavy with the weight of her pistol.

SIR O. I assure you, señora, this is the only place in Geneva where you can be perfectly happy after a perfect tea.

THE WIDOW. It is easy for you to be happy. But think of this weight continually hanging on my arm, and reminding me at every moment of my tragic destiny.

SIR O. Oh, you must allow me to carry it for you. I had no idea it was heavy. Do you keep all your money in it?

THE WIDOW. Money! No: it is this [*she takes the weapon from it and throws it on the nearest table on the Secretary's right. The pair seat themselves there*].

SIR O. Good gracious! What do you carry that for? It is against the law in Geneva.

THE WIDOW. There is no longer any law in Geneva. The Hague has abolished the Intellectual Committee, leaving my husband's murder still unexpiated. That throws me back on the blood feud. Properly this is the business of my son. I cabled him to shoot the usurping president at once. But the boy is a shameless dastard.

SIR O. A bastard!

THE WIDOW. No: I wish he were: he has disgraced me. A dastard, a coward. He has become a Communist, and pretends that the blood feud is a bourgeois tradition, contrary to the teachings of Karl Marx.

SIR O. Well, so much the better. I can hardly believe that Marx taught anything so entirely reasonable and proper as that it is wrong to shoot a president; but if he did I must say I agree with him.

THE WIDOW. But public opinion in the Earthly Paradise would never tolerate such a monstrous violation of natural justice as leaving the murder of a father unavenged. If our relatives could be murdered with impunity we should have people shooting them all over the place. Even cousins five

690

times removed have to be avenged if they have no nearer relative to take on that duty.

SIR O. Dear me! But if your son wont, he wont; and there is an end to it. A very happy end, if I may say so.

THE WIDOW. An end of it! Nothing of the sort. If my son will not shoot the president, I shall have to do it myself. The president has two brothers who will shoot me unless I stay in this ghastly Europe instead of returning to my beloved Earthly Paradise.

SIR O. To me as an Englishman, all this seems ridiculous. You really need not shoot him.

THE WIDOW. You dont know how strong public opinion is in the Earthly Paradise. You couldnt live there if you defied it. And then there is my own sense of right and wrong. You mustnt think I have no conscience.

SIR O. People have such extraordinary consciences when they have not been educated at an English public school! [To the secretary] Talking of that, have you read the Prime Minister's speech in the debate on the League last night?

THE SECRETARY [illhumoredly] Yes. Half about Harrow as a nursery for statesmen, and the other half about the sacredness of treaties. He might have shewn some consideration for me.

SIR O. But, my dear fellow, in what way could his speech have possibly hurt you? He has made that speech over and over again. You know very well that after a certain age a man has only one speech. And you have never complained before.

THE SECRETARY. Well, he had better get a new speech, and stop talking about the sacredness of treaties. Will you fellows in London never take the trouble to read the Covenant of the League? It entirely abolishes the sacredness of treaties. Article 26 expressly provides for the revision and amendment both of the treaties and the League itself.

SIR O. But how can that be? Surely the League was

created to see the Treaty of Versailles carried out. With what other object would we have joined it?

THE SECRETARY [*desperately*] Oh, there is no use talking to you. You all come here to push your own countries without the faintest notion of what the League is for; and I have to sit here listening to foreign ministers explaining to me that their countries are the greatest countries in the world and their people God's chosen race. You are supposed to be international statesmen; but none of you could keep a coffee stall at Limehouse because you would have to be equally civil to sailors of all nations.

SIR O. Nerves, my dear boy, nerves. I sometimes feel like that myself. I tell my wife I am sick of the whole business, and am going to resign; but the mood passes.

The Jew enters, in animated conversation with the quondam newcomer. The rest become discreetly silent, but keep their ears open.

THE JEW. My good sir, what is your grievance compared to mine? Have you been robbed? Have you been battered with clubs? gassed? massacred? Have you been commercially and socially ruined? Have you been imprisoned in concentration camps commanded by hooligans? Have you been driven out of your country to starve in exile?

THE NEWCOMER. No; but if the people vote for it there is no violation of democratic principle in it. Your people voted ten to one for getting rid of the Jews. Hadnt they the right to choose the sort of people they would allow to live in their own country? Look at the British! Will they allow a yellow man into Australia? Look at the Americans! Will they let a Jap into California? See what happened to the British Government in 1906 when it wanted to let Chinese labor into Lancashire!

THE JEW. Your own country! Who made you a present of a piece of God's earth?

THE NEWCOMER. I was born on it, wasnt I?

THE JEW. And was not I born in the country from

692

which I have been cast out?

THE NEWCOMER. You oughtnt to have been born there. You ought to have been born in Jerusalem.

THE JEW. And you, my friend, ought never to have been born at all. You claim a right to shut me out of the world; but you burn with indignation because you yourself have been shut out of your trumpery little parliament.

THE NEWCOMER. Easy! easy! dont lose your temper. I dont want to shut you out of the world: all I say is that you are not in the world on democratic principles; but I ought to be in parliament on democratic principles. If I shoot a Jew, thats murder; and I ought to be hanged for it. But if I vote for a Jew, as I often have, and he is elected and then not let into Parliament, what becomes of democracy?

THE JEW. The question is not what becomes of democracy but what becomes of you? You are not less rich, less happy, less secure, less well or badly governed because you are making speeches outside your Parliament House instead of inside it. But to me the persecution is a matter of life and death.

THE NEWCOMER. It's a bit hard on you, I admit. But it's not a matter of principle.

THE WIDOW [to the Jew] Do you know what I would do if I were a president?

THE JEW. No, madam. But it would interest me to hear it.

THE WIDOW. I would shoot every Jew in the country: that is what I would do.

THE JEW. Pray why?

THE WIDOW. Because they crucified my Savior: that is why. I am a religious woman; and when I meet a God murderer I can hardly keep my hands off my gun.

THE JEW. After all, madam, your Savior was a Jew.

THE WIDOW. Oh, what a horrible blasphemy! [she reaches for her pistol].

Sir Orpheus seizes her wrist. The Secretary secures her left arm.

693

THE WIDOW [*struggling*] Let me go. How dare you touch me? If you were Christians you would help me to kill this dirty Jew. Did you hear what he said?

SIR O. Yes, yes, señora: I heard. I assure you he did not mean to blaspheme. Ethnologically, you know, he was right. Only ethnologically, of course.

THE WIDOW. I do not understand that long word. Our Savior and his Virgin Mother were good Catholics, were they not?

SIR O. No doubt, señora, no doubt. We are all good Catholics, I hope, in a sense. You will remember that our Savior was of the house of King David.

THE WIDOW. You will be telling me next that King David was a Jew, I suppose.

SIR O. Well, ethnologically—

THE WIDOW. Eth no fiddlesticks. Give me my gun.

SIR O. I think you had better let me carry it for you, señora. You shall have it when this gentleman has gone.

THE NEWCOMER. Give it to the police. That woman is not safe.

THE WIDOW. I spit upon you.

SIR O. The police would arrest her for carrying arms.

THE WIDOW. Three men and a Jew against one disarmed woman! Cowards.

THE JEW. Fortunate for you, madam, and for me. But for these three gentlemen you would soon be awaiting death at the hands of the public executioner; and I should be a corpse.

THE JOURNALIST. A cadaver. Put it nicely. A cadaver.

THE WIDOW. Do you believe that any jury would find me guilty for ridding the world of a Jew?

THE JEW. One can never be quite certain, madam. If there were women on the jury, or some Jews, your good looks might not save you.

THE WIDOW. Women on juries are an abomination. Only a Jew could mention such a thing to a lady [*she gives up the struggle and resumes her seat*].

694

GENEVA

The Commissar comes in with Begonia and the Judge, of whom she has evidently made a conquest.

BEGONIA [*to the Secretary*] Good evening, boss. Cheerio, Sir Orpheus. You remember me, señora. You know the judge, boss.

THE SECRETARY. Do me the honor to share my table, your honor.

THE JUDGE. Thank you. May I introduce Commissar Posky. [*He seats himself on the Secretary's left*].

THE SECRETARY. We have met. Pray be seated.

THE JOURNALIST. Take my place, Commissar. I must get on with my work. [*He retires to the writing table, where he sits and sets to work writing his press messages, withdrawing from the conversation, but keeping his ears open*].

THE COMMISSAR [*taking the vacated seat beside the Newcomer*] I thank you.

THE SECRETARY. There is room for you here, Dame Begonia [*indicating chair on his right*].

BEGONIA [*taking it*] There is always room at the top.

THE COMMISSAR. I represent the Soviet.

THE WIDOW [*exploding again*] Another Jew!!!

THE SECRETARY. No, no. You have Jews on the brain.

THE WIDOW. He is a Bolshevist. All Bolshevists are Jews. Do you realize that if I lived under the horrible tyranny of the Soviet I should be shot?

THE JEW. I take that to be a very striking proof of the superior civilization of Russia.

THE COMMISSAR. Why should we shoot her, comrade?

THE JEW. She has just tried to shoot me.

THE COMMISSAR. We do not shoot Jews as such: we civilize them. You see, a Communist State is only possible for highly civilized people, trained to Communism from their childhood. The people we shoot are gangsters and speculators and exploiters and scoundrels of all sorts who are encouraged in other countries in the name of liberty and democracy.

695

THE NEWCOMER [*starting up*] Not a word against liberty and democracy in my presence! Do you hear?

THE COMMISSAR. And not a word against Communism in mine. Agreed?

THE NEWCOMER [*sits down sulkily*] Oh, all right.

THE COMMISSAR [*continuing*] I find it very difficult to accustom myself to the exaggerated importance you all attach to sex in these western countries. This handsome lady, it seems, has some lover's quarrel with this handsome gentleman.

THE WIDOW. A lover's quarrel!!!

THE COMMISSAR. In the U.S.S.R. that would be a triviality. At the very worst it would end in a divorce. But here she tries to shoot him.

THE WIDOW. You are mad. And divorce is a deadly sin: only Bolsheviks and Protestants would allow such an infamy. They will all go to hell for it. As to my loving this man, I hate, loathe, and abhor him. He would steal my child and cut it in pieces and sprinkle its blood on his threshold. He is a Jew.

THE COMMISSAR. Come to Russia. Jews do not do such things there. No doubt they are capable of anything when they are corrupted by Capitalism.

THE JEW. Lies! lies! Excuses for robbing and murdering us.

THE COMMISSAR. For that, comrade, one excuse is as good as another. I am not a Jew; but the lady may shoot me because I am a Communist.

THE WIDOW. How can I shoot you? They have stolen my gun. Besides, shooting Communists is not a religious duty but a political one; and in my country women do not meddle in politics.

THE COMMISSAR. Then I am safe.

BEGONIA [*recovering from her astonishment at the shooting conversation*] But dont you know, señora, that you mustnt go about shooting people here? It may be all right in your country; but here it isnt done.

696

THE WIDOW. Where I am is my country. What is right in my country cannot be wrong in yours.

SIR O. Ah, if you were a Foreign Secretary—

THE SECRETARY. If you were the secretary of the League of Nations—

SIR O. You would make the curious discovery that one nation's right is another nation's wrong. There is only one way of reconciling all the nations in a real league, and that is to convert them all to English ideas.

THE COMMISSAR. But all the world is in revolt against English ideas, especially the English themselves. The future is for Russian ideas.

THE NEWCOMER. Where did Russia get her ideas? From England. In Russia Karl Marx would have been sent to Siberia and flogged to death. In England he was kept in the British Museum at the public expense and let write what he liked. England is the country where, as the poet says, "A man may say the thing he wills—"

THE JUDGE. Pardon me: that is an illusion. I have gone into that question; and I can assure you that when the British Government is alarmed there are quite as many prosecutions for sedition, blasphemy and obscenity as in any other country. The British Government has just passed a new law under which any person obnoxious to the Government can be imprisoned for opening his mouth or dipping his pen in the ink.

SIR O. Yes; but whose fault is that? Your Russian propaganda. Freedom of thought and speech is the special glory of Britain; but surely you dont expect us to allow your missionaries to preach Bolshevism, do you?

THE COMMISSAR [laughing] I dont expect any government to tolerate any doctrine that threatens its existence or the incomes of its rulers. The only difference is that in Russia we dont pretend to tolerate such doctrines; and in England you do. Why do you give yourselves that unnecessary and dangerous trouble?

THE NEWCOMER. Karl Marx was tolerated in England:

697

he wouldnt have been tolerated in Russia.

THE COMMISSAR. That was a weakness in the British system, not a virtue. If the British Government had known and understood what Marx was doing, and what its effect was going to be on the mind of the world, it would have sent him to prison and destroyed every scrap of his handwriting and every copy of his books. But they did not know where to strike. They persecuted poor men for making profane jokes; they suppressed newspapers in England as well as in Ireland; they dismissed editors who were too independent and outspoken; they burnt the books of novelists who had gone a little too far in dealing with sex; they imprisoned street corner speakers on charges of obstructing traffic; and all the time they were providing Karl Marx with the finest reading room in the world whilst he was writing their death warrants.

SIR O. Those warrants have not yet been executed in England. They never will be. The world may be jolted out of its tracks for a moment by the shock of a war as a railway train may be thrown off the rails; but it soon settles into its old grooves. You are a Bolshevik; but nobody would know it. You have the appearance, the dress, the culture of a gentleman: your clothes might have been made within half a mile of Hanover Square.

THE COMMISSAR. As a matter of fact they were: I buy them in London.

SIR O. [*triumphant*] You see! You have given up all this Marxian nonsense and gone back to the capitalist system. I always said you would.

THE COMMISSAR. If it pleases you to think so, Sir Orpheus, I shall do nothing to disturb your happiness. Will you be so good as to convey to your Government my great regret and that of the Soviet Cabinet that your bishop should have died of his personal contact with Russian ideas. I blame myself for not having been more considerate. But I had never met that kind of man before. The only other British Bishop I had met was nearly seven feet high, an athlete, and a most revolutionary preacher.

SIR O. That is what makes the Church of England so easy to deal with. No types. Just English gentlemen. Not like Catholic priests.

THE WIDOW. Oh, Sir Orpheus! You, of all men, to insult my faith!

SIR O. Not at all, not at all, I assure you. I have the greatest respect for the Catholic faith. But you cannot deny that your priests have a professional air. They are not like other men. Our English clergy are not like that. You would not know that they were clergy at all if it were not for their collars.

THE WIDOW. I call that wicked. A priest should not be like other men.

THE COMMISSAR. Have you ever tried to seduce a priest, madam?

THE WIDOW. Give me my gun. This is monstrous. Have Bolsheviks no decency?

THE NEWCOMER. I knew a priest once who—

THE SECRETARY. No, please. The subject is a dangerous one.

THE COMMISSAR. All subjects are dangerous in Geneva, are they not?

THE JUDGE. Pardon me. It is not the subjects that are dangerous in Geneva, but the people.

THE WIDOW. Jews! Bolsheviks! Gunmen!

THE JEW. What about gunwomen? Gunmolls they are called in America. Pardon my reminding you.

THE WIDOW. You remind me of nothing that I can decently mention.

THE NEWCOMER. Hullo, maam! You know, ladies dont say things like that in my country.

THE WIDOW. They do in mine. What I have said I have said.

THE JUDGE. When the International Court was moved to action by the enterprise of my friend Dame Begonia, it found that the moment the League of Nations does any-

699

thing on its own initiative and on principle, it produces, not peace, but threats of war or secession or both which oblige it to stop hastily and do nothing until the Great Powers have decided among themselves to make use of it as an instrument of their oldfashioned diplomacy. That is true, Mr. Secretary, is it not?

THE SECRETARY. It is too true. Yet it is not altogether true. Those who think the League futile dont know what goes on here. They dont know what Geneva means to us. The Powers think we are nothing but their catspaw. They flout us openly by ignoring the Covenant and making unilateral treaties that should be made by us. They have driven us underground as if we were a criminal conspiracy. But in little ways of which the public knows nothing we sidetrack them. We sabotage them. We shame them. We make things difficult or impossible that used to be easy. You dont know what the atmosphere of Geneva is. When I came here I was a patriot, a Nationalist, regarding my appointment as a win for my own country in the diplomatic game. But the atmosphere of Geneva changed me. I am now an Internationalist. I am the ruthless enemy of every nation, my own included. Let me be frank. I hate the lot of you.

ALL THE OTHERS. Oh!

THE SECRETARY. Yes I do. You the Jew there: I hate you because you are a Jew.

THE JEW. A German Jew.

THE SECRETARY. Worse and worse. Two nationalities are worse than one. This gunwoman here: I hate her because she is heaven knows what mixture of Spaniard and Indian and savage.

THE WIDOW. Men with red blood in them do not hate me.

THE SECRETARY. You, Sir Orpheus, are an amiable and honest man. Well, I never hear you talking politics without wanting to shoot you.

SIR O. Dear me! Fortunately I have the lady's gun in

my pocket. But of course I dont believe you.

THE SECRETARY. If you had the Geneva spirit you would believe me. This Russian here: I hate him because his Government has declared for Socialism in a single country.

THE COMMISSAR. You are a Trotskyite then?

THE SECRETARY. Trotsky is nothing to me; but I hate all frontiers; and you have shut yourself into frontiers.

THE COMMISSAR. Only because infinite space is too much for us to manage. Be reasonable.

THE SECRETARY. On this subject I am not reasonable. I am sick of reasonable people: they see all the reasons for being lazy and doing nothing.

THE NEWCOMER. And what price me? Come on. Dont leave me out.

THE SECRETARY. You! You are some sort of half-Americanized colonist. You are a lower middle-class politician. Your pose is that of the rugged individualist, the isolationist, at bottom an Anarchist.

THE NEWCOMER. Anarchist yourself. Anyhow I have more common sense than you: I dont hate all my fellow creatures.

THE SECRETARY. You are all enemies of the human race. You are all armed to the teeth and full of patriotism. Your national heroes are all brigands and pirates. When it comes to the point you are all cut-throats. But Geneva will beat you yet. Not in my time, perhaps. But the Geneva spirit is a fact; and a spirit is a fact that cannot be killed.

ALL THE REST. But——

THE SECRETARY [*shouting them down*] I am not going to argue with you: you are all too damnably stupid.

SIR O. Are you sure you are quite well this afternoon? I have always believed in you and supported you as England's truest friend at Geneva.

THE SECRETARY. You were quite right. I am the truest friend England has here. I am the truest friend of all the Powers if they only knew it. That is the strength of my

701

position here. Each of you thinks I am on his side. If you
hint that I am mad or drunk I shall hint that you are going
gaga and that it is time for the British Empire to find a
younger Foreign Secretary.

SIR O. Gaga!!!

THE SECRETARY. I cannot afford to lose my job here.
Do not force me to fight you with your own weapons in
defence of my hardearned salary.

THE WIDOW [*to Sir O.*] The best weapon is in your
hands. You stole it from me. In my country he would now
be dead at your feet with as many holes drilled through
him as there are bullets in the clip.

THE SECRETARY. In your country, señora, I might have
fired first.

THE WIDOW. What matter! In either case honor would
be satisfied.

THE SECRETARY. Honor! The stock excuse for making
a corpse.

THE JOURNALIST. A cadaver.

THE WIDOW. Thank you.

THE SECRETARY. A slovenly unhandsome corse. I am
quoting Shakespear.

THE WIDOW. Then Shakespear, whoever he may be, is
no gentleman.

THE SECRETARY. Judge: you hear what we have to contend with here. Stupidity upon stupidity. Geneva is expected to make a league of nations out of political block-
heads.

THE JUDGE. I must rule this point against you. These
people are not stupid. Stupid people have nothing to say
for themselves: these people have plenty to say for themselves. Take Sir Midlander here for example. If you tell
me he is stupid the word has no meaning.

SIR O. Thank you, my dear Judge, thank you. But for
Heaven's sake dont call me clever or I shall be defeated at
the next election. I have the greatest respect for poetry
and the fine arts and all that sort of thing; but please

702

understand that I am not an intellectual. A plain Englishman doing my duty to my country according to my poor
lights.

THE JUDGE. Still, doing it with ability enough to have
attained Cabinet rank in competition with hundreds of
other successful and ambitious competitors.

SIR O. I assure you I am not ambitious. I am not competitive. I happen to be fairly well off; but the money was
made by my grandfather. Upon my honor I dont know
how I got landed where I am. I am quite an ordinary chap
really.

THE JUDGE. Then you have risen by sheer natural
ordinary superiority. However, do not be alarmed: all I
claim for the purposes of my argument is that you are not
a born fool.

SIR O. Very good of you to say so. Well, I will let it go
at that.

THE JUDGE. At the other extreme, take the case of this
passionate and attractive lady, whose name I have not the
pleasure of knowing.

THE JEW. Try Dolores.

THE WIDOW. I suppose you think you are insulting me.
You are simply making a fool of yourself. My name is
Dolores.

SIR O. I guessed it, Señora. In my undergraduate days I
used to quote Oscar Wilde's famous poem

"We are fain of thee still, we are fain.
O sanguine and subtle Dolores
Our Lady of pain."

THE JOURNALIST. Swinburne, Sir Orpheus.

SIR O. Was it Swinburne? Well, it does not matter: it
was one of the literary set.

THE WIDOW. It sounds well; but English is not my
native language. I do not understand the first line. "We
are fain of thee still: we are fain." What does fain mean?

SIR O. Ah well, never mind, Señora, never mind. We

703

are interrupting his honor the Judge. [*To the Judge*] You
were about to say—?

THE JUDGE. I was about to point out that whatever is
the matter with this lady it is not stupidity. She speaks
several languages. Her intelligence is remarkable: she takes
a point like lightning. She has in her veins the learning of
the Arabs, the courage and enterprise of the Spanish conquistadores, the skyward aspiration of the Aztecs, the self-
less devotion to divine purposes of the Jesuit missionaries,
and the readiness of them all to face death in what she
conceives to be her social duty. If we have been actually
obliged to disarm her to prevent her from sacrificing this
harmless Jewish gentleman as her ancestors would have
sacrificed him to the God Quetzalcoatl on the stepped
altars of Mexico, it is not because she is stupid.

THE WIDOW. I hardly follow you, however intelligent
you may think me. But I am proud of having Aztec blood
in my veins, though I should never dream of insulting
Quetzalcoatl by sacrificing a Jew to him.

THE JUDGE. As to the Jewish gentleman himself, I
need not dwell on his case, as he has been driven out of his
native country solely because he is so thoughtful and industrious that his fellow-countrymen are hopelessly beaten
by him in the competition for the conduct of business and
for official positions. I come to our democratic friend here.
I do not know what his business is—

THE NEWCOMER. I'm a retired builder, if you want to
know.

THE JUDGE. He has had ability enough to conduct a
builder's business with such success that he has been able
to retire at his present age, which cannot be far above fifty.

THE NEWCOMER. I am no millionaire, mind you. I have
just enough to do my bit on the Borough Council, and fight
the enemies of democracy.

THE JUDGE. Precisely. That is the spirit of Geneva.
What you lack is not mind but knowledge.

THE NEWCOMER. My wife says I'm pigheaded. How is

that for a testimonial?

THE JUDGE. A first rate one, sir. Pigs never waver in their convictions, never give in to bribes, arguments, nor persuasions. At all events you are wise enough to be dissatisfied with the existing world order, and as anxious to change it as anybody in Geneva.

THE NEWCOMER. The world's good enough for me. Democracy is what I want. We were all for democracy when only the privileged few had votes. But now that everybody has a vote, women and all, where's democracy? Dictators all over the place! and me, an elected representative, kept out of parliament by the police!

THE JUDGE. I come to our Russian friend. He must be a man of ability, or he could not be a Commissar in a country where nothing but ability counts. He has no fears for the future, whereas we are distracted by the continual dread of war, of bankruptcy, of poverty. But there is no evidence that he is a superman. Twenty years ago he would have been talking as great nonsense as any of you.

THE REST [*except the Russian and Begonia*] Nonsense!

THE JUDGE. Perhaps I should have said folly; for folly is not nonsensical: in fact the more foolish it is, the more logical, the more subtle, the more eloquent, the more brilliant.

SIR O. True. True. I have known men who could hold the House of Commons spellbound for hours; but most unsafe. Mere entertainers.

BEGONIA. My turn now. I suppose. I see you are looking at me. Well, all politics are the same to me: I never could make head or tail of them. But I draw the line at Communism and atheism and nationalization of women and doing away with marriage and the family and everybody stealing everybody's property and having to work like slaves and being shot if you breathe a word against it all.

THE JUDGE. You are intelligent enough, well-meaning enough, to be against such a state of things, Dame Begonia, are you?

BEGONIA. Well, of course I am. Wouldnt anybody?

THE JUDGE. It does you the greatest credit.

THE COMMISSAR. But allow me to remark—

THE JUDGE. Not now, Mr. Posky, or you will spoil my point, which is that Dame Begonia's sympathies and intentions are just the same as yours.

BEGONIA. Oh! I never said so. I hate his opinions.

THE COMMISSAR. I must protest. The lady is a bourgeoise: I am a Communist. How can there be the smallest sympathy between us? She upholds the dictatorship of the capitalist, I the dictatorship of the proletariat.

THE JUDGE. Never mind your opinions: I am dealing with the facts. It is evident that the lady is wrong as to the facts, because the inhabitants of a country conducted as she supposes Russia to be conducted would all be dead in a fortnight. It is evident also that her ignorance of how her own country is conducted is as complete as her ignorance of Russia. None of you seem to have any idea of the sort of world you are living in. Into the void created by this ignorance has been heaped a groundwork of savage superstitions: human sacrifices, vengeance, wars of conquest and religion, falsehoods called history, and a glorification of vulgar erotics and pugnacity called romance which transforms people who are naturally as amiable, as teachable, as companionable as dogs, into the most ferocious and cruel of all the beasts. And this, they say, is human nature! But it is not natural at all: real human nature is in continual conflict with it; for amid all the clamor for more slaughter and the erection of monuments to the great slaughterers the cry for justice, for mercy, for fellowship, for peace, has never been completely silenced: even the worst villainies must pretend to be committed for its sake.

SIR O. Too true: oh, too true. But we must take the world as we find it.

THE JUDGE. Wait a bit. How do you find the world? You find it sophisticated to the verge of suicidal insanity. This makes trouble for you as Foreign Secretary. Why not cut out the sophistication? Why not bring your economics, your religion, your history, your political philosophy up to date? Russia has made a gigantic effort to do this; and now her politicians are only about fifty years behind her philosophers and saints whilst the rest of the civilized world is from five hundred to five thousand behind it. In the west the vested interests in ignorance and superstition are so overwhelming that no teacher can tell his young pupils the truth without finding himself starving in the street. The result is that here we despair of human nature, whereas Russia has hopes that have carried her through the most appalling sufferings to the forefront of civilization. Then why despair of human nature when it costs us so much trouble to corrupt it? Why not stop telling it lies? Are we not as capable of that heroic feat as the Russians?

THE COMMISSAR. Apparently not. There are qualities which are produced on the Russian soil alone. There may be a future for the western world if it accepts the guidance of Moscow; but left to its childish self it will decline and fall like as all the old capitalist civilizations.

SIR O. Let me tell you, Mr. Posky, that if ever England takes to Communism, which heaven forbid, it will make a first-rate job of it. Downing Street will not take its orders from Moscow. Moscow took all its ideas from England, as this gentleman has told you. My grandfather bought sherry from John Ruskin's father; and very good sherry it was. And John Ruskin's gospel compared with Karl Marx's was like boiling brandy compared with milk and water.

THE JEW. Yes; but as the British would not listen to Ruskin he produced nothing. The race whose brains will guide the world to the new Jerusalem is the race that produced Karl Marx, who produced Soviet Russia.

THE JUDGE. Race! Nonsense! You are all hopeless mongrels pretending to be thoroughbreds. Why not give up pretending?

SIR O. I am not pretending. I am an Englishman: an

707

Englishman from the heart of England.

THE JUDGE. You mean a British islander from Birmingham, the choicest breed of mongrels in the world. You should be proud of your cross-fertilization.

SIR O. At least I am not a Frenchman nor a negro.

THE JUDGE. At least you are not a Scot, nor an Irishman, nor a man of Kent, nor a man of Devon, nor a Welshman—

SIR O. One of my grandmothers was a Welsh girl. Birmingham is nearer the Welsh border than a Cockney concentration camp like London.

THE JUDGE. In short, you are a mongrel.

THE WIDOW. What is a mongrel? I thought it was a cheap kind of dog.

THE JUDGE. So it is, madam. I applied the word figuratively to a cheap kind of man: that is, to an enormous majority of the human race. It simply indicates mixed ancestry.

THE WIDOW. Ah, that is the secret of the unique distinction of the upper class in the Earthly Paradise. My blood is a blend of all that is noblest in history: the Maya, the Aztec, the Spaniard, the Mexican, the—

THE SECRETARY [*flinging away his pen, with which he has been making notes of the discussion*]. You see, Judge. If you knock all this nonsense of belonging to superior races out of them, they only begin to brag of being choice blends of mongrel. Talk til you are black in the face: you get no good of them. In China the Manchus have given up binding the women's feet and making them cripples for life; but we still go on binding our heads and making fools of ourselves for life.

THE JUDGE. Yes; but do not forget that as lately as the nineteenth century the world believed that the Chinese could never change. Now they are the most revolutionary of all the revolutionists.

THE JEW [*to the Widow*] May I ask have you any engagement for dinner this evening?

THE WIDOW. What is that to you, pray?

THE JEW. Well, would you care to dine with me?

THE WIDOW. Dine with you! Dine with a Jew!

THE JEW. Only a Jew can appreciate your magnificent type of beauty, señora. These Nordics, as they ridiculously call themselves, adore girls who are dolls and women who are cows. But wherever the Jew dominates the theatre and the picture gallery—and he still dominates them in all the great capitals in spite of persecution—your type of beauty is supreme.

THE WIDOW. It is true. You have taste, you Jews. You have appetites. You are vital, in your oriental fashion. And you have boundless ambition and indefatigable pertinacity: you never stop asking for what you want until you possess it. But let me tell you that if you think you can possess me for the price of a dinner, you know neither your own place nor mine.

THE JEW. I ask nothing but the pleasure of your company, the luxury of admiring your beauty and experiencing your sex appeal, and the distinction of being seen in public with you as my guest.

THE WIDOW. You shall not get them. I will not accept your dinner.

THE JEW. Not even if I allow you to pay for it?

THE WIDOW. Is there any end to your impudence? I have never dined with a Jew in my life.

THE JEW. Then you do not know what a good dinner is. Come! Try dining with a Jew for the first time in your life.

THE WIDOW [considering it] It is true that I have nothing else to do this evening. But I must have my gun.

SIR O. [taking the pistol from his pocket] Well, as we seem to have got over the Anti-Semite difficulty I have no further excuse for retaining your property. [He hands her the pistol].

THE WIDOW [replacing it in her handbag] But remember. If you take the smallest liberty—if you hint at the

709

possibility of a more intimate relation, you are a dead man.

THE JEW. You need have no fear. If there are any further advances they must come from yourself.

THE WIDOW. I could never have believed this.

BEGONIA. Geneva is like that. You find yourself dining with all sorts.

SIR O. By the way, Mr. Posky, have you anything particular to do this evening? If not, I should be glad if you would join me at dinner. I want to talk to you about this funny Russian business. You need not dress.

THE COMMISSAR. I will dress if you will allow me. They are rather particular about it now in Moscow.

BEGONIA. Well I never! Fancy a Bolshie dressing!

THE JUDGE. May I suggest, gracious Dame, that you and I dine together?

BEGONIA. Oh, I feel I am imposing on you: I have dined with you three times already. You know, I am a little afraid of you, you are so deep and learned and what I call mental. I may be a Dame of the British Empire and all that; but I am not the least bit mental; and what attraction you can find in my conversation I cant imagine.

THE SECRETARY. Geneva is so full of mental people that it is an inexpressible relief to meet some cheerful person with absolutely no mind at all. The judge can have his pick of a hundred clever women in Geneva; but what he needs to give his brain a rest is a soft-bosomed goose without a political idea in her pretty head.

BEGONIA. Go on: I am used to it. I know your opinion of me: I am the only perfect idiot in Geneva. But I got a move on the League; and thats more than you ever could do, you old stick-in-the-mud.

THE WIDOW. Take care, señorita! A woman should not wear her brains on her sleeve as men do. She should keep them up it. Men like to be listened to.

BEGONIA. I have listened here until I am nearly dead. Still, when men start talking you can always think of something else. They are so taken up with themselves that they dont notice it.

THE WIDOW. Do not give away the secrets of our sex, child. Be thankful, as I am, that you have made sure of your next dinner.

THE JOURNALIST. What about my dinner?

THE SECRETARY. You had better dine with me. You can tell me the latest news.

THE JUDGE. I can tell you that. The trial of the dictators by the Permanent Court of International Justice has been fixed for this day fortnight.

THE REST. Where?

THE JUDGE. At the Hague, in the old palace.

THE SECRETARY. But the trial will be a farce. The dictators wont come.

THE JUDGE. I think they will. You, Sir Orpheus, will, I presume, be present with a watching brief from the British Foreign Office.

SIR O. I shall certainly be present. Whether officially or not I cannot say.

THE JUDGE. You will all be present, I hope. May I suggest that you telephone at once to secure rooms at the Hague. If you wait until the news becomes public you may find yourselves crowded out.

All except the Judge and the Secretary rise hastily and disappear in the direction of the hotel bureau.

THE SECRETARY. You really think the dictators will walk into the dock for you?

THE JUDGE. We shall see. There will be no dock. I shall ask you to act as Clerk to the Court.

THE SECRETARY. Impossible.

THE JUDGE. It seems so now; but I think you will.

THE SECRETARY. Well, as Midlander is coming I shall certainly be there to hear what he may say. But the dictators? Bombardone? Battler? How can you make them come? You have not a single soldier. Not even a policeman.

THE JUDGE. All the soldiers and police on earth could not move them except by the neck and heels. But if the

GENEVA

Hague becomes the centre of the European stage all the soldiers and police in the world will not keep them away from it.

THE SECRETARY [*musing*] Hm! Well— [*he shakes his head and gives it up*].

THE JUDGE [*smiles*] They will come. Where the spotlight is, there will the despots be gathered.

ACT IV

A SALON *in the old palace of the Hague. On a spacious dais a chair of State, which is in fact an old throne, is at the head of a table furnished with chairs, writing materials, and buttons connected with telephonic apparatus. The table occupies the centre of the dais. On the floor at both sides chairs are arranged in rows for the accommodation of spectators, litigants, witnesses, etc. The tall windows admit abundance of sunlight and shew up all the gilding and grandeur of the immovables. The door is at the side, on the right of the occupant of the chair of state, at present empty. The formal arrangement of the furniture suggests a sitting or hearing or meeting of some kind. A waste paper basket is available.*

The secretary of the League of Nations has a little central table to himself in front of the other. His profile points towards the door. Behind him, in the front row of chairs are the Jew, the Commissar and the Widow. In the opposite front row are Begonia and a cheerful young gentleman, powerfully built, with an uproarious voice which he subdues to conversational pitch with some difficulty. Next him is the quondam Newcomer. They are all reading newspapers. Begonia and her young man have one excessively illustrated newspaper between them. He has his arm round her waist and is shamelessly enjoying their physical contact. The two are evidently betrothed.

THE JEW. Do you think anything is really going to happen, Mr Secretary?

THE SECRETARY. Possibly not. I am here to be able to report from personal knowledge whether any notice has been taken of the summonses issued by the court.

THE BETROTHED. The judge himself hasnt turned up.

THE SECRETARY [*looking at his watch*]. He is not due yet: you have all come too early.

THE BETROTHED. We came early to make sure of getting seats. And theres not a soul in the bally place except ourselves.

713

Sir Orpheus comes in.

SIR ORPHEUS. What! Nobody but ourselves! Dont they admit the public?

THE SECRETARY. The public is not interested, it seems.

BEGONIA. One free lance journalist looked in; but she went away when she found there was nothing doing.

THE BETROTHED. The doors are open all right. All are affectionately invited.

SIR ORPHEUS [*seating himself next Begonia*]. But what a dreadful fiasco for our friend the judge! I warned him that this might happen. I told him to send special invitations to the press, and cards to all the leading people and foreign visitors. And here! not a soul except ourselves! All Europe will laugh at him.

THE SECRETARY. Yes; but if the affair is going to be a fiasco the fewer people there are to witness it the better.

BEGONIA. After all, theres more than half a dozen of us. Quite a distinguished audience I call it. Remember, you are the Foreign Secretary, Nunky. You are an honorable, Billikins. And I'm not exactly a nobody.

THE BETROTHED [*kissing her hand*] My ownest and bestest, you are a Dame of the British Empire. The Camberwell Times has celebrated your birthday by a poem hailing you as the Lily of Geneva; but on this occasion only, you are not the centre of European interest. The stupendous and colossal joke of the present proceedings is that this court has summoned all the dictators to appear before it and answer charges brought against them by the Toms, Dicks, Harriets, Susans and Elizas of all nations.

THE WIDOW. Pardon me, young Señor. I am neither Susan nor Eliza.

THE BETROTHED. Present company excepted, of course, Señora. But the point—the staggering, paralyzing, jolly bally breath-bereaving point of our assembly today is that the dictators have been summoned and that they wont come. Young Johnny Judge has no more authority over them than his cat.

GENEVA

THE NEWCOMER. But if they wont come, gentlemen, what are we here for?

THE BETROTHED. To see the fun when Johnny Judge comes and finds nothing doing, I suppose.

THE WIDOW. Is he not late? We seem to have been waiting here for ages.

THE SECRETARY [*looking at his watch*] He is due now. It is on the stroke of ten.

The Judge, in his judicial robe, enters. They all rise. He is in high spirits and very genial.

THE JUDGE [*shaking hands with Sir Orpheus*] Good morning, Sir Midlander. [*He passes on to the judicial chair, greeting them as he goes*] Good morning, ladies and gentlemen. Good morning, mademoiselle. Good morning, Señora. Good morning. Good morning. [*Takes his seat*] Pray be seated.

They all sit, having bowed speechlessly to his salutations.

THE JUDGE. Any defendants yet, Mr Secretary?

THE SECRETARY. None, your Honor. The parties on your left are all plaintiffs. On your right, Sir Orpheus Midlander has a watching brief for the British Foreign Office. The lady, Dame Begonia Brown, represents the Committee for Intellectual Co-operation. The young gentleman is the public.

THE JUDGE. An impartial spectator, eh?

THE BETROTHED. No, my lord. Very partial to the girl. Engaged, in fact.

THE JUDGE. My best congratulations. May I warn you all that the instruments on the table are microphones and televisors? I have arranged so as to avoid a crowd and make our proceedings as unconstrained and comfortable as possible; but our apparent privacy is quite imaginary.

General consternation. They all sit up as in church.

BEGONIA. But they should have told us this when we came in. Billikins has been sitting with his arm round my waist, whispering all sorts of silly things. Theyll be in The

715

Camberwell Times tomorrow.

THE JUDGE. I'm sorry. You should have been warned. In the International Court no walls can hide you, and no distance deaden your lightest whisper. We are all seen and heard in Rome, in Moscow, in London, wherever the latest type of receiver is installed.

BEGONIA. Heard! You mean overheard.

THE WIDOW. And overlooked. Our very clothes are transparent to the newest rays. It is scandalous.

THE JUDGE. Not at all, Señora. The knowledge that we all live in public, and that there are no longer any secret places where evil things can be done and wicked conspiracies discussed, may produce a great improvement in morals.

THE WIDOW. I protest. All things that are private are not evil; but they may be extremely indecent.

BEGONIA. We'd better change the subject, I think.

THE BETROTHED. What about the dictators, my lord? Do you really think any of them will come?

THE JUDGE. They are not under any physical compulsion to come. But every day of their lives they do things they are not physically compelled to do.

SIR ORPHEUS. That is a fact, certainly. But it is hardly a parliamentary fact.

A telephone rings on the Judge's desk. He holds down a button and listens.

THE JUDGE. You will not have to wait any longer, Sir Midlander. [*Into the telephone*] We are waiting for him. Shew him the way. [*He releases the button*]. The very first dictator to arrive is Signor Bombardone.

ALL THE REST. Bombardone!!!

The Dictator enters, dominant, brusque, every inch a man of destiny.

BOMBARDONE. Is this the so-called International Court?

THE JUDGE. It is.

BBDE. My name is Bombardone. [*He mounts the dais; takes the nearest chair with a powerful hand and places it*
716

on the Judge's left; then flings himself massively into it]
Do not let my presence embarrass you. Proceed.

THE JUDGE. I have to thank you, Signor Bombardone,
for so promptly obeying the summons of the court.

BBDE. I obey nothing. I am here because it is my will
to be here. My will is part of the world's will. A large part,
as it happens. The world moves towards internationalism.
Without this movement to nerve you you would never
have had the audacity to summon me. Your action is therefore a symptom of the movement of civilization. Wherever
such a symptom can be detected I have a place: a leading
place.

SIR ORPHEUS. But pardon me, Signor: I understand
that you are a great nationalist. How can you be at once a
nationalist and an internationalist?

BBDE. How can I be anything else? How do you build
a house? By first making good sound bricks. You cant build
it of mud. The nations are the bricks out of which the
future world State must be built. I consolidated my country as a nation: a white nation. I then added a black nation
to it and made it an empire. When the empires federate,
its leaders will govern the world; and these leaders will
have a superleader who will be the ablest man in the
world: that is my vision. I leave you to imagine what I
think of the mob of bagmen from fifty potty little foreign
States that calls itself a League of Nations.

JUDGE. Your country is a member of that League,
Signor.

BBDE. My country has to keep an eye on fools. The
scripture tells us that it is better to meet a bear in our path
than a fool. Fools are dangerous; and the so-called League
of Nations is a League of Fools; therefore the wise must
join it to watch them. That is why all the effective Powers
are in the League, as well as the little toy republics we
shall swallow up in due time.

THE ÇI-DEVANT NEWCOMER. Steady on, mister. I dont
understand.

717

GENEVA

BBDE. [*contemptuously to the Judge*] Tell him that this is a court of people who understand, and that the place of those who do not understand is in the ranks of silent and blindly obedient labor.

NEWCOMER. Oh, thats your game, is it? Who are you that I should obey you? What about democracy?

BBDE. I am what I am: you are what you are; and in virtue of these two facts I am where I am and you are where you are. Try to change places with me: you may as well try to change the path of the sun through the heavens.

THE NEWCOMER. You think a lot of yourself, dont you? I ask you again: what about democracy?

An unsmiling middle aged gentleman with slim figure, erect carriage, and resolutely dissatisfied expression, wanders in.

THE DISSATISFIED GENTLEMAN. Is this the sitting of the department of international justice?

BBDE. [*springing up*] Battler, by all thats unexpected!

BATTLER [*equally surprised*] Bombardone, by all thats underhand!

BBDE. You thought you could steal a march on me, eh?

BATTLER. You have ambushed me. Fox!

BBDE. [*sitting down*] Undignified, Ernest. Undignified.

BATTLER. True, Bardo. I apologize. [*He takes a chair from behind Sir Orpheus, and mounts the dais to the right of the Judge, who now has a dictator on each side of him*] By your leave, sir. [*He sits*].

JUDGE. I thank you, Mr Battler, for obeying the summons of the court.

BATTLER. Obedience is hardly the word, sir.

JUDGE. You have obeyed. You are here. Why?

BATTLER. That is just what I have come to find out. Why are you here, Bardo?

BBDE. I am everywhere.

THE BETROTHED [*boisterously*] Ha ha! Ha ha ha! Dam funny, that.

718

GENEVA

THE JUDGE. I must ask the public not to smile.

NEWCOMER [*who has no sense of humor*] Smile! He was not smiling: he laughed right out. With all respect to your worship we are wasting our time talking nonsense. How can a man be everywhere? The other gentleman says he came here to find out why he came here. It isnt sense. These two gents are balmy.

BBDE. Pardon me. What does balmy mean?

NEWCOMER. Balmy. Off your chumps. If you want it straight, mad.

BBDE. You belong to the lower orders, I see.

NEWCOMER. Who are you calling lower orders? Dont you know that democracy has put an end to all that?

BBDE. On the contrary, my friend, democracy has given a real meaning to it for the first time. Democracy has thrown us both into the same pair of scales. Your pan has gone up: mine has gone down; and nothing will bring down your pan while I am sitting in the other. Democracy has delivered you from the law of priest and king, of landlord and capitalist, only to bring you under the law of personal gravitation. Personal gravitation is a law of nature. You cannot cut its head off.

NEWCOMER. Democracy can cut your head off. British democracy has cut off thicker heads before.

BBDE. Never. Plutocracy has cut off the heads of kings and archbishops to make itself supreme and rob the people without interference from king or priest; but the people always follow their born leader. When there is no leader, no king, or priest, nor any body of law established by dead kings and priests, you have mob law, lynching law, gangster law: in short, American democracy. Thank your stars you have never known democracy in England. I have rescued my country from all that by my leadership. I am a democratic institution.

NEWCOMER. Gosh. You democratic! Youve abolished democracy, you have.

BBDE. Put my leadership to the vote. Take a plebiscite.

719

If I poll less than 95 per cent of the adult nation I will resign. If that is not democracy what is democracy?

NEWCOMER. It isnt British democracy.

BATTLER. British democracy is a lie. I have said it.

NEWCOMER. Oh, dont talk nonsense, you ignorant foreigner. Plebiscites are unEnglish, thoroughly unEnglish.

BEGONIA. Hear hear!

SIR O. May I venture to make an observation?

BATTLER. Who are you?

SIR O. Only a humble Englishman, listening most respectfully to your clever and entertaining conversation. Officially, I am the British Foreign Secretary.

Both Leaders rise and give the Fascist salute. Sir Orpheus remains seated, but waves his hand graciously.

BBDE. I must explain to the court that England is no longer of any consequence apart from me. I have dictated her policy for years [*he sits*].

BATTLER. I have snapped my fingers in England's face on every issue that has risen between us. Europe looks to me, not to England. [*He also resumes his seat*].

SIR O. You attract attention, Mr Battler: you certainly do attract attention. And you, Signor Bombardone, are quite welcome to dictate our policy as long as it is favorable to us. But the fact is, we are mostly unconscious of these triumphs of yours in England. I listen to your account of them with perfect complacency and—I hope you will not mind my saying so—with some amusement. But I must warn you that if your triumphs ever lead you to any steps contrary to the interests of the British Empire we shall have to come down rather abruptly from triumphs to facts; and the facts may not work so smoothly as the triumphs.

BATTLER. What could you do, facts or no facts?

SIR O. I dont know.

BATTLER. ⎫
BBDE. ⎬ You dont know!!!
       ⎭

SIR O. I dont know. Nor do you, Mr. Battler. Nor you,

Signor.

BBDE. Do you mean that I do not know what you could do, or that I do not know what I should do.

SIR O. Both, Signor.

BBDE. What have you to say to that, Ernest?

BATTLER. I should know what to do: have no doubt about that.

SIR O. You mean that you would know what to do when you knew what England was going to do?

BATTLER. I know already what you could do. Nothing. I tore up your peace treaty and threw the pieces in your face. You did nothing. I took your last Locarno pact and marched 18,000 soldiers through it. I threw down a frontier and doubled the size and power of my realm in spite of your teeth. What did you do? Nothing.

SIR O. Of course we did nothing. It did not suit us to do anything. A child of six could have foreseen that we should do nothing; so you shook your fist at us and cried "Do anything if you dare." Your countrymen thought you a hero. But as you knew you were quite safe, we were not impressed.

BBDE. You are quite right, Excellency. It was your folly and France's that blew Ernest up the greasy pole of political ambition. Still, he has a flair for power; and he has my example to encourage him. Do not despise Ernest.

BATTLER. I have never concealed my admiration for you, Bardo. But you have a failing that may ruin you unless you learn to keep it in check.

BBDE. And what is that, pray?

BATTLER. Selfconceit. You think yourself the only great man in the world.

BBDE. [calm] Can you name a greater?

BATTLER. There are rivals in Russia, Arabia, and Iran.

BBDE. And there is Ernest the Great. Why omit him?

BATTLER. We shall see. History, not I, must award the palm.

JUDGE. Let us omit all personalities, gentlemen. Allow

721

me to recall you to the important point reached by Sir Midlander.

SIR O. What was that, my lord?

JUDGE. When you were challenged as to what your country would do in the event of a conflict of interest, you said frankly you did not know.

SIR O. Well, I dont.

BATTLER. And you call yourself a statesman!

SIR O. I assure you I do not. The word is hardly in use in England. I am a member of the Cabinet, and in my modest amateur way a diplomatist. When you ask me what will happen if British interests are seriously menaced you ask me to ford the stream before we come to it. We never do that in England. But when we come to the stream we ford it or bridge it or dry it up. And when we have done that it is too late to think about it. We have found that we can get on without thinking. You see, thinking is very little use unless you know the facts. And we never do know the political facts until twenty years after. Sometimes a hundred and fifty.

JUDGE. Still, Sir Midlander, you know that such an activity as thought exists.

SIR O. You alarm me, my lord. I am intensely reluctant to lose my grip of the realities of the moment and sit down to think. It is dangerous. It is unEnglish. It leads to theories, to speculative policies, to dreams and visions. If I may say so, I think my position is a more comfortable one than that of the two eminent leaders who are gracing these proceedings by their presence here today. Their remarks are most entertaining: every sentence is an epigram: I, who am only a stupid Englishman, feel quite abashed by my commonplaceness. But if you ask me what their intentions are I must frankly say that I dont know. Where do they stand with us? I dont know. But they know what England intends. They know what to expect from us. We have no speculative plans. We shall simply stick to our beloved British Empire, and undertake any larger cares that Providence may impose on us. Meanwhile we should feel very uneasy if any other Power or combinations of Powers were to place us in a position of military or naval inferiority, especially naval inferiority. I warn you—I beg you—do not frighten us. We are a simple well-meaning folk, easily frightened. And when we are frightened we are capable of anything, even of things we hardly care to remember afterwards. Do not drive us in that direction. Take us as we are; and let be. Pardon my dull little speech. I must not take more of your time.

BATTLER. Machiavelli!

BBDE. A most astute speech. But it cannot impose on us.

JUDGE. It has imposed on both of you. It is a perfectly honest speech made to you by a perfectly honest gentleman; and you both take it as an outburst of British hypocrisy.

BEGONIA. A piece of damned cheek, I call it. I wont sit here and listen to my country being insulted.

THE BETROTHED. Hear hear! Up, Camberwell!

BATTLER. What does he mean by "Up, Camberwell!"? What is Camberwell?

BEGONIA. Oh! He doesnt know what Camberwell is!

THE SECRETARY. Camberwell, Mr Battler, is a part of London which is totally indistinguishable from any other part of London, except that it is on the south side of the Thames and not on the north.

BEGONIA. What do you mean—indistinguishable? It maynt be as distangay as Mayfair; but it's better than Peckham anyhow.

BBDE. Excuse my ignorance; but what is Peckham?

BEGONIA. Oh! He doesnt know what Peckham is. These people dont know anything.

THE SECRETARY. Peckham is another part of London, adjacent to Camberwell and equally and entirely indistinguishable from it.

BEGONIA. Dont you believe him, gentlemen. He is saying that just to get a rise out of me. The people in

723

Camberwell are the pick of south London society. The Peckham people are lower middle class: the scum of the earth.

BATTLER. I applaud your local patriotism, young lady; but I press for an answer to my question. What does "Up, Camberwell!" mean?

JUDGE. I think it is the south London equivalent to "Heil, Battler!"

BBDE. Ha ha ha! Ha ha! Good.

BATTLER. Am I being trifled with?

JUDGE. You may depend on me to keep order, Mr Battler. Dame Begonia is making a most valuable contribution to our proceedings. She is shewing us what we really have to deal with. Peace between the Powers of Europe on a basis of irreconcilable hostility between Camberwell and Peckham: that is our problem.

SIR O. Do not deceive yourself, my lord. Fire a shot at England; and Camberwell and Peckham will stand shoulder to shoulder against you.

BATTLER. You hear, Bardo. This Englishman is threatening us.

SIR O. Not at all. I am only telling you what will happen in certain contingencies which we sincerely wish to avoid. I am doing my best to be friendly in manner, as I certainly am in spirit. I respectfully suggest that if an impartial stranger were present his impression would be that you two gentlemen are threatening me: I might almost say bullying me.

BBDE. But we are. We shall not be thought the worse of at home for that. How are we to keep up the selfrespect of our people unless we confront the rest of the world with a battle cry? And—will you excuse a personal criticism?

SIR O. Certainly. I shall value it.

BBDE. You are very kind: you almost disarm me. But may I say that your technique is out of date? It would seem amusingly quaint in a museum, say in the rooms devoted to the eighteenth century; but of what use is it for impressing a modern crowd? And your slogans are hopelessly obsolete.

SIR O. I do not quite follow. What, exactly, do you mean by my technique?

BBDE. Your style, your gestures, the modulations of your voice. Public oratory is a fine art. Like other fine arts, it cannot be practised effectively without a laboriously acquired technique.

SIR O. But I am an experienced public speaker. My elocution has never been complained of. Like other public speakers I have taken pains to acquire a distinct articulation; and I have had the best parliamentary models before me all through my public life. I suppose—now that you put it in that way—that this constitutes a technique; but I should be sorry to think that there is anything professional about it.

BATTLER. Yes; but what a technique! I contemplated it at first with amazement, then with a curiosity which obliged me to study it—to find out what it could possibly mean. To me the object of public speaking is to propagate a burning conviction of truth and importance, and thus produce immediate action and enthusiastic faith and obedience. My technique, like that of my forerunner opposite, was invented and perfected with that object. You must admit that it has been wonderfully successful: your parliaments have been swept away by the mere breath of it; and we ourselves exercise a personal authority unattainable by any king, president, or minister. That is simple, natural, reasonable. But what is your technique? What is its object? Apparently its object is to destroy conviction and to paralyze action. Out of the ragbag of stale journalism and Kikkeronian Latin—

SIR O. I protest. I beg. I ask the court to protect me.

THE JUDGE. What is the matter? Protect you from what?

SIR O. From these abominable modern mispronunciations. Kikkeronian is an insult to my old school. I insist on Sisseronian.

THE BETROTHED. Hear hear!

BBDE. Take care, Ernest. This is part of the British technique. You were talking of something really important. That is dangerous. He switches you off to something of no importance whatever.

SIR O. I did not intend that, I assure you. And I cannot admit that the modern corruption of our old English pronunciation of the classics is a matter of no importance. It is a matter of supreme importance.

JUDGE. We do not question its importance, Sir Midlander; but it is outside the jurisdiction of this court; and we must not allow it to divert us from our proper business. I recall you to a specific charge of a specific crime against a specific section of the community. It is a crime of the most horrible character to drop a bomb upon a crowded city. It is a crime only a shade less diabolical to strew the sea, the common highway of all mankind, with mines that will shatter and sink any ship that stumbles on them in the dark. These abominable crimes are being committed by young men—

SIR O. Under orders, my lord, and from patriotic motives.

JUDGE. No doubt. Suppose a young man picks your pocket, and, on being detected, alleges, first that somebody told him to do it, and second that he wanted your money to pay his income tax—a highly patriotic motive—would you accept that excuse?

SIR O. Ridiculous! Remember, sir, that if our young heroes are the killers, they are also the killed. They risk their own lives.

JUDGE. Let us then add a third plea to our pickpocket's defence. He runs the same risk of having his pocket picked as you. Would you accept that plea also?

SIR O. My lord: I abhor war as much as you do. But, damn it, if a fellow is coming at me to cut my throat, I must cut his if I can. Am I to allow him to kill me and ravish my wife and daughters?

726

JUDGE. I think that under such circumstances a plea of legitimate defence might be allowed. But what has a tussle with a murderer and a ravisher to do with laying a mine in the high seas to slaughter innocent travellers whose intentions towards yourself, your wife, and your daughters, if they have any intentions, are entirely friendly? What has it to do with dropping a bomb into the bed of a sleeping baby or a woman in childbirth?

SIR O. One feels that. It is terrible. But we cannot help its happening. We must take a practical view. It is like the London traffic. We know that so many children will be run over and killed every week. But we cannot stop the traffic because of that. Motor traffic is a part of civilized life. So is coalmining. So is railway transport. So is flying. The explosions in the mines, the collisions of the trains, the accidents in the shunting yards, the aeroplane crashes, are most dreadful; but we cannot give up flying and coalmining and railway travelling on that account. They are a part of civilized life. War is a part of civilized life. We cannot give it up because of its shocking casualties.

JUDGE. But the mine explosions and railway collisions and areoplane crashes are not the objects of the industry. They are its accidents. They occur in spite of every possible precaution to prevent them. But war has no other object than to produce these casualties. The business and purpose of a coalminer is to hew the coal out of the earth to keep the home fires burning. But the soldier's business is to burn the homes and kill their inhabitants. That is not a part of civilization: it is a danger to it.

COMMISSAR. Come, Comrade Judge: have you never sentenced a criminal to death? Has the executioner never carried out your sentence? Is not that a very necessary part of civilization?

JUDGE. I sentence persons to death when they have committed some crime which has raised the question whether they are fit to live in human society, but not until that question has been decided against them by a careful

727

trial at which they have every possible legal assistance and protection. This does not justify young men in slaughtering innocent persons at random. It would justify me in sentencing the young men to death if they were brought to trial. What we are here to investigate is why they are not brought to trial.

SIR O. But really, they only obey orders.

THE JUDGE. Why do you say "only"? The slaughter of human beings and the destruction of cities are not acts to be qualified by the word only. Why are the persons who give such atrocious orders not brought to trial?

SIR O. But before what court?

JUDGE. Before this court if necessary. There was a time when I might have answered "Before the judgment seat of God". But since people no longer believe that there is any such judgment seat, must we not create one before we are destroyed by the impunity and glorification of murder?

BBDE. Peace may destroy you more effectually. It is necessary for the cultivation of the human character that a field should be reserved for war. Men decay when they do not fight.

THE WIDOW. And when they fight they die.

BBDE. No no. Only a percentage, to give zest and reality to the conflict.

THE JUDGE. Would you describe a contest of a man against a machine gun, or a woman in childbirth against a cloud of mustard gas, as a fight?

BBDE. It is a peril: a deadly peril. And it is peril that educates us, not mere bayonet fencing and fisticuffs. Nations never do anything until they are in danger.

THE JEW. Is there not plenty of danger in the world without adding the danger of poison gas to it?

BBDE. Yes: there is the danger of getting your feet wet. But it has not the fighting quality that gives war its unique power over the imagination, and through the imagination over the characters and powers of mankind.

728

GENEVA

THE WIDOW. You have been a soldier. Are you the better for it? Were you not glad when your wounds took you out of the trenches and landed you in a hospital bed?

BBDE. Extremely glad. But that was part of the experience. War is not all glory and all bravery. You find out what a rotten coward you are as well as how brave you are. You learn what it is to be numbed with misery and terror as well as how to laugh at death. Ask my understudy here. He too has been a soldier. He knows.

BATTLER. We all begin as understudies, and end, perhaps, as great actors. The army was a school in which I learnt a good deal, because whoever has my capacity for learning can learn something even in the worst school. The army is the worst school, because fighting is not a whole-time-job, and in the army they pretend that it is. It ends in the discharged soldier being good for nothing until he recovers his civilian sense and the habit of thinking for himself. No, cousin: I am a man of peace; but it must be a voluntary peace, not an intimidated one. Not until I am armed to the teeth and ready to face all the world in arms is my Pacifism worth anything.

SIR O. Admirable! Precisely our British position.

NEWCOMER. I'm British. And what I say is that war is necessary to keep down the population.

BBDE. This man is a fool. War stimulates population. The soldier may go to his death; but he leaves behind him the pregnant woman who will replace him. Women cannot resist the soldier: they despise the coward. Death, the supreme danger, rouses life to its supreme ecstasy of love. When has a warlike race ever lacked children?

THE BETROTHED. Very romantic and all that, old man; but this notion of man on the battlefield and woman in the home wont wash nowadays. Home was a safe place when Waterloo was fought; but today the home is the bomber's favorite mark. The soldier is safe in his trench while the woman is being blown to smithereens by her baby's cot. Kill the women; and where will your population be? Egad, you

729

wont have any population at all.

BATTLER. This man is not a fool. If the object of war is extermination, kill the women: the men do not matter.

BBDE. The object of war is not extermination: it is the preservation of man's noblest attribute, courage. The utmost safety for women, the utmost peril for men: that is the ideal.

THE BETROTHED. I say, Signor: do you take any precautions against assassination?

BBDE. I do not encourage it; but it is one of the risks of my position. I live dangerously. It is more intense than living safely.

NEWCOMER. Your worship: these gentlemen are talking nonsense.

JUDGE. All politicians talk nonsense. You mean, I presume, that it is not the sort of nonsense you are accustomed to.

NEWCOMER. No I dont. I am accustomed to hear statesmen talking proper politics. But this about living dangerously is not proper politics: it's nonsense to me. Am I to cross the street without looking to see whether there is a bus coming? Are there to be no red and green lights? Am I to sleep in a smallpox hospital? Am I to cross the river on a tight rope instead of on a bridge? Am I to behave like a fool or a man of sense?

BBDE. You would be a much more wonderful man if you could walk on a tight rope instead of requiring several feet of solid pavement, costing years of labor to construct.

SIR O. Do you seriously propose that we should be ruled by an aristocracy of acrobats?

BBDE. Is it more impossible than your British aristocracy of foxhunters?

SIR O. Signor: acrobats are not foxhunters.

BBDE. And gentlemen are not acrobats. But what a pity!

THE NEWCOMER. Oh, whats the use of talking to you people? Am I dreaming? Am I drunk?

BBDE. No: you are only out of your depth, my friend.

730

And now to business. Strength. Silence. Order. I am here to meet my accusers, if any.

JUDGE. You are accused, it seems, of the murder and destruction of liberty and democracy in Europe.

BBDE. One cannot destroy what never existed. Besides, these things are not my business. My business is government. I give my people good government, as far as their folly and ignorance permit. What more do they need?

THE NEWCOMER. Why am I locked out of the parliament of Jacksonland, to which I have been lawfully elected: tell me that.

BBDE. Presumably because you want to obstruct its work and discredit its leaders. Half a dozen such obstructionists as you could spin out to two years the work I do in ten minutes. The world can endure you no longer. Your place is in the dustbin.

THE NEWCOMER. I give up. You are too much for me when it comes to talking. But what do I care? I have my principles still. Thats my last word. Now go on and talk yourself silly.

BBDE. It is your turn now, cousin.

BATTLER. Do I stand accused? Of what, pray?

THE JEW [*springing up*] Of murder. Of an attempt to exterminate the flower of the human race.

BATTLER. What do you mean?

THE JEW. I am a Jew.

BATTLER. Then what right have you in my country? I exclude you as the British exclude the Chinese in Australia, as the Americans exclude the Japanese in California.

JEW. Why do the British exclude the Chinese? Because the Chinaman is so industrious, so frugal, so trustworthy, that nobody will employ a white British workman or caretaker if there is a yellow one within reach. Why do you exclude the Jew? Because you cannot compete with his intelligence, his persistence, his foresight, his grasp of finance. It is our talents, our virtues, that you fear, not our vices.

BATTLER. And am I not excluded for my virtues? I may

731

not set foot in England until I declare that I will do no work there and that I will return to my own country in a few weeks. In every country the foreigner is a trespasser. On every coast he is confronted by officers who say you shall not land without your passport, your visa. If you are of a certain race or color you shall not land at all. Sooner than let German soldiers march through Belgium England plunged Europe into war. Every State chooses its population and selects its blood. We say that ours shall be Nordic, not Hittite: that is all.

JEW. A Jew is a human being. Has he not a right of way and settlement everywhere upon the earth?

BATTLER. Nowhere without a passport. That is the law of nations.

JEW. I have been beaten and robbed. Is that the law of nations?

BATTLER. I am sorry. I cannot be everywhere; and all my agents are not angels.

THE JEW [*triumphantly*] Ah! Then you are NOT God Almighty, as you pretend to be. [*To the Judge*] Your honor: I am satisfied. He has admitted his guilt. [*He flings himself back into his seat*].

BATTLER. Liar. No Jew is ever satisfied. Enough. You have your warning. Keep away; and you will be neither beaten nor robbed. Keep away, I tell you. The world is wide enough for both of us. My country is not.

THE JEW. I leave myself in the hands of the court. For my race there are no frontiers. Let those who set them justify themselves.

BBDE. Mr President: if you allow Ernest to expatiate on the Jewish question we shall get no further before bedtime. He should have waited for a lead from me before meddling with it, and forcing me to banish the Jews lest my people should be swamped by the multitudes he has driven out. I say he should have waited. I must add that I have no use for leaders who do not follow me.

BATTLER. I am no follower of yours. When has a

Nordic ever stooped to follow a Latin Southerner?

BBDE. You forget that my country has a north as well as a south, a north beside whose mountains your little provincial Alps are molehills. The snows, the crags, the avalanches, the bitter winds of those mountains make men, Ernest, MEN! The trippers' paradise from which you come breeds operatic tenors. You are too handsome, Ernest: you think yourself a blond beast. Ladies and gentlemen, look at him! Is he a blond beast? The blondest beast I know is the Calabrian bull. I have no desire to figure as a blond beast; but I think I could play the part more plausibly than Ernest if it were my cue to do so. I am everything that you mean by the word Nordic. He is a born Southerner; and the south is the south, whether it be the south of the Arctic circle or the south of the equator. Race is nothing: it is the number of metres above sealevel that puts steel into men. Our friend here was born at a very moderate elevation. He is an artist to his finger tips; but his favorite play as a boy was not defying avalanches. As to our races, they are so mixed that the whole human race must be descended from Abraham; for everybody who is alive now must be descended from everybody who was alive in Abraham's day. Ernest has his share in Abraham.

BATTLER. This is an intolerable insult. I demand satisfaction. I cannot punch your head because you are at least two stone heavier than I; but I will fight you with any weapon that will give me a fair chance against you.

THE JUDGE. Gentlemen: you are at the Hague, and in a Court of Justice. Duels are out of date. And your lives are too valuable to be risked in that way.

BBDE. True, your Excellency. I admit that Ernest's ancestors are totally unknown. I apologize.

BATTLER. I dont want an apology. I want satisfaction. You shall not rob me of it by apologizing. Are you a coward?

BBDE. We are both cowards, Ernest. Remember 1918. All men are cowards now.

BATTLER [*rising*] I shall go home.

WIDOW [*rising*] You shall not. Here at least we have come to the real business of this court; and you want to run away from it. If a man of you stirs I shall shoot. [*Panic*].

BBDE. Hands up, Ernest [*politely holding up his own*].

THE WIDOW. Listen to me. In my country men fight duels every day. If they refuse they become pariahs: no one will visit them or speak to them: their women folk are driven out of society as if they were criminals.

BATTLER. It was so in my country. But I have stopped it.

JUDGE. Yet you want to fight a duel yourself.

BATTLER. Not for etiquette. For satisfaction.

THE WIDOW. Yes: that is what men always want. Well, look at me. I am a murderess [*general consternation*]. My husband wanted satisfaction of another kind. He got it from my dearest friend; and etiquette obliged me to kill her. In my dreams night after night she comes to me and begs me to forgive her; and I have to kill her again. I long to go mad; but I cannot: each time I do this dreadful thing I wake up with my mind clearer and clearer, and the horror of it deeper and more agonizing.

BATTLER [*flinching*] Stop this. I cannot bear it.

BBDE. Who is this woman? What right has she to be here?

WIDOW. My name is Revenge. My name is Jealousy. My name is the unwritten law that is no law. Until you have dealt with me you have done nothing.

JUDGE. You have a specific case. State it.

WIDOW. My husband has been murdered by his successor. My son must murder him if there is to be no redress but the blood feud; and I shall dream and dream and kill and kill. I call on you to condemn him.

BBDE. And condemn you.

WIDOW. I shall condemn myself. Pass your sentence on me; and I shall execute it myself, here in this court if you will.

734

JUDGE. But do you not understand that the judgments of this court are followed by no executions? They are moral judgments only.

WIDOW. I understand perfectly. You can point the finger of the whole world at the slayer of my husband and say "You are guilty of murder." You can put the same brand on my forehead. That is all you need do, all you can do. Then my dreams will cease and I shall kill myself. As for him, let him bear the brand as best he can.

JUDGE. That is the justice of this court. I thank you, Señora, for your comprehension of it.

BATTLER [*distressed by the narrative*] I cannot bear this. Order that woman not to kill herself.

BBDE. No. If she has a Roman soul, who dares forbid her?

JUDGE. My authority does not go so far, Mr Battler.

BATTLER. Your authority goes as far as you dare push it and as far as it is obeyed. What authority have I? What authority has Bardo? What authority has any leader? We command and are obeyed: that is all.

BBDE. That is true, Signor judge. Authority is a sort of genius: either you have it or you have not. Either you are obeyed or torn to pieces. But in some souls and on some points there is an authority higher than any other. Of such is the Roman soul; and this is one of the points on which the Roman soul stands firm. The woman's life is in her own hands.

BATTLER. No: I tell you I cannot bear it. Forbid her to kill herself or I will leave the court.

JUDGE. Señora: I forbid you to kill yourself. But I will sentence the slayer of your husband when his offence is proved; and by that act I will deliver you from your dreams.

WIDOW. I thank your Honor [*she sits down*].

JUDGE. Are you satisfied, Mr Battler?

BATTLER. I also thank your honor. I am satisfied [*he resumes his seat; but his emotion has not yet quite sub-*

735

sided].

BBDE. No duel then?

BATTLER. Do not torment me. [*Impatiently*] Bardo: you are a damned fool.

BBDE. [*hugely amused*] Ha ha! [*To the Judge*] The incident is closed.

An attractive and very voluble middleaged English lady enters. She is dressed as a deaconess and carries a handbag full of tracts.

DEACONESS. May I address the court? [*She goes on without waiting for a reply*]. I feel strongly that it is my duty to do so. There is a movement in the world which is also a movement in my heart. It is a movement before which all war, all unkindness, all uncharitableness, all sin and suffering will disappear and make Geneva superfluous. I speak from personal experience. I can remember many witnesses whose experience has been like my own. I——

BBDE. [*thundering at her*] Madam: you have not yet received permission to address us.

DEACONESS [*without taking the slightest notice of the interruption*] It is so simple! and the happiness it brings is so wonderful! All you have to do is to open your heart to the Master.

BATTLER. What master? I am The Master.

BBDE. There are others, Ernest.

DEACONESS. If you knew what I was, and what I am, all that you are doing here would seem the idlest trifling.

BATTLER [*shouting*] Who is the Master? Name him.

DEACONESS. Not so loud, please. I am not deaf; but when one is listening to the inner voice it is not easy to catch external noises.

BATTLER. I am not an external noise. I am the leader of my people. I may become leader of many peoples. Who is this Master of whom you speak?

DEACONESS. His beloved name, sir, is Jesus. I am sure that when you were a child your mother taught you to say "All hail the power of Jesu's name."

736

GENEVA

THE BETROTHED. "Let angels prostrate fall."

BEGONIA. Now shut up, Billikins. I wont have you laughing at religion.

BBDE. In Ernest's country, madam, they say Heil Battler. He has abolished Jesus.

DEACONESS. How can you say that? Jesus is stronger than ever. Jesus is irresistible. You can perhaps unify your countrymen in love of yourself. But Jesus can unite the whole world in love of Him. He will live when you are dust and ashes. Can you find the way to my heart as Jesus has found it? Can you make better men and women of them as Jesus can? Can——

BATTLER. I have made better men and women of them. I live for nothing else. I found them defeated, humiliated, the doormats of Europe. They now hold up their heads with the proudest; and it is I, Battler, who have raised them to spit in the faces of their oppressors.

DEACONESS. Jesus does not spit in people's faces. If your people are really raised up, really saved, it is Jesus who has done it; and you, sir, are only the instrument.

NEWCOMER [*rising*] A point of order, Mister. Is this a court of justice or is it not? Are we to be interrupted by every dotty female who starts preaching at us? I protest.

DEACONESS. It is no use protesting, my friend. When He calls you must follow.

NEWCOMER. Rot. Where are the police?

THE JUDGE. The peculiarity of this court, sir, is that there are no police. The lady is raising a point of general importance: one we must settle before we can come to any fruitful conclusions here. I rule that Jesus is a party in this case.

NEWCOMER. You are as dotty as she is. I say no more. [*He resumes his seat sulkily*].

THE JEW. A party in what capacity, may I ask? I speak as a Jew, if Mr. Battler will permit me.

THE JUDGE. In the capacity of a famous prophet who laid down the law in these words, "This commandment I

737

give unto you, that ye love one another." Are you prepared to love one another?

ALL EXCEPT SIR O. [*vociferously*] No.

SIR O. Not indiscriminately.

THE BRITISH CONTINGENT. Hear hear!

SIR O. What about the Unlovables? Judas Iscariot, for instance?

DEACONESS. If he had loved the Master he would not have betrayed Him. What a proof of the truth of my message!

BBDE. Do you love Ernest here?

DEACONESS. Why of course I do, most tenderly.

BATTLER. Woman: do not presume.

BBDE. Ha! ha! ha!

DEACONESS. Why should I not love you? I am your sister in Christ. What is there to offend you in that? Is not this touchiness a great trouble to you? You can easily get rid of it. Bring it to Jesus. It will fall from you like a heavy burden; and your heart will be light, oh, so light! You have never been happy. I can see it in your face.

BBDE. He practises that terrible expression for hours every day before the looking glass; but it is not a bit natural to him. Look at my face: there you have the real thing.

DEACONESS. You have neither of you the light in your eyes of the love of the Master. There is no happiness in these expressions that you maintain so industriously. Do you not find it very tiresome to have to be making faces all day? [*Much laughter in the British section*].

BATTLER. Is this to be allowed? The woman is making fun of us.

DEACONESS. I cannot make fun. But God has ordained that when men are childish enough to fancy that they are gods they become what you call funny. We cannot help laughing at them.

BBDE. Woman: if you had ever had God's work to do you would know that He never does it Himself. We are here to do it for Him. If we neglect it the world falls into

738

the chaos called Liberty and Democracy, in which nothing is done except talk while the people perish. Well, what you call God's work, His hardest work, His political work, cannot be done by everybody: they have neither the time nor the brains nor the divine call for it. God has sent to certain persons this call. They are not chosen by the people: they must choose themselves: that is part of their inspiration. When they have dared to do this, what happens? Out of the Liberal democratic chaos comes form, purpose, order and rapid execution.

NEWCOMER. Yes, the executions come along all right. We know what dictators are.

BBDE. Yes: the triflers and twaddlers are swept away. This trifler and twaddler here can see nothing but his own danger, which raises his twaddle to a squeak of mortal terror. He does not matter. His selfchosen ruler takes him by the scruff of the neck and flings him into some island or camp where he and his like can trifle and twaddle without obstructing God's effectives. Then comes this pious lady to bid me turn to God. There is no need: God has turned to me; and to the best of my ability I shall not fail Him, in spite of all the Democratic Liberal gabblers. I have spoken. Now it is your turn, Ernest, if you have anything left to say.

BATTLER. You have said it all in your oldfashioned way, perhaps more clearly than I could have said it. But this woman's old fairy tales do not explain me, Ernest Battler, born a nobody, and now in command above all kings and kaisers. For my support is no dead Jew, but a mighty movement in the history of the world. Impelled by it I have stretched out my hand and lifted my country from the gutter into which you and your allies were trampling it, and made it once more the terror of Europe, though the danger is in your own guilty souls and not in any malice of mine. And mark you, the vision does not stop at my frontiers, nor at any frontier. Do not mistake me: I am no soldier dreaming of military conquests: I am what I am,

739

and have done what I have done, without winning a single battle. Why is this? Because I have snapped by fingers in the face of all your Jewish beliefs and Roman traditions, your futile treaties and halfhearted threats, and the vulgar abuse you have spat at me from your platforms and newspapers like the frightened geese you are. You must all come my way, because I march with the times, and march as pioneer, not as camp follower. As pioneer I know that the real obstacle to human progress is the sort of mind that has been formed in its infancy by the Jewish Scriptures. That obstacle I must smash through at all costs; and so must you, Bardo, if you mean to be yourself and not the tool of that accursed race.

COMMISSAR. I must intervene. Are we here to discuss the Jewish problem? If so, I have no business here: my country has solved it. And we did not solve it by badinage.

BBDE. Badinage! Are our proceedings to be described as badinage by a Bolshevist?

SECRETARY. You see how hopeless it is for us to get any further. You have only to say the word Jew to Herr Battler or the word Bolshevist to Signor Bombardone, and they cease to be reasonable men. You have only to say Peckham to the representative of the Intellectual Committee of the League of Nations to reveal her as an irreconcilable belligerent. You have—

BEGONIA. Whats that he called me? It sounded awful. What does it mean, Uncle O.?

SIR O. I understood the secretary to imply that however large-minded your view of the brotherhood of mankind, you must make an exception in the case of Peckham.

BEGONIA. Okay. No Peckham for me. And mind: on that point I am a representative woman. Sorry I interrupted. Carry on, old man.

SECRETARY. I thank you, Dame Begonia. I must add, with great respect for the British Foreign Secretary, that you have only to say British Empire to discover that in his view the rest of the world exists only as a means of furthering the interests of that geographical expression.

SIR O. Surely the British Empire is something more than a geographical expression. But of course with me the British Empire comes first.

SECRETARY. Precisely. And as a common basis of agreement, this lady has proposed the policy of the Sermon on the Mount.

DEACONESS. Love oneanother. It is so simple.

SECRETARY. It turns out that we do not and cannot love oneanother—that the problem before us is how to establish peace among people who heartily dislike oneanother, and have very good reasons for doing so: in short, that the human race does not at present consist exclusively or even largely of likeable persons.

DEACONESS. But I assure you, that does not matter. There is a technique you have not learnt.

SIR O. What! More techniques! Madam: before your arrival, I was accused of having a technique. Can we not keep on the plain track of commonsense?

DEACONESS. But this one is so simple. You have spites. You have hatreds. You have bad tempers. All you have to do is to bring them to Jesus. He will relieve you of them. He will shew you that they are all imaginary. He will fill your hearts with love of Himself; and in that love there is eternal peace. I know so many cases. I know by my own experience.

SECRETARY. You are an amiable lady; and no doubt there are, as you say, other cases—

DEACONESS. Oh, I was not an amiable lady. I was a perfect fiend, jealous, quarrelsome, full of imaginary ailments, as touchy as Mr. Battler, as bumptious as Signor Bombardone—

BATTLER. Pardon. What does touchy mean?

BBDE. I am unacquainted with the word bumptious. What am I to understand by it?

DEACONESS. Look within, look within, and you will understand. I brought it all to Jesus; and now I am happy:

741

I am what the gentleman is kind enough to describe as amiable. Oh, why will you not do as I have done? It is so simple.

BBDE. It is made much simpler by the fact that you are protected by an efficient body of policemen with bludgeons in their pockets, madam. You have never had to govern.

DEACONESS. I have had to govern myself, sir. And I am now governed by Jesus.

JUDGE. Allow the lady the last word, Mr Leader. Proceed, Mr Secretary.

SECRETARY. No: I have said enough. You know now what an impossible job I have here as secretary to the League of Nations. To me it is agony to have to listen to all this talk, knowing as I do that nothing can come of it. Have pity on me. Let us adjourn for lunch.

JUDGE. Oh, it is not lunch time yet, Mr Secretary. We have been here less than an hour.

SECRETARY. It seems to me twenty years.

JUDGE. I am sorry, Mr Secretary. But I am waiting for the arrival of a defendant who has not yet appeared, General Flanco de Fortinbras, who is accused of having slaughtered many thousands of his fellow countrymen on grounds that have never been clearly stated.

BBDE. But he has not yet been elected Leader. He is a mere soldier.

COMMISSAR. Half Europe describes him as your valet.

BBDE. I do not keep valets. But in so far as Flanco is striving to save his country from the horrors of Communism he has my sympathy.

COMMISSAR. Which includes the help of your guns and soldiers.

BBDE. I cannot prevent honest men from joining in a crusade, as volunteers, against scoundrels and assassins.

JUDGE. You also, Mr Battler, sympathize with General Flanco?

BATTLER. I do. He has accepted my definite offer to Europe to rid it of Bolshevism if the western states will co-operate.

JUDGE. And you, Sir Midlander, can of course assure General Flanco of British support?

SIR O. [*rising*] Oh, no, no, no. I am amazed at such a misunderstanding. The British Empire has maintained the strictest neutrality. It has merely recognized General Flanco as a belligerent.

BBDE. Flanco will not come. I have not authorized him to come.

General Flanco de Fortinbras enters at the door. He is a middle aged officer, very smart, and quite conventional.

FLANCO. Pardon. Is this the International Court?

JUDGE. It is.

FLANCO. My name is Flanco de Fortinbras—General Flanco de Fortinbras. I have received a summons.

JUDGE. Quite so, General. We were expecting you. You are very welcome. Pray be seated.

The secretary places a chair between the judge and Bombardone. Flanco crosses to it.

JUDGE [*before Flanco sits down*] You know these gentlemen, I think.

FLANCO [*sitting down carelessly*] No. But I have seen many caricatures of them. No introduction is necessary.

THE JUDGE. You recognize also the British Foreign Secretary, Sir Orpheus Midlander.

Flanco immediately rises; clicks his heels; and salutes Sir Orpheus with a distinguished consideration that contrasts very significantly with his contemptuous indifference to the two leaders. Sir Orpheus, as before, waves a gracious acknowledgment of the salute. Flanco resumes his seat.

FLANCO. I have come here because it seemed the correct thing to do. I am relieved to find that His Excellency the British Foreign Secretary agrees with me.

BBDE. In what capacity are you here, may I ask?

FLANCO. Do I seem out of place between you and your fellow talker opposite? A man of action always is out of place among talkers.

743

BBDE. Inconceivable nothingness that you are, do you dare to class me as a talker and not a man of action?

FLANCO. Have you done anything?

BBDE. I have created an empire.

FLANCO. You mean that you have policed a place infested by savages. A child could have done it with a modern mechanized army.

BBDE. Your little military successes have gone to your head. Do not forget that they were won with my troops.

FLANCO. Your troops do fairly well under my command. We have yet to see them doing anything under yours.

BBDE. Ernest: our valet has gone stark mad.

FLANCO. Mr Battler may be a useful civilian. I am informed that he is popular with the lower middle class. But the fate of Europe will not be decided by your scraps of Socialism.

JUDGE. May I recall you to the business of the court, gentlemen. General: you are charged with an extraordinary devastation of your own country and an indiscriminate massacre of its inhabitants.

FLANCO. That is my profession. I am a soldier; and my business is to devastate the strongholds of the enemies of my country, and slaughter their inhabitants.

NEWCOMER. Do you call the lawfully constituted democratic government of your country its enemies?

FLANCO. I do, sir. That government is a government of cads. I stand for a great cause; and I have not talked about it, as these two adventurers talk: I have fought for it: fought and won.

JUDGE. And what, may we ask, is the great cause?

FLANCO. I stand simply for government by gentlemen against government by cads. I stand for the religion of gentlemen against the irreligion of cads. For me there are only two classes, gentlemen and cads: only two faiths: Catholics and heretics. The horrible vulgarity called democracy has given political power to the cads and the

744

heretics. I am determined that the world shall not be ruled by cads nor its children brought up as heretics. I maintain that all spare money should be devoted to the breeding of gentlemen. In that I have the great body of public opinion behind me. Take a plebiscite of the whole civilized world; and not a vote will be cast against me. The natural men, the farmers and peasants, will support me to a man, and to a woman. Even the peasants whom you have crowded into your towns and demoralized by street life and trade unionism, will know in their souls that I am the salvation of the world.

BBDE. A Saviour, no less! Eh?

FLANCO. Do not be profane. I am a Catholic officer and gentleman, with the beliefs, traditions, and duties of my class and my faith. I could not sit idly reading and talking whilst the civilization established by that faith and that order was being destroyed by the mob. Nobody else would do anything but read seditious pamphlets and talk, talk, talk. It was necessary to fight, fight, fight to restore order in the world. I undertook that responsibility and here I am. Everybody understands my position: nobody understands the pamphlets, the three volumes of Karl Marx, the theories of the idealists, the ranting of the demagogues: in short, the caddishness of the cads. Do I make myself clear?

BBDE. Am I a cad? Is Ernest here a cad?

FLANCO. You had better not force me to be personal.

BBDE. Come! Face the question. Are we cads or gentlemen? Out with it.

FLANCO. You are certainly not gentlemen. You are freaks.

BATTLER. Freaks!

BBDE. What is a freak?

JUDGE. An organism so extraordinary as to defy classification.

BBDE. Good. I accept that.

BATTLER. So do I. I claim it.

JUDGE. Then, as time is getting on, gentlemen, had we

not better come to judgment?

BATTLER. Judgment!

BBDE. Judgment!

BATTLER. What do you mean? Do you presume to judge me?

BBDE. Judge me if you dare.

FLANCO. Give judgment against me and you pass out of history as a cad.

BATTLER. You have already passed out of history as a Catholic: that is, nine tenths a Jew.

BBDE. The bee in your bonnet buzzes too much, Ernest. [*To the Judge*] What is the law?

JUDGE. Unfortunately there is no law as between nations. I shall have to create it as I go along, by judicial precedents.

BATTLER. In my country I create the precedents.

BBDE. Well said, Ernest. Same here.

JUDGE. As you are not judges your precedents have no authority outside the operations of your police. You, Mr Battler, are here to answer an accusation made against you by a Jewish gentleman of unlawful arrest and imprisonment, assault, robbery, and denial of his right to live in the country of his birth. What is your defence?

BATTLER. I do not condescend to defend myself.

JEW. You mean that you have no defence. You cannot even find a Jewish lawyer to defend you, because you have driven them all from your country and left it with no better brains than your own. You have employed physical force to suppress intellect. That is the sin against the Holy Ghost. I accuse you of it.

JUDGE. What have you to say to that, Mr Battler?

BATTLER. Nothing. Men such as I am are not to be stopped by academic twaddle about intellect. But I will condescend to tell this fellow from the Ghetto that to every superior race that is faithful to itself a Messiah is sent.

DEACONESS. Oh, how true! If only you would accept him!

746

JUDGE. I understand you to plead divine inspiration, Mr Battler.

BATTLER. I say that my power is mystical, not rational.

BBDE. Ernest: take care. You are walking on a razor's edge between inspiration and the madness of the beggar on horseback. We two are beggars on horseback. For the credit of leadership let us ride carefully. Leadership, we two know, is mystical. Then let us not pretend to understand it. God may choose his leaders; but he may also drop them with a crash if they get out of hand. Tell yourself that every night before you get into bed, my boy; and you may last a while yet.

Loud applause from the British section.

BATTLER. Physician, cure yourself. You need not prescribe for me.

JUDGE. This is very edifying, gentlemen; and I thank you both in the name of all present. May I ask whether this divine guidance of which you are conscious has any limits? Does it not imply a world State with Mr Battler or Signor Bombardone or the British Foreign Office at its head?

FLANCO. Certainly not in my country. A frontier is a frontier; and there must be no monkeying with it. Let these gentlemen manage their own countries and leave us to manage ours.

JUDGE. Is that your view, Mr Battler?

BATTLER. No. I believe that the most advanced race, if it breeds true, must eventually govern the world.

JUDGE. Do you agree, Sir Midlander?

SIR O. With certain reservations, yes. I do not like the term "advanced race." I greatly mistrust advanced people. In my experience they are very difficult to work with, and often most disreputable in their private lives. They seldom attend divine service. But if you will withdraw the rather unfortunate word "advanced" and substitute the race best fitted by its character—its normal, solid, everyday character —to govern justly and prosperously, then I think I agree.

JUDGE. Precisely. And now may we have your opinion,

Signor Leader?

BBDE. In principle I agree. It is easy for me to do so, as my people, being a Mediterranean people, can never be subject to northern barbarians, though it can assimilate and civilize them in unlimited numbers.

JUDGE. Has the Russian gentleman anything to say?

COMMISSAR. Nothing. These gentlemen talk of their countries. But they do not own their countries. Their people do not own the land they starve in. Their countries are owned by a handful of landlords and capitalists who allow them to live in it on condition that they work like bees and keep barely enough of the honey to keep themselves miserably alive. Russia belongs to the Russians. We shall look on whilst you eat each other up. When you have done that, Russia—Holy Russia—will save the soul of the world by teaching it to feed its people instead of robbing them.

FLANCO. Did your landlords ever rob the people as your bureaucracy now robs them to build cities and factories in the desert and to teach children to be atheists? Your country is full of conspiracies to get the old order back again. You have to shoot the conspirators by the dozen every month.

COMMISSAR. That is not many out of two hundred million people, General. Think of all the rascals you ought to shoot!

JUDGE. Pray, gentlemen, no more recriminations. Let us keep to the point of the superior race and the divine leadership. What is to happen if you disagree as to which of you is the divinely chosen leader and the superior race?

BBDE. My answer is eight million bayonets.

BATTLER. My answer is twelve million bayonets.

JUDGE. And yours, Sir Midlander?

SIR O. This sort of talk is very dangerous. Besides, men do not fight with bayonets nowadays. In fact they do not fight at all in the old sense. Mr Battler can wipe out London, Portsmouth, and all our big provincial cities in a day. We should then be obliged to wipe out Hamburg and all the eastern cities from Munster to Salzburg. Signor Bombardone can wipe out Tunis, Nice, Algiers, Marseilles, Toulouse, Lyons, and every city south of the Loire, and oblige the French, headed by the British fleet, to wipe out Naples, Venice, Florence, Rome, and even Milan by return of post. The process can go on until the European stock of munitions and air pilots is exhausted. But it is a process by which none of us can win, and all of us must lose frightfully. Which of us dare take the responsibility of dropping the first bomb?

BATTLER. Our precautions against attack from the air are perfect.

SIR O. Ours are not, unfortunately. Nobody believes in them. I certainly do not. You must allow me to doubt the efficiency of yours.

JUDGE. And your precautions, Signor? Are they efficient?

BBDE. They do not exist. Our strength is in our willingness to die.

JUDGE. That seems to complicate murder with suicide. However, am I to take it that you are all provided with the means to effect this destruction, and to retaliate in kind if they are used against you?

SIR O. What else can we do, sir?

JUDGE. I find myself in a difficulty. I have listened to you all and watched you very attentively. You seem to me to be personally harmless human beings, capable of meeting one another and chatting on fairly pleasant terms. There is no reason why you should not be good neighbors. So far, my work of building up a body of international law by judicial precedent would seem to be simple enough. Unfortunately when any question of foreign policy arises you confront me with a black depth of scoundrelism which calls for nothing short of your immediate execution.

The Leaders and the British contingent, except the Newcomer, rise indignantly.

NEWCOMER. Hear hear! Hear hear! Hear hear! SIR O.

749

Scoundrelism! BATTLER. Execution! BOMBARDONE. You are mad.

JUDGE. If you dislike the word execution I am willing to substitute liquidation. The word scoundrelism and its adjectives I cannot withdraw. Your objective is domination: your weapons fire and poison, starvation and ruin, extermination by every means known to science. You have reduced one another to such a condition of terror that no atrocity makes you recoil and say that you will die rather than commit it. You call this patriotism, courage, glory. There are a thousand good things to be done in your countries. They remain undone for hundreds of years; but the fire and the poison are always up to date. If this be not scoundrelism what is scoundrelism? I give you up as hopeless. Man is a failure as a political animal. The creative forces which produce him must produce something better. [*The telephone rings*]. Pardon me a moment. [*Changing countenance and holding up his hand for silence*] I am sorry to have to announce a very grave piece of news. Mr Battler's troops have invaded Ruritania.

General consternation. All rise to their feet except Battler, who preserves an iron calm.

JUDGE. Is this true, Mr Battler?

BATTLER. I am a man of action, not a dreamer. While you have been talking my army has been doing. Bardo: the war for the mastery of the world has begun. It is you and I, and, I presume, our friend Fortinbras, against the effete so-called democracies of which the people of Europe and America are tired.

BBDE. Ernest: you have done this without consulting me. I warned you a year ago, when you were negotiating with a relative of Sir Orpheus here, that I could not afford another war.

FLANCO. Neither can I.

All sit down gradually, greatly relieved, except Battler.

BATTLER [*rising in great agitation*] Bardo: are you

going to betray me? Remember the axis. Dare you break it?

BBDE. Damn the axis! Do you suppose I am going to ruin my country to make you emperor of the universe? You should know me better [*He resumes his seat majestically*].

BATTLER. This is the most shameless betrayal in human history. General Flanco: you owe your victory to my aid. Will you be such a monster of ingratitude as to desert me now?

FLANCO. I owe my victory equally to the aid of Signor Bombardone and to the masterly non-intervention policy of Sir Orpheus Midlander. I cannot prove ungrateful to either of them.

BATTLER. Well, traitors as you are, I can do without you. I can conquer Ruritania single-handed, no thanks to either of you. But where should I be if the British were not afraid to fight. Fortunately for me they do not believe in what they call brute force. [*He sits*].

SIR O. [*rising*] Pardon me. It is true that we abhor brute force, and are willing to make any sacrifice for the sake of peace—or almost any sacrifice. We understood that this was your attitude also. But I had the honor of informing you explicitly—very explicitly, Mr Battler—that Ruritania is, so to speak, our little sister, and that if you laid a finger on her we should—pardon me if in my indignant surprise at your breach of the peace I am unable to adhere to the language of diplomacy—we should be obliged to knock the stuffing out of you. That is our British method of meeting brute force.

BATTLER. What! You will fight?

SIR O. Fight, Mr Battler! We shall wipe you off the face of the earth. [*He resumes his seat*].

BATTLER. Then I am alone: *contra mundum*. Well, I have never failed yet.

FLANCO. Because you have never fought yet.

BATTLER. We shall see. I shall sweep through Ruritania like a hurricane.

COMMISSAR. Do so by all means, Comrade Battler. When you have finished you will settle with me how much of it you may keep.

BATTLER. What! You too! So the encirclement is complete.

SIR ORPHEUS. No! I cannot permit that expression. Outflanked if you like. Hemmed in if you will have it so. I will even go so far as to say surrounded. But encircled, NO.

NEWCOMER. It puts the kybosh on Battlerism anyhow. *The telephone rings again.*

ALL EXCEPT THE JUDGE. Hush. Let us hear the news. The news. The news. [*They listen with strained attention*]. Sh-sh-sh-sh-sh-.

JUDGE. What? Say that again: I must take it down: I do not understand. [*Writing as he listens*] "Astronomers report that the orbit of the earth is jumping to its next quantum. Message received at Greenwich from three American observatories. Humanity is doomed." Thank you. Goodbye. Can anyone explain this? Why is humanity doomed?

SECRETARY. It is intelligible enough, and very serious indeed.

JUDGE. It is not intelligible to me. Will you kindly explain?

SECRETARY. The orbit of the earth is the path in which it travels round the sun. As the sun is 93 million miles distant it takes us a year to get round.

JUDGE. We all know that. But the message says that the orbit is jumping to its next quantum. What does quantum mean?

SECRETARY. When orbits change they dont change gradually. They suddenly jump by distances called quantums or quanta. Nobody knows why. If the earth is jumping to a wider orbit it is taking us millions of miles further away from the sun. That will take us into the awful cold of

752

space. The icecaps that we have on the north and south poles will spread over the whole earth. Even the polar bears will be frozen stiff. Not a trace of any sort of life known to us will be possible on this earth.

THE JEW [*rising and hurrying to the door*] Excuse me.

SECRETARY. No use running away, my friend. The icecap will overtake you wherever you go.

JUDGE. Let him alone. The shock has made him ill.

THE JEW. No: not that. I must telephone [*he goes out*].

JUDGE [*rising*] Fellow citizens: this is the end. The end of war, of law, of leaders and foreign secretaries, of judges and generals. A moment ago we were important persons: the fate of Europe seemed to depend on us. What are we now? Democracy, Fascism, Communism: how much do they matter? Your totalitarian Catholic Church: does it still seem so very totalitarian?

FLANCO. Do not blaspheme at such a moment, sir. You tell us that nothing matters. Ten minutes ago the judgment of God seemed far off: now we stand at the gates of purgatory. We have to organize absolution for millions of our people; and we have barely priests enough to do it, even if we have no converts to deal with; and we shall have many converts. We Catholics know what to do; and I have no more time to spend trifling here with men who know nothing and believe nothing. [*He moves towards the door. He stops to hear Sir O.*]

SIR O. One moment, I beg of you. This rumor must be contradicted at all costs.

COMMISSAR. How can you contradict a scientific fact?

SIR O. It must be contradicted—officially contradicted. Think of the consequences if it is believed! People will throw off all decency, all prudence. Only the Jews, with the business faculty peculiar to their race, will profit by our despair. Why has our Jewish friend just left us? To telephone, he said. Yes; but to whom is he telephoning? To his stockbroker, gentlemen. He is instructing his stockbroker

753

to sell gilt-edged in any quantity, at any price, knowing that if this story gets about before settling day he will be able to buy it for the price of waste paper and be a millionaire until the icecap overtakes him. It must not be. I will take the necessary steps in England. The Astronomer Royal will deny this story this afternoon. You two gentlemen must see to it at once that it is officially denied in your countries.

COMMISSAR. Suppose your Astronomer Royal refuses to tell a lie. Remember: he is a man of science, not a politician.

SIR O. He is an Englishman, sir, and has some common sense. He will do his duty. Can I depend on the rest of you gentlemen?

BBDE. Can you depend on the icecap? I must go home at once. There will be a rush to the equator. My country stands right in the way of that rush. I must stop it at our frontier at any cost.

COMMISSAR. Why? Will it matter?

BBDE. I will not tolerate disorder. I will not tolerate fear. We shall die decently, stoically, steadfast at our posts, like Romans. Remember: we shall not decay: we shall stand to all eternity in cold storage. When we are discovered by some explorer from another star or another race that can live and breathe at absolute zero, he shall find my people erect at their posts like the Pompeian sentinel. You also, Ernest, must— What! Crying!! For shame, man! The world looks to us for leadership. Shall it find us in tears?

BATTLER. Let me alone. My dog Blonda will be frozen to death. My doggie! My little doggie! [*He breaks down, sobbing convulsively*].

NEWCOMER. Oh, come, old man. Dont take it so hard. I used to keep dogs myself; but I had to give it up: I couldnt bear the shortness of their lives. Youd have had to lose your little doggie some day.

Battler takes out his handkerchief and controls him-
754

self; but the Deaconess bursts into tears.

BEGONIA. Oh for God's sake, dont you start crying. You will set us all off. It's hard enough on us without that.

THE SECRETARY. Yes, maam. Take your trouble to Jesus; and set all the women a good example.

DEACONESS. But in heaven I shall lose my Jesus. There He will be a king; and there will be no more troubles and sorrows and sins to bring to Him. My life has been so happy since I found Him and came to Him a year ago! He made heaven for me on earth; and now that is all over. I cannot bear it. [*Her tears overcome her*].

NEWCOMER. Oh come come! This wont do, you know. All you people seem to think you were going to live for ever. Well, you werent. Our numbers are up; but so they were before, sooner or later. I dont complain: I havnt had such a bad time of it; and I am ready to depart, as the poet says, if it must be. In fact I must depart now and cheer up the missus. [*He rises to go*].

DEACONESS. Oh, sir, do you believe this? May it not be untrue?

NEWCOMER [*gravely*] No: it's true all right enough. If it were a priest's tale or a supersition out of the Bible I shouldnt give a snap of my fingers for it. But Science cannot be wrong. Weve got to face it. Good morning, gents.

The Newcomer goes out; and his departure breaks up the court. The Leaders and the General rise and come forward together.

DEACONESS [*to Flanco*] Oh, General, is Science always right?

FLANCO. Certainly not: it is always wrong. But I await the decision of the Church. Until that is delivered the story has no authority.

SIR O. May I suggest that you use all your influence at Rome to obtain an immediate decision from the Church against this story?

FLANCO. You shock me. The Church cannot be influenced. It knows the truth as God knows it, and will instruct us accordingly. Anyone who questions its decision will be shot. My business is to see to that. After absolution, of course. Good morning. [*He goes out*].

WIDOW. He at least has something to offer to men about to die.

COMMISSAR. Dope.

JUDGE. Why not, if they die comforted?

BATTLER. Men must learn to die undeluded.

BBDE. Flanco is dead; but he does not know it. History would have kicked him out were not History now on its deathbed.

BEGONIA. I must say I thought the general a perfect gentleman. I never wanted to kick him while he was speaking. I wanted to kick you two all the time.

THE BETROTHED. Steady, Gonny, steady! Mustnt be rude, you know.

BEGONIA. Oh, what does it matter now? As we shall all be frozen stiff presently we may as well have the satisfaction of speaking our minds until then.

THE BETROTHED. Take it easy, dear. Have a choc.

BEGONIA. No, thank you.

THE BETROTHED. I say, Uncle O: this is the first time she has ever refused a choc.

SIR O. Our valuations have changed, naturally.

THE BETROTHED. Mine havnt. You know, uncle, I think theres something in your notion of selling out and having a tremendous spree before the icecaps nip us. How does that strike you, Gonny?

BEGONIA. I dont pretend it might not have appealed to me before I represented Intellectual Co-operation. But I am a Dame of the British Empire now; and if I must die I will die like a Dame. [*She goes out*].

SIR O. Go with her, sir. And mind you behave yourself.

THE BETROTHED. Well, it does seem rather a pity. However— [*He shrugs resignedly and goes out*].

SIR O. [*to the Commissar*] Do you, sir, understand what is going to happen? My classical education did not include
756

science.

COMMISSAR. I await instructions. The Marxian dialectic does not include the quantum theory. I must consult Moscow. [*He goes out*].

SIR O. Have these men no minds of their own? One of them must consult Rome: the other must consult Moscow. You two gentlemen fortunately have no one but yourselves to consult. Can I rely on you to do your utmost to stifle this appalling news while I return to London to consult the Cabinet?

BBDE. You can rely on nothing but this. The news has just been broadcast to all the world through the arrangements made for publicity in this court. According to you, the result will be that the people will throw off all decency and repudiate all leadership. I say that the people will want a leader as they have never wanted one before. I have taught them to order their lives: I shall teach them to order their deaths. The magnitude of the catastrophe is the measure of the leader's greatness.

SIR O. You always have a speech which sounds equal to the occasion. In England that gift would make you Prime Minister. But your very excitable countrymen may run wild.

BBDE. In that case I can do nothing but fall at the head of an attempt to stem the rush. At least one man shall stand for human courage and dignity when the race expires.

SIR O. Yes: that is a very fine attitude and quite a correct one. But have you nothing better to propose than an attitude?

BBDE. Has anyone anything better to propose than an attitude?

SIR O. I suppose not; but I feel strongly that a burst of sincerity would be a great relief.

BBDE. [*to Battler*] Give him his burst of sincerity, Ernest. Cry for your dog again. Good morning, gentlemen. [*He goes to the door*].

BATTLER [*calling after him*] You will have the honor

757

of sharing my little dog's fate. But nobody will weep for you, Bardo.

BBDE. I hope not. I do not deal in tears. [*He strides out*].

BATTLER. What an actor!

SECRETARY. You should be a good judge of that. You have done a good deal in that line yourself.

BATTLER. We all have. But I claim to have done a little good with my acting. I will not have my work undone. We shall not stand in statuesque attitudes in Bardo's manner: we shall work to the last, and set an example to the new race of iceproof men who will follow us.

SIR O. Still, you know, it's no use going on making motor cars that you know will never run.

BATTLER. Yes: when the alternative is to wring our hands in despair or get drunk. We cannot work for ourselves to the last moment; but we can all work for honor. [*He goes out*].

SIR O. Wonderful luck that man has! His dog will get him into all the headlines. [*He goes out*].

JUDGE [*to the Deaconess and the widow*] Ladies: I am afraid there is nothing more to be done here.

DEACONESS [*rising*] None of you understands what this means to me, because none of you has learnt how to live. You are souls in torment, as I was until six months ago. And now I must die when I have only just learnt to live. Excuse me: I cannot bear to speak of it [*she goes out distractedly*].

JUDGE. She, at least, values her life.

SECRETARY. Yes: she belongs to some movement or other.

WIDOW [*taking her pistol from her handbag and rising*] I killed my best friend with this. I kept it to kill myself. It is useless now: God will execute His own judgment on us all. [*She throws it into the waste paper basket*]. But He is merciful; for I shall never dream again. And [*to the Secretary*] I do not belong to any movement.

758

He bows; and she goes out.

SECRETARY. Can you switch off?

JUDGE [*going to the table and turning a masterswitch*] No one can hear us now. [*Returning*] Can this thing be true?

SECRETARY. No. It is utter nonsense. If the earth made a spring to a wider orbit half a minute would carry us to regions of space where we could not breathe and our blood would freeze in our veins.

JUDGE. Yet we all believed it for the moment.

SECRETARY. You have nothing to do but mention the quantum theory, and people will take your voice for the voice of Science and believe anything. It broke up this farce of a trial, at all events.

JUDGE. Not a farce, my friend. They came, these fellows. They blustered: they defied us. But they came. They came.

HOW HE LIED TO HER HUSBAND

Written in 1904

First Performed New York 1904

LIKE many other works of mine, this playlet is a pièce d'occasion. In 1905 it happened that the late Arnold Daly, who was then playing the part of Napoleon in The Man of Destiny in New York, found that whilst the play was too long to take a secondary place in the evening's performance, it was too short to suffice by itself. I therefore took advantage of four days continuous rain during a holiday in the north of Scotland to write How He Lied To Her Husband for Daly. In his hands it served its turn very effectively.

Trifling as it is I print it as a sample of what can be done with even the most hackneyed stage framework by filling it in with an observed touch of actual humanity instead of with doctrinaire romanticism. Nothing in the theatre is staler than the situation of husband, wife, and lover, or the fun of knockabout farce. I have taken both, and got an original play out of them, as anybody else can if only he will look about him for his material instead of plagiarizing Othello and the thousand plays that have proceeded on Othello's romantic assumptions and false point of honor.

LIKE many other works of mine, this playlet is a *pièce d'occasion*. In 1905 it happened that the late Arnold Daly, who was then playing the part of Napoleon in The Man of Destiny in New York, found that whilst the play was too long to take a secondary place in the evening's performance, it was too short to suffice by itself. I therefore took advantage of four days continuous rain during a holiday in the north of Scotland to write How He Lied To Her Husband for Daly. In his hands, it served its turn very effectively.

Trifling as it is I print it as a sample of what can be done with even the most hackneyed stage framework by filling it in with an observed touch of actual humanity instead of with doctrinaire romanticism. Nothing in the theatre is staler than the situation of husband, wife, and lover, or the fun of knockabout farce. I have taken both, and got an original play out of them, as anybody else can if only he will look about him for his material instead of plagiarizing Othello and the thousand plays that have proceeded on Othello's romantic assumptions and false point of honor.

HOW HE LIED TO HER HUSBAND

I T is eight o'clock in the evening. The curtains are drawn
and the lamps lighted in the drawing room of Her flat in
Cromwell Road. Her lover, a beautiful youth of eighteen,
in evening dress and cape, with a bunch of flowers and an opera
hat in his hands, comes in alone. The door is near the corner; and
as he appears in the doorway, he has the fireplace on the nearest
wall to his right, and the grand piano along the opposite wall to
his left. Near the fireplace a small ornamental table has on it a
hand mirror, a fan, a pair of long white gloves, and a little
white woollen cloud to wrap a woman's head in. On the other
side of the room, near the piano, is a broad, square, softly upholstered stool. The room is furnished in the most approved
South Kensington fashion: that is, it is as like a shop window as
possible, and is intended to demonstrate the social position and
spending powers of its owners, and not in the least to make them
comfortable.

He is, be it repeated, a very beautiful youth, moving as in a
dream, walking as on air. He puts his flowers down carefully
on the table beside the fan; takes off his cape, and, as there is no
room on the table for it, takes it to the piano; puts his hat on the
cape; crosses to the hearth; looks at his watch; puts it up again;
notices the things on the table; lights up as if he saw heaven
opening before him; goes to the table and takes the cloud in both
hands, nestling his nose into its softness and kissing it; kisses the
gloves one after another; kisses the fan; gasps a long shuddering
sigh of ecstasy; sits down on the stool and presses his hands to his
eyes to shut out reality and dream a little; takes his hands down
and shakes his head with a little smile of rebuke for his folly;
catches sight of a speck of dust on his shoes and hastily and carefully brushes it off with his handkerchief; rises and takes the
hand mirror from the table to make sure of his tie with the
gravest anxiety; and is looking at his watch again when She
comes in, much flustered. As she is dressed for the theatre; has
spoilt, petted ways; and wears many diamonds, she has an air
of being a young and beautiful woman; but as a matter of hard
fact, she is, dress and pretensions apart, a very ordinary South

765

HOW HE LIED TO HER HUSBAND

Kensington female of about 37, hopelessly inferior in physical and spiritual distinction to the beautiful youth, who hastily puts down the mirror as she enters.

HE [*kissing her hand*] At last!

SHE. Henry: something dreadful has happened.

HE. Whats the matter?

SHE. I have lost your poems.

HE. They were unworthy of you. I will write you some more.

SHE. No, thank you. Never any more poems for me. Oh, how could I have been so mad! so rash! so imprudent!

HE. Thank Heaven for your madness, your rashness, your imprudence!

SHE [*impatiently*] Oh, be sensible, Henry. Cant you see what a terrible thing this is for me? Suppose anybody finds these poems! what will they think?

HE. They will think that a man once loved a woman more devotedly than ever man loved woman before. But they will not know what man it was.

SHE. What good is that to me if everybody will know what woman it was?

HE. But how will they know?

SHE. How will they know! Why, my name is all over them: my silly, unhappy name. Oh, if I had only been christened Mary Jane, or Gladys Muriel, or Beatrice, or Francesca, or Guinevere, or something quite common! But Aurora! Aurora! I'm the only Aurora in London; and everybody knows it. I believe I'm the only Aurora in the world. And it's so horribly easy to rhyme to it! Oh, Henry, why didnt you try to restrain your feelings a little in common consideration for me? Why didnt you write with some little reserve?

HE. Write poems to you with reserve! You ask me that!

SHE [*with perfunctory tenderness*] Yes, dear, of course it was very nice of you; and I know it was my own fault as much as yours. I ought to have noticed that your verses ought never to have been addressed to a married woman.

HOW HE LIED TO HER HUSBAND

HE. Ah, how I wish they had been addressed to an unmarried woman! how I wish they had!

SHE. Indeed you have no right to wish anything of the sort. They are quite unfit for anybody but a married woman. Thats just the difficulty. What will my sisters-in-law think of them?

HE [*painfully jarred*] Have you got sisters-in-law?

SHE. Yes, of course I have. Do you suppose I am an angel?

HE [*biting his lips*] I do. Heaven help me, I do—or I did —or [*he almost chokes a sob*].

SHE [*softening and putting her hand caressingly on his shoulder*] Listen to me, dear. It's very nice of you to live with me in a dream, and to love me, and so on; but I cant help my husband having disagreeable relatives, can I?

HE [*brightening up*] Ah, of course they are your husband's relatives: I forgot that. Forgive me, Aurora. [*He takes her hand from his shoulder and kisses it. She sits down on the stool. He remains near the table, with his back to it, smiling fatuously down at her*].

SHE. The fact is, Teddy's got nothing but relatives. He has eight sisters and six half-sisters, and ever so many brothers—but I dont mind his brothers. Now if you only knew the least little thing about the world, Henry, youd know that in a large family, though the sisters quarrel with one another like mad all the time, yet let one of the brothers marry, and they all turn on their unfortunate sister-in-law and devote the rest of their lives with perfect unanimity to persuading him that his wife is unworthy of him. They can do it to her very face without her knowing it, because they always have a lot of stupid low family jokes that nobody understands but themselves. Half the time you cant tell what theyre talking about: it just drives you wild. There ought to be a law against a man's sister ever entering his house after he's married. I'm as certain as that I'm sitting here that Georgina stole those poems out of my workbox.

HE. She will not understand them, I think.

HOW HE LIED TO HER HUSBAND

SHE. Oh, wont she! She'll understand them only too well. She'll understand more harm than ever was in them: nasty vulgar-minded cat!

HE [*going to her*] Oh dont, dont think of people in that way. Dont think of her at all. [*He takes her hand and sits down on the carpet at her feet*]. Aurora: do you remember the evening when I sat here at your feet and read you those poems for the first time?

SHE. I shouldnt have let you: I see that now. When I think of Georgina sitting there at Teddy's feet and reading them to him for the first time, I feel I shall just go distracted.

HE. Yes, you are right. It will be a profanation.

SHE. Oh, I dont care about the profanation; but what will Teddy think? what will he do? [*Suddenly throwing his head away from her knee*] You dont seem to think a bit about Teddy. [*She jumps up, more and more agitated*].

HE [*supine on the floor; for she has thrown him off his balance*] To me Teddy is nothing, and Georgina less than nothing.

SHE. Youll soon find out how much less than nothing she is. If you think a woman cant do any harm because she's only a scandalmongering dowdy ragbag, youre greatly mistaken. [*She flounces about the room. He gets up slowly and dusts his hands. Suddenly she runs to him and throws herself into his arms*]. Henry: help me. Find a way out of this for me; and I'll bless you as long as you live. Oh, how wretched I am! [*She sobs on his breast*].

HE. And oh! how happy I am!

SHE [*whisking herself abruptly away*] Dont be selfish.

HE [*humbly*] Yes: I deserve that. I think if I were going to the stake with you, I should still be so happy with you that I should forget your danger as utterly as my own.

SHE [*relenting and patting his hand fondly*] Oh, you are a dear darling boy, Henry; but [*throwing his hand away fretfully*] youre no use. I want somebody to tell me what to do.

HE [*with quiet conviction*] Your heart will tell you at the

768

right time. I have thought deeply over this; and I know what we two must do, sooner or later.

SHE. No, Henry. I will do nothing improper, nothing dishonorable. [*She sits down plump on the stool and looks inflexible*].

HE. If you did, you would no longer be Aurora. Our course is perfectly simple, perfectly straightforward, perfectly stainless and true. We love one another. I am not ashamed of that: I am ready to go out and proclaim it to all London as simply as I will declare it to your husband when you see—as you soon will see—that this is the only way honorable enough for your feet to tread. Let us go out together to our own house, this evening, without concealment and without shame. Remember! we owe something to your husband. We are his guests here: he is an honorable man: he has been kind to us: he has perhaps loved you as well as his prosaic nature and his sordid commercial environment permitted. We owe it to him in all honor not to let him learn the truth from the lips of a scandalmonger. Let us go to him now quietly, hand in hand; bid him farewell; and walk out of the house without concealment or subterfuge, freely and honestly, in full honor and self-respect.

SHE [*staring at him*] And where shall we go to?

HE. We shall not depart by a hair's breadth from the ordinary natural current of our lives. We were going to the theatre when the loss of the poems compelled us to take action at once. We shall go to the theatre still; but we shall leave your diamonds here; for we cannot afford diamonds, and do not need them.

SHE [*fretfully*] I have told you already that I hate diamonds; only Teddy insists on hanging me all over with them. You need not preach simplicity to me.

HE. I never thought of doing so, dearest: I know that these trivialities are nothing to you. What was I saying?—oh yes. Instead of coming back here from the theatre, you will come with me to my home—now and henceforth our home—and in due course of time, when you are divorced,

HOW HE LIED TO HER HUSBAND

we shall go through whatever idle legal ceremony you may desire. *I* attach no importance to the law: my love was not created in me by the law, nor can it be bound or loosed by it. That is simple enough, and sweet enough, is it not? [*He takes the flowers from the table*]. Here are flowers for you: I have the tickets: we will ask your husband to lend us the carriage to shew that there is no malice, no grudge, between us. Come!

SHE. Do you mean to say that you propose that we should walk right bang up to Teddy and tell him we're going away together?

HE. Yes. What can be simpler?

SHE. And do you think for a moment he'd stand it? He'd just kill you.

HE [*coming to a sudden stop and speaking with considerable confidence*] You dont understand these things, my darling: how could you? I have followed the Greek ideal and not neglected the culture of my body. Like all poets I have a passion for pugilism. Your husband would make a tolerable second-rate heavy weight if he were in training and ten years younger. As it is, he could, if strung up to a great effort by a burst of passion, give a good account of himself for perhaps fifteen seconds. But I am active enough to keep out of his reach for fifteen seconds; and after that I should be simply all over him.

SHE [*rising and coming to him in consternation*] What do you mean by all over him?

HE [*gently*] Dont ask me, dearest. At all events, I swear to you that you need not be anxious about me.

SHE. And what about Teddy? Do you mean to tell me that you are going to beat Teddy before my face like a brutal prizefighter?

HE. All this alarm is needless, dearest. Believe me, nothing will happen. Your husband knows that I am capable of defending myself. Under such circumstances nothing ever does happen. And of course *I* shall do nothing. The man who once loved you is sacred to me.

770

HOW HE LIED TO HER HUSBAND

SHE [*suspiciously*] Doesnt he love me still? Has he told you anything?

HE. No, no. [*He takes her tenderly in his arms*]. Dearest, dearest: how agitated you are! how unlike yourself! All these worries belong to the lower plane. Come up with me to the higher one. The heights, the solitudes, the soul world!

SHE [*avoiding his gaze*] No: stop: it's no use, Mr Apjohn.

HE [*recoiling*] Mr Apjohn!!!

SHE. Excuse me: I meant Henry, of course.

HE. How could you ever think of me as Mr Apjohn? I never think of you as Mrs Bompas: it is always Aurora, Aurora, Auro—

SHE. Yes, yes: thats all very well, Mr Apjohn [*he is about to interrupt again: but she wont have it*]: no: it's no use: Ive suddenly begun to think of you as Mr Apjohn: and it's ridiculous to go on calling you Henry. I thought you were only a boy, a child, a dreamer. I thought you would be too much afraid to do anything. And now you want to beat Teddy and to break up my home and disgrace me and make a horrible scandal in the papers. It's cruel, unmanly, cowardly.

HE [*with grave wonder*] Are you afraid?

SHE. Oh, of course I'm afraid. So would you be if you had any common sense. [*She goes to the hearth, turning her back to him, and puts one tapping foot on the fender*].

HE [*watching her with great gravity*]Perfect love casteth out fear. That is why I am not afraid. Mrs Bompas: you do not love me.

SHE [*turning to him with a gasp of relief*] Oh, thank you, thank you! You really can be very nice, Henry.

HE. Why do you thank me?

SHE [*coming prettily to him from the fireplace*] For calling me Mrs Bompas again. I feel now that you are going to be reasonable and behave like a gentleman. [*He drops on the stool; covers his face with his hands; and groans*]. Whats the matter?

HE. Once or twice in my life I have dreamed that I was

exquisitely happy and blessed. But oh! the misgiving at the first stir of consciousness! the stab of reality! the prison walls of the bedroom! the bitter, bitter disappointment of waking! And this time! oh, this time I thought I was awake.

SHE. Listen to me, Henry: we really havnt time for all that sort of flapdoodle now [*He starts to his feet as if she had pulled a trigger and straightened him by the release of a powerful spring, and goes past her with set teeth to the little table*]. Oh, take care: you nearly hit me in the chin with the top of your head.

HE [*with fierce politeness*] I beg your pardon. What is it you want me to do? I am at your service. I am ready to behave like a gentleman if you will be kind enough to explain exactly how.

SHE [*a little frightened*] Thank you, Henry: I was sure you would. Youre not angry with me, are you?

HE. Go on. Go on quickly. Give me something to think about, or I will—I will—[*he suddenly snatches up her fan and is about to break it in his clenched fists*].

SHE [*running forward and catching at the fan, with loud lamentation*] Dont break my fan—no, dont. [*He slowly relaxes his grip of it as she draws it anxiously out of his hands*] No, really, thats a stupid trick: I dont like that. Youve no right to do that [*She opens the fan, and finds that the sticks are disconnected*]. Oh, how could you be so inconsiderate?

HE. I beg your pardon. I will buy you a new one.

SHE [*querulously*] You will never be able to match it. And it was a particular favorite of mine.

HE [*shortly*] Then you will have to do without it: thats all.

SHE. Thats not a very nice thing to say after breaking my pet fan, I think.

HE. If you knew how near I was to breaking Teddy's pet wife and presenting him with the pieces, you would be thankful that you are alive instead of—of—of howling about fiveshillingsworth of ivory. Damn your fan!

SHE. Oh! Dont you dare swear in my presence. One would think you were my husband.

HOW HE LIED TO HER HUSBAND

HE [*again collapsing on the stool*] This is some horrible dream. What has become of you? You are not my Aurora.

SHE. Oh, well, if you come to that, what has become of you? Do you think I would ever have encouraged you if I had known you were such a little devil?

HE. Dont drag me down—dont—dont. Help me to find the way back to the heights.

SHE [*kneeling beside him and pleading*] If you would only be reasonable, Henry. If you would only remember that I am on the brink of ruin, and not go on calmly saying it's all quite simple.

HE. It seems so to me.

SHE [*jumping up distractedly*] If you say that again I shall do something I'll be sorry for. Here we are, standing on the edge of a frightful precipice. No doubt it's quite simple to go over and have done with it. But cant you suggest anything more agreeable?

HE. I can suggest nothing now. A chill black darkness has fallen: I can see nothing but the ruins of our dream. [*He rises with a deep sigh*].

SHE. Cant you? Well, I can. I can see Georgina rubbing those poems into Teddy. [*Facing him determinedly*] And I tell you, Henry Apjohn, that you got me into this mess; and you must get me out of it again.

HE [*polite and hopeless*] All I can say is that I am entirely at your service. What do you wish me to do?

SHE. Do you know anybody else named Aurora?

HE. No.

SHE. Theres no use in saying No in that frozen pigheaded way. You must know some Aurora or other somewhere.

HE. You said you were the only Aurora in the world. And [*lifting his clasped fists with a sudden return of his emotion*] oh God! you were the only Aurora in the world for me. [*He turns away from her, hiding his face*].

SHE [*petting him*] Yes, yes, dear: of course. It's very nice of you; and I appreciate it: indeed I do; but it's not seasonable just at present. Now just listen to me. I suppose you know all those poems by heart.

HE. Yes, by h e a r t. [*Raising his head and looking at her with a sudden suspicion*] Dont you?

SHE. Well, I never can remember verses; and besides, Ive been so busy that Ive not had time to read them all; though I intend to the very first moment I can get: I promise you that most faithfully, Henry. But now try and remember very particularly. Does the name of Bompas occur in any of the poems?

HE [*indignantly*] No.

SHE. Youre quite sure?

HE. Of course I am quite sure. How could I use such a name in a poem?

SHE. Well, I dont see why not. It rhymes to rumpus, which seems appropriate enough at present, goodness knows! However, youre a poet, and you ought to know.

HE. What does it matter—now?

SHE. It matters a lot, I can tell you. If theres nothing about Bompas in the poems, we can say that they were written to some other Aurora, and that you shewed them to me because my name was Aurora too. So youve got to invent another Aurora for the occasion.

HE [*very coldly*] Oh, if you wish me to tell a lie—

SHE. Surely, as a man of honor—as a gentleman, you wouldnt tell the truth: would you?

HE. Very well. You have broken my spirit and desecrated my dreams. I will lie and protest and stand on my honor: oh, I will play the gentleman, never fear.

SHE. Yes, put it all on me, of course. Dont be mean, Henry.

HE [*rousing himself with an effort*] You are quite right, Mrs Bompas: I beg your pardon. You must excuse my temper. I am having growing pains, I think.

SHE. Growing pains!

HE. The process of growing from romantic boyhood into cynical maturity usually takes fifteen years. When it is compressed into fifteen minutes, the pace is too fast; and grow-

774

ing pains are the result.

SHE. Oh, is this a time for cleverness? It's settled, isnt it, that youre going to be nice and good, and that youll brazen it out to Teddy that you have some other Aurora?

HE. Yes: I'm capable of anything now. I should not have told him the truth by halves; and now I will not lie by halves. I'll wallow in the honor of a gentleman.

SHE. Dearest boy, I knew you would. I—Sh! [*she rushes to the door, and holds it ajar, listening breathlessly*].

HE. What is it?

SHE [*white with apprehension*] It's Teddy: I hear him tapping the new barometer. He cant have anything serious on his mind or he wouldnt do that. Perhaps Georgina hasnt said anything. [*She steals back to the hearth*]. Try and look as if there was nothing the matter. Give me my gloves, quick. [*He hands them to her. She pulls on one hastily, and begins buttoning it with ostentatious unconcern*]. Go further away from me, quick. [*He walks doggedly away from her until the piano prevents his going farther*]. If I button my glove and you were to hum a tune, dont you think that—

HE. The tableau would be complete in its guiltiness. For Heaven's sake, Mrs Bompas, let that glove alone: you look like a pickpocket.

Her husband comes in: a robust, thicknecked, well groomed city man, with a strong chin but a blithering eye and credulous mouth. He has a momentous air, but shews no sign of displeasure: rather the contrary.

HER HUSBAND. Hallo! I thought you two were at the theatre.

SHE. I felt anxious about you, Teddy. Why didnt you come home to dinner?

HER HUSBAND. I got a message from Georgina. She wanted me to go to her.

SHE. Poor dear Georgina! I'm sorry I havnt been able to call on her this last week. I hope theres nothing the matter with her.

HER HUSBAND. Nothing, except anxiety for my welfare

775

—and yours. [*She steals a terrified look at Henry*]. By the way, Apjohn, I should like a word with you this evening, if Aurora can spare you for a moment.

HE [*formally*] I am at your service.

HER HUSBAND. No hurry. After the theatre will do.

HE. We have decided not to go.

HER HUSBAND. Indeed! Well, then, shall we adjourn to my snuggery?

SHE. You neednt move. I shall go and lock up my diamonds since I'm not going to the theatre. Give me my things.

HER HUSBAND [*as he hands her the cloud and the mirror*] Well, we shall have more room here.

HE [*looking about him and shaking his shoulders loose*] I think I should prefer plenty of room.

HER HUSBAND. So, if it's not disturbing you, Rory—?

SHE. Not at all. [*She goes out*].

When the two men are alone together, Bompas deliberately takes the poems from his breast pocket; looks at them reflectively; then looks at Henry, mutely inviting his attention. Henry refuses to understand, doing his best to look unconcerned.

HER HUSBAND. Do these manuscripts seem at all familiar to you, may I ask?

HE. Manuscripts?

HER HUSBAND. Yes. Would you like to look at them a little closer? [*He proffers them under Henry's nose*].

HE [*as with a sudden illumination of glad surprise*] Why, these are my poems!

HER HUSBAND. So I gather.

HE. What a shame! Mrs Bompas has shewn them to you! You must think me an utter ass. I wrote them years ago after reading Swinburne's Songs Before Sunrise. Nothing would do me then but I must reel off a set of Songs to the Sunrise. Aurora, you know: the rosy fingered Aurora. Theyre all about Aurora. When Mrs Bompas told me her name was Aurora, I couldnt resist the temptation to lend them to her to read. But I didnt bargain for your unsympathetic eyes.

HER HUSBAND [*grinning*] Apjohn: thats really very ready of you. You are cut out for literature; and the day will come when Rory and I will be proud to have you about the house. I have heard far thinner stories from much older men.

HE [*with an air of grieved surprise*] Do you mean to imply that you dont believe me?

HER HUSBAND. Do you expect me to believe you?

HE. Why not? I dont understand.

HER HUSBAND. Come! Dont underrate your own cleverness, Apjohn. I think you understand pretty well.

HE. I assure you I am quite at a loss. Can you not be a little more explicit?

HER HUSBAND. Dont overdo it, old chap. However, I will just be so far explicit as to say that if you think these poems read as if they were addressed, not to a live woman, but to a shivering cold time of day at which you were never out of bed in your life, you hardly do justice to your own literary powers—which I admire and appreciate, mind you, as much as any man. Come! own up. You wrote those poems to my wife. [*An internal struggle prevents Henry from answering*]. Of course you did. [*He throws the poems on the table; and goes to the hearthrug, where he plants himself solidly, chuckling a little and waiting for the next move*].

HE [*formally and carefully*] Mr Bompas: I pledge you my word you are mistaken. I need not tell you that Mrs Bompas is a lady of stainless honor, who has never cast an unworthy thought on me. The fact that she has shewn you my poems—

HER HUSBAND. Thats not a fact. I came by them without her knowledge. She didnt shew them to me.

HE. Does not that prove their perfect innocence? She would have shewn them to you at once if she had taken your quite unfounded view of them.

HER HUSBAND [*shaken*] Apjohn: play fair. Dont abuse your intellectual gifts. Do you really mean that I am making a fool of myself?

HE [*earnestly*] Believe me, you are. I assure you, on my

777

honor as a gentleman, that I have never had the slightest feeling for Mrs Bompas beyond the ordinary esteem and regard of a pleasant acquaintance.

HER HUSBAND [*shortly, shewing ill humor for the first time*] Oh! Indeed! [*He leaves his hearth and begins to approach Henry slowly, looking him up and down with growing resentment*].

HE [*hastening to improve the impression made by his mendacity*] I should never have dreamt of writing poems to her. The thing is absurd.

HER HUSBAND [*reddening ominously*] Why is it absurd?

HE [*shrugging his shoulders*] Well, it happens that I do not admire Mrs Bompas—in that way.

HER HUSBAND [*breaking out in Henry's face*] Let me tell you that Mrs Bompas has been admired by better men than you, you soapy headed little puppy, you.

HE [*much taken aback*] There is no need to insult me like this. I assure you, on my honor as a—

HER HUSBAND [*too angry to tolerate a reply, and boring Henry more and more towards the piano*] You dont admire Mrs Bompas! You would never dream of writing poems to Mrs Bompas! My wife's not good enough for you, isnt she? [*Fiercely*] Who are you, pray, that you should be so jolly superior?

HE. Mr Bompas: I can make allowances for your jealousy—

HER HUSBAND. Jealousy! do you suppose I'm jealous of you? No, nor of ten like you. But if you think I'll stand here and let you insult my wife in her own house, youre mistaken.

HE [*very uncomfortable with his back against the piano and Teddy standing over him threateningly*] How can I convince you? Be reasonable. I tell you my relations with Mrs Bompas are relations of perfect coldness—of indifference—

HER HUSBAND [*scornfully*] Say it again: say it again. Youre proud of it, arnt you? Yah! youre not worth kicking.

Henry suddenly executes the feat known to pugilists as slipping, and changes sides with Teddy, who is now between Henry and the piano.

HOW HE LIED TO HER HUSBAND

HE. Look here: I'm not going to stand this.

HER HUSBAND. Oh, you have some blood in your body after all! Good job!

HE. This is ridiculous. I assure you Mrs Bompas is quite—

HER HUSBAND. What is Mrs Bompas to you, I'd like to know. I'll tell you what Mrs Bompas is. She's the smartest woman in the smartest set in South Kensington, and the handsomest, and the cleverest, and the most fetching to experienced men who know a good thing when they see it, whatever she may be to conceited penny-a-lining puppies who think nothing good enough for them. It's admitted by the best people; and not to know it argues yourself unknown. Three of our first actor-managers have offered her a hundred a week if she'll go on the stage when they start a repertory theatre; and I think they know what theyre about as well as you. The only member of the present Cabinet that you might call a handsome man has neglected the business of the country to dance with her, though he dont belong to our set as a regular thing. One of the first professional poets in Bedford Park wrote a sonnet to her, worth all your amateur trash. At Ascot last season the eldest son of a duke excused himself from calling on me on the ground that his feelings for Mrs Bompas were not consistent with his duty to me as host; and it did him honor and me too. But [*with gathering fury*] she isnt good enough for you, it seems. You regard her with coldness, with indifference; and you have the cool cheek to tell me so to my face. For two pins I'd flatten your nose in to teach you manners. Introducing a fine woman to you is casting pearls before swine [*yelling at him*] before s w i n e! d'ye hear?

HE [*with deplorable lack of polish*] You call me a swine again and I'll land you one on the chin thatll make your head sing for a week.

HER HUSBAND [*exploding*] What!

He charges at Henry with bull-like fury. Henry places himself on guard in the manner of a well taught boxer, and gets away

779

HOW HE LIED TO HER HUSBAND

smartly, but unfortunately forgets the stool which is just behind him. He falls backwards over it, unintentionally pushing it against the shins of Bompas, who falls forward over it. Mrs Bompas, with a scream, rushes into the room between the sprawling champions, and sits down on the floor in order to get her right arm round her husband's neck.

SHE. You shant, Teddy: you shant. You will be killed: he is a prizefighter.

HER HUSBAND [*vengefully*] I'll prizefight him. [*He struggles vainly to free himself from her embrace*].

SHE: Henry: dont let him fight you. Promise me that you wont.

HE [*ruefully*] I have got a most frightful bump on the back of my head. [*He tries to rise*].

SHE [*reaching out her left hand to seize his coat tail, and pulling him down again, whilst keeping fast hold of Teddy with the other hand*] Not until you have promised: not until you both have promised. [*Teddy tries to rise: she pulls him back again*] Teddy: you promise, dont you? Yes, yes. Be good: you promise.

HER HUSBAND. I wont, unless he takes it back.

SHE. He will: he does. You take it back, Henry?—yes.

HE [*savagely*] Yes. I take it back. [*She lets go his coat. He gets up. So does Teddy*]. I take it all back, all, without reserve.

SHE [*on the carpet*] Is nobody going to help me up? [*They each take a hand and pull her up*]. Now wont you shake hands and be good?

HE [*recklessly*] I shall do nothing of the sort. I have steeped myself in lies for your sake; and the only reward I get is a lump on the back of my head the size of an apple. Now I will go back to the straight path.

SHE. Henry: for Heaven's sake—

HE. It's no use. Your husband is a fool and a brute—

HER HUSBAND. Whats that you say?

HE. I say you are a fool and a brute; and if youll step outside with me I'll say it again. [*Teddy begins to take off his coat*
780

for combat]. Those poems w e r e written to your wife, every word of them, and to nobody else. [*The scowl clears away from Bompas's countenance. Radiant, he replaces his coat*]. I wrote them because I loved her. I thought her the most beautiful woman in the world; and I told her so over and over again. I adored her: do you hear? I told her that you were a sordid commercial chump, utterly unworthy of her; and so you are.

HER HUSBAND [*so gratified, he can hardly believe his ears*] You dont mean it!

HE. Yes, I do mean it, and a lot more too. I asked Mrs Bompas to walk out of the house with me—to leave you—to get divorced from you and marry me. I begged and implored her to do it this very night. It was her refusal that ended everything between us. [*Looking very disparagingly at him*] What she can see in you, goodness only knows!

HER HUSBAND [*beaming with remorse*] My dear chap, why didnt you say so before! I apologize. Come! dont bear malice: shake hands. Make him shake hands, Rory.

SHE. For my sake, Henry. After all, he's my husband. Forgive him. Take his hand. [*Henry, dazed, lets her take his hand and place it in Teddy's*].

HER HUSBAND [*shaking it heartily*] Youve got to own that none of your literary heroines can touch my Rory. [*He turns to her and claps her with fond pride on the shoulder*]. Eh, Rory? They cant resist you: none of em. Never knew a man yet that could hold out three days.

SHE. Dont be foolish, Teddy. I hope you were not really hurt, Henry. [*She feels the back of his head. He flinches*]. Oh, poor boy, what a bump! I must get some vinegar and brown paper. [*She goes to the bell and rings*].

HER HUSBAND. Will you do me a great favor, Apjohn. I hardly like to ask; but it will be a real kindness to us both.

HE. What can I do?

HER HUSBAND [*taking up the poems*] Well, may I get these printed? It shall be done in the best style. The finest paper, sumptuous binding, everything first class. Theyre beautiful

781

HOW HE LIED TO HER HUSBAND

poems. I should like to shew them about a bit.

SHE [*running back from the bell, delighted with the idea, and coming between them*] Oh Henry, if you wouldnt mind?

HE. Oh, *I* dont mind. I am past minding anything.

HER HUSBAND. What shall we call the volume? To Aurora, or something like that, eh?

HE. I should call it How He Lied to Her Husband.

VILLAGE WOOING

A COMEDIETTINA FOR TWO VOICES
IN THREE CONVERSATIONS

Written in 1933

First Performed Dallas 1934

VILLAGE WOOING
FIRST CONVERSATION

THE *lounge deck of the Empress of Patagonia, a pleasure ship. Two of the deck chairs are occupied by* A, *a literary looking pale gentleman under forty in green spectacles, a limp black beard, and a tropical suit of white silk, who is writing and does not wish to be disturbed, and* z, *a young woman, presentable but not aristocratic, who is bored with her book. She is undressed for bathing, but is very modestly covered up with a not too flamboyant wrap.*

z. Excuse me. Could you tell me the time?

A. [*curtly*] Eleven.

z. My watch makes it half past ten.

A. The clocks were put on half an hour last night. We are going east.

z. I always think it adds to the interest of a voyage having to put on your watch.

A. I am glad you are so easily interested [*he resumes his writing pointedly*].

z. The steward will be round with the soup in half an hour. I thought we should have to wait an hour.

A. I never take it. It interrupts my work.

z. Why do you work all the time? It's not what one comes on a pleasure cruise for, is it?

A. Work is my only pleasure.

z. Oh, thats not good sense, is it? It gives me the pip to see you always sitting there over your writing, and never enjoying yourself, nor even taking a drop of soup. You should get up and have a game of deck quoits: you will feel ever so much better after it.

A. I feel perfectly well, thank you. And I loathe deck games, especially deck quoits. The slapping of those silly things on the deck destroys the quiet of the ship.

z. Oh, I see. That is why you select this end of the deck. I often wondered why.

A. Within the last fortnight you have inspected the

785

priceless antiquities of Naples, Athens, Egypt, and the Holy Land. Please occupy your mind with them until the soup comes.

z. I never cared much for geography. Where are we now?

A. We are on the Red Sea.

z. But it's blue.

A. What did you expect it to be?

z. Well, I didnt know what color the sea might be in these parts. I always thought the Red Sea would be red.

A. Well, it isnt.

z. And isnt the Black Sea black?

A. It is precisely the color of the sea at Margate.

z. [*eagerly*] Oh, I am so glad you know Margate. Theres no place like it in the season, is there?

A. I dont know: I have never been there.

z. [*disappointed*] Oh, you ought to go. You could write a book about it.

A. [*shudders, sighs, and pretends to write very hard*]! *A pause.*

z. I wonder why they call it the Red Sea.

A. Because their fathers did. Why do you call America America?

z. Well, because it is America. What else would you call it?

A. Oh, call it what you like, dear lady; but I have five hundred words to write before lunch; and I cannot do that if I talk to you.

z. [*sympathetically*] Yes: it is awful to have to talk to people, isnt it? Oh, that reminds me: I have something really interesting to tell you. I believe the man in the cabin next mine beats his wife.

A. I feel a little like him myself. Some women would provoke any men to beat them.

z. I will say this for him, that she always begins it.

A. No doubt.

z. I hate a nagger: dont you?

VILLAGE WOOING

A. It is your privilege as a woman to have the last word. Please take it and dont end all your remarks with a question.

z. You are funny.

A. Am I? I never felt less funny in my life.

z. I cant make you out at all. I am rather good at making out people as a rule; but I cant make head or tail of you.

A. I am not here to be made out. You are not here to make people out, but to revel in the enjoyments you have paid for. Deck tennis, deck quoits, shuffleboard, golf, squash rackets, the swimming pool, the gymnasium all invite you.

z. I am no good at games: besides, theyre silly. I'd rather sit and talk.

A. Then for heaven's sake talk to somebody else. I have no time for talk. I have to work my passage.

z. What do you mean: work your passage? You are not a sailor.

A. No. I make a precarious living on board ship by writing the Marco Polo Series of Chatty Guide Books. Unless I complete two thousand words a day I am bankrupt. I cannot complete them if you persist in talking to me.

z. Do you mean you are writing a book about this cruise?

A. I am trying to—under great difficulties.

z. Will I be in it?

A. [*grimly*] You will.

z. How thrilling! I have never been put in a book before. You will read me what you have written about me, wont you?

A. When the book is published you can read it to your heart's content.

z. But I should like you to get me right. After all, what do you know about me? I will tell you the whole of my life if you like.

A. Great heavens, NO. Please dont.

z. Oh, I dont care who knows it.

787

VILLAGE WOOING

A. Evidently. You would hardly offer to tell it to a perfect stranger if you cared, or if it was of the smallest interest.

z. Oh, I'd never think of you as a stranger. Here we are on the same ship, arnt we? And most people would think my life quite a romance. Wouldnt you really like to hear it?

A. No, I tell you. When I want romances I invent them for myself.

z. Oh, well, perhaps you wouldnt think it very wonderful. But it was a regular treat for me. You may think because I am well dressed and travelling de lucks and all that, that I am an educated lady. But I'm not.

A. I never supposed for a moment that you were.

z. But how could you know? How did you find out?

A. I didnt find out. I knew.

z. Who told you?

A. Nobody told me.

z. Then how did you know?

A. [exasperated] How do I know that a parrot isnt a bird of paradise?

z. Theyre different.

A. Precisely.

z. There you are, you see. But what would you take me for if you met me in a third class carriage?

A. I should not notice you.

z. I bet you would. I maynt be a beauty; but when I get into a railway carriage every man in it has a look at me.

A. I am not Everyman. Everyman thinks that every woman that steps into a railway carriage may be the right woman. But she is always a disappointment.

z. Same with the women, isnt it? If you were a woman youd know.

A. I am a woman; and you are a man, with a slight difference that doesnt matter except on special occasions.

z. Oh, what a thing to say! I never could bring myself to believe that. I know, of course, that men have their

788

weaknesses and their tempers; but all the same there is something wonderful you can get from a man that you never could get from a woman. Dont you think so?

A. Inexperienced men think there is something wonderful you can get from a woman that you never could get from a man. Hence many unhappy marriages.

z. Are you married?

A. Widower. Are you?

z. Oh, thats the first time youve asked me a question. We're getting on, arnt we?

A. No. I am not getting on with my work.

z. Youre an intellectual, arnt you?

A. What do you think you mean by an intellectual?

z. Only that you consider me no better than an idiot, and that you were a bad husband, most likely.

A. You are quite right on both points.

z. I thought so.

A. And now, please, may I go on with my work?

z. Please yourself. I'm not hindering you.

A. Thank you [*he resumes his writing*].

A pause.

z. What books would you recommend me to read to improve my mind?

A. [*shouting furiously*] Steward.

z. Oh, you shouldnt trouble the steward now. He's busy getting the soup.

A. I want him to remove my chair to the very furthest extremity of this ship.

z. I always say it's fresher under the awning at the end. You dont mind if I move too, do you?

A. If you persecute me any more I shall go overboard. Dont you see that I want to be left alone to work, and that your chatter is preventing me from working?

z. [*sympathetically*] It is annoying to have somebody talking to you all the time when you dont want to. But it's just as bad when you want to talk, and the other person wont, isnt it?

VILLAGE WOOING

A. There are three or four hundred persons on this ship. Cannot you find one of them with the same insatiable thirst for conversation as yourself?

z. Well; but we all have to make ourselves agreeable, havnt we?

A. Not at oneanother's expense. You are not making yourself agreeable to me at present: you are driving me mad.

z. My father used to say that men and women are al-always driving oneanother mad.

A. That sounds literary. Was your father a man of letters?

z. Yes: I should think he was. A postman.

A. A what?

z. A postman. A village postman.

A. Ha ha! Ha ha ha!

z. What is there funny in that?

A. I dont know. Ha ha! The postman's daughter hath ripe red lips: butter and eggs and a pound of cheese! Ha ha ha!

z. Well, I'm glad Ive amused you. But I dont think it's very polite of you to laugh at my father.

A. [*punctiliously—recovering himself*] You are right. I was rude. But a good laugh is worth a hundred pounds to me. I feel a different man. Forgive me. You see, you quoted a remark of your father's—almost an epigram—which suggested that he must have been a man of genius.

z. Well, so he was. He had a genius for walking.

A. For what?

z. For walking. When he was a child, he won a prize as The Infant Pedestrian. And would you believe it, my mother was that indoory that she grudged having to go out and do her marketing. After we had a telephone put in she never went out at all.

A. Thats strange. As she was never out and he was never in, the household should have been a quiet one; but that remark of his about men and women driving oneanother mad rather suggests the opposite.

z. So it was the opposite. She was always complaining of being lonely; and he was always at her to take more exercise. When they were not quarrelling about that, they were quarrelling about me. You see, they had great ambitions for me. She wanted me to be a parlormaid in a great house. He wanted me to be a telephone operator. He said there is no future for the great houses and a great future for telephones.

a. And you? Had you no ambition for yourself?

z. Oh, I wanted to be something romantic, like an acrobat in a circus.

a. And what actually happened?

z. I became shop assistant and telephone operator in the village shop.

a. Do village shop assistants and telephone girls—

z. Operators.

a. Pardon: operators. Do they earn enough to take cruises round the world in pleasure ships?

z. Not they. I won the first prize in a newspaper competition. My mother wanted me to save it: she said it would help me to get a thrifty husband. My father told me to blue it all in a lump while I had the chance. "You will be poor all your life," he said; "but now you have the chance of living at the rate of five thousand a year for four months. Dont miss it," he said: "see what it's like. Have your fling," he said; "for they never can take that away from you once youve had it." His idea was a walking tour, spending the nights in the best hotels; but I chose the ship because it's more dressy and more people to look at. Besides, I can get all the walking I want round the deck. At the end of the cruise back I go to the village shop without a penny.

a. Have they found out here that you are not a lady?

z. The Americans dont know the difference: they think my telephone talk is aristocratic; and the English wont speak to anyone anyhow. And lots of them are just like me.

791

VILLAGE WOOING

A. Well, how do you like living at the rate of five thousand a year? Is it worth it?

z. It is while the novelty lasts. You see, when youre at home you get tired of doing the same thing every day: the same places! the same faces! the same old round. When you get a holiday you go off in a crowded hot excursion train to the seaside and make yourself tired and miserable just because it's a change; and youd do anything for a change. But here it's change all the time until you begin to realize what it is to have a settled home and belong somewhere. I shant be sorry to get home to the shop and the telephone. I get such a dreadful lost dog feeling sometimes. Other times it seems such a foolish waste of money. And I hate wasting money.

A. Thats an extremely attractive point in your character. My wife used to waste my money. Stick to that and you will get married in no time.

z. Oh, I have had plenty of offers. But you know it's a terrible thing to be a poor man's wife when you have been accustomed to a clean decent job. I have seen so many bright jolly girls turn into dirty old drudges through getting married.

A. Dont be afraid of dirt. Mine is a clean job; but I often wish I had a dirty one to exercise me and keep me in health. Women are so set on clean collars that they make their sons clerks when they would be stronger and earn more money as navvies. I wish I was a navvy instead of writing guide books.

z. Well, whats to prevent you?

A. I am not trained to manual work. Half an hour of it would make me wish myself dead. And five minutes of my work would produce a strike among the navvies. I am only a writing machine, just as a navvy is a digging machine.

z. I dont think the world is rightly arranged: do you?

A. We must take the world as we find it. It's we that are not rightly arranged.

792

z. Thats what I mean. Well, I suppose I mustnt interrupt your work.

a. You mean that the steward is coming round with the soup at last.

z. Well, it's half past eleven, isnt it?

The steward appears with the soup and offers it to z, who seizes it eagerly; then to a.

a. No, thank you. No soup.

He buries himself in his work, unmolested.

She buries herself in the soup.

793

SECOND CONVERSATION

*I*N *a village shop and post office on the Wiltshire Downs on a fine summer morning. The counter is for general shopping for most of its length; but one end is reserved and railed in for postal business. A couple of chairs are available for customers. The goods for sale include ginger beer in stone bottles, tablets of milk chocolate, glass jars of sweets containing (inter alia) sugared almonds, all on the counter; cheese, butter, and Hovis bread handy to the scales; and, in front of the counter, a sack of apples on the floor and some string bags hanging from the rafters.*

z. [*invisible*] Th-reee ni-nnn. Sorry: no such number. Whoo-mmm do you want? Doctor Byles? One fi-fff. You are through.

A comes in. He is in hiking costume, with stick and rucksack, but wears well cut breeches (not plus fours) instead of shorts. Seeing nobody to attend to him he raps loudly on the counter with his stick. z emerges.

A. I want a packet of milk chocolate—

z. Thanks very much.

A. [*continuing*]—a couple of hard apples—

z. Thanks very much. [*She comes out through the counter to get them from the sack*].

A. [*continuing*]—quarter of a pound of Cheddar cheese—

z. Thanks very much.

A. Dont interrupt me. You can express your gratitude for the order when I have finished. Quarter of a pound of your best butter, a small loaf of Hovis, and twopennyworth of sugared almonds.

z. Anything else?

A. No, thank you.

z. Thanks very much [*she goes back through the counter to cut and weigh the butter and cheese*].

He sits down watching her deft but leisurely proceedings.

A. Do you sell baskets?

z. We sell everything. Hadnt you better have a string

794

bag? It's handier; and it packs away almost to nothing when it's empty.

A. What is a string bag? Shew me one.

z. [*coming out and taking one down*] This is the cheapest. Or would you like a better quality with a Zip fastening?

A. Certainly not. I should have the trouble of opening and shutting it, and the worry of wondering whether it would open or shut, with no compensatory advantage whatever.

z. Thats just like you. Youre not a bit changed.

A. What do you mean? I have been in this shop for less than two minutes. Why should I have changed in that time?

z. Excuse me: I shouldnt have mentioned it. Will you take a string bag?

A. Yes.

z. Thanks very much. Shall I put the rest of the order into it?

A. Of course. What else do you suppose I am buying it for? Have you any buttermilk?

z. Sorry. We dont stock it.

A. Any ginger beer?

z. Yes. We have a very good local brew.

A. Shove a bottle into the string bag.

z. Thanks very much.

A. How many times a day do you say thanks very much?

z. Depends on the number of orders.

A. Dont say it to me again, if you dont mind. It gets on my nerves.

z. It used to get on mine, at first. But I am used to it.

A. Have you a guide book of this village?

z. Sorry. Theres a leaflet in the church, written by the vicar. You are expected to put tuppence in the box for it. Excuse me; but the chocolates are tuppence, sixpence, and a shilling. Which size would you run to?

795

VILLAGE WOOING

A. It is a poor heart that never rejoices. I will have a shilling one.

z. Thanks very much.

A. Dont.

z. Excuse me: I cant help it. I say it without thinking: same as if you touched a button.

The telephone rings.

A. Someone has touched the button.

z. [*vanishing into the post office section*] What number please? Whitehall on-n-n-e two on-n-n-e two. I will ring you. Whitehall one two one two. Yes. [*She reappears*]. Thats a police call.

A. You need not point the information at me. I am not the criminal.

z. Oh, it isnt a criminal. Somebody thats been broadcasted on the wireless as lost. You know the sort of thing. Missing from his home since January the first. Last seen in a deck chair on the Empress of Patagonia talking to a female. Suffering from loss of memory.

A. How extraor— [*the telephone rings again*].

z. Excuse me. [*She vanishes*]. You are through to Whitehall. [*She reappears*].

A. You have hit on an extraordinary coincidence. I wonder whether you will believe me when I tell you that in January last I was sitting on the deck of a ship named the Empress of Patagonia, and that I was talking to a female—or rather she was talking to me. How that woman did talk!

z. And are you suffering from loss of memory?

A. Certainly not. I never forget anything.

z. Oh, then it cant be you, can it?

A. There! Can it? That woman always finished up with can it? wont it? isnt it? so that you had to answer her out of common politeness. Take care never to pick up that trick or you will be murdered some day.

z. Some people are like that. It often goes with orange colored eyes [*or whatever color her eyes happen to be*].

796

Did you notice the color of her eyes?

A. No: I never notice things like that. I am not a detective. It is people's characters that impress me; I cant tell you the color of her hair or the shape of her nose; but I can tell you that she was a most fearful nuisance. How much does all that come to?

Z. The string bag sixpence, chocolates a shilling: one and sixpence. The ginger beer is—

A. Spare me the details. Will ten shillings cover it?

Z. Oh yes, of course. You shouldnt be so careless about money.

A. [*presenting a Treasury note*] Cease preaching. Take it; and give me the change.

Z. Let me see. Eighteenpence, and fourpence for the ginger beer is one and tenpence, isnt it?

A. Have I denied it?

Z. Cheese threepence: two and a penny; butter sixpence: two and sevenpence; apples we sell by the pound. Hadnt you better have a pound?

A. How many to the pound?

Z. Three.

A. I cannot eat more than two apples at a time. Charge me for a pound; and eat the odd one yourself.

Z. Oh well, say threepence for two: thats two and tenpence, isnt it?

A. I dont know.

Z. Hovis, tuppence halfpenny. Three shillings and a halfpenny. Do you happen to have a halfpenny to save having to take fippence halfpenny in coppers?

A. I hate halfpennies: I always throw them away. Stop. I have one. Here.

Z. Thanks very much. [*Handing him his change coin by coin*] Three, four, five, seven and six, ten. Thanks very much.

A. [*pocketing his change, but remaining comfortably seated*] Dont you find it rather dull in this village shop saying thanks very much all day?

z. Well, no matter where you are you are doing the same thing all day and every day, arnt you? The only way to get it off your mind is to live in the same place and stick at the same job. Then you never have to think about it. Thats the way the people live here; and they live for ever so long: eighty's no age here. Grandfather will be a hundred and two in August. Thats because he's never had to worry about what he'll do or where he'll go. He just imagines and imagines. It's the only way to be happy and longlived.

a. But if your imagination has only one village in it it must be pretty bare. How would you like to live in a room with only one chair in it.

z. Well, if you have only one seat what more do you want than one chair? Up at the castle there are thirtysix chairs of one sort or another in the big drawing room; but Lady Flopping cant flop on more than one, can she?

a. [*pointing to the vacant chair*] May I suggest that you flop on that one while we talk?

z. [*sitting down*] Thanks very much.

a. I am not interrupting your work, I hope. There is nothing so maddening as to be talked to when you want to work.

z. Talking is part of the work in a village shop.

a. Tell me: do you ever read?

z. I used to read travels and guide books. We used to stock the Marco Polo series. I was mad about travelling. I had daydreams about the glory that was Greece, the grandeur that was Rome and all that flapdoodle.

a. Flapdoodle!

z. Well, I suppose I shouldnt call it that; but it ended in my going to Rome and Athens. They were all right; but the old parts were half knocked down; and I couldnt see any glory or grandeur different to Cheltenham. I was glad to be home again. And I had so wanted to meet the Marco Polo man and walk about with him in the ruins by moonlight and hear him go on about them!

VILLAGE WOOING

A. The Marco Polo man! The milkman! the postman! the muffin man! the Marco Polo man! Some frustrated poet, earning his crust by quoting scraps of verse to bring the Call of the East to dreaming telephone girls.

z. Operators.

A. Operators dont dream. Girls! girls of the golden west. Did that poor devil never bring you the Call of the East?

z. I'd read about it in novels and seen it on the films. They were all about moony drunkards and sheeks and the sort of girls that go dotty about them. I went right round the world to see the reality. Pretty places, of course; but the heat! and the mosquitoes! and the smells!! Travelling just destroyed the world for me as I imagined it. Give me this village all the time.

A. Had you no thrill when you stood somewhere where a poet had said "Stop; for thy tread is on an empire's dust"?

z. A guide, you mean. Theyd take the poetry out of anything; and all the time youre thinking what you ought to give them. If you fancy empires' dusts and all that sort of thing you should meet our vicar and start him talking about our standing stones, and the barrows on the downs, and the Mound. Every grain of our dust, he says, is full of history. Same everywhere, I expect.

A. Are you married?

z. No. Why? Have you any intentions?

A. Dont be in a hurry. Weve known each other less than ten minutes.

z. How much better do you think you will know me when we have talked for twenty years?

A. That is profoundly true. Still, I must think it over.

z. Nobody would ever marry if they thought it over. Youve got to take your chance, no matter how long you think.

A. You are in a hurry.

z. Well, I am past the age at which girls marry here,

799

though I'm the pick of this village. Thats because I thought all my offers over. So I have made up my mind to take the next man that asks me, provided he's reasonably suitable.

A. Do I strike you as being reasonably suitable?

z. Well, I think I have the sort of commonsense you need to keep you straight. And you being a widower know what to expect from a woman. An inexperienced man expects the earth.

A. How do you know that I am a widower?

z. You told me.

A. Did I? When did I tell you?

z. Never mind. You did. I have noticed you have a bad memory; but I have a very good one; so it wont matter.

A. Steady. Steady. I have not yet made myself liable to an action for breach of promise.

z. Dont be afraid. I'm not that sort. We dont consider it respectable here.

A. Should I get any money with you? Do you own the shop?

z. No. All the money I ever had I blued on a trip round the world. But Mrs Ward is getting too old for the business: she couldnt run it now without me. If you could afford to buy her an annuity she'd sell it.

A. I dont know how much annuities cost.

z. You will find it in Whitaker's almanac.

A. This is rather upsetting. Somehow I have always taken it for granted that when I married again I'd marry a woman with money.

z. Oh, that wouldnt suit you at all. She'd want to spend it going into society and travelling about. How could you bear that sort of life? you that never spoke to anyone on the ship and wouldnt take any part in their games and dances! When it got about that you were the Marco Polo man—the man of all our dreams as you might say—I made a bet that I'd get you to talk to me; and I had all the trouble in the world to win it.

A. Do you mean to say that we have met before? That

800

you were on that trip round the world?

z. Of course I do. But you never notice anything. Youre always reading or writing. The world doesnt exist for you. You never looked at me really. Youre shy with strangers, arnt you?

A. I am absolutely certain I never spoke to any woman on that ship. If I talk to women they always want to marry me.

z. Well, there you are, you see! The moment I set eyes on you I said to myself, "Now thats the sort of man that would suit me as a husband." I'd have said it even if you hadnt been the Marco Polo man.

A. Love at first sight: what?

z. Oh no. You know, if I fell in love with a man I'd never marry him: he could make me so miserable. But there was something about you: I dont exactly know what; but it made me feel that I could do with you in the house; and then I could fall in love with anyone I liked without any fear of making a fool of myself. I suppose it was because you are one of the quiet sort and dont run after women.

A. How do you know I dont run after women?

z. Well, if you want to know, it's because you didnt run after me. You mightnt believe it; but men do run after me.

A. Why?

z. Oh, how do I know? They dont know, themselves. But the lot of money they spend on things they dont want merely to come in and have a look at me and a word with me, you wouldnt believe. It's worth at least twenty pounds a year to the business.

A. [putting on his glasses and looking at her attentively for the first time] I shouldnt call you a pretty woman.

z. Oh, I'm not pretty. But what you might call desirable, dont you think?

A. [alarmed] No I dont think. May I explain? I am a man of letters and a gentleman. I am accustomed to as-

801

sociate with ladies. That means that I am accustomed to speak under certain well understood reserves which act as a necessary protection to both parties. You are not a lady: you are a villager; but somebody has educated you—probably the Church or the local authority—to a point at which you can impose on unobservant and unwary travellers. You have had finishing lessons on the telephone which give you a distinguished articulation: you can say Th-ree fiv-v-v-v-e ni-n-n-n instead of theree fauv nawn. But you have not acquired any of the reserves. You say what you think. You announce all the plans that wellbred women conceal. You play with your cards on the table instead of keeping them where a lady should keep them: up your sleeve.

z. Well, wheres the harm?

a. Oh, no harm. Quite the contrary. But I feel rushed.

z. What do you mean? rushed?

a Rushed. Precipitated. Carried to lengths I had no intention of going to.

z. Well, it gets you somewhere: doesnt it?

a. Yes; but where?

z. Here. Theres no mystery about it. Here, in a good business in a village shop in a quiet place, with me to keep it straight and look after you.

a. May I ask how much that expression "looking after me" includes? Let me be clear on the point. As a matter of fact I possess a small property which I could sell for enough to purchase an annuity for old Mrs Williams—

z. Ward.

a. I believe I have enough to purchase annuities for both Mrs Ward and Mrs Williams, as they are presumably both centenarians. But why on earth should I complicate the transaction by marrying you? I could pay you your present wages—

z. Salary.

a. I beg your pardon: salary. You will retain your present position as my shopgirl.

z. Shop assistant.

802

A. I beg your pardon: shop assistant. You can then make your own matrimonial arrangements, and leave me to make mine.

z. Oh, I'll make my own matrimonial arrangements all right enough. You may depend on that.

A. Excuse me: I added "and leave me to make mine." Can I depend on you for that also?

z. Well, we'll see.

A. [*angrily firm*] No: you will not see.

z. Well, what?

A. I dont know what. I will not commit myself. We'll see.

z. Just so: we'll see. It's a bargain then?

A. No: it most certainly is not a bargain. When I entered this shop half an hour ago I had not the faintest notion of buying a village shop or marrying a village maiden or any of the things you have put into my head. Have you ever read the fable of the spider and the fly?

z. No; but I used to sing a song called the honeysuckle and the bee.

A. [*resolutely*] Good morning. [*He makes for the door*].

z. [*following him with the string bag*] You are forgetting your things.

A. [*taking it*] Thank you.

z. Thanks very much.

She tempts him to kiss her.

A. No!!! [*he strides out*].

THIRD CONVERSATION

A IS now the proprietor of the shop with z as his hired assistant. The counter has been fitted with a desk at the opposite end to the post office section. At this A sits writing. He wears pepper-and-salt trousers of country cut, with an apron. He is in his shirtsleeves, and looks every inch a shopkeeper. z comes in through the post office, very fresh and matutinal.

z. Morning, boss.

A. Good morning, slave.

z. I havnt begun slaving yet. You have been at it for half an hour. Whatever on earth are you working at so hard?

A. I am making out my balance sheet.

z. Oh, you neednt do that. The accountant's clerk from Salisbury does all that when he makes out the income tax return. Youre not expected to do figures in this village. Fancy old Mrs Ward doing such a thing!

A. When I bought this shop from Mrs Ward for an annuity I found she was much clever at figures than I was. She should have been a moneylender.

z. She was. She lent a shilling for a penny a week.

A. That must have been between four and five hundred per cent per annum. Shylock would have blushed.

z. Whats the good of it when you have to give credit at the shop, and then lend the customers the money to pay you?

A. Mrs Ward should **have** gone to Geneva. International finance would have come naturally to her.

z. Thats too clever for me. Anyhow, you neednt worry over a balance sheet. The accountant will do all that for you.

A. [*rising and waving the balance sheet proudly as he comes through the counter into the public part of the shop*] This is not an accountant's balance sheet. It is a Robinson Crusoe balance sheet.

z. [*following him*] Whatever's that?

804

VILLAGE WOOING

A. Crusoe drew up a balance sheet of the advantages and disadvantages of being cast away on a desert island. I am cast away in a village on the Wiltshire Downs. I am drawing up a similar balance sheet. I propose to read it to you as far as I have got. [*He takes one of the customer's chairs*]. You can remind me of anything I have forgotten.

Z. Lets have it. [*She takes the other chair*].

A. I begin with the credit entries.

Z. Things to your own credit, you mean?

A. No, to the credit of village shopkeeping as a way of life.

Z. Oh, you are silly, boss.

A. That is a disrespectful remark. As such, it should not be made to a boss by his slave. The understanding on which I raised your salary when I engaged you as my assistant was that our relations should be completely conventional and businesslike on your side, however I might occasionally forget myself.

Z. [*rising*] Very well: you can keep your balance sheet to yourself. I will go on with the telephone call book.

A. You will do nothing of the sort. You will do what I tell you to do. That is what I pay you for. Sit down again. [*She does so*]. Now listen. [*He takes up his manuscript and reads*]. Item: I have sharpened my faculties, and greatly improved in observation and mathematics.

Z. Couldnt you put it into shorter words? What does it mean?

A. It means that formerly I always took what money was given me without condescending to count it or attempting to calculate it. I can now both calculate and count quite rapidly. Formerly I made no distinctions between grades of butter and eggs. To me an egg was an egg: butter was butter. I now make critical distinctions of the greatest subtlety, and value them in terms of money. I am forced to admit that the shopkeeper is enormously superior to the Marco Polo man, and that I have learnt more in three months in this shop than I learnt in three years in Oxford.

805

z. I cant believe that about the learning. But see how your manners have improved!

a. My manners!!

z. Yes. Why, on that ship you hadnt a word to throw to a dog; and if anyone came near you you shrank up into yourself like a hedgehog, afraid that they didnt belong to your class and wanted to speak to you without an introduction. Now it's a pleasure to hear you say "Good morning; and what can I do for you today, Mrs Burrell?" and "Have you noticed the cauliflowers today, maam? Not a touch of frost on them!" and "Sparrowgrass very good today, my lady, if you would be wanting some."

a. I positively deny that I have ever in my life called asparagus sparrowgrass to an educated customer. Of course, when people are too ignorant to know the names of what they eat, that is another matter.

z. Well, anyhow, your manners have improved, havnt they?

a. I dont know. I know that they are no longer disinterested and sincere.

z. No more they never used to be. Never easy with anybody. Now you are hail fellow well met, as you might say, with everybody.

a. The world has become a world of customers. Let me write that down. [*He pencils on the back of his balance sheet*] "Manners will never be universally good until every person is every other person's customer."

z. Youre not a real shopkeeper yet, boss. All you want is to find something clever to write.

a. Well, why not? Find enough clever things to say, and you are a Prime Minister. Write them down, and you are a Shakespear.

z. Yes; but who wants to be a Prime Minister or a Shakespear? Youve got to make a living.

a. Well, am I not making a living? I am no poorer than when I bought the shop.

z. But if the money goes as fast as it comes you cant

save anything.

A. I loathe saving. It turns human nature sour. "Cast your bread upon the waters; and it will return to you after many days."

Z. And how are you to live for the many days with nothing to eat?

A. I dont know. One does, somehow. Stop asking questions; and let us get on with the balance sheet.

Z. I speak for your good.

A. [*rising wrathfully*] The most offensive liberty one human being can possibly take with another. What business is it of yours?

Z. [*rising and facing him*] If you wont think for yourself somebody else must think for you. It's my business as much as yours.

A. Oh, indeed! Who does this shop belong to? I mean to whom does this shop belong?

Z. I get my living out of it, dont I. If it shuts up what becomes of me?

A. Well, if you come to that, what becomes of me? You can get another job. I very greatly doubt whether anyone would give me one. [*Calming down*] Can you not be content with the fact that the shop is making enough to support two people? [*He resumes his seat*].

Z. Aye; but suppose it had to support three people!

A. Why suppose? It hasnt: thats all.

Z. It's not all. If you marry a stranger there will be three. And what about the children?

A. The remedy is simple. I shall not marry.

Z. You dont know.

A. Neither do you.

Z. Yes I do. You have married once; and you will marry twice. Somebody will snap you up. You are that sort of man.

A. If a woman snaps me up she must take the consequences. She must assist in the shop. And you will get the sack.

VILLAGE WOOING

z. Oh, you are tiresome. [*She sits down, discouraged*]. But you see my point, at all events.

A. No. What point?

z. Well, that it's really cheaper to keep a wife than to pay an assistant. Let alone that you dont have to live a single life.

A. You can get rid of an assistant if she doesnt suit. You cant get rid of a wife.

z. If people thought that way, theyd never get married.

A. Precisely.

z. In this life you have to take chances.

A. I have taken them, and escaped.

z. You wont escape here. We dont hold with bachelors here.

A. You cant do without a general shop here, nor a post office. While I command both I am in an impregnable strategic position.

z. Well, I dont like to say it; but people are beginning to talk.

A. Beginning! When did they ever stop?

z. Oh, theres no use talking to you.

A. Not the slightest.

z. Oh well then, take a month's notice. [*She rises*].

A. A month's notice!

z. Yes: a month's notice.

A. A month's notice because I refuse to marry some ridiculous village maiden or illiterate widow with whom I could not hold a moment's conversation!

z. Wives are not for conversation: thats for visitors. Youve had plenty of conversation with me.

A. Leave yourself of this conversation, please.

z. Oh, very well. A month's notice.

A. Dont say that again. Utter nonsense. What have you to complain of? You are quite well off here. I purposely pay you ten pounds a year more than you could get anywhere else.

808

z. Why?

A. What do you mean, why?

z. Why do you pay me ten pounds more than you could get another assistant for?

A. Heaven only knows!

z. [*in a fury*] I'll go this very day. I'll go this very minute. You can keep my month. You dont know when youre well off. Youre selfish. I dont wonder your wife died. Did she die mad?

A. [*gravely*] As a matter of fact, she did. I am one of those unlucky men who draw the black chances in the lottery of marriage.

z. [*remorsefully*] Oh, I didnt know: I didnt indeed. I was only joking. [*She sits again*] I wouldnt have said it for the world if I'd known.

A. Never mind: I know you didnt mean it. By the way, I made an inconsiderate remark which hurt you. I did not intend that. I should have told you seriously that I pay you ten pounds more than the market rate because I value your services in the shop, and wish to offer you every inducement to stay here permanently.

z. Ten pounds extra, to stay all my life here as a single woman!

A. Not necessarily. You can get married if you wish.

z. Who to?

A. To whom? Oh, anyone.

z. Anyone in the village is good enough for me; but nobody in the village is good enough for you: is that it?

A. Dont lose your temper again.

z. I will if I like. And if you knew how near I was to putting a couple of extra words in, youd perhaps realize that a woman wants something more in life than a job and a salary.

A. I know that perfectly well. There is one thing we are all out for when we are young.

z. And what is that, pray?

A. Trouble, adventure, hardship, care, disappointment,

809

doubt, misery, danger, and death.

z. Not me, thank you. All I want is a husband and the usual consequences.

A. The same thing. Marriage is the village form of all these adventures.

z. Oh, why dont you take a more cheerful view of life?

A. I have learnt not to expect too much from life. That is the secret of real cheerfulness, because I am always getting agreeable surprises instead of desolating disappointments.

z. Well, your second marriage may be an agreeable surprise, maynt it?

A. What, exactly, do you mean by my second marriage? I have only been married once. I mean I have been married only once.

z. Well, look here? Straight, now? Is there any man in this village that would be suitable to me now that I have got used to you?

A. My dear: men are all alike.

z. You mean it will make no difference to me who I marry.

A. Very little, I am afraid.

z. And women are all alike too, arnt they?

A. [suspicious] What are you getting at?

z. If it doesnt matter who anybody marries, then it doesnt matter who I marry and it doesnt matter who you marry.

A. Whom, not who.

z. Oh, speak English: youre not on the telephone now. What I mean is that if it doesnt matter to me it doesnt matter to you either.

A. You admit, then, that it doesnt matter?

z. No I dont. It's a lie.

A. Oh!

z. Dont "oh" me. All men are not alike to me. There are men—and good nice men, too—that I wouldnt let touch me. But when I saw you on the ship I said to myself

"I could put up with him."

A. Not at all. You told me just now that you said something quite different. I believe you really said something much more rapturous. Being rather a futile sort of person I attract vigorous women like you.

Z. When you looked at me out of the corner of your eye—you looked at all the women out of the corner of your eye in spite of your keeping yourself so much to yourself—did you never say "I could put up with her"?

A. No. I said "Damn that woman: she wont stop talking to me and interrupting my work."

Z. Well, I tell you we were made for oneanother. It maynt be as plain to you as to me yet; but if it's plain to me there must be something in it; for I'm never wrong when I see a thing quite plain. I dont believe youd ever have bought this shop and given up being a gentleman if I hadn't been here.

A. Now that you mention it I believe that is true. You were one of the amenities of the estate.

Z. Well, I might be one of the amenities of the estate of holy matrimony, mightnt I?

A. Take care. You may find what you are trying to do easier than you think. About five per cent of the human race consists of positive masterful acquisitive people like you, obsessed with some passion which they must gratify at all hazards. The rest let them have their own way because they have neither the strength nor the courage to resist, or because the things the masterful ones want seem trifling beside the starry heavens and the destiny of Man. I am not one of the masterful ones. I am not worth marrying. Any woman could marry me if she took trouble enough.

Z. Thats just what I'm afraid of. If I let you out of my sight for a month I might find you married to someone else at the end of it. Well, I'm taking no chances. I dont set up to be masterful: I dont like selfish uppish domineering people any more than you do; but I must and will have you; and thats all about it.

VILLAGE WOOING

A. Well, you already have me—as an employer. And you are independent of me, and can leave me if you are not satisfied.

Z. How can I be satisfied when I cant lay my hands on you? I work for you like a slave for a month on end; and I would have to work harder as your wife than I do now; but there come times when I want to get hold of you in my arms, every bit of you; and when I do I'll give you something better to think about than the starry heavens, as you call them. Youll find that you have senses to gratify as well as fine things to say.

A. Senses! You dont know what youre talking about. Look around you. Here in this shop I have everything that can gratify the senses: apples, onions, and acid drops; pepper and mustard; cosy comforters and hot water bottles. Through the window I delight my eyes with the old church and market place, built in the days when beauty came naturally from the hands of mediæval craftsmen. My ears are filled with delightful sounds, from the cooing of doves and the humming of bees to the wireless echoes of Beethoven and Elgar. My nose can gloat over our sack of fresh lavender or our special sixpenny Eau de Cologne when the smell of rain on dry earth is denied me. My senses are saturated with satisfactions of all sorts. But when I am full to the neck with onions and acid drops; when I am so fed up with mediæval architecture that I had rather die than look at another cathedral; when all I desire is rest from sensation, not more of it, what use will my senses be to me if the starry heavens still seem no more than a senseless avalanche of lumps of stone and wisps of gas—if the destiny of Man holds out no higher hope to him than the final extinction and annihilation of so mischievous and miserable a creature?

Z. We dont bother about all that in the village.

A. Yes you do. Our best seller here is Old Moore's Almanack; and next to it comes Napoleon's Book of Fate.

812

VILLAGE WOOING

Old Mrs Ward would never have sold the shop to me if she had not become persuaded that the Day of Judgment is fixed for the seventh of August next.

z. I dont believe such nonsense. Whats it all got to do with you and me?

a. You are inexperienced. You dont know. You are the dupe of thoughtless words like sensuality, sensuousness, and all the rest of the twaddle of the Materialists. I am not a Materialist: I am a poet; and I know that to be in your arms will not gratify my senses at all. As a matter of mere physical sensation you will find the bodily contacts to which you are looking forward neither convenient nor decorous.

z. Oh, dont talk like that. You mustnt let yourself think about it like that.

a. You must always let yourself think about everything. And you must think about everything as it is, not as it is talked about. Your secondhand gabble about gratifying my senses is only your virgin innocence. We shall get quite away from the world of sense. We shall light up for one-another a lamp in the holy of holies in the temple of life; and the lamp will make its veil transparent. Aimless lumps of stone blundering through space will become stars singing in their spheres. Our dull purposeless village existence will become one irresistible purpose and nothing else. An extraordinary delight and an intense love will seize us. It will last hardly longer than the lightning flash which turns the black night into infinite radiance. It will be dark again before you can clear the light out of your eyes; but you will have seen; and for ever after you will think about what you have seen and not gabble catchwords invented by the wasted virgins that walk in darkness. It is to give ourselves this magic moment that we feel that we must and shall hold oneanother in our arms; and when the moment comes, the world of the senses will vanish; and for us there will be nothing ridiculous, nothing uncomfortable, nothing unclean, nothing but pure paradise.

VILLAGE WOOING

z. Well, I am glad you take a nice view of it; for now I come to think of it I never could bear to be nothing more to a man than a lollipop. But you mustnt expect too much.

a. I shall expect more than you have ever dreamt of giving, in spite of the boundless audacity of women. What great men would ever have been married if the female nobodies who snapped them up had known the enormity of their own presumption? I believe they all thought they were going to refine, to educate, to make real gentlemen of their husbands. What do you intend to make of me, I wonder?

z. Well, I have made a decent shopkeeper of you already, havnt I? But you neednt be afraid of my not appreciating you. I want a fancy sort of husband, not a common villager that any woman could pick up. I shall be proud of you. And now Ive nailed you, I wonder at my own nerve.

a. So do I.

z. I'm not a bit like that, you know, really. Something above me and beyond me drove me on. Thats why I know it will be all right. Dont be afraid. I cant make a fine speech about it like you; but it will be all right. I promise you that.

a. Very well. Go round to the rectory; and put up the banns. And tell the rector's wife that we got in some prime artichokes this morning. She's fond of artichokes.

z. You are sure you feel happy about it?

a. I dont know what I feel about it. Go and do as you are told; and dont ask ridiculous questions.

The telephone rings. She hastens to answer it.

z. Number, please? . . . Oh, an order. Thanks very much. . . . Yes: we have some very fine artichokes just in this morning. . . . Thanks very much: they shall be sent round directly. Oh; and theres something else—are you there? . . . Sorry to detain you: could I speak to the rector? . . . Yes: it's rather particular. It's about banns . . . banns . . . BANNS: b for beauty, a for audacity, two enns for

nonsense, and s for singing. . . . Yes, banns: thats right. . . .
Who are the what? . . . Oh, the parties! Of course. Well,
it's—

The curtain falls

In the Sunda Strait,
27th January 1933

PLAYLET ON THE BRITISH PARTY SYSTEM

from Chapter III of Everybody's Political What's What?

Written in 1944

No Performance recorded

PLAYLET ON THE BRITISH PARTY SYSTEM

PRACTICALLY nobody in these islands understands the Party System. Britons do not know its history. They believe that it is founded in human nature and therefore indestructible and eternal. When I point out that it does not exist in our municipalities they think that I am ignorant or crazy, and assure me that there are Conservative parties and Progressive parties in the municipal councils and corporations "just the same as" in Parliament, and always will be by the immutable law of political human nature.

What are the facts? Let me put them in the form of a little historical drama, as that comes easiest to me and is the most amusing.

Scene: Althorp, the residence of the Spencers, Earls of Sunderland. Present King William the Third, aged 45, of glorious pious and immortal memory, and his host Robert Spencer, the second Earl, ten years older, famous even at the courts of Charles II and James II for his complete unscrupulousness and political ingenuity. Period 1695.

ROBERT. Your Majesty has done me a tremendous honor in visiting my humble residence. As I cannot pretend to have deserved it I apprehend that there is some way in which I can be of service to your Majesty.

WILLIAM. There is. I am at my wits' end. I want advice. I am expected to save the Protestant religion in Europe from the Scarlet Woman of Rome. I am expected to save your country and my own country from the Bourbons. I am expected to do everything for everybody. And I am expected to do it all without money and without a standing army. I cannot plan my campaigns for a year ahead because this damnable British Parliament, which is elected to govern England, only wants what all Englishmen want: that is, not to be governed at all. It may leave

819

PLAYLET ON THE BRITISH PARTY SYSTEM

me at any moment without a penny and without a soldier.
France's best general, who has won all her battles for her,
has just died and left King Louis in the hollow of my
hand. And this is the moment your parliament chooses to
threaten me with a peace. It is intolerable. Damn your
parliament! I will go back to Amsterdam: better be a real
Stadtholder than a sham king. They want liberty, these pigheaded squires and knights of the shire. Well, let them
have their liberty: liberty to be broken on the wheel to
please the Pope, liberty to be the vassals of France, liberty
to go to the devil their own way and not be interfered with
by any king or council. I shall fling the crown in their faces
and shake the dust of England off my feet unless you can
shew me a way of making Parliament do what I tell it to
do.

ROBERT. I cannot do that; but I can shew you a way to
prevent Parliament from doing anything at all except vote
supplies and stave off the next election as long as it can.

WILLIAM. Can you? The only supplies I care about are
supplies of men and money to save the Protestant north
from that fat Bourbon bigot. If I cannot have them your
crown is no use to me. You can have James back again. You
know where to find him: in Louis' pocket. I daresay you
are in correspondence with him, double-faced schemer that
you are.

ROBERT. I am what the times have made me; and I
keep in correspondence with everybody: one never knows
what will happen next. But I wish I could get your Majesty's mind off the Protestant north and the army for a moment. I wish I could convince you that what you have to
fight here is not King Louis, but the British Parliament.

WILLIAM. Well, do I not know it? Am I not telling you
so?

ROBERT. Keep to that, your Majesty. Is it agreed, too,
that I am a schemer?

WILLIAM. Oh, it is: it is: by God it is!

ROBERT. Would your Majesty condescend so far as to

820

say, a fairly successful schemer?

WILLIAM. A devilishly subtle one, I should say. What then?

ROBERT. I have a scheme for dealing with Parliament, though I have never yet found a king subtle enough to understand it.

WILLIAM. Try me.

ROBERT. You, sir, are the last king on earth to understand it. But I will lay it at your royal feet. Just now you choose your ministers on their merits and capacities without regard to their parties, a Whig here, a Tory there, each in his department which you call his Cabinet, and the assembly of them forming your council, which may be called *your* Cabinet.

WILLIAM. Just so. What fault have you to find with that?

ROBERT. My advice to your Majesty is that in future you choose all your ministers from the same party, and that this party shall always be the party which has a majority in the House of Commons.

WILLIAM. You are mad. Who ever heard of such a thing?

ROBERT. All things must have a beginning, sir. Think it over.

WILLIAM. I am thinking it over. And I remember what you have forgotten.

ROBERT. What is that, your Majesty?

WILLIAM. That the majority in the House of Commons at present is a Whig majority.

ROBERT. I have not forgotten it, sir. You must at once get rid of all your Tory ministers and replace them by Whigs.

WILLIAM. But, man alive, I am a Tory. Are you out of your senses?

ROBERT. Some day the Tories will have a majority and will defeat the Whig government on some measure. You will then immediately dissolve Parliament; and when the

821

PLAYLET ON THE BRITISH PARTY SYSTEM

Tories come back from the general election with a majority you will choose Tory ministers only.

WILLIAM. But what is the purpose of this absurdity? You talk as coolly as if you were talking sense. Why are you talking nonsense?

ROBERT. If your Majesty will only deign to do what I advise, I pledge my word—

WILLIAM [*sceptically*] Hmm!

ROBERT. Pardon: I should have said I pledge my reputation as a schemer. Well, I pledge it that from the moment when your Majesty adopts this plan no member of the House of Commons will ever again vote according to his principles or his convictions or his judgment or his religion or any other of his fancies. The people will think that he is voting on toleration, on peace or war, on whether the crown shall go to the elector of Hanover if your sister-in-law's children continue to die, on the enclosure of commons or billeting or the window tax or what not; but the real question on which he will always be voting is whether or no his party shall remain in office or he himself have to spend half his property on another election with the chance of losing his seat if his opponent has a few thousand pounds more to spend than he.

WILLIAM. Dont be a fool, Robert. I should be the slave of the majority no matter how they voted. And what has all this to do with the army and the money to pay for it?

ROBERT. There would be only one way of voting about the war or about anything; and you could always count on it. No majority, Whig or Tory, dare vote for surrender to our natural enemies the French, or to the Pope.

WILLIAM. The Pope is on my side.

ROBERT. Fortunately only a few of us know that curious fact. Your best card in England is always No Popery.

WILLIAM. You are laying a trap for me. You want to make the majority in the Commons the real ruler and make the monarch a puppet. And as the majority is always led by the nose by some ambitious schemer with the gift of the gab like yourself, he would be able to dictate to me as if he were the king and I a nobody.

ROBERT. I shall never be a dictator while you live, because you, sir, will never be a nobody. But I give you this further pledge. That if you do as I advise, you will have nothing to fear from the boldest and ablest adventurer, were he Cromwell himself, or Lilburne the Leveller. He will spend half his life and most of his means in getting into Parliament; and when he at last arrives there he will have no time to think of anything but how to get into your Majesty's Cabinet. When he intrigues his way to the top of that, he will be a master of the Party game and of nothing else. He will feed out of your Majesty's hand. And the people will imagine they are free because they have a parliament. Then you can fight all Europe all the time to your heart's content.

WILLIAM. I dont understand it and dont believe it. But as I cannot go on as at present, not knowing where my next regiment or my next penny is to come from, I will try your plan until I have driven Louis back to his pigstye. And if the plan fails I will have your head off by hook or crook.

ROBERT. You shall, sir. It has been on my weary shoulders too long.

Twentyfive years elapse. William and Sunderland, having died in the same year, have been eighteen years in their coffins. Queen Anne is dead; and George the First is King. Sunderland's son Charles, aged 45, is a member of the Whig Government. Robert Walpole, aged 44, though a notable Whig Parliamentarian, leads the Opposition to the Peerage Bill. As it happens, they meet one morning in St. James's Park, where they are taking the air. Walpole is inclined to pass on with a wave of the hand; but Sunderland is determined to engage him in conversation and will not be shaken off. After the usual commonplaces he comes to his point.

SUNDERLAND. I wish I could have your support for this Peerage Bill of mine. Frankly, I fear you will defeat me

PLAYLET ON THE BRITISH PARTY SYSTEM

if you oppose it. Why not come to my aid? It is not a Party question: we are all Whigs, and all equally interested in it.

WALPOLE. How do you make that out?

SUNDERLAND. Well, is it not as plain as a pikestaff? We Whigs are above all Parliament men: to us British liberty means the supremacy of Parliament. Parliament has two rival powers to fear: the king and the voting mob. My sainted father, a grain or two of whose political genius I may claim to have inherited, rescued us from the tyranny of the mob by the Party System. He made you what you are: the greatest Party leader in the world: you owe your eminence to his invention.

WALPOLE. It costs a lot of money. Every man has his price.

SUNDERLAND. All the more reason for making sure of the cash for us, and not for the mob. But what about Parliament's other rival, the King?

WALPOLE. The king question was settled seventyone years ago.

SUNDERLAND. Nay, my dear Walpole, you cannot kill kingship with a single chop of the axe in Whitehall. The Restoration brought back the House of Lords, and the King's power to pack it by making as many new peers as he pleased at any moment. The sole purpose of the Peerage Bill is to destroy that power. It will make it impossible for the king ever to make a single peer in excess of the present number. Surely you agree.

WALPOLE. Do I? I think not. Your sainted father persuaded King William that the Party System would give him the control of Parliament. But it really gave the parliamentary majority the control of the king. That ought to suit you very well, because you have the control of the majority until I get it back again, as I shall do when I defeat your Bill.

SUNDERLAND. But why defeat us on this Bill, which is as much in your interest as in mine? You can choose some other issue.

824

PLAYLET ON THE BRITISH PARTY SYSTEM

WALPOLE. It is not as much in my interest as in yours. You are a peer: I am a commoner. You want to make the Lords supreme by breaking the king's power over them. I want the king to keep his power over the Lords, and the Commons to keep its power over the King. I can see through and through your game. I have English brains, not Dutch ones.

SUNDERLAND. You are too clever for me, I see. But consider. You are a Commoner; but you will not always be a Commoner. You will soon be one of us. You know there is an earldom waiting for you to stretch out your hand and take it.

WALPOLE. Yes, provided the King keeps his power to make me an earl. Your Bill might deprive him of that power.

SUNDERLAND. Pooh! There is always a vacancy.

WALPOLE. Even so, an earldom would be the end of me. I do not look forward to being kicked upstairs. The House of Lords is the springboard from which you plunged into politics at 21. For me it is the shelf on which I shall be laid by at three score and ten.

SUNDERLAND. That may be so in your personal case. But take the larger view. Consider the interests of the country. The Upper House, with all its faults, stands between England and the mob of rich commercial upstarts who want to make money out of her: money, money and still more money. You are not an upstart: you are a country gentleman.

WALPOLE. Yes; and you are up to the neck in this commercial South Sea madness. It will be your ruin. I warn you: it will be the end of you politically within a year from now.

SUNDERLAND. You are impossible.[*Brusquely*] Good morning. [*He walks quickly away, leaving Walpole to finish his walk alone*].